Essays on Aristotle's
Poetics

Essays on Aristotle's *Poetics*

edited by

Amélie Oksenberg Rorty

PRINCETON UNIVERSITY PRESS

Library of Congress Cataloguing-in-Publication Data

Essays on Aristotle's poetics/edited by Amélie Oksenberg Rorty.
        p.   cm.
    Includes bibliographical references.
    ISBN 0-691-06872-0 ISBN 0-691-01498-1 (pbk.)
    1. Aristotle Poetics.   2. Poetics.   3. Aesthetics, Ancient.
    4. Tragedy.   I. Rorty, Amélie.
    PN1040.A53R67   1992
    808.1—dc20   91-43905

This book has been composed in Monophoto Photina

Editorial and production services by Fisher Duncan,
10 Barley Mow Passage, London W4 4PH

Printed in the United Kingdom at the Alden Press, Oxford

For
Klara and Israel Oksenberg
and
Ruth and Natan Nevo

List of Contributors

Elizabeth Belfiore is in the Department of Classics at the University of Minnesota

Rüdiger Bittner is in the Philosophy Faculty at the University of Bielefeld, Germany

Mary Whitlock Blundell is at the Center for Hellenic Studies and the University of Washington

Wayne Booth is in the Department of English at the University of Chicago

G.E.M. de Ste. Croix is an Honorary Fellow (formerly Fellow in Ancient History) of New College, Oxford University, Great Britain

Dorothea Frede is in the Classics Seminar at the University of Hamburg, Germany

Cynthia A. Freeland is in the Department of Philosophy at the University of Houston

Leon Golden is in the Department of Classics at Florida State University

Stephen Halliwell is in the Classics Faculty at the University of Birmingham, Great Britain

Richard Janko is in the Department of Classics at the University of California at Los Angeles

Aryeh Kosman is in the Department of Philosophy at Haverford College

Jonathan Lear is in the Department of Philosophy at Yale University

Alexander Nehamas is in the Department of Comparative Literature and the Department of Philosophy at Princeton University

Martha C. Nussbaum is in the Department of Classics and the Department of Philosophy at Brown University

Deborah H. Roberts is in the Department of Classics at Haverford College

Amélie Oksenberg Rorty is at Radcliffe College and Mt. Holyoke College

Nancy Sherman is in the Department of Philosophy at Georgetown University

Jean-Pierre Vernant is Professor Emeritus of Comparative Study of Ancient Religions at the Collège de France

Stephen A. White is in The Institute for Advanced Study at Princeton

Paul Woodruff is in the Department of Philosophy at the University of Texas

Acknowledgments

G.E.M. de Ste. Croix, "Aristotle on History and Poetry," in *The Ancient Historian and his Materials*, edited by Barbara Levick (Gregg Publishing, 1975), pp. 45–58 is reprinted by permission of Gregg International, Barbara Levick and G.E.M. de Ste. Croix.

Jean Pierre Vernant, "Myth and Tragedy," originally appeared in J.-P. Vernant and P. Vidal-Naquet, *Myth and Tragedy in Ancient Greece*, trans. J. Lloyd (Cambridge, MIT/Zone Books, 1988), pp. 32–34, 36–37, 43–48; 55–69 and in Jean-Pierre Vernant, *Myth and Society in Ancient Greece* trans. J. Lloyd (Cambridge, MIT/Zone Books, 1980), pp. 203–204; 206–208; and 213–214. It is reprinted with the permission of Zone Books and Jean-Pierre Vernant.

Jonathan Lear, "Katharsis," *Phronesis*, **XXXIII**/3, (1988) 297–326, is reprinted by permission of the editors of *Phronesis* and Jonathan Lear.

Leon Golden, "Comic Pleasures," *Hermes* **115** (1987) 166–174, is reprinted by permission of Franz Steiner Verlag, Stuttgart, and Leon Golden.

An earlier version of Amélie Oksenberg Rorty, "The Psychology of Aristotelian Tragedy" appeared in *MidWest Studies in Philosophy*, 15 edited by P. French, T. Uehling and H. Wettstein (Notre Dame University Press, 1992).

Elizabeth Belfiore generously gave permission to allow the bibliography of her *Tragic Pleasures: Aristotle on Plot and Emotion* (Princeton, 1992) to serve as a base for compiling the bibliography in this volume. The editor is also grateful Mt. Holyoke College for a faculty research grant and to the Bunting Institute, Radcliffe College for its generous hospitality.

Contents

The Psychology of Aristotelian Tragedy

Amélie Oksenberg Rorty

Sophocles puts the moral of our story best, and what he says reveals the essence of Aristotelian tragedy.

> Wonders are many and none more wonderful than man . . .
> In the meshes of his woven nets, cunning of mind, ingenious man . . .
> He snares the lighthearted birds and the tribes of savage beasts,
>   and the creatures of the deep seas . . .
> He puts the halter round the horse's neck
> And rings the nostrils of the angry bull.
> He has devised himself a shelter
>   against the rigors of frost and the pelting rains.
> Speech and science he has taught himself,
>   and artfully formed laws for harmonious civic life . . .
> Only against death he fights in vain.
> But clear intelligence – a force beyond measure –
>   moves to work both good and ill . . .
> When he obeys the laws and honors justice, the city stands proud . . .
> But man swerves from side to side, and when the laws are broken,
>   and set at naught, he is like a person without a city,
>   beyond human boundary, a horror, a pollution to be avoided.

What is a tragic drama? Why are we so affected by tragedies, sobered but enlarged, seared but strangely at peace? Why do tragedies – and what we learn from them – bring us such complex, bitter-sweet pleasures?

Aristotle gives us the best explanation we have for our experiences of tragedy. But if we accept his explanation, then we must also accept a good deal of his psychology and ethics. Aristotle's characterization of a tragedy is, perhaps, all too familiar, so familiar that we misread him, replacing his intentions with ours. Tragedy is one of the poetics arts.[1] It is, he says, an imitative representation

1

(*mimēsis*) of a serious (*spoudaios*) action, dramatically presented in a plot that is self-contained, complete, and unified. The protagonists of tragic drama are admirable, not technically speaking heroes or demigods, but larger and better versions of ourselves.[2] In the finest tragedies, the character of the protagonist makes him susceptible to a deflection – to an erring waywardness – that brings disaster, producing a reversal in the projected arc of his life. The story of his undeserved misfortune arouses our pity and fear, clarifying and purifying those reactions in such a way as to bring us both pleasure and understanding. At its best, tragedy brings recognition of who and what we are. Like other forms of poetry, tragedy is more philosophic and illuminating, and so more truthful than history.

Before examining the elements of Aristotle's definition and locating them within the larger frame of his ethics and psychology, we should say something about the kind of theory he holds. Although Aristotle focuses on the formal elements of tragedy – on the best way to structure plots, his is not an aesthetic theory. The pleasures and the insights of tragedy do not rest solely or primarily in their purely formal properties, in the elegance of structural tension and balance. In the arts and crafts – as in biology and metaphysics – form follows function and purpose. The beauty and merit of any individual work – a shoe, a pot, or a tragedy – is a function of the way that its form expresses and fulfills its aims clearly and elegantly, in an appropriate medium and manner. Because they are representational, all the poetic arts include, among their various aims, that of bringing us to some sort of recognition: they fulfill their distinctive emotional aims by affecting our understanding and they affect our understanding by affecting our emotions.

Aristotle is no more a hermeneuticist than he is an aesthetic formalist. The significance of a tragic drama lies in its *mûthos* and not in the history of its interpretations. Neither self-conscious formalism nor self-conscious hermeneuticism allows for Aristotelian tragedy.[3] For whenever there is the awareness of the play of abstraction or interpretation, we implicitly grant ourselves the power – even if it is only an intellectual power – to elude the ineluctable, escape the inescapability of the tragic plot. To be sure, it is in principle possible to restructure the classical dramas, to rearrange the elements that define Aristotelian tragedy, and to vary them in such a way as to produce new plays and new genres, cousins to Aristotelian tragedy.[4] And indeed later dramatists did redirect the ends of the plays they called "tragedies": Elizabethan critics like Nevyle thought tragedies should show "Gods horrible vengeaunce for sinne:" Corneille thought they should evoke the grandeur and gravity of the diction of noble action and passion. By contrast, Lessing stressed the evocation of pity and compassion through simple, unaffected language. Schiller takes tragedy to express the tensions between the sublimity of self-legislating freedom and the pathos of human suffering.[5] From Aristotle's point of view, debates about whether these dramas are, strictly speaking, tragedies, are idle and empty. Dramatic genres are differentiated by their ends; but the ends of a work of art –

indeed the end of any *technē* – also specify the formal structures of the work. To change the form is to shift the end; to shift the end is to change the genre.

Incomplete and fragmentary as it is, the *Poetics* conjoins a number of distinct enterprises: it is, to begin with, a philosophical study intended to analyze the structures and functions of the range of poetic genres as if they were biological species. The motto of this mode is: Save the phenomena. Anatomize poetic genres by showing how the formal arrangement of their "parts" succeed in fulfilling a specific aim, that is, by showing how the structures of the works produce a certain type of response. But since the poetic genres are crafts, the *Poetics* is a book of technical advice, as well as a functionally oriented anatomy. Aristotle's advice to the tragedians is advice about how to structure dramas in such a way as to produce a specific kind of psychological and intellectual effect. This advice goes beyond telling dramatists how to conform to a model that was derived by an analysis of classical drama, as if Aristotle were a chemist who had analyzed a compound and derived the formula for producing it. Aristotle's way of saving the phenomena of tragic drama has a strongly normative turn, beyond that which is implicit in any technical advice. Indeed, his normative agenda may have so focused his analysis of classical drama that he ignored some of its important features. The motto of this mode is: save drama against Platonic attacks by showing that good tragic drama – tragic drama properly understood – can promote rather than thwart understanding, attune rather than distort the emotions it arouses. The argument of the *Poetics* is intended to show that the best effects of tragic drama derive from its representational truthfulness rather than from ecstasy; that the turn of the plot depends on human agency rather than on demonic or divine forces, on probable rather than accidental connections among incidents; that the primary emotions evoked by tragic drama are pity and fear about what can plausibly happen rather than horror or awe (*deinon*) about the way that fate (*Moira*) can, in a strange alliance with chance (*Tuchē*), intervene in the natural course of events. It is a person's character (*ēthos*), as determining his actions and choices, rather than any cosmic justice (*dikē*) or vengeance (*nemesis*) that determines his fate. It is for these reasons that Aristotle does not discuss of the role of civic and religious rituals surrounding the traditional performances of the classical tragedies; and it is for these reasons that he thinks tragedies should not represent gory and horrible deeds on stage. His view is that neither tragedy nor its essential psychological effects depend on retaining their archaic sources or forms. Nietzsche was quite right: Aristotle wanted to transform, if not actually to eliminate, any remnants of the Dionysian origins of tragedy.

Mûthos and *Mimēsis*

"*Mûthos* – a story or plot –," Aristotle says, "is the fundamental principle and soul of tragedy" (1150b2 ff.). While there is sorrow, grief, loss, and pain in life, there is tragedy only when the actions and events that compose a life are organized into a story, a structured representation of that life. A drama is not only the *mimēsis* of an action, the enactment of a story that represents actions by actions and in actions: at its best, it also brings us to an understanding of the shape (*eidos*) and boundary (*horos*) of human action. Like all representation, drama selectively condenses and structures what is presents. It reveals the inner logic and causal organization of an apparently disconnected series of events, encompassing them to form a single extended, self-contained and completed activity. A *mûthos* takes what seemed to be a set of randomly distributed points and represents them in an arc, the trajectory of a well-formed parabola, containing all (and only) the elements and causal relations that are necessary to explain what happens. The delimitation and the definition of an action – its boundaries and its essential point – are coordinate: representing the structure of an action conjoins the arc of its temporal completion with the fulfillment (or failure) of its aims or intentions. We don't know when an action has been completed, let alone whether it has been successfully completed, unless we understand its aim or purpose.

Before we can understand Aristotle's account of how drama represents action, we need to understand his theory of representation. *Mimēsis* conjoins two notions. Neither the terms *imitation* nor *representation*, taken independently of one another, fully captures Aristotle's use.[6] Consider: an actor's mask is a representational *mimēsis* of the face of a certain kind of character, that of a king or that of a shepherd, for example, as abstracted from any accidental individuating factors. A good mask enables the spectators straightaway to identify the King, the Shepherd. Similarly a portrait represents the structure (*morphē*) of an individual's features: it is successful when we can recognize that it is a representation of Pericles rather than Sophocles. A good mask represents those features that reveal what is essential to the type: presumably in showing us what differentiates a King from a Shepherd, it also shows what a king really is; in differentiating Youth and Age, tragedy from comedy, it reveals what is centrally characteristic of each.[7]

Like many other animals, we are constitutionally set to mimic the actions of those around us. It is through *mimēsis* as imitation that we first learn, acquiring the habits that form our character, as well as the skills and abilities that constitute our virtues (1103b21 ff.). When imitation works well – when our models truthfully represent the essence of what they are and what they do – we not only learn how to play, to dance, to make pots, to arrange the matters of the day, but also what playing, dancing, pottery really are, what ends guide and determine the structuring of these activities. Ideally the idiosyncrasies of the models that we imitate drop out, and what remains is a representation of the essence of the actions and activities that constitute a well-lived life.

A central step in Aristotle's defence of tragic drama against Plato's attack is his claim that tragedy produces its emotional and cathartic effects through *mimēsis*, by representing and imitating actions. Instead of seeing *mimēsis* as essentially falsifying, he sees it as capable of being correct or truthful. Every representation of an action – whether it is structured as an epic, or in history or oratory – necessarily gives that action some form, a definition and a boundary. But while interpretations are indeed perspectival, there is a truth of the matter, indeed a double truth.[8] To begin with, protagonists can be profoundly mistaken about what they are really doing. Oedipus may have believed that he married the Queen of Thebes, and so he did; but the proper description of that action – the description that should have guided his deliberation – was that in marrying the Queen of Thebes, he would be marrying his mother. Aristotle carries the correctness of actions further: however well individual agents understand their particular actions, these actions can themselves conform or fail to conform to the normative essential definitions that govern the type of action in which they are engaged.[9]

Despite their differences, Aristotle accepts a central part of Plato's account of *mimēsis*. There is no imitation or representation without selection and abstraction.[10] The representation of an object or an event sets forth the formal organization or schema (*eidos*) – the rationale (*logos*) – of the relation among its parts. A dramatic imitative representation of an action reveals the structure of the dynamic causal connections among the events that compose it. Just as a good mask truthfully represents the essential configuration of the face of a King, so the criterion for a sound or good imitation of an action is that the representation be truthful, that it captures what is essential to its typical causal structure, abstracted from the accidental and contingent features of its performance. The kinds of actions that are centrally significant to a human life – serious (*spoudaios*) actions with weighty, far-reaching consequences – have a normative structure. Such actions and activities have an objective end or point: they can succeed or fail to realize that point. Tragedies represent the way that the protagonist's serious actions – those that affect the major directions of his life and that determine his happiness – skew the essential ends of what he does, and how this error, this waywardness brings disaster. The *mimēseis* of tragic drama can be evaluated for their truthfulness: they show how the protagonist's (well-intentioned but mistaken) purposes miss the true or essential ends of his actions and how his *harmartia* brings disaster.

Many tragedies represent a tale with which the audience is likely to be familiar. The original tale is itself a mimetic representation of a legendary set of events. For such dramas – *Oedipus* is one of them – the audience does a double take, as it were. It recognizes that Sophocles is re-presenting an old tale; and it recognizes that the old tale represents the structure of a certain *sort* of action. That old story, the story of Oedipus, could also be truthfully represented – imitatively re-presented – in an epic, or in music and dance. Had Oedipus been an historical figure, the story of his actions could also have been represented in a chronicle. The appropriate structuring of a *mimēsis* varies with the aim or the purpose of the representation. While an historical treatise represents certain events and actions, it does not, by Aristotle's lights, attempt to produce a particular emotional or motivational effect on its audience. But a political orator could introduce the story of Oedipus in the course of an argument to persuade a polity to conduct a thorough investigation of a stranger's ancestry before accepting him as a ruler. He would, without distorting the original story, structure his representation of the action in such a way as to bring about a certain kind of political effect. Although the story of Oedipus is, to be sure, not an ordinary story, it is told as a tragedy – a tragedy with universal significance – when it is structured in such a way as to bring about a specific emotional and intellectual effect, by representing the story of an action that undoes a person of high energetic intelligence.

Action and the Unity of Action

What then are actions? Human actions are a species of natural motion, those sorts of motion whose sources are internal to the agent. Avalanches toss great boulders, roots of trees press through rock, animals devour one another, each acting from its own nature, to fulfill its nature. Our natural motions are also of this general kind. We differ from avalanches and animals in that some of our natural motions – those we call our actions – are structured by our intentions, our beliefs and desires. We act – we intervene to change or direct the course of events – in order to fulfill our purposes, ultimately for the sake of what we take to be our happiness (1095a14 ff.). When we intentionally and deliberately intervene in the course of events – ringing the nostril of the wild bull, snaring the light-hearted birds – we are not acting against nature. On the contrary, we are expressing our natures. We differ from avalanches and animals in that we are capable of intelligent planning and of acting voluntarily, understanding the meaning and normal consequences of what we do when it is within our power to do otherwise.

Intelligent action arranges the affairs of life in such a way as to conduce to happiness (*eudaimonia*): but a life of action and activity is more than a well-planned enterprise, one that produces happiness as if it were interest on a crafty business investment. Happiness is not an outcome or end-product of action and activity. It *is* soul actively engaged in its natural activities, doing its best at its best (1098a12 ff.). An action takes the form of an activity when it is self-contained, whole and complete, fully performed, its ends achieved in the very performance.[11] Many actions, particularly those which express basic species-defining traits, are specifications of activities or are embedded within them. Political discussion is, for example, an exercise of the fundamental activity of civic life; similarly the actions involved in botanical or animal dissection are part of the activity of scientific inquiry.

In the *Nicomachean Ethics*, Aristotle remarks that humans are in a way thought to be partially divine, or at least to share in divinity in so far as they share in *nous*, that is, in so far as they share in intelligence, in mind (1177b27 ff.). Contemplation is the most pre-eminent and perfectly formed noetic activity;

in it we fulfill what is highest and best in us, purified as it were, of all that is extraneous and contingent. Nevertheless, in so far as we act intentionally and intelligently, forming action by thought or *dianoia*, we act in a god-like way, changing the direction of what would otherwise have happened, through and because of our thought-filled and thought-directed interventions.

As we differ from animals in our capacities for thought, we differ from divinities in our susceptibilities to waywardness. We are not only capable of acting intelligently and wisely, but also of acting in error and ignorance. Unlike other animals, we can act askew, lawlessly, and although our intentions are always directed to what we believe to be good, we often do not know what is good, even for ourselves. The ends that direct our actions can be opaque to us, even when we are acting from our clearest and best understanding. Indeed, it is sometimes precisely our way of being at our clearest and best that undoes us.

Sometimes, it is the very energy and vigor of our purposiveness – the fact that we act in a focused arc of attention – that blinds or at least blurs what appears at the periphery of our intentions. There is no action without focused purpose and the energy to fulfill it; there is no focused, energetic purpose without the lively possibility of disorder, of going wrong. Even intelligent, truth-bound beliefs and well-formed desires for what is genuinely good are not sufficient to carry purposes to their realization. The successful enactment of the strongest, most intelligent desires also requires a certain kind of energy which is, at its best, confident, often indignant and sometimes courageous; at its worst, it is presumptuous and disordering.

Except for self-contained activities that are completed in the very act of performing them, we rarely grasp the structured unity of what we do. That is one of the reasons we cannot judge a person's life happy until he is dead, and perhaps some time after he is dead, when the full shape of his actions are finally revealed, their trajectories completed. The real completion of a person's life – the realization of the projects that were essential to it – does not usually coincide with the natural end of his activity in death. We do not know whether a person has been a wise parent until his children are grown; nor whether he has been a wise statesman until his policies have been in effect for some time (1100a18 ff.).

Drama reveals the form and point of the protagonist's actions, their sometimes hidden directions and purposes. In a way, we cannot see what an action really is, until we see it contextualized, embedded in the story of which it is an essential part. Until we see the completed whole in which an action functions, we cannot determine whether it has been well or ill performed, whether it succeeds or fails. An action is only partially identified and directed by the agent's intentions, by the chain of practical reasons that connect it to his general ends. These are, as it were, the logical structure of the beginning and end of his action, conceived in isolation. But even the logical structure of the agent's intentions do not give the full explanation of what he does. Those intentions must also be located in the story that reveals the causal structure of the unfolding of his interactions with other characters.[12] To be sure, in ordinary life,

we identify and evalute actions readily and quickly, without an extended investigation of the practical reasoning that formed the agents' intentions or the
stories that frame their actions. But that is because we assimilate particular
actions to a standard form, supplying the standard stories and intentions that are
implicit in our categorized perceptions. It is against the background of such
assumptions about the typical etiology and directions of action-types that we
judge particular intentions and actions to be well or ill formed, justified or
askew.[13]

The stories or plots of tragedies reveal the significant structures that unite
serious actions – actions that make a difference to how a person lives, well or ill,
happily or unhappily – into a self-contained whole, an activity. But life *is*,
according to Aristotle, activity: it is expressed in action and activity (1095a19–
20, 1098a20 ff., 1450a15 ff.).[14] By connecting the protagonist's serious actions
into a story, drama reveals the unified structure of a life. Represented *in* a unified
whole, a life can be seen *as* a unified whole, with an intelligible shape (1100b32).
That is why tragedies are of enormous and terrifying significance to us, because
they are representations of what can go wrong even in the best and most
intelligent action, go wrong not merely because chance and accident attend all
contingent events, but because of some error or misdirection in the action itself,
a deflection that brings a reversal of the very intentions that propelled it.

A plot or story presents discrete events and actions as forming a completed
and self-contained whole which can be grasped all at once, as a single activity,
lacking nothing, with its component incidents so arranged that if one of them
is removed, the whole is disturbed or destroyed (1451a7 and 15 ff.).[15] A plot
connects the incidents that compose it in three ways: (1) causally; (2) themati-
cally; and (3) by exhibiting the connections between the protagonist's character,
his thought and his actions.

(1) Aristotle puts the causal connection straightforwardly, simply and strongly:
     the events are linked, shown as happening because of one another
     (1452a2–4). To link the events in a well-ordered whole and to elicit pity and
     fear, the causal connections must be necessary or nearly so, as necessary as
     human actions can be.
(2) Repetition is the simplest type of thematic connection; ironic reversal is
     another (1452a ff.). Aristotle's example of a thematic connection is that of
     the statue of Mitys falling on his murderer (1452a10). Having saved Thebes
     by solving the riddle of the Sphinx, Oedipus must again save the city by
     solving the mystery of the source of its pollution. Blind about his real
     identity, he blinded himself when he discovered who he was; the heir
     apparent of Corinth who fled his city, he ended his days a cityless wanderer,
     a pariah, a scared suppliant. He is the solution to the mystery of the city's
     pollution; and he has become the answer to the riddle of the Sphinx, the man
     who crawled on all fours in his lamed and fettered infancy, who stood
     upright in his prime and who stumbles on a staff in the end. Antigone lived

to bury her dead; her punishment was to be buried alive. But since she deliberately did what she knew to be punishable by death, she took her own life in the tomb where Creon had condemned her. It is such patterned closures as these that give thematic unity to drama.

(3) Finally the unity of the plot is manifest in the way that each protagonist's fundamental character traits are expressed in all that he thinks, says, does (1454a2 ff.). Oedipus revealed himself kingly in all he did, in all his actions: in the images of his bold speech, in the large scope of his thoughts, in his assurance and high, quick energy; in the directions of his actions, moving always to protect his city.

Character (*Ēthos*)

Although tragedy is, according to Aristotle, about action rather than about character (1450a15 ff.), the two are coordinate (*Rhetoric* I.12. 1372 ff.). The stress of *ēthos anthrōpo(i) daimōn* now falls firmly on one side of the equation: it is a person's character rather than his *daimōn* that determines his fate. But character is expressed in choice (*prohairesis*) and choice determines action: "*eudaimonia* takes the form of action" (1450a16). While in principle a person might have some character traits that are rarely, if ever exercised, character is essentially individuated and fundamentally articulated in choice and in thoughtful action (1139a22–3; 1144b30–2).[16] Since "life is action and activity" (1450a16 ff.), tragedy that represents serious action is also a dramatic representation of the way that the protagonist's character is expressed in his fundamental choices and actions, those that affect the way that his life unfolds.

Tragedy represents protagonists who are recognizably enlarged and simplified versions of what is best in us, presented without the multiple extraneous purposes that confuse our actions. They are what we would be if we could undergo an alchemy, a purification of the elements that compose us. They have, in an exemplary form, the character traits and dispositions that are the raw materials of virtue, the intelligence that goes into *phronēsis*, the energy that goes into *andreia*, the natural affections that go into *philia*, the assurance that goes into great-heartedness. Character structures of this kind are normally stable: they are expressed in habits of perception and emotion that typically move smoothly to well-formed deliberation and action. Yet in the course of the drama, they make a terrible choice – one that is in character and voluntary, but that nevertheless involves a significant waywardness – whose consequences reverse the good fortune that would normally attend the actions of a person of their character.

It might seem as if the description of the tragic protagonist is incoherent, and the account of the tragic plot paradoxical. The pity and fear aroused by tragedy centers around the undeserved suffering of a relatively virtuous protagonist. Virtue is, by definition, self-regulating and self-correcting; and it typically brings happiness (*eudaimonia*), even in harsh circumstances (1100b22–1101a8). Yet the plot unfolds from the protagnoist's *hamartia*, a waywardness whose consequences reverses the *eudaimonia* that normally attends virtue.[17] How can virtue be subject to *hamartia*, how can it involve wayward misunderstanding? And if, as Aristotle believes, a person is at least in part responsible for his character (or at any rate, the kind of person who can be the protagonist of a tragedy is so responsible (1114b1 ff.), then how can the protagonist's suffering be undeserved?

If there is an adequate answer to these questions, it lies in Aristotle's understanding of *hamartia*. The reigning translations of that term do not help us. "Flaw" misleadingly suggests that *harmatia* is built into the protagonist's character. But if the protagonist's erring waywardness were part of his character, he would not be an exemplary figure, his suffering would not be undeserved, and we would not pity him. If, on the other hand, his *hamartia* were involuntary, purely extraneous – like an accidental illness – we would not, seeing his character in action, fear for him. In neither case would the drama be well structured or unified; in neither case, could we learn anything from tragedy; nor would it please us. Yet translating *harmartia* as "error" or "mistake" misleadingly fails to capture the dispositional character of the protagonist's *harmartia*; and in emphasizing its purely intellectual aspect, those notions also fail to capture the way that the protagonist's *harmartia* affects his *thumos* and *pathē* as well as his thoughts. Though a protagonist's *hamartia* might sometimes just involve his making a factual error, it is the sort of error that a person of his character would be typically prone to make. In combination with his character, it misleads his action. (For instance, a character given to grand postures might systematically mistake the size and importance of his family estate, and so characteristically but voluntarily treat his neighbors with untoward arrogance.) Character virtues and their susceptibilities are simultaneously cognitive *and* conative: they affect a person's passions and desires, as well as his perceptions and inferences.

In the best tragedies, the reversals of fortune that the protagonists suffer come from something central in them, not from any particular thing that they did, but from a waywardness that could not, even with more foresight or energy, have been prevented. The *hamartiai* that bring misfortune are contingent byproducts of admirable character traits, traits that are the natural basis of the virtues and that normally promote thriving. An example might help illuminate Aristotle's point: the character and skill of a corageous soldier explains his taking the sorts of risks that would normally be unwise, his charging the enemy in a way that exposes him to the danger of being wounded in battle. Still, he is not responsible for being wounded, and so we pity his suffering. But because we also admire him, we pity him in a special way, more than we might anyone who was wounded in battle. It was possible, perhaps even probable, that a courageous person like himself would, despite his skills, be more likely to be wounded than an ordinary soldier; and so although we might fear for anyone going into battle, we also especially fear for him. By contrast, we might pity someone who was accidentally wounded by a tile that fell on his head as he walked to the Agora on a windy day; but we do not fear for everyone who walks to the Agora on windy days.

It is as if *hamartiai* were like a kind of cancer: contingent growths that arise from the very activities that promote healthy physical development. Noble intentions can, often by the logic and development of their own momentum, lead to actions whose full trajectory reverses their origins. Such reversals are especially likely to occur in the interaction among several characters, each acting from the arc of his own intentions. Tragedy reveals that there is, as it were, a canker in the very heart of action. All action is formed by intelligence, to be sure; but by an intelligence directed to a relatively limited purpose. The gap of opacity, and with it the possibility of ignorance and deflection, always stands between even the best general purposes and the particular actions that actualize and fulfill them. Though it falls within the domain of the voluntary, the tragic hero's *hamartia* is an accident of his excellence: his purposes and energy make him susceptible to a kind of waywardness that arises from his character. Although the occasions that unfold the consequences of the agent's *hamartia* are contingent, they are the sorts of things which might well happen. Once they have occurred, the dramatic action that brings about the reversal of the protagonist's fortune has – in the best of tragedies – a terrible and irreversible inevitability. The focused clarity, the assurance, the vitality and energy of exemplary, excellent action – its very godlikeness – are shadowed by the misdirections that threaten their excellence. Concentration blurs what is at the periphery of attention; courage sets natural caution aside; great-heartedness carries the possibility of arrogance; a person of grandeur, with an unusual scope of action, can readily lose his sense of proper proportion, forget his finitude. Everything that is best in the protagonists make them vulnerable to their reversals: like all living creatures, they naturally strive to realize what is best in them; and it is precisely this that, as their actions unfold, undoes them.

The cancer that is at the heart of the tragic protagonist's *hamartia* often involves his not knowing who he is, his ignorance of his real identity.[18] To know who one is to know how to act: it involves understanding of one's obligations and what is important in one's interactions. The kind of ignorance that literally involves not knowing one's family is particularly dangerous because it affects all of a person's sacred, political and ethical conduct. But a protagonist can be superficially, verbally aware of who he is, and yet fail to carry that knowledge through to his conduct, acting as if he were ignorant of what he claims to know. Phaedra's passion for Hippolytus expresses a dramatic *hamartia*: her desire involves her forgetting who she is, the wife of Theseus and stepmother to Hippolytus. In a queen, such a *hamartia* endangers the whole kingdom. Of course Phaedra is not suffering from amnesia or literal ignorance. Nevertheless, her passion for Hippolytus involves her in ethical, character-based wrong-doing.

In a way, there are, in the dramatic world that is composed entirely of serious actions that affect the tenor of a life, no merely intellectual errors. When a drama is composed entirely of serious actions, even factual errors are weighty: a person who is ignorant of his lineage is likely to act improperly. Unaware of his relations and obligations to those around him, Oedipus does not, in the deepest sense, know how to behave. But Oedipus also suffers another kind of ignorance. His cleverness in answering the riddle of the Sphinx shows that he has a verbal grasp of the boundaries (*horos*) and the vulnerability of human life. Yet his contempt towards Tiresias shows that his acute awareness of his exceptional gifts has blinded him to the full significance of his answer.

In the best plots, the *peripeteia* of action – the moment that reverses the protagonist's fortunes – coincides with insightful recognition (*anagnōrisis*). Significantly, this recognition typically fulfills the ancient command to know oneself (*gnōthi seauton*) (1452a32 ff.). In recognizing that he is the son of Laius and Jocasta, Oedipus comes to himself, realizes who he is, as well as what he has done. The reversal of his fortune is his recognizing that he has violated the fundamental structures that should have directed his actions. As his ignorance was not merely an intellectual error, but a waywardness that pervaded his actions, so too his acknowledgment of his waywardness is not merely a cognitive recognition. It consists in his living out his life, a blind man wandering, "a horror, a pollution to be avoided."

Catharsis

No wonder that the reversal of intentions, the change of fortunes of those who are better than ourselves evokes pity and fear. If they are ourselves writ large, then what can happen to them, can happen to us as well. Perhaps we are as blind to what we are doing as Oedipus; perhaps we too mistake impetuous rashness for courage, presumption for righteous indignation. Perhaps we too are ignorant or forgetful of who and what we are.

What difference is there, if any, between the pity and fear that we feel in the normal course of action, and those we experience in and through tragic drama? And how can drama educate us, so that we experience pity and fear appropriately? Normally fear (*phobos*) is particular and functional; it signals danger. (*Rhetoric* II.5). The ethical and political question that the phenomena of fear raises is: what is, and what is not, worth fearing? Similarly, pity – *eleos* – is normally particular and functional: it signals that a friend or someone like ourselves has suffered an undeserved misfortune. Pity involves both distance and proximity. If the sufferer is too close to ourselves, his impending misfortune evokes horror and terror. If he is too distant, his fate does not affect us (*Rhetoric* II.8). The ethical and political questions are: whom should we pity? What should we regard as undeserved misfortune? The virtues – certainly courage and perhaps also the kind of civic friendship that is at the core of pity – involve the capacity to have the right emotional reactions at the right time, in the right way, directed to the right objects. In fact the virtues are just that – they are *hexeis* – active appropritate habits of acting and reacting. Courage, for instance, involves knowing what is worth fearing, and being able to set aside natural self-protective fears in order to act wisely on behalf of what we most prize. Similarly, appropriate pity involves knowing when misfortune is undeserved, recognizing human finitude and the limits of control and responsibility. It also involves an affective understanding of the proper domain of *philia*, our solidarity with those with whom we are bound. The psychological effects of tragedy depend on there being a strong connection between the fearful and the pitiable incidents: the audience pities the protagonist for the very reversals that they feared would attend his actions (*Rhetoric* II.8. 1386a27).

But just whom do we pity and what do we fear? The tragic hero? Ourselves? Humanity? All three, and all three in one. Like drama generally, tragedy represents intentions and actions from the agents' point of view, in their language. When they speak in the first person, the protagonists of tragic drama invite our reflective identification: after all, they are like ourselves. Because "it is easier to look at someone else than at ourselves" (*NE* 1169b33–4), the lives of the tragic protagonists will show us something about ourselves. Of course the resemblance between the protagonists and ourselves is a general one: we need not be rulers of Thebes, or even Thebans, to identify with Oedipus; nor need we be sisters or even women, to identify with Antigone. We also see the protagonists externally, taking the perspectives of the other characters and of the chorus; and we share in all their reactions.[19] So, to begin with, we feel pity and fear for the tragic protagonist, but we do not learn appropriate pity and fear by imitating exactly his emotions. For one thing, he does not pity himself: he is grieved or horrified by the unfolding of his actions. But in pitying him and fearing for him, we take the reflective spectator's point of view. He fears what may happen: we fear for him. Still when we feel for him, we see ourselves in him. In pitying the tragic protagonists, we pity ourselves; in fearing for him, we fear to suffer the kinds of reversals that he met and suffered. Since we are also essentially social and political beings, connected to others by civic *philia*, we treat the welfare of our friends and family as essential to our own welfare. Our *philoi* form a series of expanding circles, starting from the closest family and friends, to partners in a common civic project (*koinonia*), and to those who – like members of the human species – share a common form of life.[20] For the original audience, *Oedipus* may have articulated and expressed the fear that their rulers might be unwittingly dangerous; it may also have articulated and expressed pity for those exiles, who, through no fault of their own – yet because of what they were – suffered a life without their *philoi*, "without a city, beyond human boundaries, . . . a horror to be avoided" (1386ba12 ff.). The pity and the fears of that original audience are, in a way, also ours, fearing – as always we do – the actions of our rulers, and pitying the many forms that exile takes. Tragedy not only diminishes but also enlarges the scope of our pity and fear to its proper objects: to the plight and danger of those who act to change the course of events to conform to their purposes.

The issue of whether the audience's emotions are, in the end, fundamentally merely self-regarding, can be set aside. In fearing for themselves, the audience does not merely fear for themselves as idiosyncratic individuals. Their fears are simultaneously specific and general: caught up in the action of plot, they fear what seems likely to happen to the tragic hero; but since that fear also has a more general description, as a fear for the undeserved misfortunes that can attend intentional action, they also fear for their *philoi* and for themselves.

But pity and fear are aroused in order to effect a catharsis. The classical notion of catharsis combines several ideas: it is a medical term, referring to a therapeutic cleansing or purgation; it is a religious term, referring to a purification achieved by the formal and ritualized, bounded expression of powerful and often dangerous emotions; it is a cognitive term, referring to an intellectual resolution or clarification that involves directing emotions to their appropriate intentional objects.[21] All three forms of catharsis are meant, at their best, to conduce to the proper functioning of a well-balanced soul. The issue of whether tragic catharsis is expressed as a resolution of the incidents of the plot or whether it is expressed in the psychology of the audience can be set aside.[22] The psychological catharsis of the audience takes place through, and because of the catharsis of the dramatic action. A plot that has been resolved is one whose unity is revealed: the various incidents that compose it are recognized by the protagonist and by the audience to be strongly interconnected in a harmonic whole.

A harmonious soul is by no means apathetic, drained of emotion. Aristotle does not have a hydraulic or drainage-ditch model of catharsis. A room that has been cleaned has not been emptied, but brought to its proper order; a body that has been purged is not an empty sack, but one brought to its healthful functioning order, one that absorbs what is nourishing and eliminates what is not. What matters about pity and fear is that they be appropriate, directed to the right objects in the right way in the right amount at the right time (1109a20 ff.). (Consider: When a thought is well articulated and expressed, it has the proper place and weight, playing an appropriate role in a person's whole system of beliefs. In both cases, the thought and the emotion are fulfilled, brought to their appropriate psychological and intellectual functioning, by being properly focused, defined and articulated.) When pity and fear are appropriately felt, directed to the right things in the right way, according to the *logos* and the measure that is appropriate to them, they can play their natural psychological and civic functions (*Rhetoric* II.9 1386b13).

But attending even the best of tragic dramas is not, of course, sufficient to bring us to virtue. A person who has undergone a physical catharsis is only as healthy as his body can be made by purging: a purge does not cure high blood pressure or poor eyesight. So attending tragic dramas can rectify a person's pity and fear only as far as his character allows. Attending tragic dramas – experiencing a catharsis of pity and fear – cannot make an irascible person temperate. The virtues are acquired largely through active habituation and imitation. Even when tragic catharsis is combined with the insight of *anagnōrisis*, it cannot by itself make us virtuous.

The controversy about whether catharsis primarily involves an intellectual clarification or an emotional rectification shadows the controversy about whether *hamartia* is an intellectual error or a characterological flaw, and whether *anagnōrisis* is purely cognitive.[23] For Aristotle the distinction between intellectual clarification and emotional rectification is, in this sort of context, spurious and tendentious. In the domain of practical life, cognition, character and action are coordinate. Despite his repudiation of Plato, Aristotle's insistence on the separation between theory and practice does not entail a radical separation between practical reason and character. The distinction between theory and practice is a distinction between types of activities – both of them cognitive – as characterized by their methods and aims. Because the aims and methods of *epistemē* and those of *praxis* are distinct, it is possible for a good scientist to lack practical wisdom and for the *phronimos* to be a poor scientist. But the distinction between theory and practice does not imply that a person could be virtuous without practical intelligence.

The psychotherapeutic expression *working through* is a perspicuous translation of many aspects of the classical notion of catharsis.[24] In *working through* his emotions, a person realizes the proper objects of otherwise diffuse and sometimes misdirected passions. Like a therapeutic *working through*, catharsis occurs at the experienced sense of closure. In recognizing and re-cognizing the real directions of their attitudes, the members of an audience are able to feel them appropriately; and by experiencing them in their clarified and purified forms, in a ritually defined and bounded setting, they are able to experience, however briefly, the kind of psychological functioning, the balance and harmony that self-knowledge can bring to action.

And so, naturally enough, we turn to pleasure.

Pleasure

What is pleasurable about tragic drama? Unlike those Platonists who were suspicious of pleasures, Aristotle does not think that pleasure is a process or the outcome of a process: it is the unimpeded, uninterrupted exercise of a natural activity (*NE* 1153a10 ff.). The prime cases that reveal the character of pleasure are those natural species-defining characteristics which, like the pleasures of sight, are complete in their very exercise. We do not need any motivation to perform such activities, and they are, when properly performed, on their proper objects, without impediment, intrinsically pleasurable, independently of whatever else they may achieve. Even those pleasures that are relativized to pain or depletion – pleasures like those of recuperation of satisfying hunger – arise from the natural activities of the organism in healing itself or in absorbing nourishment. Properly understood, such pleasures are focused on the activity, rather than on the state produced by it.

The pleasure of an action lies in its being fulfilled, completed as the sort of

activity that it is, with its proper values achieved. Aristotle has a doubly normative conception of pleasure.[25] To begin with, pleasures are individuated and
identified by the actions and activities that they attend, and in which they are
immanent (1175b36 ff.). But actions are themselves intentionally individuated
and identified. Two persons attending the same dramatic performance may be
performing different actions in going to theater; though they may both derive
pleasure from the drama, their pleasures will differ as their intentions differ. One
may be pleased by the event, the crowds, the excitement; the other may be
absorbed in the unfolding of the drama.

But here, as elsewhere, there are norms (1176a9 ff.). The pleasures of
attending dramatic performances have proper forms and proper objects
(1462b12 ff.). Tragic drama involves and conjoins so many different kinds of
pleasure that it is difficult to determine which is primary and which accidental
(1451b7 ff.; 1448b5 ff.).[26] We take pleasure in the activities of the senses on their
natural objects: music, dance, spectacle and the declamation of rhythmical verse
are, just in themselves, pleasing to the senses. We also take a variety of pleasures
in *mimēsis* as such: in seeing and recognizing representations, and in the
tragedian's craft in forming and structuring the representation, even when what
is represented is unfamiliar, ugly or painful. But the pleasures of dramatic
mimēsis go beyond those that are generally exercised in the activities that
involve recognition. Because it represents a story that is complete in itself,
uninterrupted by the irrelevant flotsam and jetsam accidents of every-day life,
drama brings the further pleasures of the sense of closure, the recognition of
something that has been structured into a well-formed whole. The pleasures that
are specific to tragic drama are those that connect the most profound of our
pleasures – the pleasures of learning – with the therapeutic pleasures of catharsis, "the pleasure arising from pity and fear through mimesis" (1453b10–14).
Through the unity of drama, we discover that a disjointed and even a disastrous
sequence of events can be represented as ordered, with a *logos* that connects the
temporal completion of an action with its logical closure. But the representations
of the structured actions of tragic protagonists also represent us: in recognizing
ourselves to be part of the activity of an ordered world, we take delight in
self-knowledge, in the discovery that our lives form an ordered activity (*Magna
Moralia* 1213a10–26). When it is well structured and well performed, tragedy
conjoins sensory, therapeutic and intellectual pleasures. Pleasure upon pleasure,
pleasure within pleasure, producing pleasure.

Lessons and Politics

Having shown how tragedy pleases, we must now turn to what it teaches.[27]
Drama is twinned with ethics. Philosophical ethics presents an account of the
character structure of admirable agents, whose actions are well formed, reliably
successful. By analyzing the role of *phronēsis* in realizing the general ends that

constitute thriving, it reveals the logical structure of virtuous action. Drama does not, of course, supplement constructive philosophic ethics by posting a set of moralizing warnings, examples of what to avoid. Nor does it simply portray admirable nobility in the face of undeserved misfortune, so that we might be inspired to imitate it. Nevertheless its lessons are moral, and its moral lessons have political significance.[28]

It is crucial to civic life that individuals, acting for themselves, and acting as citizens on behalf of the *polis*, understand the deep and often hidden structures of the actions that are important to their thriving. To choose and act wisely, we need to know the typical dynamic patterns of actions and interactions. Later moralists – Hume for example – believed that history, rather than drama, reveals the patterns of action. But Aristotle thought we could not learn moral or political truths from history because it is, by his lights, a chronicle focused on the particularity of events, rather than on what can be generalized from them (1451b4 ff.).

Tragedies have another ethical and political dimension. Like well-formed rhetoric, they promote a sense of shared civic life, and like rhetoric, they do so both emotionally and cognitively. To begin with, the audience is united, temporarily at least, in sharing the emotions of a powerful ritual performance.[29] But tragedy also conjoins us intellectually, bringing us to be of one mind in a common world. In practical life, the trajectories of individual lives intersect, deflect or enhance one another. Although every individual's welfare is bound with that of his *philoi*, different families and commuities have their own directions, with distinctive patterns of action and reaction. By presenting us with common models and a shared understanding of the shapes of actions, tragedy – like philosophy and other modes of poetry – moves us beyond the merely individual or domestic, towards a larger, common civic *philia*.

Some say that tragedy teaches us the power of chance, of the force of contingency in determining whether the virtuous thrive. While tragedy does indeed focus on what can go wrong in the actions of the best of men, its ethical lessons are not primarily about the place of accident and fortune in the unfolding of a human life. To begin with, Aristotle says that tragedy is about what can probably or inevitably happen (1451a37 ff.). If the stressed lesson of tragedy were the disconnection between intention and action, between action and outcome, it would produce somber modesty and edifying resignation, traits that are hardly central to the Aristotelian scheme of virtues. To be sure, like all the virtues, *megalopsychia* has its shadow *hamartia*: a flaunting arrogance that forgets the straightened limits of human action. Tragic drama shows that what is central to excellence in action – what is intrinsic to the very nature of action – carries the possibility of a certain kind of arrogance and presumption. In acting purposively, we perforce discount the tangential effects of chance and accident: in the very nature of the case, intelligent action sets aside what it cannot measure. Still even if, in a general way, we somberly recognize the contingency of our lives, we cannot avoid tragedy by becoming modest or resigned: it is in our nature to strive for what is best in us. The lesson of tragedy is not that we should know more, think more carefully; or that we should be more modest and less impetuously stubborn than the protagonists of tragic dramas. Because it is no accident that excellence sometimes undoes itself, one of the dark lessons of tragedy is that there are no lessons to be learnt, in order to avoid tragedy.

Yet for all of that, the end note of tragedy – its lesson – is not that of darkest despair. The major tragic figures emerge as enlarged by what they have endured, and by the *anagnōrisis* that is a double turning of their lives, by what they have learnt from their endurance. Their fortunes are reversed in recognizing who they are and what they have done. But the mind becomes identical with what it thinks: knowledge perfects the person (*De Anima* 430a15; 431a1–8). In the nobility with which they express their recognition – a nobility which fuses character with knowledge – tragic protagonists have become their best selves. Tragedy presents a dramatic enactment of the view that is philosophically argued in the *Nicomachean Ethics*: the virtuous can retain their nobility (*kalos*) in the worse reversals of fortune, the loss of the goods – health, the thriving of their children and their city, wealth, the admiration of their fellows – that are normally central to *eudaimonia* (1100b30–3).[30] Tragedies portray the ethical doctrine that there is a sense – by no means the ordinary sense – in which the constancy of virtue, the expression of nobility in the midst of great suffering can carry its own form of *eudaimonia*, despite the loss of goods that normally constitute happiness. After all, *eudaimonia* consists in the actions of a well-lived life, as perfected as it can be. While the undeserved suffering of the virtuous elicit our pity and fear, the nobility with which they meet their reversals – a nobility manifest in their actions and speech – illuminates us. It reveals yet another dimension of the "wonders of humankind."

We, too, are transformed by what we have seen and learnt by witnessing the dramatic stories of the tragic protagonists, participating in their final recognition. Realizing what we are, recognizing our kinship with those who overreach themselves in action, we can come closer to fulfilling our natures – and our virtues – as knowers and as citizens. And since pleasure is the unimpeded exercise of a natural potentiality, our double self-realization brings a double pleasure, all the more vivid because we are united, individually and communally, in realizing that however apparently fragmented, ill-shaped and even terrible our lives may seem to us in the living, they form a single activity, a patterned, structured whole.[31]

Notes

1. *Poiēsis* is a species of craft (*technē*). Besides tragic and comic dramas, the mimetic arts include epics, dithyrambic poetry and some sorts of music. Their primary contrasts are rhetoric, history and philosophy. The mimetic poetic arts are distinguished from one another by their ends, by the objects they represent and by the means and manner of their representations (1447a14 ff.). Dramatic genres are primarily distin-

guished from one another by the types of response they attempt to evoke in their audiences, and secondarily by the differences in the structure of their representations.

2. For the sake of simplicity, I shall speak of the *protagonist* of tragic action even though Aristotle speaks primarily of agents or actors (*prattontes*) and of characters (*ēthē*) rather than of *protagonists*. *Prattontes* ambiguously refers to (1) fictional characters who, like Odysseus, might appear in the Homeric epics and also in *Philoctetus*, or (2) the dramatis personae of a specific play. *Ēthē* refers to the (1) dramatis personae of the drama, typified at the King, the Messenger, and (2) the specific character structures that affect their choices and actions as good, manly, consistent (1450b8 ff.; 1454a22 ff.).

3. We can distinguish the naive from the sentimental versions of formalism and hermeneuticism. Naive hermeneuticists can present what they take to be *the* interpretation of a work, without developing a general theory that explains and defends perspectival or historical changes in interpretations. But when critics self-consciously affirm the perspectival character of approaches – when they openly reconstruct their texts – they transform the modality of a strictly Aristotelian tragedy. The modality of the plot of an Aristotelian tragedy – the necessity or probability of its events – is central to its psychological effect. A reader who believes he is in principle entitled to reconstrue and reconstruct the tragic plot stands at a remove from the necessities of the drama. In granting himself a freedom from the necessities of the plot as it would have been experienced by the audience of classical tragic dramas, he has changed the psychology of his response.

4. For an excellent summary of the history of the influence and shifts in the discussion of tragedy, see Stephen Halliwell. *Aristotle's Poetics* (Chapel Hill, 1986). Ch. X, pp. 286 ff.

5. Alexander Nevyle, "Introduction" to *Ten Tragedies of Seneca* (Manchester, 1887), p. 162; Corneille, "Discourse," in *Pierre Corneille: Writings on the Theater*, ed. H. T. Bernwell (Oxford, 1965); Lessing, *Dramaturgie*, Essay 77, *Gesammelte Werke* (Berlin, 1968) 6: 631; Schiller, "On Tragic Drama" and "On the Pathetic" Cited by Marvin Carlson, *Theories of the Theater* (Ithaca, 1984).

6. Cf. Stephen Halliwell, *Aristotle's Poetics* (Chapel Hill, 1986), Ch. 4.

7. Cf. John Jones, *On Aristotle and Greek Tragedy* (Oxford, 1962), pp. 41 ff.

8. To be sure, everyone – the protagonists, the various members of the chorus – has his own interpretation of the action. But although he recognizes that evey representation involves interpretation, Aristotle is no egalitarian about interpretations. Like the chorus, the audience can understand the rationale of the perspectives of the various protagonists, while also recognizing that they can distort the truth.

9. Aristotle would, for instance, think that whatever the Egyptians may have believed about the matter, royal agnatic alliances do not properly qualify as mariages and that incest is a violation of the social order, even in Egypt. Confucius' view of 'the rectification of names' may illumiante Aristotle's intention. There are correct normative descriptions of marriage, of filial roles and their duties. Disorder and danger attend the violation of these structures. Because it vividly and dramatically presents the consequences of such violations, Aristotelian tragedy can be seen as an instrument in the 'rectification of names.'

10. To be sure, Plato distrusts imitations, particularly those that appeal primarily to the senses, on the grounds that they tend to distort what they represent. But not every *mimēsis* is sensory: mathematical formulae represent relations among the most general and abstract forms; and the world of becoming is an imitation of the eternal world of forms, presumably because it represents or instantiates the structure of that world.

11. The prime example of a self-contained activity is contemplation. But perception and

thought are also star examples of *energeiai*. Not every activity is completed instantaneously; and many *energeiai* are also embedded within other activities. The animal activity of self-nourishment, for instance, standardly also involves perception. Some *energeiai* – particularly those that, like nourishment and reproduction, are the expression of natural, species-defining potentialities – involve temporally sequential stages that can only be identified by reference to the self-contained, completed activity in which they appear. A action qualifies as an activity only when its end is achieved in the performance: so for instance, the activity of reproduction has not occurred unless an offspring has been produced; nor has an animal engaged in the activity of nourishment unless it has absorbed the food it ate. Sometimes an activity encompasses actions and process-movements (*kinēseis*) as its stages or segments: as for instance, the action of eating and the process of digestion are part of the activity of self-nourishment; the action of impregnation and the processes of gestation are part of the activity of reproduction. But not evey action is encompassed within, and identified by an activity; nor is the aim of every type of action intrinsic to it, fulfilled in the very performance. The aims of some actions (those involved in building a house, for example) are external, detachable from the processes that produce them. Standardly *technai* involve movement-processes; and although processes usually take time to complete, some (hammering in a nail, for example) take place virtually instantaneously, without a significant lapse of time. The primary contrast between processes and activities lies in whether their ends are extrinsic or intrinsic, and only secondarily in their temporality.

12. Although Aristotle says that Sophocles brought tragedy to its perfection by representing the interaction of several actors, he unfortunately does not discuss the interactions among the several *prattontes* of tragic drama. Can several *prattontes* perform one action? On the one hand, the close connection between *prohairesis* and responsible action suggests that however complexly developed an action might be – complex enough to encompass a whole life – actions are fundamentally only attributable to individual agents. On the other hand, Aristotle sometimes also suggests that a jury or a Council can deliberate, choose and act.

13. A homely example may illustrate the point: We do not understand why a carpenter hammered a nail just as he did, at this place, at this angle, at this place, unless we see that action embedded in the series of actions that constitutes building a certain kind of a roof. We do not know why he built that kind of roof unless we know the intentions of the architect and his client. We do not know whether he built it well, unless we know that those intentions are well formed, that they not only reflect the real needs of the client, but also correctly take into account the effects of gravity, the stress on the materials, etc.

14. The *Poetics* passage – "Tragedy is a representation not of human beings but of action and a course of life. *Eudaimonia* and its opposite consist in action, and the end [of life] is a certain sort of action, rather than a character trait . . . It is according to their actions that they live well or the reverse" – is considered corrupt by G. F. Else, *Aristotle's Poetics* (Harvard, 1957) and R. Kassel (ed.), *Aristotelis de Arte Poetica Liber* (Oxford, 1965). But corrupt or not, the direction of the passage echoes *NE* 1095a19–20, 1098a20 ff. See Halliwell, *Aristotle's Poetics*, pp. 202–207; Nussbaum, *the Fragility of Goodness* (Cambridge, 1986), pp. 500–501; and Bittner, "One Action" (this volume) for convincing arguments for its legitimacy.

15. Cf. David Gallop. "Animals in the *Poetics*," *Oxford Studies in Ancient Philosophy* (1990), 145–171.

16. Action and character are conceptually interdependent and mutually expressive. The intentionality of action assures the embedding of a character-based *prohairesis* within the identification and description of an action. For specific explanatory purposes, an

analysis can stress the one or the other. Tragic drama expresses the priority of action, while moral education traces a sequence: a child practises certain kinds of actions for the sake of developing the sort of character that typically and habitually chooses and acts in a certain way. See Halliwell, *Aristotle's Poetics*, pp. 138–67, my "The Place of Psychology in Aristotle's *Rhetoric*" in J. Cleary, *Proceedings of the Boston Area Colloquium in Ancient Philosophy* (New York, 1991–2), and the essays by J.-P. Vernant ("Myth and Tragedy," this volume) and Mary Whitlock Blundell ("*Ethos* and *Dianoia* Reconsidered," this volume) for detailed accounts of the relations between thought, character and action.

17. Waywardness is a good, though perhaps somewhat archaic and suspiciously moralistic rendering. For a summary of discussions of *hamartia* see Gerald Else, *Aristotle's Poetics* (Cambridge, MA, 1967), pp. 378–85. See J.-P. Vernant ("Myth and Tragedy," this volume) for a discussion of the conection between the characterological and intellectual aspects of *hamartia*. See Eckart Schutrumpf. "Traditional Elements in the Concept of *Hamartia* in Aristotle's *Poetics*," *Harvard Studies in Classical Philology* (1989), 137–56 for an excellent account of the relevance of the discussions of voluntary actions and *hamartia* in *NE* 5.10. Schutrumpf convincingly argues that Aristotle's account of *hamartia* reflects his understanding of juridical concepts of criminal action, particularly those involving violent death.

18. Cf. J. Peter Euben, "Identity and *Oedipus Tyrannos*", in *Tragedy and Political Theory* (Princeton, 1990).

19. See Richard Wollheim, *Painting as an Art* (Princeton, 1988), for an extended discussion of the way that we, as external observers of painting, identify with an internal observer who is represented within the painting. Wollheim's discussion can be fruitfully transposed from painting to the literary arts. The contrast between agent and observer is fundamental, and not reducible to the contrast between emotion and thought (for there is emotion and thought on both sides); nor does it reduce to the contrast between the subjective and the objective points of view: for the chorus is not always objective, and the protagonist is not always merely subjective.

20. *Politics* I.1; *NE* 1155a12–22.

21. Cf. Halliwell, *Aristotle's Poetics*, Ch. 6; Martha Nussbaum, *The Fragility of Goodness* (Cambridge, 1986), esp. 378–391; S. H. Butcher, *Aristotle's Theory of Poetry and Fine Art* (London, 1907); G. Else, *Aristotle's Poetics* (Cambridge, MA, 1967).

22. Cf. Leon Golden, "The Clarification Theory of Catharsis," *Hermes* **104** (1967) 443–446; Halliwell, *Aristotle's Poetics*, pp. 184 ff.

23. Cf. Jacob Bernays' influential "Aristotle on the Effects of Tragedy," trans. J. and J. Barnes in *Articles on Aristotle*, Vol. 4, ed. J. Barnes, M. Schofield, and R. Sorabji (London, 1979); S. Halliwell, *Aristotle's Poetics*, pp. 184–201 and Jonathan Lear, "Katharsis," (this volume).

24. See Bennett Simon, *Mind and Madness in Ancient Greece* (Ithaca, 1978).

25. Cf. my "*Akrasia* and Pleasure: *Nicomachean Ethics* Book 7," in *Essays on Aristotle's Ethics* (Berkeley, CA, 1980).

26. For discussions of the variety of pleasures that attend tragic drama, see Halliwell, *Aristotle's Poetics*, pp. 62–81 and Elizabeth Belfiore, "Pleasure, Tragedy and Aristotelian Psychology," *Classical Quarterly* **35** (1985) 349–361.

27. There is an ancient, vigorous and apparently endless debate about whether the fundamental social function of drama is that it pleases or that it teaches. As far as tragedy goes, this is a false dichotomy: it pleases by teaching; it teaches by the ways it pleases. Aristotle adds that it mostly pleases ordinary folk, implying that it pleases the wise, largely by teaching (1448b4 ff.). Presumably that is because each type gets what it looks for. Cf. Halliwell, *Aristotle's Poetics*, pp. 62—81; Else, *Aristotle's Poetics*, pp. 127–134; Butcher, *Aristotle's Theory of Poetry and Fine Art*, Ch. 4.

28. *Politics* VIII 5, 1340a15 ff. "Since . . . virtue is concerned with delighting, loving and hating correctly, there is obviously nothing more important than to learn and to become habituated to judge correctly and to delight in decent character and fine actions." When drama gives us pleasures and pains in the appropriate representations of character and actions, it will enable us to take appropriate pleasures in the real things. "Habituation to feeling pain and delight in things that are like [the thing itself] is similar to being in that same state in relation to the truth. For instance, if someone delights in looking at the image of something . . . it [will] be pleasant for him to look at the thing itself . . ."

29. Aristotle does not limit the emotional effect of tragedies to the audiences of dramatic performances: they also affect those who hear or read the story. Still, the members of an audience of a dramatic performance have the further experience (*pathos*) of a certain kind of emotional bonding.

30. I am indebted to Stephen A. White's "Aristotle's Favorite Tragedies" (this volume) for emphasizing this aspect of what we learn from the best tragedies.

31. This paper arose from a conversation with Ruth Nevo; it developed in discussions with Stephen Engstrom, Stephen Halliwell, Henry Richardson and Stephen L. White. MindaRae Amiran, Mary Whitlock Blundell, Françoise Balibar, Elizabeth Belfiore, Rüdiger Bittner, Jennifer Church, David Gallop and Jens Kulenkampff gave me helpful comments, advice I did not always follow. I am also grateful to participants in colloquia at the University of New Hampshire, the University of Oregon, the University of California at Santa Barbara and the Hebrew University in Jerusalem. An earlier version was published in *Midwest Studies in Philosophy*, Vol. 15, eds. P. French, T. Vehling and H. Wettstein (Notre Dame, IN, 1992).

Aristotle on History and Poetry
(*Poetics*, 9, 1451a36–b11)[1]

G. E. M. de Ste. Croix

In a famous passage in Chapter 9 in the *Poetics* (1451a36–b11), Aristotle disparages history (*historia*) in comparison with poetry (*poiēsis*). He begins by stating that "the function of a poet is to describe not what has happened (*ta genomena*) but the kind of thing that might happen,[2] and what is possible according to probability or necessity" (*hoia an genoito, kai ta dunata kata to eikos ē to anangkaion*). He goes on to say that the distinction between historian and poet (*historikos* and *poiētēs*) resides not in the one writing prose and other verse (for the work of Herodotus, he says, if put into verse, would still be history) but "in the fact that the one [history] describes what has happened, the other [poetry] what might happen." The conclusion he proceeds to draw is that "poetry is something more philosophic and more worthwhile (*spoudaioteron*) than history, because poetry deals rather with universals, history with particulars" (*hē men gar poiēsis mallon ta katholou, hē d' historia ta kath' hekaston legei*). And Aristotle goes on to explain what he means by "universals" and "particulars:" universal statements are about what a particular kind of man will say or do "according to probability or necessity:" particular statements are about "what Alcibiades did or had done to him."

This passage is perfectly explicit and unqualified, and it is wrong to seek to explain it away, for example by dragging in *Poetics* 23, 1459a21–24, where Aristotle refers to "our usual histories (*historias tas sunētheis*),[3] which have to set forth not one action but one period, and all that happened during that period concerning one or more persons, however disconnected the several events may have been." This passage leaves open the possibility that there may be histories of a different, less usual, kind. Some may also think here of another passage in *Poetics* 9 (1451b29–33), where Aristotle mentions that a poet who takes his subject from actual history is none the less a poet for that, "since there is nothing to prevent some historic occurrences from being such as happen in the probable and possible order of things, and it is in that aspect of them that he is their poet." But even if we take into account the possibility that in Aristotle's mind there was more than one kind of history, and that some historical events might be conceived as illustrating the possible, the probable, even the necessary, we are left with a definite assertion, in the passage in _Poetics_ 9 with which we began, about the relationship of poetry in general and history in general: poetry is more philosophic and more worthwhile than history. I fancy that most people would agree with a recent statement: "To us this seems a very strange conclusion, but it is entirely consistent with Aristotle's view-point. In real life any chain of events is influenced by chance and accident. But the poet can and should represent an ideal sequence of events, the events as they would occur according to the general rules governing human behaviour."[4] And an article on Aristotle's use of the word _historia_ expresses a view which I think most Aristotelians would hold: that in so far as _historia_ in Aristotle can sometimes mean "knowledge" rather than (as usual) "history," or "research," "enquiry," it refers to knowledge of particular facts only, not qualifying in Aristotle's eyes as a proper science, _epistēmē_.[5]

My purpose here is to argue that although our _Poetics_ passage is indeed consistent with views expressed by Aristotle when he is speaking loosely, yet if we take account of a number of important but much-neglected passages in which Aristotle defines his terms with more than usual care, we must admit that his disparagement of history is not entirely justified on his own principles, at any rate in so far as it refers to the historian whom he is likely to have had most in mind when describing history as "what Alcibiades did or had done to him:" namely, Thucydides. This will involve our taking notice of a concept which appears on numerous occasions in Aristotle but is too often ignored altogether, or given scant attention, by philosophers: _to hōs epi to polu_, which I shall consistently translate "the as a general rule." ("The usual," "normal," "habitual" would often represent the meaning well enough, but the awkward phrase I have deliberately chosen provides the nearest parallel I can think of in English to the rather curious Greek expression, which in its substantival form – not just _hōs epi to polu_, which is common enough[6] – I have not encountered outside the works of Aristotle.) It is a main aim of this essay to stimulate discussion of the rôle played by _to hōs epi to polu_ in Aristotle's thought, a question which seems to me to need a thorough investigation, by someone interested in Aristotle as a scientist and not merely as a philosopher. In the major works on Aristotle which I have consulted, I have found nothing more than passing remarks on this subject.[7]

The distinction drawn in _Poetics_ 9, between "the universal," _ta katholou_, and "the particular," _ta kath' hekaston_, is used by Aristotle in different connections and in different senses.[8] If we neglect the passages concerned with _to hōs epi to_ *polu*, we can easily suppose it to be a fundamental element in Aristotle's thought that full scientific knowledge, *epistēmē*,[9] is only of "the universal,"[10] and of "the necessary," *to ex anangkēs*,[11] something that "cannot be other than what it is."[12] These two ideas, "the universal" and "the necessary", are closely connected, as are those of "the particular" and "the accidental" or "the contingent," for universal attributes are treated as those which belong necessarily (*ex anangkēs*) to their subjects,[13] and the universal is also treated as "the always and every-where," *to aei kai pantakhou*,[14] and is contrasted with "the accidental" or "the contingent," *to sumbebēkos*,[15] which is commonly found opposed to "the neces-sary." At least, that is the way in which Aristotle's thought on the subject of *epistēmē* is commonly conceived and presented – and when it is so conceived, it can be used as part of the justification for the statement in *Poetics* 9 which we are considering, placing poetry above history: whether or not Aristotle is right in the way he characterizes poetry and history respectively, what he says will at least be consistent with his general philosophical position. In fact, however, the conception of *epistēmē* as being appropriate only to "the universal" and "the necessary" oversimplifies and seriously misrepresents the main stream of Aristotle's thinking. Even in *Poetics* 9 it will be noticed that the "universal" statements of poetry are defined as being what will happen not merely *necessarily* but also *probably* (*kata to eikos*). It is at this point that we must seriously consider Aristotle's concept of *to hōs epi to polu*, "the as a general rule," the usual, the normal, the habitual. This appears very frequently: it can be found at least in the *De Interpretatione*, in the *Analytics* both *Prior* and *Posterior*, in the *Topics*, the *Physics*, *Metaphysics Δ*, E, and K, the *De Generatione et Corruptione*, the *Generation of Animals*, the *Parts of Animals*, the *Ethics*, and the *Rhetoric*.

At the end of *Metaphysics Δ* (a book consisting almost entirely of definitions)[16] Aristotle employs a classification which is not the twofold one we have noticed already, into attributes which are either necessary or accidental (*ex anangkēs* or *sumbebēkos*), but threefold: he adds to the other two "the as a general rule". In the next book of the *Metaphysics*[17] the same threefold classification appears, and here it is specifically recognized that full scientific knowledge is possible not only of "the always" but also of "the as a general rule" (*epistēmē pasa ē tou aei ē tou hōs epi to polu*, 1027a20–21). And Aristotle adds an example: it is true as a general rule that honey-water (*to melikraton*) is useful for a patient suffering from fever. In *Metaphysics* K he is equally explicit, and again *epistēmē pasa* is either of what exists always or of "the as a general rule."[18]

In discussing the presentation of arguments, in the *Topics*,[19] Aristotle again distinguishes three types of events: not only those occurring of necessity or "as it may chance to happen" (*hopoter' etukhen*,[20] a synonym for *to sumbebēkos*), but also those which occur "as a general rule;" and elsewhere in the *Topics*,[21] as on one occasion in the *Posterior Analytics*,[22] he draws the same distinction, adding in each case to the words *hōs epi to polu* the explanatory phrase "and in most cases" (*kai en tois pleistois*). On another occasion in the *Posterior Analytics* Aristotle also introduces this threefold distinction, asserting that there can be no *epistēmē* by demonstration of chance conjunctions, for these exist neither by necessity nor as a general rule, and demonstration (*apodeixis*) is concerned with one or other of these two.[23]

Aristotle also makes use of the same threefold classification at several points in *Physics* 2.[24] First (5, 196b10–21, especially 10–13) he emphasizes that chance (*hē tukhē*) cannot be said to be the cause either of things which always happen in the same way (*ta aei hōsautōs ginomena*) or of "the as a general rule," nor can the effect of chance be identified with any of the things that come about either by necessity and always (*ex anangkēs kai aei*) or as a general rule. We can account for what exists always or as a general rule, whereas chance is in a different category (197a18–20). In another passage (7, 198b5–6), on the causes of motion, he is prepared to speak of a result following either "without qualification" (*haplōs*) or "as a general rule" under the heading of "necessity" (*anangkē*). And a little later (8, 198b34–36) he speaks of natural things like teeth as coming about in a particular way either always or "as a general rule," distinguishing them from things which arise "by chance or spontaneously" (*apo tukhēs kai tou automatou*).[25] Düring cites this passage as introducing the concept of "das statistisch Normale,"[26] and he makes an apposite reference to *De Caelo* 3.2, 301a5–9, where Aristole says that the nature (*phusis*) of things is "that which most of them possess for most of the time" (*hoian ekhei ta pleiō kai ton pleiō khronon*). There are several other passages which also need to be cited in this connection. *Generation of Animals* 1.19, 727b29–30 asserts that "it is what occurs as a general rule that is most in accord with the course of nature" (*malista kata phusin*); and 4.7, 777a18–21, ends with an identification of what is according to nature with "the as a general rule" (*to kata phusin esti to hōs epi to polu*). According to *Parts of Animals* 3.2, 663b27–29, "in studying nature we must consider the majority of cases, for it is what occurs in every case (*en tōi panti*) or as a general rule that is in accord with nature (*kata phusin*). In *Rhetoric*, 1.10, 1369a35—b2, things that happen by nature (*phusei*) are said to occur either always or as a general rule.[27] In the *Prior Analytics* 1.3, 25b14–15, Aristotle again identifies "the as a general rule" and the natural (together defining "the possible") by using the words *hosa de tōi hōs epi to polu kai tōi pephu-kenai legetai endekhesthai, kath' hon tropon diorizomen to endekhomenon*. In a rather difficult passage in *Generation of Animals* 4.4, 770b9–13, he speaks of monstrosities as occurring contrary to nature "as she is as a general rule," distinguished from "the nature which is always and by necessity;" such unnatural occurrences, he says, are to be found only within the category of "the as a general rule," of things which might have been otherwise.

In an important passage near the beginning of the *Nicomachean Ethics* (*NE*) Aristotle shows his acumen as a scientist by pointing out that in discussing some topics we are obliged to begin with *ta hōs epi to polu* and must then come to conclusions of the same order: an educated man is one who strives for that degree of precision in each branch of knowledge which the nature of the subject admits.[28]

In several contexts in the *Analytics* Aristotle employs the concept of "the as a general rule."[29] The most interesting, perhaps, is *Posterior Analytics* 2.12, 96a8–19 (especially 8–11, 15), where Aristotle opposes what is "as a general rule" to the universal (*to katholou*), defined as what happens "always and in every case."[30] There are some other pasages making use of the notion of "the as a general rule" which do not need to be mentioned separately.[31]

It is time to explain the relevance of Aristotle's concept of "the as a general rule" for the passage in *Poetics* with which we began. I am going to argue first that Aristotle, in writing that passage, must surely have had in mind precisely the historian whom many people might wish to exempt from his strictures about history dealing only with particulars: namely, Thucydides. I shall also argue that since Thucydides dealt very much with "the as a general rule" and with behavior that was characteristic of human nature, Aristotle, on his own principles, ought not to have given "what Alcibiades did or had done to him" as an illustration of the essential character of history.

When Aristotle chose that illustration, he must at least have had Thucydides in mind among others, and indeed was probably thinking mainly of Thucydides, who was the prime source of information about the earlier years in which Alcibiades played an important part on the political stage. Many scholars have found it puzzling that whereas Aristotle makes numerous references to Herodotus[32] (whom he calls *ho muthologos*, the storyteller[33]), and also makes use of his work without naming him, he never once mentions Thucydides – or, for that matter, other historians who were much read in his day, such as Xenophon, Ephorus, Theopompus, and Aristotle's relative Callisthenes, or even the early Atthidographers whose works he undoubtedly used: Hellanicus, Cleidemus and Androtion. I believe nevertheless that Aristotle had certainly read Thucydides.[34] Alcibiades of course plays a very important role in Books 5, 6, and 8 of Thucydides, who describes his activities over a period of some ten years, from 421 to 411 B.C.; and anyone referring to "what Alcibiades did or had done to him" is far more likely to have had that period primarily in mind than the remaining seven years of Alcibiades' life (nearly half of them spent in exile), the main authorities for which, in Aristotle's day, will have been Xenophon's *Hellenica* and the Oxyrhynchus historian whose continuation of Thucydides is nowadays seen to have been a main source for Ephorus.[35] There is not a very great deal about Alcibiades in Xenophon's *Hellenica*, and it seems unlikely that the Oxyrhynchus historian can have had much more to say.

We are left, then, with the probability that in his selection of a characteristic example of history Aristotle chose to speak of events the main source for which in his day (as in ours) can only have been Thucydides, the one historian who, in the opinion of most of us, is least open to the charge of merely relating particular events and failing to deal with universals, with "what might happen."

I have discussed Thucydides at length elsewhere[36] and have argued that one of the dominant ideas in his work is the consistency of human behavior, and the belief that by studying precisely how human nature has worked in a great number of actual cases one can form a good general idea of it and then proceed to deduce what is likely to happen in a particular situation with which one is confronted. Thucydides understood, as much as anyone, that the course of events is always liable to be disturbed by sheer chance (*tuchē*),[37] by the unpredictable and incalculable (*ho paralogos, to astathmēton*);[38] but he nevertheless realized that the study of past events can give understanding of how men are *likely to behave*, and can therefore provide a useful guide to action in the present. The constancy of human nature ensures that *patterns of behavior will tend to recur*. This is the origin and the justification of Thucydides' claim (1.22.4) that his own History will be "useful" and "a possession for ever." One of the most remarkable features of Thucydides' work is that its "lessons" (if such a term is permissible) are implicit in the narrative and do not need to be spelt out in the History in general terms. As one of the greatest of English philosophers said of him, "Digressions for instruction's cause, and other such open conveyances of precepts, (which is the philosopher's part), he never useth; as having so clearly set before men's eyes the ways and events of good and evil counsels, that the narrative itself doth secretly instruct the reader, and more effectually than can possibly be done by precept."[39]

My conclusion about the interpretation of our *Poetics* passage is as follows. We have seen that the rigid dichotomy which Aristotle sometimes establishes, as in *Poetics* 9, 1451b6–9, between the universal and the particular (as elsewhere between the necessary and the contingent or accidental) is often relaced by a three-term distinction, with "the as a general rule" appearing in the middle; and when this occurs, "the as a general rule" is closer to the universal and the necessary than to the particular or contingent, in that it too is conceived as an appropriate subject of *epistēmē*. Now in *Poetics* 9, 1451b8–9, Aristotle surprisingly defines the universal in terms of *probability* as well as necessity; and this surely entitles us to complain that on his own principles the distinction he ought to have drawn here was his threefold one, between, on the one hand, the universal *or "the as a general rule"* (which may indeed be concerned with probabilities), and on the other hand, the particular. If this is so, then, especially if we may take Aristotle to be thinking in the first place of Thucydides, he ought not to have written off history as dealing only with particulars, even if it does partly concern itself with "what Alcibiades did or had done to him." The poet, according to Aristotle, speaks of "what is possible according to probability or necessity." But what the poet actually *says* is concerned with a particular action: if we are to derive *epistēmē* from it, in Aristotle's sense, we have to take the further step of recognizing the general (the universal or the necessary) in the particular. Is there any essential difference in what we make of the History of Thucydides? I believe not, once we are allowed to introduce the concept of *to hōs epi to polu* and take account of the fact that that is precisely what Thucydides often offers us. Even on Aristotle's own premises, therefore, it is possible to think that his disparagement of history in the *Poetics* is not fully justified.

I prefer the explanation I have given of the *Poetics* passage to that of Pippidi, who in an interesting article published in 1948 argued that Aristotle, when he wrote the passage we are considering, was not thinking of Thucydides *as a historian.*[40] Pippidi would thus exempt the work of Thucydides from Aristotle's strictures, but only by (so to speak) transferring Thucydides from the Faculty of History, where he surely belongs, to that of Political Philosophy.

I would emphasize, in conclusion, that in *Poetics* 9 history is not absolutely disparaged: it is merely said to be less philosophic and worthwhile than poetry. To reinforce this observation it is well to recall the fact that Aristotle himself wrote a very considerable amount of what we should call historical work, even if he doubtless produced some of it with the help of pupils. First, if we may take the *Athenaion Politeia* as a characteristic example of the 158 *Politeiai* (constitutions of individual states) with which Aristotle is credited,[41] then each of these works will have begun with an account of how the constitution in question reached the form it had in Aristotle's day. He would have been entitled to say of these works that here he was not writing a mere narrative of random events, about "what so-and-so did or had done to him," but was describing the life processes of creatures, a series of human societies:[42] this, he might have said, was what he had in mind when he referred to ordinary histories as "our usual histories" in *Poetics* 23.[43] Aristotle was also responsible for the *List of Victors at the Pythian Games,* the compilation of which by Aristotle himself and his relative Callisthenes is proved beyond doubt by a Delphic inscription;[44] the *List of Olympic Victors,*[45] the genuineness of which, accepted in antiquity, is made highly probable by the certainty that Aristotle compiled a similar Pythian list; the *Didaskaliai* and *Nikai Dionysiakai,* which were also victor-lists;[46] the *Nomima* or *Nomima Barbarika;*[47] the *Dikaiomata* or *Dikaiomata Poleon;*[48] and perhaps the *Hypomnemata,* which may well have been (like the *Nomoi,* in no less than 24 Books) a joint work of Aristotle and Theophrastus, although ultimately published in the name of the latter.[49] The existence of such works is a sufficient refutation of the view that is to be found in some modern works, that Aristotle was merely a philosopher and so must not be treated seriously as a historian.[50] He evidently saw research into historical facts as a necessary condition, though not of course a sufficient condition, of full scientific knowledge of human society.[51]

I am very glad to have this opportunity of paying tribute to "Tom Brown" Stevens, whose teaching of the "Greats" pupils in Magdalen and New College whom we shared for nearly twenty years, from 1953 to 1972, was both devoted and inspiring.

Notes

1. I wish to acknowledge some useful criticisms of the draft of this essay, by G. E. L. Owen and by two other philosophers who were once my pupils in Ancient History: Edward Hussey and Terence Irwin. If I have not made the best use of their comments, the fault is entirely mine.

2. Others might perhaps translate "could happen" or "would happen."

3. I accept the MS text *sunētheis* and rather prefer the MS *einai* to Bywater's emendation, *theinai*. I need only refer to R. Weil, *Aristote et l'histoire: Essai sur la "Politique"* (Paris, 1960), pp. 163–176, esp. 170–173. As for other readings and their translations, it should be sufficient to refer to two standard works: I. Bywater, *Aristotle on the Art of Poetry* (Oxford, 1909), pp. 70–73, 305–306; and G. F. Else, *Aristotle's Poetics: The Argument* (Cambridge, MA, 1957), pp. 569–579.

4. G. E. R. Lloyd, *Aristotle: The Growth and Structure of his Thought* (Cambridge, 1968), p. 276.

5. P. Louis, "Le mot ΙΣΤΟΡΙΑ chez Aristote," *Revue de Philologie.*, Ser. 2, **29** (1955) 39–44, esp. 44 and n.1.

6. See e.g. Thucydides 2.13.3; 6.46.4; Plato, *Politicus* 294e; Isocrates 12.165; 15.271; and many other examples, including of course some in Aristotle himself, e.g. *Hist. An.* 7.3, 583b3, 8; *NE* 3.1, 1110a31–32; 8.13, 1161a27; *Rhetoric* 1.10, 1369a34; *Politics* 4.4, 1291b9–10.

7. See e.g. J. M. Le Blond, *Logique et méthode chez Aristote*, 2nd edn (Paris, 1970), p. 79 ("la curieuse notion du *hōs epi to polu*, qui joue un rôle assez notable dans les recherches d'Aristote"); I. Düring, *Aristoteles, Darstellung und Interpretation seines Denkens* (Heidelberg, 1966), as cited in n. 26 below. In some other well-known books on Aristotle I have found nothing relevant. The only treatment of the subject at length that I have been able to discover is the able article by J. Barnes, "Aristotle's Theory of Demonstration," *Phronesis* **14** (1969) 123–151 (especially 133–137), which came to my notice only when this essay was completed and overdue.

8. See e.g. *De Interpret.* 7, 17a38–b1, and other passages cited by H. Bonitz, *Index Aristotelicus* (Berlin, 1870 and Graz, 1955), p. 356b32–38.

9. Only in *Metaphysics* M 10, 1087a10–25 (a very difficult passage) does Aristotle expressly qualify this, to apply to knowledge *dunamei* rather than *energeiāi*.

10. E.g. *Posterior Analytics* 1.31, 87b37–39; 33, 88b30–31; *NE* 6.6, 1140b31–32 (cf. 10.9, 1180b15–16: *tou koinou*); *De Anima* 2.5, 417a22–23; *Metaphysics* B 6, 1003a14–15; K 1, 1059b26; 2, 1060b20–21 (*tōn katholou kai tou toioudi*); M 9, 1086b5–6; 10, 1086b33.

11. E.g. *NE* 6.3, 1139b22–23; 6, 1140b31–32. Cf. *Posterior Analytics* 1.33, 88b31.

12. E.g. *Posterior Analytics* 1.2, 71b15–16; 4, 73a21; 6, 74b6; 33, 88b30–32 ("the necessary cannot be otherwise").

13. *Posterior Analytics* 1.4, 73b26–29. On the exceptionally strict sense of *katholou* here, see W. D. Ross, *Aristotle's Prior and Posterior Analytics* (Oxford, 1949) pp. 522–523.

14. *Posterior Analytics* 1.31, 87b32–33; cf. 2.12, 96a8–9 (*aei . . . kai epi pantos*), 15 (*kai epi panti kai aei*).

15. As in *Metaphysics* Δ 9, 1017b35–18a2. Aristotle's fullest definition of *to sumbebēkos* is in *Topics* 1.5, 102b4–26.

16. *Metaphysics* Δ 30, 1025a14–21 (especially 14–15, 20–21). Many people seem prepared to accept this book as Aristotelian, even if it could originally have been a separate work; but there are those who reject it as un-Aristotelian.

17. *Metaphysics* E 2, 1026b24–37 (especially 31–33, 35–37), 1027a8–26 (especially 8–11, 15–17, 19–24, 25–26). Whether this book is actually by Aristotle is disputed. Many scholars have accepted it; and those who have seen in it the hand of a redactor

have usually accepted the material as Aristotelian, even if it has been rearranged by someone else – e.g. Andronicus, in the opinion of Düring, *Aristoteles. Darstellung und Interpretation* (n. 7), pp. 587–589, 592–593.

18. *Metaphysics* K 8, 1064b30–65a6 (esp. 1064b32–36, 1065a1–3, 3–6).
19. *Topics* 2.6, 112b1–18 (esp. 1–2, 14–15).
20. Cf. *hopōs etukhen* in *Metaphysics* K 8, 1064b36; *apo tukhēs* in *Posterior Analytics* 1.30, 87b19–27; *Physics* 2.7, 198b36–9a2.
21. *Topics* 5.1, 129a6–13.
22. *Posterior Analytics* 1.14, 79a17–28.
23. *Posterior Analytics* 1.30, 87b19–27.
24. *Physics* 2.5, 196b10–21 (esp. 10–13); 7, 198b5–6; 8, 198b34–36.
25. Cf. *De Caelo* 1.12, 283a31–b2; *De Gen. et Corr.* 2.6, 333b4–7.
26. Düring, *Aristoteles. Darstellung und Interpretation* (n. 7), p. 239, n. 372. Cf. pp. 331 and n. 262, 491 and n. 381 ("die statistische Wahrheit die gute Wahrheit ist").
27. Cf. *De Gen. et Corr.* 2.6, 333b4–7.
28. *NE* 1.1(3), 1094b19–27.
29. *Prior Analytics* 1.3, 25b14–15; 13, 32b4–10 (where it is the opposite of *to anangkaion* and *ex anangkēs*); 27, 43b32–36; *Posterior Analytics* 1.14, 79a17–22; 30, 87b19–27 (esp. 20–21, 25–27: here *to hōs epi to polu* is distinguished both from what is *anangkaion* and from *to apo tukhēs*).
30. Aristotle is very emphatic: he has *aei . . . kai epi pantos* twice (lines 8–9, 14) and in line 15 *touto gar esti to katholou, to epi panti kai aei*.
31. E.g. *De Interpret.* 9, 19a18–22; *Rhetoric* 1.2, 1356b15–17, 1357a22–32; 2.19, 1392b31–32; *Hist. An.* 6.17, 571a26–27.
32. Not only in the *Ath. Pol.* (14.4), but also in the *Poetics, Rhetoric, EE, Hist. An.*, and *Gen. An.*: see Weil, *Aristote et l'histoire* (n. 3), p. 313, n. 20, repeating the list in Bonitz, *Index Aristotelicus* (n. 8), p. 320. Add *Hist. An.* 8.18, 601b1, where most MSS have "Hesiod".
33. Aristotle, *Gen. An.* 3.5, 756b6–7. Perhaps he was thinking of such statements as the one in Her. 3.101.2, that the semen of Ethiopians is black, which he contradicts in *Gen. An.* 2.2, 736a10–13.
34. I base this belief not so much on possible parallels such as those listed by Weil, *Aristote et l'histoire* (n. 3), p. 312, n. 4 (e.g. between *Ath. Pol.* 18.4 and Thucydides 6.58.2), as on the close verbal correspondence of certain passages dealing with the events of 411 B.C. (which of course Aristotle had more reason to study when writing the *Ath. Pol.* than anything else in Thucydides), in particular (1) the references to Euboea in *Ath. Pol.* 33.1 (lines 28–29 OCT) and Thucydides 8. 96.2; 95.7; (2) *Ath. Pol.* 32.2 and Thucydides 8.68 (where the names occur in the same order and the description corresponds); (3) the characterization of the government of the Five Thousand in *Ath. Pol.* 33.2 and Thucydides 8.97.2; and (4) the 100 years in *Ath. Pol.* 32.2 (line 12 OCT) and Thucydides 8.68.4 (lines 27 ff. OCT); and most of all on the appearance in Aristotle, *Politics* 5.4, 1304b10–15, of the Thucydidean picture of the revolution of the Four Hundred, so very different from Aristotle's account in *Ath. Pol.* 29–33. (I shall argue elsewhere that the latter account reflects a change of opinion, influenced very probably by the *Apology* of Antiphon and the *Atthis* of Androtion.)
35. The best acount of Alcibiades is by J. Hatzfeld, *Alcibiade*, 2nd edn (Paris, 1951).
36. In *The Origins of the Peloponnesian War* (London, 1972), pp. 5–33. When I wrote that book I had not read A. Parry, "The Language of Thucydides' Description of the Plague," *Bulletin of the [London University] Institute of Classical Studies* **16** (1969) 106–118, who makes some useful points against the exaggerated claims of Cochrane, Weidauer, and others concerning Thucydides' intellectual debt to the Hippocratic writers and his employment of the medical vocabulary of the age, but is

himself guilty of indefensible exaggeration of the views he attacks – as when, in his last sentence, he actually accuses his opponents of trying to persuade us that Thucydides saw the great Plague of Athens as "a thing subject to rational human control"! It is on the basis of exaggerations of this sort that Parry feels able to go to the opposite pole and pretend that Thucydides did not intend his work to have any practical usefulness – a point of view which I think I have sufficiently refuted in *The Origins of the Peloponnesian War*, pp. 29–33.

37. See *Ste. Croix, Origins of the Peloponnesian War*, p. 31, n. 57.
38. See *Ste. Croix, Origins of the Peloponnesian War*, pp. 30–31, with 25 and n. 52.
39. T. Hobbes, as cited in *Ste. Croix, Origins of the Peloponnesian War*, p. 28.
40. D. M. Pippidi, "Aristote et Thucydide. En marge du chapitre IX de la *Poétique*," in *Mélanges . . . offerts à J. Marouzeau* (Paris, 1948), pp. 483–490. Pippidi would suppose that Aristotle saw in Thucydides' History "*non pas la chronique d'une guerre, quelle que fût son importance, mais un essai de philosophie politique,* fondé sur la conviction (qui était également sienne) que les mêmes causes engendrent toujours les mêmes effets" (pp. 489–490). [Pippidi's emphasis.]
41. The fullest discussion is that of Weil, *Aristote et l'histoire* (n. 3), esp. pp. 97–116.
42. Note the interesting analogy Aristotle draws between different species of animals and different forms of constitutions, in *Politics* 4.4, 1290b25–38.
43. See the beginning of the second paragraph of this essay. Contrast the attitude of Wilamowitz, *Aristoteles und Athen* (Berlin, 1893), who said that after the publication of the London papyrus of the *Ath. Pol.* Aristotle "fortan nicht mehr als Historiker gelten darf," and that he "kein geschichtlicher Forster ist" (I. 373); "in diesem Buche [the *Ath. Pol.*] wirklich geschichtliche Forschung so gut wie gar nicht steckt' (I. 308). These judgments have recently been quoted with approval by J. Day and M. Chambers, *Aristotle's History of Athenian Democracy*, University of California Publications in History, vol. 73 (Berkeley and Los Angeles, 1962), who seem to view Aristotle primarily as a philosopher who would not hesitate to make historical distortions and even inventions dictated by his *a priori* philosophical theories – a point of view with which I deeply disagree. I cannot resist quoting here the unintentionally comic remark by J. Zürcher, *Aristoteles' Werk und Geist* (Paderborn, 1952), p. 258, that Aristotle must have conceived the idea of collecting constitutions at an early stage in his development: "es passt ja sogar besser in die vorphilosophische Periode eines Mensch"!
44. M.N. Tod, *Greek Historical Inscriptions*, Vol. II, no. 187 = W. Dittenberger, *Sylloge Inscriptionum Graecarum*, 3rd edn., no. 275. For the date, see D. M. Lewis, *Classical Review*, N.S, **8** (1958) 108. See also Weil, *Aristote et l'histoire* (n. 3), pp. 133–137.
45. See Weil, *Aristote et l'histoire*, pp. 131–133.
46. See Weil, *Aristote et l'histoire*, pp. 137–139.
47. See Weil, *Aristote et l'histoire*, pp. 116–121.
48. See Weil, *Aristote et l'histoire*, pp. 127–130.
49. See Weil, *Aristote et l'histoire*, p. 130; and H. Bloch, "Studies in Historical Literature of the Fourth Century B.C.", in *Athenian Studies Presented to W. S. Ferguson (Harvard Studies in Classical Philology*, Suppl. I, 1940), pp. 355–376.
50. Cf. n. 43 above.
51. Cf. the famous passage in *Part. An.* 1.5, 644b22–5a36.

Myth and Tragedy*

Jean-Pierre Vernant

Greek tragedy is strongly marked by a number of characteristics: tension between myth and the forms of thought peculiar to the city, conflict within man, within the domain of values, the world of the gods, and the ambiguous and equivocal character of language. But perhaps the essential feature that defines it is that the drama brought to the stage unfolds both at the level of everyday existence, in a human, opaque time made up of successive and limited present moments, and also beyond this earthly life, in a divine, omnipresent time that at every instant encompasses the totality of events, sometimes to conceal them and sometimes to make them plain, but always so that nothing escapes it or is lost in oblivion. Though this constant union and configuration between the time of men and the time of the gods, throughout the drama, the play startlingly reveals that the divine intervenes even in the course of human actions.

Aristotle notes that tragedy is the imitation of an action, *mimēsis praxeōs*. It presents characters engaged in action, *prattontes*. And the word "drama" comes from the Doric *dran* that corresponds to the Attic *prattein*, to act. In effect, in contrast to epic and lyric, where the category of action is not represented since man is never envisaged as an agent, tragedy presents individuals engaged in action. It places them at the crossroads of a choice in which they are totally committed; it shows them on the threshold of a decision, asking themselves what is the best course to take. "Pylades what shall I do [*Puladē, ti drasō*]?" cries Orestes in the *choephori*[1] and Pelasgus, at the beginning of the *Suppliants*[2] reflects: "I do not know what to do; my heart is gripped in anguish; should I take action or not?" But the king immediately goes on to say someting that, taken in conjunction with the preceding lines, underlines the polarity of tragic action:

---

* Selections from J.-P. Vernant, *Myth and Society*, trans. J. Lloyd (Cambridge, MA, 1980), pp. 203–204, 206–208, 213–214, and from J.-P. Vernant in J.-P. Vernant and P. Vidal-Naquet, *Myth and Tragedy*, trans. J. Lloyd (Cambridge, MA, 1988), pp. 32–34, 36–37, 43–48.

"To act or not to act and tempt fate [*te kai tukēn helein*]?" To tempt fate: in the tragic writers, human action is not, of itself, strong enough to do without the power of the gods, not autonomous enough to be fully conceived without them. Without their presence and their support it is nothing – either abortive or producing results quite other than those initially envisaged. So it is a kind of wager – on the future, on fate and on oneself, ultimately a wager on the gods for whose support one hopes. In this game, where he is not in control, man always risks being trapped by his own decisions. The gods are incomprehensible to him. When, as a precaution before taking action, he consults them and they deign to answer, their reply is as equivocal and ambiguous as the situation on which he asked for their advice (*Myth and Tragedy*, pp. 43–44).

In contrast, tragedy creates a distance between the characters that it depicts upon the stage and the public who are its spectators. The tragic hero belongs to a different world from the world of the city and to a different age from fifth-century Athens. It is only by relegating them to a far-distant past, a legendary, other time outside the present, that the democratic *polis* can integrate into its own culture the dramas that tore apart those royal houses and the misfortunes and ancestral curses that beset them. The effect of the theatrical presentation, the costumes, the special buskins, the masks and, in sum, their larger-than-life characters was to remove these figures to the level of the legendary heroes to whom cults were devoted in the city. Yet, at the same time, by reason of the familiar, almost prosaic way they spoke and the discussions they entered into with the chorus and with each other, they were brought closer to the ordinary man and were made, as it were, the contemporaries of the citizens of Athens who crowded the stepped banks of the theater. Because of this constant tension and opposition between the mythical past and the present of the *polis* that operates within each drama and each protagonist, the hero ceases to be regarded, as he was in Pindar, as a model and becomes instead an object of debate. He is brought before the public as a subject at issue. Through the debate that the drama sets up, it is the very status of man that becomes the problem. The enigma of the human condition is brought into question, not that the inquiry pursued by tragedy, ever started anew and never completed, can find any resolution or definitive answer. Myth, in its original form, provided answers without ever explicitly formulating the problems. When tragedy takes over the mythical traditions, it uses them to pose problems to which there are no solutions.

The Greek word *muthos* means formulated speech, whether it be a story, a dialogue, or the enunciation of a plan. So *muthos* belongs to the domain of *legein*, as such compound expressions as *mutholegein* and *muthologia* show, and does not originally stand in contrast to *logoi*, a term that has a closely related semantic significance and that is concerned with the different forms of what is said. Even when, in the form of stories about the gods or heroes, the words transmit a strong religious charge, communicating to a group of initiates secret knowledge forbidden to the common crowd, *muthoi* can equally well be called *hieroi logoi*, sacred speeches. Between the eighth and fourth centuries B.C. a whole series of interrelated conditions caused a multiplicity of differentiations, breaks, and internal tensions within the mental universe of the Greeks that were responsible for distinguishing the domain of myth from other domains: the concept of myth peculiar to classical antiquity thus became clearly defined through the setting up of an opposition between *muthos* and *logos*, henceforth seen as separate and contrasting terms (*Myth and Society*, pp. 203–204).

The functional difference between speech and writing has a direct bearing on the position of myth. If the tendency of the spoken word is to give pleasure, this is because it affects the listener in the manner of an incantation. Through its metrical form, its rhythm, its consonances, its musicality, and the gestures or the dances that sometimes accompany it, oral narration stimulates its public to an affective communion with the dramatic actions recounted in the story. This magic quality of speech, which Gorgias celebrated and which confers the same kind of power upon various types of oral pronouncement – poetry, tragedy, rhetoric, and sophistry – is considered by the Greeks to be one of the specific qualities of *muthos* as opposed to *logos*. By deliberately foregoing drama and the marvelous, the *logos* acts upon the mind at a different level from an operation involving *mimēsis* or emotional participation (*sumpatheia*) on the part of the audience. Its purpose is to establish the truth following a scrupulous inquiry and to express it in a manner that should, by rights at least, appeal to the reader's critical intelligence alone. It is only when it has thus assumed the written form that a discourse, divested of its mystery and, at the same time, of its suggestive force, loses the power to impose itself on others through the illusory but irrepressible constraint of *mimēsis*. Its status is thereby changed: It becomes something "common," in the sense that this term had in Greek political vocabulary. No longer is it the exclusive privilege of whoever possesses the gift of eloquence; now it belongs equally to all the members of the community. To put a text in writing is to set down one's message *es meson*, at the center of the community – that is, to place it openly at the disposal of the group as a whole. By being written down, the *logos* is brought into the public square; like magistrates who have just discharged their duties, it must now give an account of itself before all and sundry and justify itself in the face of the objections and challenges that anyone has the right to bring against it. Thus, it can be said that the rules of political intercourse, as they function in a democratic city governed by *isegoria*, an equal right to speech for all, have also become the rules for intellectual intercourse. The internal organization of written discourse conforms with a logic that henceforward implies a form of debate in which each man fights on equal terms, through discussion and counter-argument. It is no longer a matter of overcoming one's opponent by spell-binding, or fascinating him with one's own superior power over the spoken word. It is now a matter of convincing him of the truth by gradually inducing his own internal discourse to fall into agreement, according to his own logic and criteria, with the reasons put forward in the text presented to him. Seen in this perspective, everything that had hitherto given speech the power to impress and convince its audience is now reduced to the level of *muthos*, that is to say, the stuff of the fabulous, the marvelous. It is as if discourse could only win in the sphere of truth and intelligibility by simultaneously losing out in the sphere of what is pleasurable, moving, and dramatic (*Myth and Society*, pp. 206–208).

From a tragic point of view then, there are two aspects to action. It involves on the one hand reflection, weighing up the pros and cons, foreseeing as accurately as possible the means and the ends; on the other, placing one's stake on what is unknown and incomprehensible, risking oneself on a terrain that remains impenetrable, entering into a game with supernatural forces, not knowing whether, as they join with one, they will bring success or doom. Even for the most foreseeing of men, the most carefully thought out action is still a chancy appeal to the gods and only by their reply, and usually to one's cost, will one learn what it really involved and meant. It is only when the drama is over that actions take on their true significance and agents, through what they have in reality accomplished without realizing it, discover their true identity. So long as there has been no complete consummation, human affairs remain enigmas that are the more obscure the more the actors believe themselves sure of what they are doing and what they are. Installed in his role of solver of riddles and king dispensing justice, convinced that the gods inspire him, and proclaiming himself the son of *Tuchē*, Good Luck, how could Oedipus possibly understand that he is a riddle to himself to which he will only guess the meaning when he discovers himself to be the opposite to what he thinks he is: not *Tuchē's* son at all but his victim, not the dispenser of justice but the criminal, not the king saving his city but the abominable defilement by which it is being destroyed? So it is that, at that moment when he realizes that he is responsible for having forged his misfortune with his own hands, he accuses the deity of having plotted and contrived everything in advance, of having delighted in tricking him from start to finish of the drama, the better to destroy him.[3] (*Myth and Tragedy*, p. 45).

Tragedy is not only an art form; it is also a social institution that the city, by establishing competitions in tragedies, set up alongside its political and legal institutions. The city esablished under the authority of the eponymous archon, in the same urban space and in accordance with the same institutional norms as the popular assemblies or courts, a spectacle open to all the citizens, directed, acted, and judged by the qualified representatives of the various tribes.[4] In this way it turned itself into a theater. Its subject, in a sense, was itself and it acted itself out before its public. But although tragedy, more than any other genre of literature, thus appears rooted in social reality, that does not mean that it is a reflection of it. It does not reflect that reality but calls it into question. By depicting it rent and divided against itself, it turns it into a problem. The drama brings to the stage an ancient heroic legend. For the city this legendary world constitutes the past – a past sufficiently distant for the contrasts, between the mythical traditions that it embodies and the new forms of legal and political thought, to be clearly visible; yet a past still close enough for the clash of values still to be a painful one and for this clash still to be currently taking place.

Tragedy is born when myth starts to be considered from the point of view of a citizen. But it is not only the world of myth that loses its consistency and dissolves in this focus. By the same token the world of the city is called into question and its fundamental values are challenged in the ensuing debate. When exalting the civic ideal and affirming its victory over all forces from the past, even Aeschylus, the most optimistic of the tragic writers, seems not to be making a positive declaration with tranquil conviction but rather to be expressing a hope, making an appeal that remains full of anxiety even amid the joy of the final apotheosis.[5] The questions are posed but the tragic consciousness can find no fully satisfactory answers to them and so they remain open.

This debate with a past that is still alive creates at the very heart of each tragic work a fundamental distance that the interpreter needs to take into account. It is expressed, in the very form of the drama, by the tension between the two elements that occupy the tragic stage. One is the chorus, the collective and anonymous presence embodied by an official college of citizens. Its role is to express through its fears, hopes, questions, and judgments the feelings of the spectators who make up the civic community. The other, played by a professional actor, is the individualized character whose actions form the core of the drama and who appears as a hero from an age gone by, always more or less estranged from the ordinary condition of the citizen.[6] This dichotomy between chorus and tragic hero is matched by a duality in the language of tragedy. But here already there is an aspect of ambiguity that seems to us to characterize the tragic genre. It is the language of the chorus, in the chanted passages, that carries on the lyrical tradition of a poetry celebrating the exemplary virtues of the hero of ancient times. For the protagonists of the drama the meter of the passages of dialogue is, on the contrary, close to that of prose. Even as the setting and the mask confer upon the tragic protagonist the magnified dimensions of one of the exceptional beings that are the object of a cult in the city, the language used brings him closer to the ordinary man.[7] And even as he lives his legendary adventure this closeness makes him, as it were, the contemporary of the public, so that the tension that we have noted between past and present, between the world of myth and that of the city, is to be found again within each protagonist. At one moment the same tragic character appears projected into a far distant mythical past, the hero of another age, imbued with a daunting religious power and embodying all the excesses of the ancient king of legend. At the next, he seems to speak, think, live in the very same age as the city, like a "bourgeois citizen" of Athens amid his fellows. (*Myth and Tragedy*, pp. 32–34).

As Aristotle notes, the tragic action does not unfold in conformity with the demands of a particular character; on the contrary, it is the character that must yield to the demands of the action, that is to say the *muthos*, the story, of which the tragedy is, in a strict sense, an imitation.[8]

All that the hero feels, says and does springs from his character, his *ēthos*, which the poets analyze just as subtly and interpret just as positively as might, for example, the orators or a historian such as Thucydides.[9] But at the same time these feelings, pronouncements, and actions also appear as the expression of a religious power, a *daimōn*, operating through them. Every moment in the life of the hero unfolds as if on two levels. Each would, by itself, adequately account for the *peripeteiai* of the drama, but the purpose of the tragedy is precisely to present them as inseparable. Each action appears to be in keeping with the logic of a particular character or *ēthos* even at the very moment when it is revealed to be the manifestation of a power from beyond, or a *daimōn*.

Tragic man is constituted within the space encompassed by this pair, *ēthos* and *daimōn*. If one of the two is eliminated, he vanishes. It could be said that tragedy rests on a double reading of Heraclitus' famous dictum, *ēthos anthrōpō(i) daimōn*. The minute it becomes impossible to read it equally well in the two different senses (as the syntactical symmetry allows) the formula loses its enigmatic character, its ambiguity, and the tragic consciousness is gone. For there to be tragedy it must be possible for the text simultaneously to imply two things: it is his character, in man, that one calls *daimōn* and, conversely, what one calls character, in man, is in reality a *daimōn* (*Myth and Tragedy*, pp. 36–37).

Just as the tragic character comes into being within the space between *daimōn* and *ēthos*, so tragic culpability is positioned in between on the one hand the ancient religious concepts of crime-defilement, *hamartia*, sickness of the mind, the delirium sent by the gods that necessarily engenders crime, and on the other the new concept in which the guilty one, *hamartōn* and, above all, *adikōn*, is defined as one who, under no compulsion, has deliberately chosen to commit a crime.[10] In its attempts at distinguishing the different categories of crime that fall within the competence of different courts, the *phonos dikaios, akousios, hekousios*, the law – even if still in a clumsy and hesitant manner – lays emphasis on the ideas of intention and responsibility. It raises the problem of the agent's different degrees of commitment in his actions. At the same time, within the city framework where all the citizens, following public discussions of a secular nature, themselves direct the affairs of the State, man himself is beginning to experiment as an agent who is more or less autonomous in relation to the religious forces that govern the universe, more or less master of his own actions and, through his *gnōmē*, his *phronēsis*, more or less in control of his own political and personal destiny. This experimentation, still wavering and indecisive, of what was subsequently in the psychological history of Western man to become the category of the will – as is well known, in ancient Greece there was no true vocabulary to cover willing – is expressed in tragedy in the form of an anxious questioning concerning the relation of the agent to his actions: to what extent is man really the source of his actions? Even while he deliberates concerning them deep within himself, taking the initiative and responsibility for them, does not their true origin lie somewhere outside him? Does not their significance remain opaque to the one who commits them, since actions acquire their reality not through the intentions of the agent but through the general order of the world over which the gods preside?

For there to be tragic action it is necessary that a concept of human nature with its own characteristics should have already emerged and that the human and divine spheres should have become sufficiently distinct from each other for them to stand in opposition; yet at the same time they must continue to appear as inseparable. The tragic sense of responsibility makes its appearance at the point when, in human action, a place is given to internal debate on the part of the subject, to intention and premeditation, but when this human action has still not aquired enough consistency and autonomy to be entirely self-sufficient. The true domain of tragedy lies in that border zone where human actions are hinged together with the divine powers, where – unknown to the agent – they derive their true meaning by becoming an integral part of an order that is beyond man and that eludes him. In Thucydides, human nature, *anthrōpinē phusis*, is defined in absolute contrast to religious power as represented by *Tuchē*. The two are radically heterogeneous orders of reality. In tragedy they appear rather as two opposed but complementary aspects, the two poles of a single ambiguous reality. Thus all tragedy must necessarily be played out on two levels. In its aspect of an inquiry into man as a responsible agent, it only has value as a counterpoint to the central theme. It would therefore be mistaken to focus exclusively upon the psychological element. In the famous carpet scene of the *Agamemmon*, the sovereign's fatal decision no doubt depends partly upon his wretched human vanity and also perhaps upon the guilty conscience of a husband who is the more ready to accede to the requests of his wife given that he is returning home to her with Cassandra as his concubine. But that is not the essential point. The strictly tragic effect comes from the intimate relation yet at the same time extraordinary distance between the banal action of stepping on a purple carpet with the all too human motivations this involves, and the religious forces that this action inexorably sets in motion.

The moment Agamemmon sets foot on the carpet the drama reaches its consummation. And even if the play is not quite over, it can introduce nothing that is not already accomplished once and for all. The past, the present, and the future have fused together with a single meaning that is revealed and encapsulated in the symbolism of this action of impious *hubris*. Now we know what the sacrifice of lphigenia really was: not so much obedience to the orders of Artemis, not so much the painful duty of a king not wishing to be in the wrong where his allies were concerned,[11] rather the guilty weakness of an ambitious man who, his passion conspiring with divine *Tuchē*,[12] made the decision to sacrifice his own daughter. And we know now what the capture of Troy was: not so much a triumph of justice and punishment of the guilty, rather, a sacrilegious destruction of an entire city with its temples. And in this twofold impiety all the ancient crimes of the Atreidae live again and all those that are to follow are encompassed: the blow that is to strike down Agamemmon and that, through Orestes, will eventually reach Clytemnestra too. At this culminating point of the tragedy, where all the threads are tied together, the time of the gods invades the stage and becomes manifest within the time of men (*Myth and Tragedy*, pp. 45–48).

Decision without choice, responsibility divorced from intention are, we are told, the forms that the will takes among the Greeks. The whole problem lies in knowing what the Greeks themselves understood by choice and the absence of choice and by responsibility, with or without intention. Our ideas of choice and free choice, of responsibility and intention, are not directly applicable to the ancient mentality any more than our idea of the will is, for in antiquity these notions appear with meanings and forms that are often disconcerting to a modern mind. Aristotle is a particularly significant example in this respect. It is well known that, in his moral philosophy, Aristotle is concerned to refute doctrines according to which the wicked man does not act fully of his own violition but commits his misdeed despite himself. This seems to him in some respects to be the "tragic" concept, represented in particular, in Aristotle's view, by Euripides, whose characters sometimes openly declare that they are not guilty of their crimes since, they claim, they acted despite themselves, under constraint, *bia*, dominated, violently compelled by the force of passions all the more irristible in that they are incarnations within the heroes themselves of divine powers such as Eros or Aphrodite.[13]

Socrates' point of view, on another level, is similar. For him, since all wickedness is ignorance, nobody ever does evil "willingly" (to follow the usual translation). In order to justify the principle of the personal culpability of the wicked man and to provide a theoretical basis for the declaration of man's responsibility, Aristotle elaborates a doctrine of moral action. This represents the most systematic attempt in classical Greek philosophy to distinguish according to their internal conditions all the different modalities of action,[14] from the action performed despite oneself, under external constraint or in ignorance of what one is doing (as when one administers poison, believing it to be a medicine), down to the action performed not only of one's own volition but in full knowledge of what one is doing, after due deliberation and decision. To convey the highest degree of consciousness and commitment in an action on the part of the subject, Aristotle forges a new concept. He uses the term *proairesis* – a rare term and one of hitherto indefinite meaning – giving it a precise technical sense within the framework of his moral system. *Proairesis* is action taking the form of a decision; it is the exclusive prerogative of man to the extent that he is a being endowed with reason, as opposed to children and animals, which are without it. *Proairesis* is more than *hekousion*, a word that is usually translated in French by *volontaire* (intentional or willed),[15] but that cannot really have so strong a meaning. The usual opposition in Greek, in both common speech and legal terminology, between *hekōn, hekousios* on the one hand and *akōn, akousios* on the other in no way corresponds to our own categories of "what is willed" (*volontaire*) and "what is not willed" (*involontaire*). These contrasting expressions should rather be translated as "of one's own volition" and "despite oneself." This is the sense given them by Gauthier and Jolif in their commentary on the *Nicomachean Ethics*, when they use the French terms "*de plein gré*" and "*malgré soi*."[16] To see that *hekōn* cannot mean willed intentional (*volontaire*) we have only to note that, when declaring that an act of passion is performed *hekōn* and not *akōn*, Aristotle substantiates this by pointing out that otherwise we should have to say that neither would animals be *hekontes* in their action, an expression that patently cannot have the sense of "intentionally."[17] The animal acts *hekōn*, as do men, when it follows its own inclination, under no constraint from any external power. So while any decision (*proairesis*) is an action carried out of one's own volition (*hekōn*), in contrast "what one does of one's own volition is not always the result of a decision." Thus when one acts through desire (*epithumia*), that is to say lured on by pleasure, or passionately, through *thumos*, without taking the time to reflect, one certainly does it of one's own volition (*hekōn*) but not as a result of a decision (*proairesis*). To be sure, *proairesis* also rests upon a desire, but a rational desire, a wish (*boulēsis*) informed by intelligence and directed, not toward pleasure, but toward a practical objective that thought has already presented to the soul as a good. *Proairesis* implies a previous process of deliberation (*bouleusis*). At the end of this process of reasoned calculation it sets up a choice – as the word indicates (*hairesis* = choice) – that is expressed in a decision that leads directly to the action. This aspect of choice in a practical domain, which commits the subject to action the very moment he has come to a decision, distinguishes *proairesis* firstly from *boulēsis*, the movement of which may come to nothing and remain in the pure form of a "wish" (for one may wish for the impossible), and secondly from a purely theoretical judgment that is concerned with the truth but in no way with the domain of action.[18] On the contrary, deliberation and decision only take place with regard to things that "lie within our power" that "depend on us" (*ta eph' hēmin*) and that can be effected in action not just in one single way, but in several. Here, Aristotle opposes to the *dunameis alogoi*, the irrational powers that can only produce one single effect (for example, heat can only act by heating), the powers that are accompanied by reason, *meta logou*, that are capable of producing opposite effects, *dunameis tōn enantiōn*.[19]

This doctrine presents aspects at first sight so modern that certain interpreters have seen *proairesis* as a free power to choose for the subject as he takes his decision. Some have attributed this power to reason that they understand to be the sovereign determinant of the ultimate ends of the action. Others, on the other hand, rightly stressing the anti-intellectualist reaction against Socrates and, to a large extent, also against Plato that Aristotle's analysis of action represents, have elevated *proairesis* to be a true capacity to will. They have seen it as the active faculty of determining oneself, a power that remains to the very last above the appetites directed, in the case of *epithumia*, towards what is pleasant and, in the case of *boulēsis*, to what is good, and that to some extent quite independently from the pressure desire exerts upon him, impels the subject to take action.

None of these interpretations can be upheld.[20] Without entering in detail into the Aristotelian psychology of action, we may state that *proairesis* does not constitute a power independent from the two types of faculty that, according to Aristotle, alone are at work in moral action: on the one hand the desiring part of the soul (*to orektikon*), on the other the intellect or *nous* in its practical function.[21] *Boulēsis*, desire informed by reason, is directed toward the end of the action: it is what moves the soul toward the good, but, like envy and anger, it is a part of the order of desire, *orexis*.[22] Now the function of desire is entirely passive. So the wish (*boulēsis*) is what directs the soul toward a resonable end, but it is an end that is imposed upon it and that it has not chosen. Deliberation (*bouleusis*) on the other hand belongs to the faculty that directs, that is to say the practical intellect. In contrast to the wish, however, this has no connection with the end; it is concerned with the means.[23] *Proairesis* does not opt between good and evil, between which it would have a free choice. Once an end has been decided upon – health, for instance – the deliberation consists in the chain of judgments by which reason reaches the conclusion that certain practical means can or cannot lead to health.[24] The last judgment, made at the end of the deliberation, concerns the last means in the chain; it presents it as not only possible on the same grounds as all the others but furthermore as immediately realizable. From this moment on the wish, instead of aiming at health in a general and abstract manner, includes within its desire for the end the concrete conditions by which it can be realized. It concentrates on the last condition that, in the particular situation in which the subject finds himself, effectively brings health within his grasp at that particular moment. Once the desire of *boulēsis* has thus fixed upon the immediately realizable means, action follows and does so necessarily.

This necessity immanent in every phase of wishing, deliberating, and deciding is what justifies the model of the practical syllogism that Aristotle employs to explain the workings of the mind in the process of making a decision. It is as the commentators of the *Ethics* put it: "Just as the syllogism is nothing other than the conjunction of the major and minor, the decision is nothing other than the point of junction or fusion of the desire that the wish represents and the thought that the judgment represents."[25]

Thus: "The wish is *necessarily* what it is and the judgment *necessarily* what it is and action *necessarily* follows upon their conjunction which is the decision."[26] In Aristotle's theory of moral action he is not concerned either to demonstrate or to refute the existence of psychological liberty. He never even refers to such a thing. Neither in his work nor in the language of his times can one find any word to refer to what we call free will.[27] The idea of a free power of decision remains alien to his thought. It has no place in his inquiry into the problem of responsible action either in connection with his notion of a choice made with deliberation or of an action accomplished of one's own volition.

Greek has no term that corresponds with our idea of will. The meaning of *hekōn* is both wider and has a less precise psychological sense: wider, since it is possible to include within the category of *hekousion*, as Aristotle does, any action not imposed through external compulsion, actions carried out through desire and impulse as well as actions that are the result of reflection and deliberation; and it has a less precise psychological meaning since the levels and modalities of intention ranging from a simple inclination to a plan deliberately decided upon remain confused as the term is employed in common usage. There is no distinction between the intentional and the premeditated: *hekōn* has both meanings.[28] As for *akōn*, as Louis Gernet pointed out, it associates all kinds of ideas that, from the point of view of psychology, should be carefully distinguished right from the start. The single expression of *phonos akousios*, referring to the murder committed despite oneself, can mean now a total absence of guilt, now mere negligence, now a positive lack of prudence, now even a more or less fleeting impulse or the quite different case of homicide committed in legitimate self-defense.[29] The fact is that the *hekōn–akōn* opposition is not the fruit of disinterested reflection on the subjective conditions that make an individual the cause responsible for his actions. It is rather a matter of legal categories that, at the time of the city-state, were imposed by the law as norms for common thought. Now the law did not proceed on the basis of a psychological analysis of the varying degrees of the responsibility of the agent. It followed criteria designed to regulate, in the name of the State, the exercise of private vengeance, by drawing distinctions, in accordance with the varying intensity of emotional reaction aroused in the group in question, between the various forms of murder calling for different legal sentences. Dracon is believed to have given Athens, at the beginning of the seventh century, an organized system of courts competent to judge crimes of bloodshed. They covered a number of grades of gravity arranged in descending order according to the strength of collective feeling regarding the excusability of the crime. In this system the *phonos hekousios* included within a single category all murders calling for the full penalty and these fell within the competence of the Areopagus. The *phonos akousios* included excusable murders, which were the province of the Palladion, while the *phonos dikaios* covered justifiable murders, which were the concern of the Delphinion. This third category, even more than the other two, associates together actions that, from the point of view of the psychology of the agent, are extremely heterogeneous. In effect it applies to all cases of murder that custom, for various reasons, fully exculpates and considers unquestionably legitimate. These range from the execution of the adulterer to homicide committed accidentally in the course of public games or in warfare. It is clear then that the distinction made in law by the semantic opposition between *hekōn* and *akōn* is not, in the first instance, founded upon a distinction between what is willed and what is not willed. Rather, it rests upon the differentiation that, in particular historical conditions, the social conscience establishes between actions that are altogether reprehensible and those that are excusable. The two groups are set alongside that of legitimate actions and are seen as representing two antithetical values.

We must furthermore bear in mind the basically intellectualist character of the entire Greek terminology for action, whether it be a matter of the action performed of one's own volition or the one performed despite oneself, the action for which the subject is responsible or the one for which he is not, the action that is reprehensible or the one that is excusable. In the language and mentality of the ancient Greeks, the concepts of knowledge and of action appear to be

integrally connected. Where a modern reader expects to find a formula expressing will he instead finds one expressing knowledge. In this sense Socrates'
declaration, repeated by Plato, that wrongdoing is ignorance, a lack of understanding, was not so paradoxical as it seems to us today. It is in effect a very
clear extension of the most ancient ideas about misdeeds attested in the pre-legal
(*préjuridique*) state of society, before the advent of the city-state. In this context
a misdeed, *hamartéma*, is seen at the same time as a "mistake" made by the mind,
as a religious defilement, and as a moral weakness.[30] *Hamartanein* means to
make a mistake in the strongest sense of an error of the intelligence, a blindness
that entails failure. *Hamartia* is a mental sickness, the criminal who is prey to
madness, a man who has lost his senses, a *demens, hamartinoos*. This madness
in committing a misdeed or, to give it its Greek names, this *atē* or *Erinus*, takes
over the individual from within. It penetrates him like an evil religious force. But
even while to some extent it becomes identifed with him, it at the same time
remains separate, beyond him. The defilement of crime is contiguous and attaches
itself, over and beyond the individual to his whole lineage, the whole circle of his
relatives. It may affect an entire town, pollute a whole territory. A single power
of evil may embody the crime and its most distant beginnings in the criminal and
outside him too, together with its ultimate consequences and the punishment for
which it rebounds from one generation to the next. As Louis Gernet points out,
in such circumstances the individual as such is not the main factor in the crime.
"The crime exists outside him, it is objective." In the context of religious thought
such as this in which the action of the criminal is seen, in the outside world, as
a daemonic power of defilement and, within himself, as an error of the mind, the
entire category of action appears to be organized in a different way from our
own. Error, felt to be an assault on the religious order, contains a malignant
power far greater than the human agent. The individual who commits it (or, to
be more precise, who is its victim) is himself caught up in the sinister force that
he has unleashed (or that exerts itself through him). The action does not emanate
from the agent as from its source; rather, it envelops him and carries him away,
swallowing him up in a power that must perforce be beyond him since it extends,
both spatially and temporally, far beyond his own person. The agent is caught
in the action. He is not its author; he remains included in it. Within such a
framework there can clearly be no question of individual will. The distinction
between what is intentional and what is enforced in the action of the subject does
not even make sense here. How could one of one's own volition be misled by
error? And once it has been committed how could the *hamartia* possibly not carry
its punishment within itself, quite independent of the intentions of the subject?

With the advent of law and the institution of the city courts, the ancient
religious conception of the misdeed fades away. A new idea of crime emerges.[32]
the rôle of the individual becomes more clearly defined. Intention now appears
as a constitutive element of the criminal action, especially in the case of
homicide. The divide between the two broad categories of *hekōn* and *akōn* in
human behavior is now considered a norm. But it is quite clear that this way of

thinking of the offender is also developed within the framework of a purely intellectualist terminology. The action performed fully of one's own volition and that which is performed despite oneself are defined as reciprocal opposes in terms of knowledge and ignorance. The word *hekōn*, of one's own volition, comes to include the idea, in its pure and simple form, of intention conceived in general terms and without analysis. This intention is expressed by the word *pronoia*. In the fragments of the Draconian code that have come down to us the expression *ek pronoias* replaces *hekōn*, standing in opposition to *akōn*. In fact the expressions *ek pronoias* and *hekōn ek pronoias* are exactly synonymous. *Pronoia* is a mode of knowledge, an act of the intellect made before the action, a premeditation. The culpable intention that makes the act a crime is seen not as a will to do evil but rather as a full knowledge of the situation. In a decree from the Hecatompedon, which is the most ancient legal text to have come down to us in its original form, the understanding of the new requirements for subjective responsibility is expressed by the word *eidōs*; to be at fault it is necessary for the offender to have acted "knowingly".[33] Conversely, *agnoia*, ignorance, which previously constituted the very essence of the misdeed, now stands in opposition to *hekousion* and comes to define the category of crimes committed despite oneself, *akōn*, without criminal intention. Xenophon writes: "Misdeeds that men commit through *agnoia* I hold all to be *akousia*."[34] Plato himself was obliged to recognize alongside "ignorance," which for him was the general cause of crime, a second form of *agnoia* that was more strictly defined and became the basis for the misdeed performed without criminal intention.[35] The paradox of an *agnoia* that is both the constitutive principle of the misdeed and at the same time excuses it by expunging it is also to be found in the semantic evolution of the words related to *hamartia*. The evolution is twofold.[36] On the one hand the terms come to carry the notion of intention: one is only guilty, *hamartōn*, if one has committed the criminal action intentionally; anyone who has acted despite himself, *akōn*, is not guilty, *ouk hamartōn*. The verb *hamartanein* can designate the same thing as *adikein*: the intentional crime that is prosecuted by the city. On the other hand, the concept of the intentional that is implied in the primitive idea of a mistake made through a man's blindness also bears fruit as early as the fifth century. *Hamartanein* comes to apply to the excusable misdeed where the subject was not fully aware of what he was doing. As early as the end of the fourth century *hamartēma* comes to be used to express the almost technical idea of the unintentional crime, the *akousion*. Thus Aristotle sets it in opposition to the *adikēma*, the intentional crime, and to the *atuchēma*, the unforeseeable accident that has nothing to do with the intentions and knowledge of the agent.[37] Thus this intellectualist psychology of the intention makes it possible, over several centuries, for two contradictory meanings to coexist within the same family of terms: to commit a misdeed intentionally and to commit it unintentionally. The reason for this is that the notion of ignorance operated at two quite different levels of thought in quite different ways. On the one hand it retained the earlier association of sinister religious forces that can overtake a man's mind and render him blind to evil. On the other, it had already acquired the positivist sense of an absence of knowledge regarding the concrete conditions in which an action is perpetrated. The ancient kernel of myth remains sufficiently alive in the collective imagination to provide the schema necessary for what is excusable to be represented in a way in which, precisely, it is possible for "ignorance" to assume the most modern of meanings. But on neither of the two levels of meaning for this term, which is, as it were, balanced between the idea of ignorance that causes the misdeed and that of ignorance that excuses it, is the category of will implied.

Another type of ambiguity appears in the compound forms of the *boul*- family, which are also employed to express different modalities of the intentional.[38] The verb *boulomai*, which is sometimes translated as "to will" (*vouloir*), is used in Homer less frequently than *thelō* and *ethelō*. It has the meaning of "to desire," "to prefer." In Attic prose it tends to supplant *ethelō* and means the subject's own inclination, his intimate wish, his personal preference, while *ethelō* takes on the specialized meaning of "to consent to" and is often used with an object that is the opposite of that which is the subject's own inclination. Three nouns connected with action were derived from *boulomai*: *boulēsis*, desire, wish; *boulēma*, intention; and *boulē*, decision, plan, council (in the sense of the ancient political institution). It is clear that the group of terms lies somewhere between the level of desire or spontaneous inclination and that of reflection, intelligent calculation.[40] The meaning of the verbs *bouleuō* and *bouleuomai* is less equivocal: to sit in council, to deliberate. We have seen that in Aristotle *boulēsis* is a kind of desire; so, in so far as *boulēsis* means inclination or wish, its meaning is not so strong as actual intention. On the other hand the meaning of *bouleuō* and its derivatives *boulēma*, *epiboulē*, *proboulē*, is stronger. They indicate premeditation or, to translate the Aristotelian term *proairesis* more precisely, the predecision that, as Aristotle stresses, implies two associated ideas: on the one hand that of deliberation (*bouleuomai*) through calculation (*logos*) and reflection (*dianoia*) and, on the other, the idea that this has taken place at some previous point in time.[41] The notion of the intentional thus oscillates between the spontaneous tendency of a desire and intelligent premeditated calculation. In their analyses the philosophers distinguish and sometimes oppose these two poles but the way the words are used makes it possible to move from one to the other or to shift between them. Thus, in the *Cratylus*, Plato connects *boulē* with *bolē*, a throw. His reason for doing so is that *boulesthai* (to wish) means *ephiesthai* (to incline toward) and he adds that *bouleusthai* (to deliberate) also does. In contrast, *aboulia* (lack of reflection) consists in missing the target, in not achieving "what one desired [*ebouleto*], that on which one has deliberated [*ebouleueto*], that toward which one was inclined [*ephieto*]."[42] Thus not only wishing but also deliberating implies a movement, a tension, a spurt of the soul toward the object. This is because, in the case of inclination (*boulomai*) as in that of reasoned deliberation (*bouleuō*) the truest cause for the subject's action is not to be found in the subject himself. He is always set in movement by an "end" that directs his behavior as it were from outside him, namely either the object toward which his desire spontaneously reaches out or that which reflection presents to his thought as something desirable.[43] In the former case the intention of the agent appears to be linked with and subject to the desire; in the latter, it is impelled by his intellectual knowledge of what is best. But between the spontaneous movement of desire and the intellect's vision of the good, there seems to be no area where the will could find its own particular field of application and where the subject, in and through his own action of willing, could become the autonomous center for his decision, the true source of his actions.

How should we understand Aristotle's declarations to the effect that our actions lie within our power (*eph' hēmin*), that we are the responsible causes for them (*aitioi*), that man is the origin and father (*archē kai gennētēs*) of his actions as of his children?[44] They certainly indicate a desire to root actions deep within the subject, to present the individual as the efficient cause of his action so that wicked men or those who lack self-control may be held responsible for their misdeeds and may not invoke as an excuse some external constraint of which they claim to be the victims. Nevertheless, we must interpret the expressions used by Aristotle correctly. He writes on several occasions that a man's actions "depend upon himself." The exact meaning of this "*autos*" becomes clearer if it is compared to the expression in which he defines living creatures as being endowed with the power "of moving themselves." In this context *autos* does not have the meaning of a personal self nor of a special faculty possessed by the subject to control the interplay of the causes that operate within him.[45] *Autos* refers to the human individual taken as a whole, conceived as the sum total of the dispositions that make up his particular character or *ēthos*. Discussing the Socratic theory that wickedness is ignorance, Aristotle points out that men are responsible for this ignorance; it depends upon them, lies within their power (*ep' autois*), for they are free (*kurioi*, literally "masters") to do something about it. He then dismisses the objection that the wicked man is, precisely by reason of his wicked state, incapable of doing such a thing. He declares that the wicked man is himself, by reason of his dissolute life, the responsible cause (*aitios*) for finding himself in this state. "For in every domain, actions of a certain type produce a corresponding type of man."[46] The character or *ēthos* that belongs to every kind of man depends upon the sum total of dispositions (*hexeis*) that are developed by practice and fixed by force of habit.[47] Once the character is formed the subject acts in conformity with these dispositions and would be unable to act in any other way. But, Aristotle says, prior to this he was free (*kurios*) to act in various ways.[48] In this sense, if the way in which each of us conceives the end of his action necessarily depends on his character, his character also depends on himself since it has been formed by his own actions. At no moment, however, does Aristotle seek to found upon psychological analysis the capacity possessed by the subject to decide to do one thing rather than another while his dispositions were not yet fixed, and thus to assume responsibility for what he would do later on. It is difficult to see how the young child, without *proairesis*, could have any more power than the grown man to determine himself freely and to forge his own character. Aristotle does not inquire into the various forces that are at work in the formation of an individual temperament, although he is not unaware of the role of nature or of that of education or legislation. "It is therefore of no meager importance that we should have been brought up with such-or-such habits; on the contrary this is of sovereign importance, or rather everything depends on this."[49] If everything depends on this, the autonomy of the subject fades away in the face of the weight of social constraints. But Aristotle is unconcerned: his point was essentially a moral one, so it is enough for him to establish between the character and the individual seen in the round the intimate and reciprocal link that is the basis for the subjective responsibility of the agent. The man is "father" of his actions when their origin, *archē*, and their efficient cause, *aitia*, are to be found "in him." But this inner causality is only defined in a purely negative fashion: whenever an action can be asigned no external source of constraint, it is because the cause is to be found "in the man" because he has acted "voluntarily," "of his own volition," so that his action can legitimately be imputed to him.

In the last analysis Aristotle does not refer the causality of the subject, any more than his responsibility, to any kind of will power. For him it depends upon an assimilation of the internal, the spontaneous, and what is strictly autonomous. The confusion of these different levels of action shows that even if the subject has already taken on his own individuality and is accepting responsibility for all the actions that he performs of his own volition, he remains too much bound by the determining factors upon his character and too closely welded to the internal dispositions of his nature – which control the practice of vice and virtue – for him to emerge fully as the seat of personal decision and to assume, as *autos*, his full stature as agent (*Myth and Tragedy*, pp. 55–69).

Notes

1. *Choëphori*, 899.
2. *Suppliants*, 379–380.
3. Cl. R. P. Winnington-Ingram, "Tragedy and Great Archaic Thought" in *Classical Drama and its Influence* (London, 1965), pp. 31–50; and as regards the same problem in Aeschylus, A. Lesky, "Decision and Responsibility in the Tragedy of Aeschylus." *Journal of Hellenic Studies* **86** (1966) 78–85. As Lesky notes, "freedom and compulsion are united in a genuinely tragic way," because one of the major features of Aeschylus' tragedy is precisely "the close union of necessity imposed by the Gods and the personal decision to act."
4. Only men can be qualified representatives of the city; women are alien to political life. That is why the members of the chorus (not to mention the actors) are always and exclusively male. Even when the chorus is supposed to represent a group of young girls or women, as is the case in a whole series of plays, those who represent it are men, suitably disguised and masked.
5. At the end of Aeschylus' *Oresteia*, the establishment of the human court and the integration of the Erinyes into the new order of the city do not entirely do away with the contradition between the ancient gods and the new ones, and between the heroic

past of the noble *gene* and the present of the democratic Athens of the fifth century. Certainly, a balance is achieved, but it rests upon a number of tensions. Conflict persists, in the background, between contrary forces. To this extent the tragic ambiguity is not removed: ambivalence remains. Remember, for instance, that a majority of human judges pronounced a vote against Orestes, for it was only Athena's vote that made the two sides equal.

6. Cl. Aristotle, *Problemata* 19, 48: "The characters on the stage imitate heroes, and among the ancients the leaders alone were heroes, and the people, of whom the chorus consists, were mere men" (Ross/Forster translation).

7. Aristotle, *Poetics* 1449b24–28: The iambic, we know, is the most speakable of metres, as is shown by the fact that we very often fall into it in conversation, whereas we rarely talk hexameters, and only when we depart from the [conversational] tone of voice." (Ross/Ingram Bywater translation).

8. Aristotle, *Poetics* 1449b24, 31, 36; 1450a15–23; 1450a23–25 and 38–39; 1450b2–3.

9. On this aspect of tragedy and on the heroic nature of Sophocles' characters, cf: B. Knox, *The Heroic Temper: Studies in Sophoclean Tragedy* (Berkeley and Los Angeles, 1964).

10. In the formula that Aeschylus puts into the mouth of the leader of the Chorus (*Agememnon* 1337–8), the two contrary concepts are to some extent superimposed or confused within the same words. Because it is ambiguous, the phrase does indeed lend itself to a double interpretation: *nun d'ei proterōn aim' apoteisē* can mean: "And now, if he must pay for the blood that his ancestors have shed," but also: "And now, if he must pay for the blood he has shed in the past." In the first case, Agamemnon is the victim of an ancestral curse: he pays for crimes that he has not committed. In the second, he expiates crimes for which he is responsible.

11. Cf. *Agamemnon*, 213.

12. Ibid., 187: *empaiois tuchaisi sumpveōn* On this line cf. the commentary of E. Fraenkel, *Aeschylus, Agamemnon*, (Oxford, 1950), Vol. II, p. 115, that refers back to line 219, pp. 127–128.

13. Aristotle, *Nicomachean Ethics* (*NE*) 3, 1110a28 and the commentary by R. A. Gauthier and J.-R. Jolif, (Louvain-Paris, 1959), pp. 177–178.

14. Ibid., ". . . it is our internal decisions, that is to say our intentions, rather than our exterior actions, that enable our characters to be judged," (1111b5–6); cf. also *Eudemian Ethics*, 1228a.

15. Translator's notes: this French term is stronger than the English "voluntary" or "willing," meaning rather "what is willed" or "intentional."

16. Gauthier and Jolif, Vol. II, pp. 169–170.

17. *NE*, 1111a25–27 and 1111b7–8.

18. Ibid., "For choice [*proairesis*] cannot relate to impossibles and if anyone said he chose them he would be thought silly; but there may be a wish even for impossibles e.g. for immortality" (Ross translation: 1111b20–23). "For mind as speculative never thinks what is practicable, it never says anything about an object to be avoided or pursued," *De Anima*, 432b27–28.

19. *Metaphysics*, 1046b5–10; *NE*, 1103a19–b22.

20. Cf. Gauthier and Jolif, Vol. II, pp. 217–220.

21. Cf. *NE*, 1139a17–20.

22. Ibid., 1139b2–3, "For good action is an end in the absolute sense and desire aims at this."

23. Ibid., 1113b3–5, "The end then is what we wish for, the means what we deliberate about and choose"; 1111b26: "wish related rather to the end, choice to the means."

24. Ibid., 1139a31: "The origin . . . of choice is desire and reasoning with a view to an

end." Cf. the commentary by Gauthier and Jolif, Vol. II, part 2, p. 144. On the role
of desire and of the *nous praktikôs* in choice and decision, on the order of ends and
means in the framework of an Aristotelian moral philosophy of *phronēsis*, cf. E. M.
Michelakis, *Aristotle's Theory of Practical Principles* (Athens, 1961), ch. 2, pp. 22–62.

25. Cf. Gauthier and Jolif, pp. 202 and 212. Cf. *NE* 1147a29–31: "For example, let us
take a universal premise: *One must taste everything that is sweet*, together with a
particular case that falls within the general category: *this food before us is sweet*. Given
these two propositions, if one can and is not prevented from doing so, one must
necessarily [*ex anankēs*] immediately accomplish this action of tasting."

26. Gauthier and Jolif, p. 129.

27. Cf. Gauthier and Jolif, p. 217. The term *eleutheria* (*NE*, V, 1131a28) "at this period
refers not to psychological freedom but to the legal condition of a free man as opposed
to that of a slave; the expression "free will" only appears in the Greek language very
much later when *eleutheria* acquires the sense of psychological freedom. It was to be
to autezousion (or *hē autezousiotēs*), literally, self-control. The earliest instance occurs
in Diodorus Siculus, 19, 105, 4 (first century A.C.) but it does not have its technical
sense here. The latter is already firmly established in Epictetus (first century A.D.),
who uses the word five times (*Discourses*, 1, 2, 4; IV, I, 56; 62; 68; 100); from this
date onwards the word is fully accepted in Greek philosophy." The Latins later
translated *to autezousion* as *liberum arbitrium*.

28. L. Gernet, *Recherches sur le Développement de la Pensée Juridique et Morale en Grèce*
(Paris, 1917), p. 352.

29. Ibid., pp. 353–354.

30. Ibid., pp. 305 ff.

31. Ibid., p. 305.

32. Ibid., pp. 373 ff.

33. Cf. G. Maddoli, "Responsibilità e Sanzione nei "Decreta de Hecatomepedo"," *I.G.*, I²,
3–4, *Museum Helveticum* (1967), I–II; J. and L. Robert, *Bulletin Épigraphique, REG*
(1954), no. 63 and (1967), no. 176.

34. *Cyropaedia*, III, I, 38; cf. L. Gernet, *Recherches*, p. 387.

35. *Laws*, IX, 863c.

36. Cf. L. Gernet, *Recherches*, pp. 305, 310 and 339–348.

37. *NE*, 1135b ff.

38. L. Gernet, *Recherches*, p. 351; Gauthier and Jolif, pp. 192–194; P. Chantraine,
Dictionnaire Étymologique de la Langue Grecque (Paris, 1968–80), Vol. I, pp. 189–190.

39. *NE*, 1112a17.

40. In Aristotle, *proairesis*, as a deliberate decision of practical thought, can be defined
either as a desiring intellect, *orektikos nous*, or as an intellectual desire, *orexis dianoe-
tikē*, *NE*, 1139b4–5, together with the commentary by Gauthier and Jolif.

41. *NE*, 1112a15–17.

42. *Cratylus* 420c–d.

43. If Aristotle declares that man is the principle and cause (in the sense of efficient cause)
of his actions, he also writes: "For the originating causes of the things that are done
consist in the end at which they are aimed," *NE*, 1140b16–17.

44. Cf., for example, *NE*, 1113b17–19.

45. Cf. D. J. Allan, "The Practical Syllogism," *Autour d' Aristotle* (London, 1955), who
stresses that *autos* does not have the sense of a rational self opposed to the passions
and wielding its own power over the latter.

46. *NE*, 1114a7–8.

47. On the correspondence of the character, *ēthos*, and the desiring part of the soul and
its dispositions, cf. *NE*, 1103a6–10 and 1139a34–35.

48. *NE*, 1114a3–8 and 13–21.

49. Ibid., 1103b24–25; cf. also 1179b31 ff.

Acting: *Drama* as the *Mimēsis* of *Praxis*

Aryeh Kosman

To the memory of Paul Desjardins, who loved both philosophy and poetry.

Like poetry in general, tragic poetry is a form of mimesis; so Aristotle tells his readers at the beginning of the *Poetics*. He then goes on to describe tragedy more particularly (in what seems to be more or less a definition of the genre) as the mimesis of an action: *estin oun tragōdia mimēsis praxeōs*.[1] As part of the same account, Aristotle also describes *mythos* or plot (which he styles the "soul" of a drama, that is, the cause of its being what it is) as the mimesis of an action.[2] This characterization of tragedy as mimetic, and specifically as mimetic with respect to a praxis, is repeated several times in the course of the *Poetics*, and much of what Aristotle has to say about tragic poetry seems to depend upon it.[3] In this essay I offer some reflections on both parts of this characterization, on the view that tragedy is mimesis and on the view that it is the mimesis of praxis.

I

It would be hyperbole to attribute to Aristotle a *theory* of mimesis; there is no thematic discussion of the nature of imitation in the Aristotelian corpus such as we find, for example, in Plato. But it should be clear from the prominent place accorded mimesis in the *Poetics* (and should be expected given the prominent place that mimesis enjoys in Plato's discussions) that the concept is an important one for our understanding of Aristotle's account of tragic poetry. We may begin by noting the generality of Aristotle's claim: at the beginning of the *Poetics* mimesis is said to comprise *all* forms of poetry.[4] In thus characterizing all poetry as mimesis, Aristotle appears to diverge sharply from the account of mimesis that

51

we find early in Plato's *Republic*. Socrates, speaking with Adeimantus about what kind of poetry will and will not be allowed in their fantastic political utopia, there distinguishes between two modes of *lexis* or styles of poetic discourse.[5]

On the one hand, poets may accomplish their ends by what he calls *haplē diēgēsis*, straight narration or narration proper. This mode is one in which, as Socrates says, "the poet himself speaks, without attempting to turn our attention elsewhere as though someone else than he were the speaker."[6] On the other hand, poets may use what Socrates calls *mimēsis*, using the word which Aristotle in our text applies to poetry in general. A poet is said to employ *mimēsis* when he imitates or takes on the *persona* of someone else, speaking as though he were that person, creating a fictional voice through which his discourse is accomplished.

Socrates illustrates the difference between diegesis and mimesis by reminding Adeimantus of an early scene in the *Iliad*. The poet, having first described in narrative Chryses' approach to the Achaeans, then adopts the mimetic style; he "speaks as though he himself were Chryses, trying as hard as possible to make it seem to us that it is not Homer who is speaking, but the priest, an old man."[7] Socrates proceeds to show Adeimantus (after first warning him that he is no poet) what it would be like if Homer had spoken *without* mimesis. He offers this narratized version of the Homeric episode: "When the priest came, he prayed that the gods should grant them the capture of Troy and their safety, but that they should release his daughter, accepting the ransom and honoring the god."[8]

The distinction that Plato has Socrates here draw reminds us of how particular the notion of mimesis is in these contexts; it refers quite specifically to the poet's creation of a fictional voice. Mimesis is not (at least in these first books of the *Republic*) a feature of art in relation to the real world represented in art, nor a feature of discourse in relation to reality represented in discourse; it is not, in other words, described by a theory of how art in general or literary language in particular mirrors the world by representation. It is rather a feature of literary discourse in terms of the relation between poet and fictional voice, between dramatist and dramatic character, between author and *persona*.[9]

In claiming that *all* poetry is mimesis, it appears that Aristotle undermines Socrates' distinction and enlarges considerably his notion of mimesis. This impression is strengthened by Aristotle's later classification of mimetic modes. Chapter 1 of the *Poetics* differentiates mimesis in three respects; instances of mimesis may differ from one another either in medium, or in object, or in manner: *ē tō en heterois mimeisthai ē tō hetera ē tō heterōs kai mē ton auton tropon*.[10] In Chapter 3, the third respect is elaborated; it is possible, Aristotle writes, for the poet "to imitate by the same means the same objects either (1) sometimes narrating, sometimes becoming someone other than himself, as Homer does, or (2) by remaining himself without changing, or (3) entirely by acting, that is, playing out the parts [*prattontas kai energountas tous mimoumenous*]."[1]

The distinction between (2) and (3), presented in the *Poetics* as a distinction in *kinds* of mimesis, is precisely Socrates' distinction between what is not and what is mimetic, between diegesis and mimesis, and (1), which is for Aristotle a composite form of mimetic poetry, is for Socrates a hybrid of nonmimetic and mimetic poetic discourse.

Socrates' distinction then, lives on in the *Poetics* only as a distinction of style within mimesis. But it does live on; and we may indeed discern a continuation of Plato's more restricted understanding of mimesis in Aristotle's praise of Homer as superior to other epic poets, although now the poles of valuation appear reversed. Homer, Aristotle writes, "deserves praise especially because he alone among the poets does not lose sight of what he must say in his own person; for in his own person, a poet ought to say as little as possible, since when doing that he is not a *mimētēs*."[12]

In so far as Aristotle, despite his more general characterization of all poetic discourse as mimetic, thus perpetuates the narrower Platonic understanding of mimesis, his account of mimesis may be subject to some of the same criticisms that have been directed against Plato. Gérard Genette, for example, argues that in poetry the narrower concept of mimesis can account for nothing other than the occasional reported speech. For in language nothing can be *imitated* in the narrower sense other *than* language itself, and such imitation finally collapses into mere reproduction: not the *representation,* but the unadorned *presentation* of speech.[13] The general point is made early in modern discussions of mimesis; consider this observation of an eighteenth century English scholar:

> There seems to be but *one* view in which Poetry can be considered as *Imitation,* in the strict and proper sense of the word. If we look for both *immediate* and *obvious* resemblance, we shall find it only in DRAMATIC – or to use a more general term – PERSONATIVE Poetry; that is, all Poetry in which, whether essentially or occasionally, the Poet personates; for here, *speech* is imitated by *speech.* The difference between this, and mere narration or description, is obvious. When, in common discourse, we *relate,* or *describe,* in our own persons, we *imitate* in no other sense than as we raise *ideas* which resemble the things related or described. But when we speak *as another person,* we become mimics, and not only the ideas we convey, but the words, the discourse itself, in which we convey them, are imitations; they resemble, or are supposed to resemble, those of the person we represent.[14]

In Genette this point becomes a critique of "personative" mimesis, and a critique which (ironically, given Socrates' manifest intent,) is an attempt to reclaim narrative at the expense of the dramatic; thus notice how Genette's argument ends with a celebration of diegesis: "the truth is that mimesis in words can only be mimesis of words. Other than that, all we have and can have is degrees of diegesis."[15]

Such projects of reclamation are what we might expect from a critical tradition whose central concern has been with narrative, and which often sees itself as engaged in reversing the Jamesian Anglo-American valuing of the mimetic–dramatic over the narrative, of *showing* over *telling.*[16] But the issue in fact is a deeper one; for questions of the relative place of stylistic strategies in fictional discourse (in the contemporary argument most notably in the novel) are here subsidiary to larger theoretical issues to which the question of mimesis is relevant.

To follow Aristotle in classifying diegesis as one of the modes *of* poetic mimesis rather than classifying it in opposition to mimesis, as Socrates appears to do in the Platonic dialogues, is not to argue that narrative is *per se* an act of mimesis. It is only to claim that narrative and mimesis are contingently related; narrative can be mimetic, but need not be. We will be prevented from seeing this contingency if we think of mimesis in the broader sense as an activity by which a mode of discourse is made to represent a nondiscursive reality; for then narrative will indeed become the privileged and indeed paradigmatic mode of poetic discourse. This is in fact how Genette views mimesis and what leads him to his critique of the Platonic understanding of mimesis as dramatic:

> If we call poetic imitation the fact of representing by verbal means a non-verbal reality and, in exceptional circumstances, a verbal reality (as one calls pictorial imitation the fact of representing in pictorial means non-pictorial reality and, in exceptional circumstances, a pictorial reality), it must be admitted that imitation is to be found in the . . . narrative lines [of the *Iliad*] and not in the . . . dramatic lines, which consist simply in the interpolation, in the middle of a text representing events, of another text directly taken from those events.[17]

This understanding of the nature of mimesis naturally makes Plato's distinction between mimesis and diegesis problematic, while at the same time elevating narrative to a privileged place above the dramatic as the most obvious mode of poetic mimesis. The theoretical issues concerning mimesis which emerge on such an understanding will then concern questions of the power of discourse to represent the nondiscursive and questions concerning the modes of such representation: issues of realism and verisimilitude, of referentiality and illusion, and most abstractly of the relative priority of word and world in the commerce of representation.[18]

But these are not the issues and this is not the understanding of mimesis which informs either Plato's discussion or Aristotle's more general characterization of poetry as mimetic. For Plato and Aristotle, mimesis is not primarily a feature of discourse in its relation to a nondiscursive reality that it represents; it is not, in other words, a mode of radically symbolic, that is, noniconic, representation. For Plato, it is, as we saw, initially a feature of literary discourse in terms of the relation between poet and fictional voice, or more generally between dramatist and dramatic character or between author and *persona*. In the mimetic mode of lexis, the poet, by an act of impersonation, submerges his being with and beneath that of a fictional *persona*. This sense of mimesis is clearly tied to a mode of what is more strictly *imitation*. The larger sense of mimesis which then derives from this narrower sense and which remains operative for Plato and Aristotle is that of mimesis as *iconic* representation.

In this sense, Genette's criticism may be viewed more revealingly as the expression of a theoretical concern above all with structures of noniconic signification, with the rôle that the arbitrary sign plays in the economies of human cognition and creativity. Such a concern may be more faithful to the preoccupations of modern aesthetic theory, for which mimesis has come to figure the absolutely creative and not merely imitative powers of human thought and discourse. But for an understanding of ancient theories of mimesis, we may need to forsake that faithfulness in order to reclaim the iconic sense of mimesis common to Plato and Aristotle.

To reclaim that sense is not to disparage the creativity of noniconic signification, nor therefore to disparage the importance of narrative in the economy of human poetic activity. Our instinct for mimesis, marked by Aristotle as "natural to humankind,"[19] is not in competition with what is undoubtedly our more unique and fundamental capacity to manipulate arbitrary symbols and to invest them with meaning. But these are distinct capacities,[20] and it may be that the capacity for iconic representation is as central to our specifically *artistic* and *fictionalizing* activities as are the capacities that make possible narrative and our more general symbolic activities.

II

It may be appropriate, therefore, to think of mimesis as a richer concept for our understanding of literary art than is apparent from the narrow stylistic context early in the *Republic*. We may discern in mimesis a characteristic feature of poetic or of literary or fictional discourse in general, a feature which may be thought to distinguish literary from more ordinary modes of discourse.

In a literary work, an author has created one or several fictional *personae* who perform speech acts within the fictional world of the work. The author, however, performs no such speech acts in her own person, although she performs creative acts involved in making the linguistic artifact that is the work. But it is only the *personae*, that is, the characters created by the author, who perform first order locutionary acts and who speak within the work. From the point of view of the reader or author *outside* the literary work, these speech acts must therefore be thought of as mimetic or imitative.

The description of literary discourse as mimetic may indeed seem most appropriate to *drama*, where full-blown impersonation is encountered. This view is entertained in the *Republic* where Adeimantus, in the heart of his discussion with Socrates concerning mimesis, speaks as though mimesis were uniquely a feature of the dramatic genre.[21] So it was often understood in antiquity; Proclus for example *glosses* dramatic as mimetic, referring to the *Republic's* first category of lexis as "*to men dramatikon kai mimētikon*, the dramatic or mimetic."[22]

One may understand what draws us to think of the mimetic as uniquely dramatic; but it is not because mimesis applies uniquely to the *genre* of dramatic literature. For a theory of literature as mimesis does not apply selectively to one genre and not to another, to drama, for instance, and not to lyric poetry; such a theory offers itself as a theory of literature in general, a theory which derives from the status of literary discourse itself.

Distinguishing among literary genres as mimetic and nonmimetic confuses specific stylistic and generic features of art with features of art in general. The fact that any object may become mimetic merely by being proclaimed or taken as mimetic by an artist or aesthetic subject has to do with the ontology of art; it cannot be true of this or that artistic genre and not another. Duchamps' bicycle wheel is no more or less mimetic than a Donatello or a Henry Moore, nor than a Brueghel or a Mondrain. In the same way, a theory of literature as mimesis has to do with the nature of literary discourse itself and therefore of literature in general, not with the nature of any *particular* genre of literature.

In some cases the mimetic nature of nondramatic literature will be obvious. Think of the poems of Browning; here the author characteristically creates a fictional voice distanced ironically both from himself and from the "meaning" of his poem. But although the *distance* between author and *persona* may be particularly striking in this case, the ontological *distinction* is not unique to it; it is equally true for any instance of poetic discourse.

Compare for example Wordsworth; the historical poet Wordsworth and the poetic voice which speaks in his poems are not the same person, even though their lives are strikingly similar. Wordsworth the poet lived in an historical place and time continuous with ours, but the poetic *I* which speaks in one of his poems lives in a place and time which is part of the fictional world invoked by that very poem which Wordsworth has created; it is thus in a sense a world generated by words. What is created in these poems, and equally in the poems of a poet such as Anne Sexton or Robert Lowell, who might seem to us on first thought to be speaking directly in their poems, is a fictional *persona*, a *persona* who greatly resembles the person of the author, but who is ontologically distinct from it. Such personae are the primary characters of fictive discourse; they live in fictional worlds to which we have access only through their fragmentary incursions into our world. A poetic voice – a fictive character – is thus part of a fictional world, elements of which correspond to the mimetic residue, so to speak, in our world that constitutes an art work; but a character has no direct connections into our world, and we have no access into his save through the small fixed window art provides.[23]

These facts, I am claiming, follow from the nature of literary discourse itself rather than from a special feature of certain poetry. It follows therefore that every *narrative* voice in a work of literature is also part of a fictional world created by its author. The narrative voice in *War and Peace*, for example, is authored by Tolstoy, but it is not the voice *of* Tolstoy; it is a voice which lives within the fictional world created by the novel and ultimately by the novel's author. An act of narrative, therefore, like any action (or indeed like any other entity) can be mimetic or not.

These reflections about narration and mimesis have been in the service of revealing a view of poetic activity which is founded on more than the concern with the arbitrarily signifying powers of language. The more, I have argued, is iconic imitation, mimesis. A poet in this sense is not primarily a creator of things that imitate; it is the poet himself who is an imitator in that she makes imitation things. It is not, in other words, that the poet is an imitator because she creates a piece of discourse that imitates a non-discursive reality; she is an imitator because she imitates a speaker speaking about reality, though it is not her reality, but the reality of that fictional speaker's fictional world. It is this relation between the poet and the speaker that is the primary imitative relation. The poet creates an imitation speaker who makes real speeches in the imitative world, "imaginary gardens with real toads in them," as Marianne Moore once put it, not imaginary toads in gardens that are real. The fact that poetry is imitation does not mean that poetry imitates, but that it, like all literary discourse, is the internal object of an act of imitating.

III

The generality of Aristotle's claim, therefore, is a fruitful one, not in that it depicts art as a mirror of the world, but in that it reminds us of the iconicity, the fictionalizing modality of artistic representation.

But the critique of mimesis with which we began may still interest us; for if even narrative is mimetic in an iconic sense, it follows *a fortiori* that drama is also iconic. Thus the observation that poetry as speech can be strongly mimetic only *of* speech has as its correlate the fact that tragedy can be iconic of action only if the mimesis is itself an action. So Twining, in his discussion of imitation cited above, observes that: "In the poem itself nothing but *words* can be immediately copied. Gravina says well, Non *è imitazione poetica* quella, che non è fatta *dalle parole*." But in the same context, he notes that: "the drama, indeed, is said also to imitate *action* by *action*; but this is only in actual representation, where the players are the immediate imitators."[24] Drama, in other words, does not describe action, but re-presents it; a drama is a mimetic action.

So if tragedy is a mimesis of action, its medium in turn is itself action, but mimetic action. This fact is made clear in the further elaboration of Aristotle's definition of tragedy at the beginning of Chapter 6. Tragedy, we recall, is there defined as the mimesis of an action; the action, Aristotle then continues, must be serious (*spoudaios*) and it must be an action which is complete although taking place over time: *teleias megethos ekhousēs*.[25] The mimesis in turn is said to be accomplished in "sweetened" language, by which Aristotle explains he means language such as we might call *poetic* language, and it is to be: "*drōntōn kai ou di apangelias* – by means of acting and not by means of narration."[26]

The requirement that a drama be acted[27] and not narrated is one that we recognize; it is the requirement that it be *dramatic*. But the word of interest here is the word that gives rise to its being called dramatic in the first place, the word *drōntōn*. This word is an inflected form of *dran*, which Aristotle has earlier reminded his readers is the Doric for *to act*, equivalent to Attic *prattein*.[28]

To describe a tragedy thus as *acted* is to make clear that the medium of the mimesis of an action is itself an action. But in using a term which is equivalent to but distinct from the standard Attic term for action (and which moreoever has the deep connections to the poetic and linguistic conventions of tragedy that *dran* enjoys) Aristotle makes clear that it is an action of a special and peculiar character. It is an action which is an instance not of *prattein* or *praxis*, but of *dran* or *drasis*, and its internal product is therefore not a *pragma* or *praxis*; it is a *drama*. We may describe such action using a scholastic distinction as *formally* a drama and *objectively* a praxis, and this way of putting the difference reveals the logical tie which the subtitle of this paper is meant to invoke; it is a *drama* because it is the mimesis of a *praxis*.

That a drama is a mimetic representation of a praxis was earlier made clear by Aristotle when he contrasted different modes of poetry with reference to the distinctions drawn in the first three chapters of the *Poetics*. Let us recall that contrast. One the one hand, Aristotle notes, Sophocles is an imitator of the same sort as Homer, for both imitate what is serious; but on the other hand he is an imitator of the same sort as Aristophanes, for "*prattontas mimountai kai drōntas amphō*: both imitate actors [*prattontas*] and actors [*drōntas*]."[29]

The sense here surely demands that the second likeness, that between Sophocles and Aristophanes, should be in terms of the *mode* of mimesis (the *tō heterōs kai mē ton auton tropon mimeisthai* of Chapter 1) in contrast to the first likeness, that between Sophocles and Homer, which is clearly presented in terms of the *object* which the mimesis is a mimesis *of* (the *tō hetera mimeisthai* of that chapter). But it may seem hard to find that contrast in the received text. Casaubon therefore suggests that we should read *prattontes* and *drōntes*, making them the subject and not the object of *mimountai*.[30] The difficulty is equally clear a few lines later, where Casaubon also emends. The manuscripts given *hothen kai dramata kaleisthai tines auta phasin, hoti mimountai drōntas*; Casaubon again suggests that we read *drōntes*, so as to yield, as it were: it is for this reason that they are called *acts*, because it is *actors* who do the imitating.

Casaubon's concerns are understandable, and his emendations, although they demand a tortured construction of the Greek, produce a text consistent with our observation that the mimesis of an action is itself an action. But they may be seen as unnecessary, and their dificulties avoided,[31] if we recall that *mimeisthai* carries with it the sense of acting a role, that is, playing a part.[32] In such cases, the object of mimesis is the *internal* and not the *external* object imitated. It is this very doubleness of mimesis – the fact that dramas (or more properly dramatic authors and actors) imitate praxis-acting persons by imitating dramatic-acting characters – that is captured in Aristotle's requirement: *prattontas mimountai kai drōntas* – they imitate agents acting, that is, you understand, *acting*.

We may express this fact in a Sassurian way: Casaubon wishes to prevent

Aristotle's phrase from capturing the *external referent.* He therefore reads the phrase as referring to the *physical signifier* (that is, to the actual flesh and blood actors), whereas what we want is reference to the *signified* (that is, to the dramatic characters). These are subtle distinctions and characteristically difficult to make; compare the difficulty I noted above with confessional poets. Sometimes the difficulty is expressed in our desire to say, for example, that John Wayne always plays John Wayne, or Marlon Brando Marlon Brando. The cinema in particular may lead to this temptation, or rather, as we should say, to this intriguing artistic possibility; it is what allows actors like Brando to play themselves in ways that lead to interesting intertextuality in the film medium.

Perhaps we can become clearer about the relation between praxis and drama by considering a representative action. Here is one for example: a man is hiding behind a curtain in a room in which another man is speaking to a woman, and when the first man moves, the second, taking him for a much hated adversary, stabs him through the curtain. Imagine this action being enacted on stage as part of a drama; imagine, in other words, that it is an *act* and not simply an action. On a September evening at Drury Lane Theater, we witness this acted action; we watch Mr. Garrick acting Hamlet stabbing Polonius, acted by Mr. Cibber.

How shall we describe what we see? Here are three descriptions: (1) Mr. Garrick runs a stage rapier through a curtain, carefully avoiding hitting Mr. Cibber, but so as to give the audience the illusion of one man stabbing another through a curtain. (2) A character named Hamlet (one of the *dramatis personae*) kills another character named Polonius. (3) Hamlet kills Polonius.

I suggest that it is fruitful to think of these three formally distinct but materially intertwined actions in this way: (1) describes a real action in the real world. (2) describes a mimetic action in the real world. (3) describes a real action in the mimetic world, that is, in the world which is projected from the actions and speeches we witness. Description (1) concerns the art of acting, and is importantly though subtly distinct from (2); to confound the two is a common confusion, and may be at the heart of much misunderstanding of the structure of mimesis, as well perhaps as of our distrust of the mimetic and of those who enact it.[33] But, nevertheless, (1) and (2) are in a sense aspects of the same ontological complex (as signifier and signified are aspects of a single sign).

The relations between (2) and (3) are even more subtle and more difficult to sort out. But the central point is the point above, that mimesis takes two different but logically related objects, one of which might be thought to be an internal object, the other not. The relationship is thus perhaps an instance of the inveterately philosophically perplexing relationship between the internal and external objects of intentional states. I see a sight: for example, Philadelphia. In a sense it follows that Philadelphia is a sight (e.g. for sore eyes); but it certainly does not follow that I live in a sight, or that William Penn founded a sight. We may try to guard against the inanity of such inference by the careful use of expressions like "the sight of Philadelphia." Matty Groves hears a sound; it must be Lord Arling and all his men. But again it does not follow that poor Matty was slain by a mere sound, and again we may try to guard reason with protective phrases like "the sound of Lord Arling and all his men."

To trace the history of these and other moves, and of the attempts to deal with the larger issues behind them, is to trace the complex history of philosophy's (necessary) concern with the nature of *appearance*. The masters of philosophical discourse on this topic include (among others and with varying degrees of attention to its ontological and epistemological dimensions) Plato, Berkeley, Hume and Kant. A central curiosity about Aristotle is the fact that his name does not appear on this list; why is this question so relatively unaddressed in his writings? Why is Plato's virtual obsession with *image* not matched in Aristotle's thought?

One possible answer is that Plato's concern with the imaged and its image (his concern with the complex modalities of Socrates' divided line) is translated into Aristotle's concern with the *latent* and the *manifest*, with power and its corresponding actualizing activity. The medium of such translation may be the duality of *inner* and *outer*; recall that in the *Republic* this duality figures precisely the relation between a virtue and its expression that comes to be understood by Aristotle in terms of *hexis* and *energeia*.

But it may be equally revealing that Aristotle does express this concern, but expresses it almost uniquely in the context of his discussion of *fictional mimesis*. It may be no accident, in other words, that the *Poetics* is not part of the *Metaphysics*, and that there is no Aristotelian work that weaves together the issues of *being* and *mimetic representation* as the *Republic*, for example, does.

IV

It may be of interest to reflect further on this fact. Aristotle, we have seen, uses two different Greek words to refer to the mimetic and its object, but points to the affinity of these words to reveal the corresponding affinity of their referents, the reciprocal filiation of drama and praxis. We use one word – the word *act* – to do the job of Aristotle's (that is, Greek's) two words. This fact gives to a later master a wonderful device for the deep and significant word-play on the complex senses of "act" that we find in *Hamlet*.[34] When Polonius pairs "devotion's visage" with "pious action" as means by which "we do sugar o'er The devil himself" we hear the complexities inherent in the concept of acting, as when the grave-digger points out that "an act hath three branches – it is to act, to do, to perform."[35]

Shakespeare's punning mirrors more than his concern with theatricality as a figure of life. It reveals a respect in which all moral action is in a sense mimetic. I do not mean this simply in the sense that dramaturgical theories of action reveal to us. There is a further fact about the relation of action to virtue that is here invoked, the fact that in acting, we may merely be acting. When Hamlet counsels his mother to "assume a virtue, if you have it not,"[36] this fact is registered. It is a fact about virtue and action for any moral theory which, like that of Plato and Aristotle, is founded on the *good*, that is, on the centrality of *virtue*; for such a theory, action in itself is morally thin. Recall Aristotle's remark that although "actions [*pragmata*] are said to be just or moderate when they are the sort of acts which a just or moderate person would perform [*praxeien*], a person is not just or moderate who performs these actions [*ho tauta prattōn*], but who also acts as the just or moderate act."³⁷

On a moral theory of this sort, the moral status of any given action is thus by itself only contingently related to virtue. We may of course avoid this difficulty simply by abandoning a virtue ethic, and concerning ourselves only with *action*, since according to a moral theory founded on the *right*, that is, on the centrality of *action* alone, merely to act correctly in each given situation may be sufficient for moral success. But it is a critical fact for a virtue-based theory of ethics that a virtuous person can thus be impersonated by someone who is merely, as we might say, *acting*.

Hamlet's advice to Gertrude has another more familiar Aristotelian ring to it. For the assumption of virtue, by itself a mere act, is, when repeated, the instrument by which virtue is produced: "*ek tou pollakis prattein ta dikaia kai sōphrona [hai aretai] periginetai* – [virtue] comes about from repeated just and modern actions."³⁸ Virtue, in other words, is itself shaped by the impersonation of the virtuous. We know from Plato's sensitivity to the dangers of mimesis how double-edged this fact is; for it is not only virtue but vice as well which is engendered by impersonation. These dangers were not overlooked in the Elizabethan fascination with acting; witness Ben Jonson: "*I have* considered, our whole life is like a *Play*; wherein every man, forgetfull of himself, is in travaile with expression of another. Nay, wee so insist in imitating others, as wee cannot (when it is necessary) returne to our selves; like Children, that imitate the vices of *Stammerers* so long, till at last they become such; and make the habit to another nature, as it is never forgotten."³⁹

The complex modalities of acting that are revealed in these facts are mirrored in a corresponding complexity in the meaning of *mimēsis*. For in the tradition to which Aristotle is heir, *mimēsis* and *mimeisthai* can clearly bear the meaning of a nonfictional impersonation, as well as the more standard sense of artistic impersonation. So we find it, for example, in Democritus: "it is necessary either to be good or to impersonate the good [*agathon ē einai khreōn ē mimeisthai*]"⁴⁰ or "it is difficult to imitate bad people [*mimeisthai tous kakous*] and not to wish to imiate good people."⁴¹

Similarly, Xenophon, discussing the charges brought against Socrates, asks:

> how could he, given his character, have made others either impious or lawbreaking or gluttonous or sexually intemperate or lazy? In fact, he kept them from these vices, making them desire virtue and leading them to expect that if they took care of themselves, they would become decent and respectable people. To be sure, he never claimed to be a teacher of such excellence, but by being a model of it [*phaneros einai toioutos*], he gave his followers the

> hope that by becoming imitators of him [*mimoumenous ekeinon*], they could
> aquire it.[42]

In similar vein, the author of the *Rhetoric to Alexander* urges that children
"imitate the actions of their fathers – *mimeisthai tas tōn paterōn praxeis*."[43]

Above all, it is this power of imitation to mould character which creates the
dangers to which Plato constantly alerts his readers, and which is the foundation
of the Socratic critique of mimesis, the critique personified in the depiction of the
sophist as a practitioner of the *doxomimetic art*.[44]

But once again, no such discussion of this dimension of mimesis occurs in
Aristotle. With few exceptions, the Aristotelian treatment of mimesis is uniquely
in the context of poetry; it concerns itself almost exclusively with mimesis as a
mode of fictional representation.[45] It is as though Aristotle has carefully pruned
from his discussion all senses of mimesis which might involve direct preparation
for or actual connection with the affective and practical aspects of an agent's life.
Mimesis with all its rich complexity has been channelled by Aristotle into the
single context of artistic representation, condensed and intensified by being
limited to the fictive contexts of poetry.

V

Recognizing the degree to which Aristotle's use of the term *mimēsis* is restricted
to dramatic representation should remind us again of how important the notion
of mimesis is to his account of tragedy. Nietzsche complained of the fact that

> Never since Aristotle has an explanation of the tragic effect been offered from
> which aesthetic states or an aesthetic activity of the listener could be
> inferred. Now the serious events are supposed to prompt pity and fear to
> discharge themselves in a way that relieves us; now we are supposed to feel
> elevated and inspired by the triumph of good and noble principles, at the
> sacrifice of the hero in the interest of a moral vision of the universe. I am sure
> that for countless men precisely this, and only this, is the effect of tragedy,
> but it plainly follows that all these men, together with their interpreting
> aestheticians, have had no experience of tragedy as a supreme *art*.[46]

Nietzsche's plea that tragedy be understood as an art accords with our
recognition that Aristotle's account is elaborated in the context of his description
of tragedy as mimetic poetry. This fact of course leaves open the critical and
interesting question of the relationship between the peculiar pleasure appropriate to tragedy and the pleasure which, Aristotle tells us, we take in mimesis
itself.[47] While these two pleasures may not be the same, it remains true that we
can understand the tragic pleasure only if we keep in mind that tragedies are
mimetic.

What is the force of the mimetic nature of drama for our understanding of
tragedy? We may begin by reminding ourselves of this fact about mimetic

representation: we do not experience emotions in a theatrical context in the same way that we might be expected to experience them in real life. Our emotional responses to tragic events witnessed on stage, that is, to events mimetically represented in tragic poetry, are not the same as the responses which would be appropriate if we were to encounter such events in a nonmimetic situation.

Nor for Aristotle can they be; for he holds that the effect of witnessing tragedy is at once pleasurable and associated with the experience of fear and pity. But the experience of fear and of pity are not in themselves pleasurable; so how can the otherwise painful experience of fear and pity yield *pleasure?* It is the ability of tragic drama to cause this to happen that makes it such a miracle of rare device, its ability to raise a sunny dome of pleasure upon the icy caves of terror and commiseration.

One source of this ability lies precisely in the fact that the theater is an arena of *mimetic* representation. As such, it is a context in which emotions are *experienced,* but without their ordinary connection to the rest of our affective and practical lives. And not surprisingly; for the events that occasion these emotions are not happening to anyone who lives where we live. I do not mean that they are not happening to anyone in our *neighborhood,* but that they are not happening to anyone in our *world;* the deep ontological otherness of the fictional thus enables us to experience these emotions, as it were, *dispassionately.* Our awareness that we are not to rush down the aisle to prevent Hamlet's stabbing of Polonius, an awareness which is an important element in our grasp of the mimetic, has its emotional counterpart in our ability to experience fear and pity in the context of the theater without the affective consequences and connections that accompany fear and pity in the contexts of, as we say, real life.

We may wish, on such a view, to think of the uses of tragic poetry, and indeed of art in general, as analogous to the uses of ritual, not simply to intensify and enforce structures of communal life, but in addition to provide contexts of sanctuary in which dangerous activities of such intensification and ordering can be carried out.[48] By virtue of its mimetic nature, tragedy marks off a sacred space in which we are allowed to experience emotions safely; it enables us to confront terrible possibilities and the fears which they inspire, fears we cannot painlessly nor therefore easily admit in the ordinary contexts of our life. All of this is accomplished because dramatic action is *drama,* that is, because it is *mimetic* action.[49]

VI

We might thank that Aristotle sees tragedy as enabling us, by providing a context of mimesis such as I have described, to experience safely and thus to allay a more general and abstract fear: the fear that we may be subject to the sorts of terrible events represented in tragic poetry.[50] In a sense this is true. But the more general fear which tragedy allows us to confront is not, on Aristotle's view, the fear that we may find ourselves in situations specifically identical to those of tragic protagonists; it is not, in other words, the fear that we might be led to slay our fathers or sacrifice our daughters. What we fear on Aristotle's view, I think, is far more general than the particular family troubles (if we may so under-describe them) of Agamemmon's or Oedipus' lives. It is rather the common feature of (tragically represented) action that derives from the universal possibility of *hamartia*: the general liability of action to mishap, and the consequent fragility of happiness and frailty of moral character and choice.

When we think of tragic action in this light, I shall now suggest, we may begin to have a different appreciation of the second aspect of Aristotle's theory with which we began, the centrality of praxis to his understanding of tragedy and the force of his repeated emphasis that tragedy is a mimesis specifically of praxis. I do not mean to argue that the linked vulnerability of action and happiness is a unique focus of Aristotle's interest in the *Poetics*; that work is too ample in scope for there to be a single focus. Aristotle's interest in tragedy, like his interest in so many things, has many sources. At one level the *Poetics* is simply an expression of his seemingly indefatigable curiosity concerning whatever he finds about him, and particularly concerning the institutions of the *polis*. Perhaps at the most basic level, it is simply another theoretical treatise, this time about drama and the institutions of dramatic poetry which, Everestlike, were there to write a theoretical treatise about.

I mean to argue simply that in the *Poetics*, we may see Aristotle's fascination with how the plots of tragedy (particularly in his favorite example of *Oedipus the King*) reveal the complex problems involved in our understanding of praxis and, more importantly, the complexities in praxis itself that generate those problems. It is this fascination, I think, that is revealed in his repeated emphasis that tragedy is a mimesis, and a mimesis of praxis.

We have seen one aspect of this emphasis in remarking how the fragile relationship between action and virtue is registered in the mimetic status of tragic action; for mimesis, I have suggested, figures the unreliability of that *impersonation* by which virtue is acquired. But the more characteristic obsessions of Greek tragedy concern the nature of praxis itself rather than the relation of praxis to virtue. What is important here, I shall suggest, is the ambiguity of action.

Note first that actions are multiply individuated; a particular set of an agent's bodily motions, that is, may be thought of as any one of a number of actions. At one level, this multiplicity of action follows simply from a more general ontological multiplicity which Aristotle recognizes. In the *Metaphysics*, for example,[51] he remarks on the unity of an individual *entity* which under different descriptions exhibits different *beings*. His argument there relies on a simple fact central to his ontology: the fact that any single individual entity may be introduced under a plurality of descriptions, each of which determines one of a plurality of different *beings*. This inversion of the more conventional form of the one and the many, central to the thinking of both Plato and Aristotle, is equally applicable to actions. There are, in other words, "alternative descriptions of the same action,"[52] witness Aristotle's discussion concerning actions as voluntary and involuntary at the beginning of Book III of the *Nicomachean Ethics*.[53] It is this multiplicity of human action – what one scholar has called "the doubleness of the deed" – that results in the phenomenon of "tragic conflict", a phenomenon which may be thought to characterize much of the central action of tragedy.[54]

This view of the tragic dimensions of action, however, takes as its paradigm such tragedies as *Agamemnon* and *Antigone*, dramas in which the protagonist's performing an action under one description entails choosing it as well under other equally applicable descriptions: "We [see] what an important part in Aeschylus' dramas the ambiguity of human action plays. It can be the fulfillment of a duty, obedience to a divine order; and yet at the same time be a dreadful crime."[55] But it is instructive that Aristotle takes as his paradigm *Oedipus the King*; for this fact suggests that it is a different ambiguity in actions which interests him.

This ambiguity is not lateral, between a series of coextensive and equally applicable descriptions, but categorical, between two fundamentally different modes of capturing and individuating actions. On the one hand, an action is the object of the intentional states of a deliberative and choosing agent; it is what we do in the sense that it is what we are about and what we take ourselves to be doing. On the other hand, however, an action is an act; it is what we do in the sense of what emerges as the result of our intentional activity.

What is revealed in tragedy is the ever-present possibility of a fracture between these two aspects of action. Tragic lives figure the chance of rift between actions understood as the expressions of the character and intentional choices of moral agents and actions as events in an objective world outside the control of such agents, actions with a life of their own which thus transcends the intentions and plans of their authors. But perhaps more central to Aristotle's concern is what follows from this fact: the distinction between guilt and blameworthiness, and more critically, the power of an institution like tragic poetry to help us come to terms with the terrible weight of that distinction and of the fault line in our practical lives on which it rests.

In the background of the *Poetics*, we may thus witness Aristotle's interest in questions of moral action. But these questions concern, as it were, the pathology of such action; his attention here is on the ways in which our deliberations, choices, and moral plans may ultimately prove feckless or offer us no safe choice, and of the fear and pity which are occasioned by the recognition of this fact. At our best, acting out of good character and with good deliberation, we often will, at one crossroad or another in our lives, act in ways that bring about our downfall, killing men whom we take to be brigands, but whom the gods, in their diffident cunning, know to be our fathers.

The fears occasioned by this recognition, as I have urged, are more general than the fear that we might kill our fathers; they are the fears that lie at the heart of our recognition that goodness of character and excellence of deliberation cannot guarantee our happiness, that actions good from the point of view of the agent may nonetheless, through no fault of the agent, be revealed as bad in that very world in which they are enacted.

These fears show the *Poetics* as the sequel to the *Ethics*, a sequel that reveals the terrifying frailty of virtue and the vulnerability of the happiness that we, correctly and for all the right reasons, aim at in the cultivation of such virtue. Behind these fears is thus the fact of human vulnerability, a fact that derives from the very structure and nature of human action and the tenuous relation between virtue and happiness which in turn results from that nature; tragic poetry, precisely because it is mimetic, provides a context in which these fears may be experienced in ways detached from the painful and paralyzingly frightful modes of experience in our daily life. But because they are not like the fear that I might slay my father – a fear which, however much it may reveal the deeply conflicted feelings that I harbor toward my father, is at once remote and neurotic – these fears are associated with the darker and more pervasive recognition of human limitation that is central to tragedy.

The nature of that limitation, on Aristotle's understanding of tragedy, is specific. For tragedies, on his view, mimetically represent the actions of human beings who are basically good, and who, moreover, have on the whole deliberated and chosen well, but who have ended up acting badly. The fear and pity which tragedy occasions are wed precisely to this recognition that goodness of character and goodness of deliberation can lead, not simply to disastrous *consequences*, but to disastrous *actions* on the part of an agent. It is the recognition of a strain of insouciant refractoriness to human agency that is woven into the very fabric of action itself, a recognition of the inability of agents to guarantee their well-being and happiness even when they attempt, *correctly*, to found that well-being and happiness on the cultivation of moral virtue and deliberation.

VII

These reflections should lead us to practice extreme care when we try to understand Aristotle's apparent and cryptic promise, at the end of the definition we cited above, that tragedy may effect a *catharsis* from these very fears that it occasions.[56] We ought not to read this promise to mean that tragedy may relieve us of these fears by revealing a deeper rationality and order of the world in which human agency operates, a perspective from which that world may be absolved and its fundamental goodness reaffirmed.[57]

For such a reading, I think, would blunt Aristotle's view that tragedy reveals to us a critical fact (though perhaps not the most important fact) about human agency: the fact that happiness is subject to vicissitude in a manner that neither character nor virtue nor deliberation can ultimately guard against. Aristotle means neither to deny that fact nor to characterize tragic poetry as denying it.

He rather thinks of tragedy as a human institution designed to help us accept it. We may think of such acceptance as ultimately restorative of our trust in the world, but it is not founded for Aristotle on a palliation of the tragic truth about the efficacy of human agency in that world.

Nor is it founded on a relief effected by simple emotional purgation. This fact may reveal one final respect in which it is helpful to remember that tragedy is a form of mimesis, the respect in which attention to the mimetic nature of tragic action might allow a new appreciation of *catharsis* both as lustrative rather than merely purgative and as objective rather than simply a feature of audience response.

Despite (or perhaps because of) the intense and voluminous discussion it has received, the exact sense of *catharsis* in its cameo appearance in the *Poetics* may well continue to elude us. But much of the controversy, and in particular the familiar opposition between lustrative and purgative interpretations, may be unnecessary; to stress the lustrative sense of *catharsis* is not *per se* to deny its purgative sense, for lustration is a purging of the purified object from its impurities and pollutions.[58] It is certainly this lustrative sense that we find prominent in Plato[59] (a fact which may help to balance the antilustrative weight characteristically given the single discussion of *catharsis* in the *Politics*).[60] But in any case, it seems to me that the opposition between these senses, as well as the vexed question of exactly where the *catharsis* takes place,[61] may seem less pressing when we attend to the mimetic character of tragic poetry.

We may see the *catharsis* which takes place in the theater as kin to those rituals of purification which effect atonement for agents who have acquired an objective guilt through no fault of their own or as the result of actions whose moral ambiguity is incommensurable with their guilt. Such purification is sometimes mimetically represented on stage. The witty ablution of Orestes and of a god that is at the heart of Iphigenia's ruse in *Iphigenia among the Taurians*[62] is perhaps the most straightforward instance, although Aristotle's description of the plot of which it is a part reads uncannily like an allegory of tragedy itself, culminating in a "*sōtēria dia tēs katharseōs*" – salvation by purification.[63] But we may think of more subtle cases. Something happens in the course of *Oedipus at Colonus* that allows Oedipus to characterize himself as now being *catharos*;[64] the *Oresteia* is in one sense a representation of the *polis* as the developed succesor to simpler institutions of purification by which Orestes may be not only cleansed from bloodstain but also released from the wearying and repetitive violence based upon an economy of blood vengeance.

We may, however, think of the purification as taking place not in praxis, but in drama, not, that is to say, in action mimetically represented, but in the acting which mimetically represents that action.[65] It is here, I think, that the double emphasis of Aristotle's theory is important; tragedy is the mimesis of praxis *drōntōn*: action acted. It is here that we might imagine the hero of *Oedipus the King* receiving in the mimetic action of drama the forgiveness and cleansing of guilt denied him in the praxeis of his life, missing in his own (fictional) real-life role of *pharmakon*.

Such *catharsis* is achieved through the *apodeixis* in action of the events in all their complexity, and the resultant excitement in the compassionate audience of the fear and pity which are the occasion both of Oedipus' staged purification and of the audience's sympathetic purification. Through the ritualized and for- malized action of tragic poetry, we as audience are thus enabled to participate in the restorative capacities of human society to forgive and thus to heal the guilty sufferers of tragic misaction. And in so far as we are able to identify with Oedipus, for example, and to do so by the very fear and pity we experience at the witnessing of his fate and which is the occasion of his theatrical purification, we are at the same time relieved of the more painful (and potentially paralyzing) aspects of the general fear we feel at the possibility of that identification; we achieve, like Orestes, a salvation through purgatory, a *sōtēria dia tēs katharseōs*.

The power of mimesis to effect an almost magical salvation for those who share in and witness it is, it seems to me, part of the mysterious force of the dramatic. Its recognition is not limited to ancient theory; consider this descrip- tion, by a thinker some seven hundred years later than Aristotle, of Christian mimetic rites:

> O strange and wondrous thing; we did not really die, nor were we really buried, nor did we really rise again after being crucified; but although the mimesis was a representation, the salvation was a reality [*en eikoni hē mimēsis, en alētheiai de hē sōtēria*]. Christ actually was crucified and actually was buried and truly rose again, and all of this has been graciously given us in order that we might, by participating through mimesis in his sufferings, gain salvation in reality [*tē mimēsei tōn pathēmatōn autou koinōnēsantes alēthieai tēn sōtērian kerdēsōmen*].[66]

VIII

The *Poetics* may be seen as the sequel to the *Ethics* and the *Politics* in a deeper sense than that in which it continues philosophical interests central to the theory of human action in these works. For more importantly, the *Poetics* continues the vision developed in these companion volumes of the polis, or more generally of organized social and communal activity, as the source of our capacity to live satisfying and fulfiling human lives.

Both the *Nicomachean Ethics* and the *Politics* see civic life as the matrix in which virtue may be formed and nurtured as means to the achievement of human happiness and well-being. In tragedy our gaze is directed upon the vulnerability of that well-being, and we are invited to acknowledge the fears occasioned by that vulnerability. These are the realistic fears that politically nurtured virtue may not always be sufficient for the well-being at which it aims, and that our happiness is subject to the stern and seemingly irrational control of a destiny which may at any moment sunder the tenuous connection between virtue and well-being, a destiny which is the result neither of some inner flaw of character nor of some external *daimōn* of ill-fortune, but of the very actions that we have thoughtfully and courageously chosen.[67]

The *Poetics* offers us the hope that we may be able, by acknowledging these fears, to cleanse our affective lives of their pollution, and be restored to the fellowship of parlous human agency. And that cleansing, the *Poetics* suggests, may be accomplished through the agency of institutions which are themselves artifacts of human cultural life, institutions and artifacts rooted in the human capacity for mimesis.

Notes

1. *Poetics* 1, 1447a13 ff; 6, 1449b24.
2. *Poetics* 6, 1450a37; 1450b3; for *psychē* as cause of being, see *Metaphysics* V. 8, 1017b16.
3. *Poetics* 6, 1449b36; 1450a16; 1450a37; 1450b3; 7, 1450b24; 8, 1451a31; 9, 1451b29; 1452a2; 11, 1452b1; 23, 1459a17.
4. *Poetics* 1, 1447a13–16.
5. *Republic* III, 392D.
6. *Republic* III, 393A6 f.
7. *Republic* III, 393A8 ff.
8. *Republic* III, 393D8 ff.
9. I have discussed this distinction at greater length and tried to sketch its implications for our understanding of Plato in "Silence and Imitation in the Platonic Dialogues" in *Methods of Interpreting Plato and his Dialogues*, eds. J. C. Klagge and N. D. Smith, (1992 Supplementary Volume to *Oxford Studies in Ancient Philosophy*), pp. 73–92. There I argue that in fact the Socratic distinction is by no means Plato's considered view on this issue; mimesis is far more general and far more integral to Plato's views than the argument of Socrates in this context might lead us to believe. In this respect, Aristotle's recognition that all modes of poetic discourse, both narrative and dramatic, are mimetic, is in keeping with Plato's deeper intentions. I also argue that the account of *mimēsis* in Book III of the *Republic* extends into Book X.
10. *Poetics* 1, 1447a17 f.
11. *Poetics* 3, 1448a20 ff.
12. *Poetics* 24, 1460a5 ff.
13. G. Genette, "Discours du récit," in *Figures III*, (Paris 1972), published in English translation as *Narrative Discourse*, trans. J. Lewin (Ithaca, 1980), 164.
14. T. Twining, *Aristotle's Treatise on Poetry Translated; With Notes on the Translation, and on the Original; and Two Dissertations, on Poetical, an Musical, Imitation* (London 1789; reprinted New York, 1971), 20 f.
15. Genette, *Narrative Discourse*, 164.
16. The central manifesto of the view under attack is P. Lubbock, *The Craft of Fiction*, (New York, 1921). It is instructive to compare W. Booth. *The Rhetoric of Fiction* (Chicago, 1961). Booth is cited by Genette as an internal critic of the valuing of mimesis (*Narrative Discourse*, 163); this strikes me as a misreading of Booth's larger argument, which asks how the rhetorical force of fiction operates in spite of the pervasive fact of mimesis. Booth's concern is not with the author, but with what he calls the "implied author," and that is a concept which lives in the field of mimesis.
17. G. Genette, "Frontières du récit, in *Figures II* (Paris, 1962), 53 f., published in English

translation as "Frontiers of Narrative," in *Figures of Literary Discourse*, trans. A. Sheridan (New York, 1982), 31.

18. See for example A. D. Nutall's plea for a realist aesthetic in *A New mimesis: Shakespeare and the Representation of Reality* (London, 1983), 181; "The new mimesis is a new theory, and its essence is the reconciliation of form with veridical or probable representation."

19. *Poetics* 4, 1448b5 ff.

20. Although we may wish to explain the one in terms of the other, as R. Girard for example argues that mimetic desire is the originary principle of structures of signification.

21. *Republic* III, 394D5 ff.

22. Proclus, *In Platonis Rem Publicam commentarii*, ed. W. Kroll (Leipzig, 1899), 14.20.

23. "Think for instance, of a striding statue; imagine the purposeful inclination of the torso, the alert and penetrating gaze of the head and its eyes, the outstreched arm and pointing figure; everything would appear to direct us toward some goal in front of it. Yet our eye travels only to the finger's end, and not beyond. Though pointing, the finger bids us stay instead, and we journey slowly back along the tension of the arm. In our hearts we know what actually surrounds the statue. The same surrounds every other work of art: empty space and silence." W. Gass, "The Concept of Character in Fiction," in *Fiction and the Figures of Life* (Boston, 1979), 49. The operative word here is "actually;" it must mean "in this, and not the statue's fictional, world." For what surrounds the statue in its fictional space is a world, the world which contains among other things the object of the statue's pointing, the object of its intention. Indeed, it is by the "pointing" of those elements of a work of art common to its world and ours that it reveals to us the existence and nature of that part of its world hidden from us, the world behind the scenes. When a character looks offstage, we know that something is there. But we don't turn around in the theater to search for it, since it isn't *there*; it is just beyond our sight in another world, a world of which we're allowed only a glimpse.

24. Twining, *Aristotle's Treatise on Poetry*, 21. Twining's reference is to G. Gravina, *Della ragion poetica libri due e Della Tragedia libro uno* (Venice, 1731).

25. The stipulation is important, since an action may be complete without taking any time: *Poetics* 7 1450b25: *estin gar holon kai mēden ekhon megethos*. See Aristotle's explanation at *Nicomachean Ethics* (*NE*) X.5, 1174a14 ff.

26. *Poetics* 6, 1449b26–27.

27. This requirement is independent of the thorny question of whether Aristotle thought that tragedy must be actually performed on stage.

28. *Poetics* 3, 1448b1.

29. *Poetics* 3, 1448a27.

30. I. Casaubon, *De Satyrica Graecorum Poesi et Romanorum Satira* (Paris, 1605), Ch. 3.

31. For a discussion of these difficulties, see R. Dupont-Roc and J. Lallot's edition of the *Poetics*, Aristotle, *La Poétique, le text Grec avec une traduction et des notes de lecture* (Paris, 1980), 162.

32. See for example Aristophanes *Thesmorporiazusae* 851 in which Mnesilochus' playing the part of Helen is described by the verb *mimēsomai*, or *Plutus* 290, in which Cairo leads a rendition of a Cyclops play *ton Kuklōpa mimoumenos* – playing the part of the Cyclops.

33. See the various remarks about attitudes towards actors in J. Barish, *The Antitheatrical Prejudice* (Berkeley, 1981).

34. See M. Mack's remarks about "act" as *Hamlet's* "radical metaphor" in "The World of 'Hamlet'," *The Yale Review* XLI (1952) 502–523, and more generally A. Righter, *Shakespeare and the Idea of the Play* (London, 1962).

35. *Hamlet* 3.1.47, 5.1.11.
36. *Hamlet* 3.4.161.
37. *NE* II. 4, 1105b5 ff.
38. *NE* II. 4, 1105b4 f.
39. B. Jonson, *Timber: or Discoveries* (§§ 1093–1098), ed. R. S. Walker, (Syracuse, NY, 1953).
40. Democritus, DK B39, Stobaeus, III. 37.25.
41. Democritus, DK B79.
42. Xenophon, *Memorabilia* I.ii.2–3.
43. *Rhetoric to Alexander,* 1422a30 Cf. also the Aristotelian *Problems* XXIX. 10, 951a7.
44. *Sophist,* 267 E1.
45. The exceptions are these: in the *Meteorology* IV, 381b6, the fact that cooking helps digestion is described as an instance of art imitating nature; the mimetic powers of parrots and similar birds are mentioned in the *History of Animals* VIII. 12, 597b24 ff., while the ape's palm is said to imitate a heel in II. 8, 502b9; at *Politics* II. 10, 1271b22, the Spartan constitution is said to imitate the Cretan.
46. F. Nietzsche, *The Birth of Tragedy* (§ 22), trans. W. Kaufmann (New York, 1967), 132.
47. *Poetics* 4, 1448b8 ff.
48. Think of M. Gluckman's theories of rituals of rebellion: *Rituals of Rebellion in South-East Africa* (Manchester, 1954).
49. A similar view is suggested by J. Lear, "*Katharsis,*" *Phronesis* **XXXIII** (1988), 297–326; J. Lear, "Katharsis" (this volume).
50. In the article in *Phronesis* noted above, Lear suggests that it is an important element in the Aristotelian view of tragedy that an audience should believe in its susceptibility to the events shown on stage. "A normal, educated audience", he writes, "going to a performance of a good tragedy, believes that the terrible events portrayed – infanticide, parricide, matricide, the tearing apart of the most primordial bonds of family and society – could happen to them" (321). I find this suggestion both correct and misleading. Aristotle indeed expects the audience of a tragedy to believe in its susceptibility to the events mimetically represented in tragedy, but not, as I shall suggest, qua those specific events.
51. *Metaphysics* Z 1031a19 ff.
52. See D. Davidson, e.g., "Agency," in *Agent, Action, and Reason,* ed. Binkley, Bronaugh, and Marras (Toronto, 1971), and "The Logical Form of Action Sentences," in *The Logic of Decision and Action,* ed. N. Rescher (Pittsburgh, 1967). Both are reprinted in *Essays on Actions and Events* (Oxford, 1980), 43–61 and 105–122. In a sense, the argument I am here proposing about tragedy is a meditation on Davidson's outrageous claim in the former essay (59) that "we never do more than move our bodies: the rest is up to nature."
53. This fact follows from the very possibility of mimetic representation and from the question of how an action is to be mimetically represented; as P. Ricoeur puts it: "If human action can be recounted and poeticized, in other words, it is due to the fact that it is always articulated by signs, rules, and norms. To use a phrase from C. Geertz, human action is always symbolically mediated." "Mimesis and Representation," *Annals of scholarship* **II** (1982) 19.
54. See A. Lesky, "Decision and Responsibility in the Tragedy of Aeschylus," *Journal of Hellenic Studies* **86** (1966) 78–86, reprinted in *Greek Tragedy: Modern Essays in Criticism,* ed. E. Segal (New York, 1983), 13–23: "Many human actions have a double aspect – this holds true if not for all human actions, at least for all those which presuppose a decision. To protect the suppliants means disregarding the interests of the city; by giving preference to these, the king would prove his sense of responsibility towards the Polis, and yet he would gravely sin against Zeus, who protects the

fugitives" (16). "Thus, the deed of Eteokles, too, reveals the twofold aspect of human action; the king's defense of Thebes, which proves his heroism, becomes at the same time the terrible crime of fratricide" (20). See also M. Nussbaum, *The Fragility of Goodness* (Cambridge, 1986), 25 ff.

55. Lesky, "Decision and Responsibility," 22. Both Lesky and Nussbaum take these plays as paradigmatic.

56. *Poetics* 6, 1449b27 ff.

57. Such a view is in Lear, *"Katharsis"*, who takes Aristotle to offer a view of tragedy as recuperative cosmodicy. "In Aristotle's conception of tragedy, the individual actor takes on the burden of badness, the world as a whole is absolved" (325); "Even in tragedy, perhaps especially in tragedy, the fundamental goodness of man and world are reaffirmed," (326).

58. See E. Rohde, *Psyche: The Cult of Souls and the Belief in Immortality among the Greeks*, trans. W. B. Hillis (London, 1925), 294 ff.

59. Witness the pervasive presence of this sense of *catharsis* in the argument of the *Phaedo*, as also in the *Laws* 1831A inter alia. The characteristically Platonic extension of *catharsis* at *Phaedrus*243A to deal not simply with mistaken action but with mistaken mythological belief is connected with a much larger view of the philosopher's office as one of cleansing the city of the impurities of ignorance and error. See the beginning of the *Euthyphro*, where *aphosiōsis* is analogous to *catharsis*; and note the strong resemblances between the situation there and the situation at the beginning of *Oedipus the King*. For the analogy between *hosion* and *catharmos*, see Rhode, *Psyche*, 233.

60. *Politics* VIII 7, 1341b32 ff.

61. That is, whether in the audience, or on the stage as according to the now unpopular theory of G. R. Else, *Aristotle's Poetics: The Argument* (Cambridge, 1957). See also L. Golden, "Catharsis," *Transactions and Proceedings of the American Philological Association* **93** (1962) 51–60.

62. Euripides, *Iphigenia among the Taurians* 1030 ff.

63. *Poetics* 17, 1455b15.

64. Sophocles, *Oedipus at Colonus* 548.

65. Lear, who finds Else's view "highly implausible," presents what is to me a very convincing argument for its plausibility in the distinction he draws between objective and subjective katharsis; Lear, *"Katharsis,"* 319, n. 79.

66. Cyril of Jerusalem, *Mystagogical Catacheses* II.5, in *St. Cyril of Jerusalem's Lectures on the Christian Sacraments*, ed. F. L. Cross (Crestwood, NY, 1986), 20.

67. It would be fruitful here to consider further the relation between *ēthos* and *daimōn*, character and destiny, in relation to Aristotle's project of so refining character as to lead to a life which is well-daimoned. Think of Heraclitus' enigmatic remark (DK B119) that *ēthos anthrōpōi diamōn* – character is destiny – and R. P. Winnington-Ingram's comments upon its "syntactic reversibility" in "Tragedy and Greek Archaic Thought," *Classical Drama and its Influence*, ed. M. J. Anderson (New York, 1965), 37, 47; see also J.-P. Vernant, "Tensions and Ambiguities in Greek Tragedy," in *Myth and Tragedy in Ancient Greece*, trans. J. Lloyd (New York, 1988), 35 ff.

Aristotle on *Mimēsis*

Paul Woodruff

Modern readers are often dismayed to find that Aristotle classified poetry, music, and dance under a heading that is usually translated "imitation." We take some comfort in blaming this usage on Plato, who put poetry under this heading in order to condemn it, and we expect Aristotle to defend poetry by providing us with a new, more positive, and even (dare we hope?) more modern understanding of "imitation." The comfort begins to turn cold, however, when we find that *mimēsis* – the Greek word commonly translated "imitation" – has an independent life in Aristotle. It is neither a throwback to Plato nor a precursor of modern theories of fiction. It has little to do with the problem of truth in poetry, and a great deal to do with explaining the effects poetry has on its audience.

Altogether, Aristotle's theory of poetry translates poorly into the idioms of modern criticism, and there is no help for this. *Mimēsis* and its Greek cognates defy translation. Besides "imitation," we find in English such renderings as "image-making," "imitation," "representation," "reproduction," "expression," "fiction," "emulation," "make-believe," and so forth. As any of these would beg important questions of interpretation, we shall have to be content with transliteration for discussions such as this. Mimesis is the production of *mimemata*; and though "images" is almost right for *mimemata*, we shall leave that word in Greek as well. I shall also use the adjective *mimetic* for any procedure of mimesis.

So stricken have we been by Plato's war on the tragedians that we keep wanting to read the *Poetics* as a definitive counter-offensive, and we keep trying to frame Aristotle's theory in Platonic terms, as a response to Plato. This is especially inviting in the case of mimesis, a term which Plato defined and which Aristotle did not. It seems natural to suppose that Aristotle took Plato's notion of mimesis, stretched it into something rather like the modern notion of fiction, and so found his way to the sort of answer we would like to give to Plato.[1] Now I think this is entirely wrong-headed: there is no good internal evidence that

Aristotle was driven in the *Poetics* by the need to answer Plato, and this is especially clear in the case of mimesis. What Aristotle has to say on mimesis is almost entirely free of Platonic influence; what he shares with Plato does not go much beyond their common language. Mimesis in Aristotle does stretch to accommodate itself to Aristotelian theory, but the result is light-years away from modern concepts such as fiction, representation, and expression.

The first part of this essay tries to develop a more exact understanding of Aristotelian mimesis, and to demonstrate its independence from Plato. The second part addresses the problem of deception in mimesis. The third develops a speculative account of mimesis in Aristotle, and applies this to difficulties that arise in connection with Aristotle's larger account of poetry. What relation does a product of mimesis bear to its object – to that of which it is a *mimema*? How can our emotions be aroused by made-up actions and characters? Whom do we fear, whom do we pity, when we watch mimetic drama or read mimetic poetry? How can our emotions be engaged by a process that aims at what is universal in human behavior? How, on Aristotle's theory, can deception through mimesis be benign?

I. *Mimēsis* in Plato and Aristotle

Aristotle used the word *mimēsis* and its cognates generously, without the pejorative connotation Plato attached to it, and in a wide variety of contexts. As most scholars have observed, this broader understanding of mimesis is part of Aristotle's more positive view of poetry. The word *mimēsis*, however, is as obscure in Aristotle as it is in other ancient authors. It is not just that modern languages fail to furnish precise equivalents. The problem is deeper: Aristotle is no clearer than his predecessors as to what place mimesis has in the family that includes likeness, image, sign, reproduction, impersonation, and the rest.

Mimēsis seems to be a technical term in the *Poetics*, and so ought to be used with reference to one focal meaning. From its debut at 1447a16 in defining the species of poetry (see also 47b15 and 51b28), to its last bow at 62b5, mimesis is brought on to settle one issue after another, as if its meaning were clear from the beginning. Yet readers do not know exactly how it settles things, and are unable to agree on a focal meaning for the term. Artistotle does not appear to be consistent in his discussions of mimesis. A particular worry is his apparent tendency to fall back on the Platonic concept from time to time: Aristotle seems occasionally not to have entirely freed himself from the influence of his teacher on mimesis. And as he nowhere stops to define the term, we are left to infer from the variety of contexts a variety of meanings the term seems to have had for Aristotle.

A. Plato's legacy

In Plato's work *mimēsis* is often understood to involve deception, and is very often used pejoratively of arts or crafts which Plato considers harmful or at least inferior. When Plato does not use the term pejoratively he uses it as part of a metaphysical theory. Yet neither the pejorative nor the metaphysical use surfaces in the *Poetics*, though most scholars hear echoes of Plato there. What is even more remarkable, Aristotle makes no mention of any differences he may have with Plato on mimesis.

Not even Plato is entirely consistent on the subject of mimesis. Book III of the *Republic* treats it as impersonation, Book X as image-making, and although these are not the same, both seem to be inherently dangerous processes. Plato cannot think that mimesis is intrinsically bad, however, for he treats it elsewhere more positively.

1. Impersonation

In Book III of the *Republic*, Plato defines mimesis in poetry as impersonation: "to liken oneself to another either in voice or in appearance is to make a mimesis of the person to whom one likens oneself" (*Republic* 393c5, cf. *Sophist* 267a). Plato distinguishes mimesis from narrative (392d5), and illustrates mimesis with an example of direct discourse in Homer: when Homer gives the speech of Chryses (at *Iliad* I.17 ff.), he "tries his best to make us think that the speaker is not Homer, but a priest, and he an old man" (393b1–2). Here Plato is clear that it is the author who impersonates the speaker in direct discourse; later in the same passage he will treat the performer as the impersonator. An adequate account of mimesis as impersonation will have to explain why Plato treats these two cases in the same way.

Plato holds that mimesis so defined aims at a kind of deception. In the case Plato cites, it aims to make its audience believe what is not the case: that the author of the lines beginning at *Iliad* I.17 is an elderly priest, when in fact it is Homer. A performer of the same lines – and the lines would have been encountered most frequently in performance – would aim at a double deception: to make the audience believe that he himself is an elderly priest and that this priest is the author of the lines, when in fact he is not an elderly priest, and the lines are Homer's.

In this context, unlike Book X, Plato does not take either narrative or indirect discourse to be mimetic and therefore deceptive in aim (394a). This gives Plato three modes of poetry: pure mimesis (direct discourse) in tragedy and comedy, pure narrative in dithyrambs, and a mixture of the two in epic (394c, 392d). Because he holds that poetry can be made without mimesis, Plato can bar mimetic poetry from education without barring poetry altogether (398a).

The danger Plato sees in mimetic poetry is not deception as such, and he is not afraid that the audience will be deceived by mimesis. No audience is deceived by such things, as Plato well knows. Everyone knows Homer wrote the poem. And even if the audience were beguiled into thinking that the speaker is an elderly priest, they may still be undeceived by what he says. It is not part of Plato's thesis in Book III that mimesis disables the ability of an audience to judge what is said. The trouble with mimesis is that it *aims* at deception concerning the identity of the speaker, and it entices us to do the same: the poet "tries his best to make us think" what is not the case, and so must the performer. Here is the kernel of Plato's concern. It is not that we are really likely to be taken in by a deception, but that we may be beguiled into becoming performers, and therefore into taking deception as *our* aim; and this is morally an unhealthy aim to take.

The difference between mimetic and narrative poetry is of greater importance to Plato than it could be to modern readers of poetry, because Plato belonged to a culture in which poetry was written to be performed. Ancient Greek education depended heavily on the recitation or performance of poetry by upper class youngsters, and Plato was afraid that students would tend to become like the characters they impersonated if they performed mimetic poetry. Certainly ancient poetry teems with characters we would not want our children to emulate. Another reason Plato condemned mimetic performance is this: each student must learn to play only his own role and to avoid all others, if justice is to be preserved in the city; but a course of mimetic performances will require each student to take many parts, and this would be bad practice for the life of a guardian.

It is important to observe that the distinction between history and poetry, which looms large in modern scholars' readings of *Poetics* 9, means nothing to Plato. His criticisms of mimesis in Book III would apply whether or not the subjects were historical: if an audience is led to think that a performer is Chryses, they are as much deceived if Chryses is historical as they are if he is a product of fiction.

2. *Image-making*

Plato seems to understand mimesis differently in Book X of the *Republic*, where he uses the example of the production of images in a mirror (596d) to illuminate the production of images by painters, and, in turn, the production of poems by Homer and the tragedians. Here he drops his earlier distinction between narrative and non-narrative forms, and builds a line of criticism aimed at poetry in any form. He treats mimesis as image-making not to show that it is deceptive as to content, but to show that a mimetic artist can succeed on his own terms without full knowledge of the original object.

The painter–poet analogy is supposed to drive home his point (new in Book X) that dramatic mimesis is deceptive if it makes an audience believe that it is based on knowledge of its subject (598c). It would be absurd if a painter who can produce a convincing image of a bridle could thereby persuade us that he knew how the the bridle should be made if it is to serve its purpose well. Plato argues that the same should be said of a poet. Poets, Plato claims, present themselves as the moral teachers of Greece: a poet who produces a convincing representation of a general does, at the same time, persuade his audience that he knows how a general should be educated if he is to serve his purpose well. Painters, of course, do not successfully deceive in the relevant way: no one entrusts them with the manufacture of bridles or the education of cobblers, no matter how convincing their pictures of bridles or cobblers. Only children and fools are taken in by a painting (598c). But poets do deceive and are entrusted with moral education. The point of the painter-poet analogy is to show how silly the Greeks are to be taken in by poetry, when they are not deceived by painting, at least not in the same way or to the same degree.

Again, as in Book III, the danger is not that we may be taken in by false content in poetry. Indeed, the poem – like the painting – might be an excellent representation of its object, and may convey any number of true beliefs. The danger Plato brings up in Book X is that we may be taken in by claims that the poet has a certain sort of knowledge. The context makes it clear what knowledge this is – knowledge of how to design a state and how to educate young men in virtue. A poet might publish convincing and even accurate portrayals of virtue, and still not have this knowledge. Just so, a leader might achieve great success on the basis of true beliefs about statecraft without having the sort of knowledge that would enable him to teach. Plato's criticism of the poets in Book X is an extension of Socrates' famous resolve never to let a pretension to knowledge go untested by the elenchus.

Book X does not limit mimesis to impersonation or even to performance: a purely narrative representation of a general would be subject to the same Platonic criticism, and so would a dramatic representation of a general in a script that has not been performed. Still, Plato is most critical of mimetic drama in performance, for it is this that most bewitches our power to judge between reality and illusion, and most strengthens our nonrational responses. Again, as in Book III, it makes no difference whether this is fact or fiction: as far as we can tell, a convincing drama about Pericles could be just as dangerous as one about a generic general. Aristotle's distinction in *Politics* 9 has no purchase here.

3. Reproduction

Plato is more positive about mimesis in other contexts. In the *Laws*, mimesis is a kind of reproduction that can be accurate (668b); in the *Timaeus* it is the ideal relation between thought or speech and the divine reality of the Forms (47bc); and in the *Statesman* the laws are mimemata of the truth that is known by experts; they are therefore a very good thing, though second best to direct rule by the experts themselves (300c, cf. *Laws* 817b). All of these positive uses of mimesis depend on the idea that a product of mimesis should have at least some of the good qualities of the original object. Sound thought, for example, is a mimema of reality in virtue of having some of the stability of the intelligible world. Thus a mimema can serve a useful purpose so long as its limitations are known.

This is not really a third theory of mimesis, for it can be absorbed by either the impersonation or the image-making view; but it is a new emphasis. Plato's argument in *Republic* III depends on assuming that mimesis can reproduce objectionable features of the original, and so interfere with the proper education of the young. In *Republic* X, again, Plato's case against mimesis depends on his observation that by reproducing selected features of an object, mimesis gives a false impression of knowledge.

Mimesis in Plato, then, is the reproduction of at least some of the qualities of an original, either through impersonation or image-making, sometimes with the aim of deceiving its audience, and sometimes not. In itself, it is neither a good nor a bad thing to do.

B. Mimesis in Aristotle

Outside the *Poetics*, there are the slightest hints of a theory of mimesis. The *Physics* presents us with the engaging idea that a profession (*technē*) like medicine or architecture works like nature in that both *technē* and nature subordinate their products teleologically, for the sake of ends (194a21); and this relation between *technē* and nature he describes as mimesis. Later he will add, in a similar context, that *technē* completes nature by bringing about through mimesis what nature was unable to accomplish (199a15). Nature means us to be healthy, for example, but does not always succeed; medicine can intervene to bring about the effect at which nature had aimed. Medicine and nature, in this account, are alike in two ways: they produce the same ends, and they do so in the same way, by subordinating each thing they do to the ends at which they aim. Mimesis here has nothing to do with imitation or representation; it produces health, rather than a simulacrum of health. On the surface, there is no point of contact between this sort of mimesis and the sort Plato discussed, and little connection with Aristotle's own more representational treatment of mimesis in poetry and music, though there may be some resonance at a deeper level between the sorts of mimesis.[2] One possibility to keep in mind is that medicine must at some stage simulate nature. If medicine is to intervene and then let nature carry on the natural process of maintaining health, it must arrange for nature to take some medical artifice as if it were natural; that is, it must produce an artificial effect that merges smoothly in the health-promoting course of nature.[3] There is a sort of benign deception implicit in this process. We shall see whether this idea is useful in explaining mimesis in poetry and music.

In the *Poetics*, Aristotle considers mimesis under three headings: media, objects, and modes. The media of mimesis include dance, music, painting, and poetry; the objects include things as they are, things better than they are, and things worse than they are. The modes include narrative and drama – and, perhaps, impersonation as well.

1. Modes of mimesis in Aristotle
An echo of Plato's threefold classification in *Republic* III may sound in Aristotle's taxonomy of the modes of poetry, which can be read in two ways (1448a2–24):

1. (*Twofold reading*) It is possible to make a mimesis of the same object in

the same medium either (a) through narration (either (i) by becoming someone else as Homer does or (ii) by just being onself and not changing), or (b) through representing characters actively doing things.

2. (*Threefold reading*) It is possible to make a mimesis of the same object in the same medium either (c) through narration [sometimes] becoming someone else as Homer does or (d) by just being oneself and not changing, or (e) through representing characters actively doing things.

Most editors prefer (1) simply as a reading of the Greek text; but scholars who wish to hear an echo of Plato's theory in this passage prefer the triparite reading.[4] If the passage echoes Plato, however, it does so faintly and through a serious confusion, because Aristotle regards all – or both – of the modes he discusses to be modes of mimesis, whereas Plato restricts mimesis in Book III to impersonation. Specifically, the second category (a (ii) or d) corresponds to Platonic narrative, but would not be mimetic under Plato's classification. The third category (b or e) is neither narrative nor explicitly involves impersonation, and has no place in Plato's scheme at all. The first category (a (i) or c) may be Plato's mixed class of narration interrupted by impersonation; but to take it this way requires us to understand more than is given us in the text, and a word like "sometimes" must be supplied.[5] Furthermore, the impersonation that does interest Aristotle in the present passage must – by the grammar of the sentence – be a kind of narration, and this is impossible on the Platonic model. It is more likely that the impersonation of this passage really is a sub-mode of narration, namely, narration through a fictive narrator – a device for which Homer is especially famous in the *Odyssey*. If this reading is right, then there is no echo here at all of Plato's view of mimesis as impersonation, by the author, of a non-narrative speaker.[6] In any case, the argument against the reading I propose depends on assuming that Aristotle is following Plato, which is the point at issue. So far, then, Aristotle pays little homage to Plato's narrow understanding of mimesis as impersonation. The distinction we have is between narrative and dramatic modes, with two subordinate modes of narration, depending on whether the poet tells the story in his own or in an assumed voice.

Just once in the *Poetics* mimesis appears to be confined to impersonation on the narrow model of *Republic* III. In *Poetics* 24, Aristotle praises Homer for his use of direct discourse: "the poet should speak as little as possible in his own person, for doing this is not what makes him a *mimetes*" (1460a7–8). The passage stands out in the *Poetics* as uniquely Platonic, and, in the view of one scholar, playfully so.[7] Every other relevant text in the *Poetics* implies that mimesis may or may not involve dramatic impersonation. So, for example, Aristotle makes a similar point about Homer in *Poetics* 4 by saying that his mimesis, by contrast with that of other epic poets, is dramatic (1448b35) – and this presupposes that mimesis can fail to be dramatic.

Indeed, a poetic text is equally mimetic whether or not it is performed. Whereas the effects of mimetic poetry that concern Plato in *Republic* III are directly linked to performance, Aristotle's discussion of mimesis in tragedy is quite independent of its potential for performance. A mimesis of an action is not necessarily an enactment – hence the need to specify action at 1449b26 – and it seems that a story alone counts as mimesis of an action (1450a4). If a poet has done her work well, her audience will be moved to pity and fear merely by hearing what happens in the play (1453b3–7). Aristotelian mimesis can be entirely literary, and requires nothing like enactment in the strict sense (Somville, *Essai sur la Poétique d'Aristote*, p. 52).

2. Media

Aristotle's theory of mimesis must make room for the making of visual images as well, though he need not give it pride of place as Plato does in Book X of the *Republic*. He treats it not as a mode or kind of mimesis, but as a medium. Painted images are of course mentioned in *Poetics* 1, and images (*eikones*) crop up again in *Poetics* 4 to explain our pleasure in mimesis (1448b11 ff.). In *Poetics* 2 and 25, also, Aristotle uses the analogy of poets to painters to make the point that objects can be represented as better than they are, worse, than they are, or just the same (1448a5 ff., 1460b8 ff.). Although Aristotle thinks of mimesis through color and form as the same sort of thing as mimesis through speech, rhythm, and melody, he does think that different objects can be represented in different media, and different effects achieved. We shall see, for example, that painting is less well adapted than poetry to the mimesis of character than poetry is, while it is better adapted for conveying information.

There is also mimesis by music without words, and there is mimesis by rhythm without music. This raises a problem: how can mimesis in dance, melody, or painting be carried out in all of the Aristotelian modes? In none of these media can mimesis be narrative in the usual sense; and only in some can it be dramatic. Dance and painting can represent action, but it is hard to see how this can be done by music without words. Perhaps Aristotle has forgotten the nonpoetic media when he introduces the modes, or perhaps he intends these modes to apply only to the medium of poetry. In any case, we must recognize that an adequate Aristotelian account of mimesis should accommodate all of the media he mentions in *Poetics* 1.

3. Objects

By "object" I mean what is referred to by the grammatical object of *mimeisthai*, the verbal cognate of *mimēsis*. It appears that mimesis can take as its objects characters, passions, or actions; but that the chief object of mimesis is people in action (*Poetics* 1 and 2). Aristotle makes two interesting points about objects of mimesis, of which the first seems fairly general, and the second is specific to tragedy.

(a) Objects that are made up. The people whose actions are the objects of mimesis

must be better than we are, the same, or worse (*Poetics* 2, cf. 1460b8 ff.). Aristotle borrows from Plato the idea that mimesis has people in action as its object (*Republic* X 603c4); but the division into three moral classes is his own, and leads, as we shall see, to a very un-Platonic consequence.

It is not clear who "we" are supposed to be; but "people of our time" evidently refers to the same group (1448a18). Those who are better are evidently those from the past – people who have the heroic names of myth-or-history (which Aristotle treats as a single genre). The actions of such people are the chief stuff of tragedy, though some tragedies use names and actions that are entirely made up (1451b15 ff.). The people who are worse are always entirely made up by comic poets, while the people who are at our level are particular people of our time who are picked out by the iambic poets for satire (1451b11 ff., 1449b8). It follows that the object of poetic mimesis can be entirely made up by a poet. The object of mimesis can be a fiction.

Here Aristotle diverges considerably from Plato, who treats mimesis consistently as having objects that are either real or – in the case of poetry and painting – as having objects that are themselves mimemata of real things. Mimesis in Aristotle, then, cannot be anything like *imitation*, which in modern usage implies the existence of something real which is imitated. We speak of imitation flowers and fake flamingos, but not of imitation goblins or fake fairies, because there are no goblins or fairies. Again, mimesis in Aristotle cannot be the same as fiction. The comic poet does indeed produce fiction – he makes up events and characters (the word for doing that is simply *poiein*); but then he accomplishes a mimesis which has as its object precisely the fiction that he has made up. If mimesis were fiction then it would make no sense to say that it can take fiction as its object. But if fiction is the making up of people and events, and if that is what a poet does, then what in the world could mimesis be? What role is left for mimesis if fiction is prior to it? Aristotle's way of speaking implies that there is a difference between simply making up actions, and producing a mimesis of actions that have been made up. A speculative hypothesis to which I shall return: the difference is that mimesis affects us, while simply making things up – without mimesis – does not. To produce a mimesis of a fiction is to give to that fiction the power of engaging our attention and our emotions almost as if it were real.

(b) Universals. Specifically tragic mimesis has as its object an action that is complete and whole, and has a certain magnitude; the main idea is that this action consists of smaller actions (*pragmata*) arranged in accordance with certain general principles (*Poetics* 7–9, cf. 1450a15 ff.). "The poet's job is to tell not what has happened, but the sort of thing that could happen – what is possible in accordance with probability or necessity" (1450b36–8). Poetry is more philosophical than history because it aims at universals of the form "this kind of speech or action belongs to that kind of person, by probability or necessity" (1451b8–10, cf. 1449b8). It makes no difference whether the events to be represented are historical, mythical, or fictional; mimesis of actions is poetic

so long as the actions are governed by probability or necessity (1451b29–32). As these are human actions, necessity in the strict sense does not seem appropriate: the probable is what happens "for the most part" (*Rhetoric* I.ii.15), and it is to this that Aristotle regularly appeals (e.g. 1455b10).

What is the connection between poetic mimesis and universals? Aristotle consistently says that the poet takes *actions* as his objects (as at 1451b29), and he very clearly does not say that the poet takes universals as his objects, though this might seem to afford him an elegant reply to *Republic* X. In fact, however, the universals that concern poetry are not at all like the objects of Platonic knowledge (see G. Else, *Aristotle's Poetics*, p. 35), and there is nothing here that Aristotle could offer as a direct answer to Plato's concern.

Aristotle's discussion of universals in poetry is fertile ground for the reading-in of modern theories, a practice usefully discussed by Halliwell (*The Poetics of Aristotle*, pp. 109–111). Aristotle means at least that a poet should make sure the actions she represents are appropriate to her characters; but he must mean more than this: the poet "says what sort of things can happen;" she "aims at" universals, though she sticks in proper names. Plainly, Aristotle's poet takes as her material – in some sense of material – a set of generalizations about human behavior. But she does not take these generalizations directly as the objects of mimesis. Why does Aristotle resist the temptation here to say that poetic mimesis is the mimesis that takes universals as its objects? I offer the speculative suggestion that poetic mimesis in Aristotle's theory can take only a particular action as its object, because only particular actions can arouse pity or fear. Although a poet must have universal probabilities in mind when she writes tragedy, she must make us feel as if we were witnesses to particular events, if she is to affect our emotions; and this would seem to require that the objects of tragic mimesis be particular actions. If so, what is the role of universals in mimesis? Aristotle leaves us to speculate on this, a task I shall take up in Section II.C.

The object of poetic mimesis, then, is an action that may or may not be fictional but must in any case bear a certain relation to universals dealing with human behavior.

C. Consistency

We have seen that there is tension at the first level of interpretation of Plato's *Republic* between two views of mimesis – as impersonation and as image-making – and that these two views generate in turn narrower and wider bans on poetry. Nothing like this tension surfaces in the *Poetics*, or, indeed, in any other text in which Aristotle treats mimesis; from what we have seen so far we have no reason to doubt that a unified Aristotelian account of mimesis could be given. Halliwell has to labor to find an instability in the *Poetics'* treatment of mimesis between image-making and enactment (*Aristotle's Poetics*, esp. 130 ff.), and he succeeds only because he has assumed a stronger Platonic influence on the *Poetics* than is warranted (Janko, "Review of Halliwell (1989)," p. 154).

It turns out that Aristotle is neither echoing Plato on mimesis (except perhaps at 1460a8) nor directly answering Plato's mimesis-based criticism of the poets. Aristotle's independence from Plato on this score is underlined by his silence concerning Plato's use of the analogy of painting with poetry to show the ignorance of poets, and by his failure to answer the charge that poetry is deceptive.

Yet mimesis in poetry *is* deceptive, as Aristotle implies more than once in the *Poetics*, and this makes it hard for us to see how poetic mimesis can be at all like the sort of mimesis that works hand in hand with nature. We need to look closely at the kind of deception that is involved in poetry.

II. Mimesis and Deception

Although Aristotle ignores the sort of deception that worried Plato about poetry, his sort of mimesis is still deceptive. Perhaps this is inevitable. The tradition that poetry is inherently deceptive is an ancient one, and apparently made no one but Plato and perhaps Xenophanes uneasy. Aristotle, as we shall see, falls squarely into the tradition that does not apologize for the deceptive character of poetry. To this, the most famous of Plato's canards against poetry, Aristotle does not even deign to answer.

"Poets tell many lies," says Plutarch, citing a proverb, and elsewhere reports that Gorgias said that a poet who deceives is wiser than one who does not.[8] Philostratus presumably records an older view when he claims that it is pleasant and harmless to be affected by things that do not exist as if they did (*Proemium* 391k4). It is Plato who rasies the alarm about deception in poetry. As we have seen, he has two concerns: first that students should not become deceivers, and second that none of us be taken in by pretensions to expert knowledge either on the part of poets or by poets on behalf of their characters (*Republic* 598c, cf. *Sophist* 267c). In his criticisms of poetry as mimesis, Plato is not concerned with the specific content of a poem: even if what is said in a poem is entirely true, Plato's concerns about its deceptive power remain. We might still be corrupted by performing it, and we might still wrongly think that its good qualities are due to knowledge.

Aristotle is not sensitive to either of these concerns. He does not address the ethical issue of the effect of impersonation on performers at all. As for the pretensions of poets to knowledge, Aristotle gives us texts in which we can find the germ of an answer to Plato (especially *Poetics* 4, 9, and 25), but he does not face the issue squarely.

A. Deception regarding content

In fact, the *Poetics* says nothing explicit about deception; it merely implies that poetry can be deceptive in content and, as we shall see, in the way it engages our emotions. The clearest case has to do with the content of poetry – with the deception that occurs when an audience is led to believe in the probability of events that could not have happened. In several contexts, and especially in his chapter on problems (*Poetics* 25), Aristotle recognizes implicitly and applauds the deceptive power of mimesis:

> In general one should deal with impossibilities by appealing to composition, or to what is better, or to common opinion. As for composition, one should prefer what is convincing but impossible over what is unconvincing but possible.
>
> (1461b9–12, cf. 1460a26 and 1460a13 ff.)

A poem that takes an impossible sequence of events and makes it convincing does so through deceiving its audience, by making them believe that certain events have taken place, or could have taken place, when in fact it is impossible that they could have taken place.

Aristotle's treatment of this theme seems to imply that by the standards appropriate to poetry, deception of this sort is not a vice. Aristotle does not call attention to this as a point about deception; and in any case this could not be a serious answer to Plato, for Plato never criticized mimesis for being deceptive in this way. Plato does, of course, criticize poets for being wrong about gods and heros, but this has nothing to do with the mimetic character of the poems in question. The closest Aristotle comes to an answer on this score is in his discussion of correctness in poetry, where he says that being right about subject matter is only *incidentally* part of a poet's job:

> And besides, there is not the same correctness in politics as in poetry, nor in any other *technē* as in poetry. But two kinds of failure belong to poetry proper: one is essentially poetic, the other merely happens to be so. If someone intended a mimesis [of something to be correct, but failed through] incompetence, then this would be a failure of poetry itself; but if he intended to do this incorrectly – to show a horse with both right legs thrown forward, for example – then that failure would belong to the particular *technē*.
>
> (1460b13–19)

A product of mimesis is a thing in its own right, but is also *of* something else. A poet who is good at mimesis in itself may still misrepresent his subject matter, if he is not well informed about that or does not intend to represent it accurately. This useful distinction between mimesis and the particular *technai* goes beyond anything Plato says on the subject of error in poetry, for it allows us reasons for praising poets who get things wrong; but it does not allow inaccurate poets to escape all criticism. The passage does not isolate poetry from real-world concerns, or judge poetry merely by its own autonomous standards. A *technē* like politics has one standard of correctness, its own; and a statesman can go wrong in just one sort of way. But a poet can go wrong in two sorts of ways, and poetry is to be judged by two standards, one belonging only to poetry as such, the other to the body of knowledge (*technē*) which governs the subject covered by the poet, and which therefore incidentally governs the poet himself (cf. *Magna Moralia* 1190a31). The passage does not imply that the poet need not know anything of the subject of his poem – only that he need not know this *qua* poet. It is a common error among scholars to read into this passage a reply to Plato's criticism of poetry (e.g. Lucas, *Aristotle Poetics*, p. 235). But in order to answer Plato, Aristotle should address the specific dangers that accompany mimesis on Plato's view, and this he does not do. Though 1461b9–12, for example, does license some inaccuracies and deceptions, it does so merely by appealing to the principle that poetry should above all be convincing. Plato knew poets worked on such a principle; that is why he was afraid they would appear to be experts on subjects about which they knew only how to convince. But this fear is not addressed by Aristotle. As the passage is not marked by any clear allusions to the *Republic*, it should not be taken as Aristotle's response. Aristotle has provided us with elegant replies to Plato on other topics; it is kinder to see the present passage in another light: like Gorgias before him, Aristotle seems to think it obvious and unproblematic that a poet ought to deceive, and that his audience ought to be taken in at some level. Aristotle goes beyond what we know of Gorgias's theory not because he has attended to Plato's concerns, but because he has advanced independently towards his own theory of the effects of poetry on an audience.

B. Deception and the emotions

Poetry must engage our emotions through events which are merely represented on stage and which are in some cases purely fictional. This implicates the poet in a sort of deception that Aristotle does not recognize explicitly.[9]

In the case of tragedy we can easily see the complexity of the matter. Tragedy succeeds only in so far as it elicits the emotions of pity and fear, and these emotions (we are told in the *Rhetoric*) are felt on the presentation of something that is destructive or painful. According to the *Rhetoric*, in order to feel pity or fear one must have the impression that an action is taking place which is painful or destructive; but on the tragic stage, in fact, nothing is destroyed, and the actors do not necessarily feel pain on account of the actions they represent. So it appears that the audience or reader must believe what is not true in order to be affected properly by a tragedy.

On the other hand, the audience does know that nothing truly painful or destructive is taking place on stage; otherwise they could not take pleasure in the performance. Generally, on Aristotle's theory, we can take pleasure in mimesis precisely because we are not deceived by it; we can take pleasure in an image of a lion, for example, because we know that it is an image and not a lion (1448b9–15). If that is so, then how can the proper experience of tragedy depend on our being deceived by it? Part of the answer is that tragedy and painting have rather different effects according to Aristotle, and that tragedy has an emotional effect far greater than that of painting; but this is not the whole story. However tragedy affects us, it should not send us running from the theater in fear and horror at the ghastly doings inside. The horror that drove King Claudius from the theater was not horror at the murder of Gonzago.

Apparently we must believe at the same time that an evil is taking place and that it is not. The poet must make us respond to events represented on stage as if they are actually happening, so as to evoke fear and pity, and as if they are not, so as to cause pleasure rather than pain. Our challenge is to give accounts of mimesis and the emotions that will explain how this is possible.[10]

C. Deception and universals

A related difficulty emerges from the fact that most emotions are elicited by particular events and people, while Aristotle seems to say that poetry aims at universals (*Poetics* 9). On this theory a poet must be able to convey universal truths to her audience, while eliciting an emotional response normally reserved for the experience of particular events. We will have to ask whether this can be done without some form of deception.

Aristotle distinguishes between hatred and anger in this way: hatred (*misos*) is directed against classes of people, such as thieves; while anger (*orge*) is directed against particular persons who are perceived as causing pain (*Rhetoric* II.iv.31). Pity and fear are more like anger than hatred; they are elicited by impressions (*phantasiai* – *Rhetoric* II.v, II.viii); and these, it seems, must be of particulars, since we do not have impressions of universals. And this seems to be right about the emotions: if the fear of death makes your blood run cold, it is the fear of a particular death – your own, or perhaps that of someone near to you – that does this. Death in general (unless personified) is not the sort of thing that can make a vivid enough impression on me to cause genuine fear or pity.

Here is an example to illustrate the point. Aristotle would accept the *Phaedo* as a case of mimesis (though not as a case of poetry), since it is a Socratic *logos*, and this presents vividly the death of a particular man, Socrates. The emotions evoked by this scene are an intense mix of admiration for Socrates, pity for his grieving comrades, and anger at those who caused his death. The mere occurrence of these emotions – to say nothing of their intensity – depends on our believing at some level that the event Plato described really happened, and happened in a particular place to a particular man at a particular time. Although we know that what Plato wrote about Socrates is mostly fiction, we cannot so easily dismiss the elements in his story that move our emotions. At the time we are moved by them, we do believe in them, at least at some level. Now medical science tells us what Plato and his audience all surely knew, that death by hemlock poisoning is an agony not at all like the cessation of warmth Plato describes easing its way up Socrates's limbs. Plato is making a general point about what death is to a philosopher, and not recording the scene that took place on Socrates's last day. But no statement of the universal truth would affect us in the way Plato's scene does; knowing this, Plato makes an impossible scene convincing and affecting. He makes us appreciate a philosophical point which is arguably true — that death is nothing to a philosopher; but in doing so he makes us accept as history an account that is literally false. The passage is complex irony on a grand scale – deep truth dressed up as superficial falsehood. What the writer aimed at was the deep truth, and what aroused our emotions was the superficial falsehood. We recognize the general point, and are affected at the same time by the particular event. This is the possibility Aristotle intimated in *Poetics* 9, that a writer can tell us universal truths about human behavior and, in doing so, produce a mimema of an action that is both fictional and particular.

What is the relation of universal to particular in mimesis on this account? Aristotle does not say. Perhaps mimesis starts with a particular object, and then calls our attention to the universal that is exemplified by that particular. At best, mimesis reproduces only selected features of its object, and in doing this may reduce its object to what Redfield calls "form." "Imitation," he says, "is the discovery of form in things." Without attempting to pry form out of the object that has it, mimesis arises "from some inclusive, if schematic, intuition of the patterns found in experience."[11] This insight is especially helpful in explaining how we can learn from a mimema what we might not be able to learn from its object. If I came upon a lion in the veldt, I would probably be too occupied with running, and too preoccupied with fear, to learn much about lions. But if I see a lion in a picture, I can study it dispassionately and at leisure. The picture selects just those points about lions that I need to know, and makes the task easy for me. Generally, mimesis can present us with images that reveal the form that is common to a certain species; and this appears to be the point of *Poetics* 4. In such cases, mimesis carries the mind of its audience from the particular image to a universal truth which is instantiated by it, and does so partly by disabling the emotional response we would normally have to the object.

Although painting and various other types of mimesis can work in this way, tragic mimesis plainly cannot. The emotions that retard learning in the case of the lion-painting are precisely what is wanted in the case of Aristotelian tragedy. If painting calls our cognitive attention to what is universal in a general case, tragedy summons up our emotions on behalf of particulars that are contrived to represent a general pattern. Tragic mimesis must bypass not our emotions, but the cognitive power that normally keeps them in check, so that we may be led to experience emotions on behalf of characters and events that our minds could dismiss as unreal. The difference is this: a painter, with his eye on a particular specimen, can produce an image that reveals the universal form of lions; a poet, contemplating a universal truth about human behavior, can invent actions and characters that illustrate those, and then contrive to engage the emotions of his audience with these inventions as if they were particular and actual. Aristotle makes it clear in *Poetics* 17 that this is the order of composition for a poet: start with the universal (so as to be sure not to violate what is probable), and then add the particular names and circumstances. Poetry and painting seem to work mimetically in opposite directions: painting towards, and poetry away from, the universal. Mimesis in Aristotle is broad enough to accommodate both kinds of processes.

A speculative hypothesis: Mimesis in poetry takes universals and dresses them up with particular names and episodes so as to enable them to play the part that particular people and events normally play in our emotional lives. A writer can make us respond to universal types of events and characters as if they were particulars, and this involves a kind of deception that is especially clear in the case of the death of Socrates. The important truth in a poem is too general to engage our emotions; and the particulars are often too severely constrained by the facts to illustrate the general point. If a poem is to represent universals, therefore, and if these are to be at all affecting, then the poet will have to represent them to us in the guise of particular events and characters. I am not saying that poets do this consciously, or even that Aristotle says that poets do this – only that it is a consequence of Aristotelian theory that poets do arrange to make universals affect their audiences in ways that are normally reserved for particulars.

We have already seen that Aristotelian tragedy makes us respond emotionally to representations as if they were real, and that this involves one kind of poetic deception. Now we see that a second, more subtle, kind of deception is involved in tragedy: in so far as a tragedy represents universals, it makes us respond to them as if they were particulars. Aristotle nowhere recognizes the need for either kind of deception in poetry, but both are consequences of his theory of poetry, taken with his theory of the emotions. These are benign consequences, and would give him no reason to turn back and change his views on poetry or the emotions; but they are deceptions nonetheless. This result invites us to consider whether poetic deception has anything in common with the benign form of deception we encountered earlier, in connection with the simulation of nature by medicine.

D. Benign deceptions

Aristotle knew that poetry could deceive, and that sometimes it ought to do so; but defenders of poetry might be upset at my use of the word "deception" for what is the usual stock-in-trade of poets. I take it that any process that causes us to believe what is not the case – at any level – is deceptive. Generally, neither Plato nor Aristotle was opposed to deception as such. Plato has no quarrel with the good lie; his objections to mimesis are subtle, as we have seen, and have nothing to do with the deceptive content of a poem, although he has independent reasons for objecting to the content of many poems. Aristotle does not take Plato's concerns to heart, but accepts without defense a concept of mimesis that is inherently deceptive, at least in the case of poetry.

In my sense of "deception," a poet can deceive her audience without misleading or intending to mislead them. I do not really believe that Oedipus has plucked out his eyes here and now; but while watching an effective production of the play

I feel as if I did hold that belief, and, indeed, at some level I do believe this. Otherwise I could not be moved. But I am not misled, because the deception does not affect my deep beliefs.

Deception that does not affect deep beliefs is on the way to being a deception-like process that does not affect belief at all. I shall call this process "functional deception." Consider what happens when I use my desktop mini-computer to emulate a mainframe terminal. Then my desktop model does what is normally done by a terminal, but it is not a terminal. The mainframe computer responds to my desktop model just as if it were responding to the terminal for which it was designed; but my desktop model is not the terminal for which it was designed, and so the mainframe is taken in, and functionally deceived. In a similar sense, a predator may be deceived by a harmless beetle that carries the markings of a poisonous species: such markings were designed to deter predators from eating poisonous meals; but these markings simply deter predators. Neither the computer nor the predator need have any conscious beliefs in order to be deceived. Both are seduced by cases of functional deception.

III. A New Theory of Mimesis

We have seen that mimesis in Aristotle is either narrative or dramatic in mode, that it can occur in a variety of media from music and dance to painting, poetry and the theater, and that it can take as its objects people as they are, people as they ought to be, or people as they ought not to be. We have also come to realize that the texts do not determine a single account of mimesis. We shall have to speculate.

It would be good to be able to give a definition of mimesis that would serve in all of Aristotle's contexts. No simple account of mimesis can explain why Aristotle classifies so many different arts under this heading; but the definition we want should do so. A second condition on successful definition is this: we have seen that mimesis selects certain features of its object to be reproduced in the mimema. What is the principle of selection? We often borrow the features of one thing and give them to another: when is this process a case of mimesis? An account of mimesis ought to answer these questions. Third, our account of mimesis should explain why it is deceptive in the ways that it is, and why those sorts of deception can be benign.

A. What mimesis is not

Aristotelian mimesis is not the same as imitation or fiction or reproduction or representation or make-believe; it is not expression; and it is not even the making of images or likenesses. Although to do some of these things may be a kind of mimesis, none of them goes to the heart of the matter.

We have already seen one reason why mimesis is not the same as imitation:

unlike imitation, mimesis can take pure fiction as its object. "Imitation" will not work in all contexts, in any case: in no ordinary English sense is narrative imitative, yet narrative is a mode of mimesis in Aristotle. "Emulation" is better than "imitation" for some contexts, but it too fails for the narrative mode.

Again, mimesis is not fiction, since it can take a fiction for its object. Mimesis is something that is added to fiction, probably with the aim of making it believable and affecting.

Mimesis in Aristotle is something like make-believe. Walton has shown how useful a model there is in child's play for understanding the various arts Aristotle considers mimetic (Walton, *Mimesis as Make-Believe*). Still, mimesis is not the same as make-believe, though it does aim to make us believe certain things. Our response to mimesis may involve make-believe, in so far as we are in cahoots with the artist – like adults joining a child's game of make-belive. But what the Aristotelian artist does to draw us in, so that we accept at some level the truth of his work, and are moved by it – that is the heart of mimesis. The model of make-believe will not by itself explain this power of mimetic poetry to affect us.

The case of reproduction is complicated. In one sense, mimesis is reproduction; in another it is not. Reproduction in the full sense is not mimesis at all. There is a weak sort of reproduction that Plato identifies as a kind of mimesis: the reproduction of the qualities and proportions of an object in musical form (*Laws* 668b); but this is far from being a process that would truly reproduce an object. If a bridlemaker makes a new bridle on the model of an old one so as to get the right fit, he is not a mimetic artist but a bridlemaker, and the horseman who purchases a bridle reproduced in this way is in no way deceived if he thinks he has bought a bridle. Although the maker imitates his model, his product is not an imitation bridle. Reproduction in the full sense is never the sort of mimesis we are investigating.

But what of the sort of reproduction we encountered in Plato, that passes some qualities of the original on to the product? It probably is fair to say that every case of mimesis involves this sort of reproduction, and that every *mimema* has some features that belong also to its original. But not every case of feature-sharing is mimesis, for I have many of my mother's physical features, but I am not her mimema nor was meant to be. In any case an adequate account of mimesis as feature-sharing would have to explain which features must be shared for a given case of feature-sharing to turn out to be mimesis.

Mimesis is not the same as representation, because only some representations may be mimetic. The word "representation" is widely used to translate *mimēsis* in certain contexts, but it is not helpful in elucidating the ancient texts. Representation is at least as difficult a concept in modern philosophy as mimesis is in classical thought, and we achieve no advantage in clarity by translating the word in this way. Furthermore, we can always ask of a representation whether or not it is mimetic. Symbols, too, represent; but symbols are not mimetic, and have nothing to do with Aristotle's theory of poetry.[12]

Mimesis is not expression, although it is tempting to translate "mimesis" this way when it is used for the sort of mimesis that is accomplished by music and dance. There is nothing wrong with this rendering as a device for producing a readable English translation, but it papers over one of the main difficulties about mimesis, which is to explain how it can have the broad range that Aristotle assigns to it – how music and dance and painting and poetry can all be mimetic.

Nor does it explain mimesis to say that it is the production of likenesses or images, though this is the closest of the candidates we have reviewed thus far, for Aristotle does gloss *mimema* as *image* (*eikon*) and as *likeness* (*omoioma*). We have no trouble taking "image" as equivalent to *mimema* when Aristotle is speaking of painting (1448b11); but when he is speaking of music, we simply do not know what he means by "likeness," which he treats in this context as a synonym for *mimema* (*Politics* 1340a18, a39). We may say that a piece of music is *like* an emotion or a virtue, or a character,[13] but it is not at all clear what we mean by saying such things, and that is what we want a theory of mimesis to explain.

B. Mimesis as functional deception

The hard cases for a definition of mimesis are music and dance. Here I shall propose a definition that works for music, and then ask if this can cover all the media in which mimesis occurs.

Aristotle says he knows that music contains likenesses of virtue and vice because he observes that our characters are changed when we listen to music (*Politics* 1340a22, a41). Why should this prove his point? In the *Problemata* he gives a sketchy explanation of the likeness of melody and rhythm to character. Melody and rhythm are motions, and so are actions; both kinds of motion, when perceived, set up corresponding motions in the mind of the audience.[14] So far this would seem to explain only the likeness of music to actions. Where does character come in? Actions are both indicative and formative of character: the music that corresponds to a given type of character simulates that character in the listener by setting up appropriate motions in his soul. Listening to heroic music, I feel heroic rhythms pulsing through my soul, and these are just the motions I would feel if I were a hero engaged in an heroic action, and these are the motions to which, if I had an heroic character, I would become accustomed. This music, then, is like an heroic character – it does for me what it would do for me to have that character; and if I listen to such music regularly, my soul will become accustomed to motions of that kind, and I will in fact develop an heroic character.[15]

This suggests a general answer to the problem of defining *mimēsis*. Mimesis is the art of arranging for one thing to have an effect that properly belongs to another: *M is a mimema of O just in case M has an effect that is proper to O*. Mimesis is, in effect, an intervention in natural causal processes. The usual way to feel or to become heroic has nothing to do with music; but music can be contrived in such a way that it has this effect. What goes for music goes for dance, as both are supposed to be kinds of motion.

This theory depends on the idea that there is a natural order in which mimesis can intervene. One reason mimesis has been hard for modern thinkers to digest is that it belongs to a nest of concepts that are intrinsically teleological. Mimesis is best understood as a goal-directed activity; specifically, it is an activity that aims at producing effects that are normally achieved by other means; but this makes sense to you only if you think of objects and their effects as somehow being designed for each other. Mimesis breaks the natural order of design and effect. That is why it is wonderful and exciting, and that is why it gives us a safe way to learn facts about lions – through pictures – and a pleasant way to develop courageous habits of mind – through music or dance.

1. The range of mimesis

It should now be clear why mimesis includes music and dance, but we still need to explain why it includes poetry only if it is governed by what is probable, and therefore does not include all fiction. Fiction invents, but mimesis allows those inventions to have effects that are normally reserved for actual experiences. It is not enough for a mimetic poet to make up characters and actions; she must also make them convincing and affecting. She must, in other words, endow her creations with something like the power to affect us that they would have if they were real. Fiction is mimetic not in so far as it is made up, but insofar as it is probable enough to trigger our emotions.

But what about pictures? Aristotle on the whole does not think that pictures arouse emotion or depict character,[16] yet they are mimetic according to his standards in the *Poetics*, and they do satisfy the proposed definition. Pictures do have some of the effects that normally belong to their originals: the lion picture gives us information we would otherwise have to obtain at some risk from the lion himself; but the picture is safer and less emotionally demanding. Information in ideas can, according to Aristotle, have the same effect on us as perceptions;[17] but it cannot be the case that every idea has the same effect that the corresponding thing would have. Otherwise, the lion-picture would pack the emotional wallop of its original.

2. The selectivity of mimesis

Mimesis does not aim at the same sort of effect in every case; but it does in every case aim at an effect, and that explains the selection of features that are reproduced in mimesis. The reason I am not a mimema of my mother, though I share a number of features with her, is that I was not produced to have an effect that is properly hers; and the physical features we have in common have nothing to do with my ability to function in her place. (This ability might be granted me by the law for very different reasons.) A mimema takes on just those features of its object – or takes on a likeness of just those features – which it needs to take over the effect at which it aims. The non-poisonous beetle, for example, need only carry the marking that deters predators in order to be a mimema of its poisonous cousin; the lion-picture need only represent the lion features about which it seeks to inform us; and the tragic play need show us only enough of the invented lives of its characters to arouse the desired emotions.

3. *Benign deception?*

We now have to ask whether this definition clears up the various problems I raised earlier about mimesis and deception.

Let us begin with the difficulty about deception and the emotions: if tragedy is to have its effect on us, it must move us in ways we are normally moved only if we have certain beliefs; but in this case we do not really have those beliefs. For example, if I am to pity Agave, I must react as if I believed she had just now torn her son to pieces; but Agave has not just now torn her son to pieces. This is only a play, as I well know; if I had not known this, I would long since have called the police. In such a case, mimesis interferes with the normal process by which belief leads to emotion. It is as if mimesis deceives my emotions without deceiving me: it provides me with an impression to which I do not assent, but which moves me as if I did.

In the case of tragedy, the mimetic poet produces a script about certain actions. If you believed that those actions were happening, on Aristotle's theory of the emotions, you would have certain emotions. Of course in reading the script or seeing it performed, you do not believe that those actions are actually happening, but you are made to feel the emotions that you would feel if you did have those beliefs. In other words, the script has the same effect on you that the actions would have had, if you had believed they were taking place. In this way the poet's mimesis is aimed at producing a result that is normally achieved by other means.

Most important for Plato is the way in which belief is overridden by the mimetic process: actions that normally cause emotions affect you in this way only when you have certain beliefs about them; but it seems that an effective tragedy elicits those same emotions regardless of what you really believe. Thus mimesis has the effect of disabling our intelligence; it bypasses the conscious beliefs through which intelligence is usually able to control emotional responses.

The reason this does not disturb Aristotle as it does Plato is not given in the *Poetics*, but in the *Ethics*: we should aim at a sound emotional life not merely by controlling our conscious beliefs, but also by controlling the sorts of persons we turn out to be. We are responsible for the moral condition we are in, and this governs the emotions that a given impression elicits in us, and it even governs the impressions we can be given. In some sense, we are responsible for the impressions that we have.[18] Mimesis of O gives us the sort of impression we would have if we were having an experience of O; but that sort of impression is partly a product of our moral character. Mimesis intervenes between me and actual experience in a particular case; but never (*pace* Plato) between me and the moral character I have developed over the years, which equally affects my response to first-hand experience and my response to an experience that is simulated by mimesis.

Notes

1. This approach is so much the consensual one that Janko and Halliwell agree on it, though Janko does not agree that Aristotle is guided throughout by the Platonic notion (Stephen Halliwell, *Aristotle's Poetics* (London, 1986) with Richard Janko's review of the same, *Classical Philology* **84** (1989) 154). The approach is wisely rejected by P. Somville in (*Essai sur la Poétique d'Aristote* (Paris, 1975), pp. 48 ff. For useful summaries of treatments of mimesis see Somville, pp. 45–54, and, more recently, Halliwell, pp. 110 ff.

2. P. Somville, *Essai sur la Poétique d'Aristote* (Paris, 1975), p. 48.

3. Similar merging of *technē* and nature occur in other *technai*, though the point depends on a broader view of nature than comes naturally to us. On an Aristotelian view, the building of houses is as natural for us as is city-dwelling, and the *technē* that goes into this should merge as naturally as medicine does in the natural process of human life.

4. D. W. Lucas adopts the twofold reading in *Aristotle Poetics* (Oxford, 1968), p. 67, as does Richard Janko in *Aristotle Poetics* (Indianapolis, 1987), p. 72. Stephen Halliwell adopts the threefold reading in *The Poetics of Aristotle*, (London, 1987), p. 77.

5. Halliwell's translation, "first, by alternation between narrative and dramatic impersonation" would seem to require either *hote de* or *allote* before *heteron ti gignomenon* (Stephen Halliwell, *The Poetics of Aristotle*, p. 33); I have captured this by supplying "sometimes." Without some such addition, the "mixed" reading of this classification will be lost.

6. Else achieves the same result by taking this category to be a Platonizing interpolation: G. Else, *Aristotle's Poetics: The Argument* (Cambridge, MA, 1957), pp. 90 ff.

7. R. Janko, *Aristotle Poetics*, p. 142; "Review of Halliwell (1986)," *Classical Philology* **84** (1989) 154.

8. The proverb is from "How the Young Man Should Study Poetry," Plutarch, *Moralia* 16A (available in Vol. I of the Loeb series, trans. by F. C. Babbitt, (London, 1927), pp. 74–197). The testimony on Gorgias is found in his "Were the the Athenians Famous in War or in Wisdom?" *Moralia* 348C (Babbitt, Vol. IV (London, 1936), pp. 492–527).

9. This is closely related to the sort of deception Plato feared, which disabled the watcher's judgment (*Republic* 605b) and incited him to emotions of which he would have been ashamed in real life (605c–d).

10. Aristotle does not seem aware of the difficulty, though I think he has the theoretical machinery he would need to deal with it. (For recent attempts at solving such problems, see R. Scruton, *Art and Imagination* (London, 1974); K. Walton, *Mimesis as Make-Believe* (Cambridge, MA, 1990), pp. 240 ff; B. H. Boruah, *Fiction and Emotion; a Study in Aesthetics and the Philosophy of Mind* (Oxford, 1988), pp. 64–74); and N. Carroll, *The Philosophy of Horror; or Paradoxes of the Heart* (London, 1990), pp. 60–88).

11. J. M. Redfield, *Nature and Culture in the Iliad: The Tragedy of Hector* (Chicago, 1975), pp. 54 ff.

12. On this see S. H. Butcher, *Aristotle's Theory of Poetry and Fine Art*, 4th edn (London, 1911), pp. 124 ff., who follows Teichmüller, *Aristotelisches Forschungen*, Vol. II (Halle, 1869, repr. Aalen, 1964), pp. 145–154.

13. "In tunes themselves there are *mimemata* of types of character, and this is evident, for right away there are different natural harmonies, so that listeners are affected in

different ways . . ." (*Politics* 134a38 ff., cf. *Problemata* 919b26). The idea that music can serve in the mimesis of character is at least as old as Plato (e.g. at *Republic* 399a ff., *Laws* 812c).

14. *Problemata* 919b26 ff. and 920a3 ff. For the link between motion and emotion, see *De Anima* 403a16.

15. I am indebted to Victor Caston, who helped me reach my understanding of this passage.

16. *Poetics* 1340a32 ff., cf. *Poetics* 4 and *Problemata* 920a3 ff.; the related passage, 919b26 ff., seems to give more scope to painting, however, as does *Poetics* 1450a27.

17. "Impressions and percusions and ideas cause alterations, for perceptions are really a kind of immediate alteration, and having impressions or ideas has the effect of the things themselves. For in a certain way the form in our ideas of something warm or cold or pleasant or fearful turns out to be very like each of these things, which is why we shiver and are afraid when we have only had an idea." (*De Motu* 701b16–22, cf. 702a17–19).

18. *Nicomachean Ethics* 1114a25–b3; R. J. Hankinson, "Perception and Evaluation: Aristotle on the Moral Imagination," *Dialogue* XXIX (1990) 60.

One Action

Rüdiger Bittner

1

Aristotle says in the *Poetics* that tragedy represents "one action which is whole and complete and has beginning, middle and end" (1459a19–20). "One action" means here just one action, no more and no less than one. That there should not be less than one action is further emphasized by "whole:" the action must be represented in full, no part of it should be missing. "Complete" in turn makes a claim implicit in wholeness: the action must be carried through to its end, no loose threads should be left. "Having beginning, middle and end" is equivalent to wholeness: tragedy represents one action from A to Z. On the other hand, that there should not be more than one action is insisted upon in the criticism of those who try to give their work unity by centering it on one character: "the actions of this one person will be many, and from them no one action will arise" (1451a18–19) – which is to say that one action, and not many, ought to arise. But to understand what is required by saying that tragedy should contain no more or less than one action, it is necessary to understand, first of all, what one action is. This is not clear. It is not clear, that is to say, what it takes for an arbitrary segment of a person's acting to qualify as one action.

2

To find out is of interest for both the playwright and the dramaturg. They would get a conceptual grip on one of the things they are aiming for, according to Aristotle, when they write or edit a text for the stage. In fact, perhaps not only according to Aristotle they are aiming for it. While talk of Aristotelian unities is definitely out of fashion in the theaters these days, the playwright and the dramaturg may actually be pursuing the thing that Aristotle has in mind here. After all, it is certainly considered a defect in a play or in a performance if it lacks coherence, if it falls apart. Not unity of action, but only some overly narrow conception of it, may have become obsolete in modern theater. All the more important it is, then, to be clear about what unity of action really amounts to.

3

The question is of interest for moralists, too. Indeed, for moralists in a broad sense of the term: anyone offering guidance in terms of rules for somebody's conduct in general assumes an understanding of what one action is. This is so because individual actions form the universe of discourse over which the rules range. Rules enjoin summarily every action of a certain quality. For example, the odd rule in the *Nicomachean Ethics* "to taste everything sweet" (*NE* 1147a29),[1] or what Kant calls a maxim like "to increase my wealth by any safe means,"[2] select all the tastings of sweets and all the safe increasings of one's wealth and require the agent to execute one of these whenever such an action becomes available. But the actions enjoined are selected from the range of actions in general, i.e. from the range of individual actions. Thus, to know what fills the pool they are selecting from, moralists should be interested in learning what one action is. To be sure, failure to know this will not prevent them from setting up rules. But without an account of what one action is, they do not know what they are talking about.

4

It may be suspected that the playwright and the moralist, using the same word "action," are nevertheless dealing with different things. It may be suspected, that is, that Aristotle's statements about actions in tragedies are irrelevant to actions in life. But the very fact that he is using the same word in the *Poetics* and in the *Ethics* makes this improbable; and freely referring to various tragedies in the *Ethics*,[3] he shows that he does not recognize a gap between the two genres: what tragedy represents and *Ethics* investigates is the same sort of thing. Indeed, tragedy would be irrelevant otherwise. It is true, actions in tragedy are usually larger than actions in life: they have more complications and weightier consequences, and involve individuals of higher rank. But that they are large is what makes them worth putting on the stage. It does not make them different in kind.

5

Distinct actions need not be temporally separate. Stuart Hampshire may be right in suggesting that the entire conscious life of a human being can be covered with correct answers to the question: "What is the person doing right now?" with no gap occurring between what these answers describe.[4] Acting being uninterrupted, then, actions cannot be distinguished as pieces of acting separated by non-acting in between. However, continuity does not preclude individuation, or we could not speak of mountains or waves. So with mountains as a model, a person's acting can be represented on Hampshire's view as a hilly landscape, every point of which belongs to some mountain. (There are no valleys.) The question, then, is: a mountain stands out as such by height; by what does an action stand out as an action?

6

By being meaningful. The doings of a person coalesce into individual actions discrete by virtue of separately making sense. One action is what you get if you cut a person's doings into the smallest still meaningful parts. One action is the unit of meaningful activity.

7

On any day, ordinary people take up a number of things which make sense independently of each other: they are engaged in several actions. For example, having breakfast in the morning is one thing, working on the manuscript of "One Action" is another, even though it should be true that the former is helpful or even indispensable for the latter. Tragedy, by contrast, represents one and only one action. This means that everything done within the play, including in particular everything said in it, together forms just one piece of meaningful activity. Suppose, for example, that this is the action of Sophocles' *Ajax*: "Ajax kills himself from regret over his fury after being refused the arms of Achilles."[5] If *Ajax* is indeed a tragedy, then Ajax' killing himself from regret over his fury after being refused the arms of Achilles is a piece of meaningful activity, it is the smallest such piece occurring in the play, and everything happening in the play is part of it. At one point, Ajax requests to see his son. Strictly speaking, this is not an action of his. it is just a part of the one action he is engaged in, that of killing himself from the motive described. So to say that what Ajax is doing at this point is asking to see his son would be as misleading as to say of somebody that he is pushing his arm at such and such an angle into the air, when what he is doing is pulling on his coat to go for a walk. The idea is, to identify correctly the action somebody is engaged in you have to cut the mass of his doings at the joints,[6] i.e. at the boundary lines of meaningful pieces of activity. This also explains why characters in tragedy never have breakfast. This is not because having breakfast is too lowly an activity, for in fact there is nothing contemptible about it. It is because having breakfast is not the sort of thing to be part of an action like killing oneself from the motive mentioned. Having breakfast is bound to be a different story, and that is just what tragedy does not permit.

8

If tragedy represents one and only one action, actions with more than one agent need to be admitted. It is not, after all, the hero's doings only that appear on stage. But that seems to be right anyway. If limits of meaning determine unity of action, then often enough one action will cut across the boundaries of individuals' agencies, outside tragedy as well as inside. If the two of us carry a heavy table together, we do not each have one action apart. Since what each of us is doing makes sense only together with what the other is doing, the action is the whole thing, our carrying the table, and what each of us does individually forms a part of that. So for tragedy. Appearance notwithstanding, Ajax' killing himself from regret over his fury after being refused the arms of Achilles involves not just Ajax, but the other characters of the play too, even the chorus: they are all engaged in this action, his killing himself from that motive. And there may be truth in that. Sometimes it does take two, at least two, to kill oneself.

9

The contrast invoked here between a piece of meaningful activity and mere doings may become clearer with the following image. There is a game: people dance, but suddenly the music is interrupted, and they are suppposed to remain frozen in whatever position they were in at this moment; the point being that these positions can look quite funny. Now they are funny because they make no sense: they look odd even though they are parts of ordinary, perhaps even graceful movements. (Sometimes photographs, for instance of people speaking, have a similar effect.) So there is a contrast here, between a movement resulting in that odd position and another one, the turn of the dance or the whole dance, of which the former is a part and which has nothing odd about it. Transferred from such a dance to activity in general, this is the contrast referred to above. You can cut the film of a person's doings anywhere, but with many cuts what you get is practical mumbo jumbo and with some only you get pieces of activity which make sense. It is the same as with objects. You can cut the stuff around in many ways, but with most cuts what you get is nothing sensible, while with others you get objects which make sense. Corresponding in the range of objects to what that game does for movements, there is a poem by Christian Morgenstern reporting that a knee is travelling in solitude through the world, "it is a knee and nothing else." Again, this is funny because absurd: a sheer knee, which is not anybody's knee, but just a knee, makes no sense.

10

This interpretation of Aristotle's one action requirement is supported by his comparison between an action and an animal. The passage quoted at the beginning, which says that tragedy represents one action which is whole and complete and has beginning, middle and end, continues with the words: "so that it give the proper pleasure like an animal one and whole."[7] An action one and whole is similar to an animal one and whole in that both are the smallest still meaningful parts of the respective realm, of the whole range of acting the one, of the whole range of animal life the other. Actions have beginning, middle and end the way animals have forelimbs and hindlimbs, because that is what it takes to be a full member of the domain in question. Actions and animals are alike in being the genuine citizens of their fields.

11

The interpretation also helps to explain the phenomenon of what is called tragic necessity. A successful tragedy often gives the impression: it was inevitable. Aristotle mentions repeatedly that in tragedy things happen according to what is probable or necessary.[8] But the necessity involved here is not imposed by an alien power crushing human endeavor. Nor is it fate, predetermining the course of events. It is a necessity immanent to the action. All that is happening is tied together by its constituting this sort of action.[9] Not consequences, strictly speaking, are inevitable, since consequences are something distinct from what they are consequences of. Not punishment is imposed on the hero, for the same reason. It is all the one action that takes its course, and the suffering at the end is part of it. Admittedly, doubts arise at this point whether under such strict conditions of immanence there exist any tragedies worth the name. For one thing, it is not clear that divine intervention can in every case be vindicated as a genuine part of the action represented, even if in some cases it certainly can. For another, it is not clear whether the bloody end of tragedies is always just the conclusion of their action. It is not clear that Antigone's killing herself in the cave is really the final part of her burying Polyneices, and not just something she does in a situation which is brought about in part by her burying him. It is not clear that Oedipus' blinding himself is the conclusion of his killing his father and marrying his mother, rather than his reaction to learning that this is what he did. Perhaps there is just one tragedy living up to Aristotle's exacting standards for unity of action, namely Jean Racine's *Bérénice* of 1670, a play of passionate love prevented from fulfillment by reasons of state and ending with the separation of the three main characters, a separation all the more smarting as it is fully understood by each of them. This is a dénouement that works without any additional prompting or reaction, it just completes the play's business. However, doubts about the applicability of Aristotle's theory so interpreted do not undermine the credibility of the interpretation. Some divergence between what Aristotle claims tragedy is and what tragedy actually was has to be recognized in any case.[10]

12

A difficulty of the present interpretation is that, taking literally Aristotle's requirement that tragedy represent just one action, it denies that any particular event within the play, like Ajax' requesting to see his son, can be considered an action. This is hard to accept, given ordinary ways of speaking both about life and plays. The traditional reading of Aristotle's doctrine responds by pleading ambiguity: "action" (that is, *praxis*) refers, in the *Ethics* and sometimes in the *Poetics*, to some individual thing done, and it refers, at other places in the *Poetics*, to "the organized totality of a play's structure of events."[11] In Stephen Halliwell's words, "a plot-structure contains both several, individual actions, and one composite or total 'action'."[12] But this is unsatisfactory. First, the ambiguity is only postulated, not found. Indeed, when Aristotle writes at the beginning of Chapter 8 of the *Poetics* "the actions of one individual are many, out of which no one action arises," this is evidence against the alleged ambiguity:[13] if "action" is ambiguous, it is perfectly possible for one action to arise from many actions. Second, once the one action of a play is a different kind of thing than the individual actions of ordinary agents, it is unclear what the criteria of unity for the composite action are. When does, and when doesn't, a play exhibit one "organized totality" of the structure of its events? Halliwell, following the traditional doctrine of unity of action, holds that "the causal and consequential relations between the actions or events of a tragedy" constitute the structure which is *the* action of the play.[14] But this is too weak: lots of things are causally and consequentially related which still would not qualify for an organized totality of events. The traditional doctrine has been so unrewarding precisely because it failed to spell out in full what is needed for unity of composite action. Despairing of this task, the present interpretation discards the distinction between actions and composite action and claims that the action of a tragedy has the same unity as ordinary actions have, that of being a piece of meaningful activity.

13

If, then, the interpretation offered here seems correct, the doctrine so interpreted should nonetheless be rejected. The crux is just this central idea of a piece of meaningful activity. The idea is clear enough to give content to the assertion that this is what underlies Aristotle's one action requirement. The idea is not clear enough to be itself acceptable. There is nothing, no object, no piece of activity, nor anything else, which just by itself makes sense; or at least we do not know what this would mean. It is unclear, and hopelessly so, what it is for something, say a piece of activity, to be simply a meaningful entity, and not only to fit into some framework, to be useful for some purpose, to give somebody a clue and the like. To put the point negatively, it is unclear by contrast to what some stretch of activity can be qualified, or disqualified, as practical mumbo jumbo. This being unclear, however, the suspicion arises that such qualifications get distributed according to mere familiarity and unfamiliarity; that the way we have become accustomed to carve up the field of activity has been turned into the way the field divides itself. Gustav Mahler is reported to have said that tradition is mere sloppiness. In the spirit of this remark it may be said that meaningful being is mere lazy thinking.

14

So there is no satisfactory account of "one action" on Aristotelian lines, since, according to the argument so far, Aristotle needs an idea of units of meaningful activity for that, and this idea is inaccessible. To be sure, we talk of actions, of one action, of different actions. But the individuation underlying such talk is not provided by the field of activity to be individuated. It depends on the needs of the describer in the context at hand. Thus in particular we can learn to recognize what sort of segment of doings Aristotle calls "one action." But this is just to acquire familiarity with one established habit of speaking about people's doings, with one way of lazy thinking. It is to learn a bit of Aristotelian. It is not to come to know what one action is, nor does it presuppose such knowledge. Nothing simply is one action. Any piece of activity may be treated as such. "Whatever we are willing to recognize as an entity at all may be construed as an individual," Nelson Goodman wrote: that principle holds for actions as well as for objects.[15]

15

It is not unity of action, then, towards which playwright and dramaturg are working. Unity of action is too cheap, anything may be said to have it; or else it is incomprehensible. Incoherence on the stage does not consist in a failure to represent one and only one of those segments of people's doings which constitute pieces of meaningful activity. It consists in a failure to represent a segment of people's doings which, given the relevant assumptions and expectations of its audiences, cannot fruitfully and comprehensively be understood. August Strindberg's *Ett drömspel* is by Aristotle's, and also by traditional Aristotelian, standards a hotchpotch of actions. But through the very diversity of what are traditionally called individual actions, through separating, joining, overlaying them, making them reflect and oppose each other, the play achieves a rich and comprehensive picture. What makes the play incoherent in the end is not the plurality of traditionally so-called actions. It is Strindberg's half-hearted attempt to tie things together with some traditional dramaturgy, namely with a story of God Indra's daughter descending to earth to see how humans live. This attempt at coherence makes the play incoherent, for now we do not know any more what is going on, a play of dreams or the journey of Indra's daughter. This is also what is bad about incoherence, on the stage as well as in theories: there is no way to tell what all in all has been said. Playwright and dramaturg find a task, then, which is neither trivial nor impossible. There are no material restrictions for their work. Any part and any combination of parts of what people are doing is permitted. (Samuel Beckett went quite far in cutting artificial slices out of what would be called an individual action: with remarkable success.) The task is to make the whole thing comprehensible and telling, however artificially it may be composed. Not that this is the only task. It is the one replacing Aristotle's one action requirement.

16

What if this just *were* Aristotle's one action requirement? The interpretation of "one action" offered here (Section 6–9) may be suspecting too much metaphysics in Aristotle's conception. He may not have thought that actions are the true inhabitants of the world of doings. He may just have thought that playwrights need to get their act together, and not anything can follow anything in a well-composed play.[16] Perhaps it is only the Aristotle of French classicism who finds fault with Strindberg and Beckett. The author of the *Poetics* is perfectly happy with them.

17

He couldn't be. Two reasons were touched upon already. First, actions are compared to animals (Section 10), and animals are the paradigm of true inhabitants of the world. Second, action in the *Poetics* and in the *Ethics* is the same thing (Section 4), but action in *Ethics* is considered the individual in the world of doings.[17] So "one action" does mean more for Aristotle than a composition of doings which can fruitfully be understood. Another reason against the present objection lies in the term "representation" ("mimesis"). Such talk makes sense only if there are entities of the relevant kind around in the world which can get represented in a representation. "Mimesis" is at best an unattractive metaphor and at worst a meaningless term if what undergoes "mimesis," one action, is considered, not something found, but something construed. "Mimesis" needs real things. It carries the metaphysics right with it.

18

As for the moralist (Section 3), he has to change his ways, too, deprived as he is of a substantive notion of "one action" (Section 13). Moral rules go, with the word "moral" understood in the broad sense mentioned (Section 3). This is not because of general Wittgensteinian worries about what counts as following a rule, nor because of specific doubts about the acceptability of rule-following in morals.[18] It is because moral rules range over individual actions, and the membership of this class is undetermined. Technical rules are safe, for they can be defined over a restricted field the concept of which carries a principle of individuation with it. "When installing a lamp, take out the fuse," this rule prescribes to do only such lamp-installings as are preceded by a taking out of the fuse. Here there is no difficulty because we know well enough what one lamp-installing is as opposed to another. But moral rules and general rules of prudence do not restrict themselves to classes of specific actions. They address the agent in whatever he does.[19] "*Quidquid agis prudenter agas et respice finem*," the old saying goes: whatever you do, act with prudence and keep in mind the consequences. And similarly, there is not a specific range of actions, say proceedings in court, for which justice is required, and another, military action say, which calls for courage. The requirements of justice, courage and the like are supposed to be in force across the board. But what this board consists of, individual actions, turned out to be unclear. So moral guidance needs to express itself other than in rules defined over the range of actions.

19

The moralist Aristotle recommends virtues. This seems to be good advice, especially if, contrary to Aristotle's view, agents do not produce individual actions, but simply are acting, which acting may be divided *ad libitum* into pieces called actions. Acting is of this or that kind, goes this way or that, presents a physiognomy over a shorter or longer period of time. Thereby it shows, the idea would be, traits of character, i.e. ways in which the agent is constituted as an agent. Traits of character are not identical with physiognomies of acting, they underlie them.[20] Hence Aristotle's standard expression "activity according to virtue,"[21] rather than something like "virtuous activity." The character trait is not a quality of the acting itself, it is a quality of the agent which the acting normally follows and thereby shows. Now the praiseworthy among the character traits are the virtues.[22] It is of them that moral discourse speaks. Talk of them can well be accommodated in a framework that does not have a substantive notion of individual actions.

20

To make a virtue conception of morality more precise and to defend it against objections is no part of the present task.[23] But another question arises here which is. According to Aristotle's *Ethics*, moral excellence is located primarily in

character traits, only derivatively in actions. Deliberate choices, we are told at
NE 1111b6, distinguish characters better from one another than actions do: that
suggests that to distinguish characters, not actions, is what we are primarily
after in moral consideration of people. *NE* 1103a14–b25 says that it is through
appropriate activity that character traits are acquired. That suggests that to have
certain character traits, not to produce certain actions, is the moral fulfillment.[24]
In many places Aristotle explains what is the right thing to do by reference to
what a person of virtue would do.[25] That suggests that it is the person's character, not his actions, to which moral qualities are ascribed primarily. But then
why does the *Poetics* not allow, indeed recommend, plays centered on character
rather than on action? Why does it exclude plays held together only by the
central figure (Section 1)? Why not have what Aristotle would call many
actions, in which the agent's character traits could be shown as expressing or
as forming themselves? It would seem that such a play is more Aristotelian,
closer to the doctrines of the ethical writings, than the one action plays he
advocates in the *Poetics*. Ibsen's *Peer Gynt*, Wedekind's, and Alban Berg's, *Lulu*,
Brecht's *Mutter Courage*, these rather than *Oedipus* should be Aristotle's favorite
plays.

21

If there is an answer to this query in Aristotle, it occurs in an obscure, and
possibly corrupt, passage, which in one version, literally translated, reads as
follows: "Tragedy is a representation not of individuals, but of an action and life
and happiness and the unhappiness is in the action, and the aim is an action,
not a quality; people have some quality according to the traits of character, but
they are happy or the opposite according to the actions" (1450a16–20).
Rudolph Kassel's edition rejects the text from "and happiness" to "the actions."
Strong as the philological grounds for doing so may be, it is hard to imagine them
outweighing the sheer need for an argument at this point. As Hans-Jürgen Horn
has shown, eliminating the disputed text leaves the proposition of the first
one-and-a-half lines unsupported.[26] To avoid that, some way of making sense of
the passage has to be found.

22

Assuming with one manuscript that "happiness" in the second line of the
quotation above is a nominative, not a genitive, and assuming accordingly that
the text should be read with a comma after "life," the key to an understanding
lies in the clause: "happiness and unhappiness is in the action." Horn interprets:
happiness and unhappiness are aims of action; an aim is part of that of which
it is an aim; thus, happiness and unhappiness are in the action, they are action;

so if tragedy is about happiness and unhappiness, it must be about action.[27] This reasoning is unsatisfactory. First, it does not make sense of the fact that Aristotle says both happiness and unhappiness are in the action; for while happiness may be the aim of action and unhappiness may be its actual result, unhappiness is not an aim of action and thus could not be said on the basis of the present reasoning to be in the action. Second, the sense in which happiness is action turns out to be thin. If happiness is action already by being the aim of action, then presenting a picture of somebody's state of happiness which is due to his actions would be sufficient for a play to be about action. For Aristotle, happiness is action in a stronger sense: the activity itself is the human fulfillment. Third, there is no reason to assume that tragedy is about happiness or unhappiness. It is about changes in happiness (1453a9, 1455b26–28). Yet to these changes Horn's reasoning does not refer. Martha Nussbaum interprets: happiness and unhappiness consist in action, not in merely having good qualities; tragedy shows "what is supremely valuable about human life;" thus, tragedy portrays people acting, not just having such and such qualities.[28] This reasoning is not successful either. First, happiness does consist, according to Aristotle's *Ethics*, in activity (*NE* 1098a5–18), but why should unhappiness? Ivan Gontscharow's Oblomow, who does nothing at all, must be, from Aristotle's point of view, a thoroughly unhappy creature. If it is replied that no human being can fail to be active, then the point about the activity involved in happiness becomes trivial, as it should not. Second, as with Horn, there is no reason to think that tragedy is a representation of happiness. Third, the reasoning misses the point at issue. It need not be demonstrated that tragedy does not represent mere characters, but shows them in activity. A story which is being enacted (1449b26–27) could hardly fail to do so. After all, when Aristotle denies that tragedy represents individuals, he does not mean, either, that in a tragedy there are only actions and no individuals on the stage. It needs to be demonstrated that tragedy, which represents active individuals in any case, does so by centering on one action rather than on one individual and his character.

23

Here is another interpretation. The key clause means: happiness and unhappiness depend on the action.[29] Taking "aim" in the following clause, just as a few lines further down (1450a22), to refer to the aim of tragedy, not to the aims of the tragedy's characters, the reasoning goes as follows: tragedy represents not individuals, but an action and life. This is because on the action depend happiness and unhappiness. So the point of tragedy is some action, not the quality of an agent. According to their character traits people have only such and such qualities, but according to how they act they become happy or the opposite. The reasoning has nothing to do with ethics, the point is, rather, dramatic effectivity. Aristotle draws attention to the fact that tragedies lead their heroes to a point

where what is at stake for them is all their happiness and unhappiness. Oedipus'
weal and woe, for example, lie in what the shepherd is going to say in line 1171,
as indeed both Oedipus and the shepherd recognize. Antigone puts not only her
life, but the meaning of her life at stake in burying her brother, because she is
thereby stepping outside the ethical order of the city. Penthesilea in Heinrich von
Kleist's play gives expression to the situation of tragic heroes in general, when
she says: "My all I have set on this throw, and there the dice lie which decide,
there they lie, I have to understand it – and also that I lost" (l.1305–1307).
Actually, this feature of tragedies is recognized in the common use of the term
"tragic." Accidents are called tragic, not chronic diseases, because the former,
not the latter, are supposed to decide in one stroke over the agent's happiness.
Now what Aristotle is arguing is that this compression of all the happiness and
unhappiness of the agent into what is being decided now requires centering the
play on one action. And he is right there. A play built around one figure like the
ones mentioned, *Peer Gynt, Lulu, Mutter Courage*, does not give this impression
of everything standing on a razor-edge,[30] because its many actions, in Aristotle's
sense, make each of them partial and undecisive.

24

To have all the happiness and unhappiness of the agent be at stake in the
dramatic moment is required, in turn, to produce the effect of tragedy, the right
sort of pity and fear. Disaster is grandly gripping and spectacular if, all the time
still uncertain, it then crushes its victim with one blow. To see things on the
brink of catastrophe is frightening and to see people routed in one moment is
pitiful in a stirring, elating way, whereas assured ruin and piecemeal and slow
decay are dejectingly sad. People sometimes speak of having had "a good cry."
Tragedy affords in a similar way a good fright and a good surge of pity. This is
what "catharsis" comes to. Just as a purge, initially an unpleasant experience,
makes you feel better after all, so undergoing the seemingly unpleasant affections
of pity and fear leaves you with high spirits in the end. But it does so only if the
objects of pity and fear are of the suitable kind, grand and elevating. Part of what
makes them so is that compression into one action.

25

It may also be part of why tragedy is over. I used to erect a tower as high as
possible with my building blocks and then, with one of the bottom pieces
removed, to collapse it at one blow. There is something similarly childish about
tragedy. There is something childish about these constructions of mothers
killing, or nearly killing, their unrecognized sons (1454a4–7), sons marrying
their mothers, heroes killing themselves from regret over their fury. What is

childish is the supposition that a human life can be gathered into the one action, can be exposed in its totality to happiness and destruction, and can be felled or saved in one stroke. The point here is different from the one made above (Section 14): that Aristotle has no viable account of what one action is. That point concerned the theory of tragedy. The present point concerns tragedy. Even without an account of "one action" we do recognize what Aristotle calls so, when we see it (Section 14). Thus we can say, not only that Aristotle's theory of tragedy needs the concept of one action, but that tragedy is itself built around what Aristotle calls "one action." And the point is that tragedy is built around it to its detriment. It makes for false dramatization. We have learnt, on the theater and otherwise, that we are dispersed beings. We are too fragmentary for tragedy; and "fragmentary" is not even the word, since it suggests a deficiency. In fact the totality of the tragic hero is not something we lack, it is an illusion. There is no such thing as one's all that could be put at stake. The decision in tragedy is void: we do not stand nor do we fall because, unlike the towering hero, we are many places. Tragedy errs.[31]

Notes

1. W. F. R. Hardie, *Aristotle's Ethical Theory* (Oxford, 1968), p. 240, considers this a rule. J. Cooper, *Reason and Human Good in Aristotle* (Cambridge, MA, 1975), p. 56n., disagrees.
2. I. Kant, *Kritik der praktischen Vernunft*, § 4, Remark. On Kant's concept of a maxim, see O. O'Neill, "Universal Laws and Ends-in-themselves," in *Constructions of Reason* (Cambridge, 1989), esp. pp. 128–131.
3. See *NE* 1111a11–12; 1146a19–20; 1148a32–34; 1150b6–9.
4. S. Hampshire, *Thought and Action* (New York, 1959), p. 75.
5. This summary is taken from J. Racine, Preface to Bérénice, in *Théâtre de 1668 à 1670* (Paris, 1929), p. 176.
6. See Plato, *Phaedrus* 265e1–3.
7. 1459a20–21. See also the similar passage 1450b34–1451a6.
8. 1451a12–13, 37–38, b8–9.
9. At 1450b27–31 Aristotle describes the necessity connecting the parts of a tragedy as implied by the wholeness of its action.
10. See S. Halliwell's introduction to his translation and commentary of the *Poetics*: S. Halliwell, *The Poetics of Aristotle* (Chapel Hill, NC, 1987), pp. 9–16.
11. S. Halliwell, *Aristotle's Poetics* (London, 1986), p. 141. P. Corneille already distinguishes in this way: "the expression 'unity of action' does not mean that tragedy presents only one action on the stage. That action which the poet chooses as his subject must have beginning, middle and end; and these three parts are not only as many actions feeding into the principal one, but in addition any of these may contain several subordinated ones." (*Trois discours sur le Poème dramatique*, ed. L. Forestier (Paris, 1982), p. 124). A similar view is held by the anonymous author of a French translation and commentary on Aristotle's *Poetics* (Paris, 1692), p. 119.
12. S. Halliwell, *The Poetics of Aristotle*, p. 104.
13. Rather than for it, as Halliwell claims: *Aristotle's Poetics*, p. 143; *The Poetics of Aristotle*, p. 104.
14. S. Halliwell, *Aristotle's Poetics*, p. 144. For the claim that this is traditional doctrine,

see e.g. *Monsieur Bossu's Treatise of the Epick Poem, Made English by W. J.* (London, 1719), p. 142, where a failure to follow Aristotle's principles is described in these terms: ". . . the Action would have been double and *Episodical*: Because the first *Episode* would not have been the Cause of the second, nor the second a Consequence of the first."

15. N. Goodman, "A World of Individuals," in *Problems and Projects,* (Indianapolis, IN, 1972), p. 157. On this point see also G. E. M. Anscombe, "Under a Description," *Nous* **13** (1979) 225.

16. See for instance 1450b32–33.

17. See in particular *NE* 1113b18.

18. See on this topic G. J. Warnock, *The Object of Morality* (London, 1971), pp. 50–70.

19. Kant's distinction between categorical and hypothetical imperatives can perhaps be reconstrued on these lines. See my article: "Hypothetische Imperative," *Zeitschrift für philosophische Forschung* **34** (1980) 210–226.

20. Evidence for this is *NE* 1098b33–1099a3.

21. For instance *NE* 1098a16–17.

22. See *NE* 1103a9–10.

23. See the recent volume of *Midwest Studies in Philosophy: Ethical Theory, Character and Virtue,* eds. P. French, Th. Uehling and H. Wettstein. (Notre Dame, IN, 1988).

24. See here also *NE* 1105a21–b5.

25. See for instance *NE* 1105b5–9, 1140a24–b13.

26. H.-J. Horn, "Zur Begründung des Vorrangs der "praxis" vor dem "ethos" in der aristotelischen Tragödientheorie," *Hermes* **103** (1975) 292–299.

27. *ibidem,* p. 294–299.

28. M. Nussbaum, "The fragility of goodness," in *Luck and Ethics in Greek Tragedy and Philosophy* (Cambridge, 1986), pp. 378–383; the quoted phrase is on p. 381.

29. For this meaning of "en" see Section AI6 of the entry in the dictionary of Liddell and Scott, with references. *Iliad* XVI 630 is a particularly apt one for the present context. E. Schütrumpf, *Die Bedeutung des Wortes "ethos" in der Poetik des Aristoteles* (Munich, 1970), p. 97, gives a hint in the direction advocated here.

30. Indeed, this was one of Brecht's reasons to shun the dramaturgy of one action.

31. Help, criticism and encouragement I received from Celène Abramson, Hajo Kurzenberger, Amélie Oksenberg Rorty and Nancy Schauber. I am grateful.

Plot Imitates Action:
Aesthetic Evaluation and Moral
Realism in Aristotle's *Poetics*

Cynthia A. Freeland

O vain is man
Who glorieth in his joy and hath no fears
While to and fro the chances of the years
Dance like an idiot in the wind!
And none by any strength has his own fortune.

Hecuba, *The Trojan Women*[1]

It is well-known that one of Aristotle's aims in the *Poetics* was to defend tragedy against Plato's moral critique in *Republic* X. It is perhaps less well recognized that Aristotle himself used moral criteria to identify good or bad tragedies as such, that is, as good or bad examples of the sort of works of art they are. In this essay I shall examine Aristotle's *Poetics* as an instance of a more general tradition of philosophical moralizing about art.

Aristotle's approach to tragedy rests on three fundamental bases: first, aesthetic naturalism – a naive understanding of *mimēsis* a realistic imitation of life; second, moral realism – a commitment to the existence of objective moral truths, and to a certain conception of moral tragedy; and third, essentialism – a functionalist account of tragedy as an artistic genre. A central notion that figures into each of these presuppositions is Aristotle's view that plot is the key element of tragedy, because plot imitates action. In Section I, which addresses Aristotle's aesthetic naturalism, I shall discuss the central role of plot in tragic mimesis. In Section II I shall explain what I mean by Aristotle's moral realism, and I shall describe the notion of moral tragedy that applies within the *Poetics*. In Section III I explore Aristotle's essentialist picture of tragedy, focusing on his account of the paradigm tragic plots. In my conclusion (Section IV) I shall discuss limitations of Aristotle's moralizing criticism of tragedy.

111

I. Plot as Imitation of Action

In the *Poetics* Aristotle places central emphasis on action and plot. Plots are artifacts constructed by tragic poets within constraints of a kind of realism of intended representation of actions (51b27–9). Aristotle is certainly aware of the poet's creative role in plot construction. Yet a tension arises between the idea that poets have the freedom to arrange and cast events in a "subjective" way in their plots, and the idea that the pattern of events depicted in those plots must be "objective," somehow "out there" as a reality the audience experiences through the vehicle of plot.

Aristotle defines plot as the imitation of action (*mimēsis praxeōs*).[2] From the fact that plot directly mirrors reality, he infers that plot is the key ingredient or even the "soul" of tragedy. He argues for the pre-eminence of plot in tragedy simply by noting the pre-eminence of action in life (50a15–22).

The emphasis on plot in the *Poetics* reflects what I will describe below as Aristotle's moral realism. In his ethics Aristotle articulates an account of human good in the context of how things really are in the world. Central to the *Ethics'* account is, of course, the view that happiness, our ultimate aim, resides in actions. Regardless of whether the *Poetics* directly follows upon or reflects the moral theory of either of the ethical treatises, it presupposes a moral realism of the sort Aristotle developed in his ethical writings. Aristotle also asserts something like the *Ethics'* view when he comments in *Poetics* 6 that action springs from thought and character, and "on actions again all success or failure depends" (50a1–3).

Tragedy "imitates" action, but it does so in ways that are more complex and abstract than is usually recognized, or than Aristotle himself seems to have recognized. Tragedy is a multimedia art, but Aristotle regards it first and foremost as a verbal art, the art of constructing or writing the plot. To focus further attention on the artificiality or constructedness of plot, and on the poet's selectivity in making decisions about his plot, I shall discuss various questions concerning tragic action in relation to plot.

Aristotle characterizes tragedy as a certain sort of imitation which is distinguished according to its "media," "objects," and "manner" (47a16–18). He proceeds to specify that (1) language and accessories are the means of tragedy, (2) a serious action (and agents) are its object, and (3) dramatic form is its manner. Let us consider (2) and (3) in more detail. Strictly speaking, of course, the tragic poet uses actors as part of his manner of imitating. Aristotle usually writes in this way, although at times he suggests instead that it is the actors who "make" the imitation (e.g. at 49b31). When he speaks of actors, there is an ambiguity between the players and the agents of the depicted play: his word *prattontes* shifts back and forth between these senses.[3] The analogy Aristotle draws between the narrative techniques of tragedy and of epic verse is helpful here. He says that the tragic poet employs just dramatization, while Homer imitates "by narrating part of the time and dramatizing the rest of the time"

(48a21–23). That is, Homer gives his audience various characters who speak as if they were involved in the story's action, often simply by adopting the narrative thread, as Odysseus does, for example, in *Odyssey* IX through XII. Again, Homer, author of the characters' lines, must be distinguished from the rhapsode who reads or recites them. Rhapsodes' enacting does not involve imitating in the sense of "mimicking" such typical epic deeds as dining, seducing, murdering, or escaping. At most, rhapsodes might imitate the emotions and speeches of the presumed agents or participants in these epic acts. Actors function similarly as the tragic poet's means of presenting his story; they take on characters' parts in a more consistent and prescribed fashion.

The tragic actor's representation of a plot, like the rhapsode's, amounts to taking on and reading parts rather than actual mimicking. This has often been remarked upon in connection with the central tragic acts, such grisly deeds as Oedipus' self-blinding or Medea's infanticide, which take place offstage due to some presumed delicacy of sensibility.[4] It is less often noted, but equally true, that in general the action in tragedy occurs offstage, and, like epic action, it is presented to the audience by a kind of stylized narration rather than by direct imitation (mimicking).[5] One can, to be sure, think of examples of actions that were presumably mimed or symbolically enacted onstage, but ordinarily the acts of tragedy were imitated by actor-readers pretending to be certain characters undergoing certain experiences. We, the audience, experience exciting narrations by actors, in a sequence, of the story of a tragedy.[6]

It is clear, then, that Aristotle's notion of the "imitation of action" is a rather abstract one involving considerable artificiality. Yet I think he regarded plot as quite apparent and natural in its functioning as imitation, claiming that the true pleasure of an imitation derives largely from our ability to recognize it as such, as an imitation.[7] We enjoy comparing the image to the real object it imitates in virtue of our prior knowledge and experience of the thing being represented: "For if one has not seen the thing [that is represented] before, [its image] will not produce pleasure as a representation, but because of its accomplishment, colour, or some other such cause" (48b15–19).

It is especially difficult to see how this "knowing-beforehand" requirement might be applied to the tragic plot. Consider the parallel problem of how the Greeks would recognize a statue of Apollo as the representation of this god. The viewer's interpretation and identification of the statue as one of Apollo can only rely on comparison with the god as he "really is" by invoking other images – familar representations, known symbolic associations, etc. Similarly, the story told by a tragic plot concerns actions which only "exist" for an audience's inspection and comparison in the form of other, previously known and familiar, stories. No doubt for an Athenian audience part of the pleasure of certain plays lay in comparing the treatment of the story in a new version to that of a previous version. Realism of plot turns out to be more a matter of intertextuality than of comparison with "similar" examples from daily life.

Aristotle expects tragic poets to generalize and portray a certain sort of action or course of events (51a37–b32), and the audience is presumed capable of assessing whether the depicted events "are possible in accordance with probability or necessity" (51a38). Aristotle supposes that poets often choose plots from the traditional stories precisely because then they'll have this feature – since "things which have happened are obviously possible, they would not have happened, if they were impossible" (51b17–18). Strangely, though, he asserts that, though history obviously involves what has happened, it may still lack the requisite feature of probability. Poets may still choose to treat some historical events, "since there is no reason why some historical events should not be in conformity with probability," (51b29–32). Notice how in these cases the poet, not the historian, has become the arbiter of probability in human affairs!

In recent years Nelson Goodman in particular has challenged the naive view that artworks represent reality in virtue of some "natural" resemblance to it.[8] He emphasizes that representation is achieved not through natural resemblances but rather through the audience's decoding of a complex symbol system. Realism is a matter of familiarity with the relevant symbol system. Additionally, Goodman has argued that artworks achieve the effect of realism because they actually help us construct our world, by showing us how to experience or "see" it.[9] Aristotle's point about the respective probabilities of literature and history comes close to this conclusion but by a different path; he thinks poetry is superior because it better captures how reality ought to be: more intelligible and predictable than it in fact is when compounded with contingency and accident.

It may seem strange to think of the *Poetics* as an early tract on realism in art. I believe, nonetheless, that Aristotle does build his account of the centrality of plot upon what he takes to be certain natural and inevitable resemblances between poetic representation and a certain idealized conception of reality. But in fact his commonplace guidelines about realism in plot record conventions. To show this I shall examine several of the most fundamental, obvious, and commonsense requirements he notes for "the action" to be represented in a tragic plot.

In the opening of Chapter 7 Aristotle lays down the most basic requirements on tragic action, arguing that it must be complete (*teleia*), whole (*olē*) and of a certain magnitude (*echousē ti megethos*) (50b24–27). Of these, wholeness is most significant, implying a special sort of unity and continuity (cf. 50b27 ff.). He insists straightforwardly that the unity of an imitation is a direct function of the unity of its object (51a30–31). Since the relevant object represented in tragedy is, of course, the tragic action, Aristotle's attention next turns, naturally, to questions about the unity of the represented action in tragedy.

A plot is unified if it represents one action; but what makes this represented action one? Is an action one if it is done by one agent, has one effect, or occurs within some one fairly narrowly specified stretch of time? In the *Poetics* treatment of this topic Aristotle largely avoids difficult metaphysical questions about the criteria for identifying actions.[10] He hints that one act presupposes one agent, but denies, at 51a15 ff., that this alone is enough to make the action unified. He does believe that a single action requires a fairly narrow timespan (49b13–14). For the most part Aristotle zeroes in on "the action" of a tragedy by saying that the story must have an internal coherence. Thus he says that tragedy, like epic, ". . . should be based on a single action, one that is a complete whole in itself, with a beginning, middle, and end, so as to enable the work to produce its own proper pleasure with all the organic unity of a living creature" (59a18–21). More specifically, the tragic plot becomes unified through representing some one course of action undergone by one agent in a narrow stretch of time, wherein the agent's condition in life is altered and reversed, as he progresses from either happiness or unhappiness to its contrary state (51a11–15). The action of a tragedy is also said to be single if it cannot have any part removed without the whole being disrupted (51a31–34). (But this requirement seems implausibly stringent in light of his recognition that plot will almost always be extended by the use of episodes (55a34 ff.).)

Clearly Aristotle holds that all plots have a temporal course. More specifically, Aristotle infers from this resemblance to the temporal sequencing of life that plots must have a beginning, middle, and end. What could seem more obvious? Lives have a beginning, middle, and end. But notice how schematic the relevant kind of imitation of life is. Aristotle says that plots are not to begin or end at just any point whatsoever. Plot must artificially designate a certain event as a beginning ("that which of itself does not of necessity follow something else, but after which there naturally is, or comes to be, something else" (50b27–28): but just what in a person's life "does not of necessity follow something else" – at the very least birth?). When does one begin in telling the story of Oedipus? If Sophocles' version of the tragedy presupposes various background events, then when does it actually begin? Aristotle's remark that the dramatist may omit portions of these stories that lie "outside the plot" (Chapter 24) is not helpful, for his ideas on this point seem quite arbitrary. In the same way, plot selects other events as middle and end of the story, thus artificially making clear the delineation of a teleological pattern of choice/effects/consequences.[11]

This teleological feature of plots should not be ignored. Aristotle argues that plot is "the origin and as it were the soul" of tragedy (50b38–39), and we should understand this not simply as stating that plot is an organizing principle of tragedy: plot like an animal's soul provides a play with its essential identity, function and purpose. The purpose of tragedy, as we saw earlier, is the representation of action. It has the aim of showing how lives come out in the end, and "the end [of life] is a sort of action, not a quality; people are of a certain sort according to their characters, but happy or the opposite according to their actions" (50a17–19).

What does Aristotle have in mind, then, when he speaks of the represented action of a tragedy? In the *Ethics* he shifts between broad and narrow uses of the key term for "action" (*praxis*).[12] In the broader, nontechnical sense, action is any self-directed movement; children and animals as well as adults are capable of such "voluntary" action (cf. III, 2, 1111b8–9). In the narrower, more strict sense of the term, an action is a manifestation of choice (*prohairesis*) or rational deliberation about ends (1111b8–10; 1094a1–2; 1139a31). Aristotle says once that action is its own end (1104b6–7), referring presumably to this sort of morally deliberated action of adults. Children, animals, and characterless adults do not "act" in this more restrictive sense of the term (cf. VII, 3, 1146b23–24, on the weak-willed person). In the *Poetics* Aristotle's use of the term *praxis* also vacillates among various senses. Sometimes the notion is extremely broad. In Chapter 8 he praises Homer, for example, for constructing the plots of the *Iliad* and the *Odyssey* around the representation of "a single action (*peri mia praxin*)" (51a28–29). Yet when he summarizes the plot or story of the *Odyssey* later, in Chapter 17, it clearly involves what would seem to be numerous particular *praxeis*, often called merely "incidents" (*pragmatōn*) (50a5, 55b16–23). Nevertheless, Aristotle calls epics "as far as possible representations of a single action" (62b10–12).

At other times, when Aristotle discusses the tragic action of a play he does seem to have in mind a more restricted notion of *praxis*; that is, he seems more to have in mind the *Ethics*' technical notion of an action which manifests choice. This is reasonable, for through this sort of action characters define themselves and become happy or unhappy. It would also account for why it makes sense to say that characters are included "on account of" or "for the sake of" the actions (50a20–22); in the *Ethics* view, character helps to clarify choice, which in turn clarifies *praxis* in the narrow, more technical sense (see also 50b8–9).

Though there is then some ambiguity in Aristotle's descriptions of action in the *Poetics*, what is crucial to keep in mind is the tension between constructed plot and depicted reality. The poet constructs plot by selecting an abstract pattern of words and speeches. The audience recognizes these speeches as depictions of actions, by decoding a highly complex symbol system involving elevated language, mime, character, narration, and intertextuality with the previous literary tradition. Plot is artificial; even to select the apparently innocuous structuring of action by a beginning, middle, and end the poet artificially isolates just part of a depicted life, making the actions' preconditions and consequences more clearly visible than they are ever likely to be in real life. Nevertheless, the represented action is to be understood and evaluated by the audience as though it were real – and revealing consequences that are like those that could occur in reality: "As for whether someone's saying or action is fine or not so fine, one must consider not only what was said or done itself, to see whether it is good or inferior, but also the person saying or doing it, and to whom, at what time, by what means and to what end, e.g. whether it is to bring about a greater good, or to avert a greater evil" (61a4–9).

To carry out such a refined ethical assessment the audience must come equipped with a theory about the reality of human behavior, its motives and ends – a theory like that provided in Aristotle's *Ethics*.

II. Aristotle's Moral Realism

I now wish to take up the topic of "moral tragedy." Aristotle's views in the *Poetics* reflect his moral realism: the sorts of circumstances that a tragic poet might depict in a plot must resemble particular patterns or possible relations among events in reality, which have an actual moral status – that is, moral judgments can truthfully be made about them. I suppose that the *Ethics* understands moral tragedy to occur only in certain sorts of cases. Thus if the *Poetics* directs poets to represent the world as it is, they will be constrained by facts about these sorts of cases. In this section I shall explain Aristotle's notion of moral tragedy, and in my next section I shall show that he held that it is the natural aim of literary tragedy to depict just such sorts of objective moral relations.

Aristotle in his *Ethics* admitted that life can offer impediments to happiness, even for someone virtuous:

> Now many events happen by chance (*kata tuchēn*), and events differing in importance; small pieces of good fortune or of its opposite clearly do not weigh down the scales of life one way or the other, but a multitude of great events if they turn out well will make life happier . . . while if they turn out ill they crush and maim happiness (*to makarion*); for they both bring pain with them and hinder many activities. (*NE* 1100b22–30 *passim*)

Let me call this provisionally an admission that there is "moral luck." Recently both Bernard Williams and Thomas Nagel have written on this notion; moral luck involves circumstances that the world places one in that can affect the success and evaluation of one's fundamental endeavors.[13] Nagel defines this notion as follows: "Where a significant aspect of what someone does depends on factors beyond his control, yet we continue to treat him in that respect as an object of moral judgment, it can be called moral luck" (p. 26).

Nagel concludes that even when moral luck does not affect our intentions or even our virtues, it can alter our happiness and our views of ourselves as moral agents. Williams' treatment of moral luck emphasizes retrospective justification and feelings of regret. For example, the driver of a truck who has killed a child through sheer bad luck will feel a certain sort of regret, agent-regret, that is different from, and stronger than, the regret felt by a spectator. An agent will feel more regret (in particular "agent-regret") if bad luck affecting a project involved the possibility of failure in relation to that project itself. Williams writes, "In these cases, the relevant consciousness of having done the harmful thing is basically that of its having happened as a consequence of one's acts, together with the thought that the cost of its happening can in the circumstances fairly be allocated to one's account" (p. 28).

Though I believe that there is some room in the *Ethics* for moral luck, I doubt that it extends very far. Aristotle insists that a good character is largely under a person's control. This is why he says that a good man like Priam can never do base or evil deeds, and can never become truly unhappy (1100b33–35).

Even in his sorrows Priam's nobility will "shine through" (1100b30–31). On Aristotle's own account, Priam's happiness was marred because complete happiness involves not just virtuous activity but also external goods or "goods of fortune" – factors such as health, the welfare of friends and loved ones, noble birth, wealth, or good looks. Possessing and preserving the goods of fortune is affected by factors beyond a person's control, though these goods can make a difference to happiness (1101a14–16).

Now, there are various ways of understanding the role of goods of fortune in a happy life, depending on the extent to which an agent cares about these goods in their own right.[14] But in any case, Aristotle's ethics can accurately be said to allow that tragedy occurs when a good person is prevented from being happy through the loss of external goods. This loss of happiness is a misfortune, and it is worth noting that Aristotle does speak of misfortune (dustuchia) as the most natural and fitting outcome of a literary tragedy.[15]

Moral luck can operate in ways that are more or less intrinsic to a good person's projects, regardless of whether external goods are valued in themselves. In some cases the agent may feel responsible for having done things that led to unhappiness, even though he does not see himself or the acts he has done as evil. In such cases pity is an appropriate response on the spectator's part, the response of thinking and feeling that the person has suffered undeservedly. But Aristotle appears to regard moral luck as a significant phenomenon worth discussing only in cases in which it intervenes in a well-advanced life plan like that of Priam. So he does not consider, for example, cases of bad moral luck that are more purely extrinsic, like that which befell Astyanax at Troy.

Now in the Poetics I believe that Aristotle also builds an account of literary tragedy that presupposes that the paradigm plots will depict only certain sorts of moral luck, in particular, cases in which this luck seems integrally involved with a mature agent's projects. In other words, he presupposes a certain kind of real phenomenon, moral tragedy, is the subject of literary tragedy. The pattern selected for tragedy is narrower and more specific than undifferentiated moral luck. First, Aristotle's criteria for the subjects of a tragedy will exclude pure victims like Astyanax. Next, Aristotle rules out both plots concerning a thoroughly bad person and those concerning a good person who changes into a bad person. He explicitly claims that it would be "revolting" (miaron)[16] to use a plot structure which depicts the downfall of a good person (1452b34–36).[17] It is not horrifying to show that an imperfectly good person can make a mistake and subsequently experience impediments, constraints, or the loss of happiness due to moral luck. Tragedy may precisely involve a person who's trying very hard to be good but who fails. But Aristotle wants to rule out tragedies depicting the most extreme cases of moral luck, cases in which a truly good person fails to win happiness. The only times that this is countenanced by Aristotle will involve plots showing an act done in ignorance. In both the Ethics and the Poetics Aristotle thus retains a good part of the Socratic view that we are responsible for faring well or ill. Though to be sure, the world may impose its limitations and impediments, for Aristotle this is not the stuff of tragedy.

The *Poetics* emphasizes that tragic dramas do or should represent effects of a specific kind of agent-centered moral luck. It seems quite clear to me that Aristotle's conception of tragic action in the *Poetics* does draw distinctions among types of moral luck. That is, he simply does not countenance plots in which (bad) moral luck of a purely extrinsic type is the key factor. When he says in the *Poetics* that the change in fortune of a tragedy will occur owing to a frailty or mistake (*hamartia*) of the hero, he is emphasizing that tragic unhappiness requires the agent's contribution; think for instance of Deianeira trying to win Heracles back through the centaur's magical love potion. A hamartia, then, is a mistake which turns out to mar or destroy one's happiness – but merely an error, not vice or the loss of good character. Indeed, Aristotle does insist on the centrality of this particular variety of moral luck to tragedy. This means that he rules out both passive heroes who do not act but simply suffer, as well as persons whose mistaken choice signals a real flaw in character.

Aristotle's emphasis on the tragic hero's choice and action seems to create problems for certain sorts of plays which we might call victim tragedies, like *The Trojan Women*. This play's episodic structure depicts a series of characters and their misfortunes, and the tragic heroines seem not to have made choices that crucially led to their downfall in the way Oedipus' choices did. Aristotle would probably not be much troubled by the charge that his account does not encompass all tragedies. "If my account does not fit certain tragedies," he would remark, "then so much the worse for those tragedies."

III. Essentialism and The Evaluation of Tragedy

A. Plot patterns

I can now begin to sketch Aristotle's view of the relationship between the definition of tragedy and the evaluation of tragedies. Aristotle approaches the study of poetry as the scientist he is. His account of tragedy is an essentialist one; he speaks of giving an account of its being or essence (*horon tès ousias*, 49b20). Tragedy has a particular nature, a set of constitutive necessary properties. He construes it as a product of natural human causes (48b4–5) with a natural development into its own form; it halted when it had attained its own nature (49a15). On analogy with living beings, tragedy also has an inherent nature, a quasi-soul – its plot (50a38–39).

Plot is the means by which tragedy accomplishes its natural aim, the representation of certain kinds of action and passion. Although plot is constructed and hence artificial, it represents events which the audience interprets as real: they "see through" the plot to moral and causal relationships between sorts of real events, and respond to these relationships with their peculiar response of catharsis. I shall say more about this response in Section III B below; first it is important to see how Aristotle's guidelines for plot construction advise the poet to represent certain sorts of people, acts, and outcomes. In particular tragic playwrights represent moral tragedy. To the extent that Aristotle holds that tragedy should present a particular vision of moral reality, he lays the groundwork for his moralizing approach to the evaluation of tragedies.

Two key methodological issues from Aristotelian science and metaphysics should be kept in mind by readers of the *Poetics*. Aristotle tends to draw what we would regard as *normative* inferences from the data, even in the so-called "pure" sciences like biology. That is, he draws conclusions about things' natural functions or goods.[18] Even within biology he sets up analytic categories in a prescriptive-sounding way. This is so despite the second key fact, that Aristotelian essentialism allows for wide individual variations. An individual mammal may lack some essential characteristic of its species. Defective individuals are types of monsters, and sometimes Aristotle even refers to an entire species as defective or as "monsters" (*terata*) because they lack some feature that is essential relative to their overall genus.[19] What all this means is that Aristotelian essentialism permits application of the term "tragedy" to dramas whose plots do not fulfill the desiderata of a genuine or paradigm tragedy. A play can count as a tragedy even if it depicts the wrong sort of hero, the wrong sort of circumstances or choices, and so on. Aristotle would probably say that such tragedies are defective, comparable to monsters in the biological realm.

Aristotle's fundamental typology of tragedies is based upon an analysis of plot structures. Plot, that schematic pattern of choice–action–consequence, is so all-important that Aristotle believes we can respond in an appropriate way even to the merest outline of a play's story (53b3–7, 62a11–13). Unfortunately, Aristotle offers two distinct and apparently conflicting sets of guidelines for construction of excellent tragic plots.[20] In the first of these, in Chapter 13, he begins by asking what poets should aim at and avoid in constructing plot, so as to enable tragedy to achieve its function (*pothen estai to tēs tragōdius ergon*, 52b29–30). He identifies as the most tragic plot patterns those depicting a hero whose life becomes unhappy or who experiences misfortune and who is initially good, though not perfectly virtuous (53a7–8; cf. 15, 54a16–17). The hero's fortunes change through some error, weakness or frailty (hamartia), rather than through sheer vice or depravity (53a8–10). The plot of the *Oedipus Tyrannos*, then, is the "finest" according to this chapter's ranking. More precisely, he says that "the tragedy which is finest according to the [principles of the] art results from this structure" (53a22–23), and also that these plots are the "most tragic" (*tragikōtatai*, 53a27–28).

In Chapter 14 Aristotle provides a more complicated discussion, describing how various distinct poles can be combined to create possible types of plot-patterns which achieve the end of depicting the terrifying and the pitiable. The first pole involves the direction of the reversal depicted: in "happy ending" stories, the hero's fortunes improve, whereas in sad tales, the progress goes downhill. Other poles concern whether the central act or tragic deed is "either

. . . done or not done, and either knowingly or unknowingly" (53b36–37). He argues that the best sort of tragic plot depicts a happy, fortunate individual who almost does something truly terrible (not through vice, but by mistake), becomes very unhappy at realizing this, but at the last minute is saved or devises an escape (54a4–8). This means that the *Iphigenia in Tauris* (*IT*) not *Oedipus Tyrannos*, exemplifies the type of plot Aristotle deems superior in Chapter 14.[21]

Why is the plot structure of the *IT* referred to as the "most powerful" (*kratiston*)? My suggestion is that Aristotle prefers this plot-pattern for its depiction of the moral order as more rational and less ultimately subject to moral luck. Aristotle's ranking in Chapter 14 looks as though it reflects a clearly descending order of degrees of moral innocence. That is, better plots involve less contamination by moral luck. That Iphigenia should sacrifice her brother would be shocking; should she do so in ignorance it would be somewhat less so; best of all is that she almost do it but have luck work in her favor rather than against her, so as to prevent such a moral tragedy. This also explains why Aristotle assigns last place on his list to those plots in which a person actually chooses an evil deed knowing that he is doing so. Such people deserve less pity, so the plots about them are less tragic. In the *Oedipus*, on the other hand, more than in the *IT*, the audience may be confused about Oedipus' moral status, because he is contaminated by his crime – despite having done it unwillingly.

Though in Chapter 13 Aristotle recognizes that tragedy concerns moral tragedy, he still, in chapter 14, gives highest praise to plots in which moral tragedy is averted. This is true in spite of the fact that his focus in this chapter is on plots suitable for arousing the tragic emotions and producing a catharsis. He ultimately ranks plots, then, according to his estimation of the acceptability of their moral messages. After describing the four plot structures in Chapter 14 he doesn't say, "But a type IV plot could be a great tragedy if used by a writer along with fabulous imagery and language and characterization, or if it is somehow otherwise extremely thought-provoking." In fact, he warns us away from tragedies that try to utilize other means to achieve catharsis, e.g. distraction by "spectacle" (*opsis*) (53b1–3); furthermore, a play without plot is like a drawing without outline or shape; it can only be appreciated for its pretty colors, not for anything it represents (50a38–b4). Certainly he recognizes such nonmoral aspects of plots as their believability, along with such "aesthetic" features of tragedies as their sets, costumes, and gorgeous language. He acknowledges there is a diverse range of tragedies and makes no move to censor those he might regard as defective, even ones with the sort of plot he considers "shocking." But neither does he supply any reasonable account of the grounds for appreciation of such plays.

Thus, despite differences between Chapters 13 and 14, I want to emphasize that in both chapters the recommended tragic plots involve an artificially selective focus on one agent and one deed. The tragic plot abstracts from the concreteness of life and delivers a clearly unified pattern of well-defined antecedent circumstances – choice – consequences. Our focus is riveted on one person and we see her fate, his choices, and their ultimate outcome. At another level of artificiality, the sort of tragic downfall depicted is sharply constrained to a certain weakness, ignorance, or frailty. In other words, the tragic plot should be constructed so as to present a specific kind of moral luck, what I earlier called (following Nagel and Williams) agent-centered moral luck. Neither of the patterns recommended in Chapter 13 or Chapter 14 allow for the constrution of an excellent, powerful tragedy based upon extrinsic bad luck, the kind that involves loss of goods of fortune through no action of one's own. In effect this means that his criteria rule out a tragedy like *The Trojan Women*. The losses incurred by Hecuba and Andromache in *The Trojan Women* are not represented in that play as having been brought about by their own actions or frailties. Tragedy ought to depict only certain people, certain circumstances, certain outcomes – those in accord with Aristotle's moral views. Otherwise it will fall short of its aim, truth.

B. Catharsis

Aristotle's evaluations of plot construction are grounded in his view of tragedy's essential aim – to produce catharsis. The audience judges that the depicted events are ones that are pitiable and fearful, and accordingly, they actually feel pity and fear; and from these there arises a catharsis. In such a case audience members take pleasure from their awareness that they are responding to a play, or a depiction; but the plot which facilitates catharsis works by receding into the background and letting the events speak for themselves. The tragic emotions of pity and fear that are essential to catharsis fundamentally involve certain moral judgments. Pity in particular requires feeling/judging that a good person, someone like ourselves, suffers something undeserved. The notion of catharsis has proved notoriously elusive. Here I shall confine myself to considering two broad lines of interpretation, the cognitivist and the emotivist accounts.[22] On either of these plausible views, I want to show, Aristotle's moral realism proves crucial to his aesthetic evaluations.

According to the cognitivist, catharsis does involve feeling, but more importantly it requires making appropriate intellectual judgments about particular deliberative decisions represented in tragedy. As Martha Nussbaum, a recent defender of this line of interpretation, explains it, when the audience responds to the depicted events of a play with the emotions of pity and fear, they think and learn, and they come to draw appropriate judgments concerning the moral issues and problems represented in the play.[23] In general, according to Nussbaum, catharsis provides a broad sort of emotional/intellectual "clarification concerning who we are . . . [and] an appropriate practical perception of our situation" (p. 391).

On a cognitivist account the catharsis of a play derives from our recognition and contemplation of moral truths addressed in it. But it is not altogether clear just how on the cognitivist account moral truths are located in artworks, including plays. Nussbaum aims at interpreting the ancient tragedians as important moral thinkers who reflected seriously on the possibility of failure in our fundamental moral enterprises. At times she suggests that they did so by presenting fairly specific moral truths in their plays. She argues that the tragic poems "[embody] in both their content and their style a conception of human excellence" (p. 13). This conception would have to contain some quite definite theses about virtue, reason, happiness, and so on – theses Nussbaum believes turn out to be similar to Aristotle's.

An important distinction enters into play here that must be noted. Artworks may function cognitively (on a broad view) by stimulating thought, or on the other hand (on a narrower view) by presenting and defending theses. Nussbaum overall seems to defend a broad cognitivist interpretation of catharsis; she understands it as requiring a general perception and reflection upon serious moral issues. This broad interpretation is an attractive one. It recognizes that plays have various aesthetic dimensions distinct from their subject matter or moral content. We can attend to and appreciate such factors as psychological realism, plausible plots, and effective characterization as positive considerations, along with vaguer features like complexity and depth of insight. These factors are distinct from, though of course they could subserve, the end the cognitivist attributes to tragedy, prompting moral thought and clarification.

I believe, however, that the broad cognitivist interpretation of catharsis goes astray, in failing to take seriously Aristotle's own narrower thought about what was requisite for moral clarification: a depiction of moral truth. The features mentioned by Aristotle in his recommendations for plot construction, such as varying degrees of responsibility or of external fortune's involvement, conditions of knowledge or ignorance, etc., result in a proposed evaluation of tragedies based on a moral realist assessment, where the moral realism in question is that of his own ethics. It is easy to disagree with Aristotle, and to argue that the kind of play he places at the bottom of his list in Chapter 14, viewing it with moral repugnance, might appear to offer superb opportunities for catharsis understood as intellectual clarification. Conversely, there may seem to be little reason to praise some of the tragedies Aristotle prefers.

Still, if tragedy is "part of ethical investigation," to use Nussbaum's own terms, (pp. 13–14), then we should assess tragedies as we would other moral situations. True, to interpret the plays we must respond to them as complex works of art, in emotional and intellectual ways, recognizing that as literary works they employ special techniques of poetic language and dramatic characterization. But to evaluate these works – to react with our own catharsis – involves making a kind of moral judgment. Aristotle himself writes as though our evaluation of deeds done in tragedies will proceed in just the same way as if we were presented with those deeds in reality (61a4–9). Inevitably we must reject or criticize plays with questionable plots, alternative moral visions, or even unclear moral messages. It would be absurd to argue that such tragedies offer catharsis, genuine and valuable moral clarification. Whatever the merits of broad cognivitism as an account of the intellectual contribution of tragedies in themselves, Aristotle's own view was narrower. The audience's emotional/theatrical response to tragedies as artworks is to arrive at a form of moral insight, but I have argued that this moral insight could not, on Aristotle's own criteria, be an appropriate response to certain sorts of plots, because those plots do not depict a moral vision Aristotle accepts.

A second important line of interpretation of catharsis is the emotivist view. The emotivist reasons against the cognitivist that the pleasure of catharsis is not in and of itself the pleasure of learning or thinking something, but rather of seeing and feeling something. Though audience members may exercise cognitive skills in viewing and reacting to a tragedy, this is not the real pleasure of tragedy. In a recent extended defense of this line of interpretation, Jonathan Lear emphasized that tragedy provides the audience with an opportunity to make bits of its moral knowledge more concretely felt, by bringing home that something they know intellectually or in the abstract really could occur.[24] The strongly felt emotions appropriate to these unlikely but possible situations are ultimately pleasureable because one feels the nobility of the human who survives such an extreme situation.

On this emotivist line of interpretation, what is emphasized is the audience's awareness of the mimetic relation between the depicted events, with their "objective pathos," and the audience's aesthetic response, "subjective pathos" (321). Pleasure must be taken in the play as mimesis. While I agree with Lear that the audience does respond to tragedy as to life – because in life there would be no pleasure in the relevant observations (307–309) – I also think that the audience does not respond to tragedy as real, because otherwise it would not feel the pity and fear through which catharsis occur at the depicted events. Even though the emotivist interpretation of catharsis does not stress knowledge, it still places great weight on the idea that tragedy itself presents truths of a sort, or in other words, certain sorts of depictions of reality. So Lear seems to recognize what I have described above, the fact that Aristotle advises poets to construct plots so as to conform with his fundamentally optimistic view of human activity:

> The world of tragic events must, Aristotle repeatedly insists, be rational. The subject of tragedy may be a good man, but he must make a mistake which rationalizes his fall. . . . For the point of tragedy, in Aristotle's eyes, is not to portray a world in which a person through no fault of his own may be subject to fundamentally irreconcilable and destructive demands. (p. 325 *passim*)

A similar faith in Aristotle's optimistic vision of moral reality seems to underlie Lear's conviction that the audience can enjoy tragedy because in it they see that, despite suffering and horror, the world remains a rational, meaningful place offering a sphere for meaningful human response. But Lear's account provides no meaningful scope of operation for catharsis in response to scenarios in which people lose their dignity through no fault of their own: in which they are crushed beneath forces of evil or of fate. The emotivist account cannot explain how we would get a catharsis from watching someone crying like Hecuba in *The Trojan Women*: "Weep now, and mourn for me, my women./ Fortune has flung me to the bottom of her wheel/And I am ruined."[25] I mention this point not as an objection to the emotivist account, but rather to show how it results in a limitation curiously parallel to the cognitivist's: it fails to explain how catharsis is provided by certain tragedies like *The Trojan Women*. This could indicate that it is flawed as a proposal of what Aristotle had in mind by catharsis; but alternatively, and more plausibly I believe, it shows that Aristotle's own account is not intended to encompass a play such as this, simply because he regarded it as an inferior example of its kind.

IV. Conclusion

I have identified three central assumptions of the *Poetics* which, taken together, form the basis for Aristotle's moralizing approach to the evaluation of tragedies. First was his aesthetic naturalism, the belief that art in general, and poetry in particular, represent reality and life by direct mimesis, a kind of simple mirroring. Plot is the central component facilitating the mimesis of key points in human life: choice, action, happiness, and unhappiness. Second, Aristotle is a moral realist: a metaphysical view of human nature undergirds his moral epistemology and his belief that we may achieve truth in our moral assessments of characters and actions. Ethical reality encompasses certain types of moral luck; if this moral luck is in some way integral to a person's own projects and follows upon a hamartia, then the resulting downturn in fortune is a moral tragedy. Third, Aristotle adopts an essentialist account of literary tragedy as a naturally occurring phenomenon with intrinsic necessary properties and a specific aim. To achieve its natural aim of evoking catharsis in its audience, a tragic plot should represent situations of moral luck, by depicting certain types of characters, situations, choices, actions, and outcomes. A tragedy which fails to follow these guidelines will *ipso facto* be less effective at its natural work, and hence a less good representative of its kind.

The basic ideas that figure into Aristotle's argument and subsequent evaluative guidelines are so interwoven that they prove difficult to isolate and consider critically. But since all three are crucial to the nature and success of his enterprise in the *Poetics*, they must be examined independently. The most serious criticism of Aristotle's first tenet can be stated by adopting a viewpoint like Nelson Goodman's. Recall Goodman's point that art creates or forms our vision of life; plot constructs rather than mirroring an orderly and intelligible reality. In Section I above I described the tension between Aristotle's view that tragic imitation is direct and natural, and various artificial or conventional constraints he imposes on plot in order to satisfy his realist conceptions of tragedy's aims. For example, plot provides greater intelligibility and coherence than life itself by focusing on a sequence of events connected by probability or necessity, representing the sequence as whole and complete with a natural starting place and an inevitable conclusion. Further, realism in the tragic plays was more a matter of intertextuality and tradition rather than the direct comparison with reality that Aristotle seemed to recognize.

The limitations of Aristotle's aesthetic naturalism are partly due to the specificity of the genre he was analyzing. Aristotle's naive realism would be hard pressed by developments in subjective narrative, stream of consciousness, and temporal manipulation in literary works by authors like Faulkner or Woolf, or in films by Resnais, Altman, and others. But there were variations in genre and narrative that he himself recognized. Thus, he noted that epic, which is longer than tragedy, permits the representation of many actions occurring at the same time (59b26–28). Obviously such a narrative must be structured in a more complicated way than tragedy. Aristotle seemed immediately to feel the temptation to compare genres so as to assess primacy, as if they shared one aim (62b13–14). Accordingly, he criticized epic as less unified, more episodic, less vivid, and more diffuse. Some might say instead that epic is more life-like than tragedy in view of these factors, since life itself is more like a random series of unconnected events.

Related issues lead to more pressing questions about the adequacy of Aristotle's conceptualization of tragedy itself. Consider briefly how feminist criticism, for example, might challenge the innocence of his commitments to certain sorts of plot. Aristotle's pronouncements about women's defects and limitations in his *Politics* and biology are well-known targets of feminist criticism.[26] His views on women's character and mode of rationality are clearly relevant to the accounts of character and action so central in the *Poetics*, and surface for instance in his remarks that a woman's character must not be too good (54a20–22) or too clever or brave (54a23–24). But beyond this, sexism may have infiltrated Aristotle's conception of that complex interrelation among the hero, his goodness, hamartia, and downfall which constitutes tragedy. That is, his criteria for well-structured plots downgrade at least two varieties of women's tragedies. I speak of "women's tragedies" not just in the sense of plays depicting female protagonists, but ones that represent a kind of generalized misfortune and victimization, rather than the agent-centered moral luck that Aristotle considers essential to moral tragedy.[27]

Aristotle's teleology of plot presupposes an active, responsible hero who has a definite social context. The poet abstracts from the flux of life, selecting just a few from among a character's actions as dramatizable, denying the concrete reality of lived experience. Aristotle highlights the hero's individual freedom and power to affect his life. On his criteria it is hard to see how a play like *The Trojan Women* could count as a good tragedy – or indeed, how it counts as a tragedy at all. There is a clear difficulty in identifying "the action" of this play. The play has a certain unity, but it is simply the unity of victimization and unrelieved suffering. The play does not depict some mistake or hamartia on Hecuba's part (unless her mistake was simply marrying and bearing children in the first place). Like the other characters in the play, Hecuba suffers because she is female, in her case, wife and mother. They suffer in a way appropriate to women whose fates are decided as a consequence of powerful men's deeds.[28] The play that dramatizes their misfortunes is purely episodic (translator Neil Cury says in his introduction "*The Trojan Women* scarcely has a plot"[29]). On Aristotle's criteria for constructing a good plot it also runs dangerously close to the risk of being "repulsive" through showing unmitigated disasters befalling good people.

A second category of "women's plots" may be found in those ancient tragedies depicting women (and virgins in particular) as favored sacrificial victims. This topic has been treated in Nicole Loraux's recent book, *Tragic Ways of Killing a Woman*.[30] Loraux points out that being a sacrificial victim was a role somehow more appropriate to a women than to a man in tragedy. She also pursues more specific issues concerning how the woman's body is treated in tragedy, how women and men may kill themselves in tragedy, and so on. It emerges that there were important differences in plot structures centered around men and women. Loraux remarks: "In itself the setting of women on the stage was already an excellent opportunity for the Athenian citizen to ponder the difference between the sexes. It was a chance to state the difference before obscuring it, and then to find it again, all the richer for having been obscured, and more firmly based for having been finally reaffirmed" (p. x).

Though men and women do get represented and treated differently in tragic plots (and it would be surprising if they did not), Aristotle does not notice this fact. My claim is that his emphasis on choice and action preselects plots that are more likely to concern the "important," i.e. state or political decision-making of men rather than the domestic sphere appropriate to women. Moral luck or fate itself strikes the genders in significantly different ways. We may rush to excuse Aristotle for not having regarded tragedies as gender-specific, because we might ourselves balk at the thought. We can think of important women protagonists in ancient tragedies, strong women who did indeed make significant choices. But there are nevertheless questions to be raised concerning general differences between roles of female and male protagonists in ancient tragedies – how they met their specific tragic ends.

The second fundamental assumption Aristotle makes about tragedies involves his moral realism. Tragedies aim to present views that are somehow "true." Aristotle holds a certain view in his ethics about the relations among virtue, happiness, and moral luck. On his view, moral luck may impede virtuous persons' pursuits of happiness by affecting their possession of the goods of fortune (but not their characters). This leads Aristotle to think of tragedy in a certain way. His definition of tragedy as a literary genre in the *Poetics* describes it as an artificial enactment of this sort of moral vision in the created medium of a play, accomplished in particular through plot. Aristotle thought that in general the tragedies known to him had in fact aimed at just such a depiction of reality, and that they ought to.

To the extent that Aristotle's analyses and criticisms of tragedy hinge upon his own moral views, they can be damaged by any independent critisism of those views. Aristotle's second basic supposition can be criticized in a variety of ways. I suggested above, for example, that Aristotle's own verdicts on plays can strike us as narrow and restrictive, or just plain wrong. The *Medea*, for example, has a plot Aristotle must surely condemn, yet this play is an extraordinarily effective tragedy with continuing relevance; on the other hand the play that Aristotle and the Athenians admired, the *Iphigenia in Tauris* can be seen as bearing the morally repugnant message that some kinds of people are fundamentally more civilized than others, so that these people's fate is of more concern to us (and to the gods) than that of the barbarians.

I think that the most significant limitation of this second of Aristotle's suppositions is that it confines artists to articulating or confirming moral truths we already know, rather than revealing difficult moral problems or raising moral issues in a significantly original and challenging way. As I have interpreted Aristotle, tragedies are best if they present a certain picture of the relations among virtue, reason, happiness, and so on. But on an alternative view, artists could be acknowledged to have a more genuine, original, and creative role in addressing moral issues.[31] They may not only present situations which we can view as concretized examples for our pleasure and edification, but raise questions or pose real problems, jarring our current sensibilities and categories. Despite the fact that Aristotle showed a greater openness to tragedy than Plato, I see no evidence that he granted poets can have this sort of groundbreaking role in the moral arena.

The third and final of Aristotle's basic presuppositions is his essentialist account of tragedy as a genre. The validity of this sort of account is restricted by its methodological and metaphysical assumptions. Even granting that we are sympathetic to the claim that, as a particular genre situated in a particular culture and era, tragedy had an essence, still, Aristotle could be wrong about that essence. In fact, it is rather difficult to say how Aristotle arrived at his own account of this genre's "essence." Was it a quasi-scientific conclusion drawn from the mass of empirical data – from the existing corpus of plays; or was his essentialism more prescriptive? Would he have said that his account possessed objectivity not in the way that scientific accounts of the essence of thunder or dolphins do, but rather in the way that he thinks our ethical judgments do?

Forgetting metaphysical disputes over essence, we can ask about the merits of Aristotle's *Poetics* as a foundational example of genre criticism. In Aristotle's case this led naturally to a problematic ranking of the merits of various genres, but it need not. Purposiveness will probably be the key difficulty in any proposed account of a genre's nature. In Aristotle's time there were clear civic and ritual roles for tragedy. Though his description of tragedy's function included mention of the activity of the poet, various criteria about the product, and the response of the audience, it neglected to consider tragedy as socially grounded in ritual, either civic or religious. He also fails to explore its economic underpinnings or the political themes so often lurking just beneath the surface. To this extent he falsifies the aim of tragedy by over-aestheticizing it – like a commentator on Gothic cathedrals who mentions innovations in structure, light, and airiness, while forgetting to discuss the cathedral's role in a city's economy, political structure, and religious life.

Even if a plausible, socially situated account of the role of an artistic genre in a culture can be formulated, the philosopher's role in relation to the practitioner of a genre with moral aims remains problematic. In articulating the moral purpose of a genre the philosopher lays out an account that bears relation to serious moral issues. Who is to be the arbiter of truth here, the moral philosopher or the artist? When should the innovator be criticized for a departure from genre, and when for a moral failing? Traditionally, philosophers have had a key role to play in laying out and defending a view of morality. But on the other hand, this may make them poor commentators on an art whose vision seems restricted or alien to their own.

Continuing debate about art and morals shows that these questions are far from settled. The lessons to be learned from Aristotle are moderate. His evaluation approach has the plausibility it does because it rests on three interconnected assumptions which he works to defend: assumptions about the nature of art in general, about morality, and about the genre of tragic poetry in particular. But of course these assumptions are not impervious to criticism; the first in particular has been vigorously debated. In light of the perennial problem of defining "art" in general, the moralizing approach would seem to get its best grounding in independent accounts of morality and of the nature and aims of a particular artistic genre. Of course, the chief question for a philosopher attempting to work out such accounts will be whether to place primacy on a vision of moral truth, or instead on artistic expression, independence, and creativity. Can the philosopher committed to a moral position reasonably grant artists the power independently to formulate, reflect on, and even beyond this, resolve moral questions?

As we have seen, sadly, in late twentieth century America, moralists often seem to be the people who are least willing to accept and acknowledge experimental contributions made by artists. Of course our current cultural context of debates about art and morality is quite different from that of the *Poetics*, including as it does such diverse facts as the Constitution's protection of art as free speech, the much-diminished role of the philosopher as moral spokesman in the public arena, and the operation of most art production within a free market economy. Aristotle's greatest limitation as an art critic may be (like Plato's) his strength as a moralist who has his own deep and enduring moral commitments. This seems to have left him unwilling to risk admitting a truly creative role for the artist in articulating or resolving moral issues. It seems then that, as in *Republic* X, so also in the *Poetics*, art was just too much of a threat – as it apparently continues to be today.[32]

Notes

1. Euripides, *The Trojan Women*, 1203–1206. Translated by G. Murray in W. J. Oates and E. O'Neill, Jr., *The Complete Greek Drama*, 2 vols (New York, 1938).

2. The text I use of the *Poetics* is D. W. Lucas, *Aristotle: Poetics* (Oxford, 1983), recognizing suggestions of others, such as M. Nussbaum, *The Fragility of Goodness, Luck and Ethics in Greek Tragedy and Philosophy* (New York, 1986) and R. Janko (trans.) *Aristotle: Poetics* (Indianapolis, IN, 1987). I use Janko's translation of the *Poetics*, and T. Irwin's translation of the *Nicomachean Ethics* (Indianapolis, IN, 1986).

3. D. W. Lucas, *Aristotle: Poetics*, emphasizes that this is so depite the fact that the term does not designate the acting of stage actors as it can in English. See his note on 48a1, pp. 62–63; also on 49b37, p. 99 and on 50a21, p. 102. Compare Halliwell's to Janko's translations (S. Halliwell, *The Poetics of Aristotle*, trans. and comm. (Chapel Hill, NC, 1987), p. 37; R. Janko, *Aristotle: Poetics* p. 9) of 50a20–22 for an example of the ambiguity in Greek being decided one way or the other by the translator.

4. On this see G. Else, *Aristotle's Poetics: The Argument* (Cambridge, MA, 1957), p. 607.

5. D. Pozzi discusses an example of ritual enactment appropriate to tragic narrative's performance aspects in "The Metaphor of Sacrifice in Sophocles' *Antigone* 853–856, *Hermes* 117 (1989) 500—505.

6. See N. Loraux, *Tragic Ways of Killing a Woman*, trans. A. Foster (Cambridge, MA, 1987), pp. ix–xi on particular reasons for enactment of women's deaths in tragedy through narrative.

7. A. Danto, *The Transfiguration of the Commonplace* (Cambridge, MA, 1981) emphasizes this requirement is an important part of Aristotle's aesthetic theory with continuing relevance (pp. 13–15).

8. N. Goodman, "Reality Remade," in *Languages of Art. An Approach to a Theory of Symbols*, 2nd edn (Indianapolis, IN, 1976).

9. N. Goodman, *Ways of Worldmaking* (Indianapolis, IN, 1978), esp. Chs 1 and 7.

10. See D. Charles, *Aristotle on Action* (Ithaca, NY, and London, 1984) and C. Freeland, "Aristotelian Actions," *Nous* (1985) 397–414 on Aristotle's metaphysics of actions. By contrast, in *Physics* V, 4 Aristotle provides quite precise criteria for identifying changes (*kineseis*).

11. Compare Trinh T. Minh-ha's comments on storytelling in nonwestern cultures: "A story in Africa may last three months. The storyteller relates it night after night, continually, or s/he starts it one night and takes it up again from that point three months later" Trinh T. Minh-ha (*Woman, Native, Other: Writing Postcoloniality and Feminism* (Bloomington, IN, 1987), p. 143).

12. Irwin describes three distinct uses of *praxis* in the *Ethics* (T. Irwin, "Permanent Happiness: Aristotle and Solon," *Oxford Studies in Ancient Philosophy* (1985) 89–124). My two uses correspond to the first two he lists.

13. See Bernard Williams, "Moral Luck," *Proceedings of the Aristotelian Society* Suppl. Vol. L (1976) pp. 115–135, and Thomas Nagel, "Moral Luck," in *Mortal Questions* (Cambridge, 1979), pp. 24–38. Nussbaum, *The Fragility of Goodness*, argues Aristotle has more room for moral luck in his ethics. I shall have further occasion to refer to her view below.

14. Cooper interprets Aristotle as arguing that goods of fortune are best understood as means enabling one better to achieve happiness, but not themselves essential or intrinsic parts of happiness (J. Cooper, "Aristotle on the Goods of Fortune," *The Philosophical Review* XCIV (1985) 173–196). Irwin, "Permanent Happiness," offers a broader interpretation in which goods of fortune figure more centrally into a person's life projects, and may have value in and of themselves.

15. In Chapter 8's summary of plot patterns in 51a13–14 as well as in Chapter 13's

account of various sorts of reversals in plots, he repeatedly speaks of changes in fortune, from *eutuchia* to *dustuchia*, and not of changes from happiness (*eudaimonia*) to its opposite. Texts of the *Poetics* usually suppress as non-Aristotelian the term "*kakodaimonia*" which appears at 50a17; Nussbaum follows Else, Lucas and others in taking the more likely possibility here to refer simply to "the opposite" of *eudaimonia* (Nussbaum, *The Fragility of Goodness*, p. 500, n. 2). This still leaves some unclarity about how Aristotle would understand the opposite of happiness in the *Poetics*. *Eudemian Ethics* VIII, 2 is relevant on this topic; see also the commentary in M. Woods (trans.) *Aristotle's Eudemian Ethics, Books I, II, and VIII. Translated with a Commentary* (Oxford, 1982), pp. 176–183.

16. For discussion of this important term see G. Else *Aristotle, Poetics*, trans. with intro. (Ann Arbor, MI, 1970), pp. 97–99.

17. T. Irwin points out in 'Review of Martha Nussbaum's "The Fragility of Goodness",' *Journal of Philosophy* (1988) 376–383, that this is a key passage Nussbaum (*The Fragility of Goodness*) neglects. Irwin also notes that "In denying that the happy person could ever become wretched, Aristotle rejects a universal assumption of the tragedians . . ."

18. On this see T. Irwin, "The Metaphysical and Psychological Foundations of Aristotle's Ethics," in *Essays on Aristotle's Ethics*, ed. A. O. Rorty (Berkeley, CA, 1980), pp. 35–53.

19. See A. Gotthelf (ed.), "Notes Toward a Study of Substance and Essence in Aristotle's *Parts of Animals* II–IV," in *Aristotle on Nature and Living Things* (Pittsburgh and Bristol, 1985); G. E. R. Lloyd, *Science, Folklore, and Ideology* (Cambridge, 1983); and P. Pellegrin, *Aristotle's Classification of Animals. Biology and the Conceptual Unity of the Aristotelian Corpus*, trans. A. Preus (Berkeley, CA, 1987).

20. Here my account is indebted to S. White, "Aristotle's Favorite Tragedies" (this volume).

21. Winkler provides alternative insights into Aristotle's preference for such a plot (J. Winkler, "An Oscar for Iphigenia" in *The Ephebe's Song: Athenian Drama and the Poetics of Manhood* (Princeton, 1990).

22. I cannot undertake here to examine other interpretations such as a more crude purificationist account or the subtle account offered by Else.

23. See Nussbaum, *The Fragility of Goodness*, "Interlude," esp. pp. 383–385.

24. J. Lear, "Katharsis," *Phronesis* **XXXIII**/3 (1988) 297—326.

25. Trans. N. Curry, *Euripides: The Trojan Women* (Cambridge, 1981).

26. See for example Lange in S. Harding and M. B. Hintikka, *Discovering Reality: Feminist Perspectives on Epistemology, Metaphysics, Methodology and Philosophy of Science* (Dordrecht, 1983); C. Freeland, "Nourishing Speculation: A Feminist Reading of Aristotelian Science," in *Critical Feminist Essays on the History of Western Philosophy*, ed. Bar on Bat-Ami (Albany, NY, 1992); and N. Tuana, "Aristotle and the Politics of Reproduction," also in *Critical Feminist Essays*.

27. I discuss the related issue of "reading as a woman" in C. Freeland, "Revealing Gendered Texts," *Philosophy and Literature* 15 (1991) April, pp. 40–58.

28. Long remarks (p. 365) in a review of Nussbaum, *The Fragility of Goodness*, discussing the decay of Hecuba's character in the Hecuba, "This [the damage to noble character chance can inflict] . . . is more a failure of tragic heroines . . . than it is of heroes" (A. A. Long, "Review of Martha Nussbaum's *The Fragility of Goodness*," *Classical Philology* **83** (1988) 361–369).

29. Curry, *Euripides: The Trojan Women*, p. 4.

30. Loraux, *Tragic Ways of Killing a Woman*. See also H. Foley, *Ritual Irony, Poetry and Sacrifice in Euripides* (Ithaca, NY, 1985), and M. Gagarin, *Aeschylean Drama* (Berkeley, CA, 1976).

31. Nussbaum, *The Fragility of Goodness*, seems to have something like this in mind, particularly when she argues that the tragic poems "[embody] in both their content and their style a conception of human excellence" (p. 13).

32. Earlier versions of this essay were presented as part of the SAGP program at the Pacific APA meetings in 1989 and at the University of Texas at Austin. Many people generously provided comments on earlier versions, and I am glad to thank them here: Michael Gagarin, Charles Kahn, Donald Morrison, Martha Nussbaum, Dora Pozzi, and Gregory Vlastos. Terence Irwin offered particularly challenging comments. I am also grateful to Bill Nelson for helpful discussions of moral luck, and to Stephen White for sharing his unpublished paper with me.

Outside the Drama: The Limits of Tragedy in Aristotle's *Poetics*

Deborah H. Roberts

In Chapter 7 of the *Poetics* (1450b26–31), Aristotle notes that the action of which a play is an imitation must be whole, that is, must have a beginning, a middle, and an end; a beginning, he goes on to say, is that which does not follow naturally or necessarily from anything else, and an end is that from which nothing else follows. This claim often strikes readers at first as obvious and then as untrue. What Aristotle says seems obvious in the sense that a play's action has in fact a duration limited in time; it starts and it stops. It seems untrue in the sense that there appears to be a great deal that precedes the actual beginning of many Greek tragedies, and that tragedies often end with some indication that there is more to come; furthermore, what precedes is often causally connected with the events of the play itself, and what follows often constitutes the later ramifications of an outcome only partially revealed on stage.

It is, of course, precisely the fact that the plot of any literary work implies continuing action which takes place before and after the events narrated that makes Aristotle's claim subtler than at first appears. Recall Henry James's often-quoted remarks in the Preface to *Roderick Hudson*: "Really, universally, relations stop nowhere, and the exquisite problem of the artist is eternally but to draw, by a geometry of his own, the circle in which they shall happily appear to do so."[1] Recent work on closure has complicated our ideas about this geometry, that is, about how literature achieves what Frank Kermode calls "the sense of an ending."[2] The problem of creating beginnings and endings that seem genuinely to begin and to end is particularly prominent in the case of Greek tragedy, which like much of ancient literature took its plots primarily from a body of stories that were continuous with each other and to some extent known to audience or reader.[3]

Aristotle's account in the *Poetics* recognizes that any given work is selective and therefore limited in relation to the larger myth – indeed, insists that it must be so. An action (epic or tragic) with a proper beginning, middle, and end will in Aristotle's terms be a whole. But Aristotle makes clear that an action that is itself a whole may also be selected from a larger whole, in keeping with requirements of unity and of size. An epic or tragic plot must have unity, and cannot therefore include (for example) all the events of an individual's life (8.1451a16–30); the natural limit of a plot's length (for both tragedy and epic) is one that allows that plot to be clearly grasped (7.1451a3–6, 23.1459a32–34, 24.1459b18–20). Where even epic is limited in what it can actually include, tragedy – both shorter and more compact – is more radically so.[4]

Aristotle further recognizes the limits of tragedy by several times noting that there are events that occur outside: outside the drama, outside the tragedy, outside the story or plot. In these passages, Aristotle is not speaking of the world outside the drama, that is, the world of the audience, the nonfictive world, but rather of some part of the larger story from which the play draws its plot.[5]

For some scholars, the limits Aristotle puts on the tragic plot by relegating certain events to "outside" point to other limits Aristotle imposes on the subject matter of tragedy and ultimately to the limits – or limitations – of Aristotle's imagination as a critic tragedy, limits based in his profound rationalism.[6] But Aristotle's rationalism, properly appreciated, is itself at times as revelatory as any leap of the imagination, and it may be rewarding to consider the implications even of some of his less fully developed ideas. His concept of what is outside the drama has implications for our understanding of the nature of dramatic limits and of audience response.

I

Aristotle refers to what is in some sense "outside" in six passages in the *Poetics*. Of these, three are concerned with the action of the play, one with the audience's knowledge, and two with the presence in the play of the irrational or inexplicable.

A. Action

(1) In a discussion of actions that arouse pity and fear (14.1453b29–34), Aristotle gives as an example the Sophoclean Oedipus' unknowing murder of his father, but notes that this is in fact outside the drama (*exō tou dramatos*).

(2) In his discussion of the way to set out a plot in general terms before the addition of names and episodes (17.1455b2–15), Aristotle gives as his first example an outline of an *Iphigenia* which is in all essentials Euripides' *Iphigenia in Tauris*; the divine command and the purpose that lie behind the

arrival of the central character's brother (Orestes) are said to be outside the plot or story (*exō tou muthou*) (1455b6–9).[7]

(3) In his account of plot-complication (*desis*) and denouement (*lusis*), Aristotle notes that the plot-complication of a tragedy includes the things outside (*exōthen*) and some of the things within (18.1455b23–26). It seems safe here to take "outside" as the equivalent of "outside the tragedy," since tragedy has just been mentioned. The example given is a lost play (the *Lynceus* of Theodectes) and Aristotle specifies no events in that play as outside, merely alluding to the things that have occurred beforehand (*ta propepragmena*).

B. Knowledge

(4) After commenting that the denouement should come from the plot itself, Aristotle notes (15.1454a37–1454b6) that the *deus ex machina* (*apo mēchanēs*) should not be used, as in Euripides' *Medea*, to bring about a play's resolution, but only for "the things outside the drama" (*ta exō tou dramatos*), that is, for things which happened either before or after the play, are inaccessible to human knowledge, and must therefore be revealed by a god.[8]

C. The irrational

(5) Aristotle adds to his remarks on the *deus ex machina* that there should be nothing irrational (*alogon*) in the play's events, or if there is, it should be outside the tragedy (*exō tēs tragoidias*), as in Sophocles' *Oedipus* (15.1454b6–9). This allusion will be explained only later, in Chapter 24. That "outside the tragedy" is here equivalent to "outside the drama" is made clear both by the identification elsewhere of the two terms and by the wording in Chapter 14, which contrasts a play in which something happens outside the drama with two in which the same thing happens in the tragedy itself.

(6) In stressing the importance of plausibility (24.1460a27–32), Aristotle again (as in Chapter 15) consigns what is irrational (*alogon*) to outside, here *exō tou mutheumatos*.[9] What *mutheuma* seems to mean is the plot as enacted or represented – essentially the equivalent of the drama. This interpretation is supported by the opposition in this passage between what is outside the *mutheuma* and what is in the drama; *mutheuma* is used here in place of *drama* because Aristotle is speaking of epic as well as of drama.[10] He here clarifies his earlier reference to something *alogon* in the *Oedipus*: it is Oedipus' ignorance of how his predecessor died that is both outside and hard to account for.

Of these references to what is outside some poetic boundary, all but one (the example of Orestes from Chapter 17) are stated in terms that seem in this context to be equivalent: something is outside the drama, the tragedy, or the story as represented. All Aristotle's examples of things outside are things that have actually been mentioned inside the drama; he does not cite any events that might have been known to the audience from other sources but are not mentioned in the play.[11] None of Aristotle's instances of what is outside the drama involves a report of something that is supposed to have occurred in the course of the play, rather than before or after. Nor does he include in his category allusions to stories that are parallel to the play's story, the sort of mythic exempla usually found in choral odes. What is outside the drama, then, appears to be anything continuous with the action of the play that occurs before or after the play as staged and is mentioned in it.

But the example from Chapter 17 complicates matters. If *muthos* here (like *mutheuma* in Chapter 24) refers to the plot as represented and is thus also essentially the equivalent of "drama," then not all reported events that precede the play's beginning count for Aristotle as outside the drama. For here he appears to include in the plot Iphigenia's past history but not Orestes'; yet neither is enacted within the play, and both must presumably be recounted.[12] Unless there is some other reason for the different treatment of the two, *muthos* must then be distinct from (and more inclusive than) drama.[13] The past history of Iphigenia is part of the *muthos*, that is, of the plot in a larger sense (and thus included in the general outline), but not part of the drama. The background of Orestes' arrival is less essential to the *muthos* in this sense, since he could presumably have been made to arrive for some other reason; it is therefore outside both drama and plot.

It is hard to be confident of a reading based on a particular understanding of *muthos*, given the great variety of ways in which Aristotle uses the word.[14] But such a distinction is consistent with our other passages. What is outside the drama may count as among the play's events in some sense (*en tois pragmasin*, 15.1454b6–7), and may in fact be a crucial antecedent to the play, as is Oedipus' killing of his father (14.1453b30–32). The claim in Chapter 18 that a play's actual plot-complication will normally include things outside the drama makes it explicit that something may be essential to the plot's construction and development and still be considered outside the tragedy. The beginning of the plot and the beginning of the play are not necessarily the same.

What is outside the drama, then, precedes or follows the play's action and is reported in the play, but something outside the drama may be (though it need not be) a part of the plot or story. This view has an intuitive appeal; most readers think of Oedipus' killing of his father (for example) as in some sense a part of the plot of the *Oedipus Tyrannus*. It is also in keeping with the dominant approach in current narrative theory, for which everything connected with the story line that is actually mentioned is part of a play's story (its events, what it tells) and is simply given in a different order in the discourse or narrative that is the play itself.[15]

II

But if what is outside the drama may be part of the plot, which is after all the soul of tragedy, why does Aristotle continue to invoke an apparently secondary distinction between what is inside and what is outside the drama?[16]

Taken together, the passages that refer to this distinction reflect the general importance of boundedness and selection for Aristotle, in the *Poetics* as elsewhere in his writings.[17] The unity of the plot is his central concern, but the drama as staged has its own limits, and these are marked in part by what is excluded.

The passages in which the issue is action outside the drama suggest, as it were, the limitations of the drama's limits and the subordination of staged drama to plot. That is, it is by noting that an action central to the plot may be outside the drama (14.1453b29–34), and that the plot-complication will normally include events outside the drama (18.1455b23–26) that Aristotle makes the point (albeit in passing) that the staged drama and the plot are not the same thing and that the latter crosses the bounds of the former.

Since some events crucial to the plot (as well as much ancillary information) will be outside the drama, these must be made known to the audience in some way other than by enactment; the passage in which the issue is knowledge of what is outside the drama points to one such way. Aristotle's comment (in his critique of the *deus ex machina*, 15.1454a37–1454b6) that the gods provide knowledge of earlier or later events inaccessible to humans suggests that divine prologues and epilogues serve the function which in an epic (or a novel) is often served by a narrator, the function of providing knowledge that the audience must have in order to understand the story, and that only a god (or a narrator) could have.

Such knowledge of what is outside the drama itself helps constitute the limits of the drama, since it tells where both plot and play begin and end and thus helps the audience grasp the work as a whole.[18] Aristotle makes a related point in the *Rhetoric* (3.14.1415a17–33), noting that as in speeches and epics the exordium lets the hearers know something of the subject in advance, so tragic poets make clear what a play is about – either immediately, like Euripides, or at some point in the prologue, like Sophocles.[19] Such knowledge is critical because "what is unbounded/undefined (*aoristos*) leads one astray" (3.14.1415a14).[20]

III

So far I have been considering what is "outside the drama" from the perspective of the boundary it defines. But what is outside the drama may also be said to constitute a region or area, and that there is something distinctive about this region is suggested by the passages (15.1454b6–9, 24.1460a27–32) in which Aristotle relegates to outside the drama an otherwise undesirable element he calls the *alogon*, variously rendered as the inexplicable, the improbable, or (most often) the irrational.

Even when, in the later chapters of the *Poetics*, Aristotle's initial exclusion of the *alogon* (15.1454b6–7) is qualified, the presumption remains that the irrational is best done without. Epic is more likely than tragedy to accept the irrational, which is the chief element in the amazing, because in epic we do not actually see the events in question (24.1460a11–17; Aristotle's example here is the surprising restraint of the other Greeks during Achilles' pursuit of Hector at *Iliad* XXII.205–7). But even in epic the irrational is undesirable; as a general rule, a story (*logos*) should not be made up of irrational (*aloga*) parts. It should contain nothing irrational, but if it does, the place for it is outside the represented story (24.1460a27–37). Again, one may defend the irrational against critics (25.1461b14–25) either by appealing to "what people say" or by arguing that it is likely that unlikely things should sometimes happen; nonetheless, one should not unnecessarily introduce something irrational for no purpose.[21] Why does Aristotle tell us that there should as a rule be nothing irrational in the story or events, and that if there is, it should be outside the drama or story as represented?

IV

Does this exclusion of the irrational, as some have thought, spring primarily from a more basic wish to exclude the divine or supernatural?[22] On such a view, the critique of the use of the *deus ex machina* in Chapter 15 is a rejection of any significant involvement of the gods in the dramatic action itself,[23] and the description of the god's (Apollo's) sending of Orestes in the *Iphigenia in Tauris* as "outside the plot" (Chapter 17) similarly reflects a rejection of divine agency.[24]

In fact, Aristotle has little to say about the role of the gods in tragedy, and this omission has often disturbed readers.[25] But it is not to the use of the gods *per se* that Aristotle objects in Chapter 15. Medea's appearance in her divine chariot at the end of Euripides' play is a surprise, and most modern readers would see it as a typical and successful instance of Euripides' playing with the audience's expectations. But it is a surprise for which the drama hardly prepares us, and it is for this reason that Aristotle disapproves of it. There are other instances of divine intervention in tragedy whose abruptness would be likely to meet with Aristotle's disapproval, most notably the sudden arrival of Apollo in Euripides' *Orestes* to solve what appears on the human level to be a hopeless conflict. But there seems to be no reason in Aristotelian terms why the gods may not be used in the action when their arrival is called for by a plot in which they have previously had some involvement (Hermes in Aeschylus' *Prometheus* or Artemis in Euripides' *Hippolytus*) or when they are fully involved in the action throughout (Apollo and Athena in Aeschylus' *Eumenides* or Dionysus in Euripides' *Bacchae*). Nor does the fact that Aristotle cites "a standard mode of involvement of a deity in the action of the *Iliad*"[26] necessarily suggest that he is critical of all divine involvement; Athena's intervention in *Iliad* II, like the intervention of some gods *ex machina*, is a case of divine interference in something that would otherwise have gone in an entirely different direction; without her, the Greeks would have returned home "contary to fate."[27] What Aristotle objects to, in tragedy or in epic, is divine action that is inadequately prepared for and inadequately connected with the rest of the action.[28]

Nor is the exclusion from the plot of Orestes' reason for coming to the land of the Taurians (Chapter 17) a rejection of the divine. It is difficult to be certain of Aristotle's grounds for this exclusion, but it can be plausibly argued that he sees Orestes' arrival but not the reason for it as integral to what is essentially Iphigenia's story. Halliwell rejects the view that what lies behind Orestes' arrival is excluded simply as inessential to the plot, arguing that if that were so, his arrival would appear to constitute just the sort of "unintelligible coincidence" to which Aristotle objects elsewhere.[29] But the omission of Orestes' motive at this stage does not mean that the play in its final form would lack such a motive (any more than the omission of names means the characters would lack names); it means simply that the particular motive given in Euripides' version is not essential to the plot as outlined. The mention of Polyidus' version of the recognition makes it plain that although this general outline is based on Euripide's play, it is not identical with it, and one can easily conceive of a play in which Orestes comes for quite other reasons.[30]

Furthermore, although there is no mention of the god's playing an active role in the story of Iphigenia as given here,[31] the comment that she disappeared in a manner mysterious (*adēlōs*) to those who had sacrificed her suggests an action that cannot be explained in human terms and that is nonetheless counted as part of the story or plot as outlined. It is therefore difficult to make the presence or absence of the supernatural the feature that distinguishes Iphigenia's arrival (inside the plot) from Orestes' arrival (outside the plot). Finally, in the outline of the *Odyssey* that follows Aristotle seems to have no problem with the role of Poseidon.

Under certain conditions Aristotle even welcomes the presence in tragedy of action inexplicable in human terms. At 9.1452a1–12 he singles out for praise events which cause amazement because they occur contrary to expectation but in a causal sequence (*para tēn doxan di' allēla*). As an example (taken not from tragedy but from life) he cites the statue of Mitys, which killed Mitys' killer by falling on him. Such events, says Aristotle, do not seem to come about by chance. Note, then, that here is something which is praiseworthy in part because it follows in likely sequence (or at least in the semblance of likely sequence) even though it cannot be explained in purely human terms.[32] Unexpected but fitting events in tragedy may well involve the divine, for example in the form of the unexpectedly fulfilled oracle. Compare Aristotle's acceptance of such events – magical but nonetheless logical – with his rejection of Medea's magical but unmotivated departure in a chariot or of Oedipus' ordinary but unlikely ignorance about his predecessor's death; such a comparison serves to support the view that Aristotle really objects not to the supernatural *per se* but to the unmotivated or unlikely, whether divine or human in origin.[33]

In tragedy itself the more magical aspects of divine activity are usually located outside the central action and offstage; such aspects of the divine seem to play a secondary role in tragedy for the tragedians themselves. If, then, Aristotle has some special difficulty with irrational *divine* action (as opposed to the irrational in general), he may simply be reflecting an exclusion already dominant in tragedy, rather than excluding out of an obstinate secularism what is really central to the genre, that is, the mysterious but somehow ordered role of the gods in the way things are.

But Aristotle does not even seem to have any such special difficulty with the irrational involvement of the gods. Indeed, with the possible exception of Medea's departure *ex machina*, all the examples Aristotle actually gives of the objectionable *alogon* have to do with instances of human rather than divine behavior. It is *alogon* that Oedipus does not know how his predecessor died (Chapters 15, 24), and that Aegeus suddenly appears in Corinth in Euripides' *Medea* (Chapter 25),[34] but in neither case does Aristotle suggest the involvement of the gods. Aristotle's two remaining examples of dramatic *aloga* (Chapter 24) are harder to interpret, but no one has suggested that there is anything supernatural about either of them. The reporting of the Pythian games in the *Electra* is variously read as constituting an anachronism or as entailing an unlikely delay in the news. The case of the man who comes without speaking from Tegea to Mysia seems irrational because of the unlikelihood of someone making such a journey in silence. Nor do the two examples from epic (24.1460a11–16, 35–36) have any clear connection with divine activity: the gods are not involved either in Achilles' unassisted pursuit of Hector or in the putting ashore of Odysseus on Ithaca in *Odyssey* XIII, presumably an *alogon* because he fails to wake up when the Phaeacians leave him there.[35]

That Aristotle's own views of the divine are quite different from those of epic and tragedy is no problem; he evidently considers it appropriate to speak of the gods in various ways to suit various contexts. The *Rhetoric*, for example, reflects traditional views of the gods where other works call them into question.[36] And surely poetry can use tradition as rhetoric does; in Chapter 25, Aristotle offers the response "that's what people say" as a defense against those who object to stories about the gods in epic. Indeed, Aristotle uses a traditional view of the gods to justify his explicit approval of one form of divine involvement: the *deus ex machina* should be used to provide knowledge of past and future, "for we attribute to the gods the capacity to see all things" (15.1454b3–6).[37]

Chapter 25 provides further evidence for Aristotle's willingness to retain the traditional divine framework in the world of poetry. He twice mentions a way of rationalizing divine activity, but in neither case does the rationalization entail an explanation in human terms: although the gods drink no wine, Ganymede may be said to pour wine for Zeus if we understand this metaphorically

(1461a29–31); if we change the accent of a verb, it was the dream of Zeus sent to Agamemnon in *Iliad* II that lied, not Zeus himself (1461a22).[38] These corrections demand not that the gods be explained away but that the world of the gods make sense in itself; as we know, the gods drink nectar, and what Zeus says should be valid.[39] The fragmentary evidence for the lost *Homeric Problems* presents a similar picture.[40] Aristotle is here concerned with apparent contradictions, factual difficulties, and implausible behavior in the Homeric poems; those problems that have to do with the gods are almost all problems of consistency or probability within the poem or the tradition, not problems with the divine presence *per se*. Most striking is Aristotle's treatment of one of the relatively rare instances in Greek literature in which a portent involves not merely a significant natural event (two eagles chase a pregnant hare, an eagle carries off and drops a snake) but an event which is supernatural; at *Iliad* II.308–319 Odysseus recalls an omen in which a snake eats eight nestlings and their mother and then is turned to stone by Zeus. What troubles Aristotle about this passage is not any implausibility in the magical transformation itself, but rather Calchas' failure to interpret that transformation, apparently the most portentous feature of the omen.[41]

Aristotle, then, does not actually treat the role of the gods as central to tragedy (or epic) in his own account, but neither does his account require a rejection of their role. Discourse about the gods is for Greek tragedy and Greek culture generally the language in which human experience and human action are expressed; Aristotle can allow tragedy to continue speaking that language while himself analyzing experience and action in his own terms.

V

What then is the significance of the irrational or *alogon?* Aristotle's examples suggest for the most part either a kind of commonsense implausibility (the unlikely ignorance of Oedipus, the surprising behavior of the other Greeks during the pursuit of Hector) or a lack of dramatic connectedness (the coincidental arrival of Aegeus, the unprepared for departure of Medea).[42]

Whatever we make of the *alogon*, however, we must ask the further question: why does it make sense in Aristotle's view for the poet to locate what is irrational outside the drama? Part of the explanation is suggested by the contrast between epic and drama at *Poetics* 24.1460a11–17, where epic is said to admit the irrational more readily than drama because in epic we do not actually see the action; the restraint of the other Greeks as Achilles chases Hector would be ridiculous if the action were actually performed on stage, but its absurdity escapes notice in epic. Compare the importance given to the visual in tragedy at 17.1455a2–29, where it is said that in constructing plots the playwright must be careful to place what is happening before his eyes; otherwise he may find himself introducing into the action contradictions that would escape the notice of someone who did not *see* them but will bother an audience when actually staged.

In both passages, some problem goes undetected (the verb is *lanthanein*) by one who does not actually see the action staged. Aristotle is here stressing not our diminished emotional response to the merely heard, but our weakened apprehension of it. We are not only less bothered by oddities in action we do not see; since such action is less striking, we actually fail to notice what is odd about it.

Something irrational or inexplicable may then affect us more strongly when we actually see it, and will therefore be more acceptable if it is ouside the drama and thus (as in epic) only heard.[43] But this explanation does not work equally well for all cases of the *alogon*. The pursuit of Hector and the landing of Odysseus might well be more implausible on a stage. It is harder to see how Aegeus' arrival in the *Medea* (whether it is understood as coincidental and thus unmotivated by the plot, or as absurdly off-course and thus offensive to common sense) would be less implausible if not seen. And consider Aristotle's main example of something irrational outside the drama, that is, Oedipus' ignorance of how Laius died. Why would the general implausibility of this ignorance – is it likely that a man would accept a recently vacated throne without asking how his predecessor died? – be more or less striking depending on whether or not the audience saw presented the failure to seek information? And what exactly would it mean to *see* such a failure?

What is important in this case is not so much the difference between what is seen and what is merely heard *per se* as the related difference (one Aristotle stresses in Chapter 3) between what is enacted and what is merely narrated. The crucial feature of that difference for our purposes is this: what is narrated can be more selective than what is enacted, and therefore omissions in narrative may be less noticeable. This comment may at first seem surprising, since in some sense tragedy is more selective than epic, constrained by limitations of size and staging. Once one has chosen to enact an event, however, that enactment cannot be elliptical in the way that narrative can.[44] If Oedipus tells us he never knew how Laius died, he need say nothing about the context that reveals this surprising lack. But if Sophocles had actually portrayed a Theban delegation offering the throne to Oedipus and explaining that their own king had recently died, the absence of an important question between the offer and the acceptance would be more apparent.

Indeed, since throughout the *Poetics* Aristotle stresses the fact that it is the structure of events in likely or necessary sequence that is chiefly productive of audience response, the difference between the fully enacted and the merely narrated should be as important for audience response as the difference between what is seen and what is heard. If what is seen is more striking than what is heard, and therefore commands our powers of attention more fully, what is enacted is less selective than what is narrated, and therefore makes a greater demand on our powers of connection.

But several times in the *Poetics* Aristotle seeks to diminish the importance for tragedy of what we see, that is of staging or enactment. He tells us in Chapter 6 that the effect (*dunamis*) of tragedy may be achieved without staging (1450b18–20); later he comments that in the work of the best poets, pity and fear result from the plot and not from the spectacle (14.1453b1–7), and that if the plot is well constructed we should be able to experience pity and fear, even without seeing the play, by hearing of its events. Finally, although spectacle may make our pleasures especially vivid, that very vividness can be achieved by a reading as well as by enactment (26.1460a15–18). What is important, then, for audience response is not the difference between what is enacted and what is narrated, but the difference between what is *written to be enacted* and what is narrated or written to be narrated. Such an account receives support especially from the passage in Chapter 26, in which the spectacle seems to create an effect that is somehow present even when the play is only read.

Even this distinction, however, is not without difficulties in the context of the *Poetics* as a whole. Epic is a narrative genre, yet Aristotle makes it clear that epic has almost as strong an effect on the audience as tragedy, and that its events too must be connected; in epic too the irrational is undesirable, even if it is more acceptable there than in tragedy.

What is implicit here is that the more closely narrative approximates to drama (a desideratum suggested by Aristotle's praise of Homer in Chapter 24 for being more mimetic in the dramatic sense than other epic poets), that is, the more vivid and more detailed its narration, the more it will evoke the same response as drama, and the less freely it will admit of the marvellous and the irrational or absurd. If the audience heard Oedipus (or a narrator) telling the story of his taking the throne as fully as he tells the story of his encounter with Laius, it might well have as much difficulty with the narration as with an enacted version. Perhaps, then, the crucial limitation on what is outside, the limitation that makes it an appropriate home for the irrational, is not *that* it is narrated so much as *how* it is narrated.

The view that an audience is similarly affected by what is actually seen, what is made vivid, and what is narrated in a complete way gains support from Aristotle's *Rhetoric*.[45] In *Rhetoric* II.8.1386a34 Aristotle describes speakers who arouse pity by using gesture, voice, and dress to place events before the hearers' eyes either as just having happened or as about to happen. Here, clearly, the greater effect is due to a kind of dramatic enactment, and the events described are placed before the eyes in a sense only once removed from the literal. Elsewhere in the treatise, however, Aristotle suggests that a certain kind of verbal presentation alone may have the same effect; in III.11.1411b24, he explains that things may be placed before the eyes by expressions that signify actuality – in particular by metaphors that animate what they describe. Here, the bringing before the eyes, itself metaphorical, results from vivid narration rather than from dramatic mimesis. That what is important is not so much *that* something is narrated as *how* it is narrated is further supported by a third passage from the *Rhetoric*. In III.16.1417a12–16, in the course of a discussion of narrative in oratory, Aristotle recommends that one should relate past events as having happened (*pepragmena*) unless their being described as happening (*prattomena*) will effect either pity or fear.[46] As an example, he cites the long story Odysseus tells to Alcinous in *Odyssey* IX–XII, which as told to Penelope in *Odyssey* XXIII takes only sixty lines; the point is the contrast between the first version, told at length as happening, and the second, told in summary form as having happened. Aristotle supplies two more examples which are instances of the summary ("having happened") form; one of these is the unknown Phayllus' treatment of the epic cycle (presumably an epitome), the other, tellingly for our purposes, the prologue to an *Oeneus* plausibly identified as Euripides'.[47] A story told as happening has a considerably different effect from one told as completed, and it is the former that elicits the traditional tragic response.

Aristotle's location of the *alogon* outside the drama, then, has to do not with his supposed discomfort with traditional beliefs but with the much more fundamental issue of audience response, and suggests that an audience will understand and react differently to what is outside the drama for reasons that have to do with its mode of narration.

Let me sum up what has been argued so far: (1) By "things outside the drama" Aristotle means events that precede or follow the drama and are reported in it. He does not count all such events as outside the plot; indeed, he makes it explicit that although what is outside the drama may be merely background, it may also be a part of the plot. It seems likely that something with a strong causal connection to the staged action (such as the murder of Laius by Oedipus) is outside the drama but inside the plot, whereas something that Aristotle takes to be incidental to the central praxis (the command that brings Orestes to the land of the Taurians) is outside the plot as well. (2) The identification of certain things as outside derives partly from a general concern in the *Poetics* with boundedness and selection. (3) This identification also reflects an interest in the different effect on the audience of what is outside the drama. Partly because it is reported and not seen, and partly because it is less fully represented than events that are enacted, what is outside the drama not only affects the audience less strongly[48] but (we may conclude from Aristotle's treatment of the *alogon*) elicits its critical attention less fully than the drama itself. Since, however, vivid and detailed narration (a story told "as happening") may approximate the effect of dramatic enactment, it seems possible that Aristotle would not identify as outside the drama something so recounted.

VI

Tragedy must frequently refer to earlier or later events without staging them, and some of these events are crucial to the plot. The tragedians exploit this generic constraints as they do others, developing the relationship of staged drama to larger myth in a variety of ways. Aristotle's scattered remarks on what is outside the drama reflect the basic fact of tragedy's reference to past and future events but do not constitute anything like a theory of this rich feature of tragic narrative; they are neither comprehensive nor analytic. Nevertheless, his outside/inside distinction both takes account of a central problem for the tragedians and reflects a significant variation in the way they deal with events not staged, a variation which has implications for audience response.

Consider the range of references in extant tragedy to action before or after the events staged. In the parados of Aeschylus' *Agamemnon*, the chorus recount events from ten years before the play with a declared confidence in the nearly magical efficacy of their own singing. They are selective in the manner characteristic of Greek lyric, but can surely be said to bring what they tell before our eyes. Here is how they tell the sacrifice of Iphigenia:

> Her supplications and her cries of father
> were nothing, nor the child's lamentation
> to kings passioned for battle.
> The father prayed, called to his men to lift her
> with strength of hand swept in her robes aloft
> and prone above the altar, as you might lift
> a goat for sacrifice, with guards
> against the lips' sweet edge, to check
> the curse cried on the house of Atreus
> by force of bit and speech drowned in strength.
>
> Pouring then to the ground her saffron mantle
> she struck the sacrificers with
> the eyes' arrows of pity,
> lovely as in a painted scene, and striving
> to speak – as many times
> at the kind festive table of her father
> she had sung, and in the clear voice of a stainless maiden
> with love had graced the song
> of worship when the third cup was poured (227–247).[49]

Such vivid and detailed treatment of past events may be found in Sophocles and Euripides as well, but is less common. More typical of Euripides are the explanatory prologue and the parting speech by a *deus ex machina*, where what is told tends to take the form not of detailed descriptive narrative but of summary. Such summary rarely has the rhetorical effect of placing something before our eyes, confining itself to giving us the facts as facts, though not necessarily without emotion. Here again is the sacrifice of Iphigenia, this time from the *Iphigenia in Tauris*, narrated in the opening speech by Iphigenia herself:

> I came to Aulis, wretched I. I was caught and held
> above the death-pyre, and the sword was ready to kill.
> But Artemis stole me away, and gave to the Achaians
> a fawn in my place, and carried me through the bright air
> to this land of the Taurians, and settled me here (26–30).[50]

Such prologue speeches seem clear instances of what Aristotle calls in the *Rhetoric* presenting things as having happened (*pepragmena*) rather than as happening (*prattomena*); recall that one of the examples given there was in fact a prologue, probably from a Euripidean play. The flatness and sameness of such speeches was an object of mockery already in antiquity; witness Aristophanes' parody in the *Frogs* (1198–1247).

A third mode of reference to past and future is particularly characteristic of Sophocles. What preceded the action of the play is introduced gradually and piecemeal, in the form of references to the past by various characters rather than full-scale accounts; the future too is more often alluded to that narrated in full. References to past and future are often so conditioned by a given character's perspective and by the particular discursive context that our sense of past and future is incomplete. In Sophocles' *Electra* the story of Iphigenia's sacrifice is told in typically Sophoclean fashion, introduced by characters as a briefly told part of their versions of events. Thus, Clytemnestra, defending her killing of Agamemnon as just, says:

> This father of yours, your constant lamentation,
> Alone of all the Greeks was bold enough
> To sacrifice your sister to the gods.
> The pain he suffered over her was not the same
> As mine – he only sowed, while *I* gave birth (530 ff.).[51]

Electra's response tells more of the background to the sacrifice (558–574), but still as part of an argument, and the sacrifice itself is mentioned as briefly as possible (573); again, as with the Euripidean example above, the events are clearly related as having happened, not as happening.

In contrast with Aeschylus, then, both Euripides and Sophocles – although in different ways, indeed almost opposite ways – frame what is beyond the play as being distinctively outside. So it is not surprising that Aristotle's examples of what is outside include the Euripidean and the Sophoclean modes but not the Aeschylean. This may be because in general Aristotle pays less attention to Aeschylus than to the other two tragedians, but it may also have to do with the way in which Aeschylus presents the material in question. His more visually detailed accounts of preceding events seem likely to evoke the sort of audience response evoked by dramatic action; they bear as well some resemblance to messenger speeches, which Aristotle nowhere treats as instances of what is outside. Where Aristotle does count as outside the drama an event told with some detail and vividness, namely Oedipus' killing of his father,[52] he excludes this event from the drama almost as an afterthought (14.1454a29–32); his treatment displays ambivalence about the place of this deed in the tragedy, an ambivalence that has to do not only with its centrality in the plot but also with the dramatic force with which it is narrated.

Varied modes of narration make events seem to varying degrees a part of the drama, and evoke varying responses from the audience. A tragedian may exploit the possibility of variation in order to evoke different responses from the audience; Aeschylus' treatment of Iphigenia's sacrifice will again serve as an example.

In the *Agamemnon*, the sacrifice of Iphigenia is recounted in detailed and vivid terms up until the moment when the chorus can no longer bear to describe what happened; there are a number of further references to Iphigenia in the text (1415–1418, 1432, 1525–1529, 1555–1559) and she is kept carefully on our mind by Clytemnestra's words. In the next play of the trilogy, however, the *Choephori*, Iphigenia is never mentioned by name; the clearest reference to her and to her story occurs in line 242, when Electra, explaining to Orestes that she feels for him all the love she might have given the rest of her family speaks of her "sister who was pitilessly sacrificed." The story is here, in epitome, and so is a judgment on the story. But there is no effort to concentrate the audience's attention on that story, to make the audience understand it as part of a sequence of events, or to bring it vividly before their eyes. The sacrifice which was in all but staging a part of the drama of the *Agamemnon* is here clearly outside the drama.

Iphigenia's presence is still further diminished in the last play of the trilogy; her sacrifice is not mentioned at all, and seems to be quite outside the plot. Of course, given that the three plays form a trilogy, to be seen together, the audience will recall the events (seen and narrated) of the earlier plays while watching the later. But each of the plays has a unity of its own, with a beginning, a middle, and an end, and the fact that we obviously retain knowledge from the earlier plays only makes more interesting the fact that the shift in treatment of the Iphigenia story changes the degree to which we respond to it as part of the play we are currently watching. What is important is not so much what we know or even how recently we thought of it as the way that knowledge is structured and called to mind. The play itself shows us what we are to treat, by a selective act of attention, as truly part of the play.

A final question: to what extent do the extant tragedies follow Aristotle's rule that the *alogon* should if possible be kept outside the drama?[53] Are there many examples of irrational or absurd events in what is merely narrated? In fact, and perhaps this is Aristotle's point, I have not noticed many – except the ones that Euripides shows us. For although it is true that Euripides does to some extent seem to locate the irrational or unlikely outside the drama (in prologue, in epilogue, or in choral reminiscence) he seems positively to call our attention to it, deliberately arousing the skepticism, discomfort or laughter that Aristotle implies would naturally be weakest in us at such times. "Seems" is too mild; sometimes Euripides explicitly draws our attention to implausibilities in the background story: could a woman be born from an egg, or the sun go backwards in response to human wrong?[54] Nor is it only in what is outside the drama that Euripides reveals and questions the *alogon*; the case that most seems to fit Aristotle's description of the irrational is virtually flung in our face by Euripides in his famous parody of the Aeschylean scene in which Electra becomes aware of Orestes' presence by a series of unlikely signs.[55] But this may only be to say that Euripides is the most important pre-Aristotelian critic of tragedy.[56]

VII

I conclude by setting these comments about the limits or boundaries of drama in a larger context – outside the drama in quite another sense. It is a common-place of contemporary narratology that we seek to give narrative structures to our lives as well as to our fictions, and that our desire for bounded narratives is in part a way of dealing with our inability to be fully aware of either our own beginning or our own end, let alone what precedes and follows.[57] Greek culture generally, and tragedy in particular, show a concern both with escaping the boundedness of the human perspective (consider the role of oracles) and with establishing boundaries (consider the role of oracles). And the wisdom of Herodotus' Solon, that we may call no one happy until death, suggests that we require to know the boundaries within which we are to judge the worth of human life.[58]

In *Nicomachean Ethics* I.11, in the context of his discussion of happiness, Aristotle turns to a discussion of Solon's view, and asks whether happiness can be affected by things that happen after death. After noting that we are in any case variously affected by different things that happen to us, he concludes that the happiness of the dead may be affected by the experiences of their descen-dants, but not very much, and makes the following comparison: it makes more difference whether suffering happens to the living or the dead than whether terrible events are presupposed by the drama or presented onstage (1101a32 ff.).

This analogy suggests the way in which we give varying qualities of attention and significance to what is within and without boundaries, and points not only to Aristotle's own concern with boundaries but to our human preoccupation with boundaries in literature and in life. I am not suggesting that these connec-tions are explicit either here or in the *Poetics*, but that here as elsewhere Aristotle's eye for similitude – the eye not only of the philosopher, but of the dream interpreter and the maker of metaphors[59] – points us beyond the connec-tion he sees to connections that perhaps for him remain outside the range of vision.[60]

Notes

1. Preface to *Roderick Hudson*, rpt. in *The Art of the Novel*, ed. R. P. Blackmur (1907; New York, 1962), 6. D. W. Lucas (comm., *Aristotle's Poetics*, Oxford, 1968) cites James ad 1450b24. The text of the *Poetics* used here is R. Kassel's Oxford Classical Text (Oxford, 1965).
2. F. Kermode, *The Sense of an Ending* (Oxford, 1966). See also B. H. Smith, *Poetic Closure* (Chicago, 1968), D. P. Fowler, "First Thoughts on Closure: Problems and Prospects,"

Materiali e discussioni per l'analisi dei testi classici **22** (1989) 75–122, and bibliography cited in Fowler.

3. Cf. Lucas, *Aristotle's Poetics* (ad 1451b26). It is unclear exactly how well known the stories were. Aristotle himself suggests that the main lines of the narrative must be respected (14.1453b22–26) but notes also that one need not base tragedies only on traditional stories, since "even what is familiar is familiar only to a few but pleases everyone" (9.1451b25–26). Audience knowledge probably varied considerably, with the basic facts of certain central stories known to most though not all.

4. Cf. also 9.1451b37–39 on playwrights who stretch the plot by adding episodes. In the course of the *Poetics* Aristotle discusses size from three different perspectives: the length of time a work takes in performance (7.1451a6–9), the length of the play or epic itself on what might now be called the level of discourse (passages cited here and 7.1451a9–15), and the length of the story the play or epic tells (5.1449b12–16, 7.1451a11–15). Epic is said in Chapter 5 to be, like early tragedy, unlimited in time; given the comparison with tragedy and what is said later, this clearly refers only to the duration of the story, that is, of the events narrated. On the relation of these different levels see esp. R. Dupont-Roc and J. Lallot, trans. and comm., *Aristote, La Poétique* (Paris, 1980) ad. loc.

5. Recent developments in narrative theory have led to heightened interest in the narratological aspects of the *Poetics*. See for example E. Downing, "Hoion Psychê: An Essay on Aristotle's Muthos," *Classical Antiquity* **3** (1984) 164–178; Dupont-Roc and Lallot, *Aristote, La Poétique*; S. Halliwell, *Aristotle's Poetics* (London and Chapel Hill, 1986); S. Halliwell, trans. and comm., *The Poetics of Aristotle* (London and Chapel Hill, 1987); P. Ricoeur, *Time and Narrative*, Vol. 1, trans. K. McLaughlin and D. Pellauer (Chicago and London, 1984), trans. of *Temps et Récit*, Vol. 1 (Paris, 1983). Halliwell's treatment of Aristotle's "outside the drama" is the most thorough to date.

6. See esp. Halliwell, *Aristotle's Poetics*, and *The Poetics of Aristotle*.

7. The variation in terminology is rendered doubly problematic by textual debate. Kassel's text gives the manuscript reading, and brackets (following W. von Christ) the words most frequently left out (*dia tina aitian exō tou katholou*). If we accept this emendation, we read that the fact that the god commanded the brother to come, and the purpose of his doing so, are outside the plot or story (*exō tou muthou*); if we leave the text unemended (so most recently R. Janko, *Aristotle, Poetics I with the Tractatus Coislinianus*); (Indianapolis, 1987) and Dupont-Roc and Lallot, *Aristote, La Poétique*), we learn in addition that the god gave his command for some reason outside the general sketch (*exō tou katholou*). Depending on our choice, either the general background of Orestes' arrival is outside the *muthos*, or that general background is outside the *muthos* and contains an element which is outside the general outline as well. Those who try to distinguish the *katholou* from the *muthos* run into difficulties not so much because of theoretical problems as because it is difficult to see the cause of the oracle as having a different status from the oracle itself and the purpose of the god in sending Orestes. The duplication of "outside" in one speech is awkward, even for the *Poetics*; stranger still is that the "outside" apparently more relevant to the subject here under discussion – "outside the general outline" – is the one introduced parenthetically. See Dupont-Roc and Lallot and Janko ad loc. for the most interesting attempts at interpreting the ms. text.

8. This section of Chapter 15 appears to deal with some concerns of plot that intrude briefly on a larger discussion of character; on the problem of the passage's relation to what proceeds see the various commentators ad loc. Aristotle is here using the term *apo mēchanēs* (literally, "from the crane") in an extended sense, to cover other sorts of (sudden) divine intervention as well (see Lucas, *Aristotle's Poetics* ad loc., and cf. Else, *Aristotle's Poetics* (Ann Arbor, MI, 1967), 470–473 for a different view).

9. The topic here is ostensibly epic, but the constraint seems to apply to either genre, and Aristotle's examples are mostly drawn from tragedy, in which he thinks the presence of the *alogon* is more problematic.

10. See on this point esp. Janko, *Aristotle Poetics I* and Dupont-Roc and Lallot, *Aristote, La Poétique.* The term *mutheuma* occurs nowhere else in the *Poetics*, and all the other examples of its use seem to be considerably later. The word is sometimes taken (by Lucas, *Aristotle's Poetics*, for example, ad loc.) as the equivalent of *muthos* (see E. Downing), "Hoion Psyche: An Essay on Aristotle's Muthos," *Classical Antiquity* 3 (1984) 164–178).

11. E.g. Laius' rape of Pelops' son Chrysippus, long before the events of Sophocles' *Oedipus Tyrannus*, or Heracles' fatal second marriage, to Deianeira, after the events of Euripides' *Heracles.*

12. See Euripides' play, 1–66, 77–93; even if we envision a somewhat different play, the way Aristotle speaks of Iphigenia's past suggests that it is not actually enacted.

13. O. B. Hardison (*Aristotle's Poetics*, trans. L. Golden, 2nd edn (Tallahassee, FL 1981), ad loc.), takes *logos* (1455a34, rendered as "argument") as the larger, more inclusive term, and *muthos* as the less inclusive; his discussion is interesting but not altogether convincing. For a different reason for Aristotle's exclusion of Orestes' past, see below on Else, *Aristotle: Poetics* and Halliwell, *Aristotle's Poetics.*

14. Again, see Downing, "Hoion Psychē."

15. See (for example) G. Genette, *Narrative Discourse: An Essay in Method*, trans. J. E. Lewin (Ithaca, 1980), trans. of "Discours du récit," *Figures III* (Paris, 1972), and T. Todorov, "Les catégories du récit littéraire," *Communications* 8 (1966) 125–151. For a helpful general account of issues and terminology in narrative theory, see S. Chatman, *Story and Discourse: Narrative Structure in Fiction and Film* (Ithaca, 1978).

16. Cf. Halliwell, *The Poetics of Aristotle*, ad Ch. 18; he sees Aristotle's distinction as even more problematic than I have suggested here. On his response to this question, see below.

17. Dupont-Roc and Lallot, *Aristote, La Poétique* (ad 1450b37) cite *Politics* VII, 1326a33 ff. and its limitations on the best city-state, *Metaphysics* 1078a36 on the beauty of mathematical entities in virtue of order, symmetry and limitation (*to horismenon*). Cf. also Aristotle on *exō tou pragmatos* in the *Rhetoric* and his complex and interesting discussion of what is *exō tou ouranou* in *De Caelo* I, 9.

18. Cf. 24.1459b18–20. When Iphigenia speaks the prologue to Euripides' *Iphigenia in Tauris*, she tells us, among other things, both where the plot begins (with her sacrifice, according to Aristotle's outline in Ch. 17) and where the play begins (many years later, the morning after her dream about Orestes).

19. What is made known may be the general topic (as in the epic examples given), but it may also be information from the past, as in Sophocles' "my father was Polybus" (Sophocles' *Oedipus Tyrannus* 774, not the prologue in any usual sense).

20. Cf. also *Poetics* 23.1459a17–21 on the importance of wholeness and unity for the production of the proper pleasure (*oikeia hēdonē*) of a work.

21. There is one further reference to the *alogon* at 25.1461a35–1461b9, a description of critics who unreasonably make assumptions about what an author means and then criticize him for it; this passage may serve as a caution to Aristotle's own critics.

22. See esp. Else (*Aristotle: Poetics*, ad Chs. 15, 17; cf. also 306), Halliwell, *Aristotle's Poetics* (231–234 and Ch. 7 *passim*), and Halliwell, *The Poetics of Aristotle* (11–15 and *passim*); cf. also Dupont-Roc and Lallot, *Aristote, La Poétique* (ad 15.1454b8). Halliwell gives a particular prominence to the association between the inside/outside distinction and the *alogon*; in fact, for him this association points to the orientation

that explains Aristotle's insistence on a separation between outside and inside. Aristotle's emphasis on tragedy's connectedness in terms of purely human action means that he cannot accept the irrational elements that are a part of the role of the divine in tragedy. Halliwell's wording is telling: Aristotle "deliberately reinterprets the possibilities of tragic drama so as to make the religious ideas of myth *marginal* [my italics] to its purpose" (*The Poetics of Aristotle*, 12).

23. For Halliwell it is the inclusion of an example from epic that "indicates what we might anyway infer from the repeated insistence on the principles of coherent plot-construction: that Aristotle's ideal of dramatic action does not readily permit the intervention of divine agency in any form, except "outside the plot" – which is where, we note, the "irrational" in general belongs" (*Aristotle's Poetics* 231, and cf. *The Poetics of Aristotle*, ad loc.). Else, *Aristotle: Poetics* (463–475) reads *Aulidi* for *Iliadi*, thus replacing a reference to epic with another to Euripides, but he too reads the passage as "a warning that the gods are not to be tolerated in the tragic action in any organic capacity" (475).

24. Halliwell, *Aristotles Poetics*, 232 and cf. his comm., *The Poetics of Aristotle* ad loc.; Else, *Aristotle: Poetics* ad loc., 507–508.

25. See Halliwell, *Aristotle's Poetics*, p. 233 n. 42 for bibliography on this issue.

26. Halliwell, *Aristotle's Poetics*, p. 231.

27. *Iliad* II.155. Athena wrenches the story back to its required and traditional sequence much as Apollo does in Euripides' *Orestes* or Heracles in Sophocles' *Philoctetes*. Aristotle seems to have commented on this intervention in his *Homeric Problems* (see V. Rose, *Aristotelis Qui Ferebantur Librorum Fragmenta* (Leipzig, 1886), fr. 142) but it is not altogether clear how much of the discussion in this fragment and its larger context is Aristotle's own; see n. 41 below.

28. Cf. Hardison, *Aristotle's Poetics*, ad loc.

29. That is, it would be an *alogon* like the arrival of Aegeus in the *Medea* (25.1461b21); Halliwell, *Aristotle's Poetics* 232.

30. Cf. Janko, *Aristotle, Poetics* I., ad loc.; cf. also Else, *Aristotle: Poetics*, ad loc. (508) on the significance of understanding "the priestess's brother" here rather than "Orestes."

31. Aristotle mentions the custom of sacrificing strangers to the (unnamed) goddess. Halliwell notes the absence from this outline of Athena's concluding intervention (*Aristotle's Poetics*, 232).

32. Halliwell (*The Poetics of Aristotle*, ad Ch. 9, 111) sees the sort of thing described here as still falling short of the "deep and final inscrutability" tragedy in fact involves. But although Aristotle shows no particular interest in the deep and inscrutable action of the gods we also have no clear evidence that he objects to such action.

33. Cf. Hardison, *Aristotle's Poetics*, ad Ch. 15, 209–210.

34. This is apparently what Aristotle has in mind when he says "as Euripides uses Aegeus."

35. Some scholars (cf. Hardison, *Aristotle's Poetics*; Else, *Aristotle: Poetics*; and Lucas, *Aristotle's Poetics*, ad loc.) suggest that the irrational elements in the casting ashore include the Phaeacian's magical boat and Poseidon's turning that boat to stone. But the former is not at all stressed in the actual putting ashore (the Phaeacians row in), and the latter is a separate matter.

36. Compare (for example) *Rhetoric* II.22.7–8 and *NE* I.12.3 on praising the gods; cf. also *Rhetoric* II.5.21 and II.17.6.

37. For Halliwell's view of the necessary limitations on Aristotle's acceptance of traditional religion in poetry, see Halliwell, *Aristotle's Poetics*, 233.

38. See Lucas, *Aristotle: Poetics*, ad loc. on this interpretation of Aristotle's highly elliptical remark.

39. The gods are not of course consistent truth-tellers in Greek tradition but there is at least as strong a stress on the force of Zeus' word as on divine deception.

40. See Rose, *Aristotelis qui Ferebantur Librorum Fragmenta* (Leipzig, 1886), frs. 142–179.

41. Fr. 145; cf. frs. 142, 149, 153, 163, 170, 171, 172, 174, 175, 178. Fr. 175 is the sole example of allegorical treatment; the rationalization Janko (*Aristotle: Poetics I*, ad 1454b2) cites as part of fr. 142 (not actually included in Rose's fragment, but drawn from its context) may or may not be Aristotle's; see W. Dindorf, *Scholia Graeca in Homeri Iliadem*, Vol. 3 (Oxford, 1877), 91–92, and H. Schrader, *Porphyrii Quaestionum Homericarum ad Iliadem Pertinentium Reliquias* (Leipzig, 1880), 24–25.

42. It is sometimes hard to tell into which category a particular example falls: some commentators think that Aegeus' arrival is an *alogon* because it is not motivated within the plot, others that it is simply unlikely that a man should return from Delphi to Athens by way of Corinth.

43. Cf. (somewhat differently) Dupont–Roc and Lallot, *Aristote, La Poétique*, ad 15.1454b8.

44. Cf. S. Chatman on the difference between novel and film narrative (*Story and Discourse: Narrative Structure in Fiction and Film* (Ithaca, 1978)).

45. In the relevant passages from the *Rhetoric* Aristotle stresses the emotional response, but it is clear that he is also talking about the degree to which (and the way in which) the audience really takes in what is heard.

46. See the Cope and Sandys edition for this interpretation. The proper translation of this passage is much debated; I have seen no version that makes better sense than Cope's (E. M. Cope and J. E. Sandys, *The Rhetoric of Aristotle*, 3 vols (Cambridge, 1877)).

47. On these examples see Cope and Sandys, *The Rhetoric of Aristotle*, and M. Dufour and A. Wartelle, *Aristote, Rhétorique*, Vol. 3, (Paris, 1973) ad loc.

48. See Lucas, *Aristotle's Poetics*, ad 1454b7.

49. Trans. R. Lattimore, *The Complete Greek Tragedies*, eds. D. Grene and R. Lattimore, Vol. 1 (Chicago, 1953).

50. Trans. R. Lattimore, *Euripides, Iphigenia in Tauris* (London, 1974).

51. Trans. W. Sale, *Electra by Sophocles* (Englewood Cliffs, NJ, 1973).

52. Sophocles' *Oedipus Tyrannus* 800–813; the terrifying restraint of the narration gives this factual account its own vividness.

53. Modern scholars share Aristotle's concern with the inexplicable or irrational as a problem in the drama itself – witness the endless articles on the double burial in the *Antigone*, and other such matters – but often suggest (the opposite of Aristotle's view) that it is precisely when such irrational actions *are* staged that an audience is least likely to notice such problems; what is peculiar will go unnoticed as the drama holds our attention.

54. See *Helen* 257–259, 17–21, *Electra* 737–745; cf. also *Bacchae* 286–297.

55. *Electra* 518–544.

56. Euripides allows his characters to be more critical of unlikely divine action than Aristotle is; he often problematizes these criticisms at the same time, as for example in the *Heracles*, where the hero expresses at 1340–1346 disbelief in the sort of divine misbehavior which is part of this very play's background, calling the tales of such misbehavior "wretched stories of the poets."

57. See for example P. Brooks, *Reading for the Plot* (New York, 1984), esp. his discussion (in Chs. 1, 4) of W. Benjamin's "The Storyteller [Der Erzähler]," *Illuminations*, trans. H. Zohn (New York, 1969). Cf. also Kermode, *The Sense of an Ending*.

58. Herodotus, *Histories* I.32.
59. See *Poetics* 22.1459a5–8, *On Divination in Sleep* 464b6–7.
60. This paper is based on one presented at the Princeton Colloquium on Classical Philosophy in December 1989; earlier versions of small parts of it were presented at the Comparative Drama Conference at the University of Florida at Gainesville and at an NEH Summer Institute on Language in the Greek Enlightenment. I am grateful to Mark Griffith, my commentator at Princeton, and to the other participants in these occasions for their comments and questions.

Ēthos and *Dianoia* Reconsidered

Mary Whitlock Blundell

"Alas, what shall I do?" This question reverberates through the pages of Greek tragedy. The action contemplated is rarely a trivial one, and usually calls for a serious moral choice with far-reaching consequences for the self and others. In situations of this kind, a decision to act is seldom reached without extensive deliberation or debate. The prominence of such purposeful choice and action in the drama doubtless influenced Aristotle's definition of tragedy as an "imitation of action (*praxis*)" (*Poetics* 1449b24). Aristotelian *praxis* is not just any sort of action, but the kind of purposefully chosen deed that is so often central to tragedy.[1] The moral and intellectual qualities that give rise to such action are aspects of a person's *ēthos* and *dianoia*, "character" and "intellect," and as such fall within the purview of Aristotle's *Ethics*. But *ēthos* and *dianoia* also form two of the essential "parts" of tragedy, following only plot in significance. Their presence and importance follow directly from the definition of tragedy as the imitation of *praxis*.[2] For an adequate representation of *praxis* must include the characteristics that give rise to such action – the tragic actors must "include characters on account of the actions" (1450a21–22). The necessity for dramatic *ēthos* and *dianoia* is accordingly derived from the nature of human action as such (1448a1–4, 1449b36–38).

The interrelation between *ēthos*, *dianoia* and *praxis* in the *Poetics* can only be understood against the background of the *Ethics*. Tragedy, however, is not just the imitation of *action*, but the *imitation* of action, using speech as its most prominent medium (the others are rhythm and melody) (1447a21–22, 1447b24–27). The poet must not only know what a good or bad person is like, but be able to portray this persuasively, employing the resources of language to reveal (whether explicitly or by inference) the presumed personal qualities of the agent. We may therefore expect Aristotle's *Rhetoric*, as well as his ethical writings, to illuminate his theory of tragedy.[3] Indeed, if we are to succeed in elucidating the relationship between tragic *ēthos* and *dianoia*, we have little choice but to turn to these other works for help, since the *Poetics* itself offers virtually no guidance.[4] The interconnection between these three areas of Aristotle's thought is confirmed by the way he treats tragic characters as indistinguishable in important respects from living people. In the *Poetics* he often speaks of dramatic figures as if they were real persons, who must have appropriate qualities of character and intellect in order to undertake purposeful action. Conversely in the ethical and rhetorical works he regularly illustrates his argument with characters from literature, especially epic and tragedy.

In the *Nicomachean Ethics* (*NE*), the distinction between *ēthos* and *dianoia* is central to Aristotle's theory and plays a structural role in its elaboration. At the end of Book I, human excellence is divided between the excellences of character (such as courage and self-control) and those of intellect (such as wisdom and cleverness), and the bulk of the work is organized around this dichotomy.[5] *Ēthos* in this sense is said to belong to the irrational part of the soul, whose only participation in intellect is a passive ability to heed the commands of reason.[6] But complete excellence of character also turns out to involve the intellectual excellence of practical wisdom (*phronēsis*).[7] *Phronēsis* guides the process of deliberation (1141b8–12), and hence plays an essential role in purposeful choice (*prohairesis*), which in turn is the moving cause of *praxis* (1139a31–32). *Prohairesis* requires both *dianoia* and *ēthos* (in the narrow sense) (1139a33–35), and is involved in the definition of excellence of *ēthos* (1106b36, 1139a22–23). It is *prohairesis* that makes us "of a certain kind" (1112a1–2), and by *prohairesis* that we judge a person's *ēthos* (1111b5–6).[8] Correct *prohairesis* and complete (as opposed to "natural") excellence of *ēthos* require the cooperation of *phronēsis* with excellence of *ēthos* (in the narrow sense).[9] So in addition to the narrow usage most characteristic of the *Ethics*, there is a broader sense of *ēthos* which involves the intellectual excellence of *phronēsis*. Theoretical wisdom, the other main branch of intellectual excellence, plays no part in deliberation and choice, and hence is not associated with *ēthos*.

To these two conceptions of *ēthos* in the *Ethics* we may add a third. *Ēthos* and related words are used not only for the fully developed excellences of character and their opposites, but also more loosely for a variety of related states and capacities.[10] These include the undeveloped character of the young (*NE* 1179b7–10, 29–31; cf. *Eudemian Ethics* (*EE*) 1236a40), and the irrational "natural" excellences which are present from birth and may be found in children and even animals (*NE* 1144b4–17). In mature adults, *ēthos* may be used in connection with such conditions as self-control (or its absence) (*NE* 1145a16–17), and a sense of shame (*EE* 1233b16–18, 22–25), neither of which is strictly speaking an excellence (*NE* 1128b10–11, 1145a35–b2). This breadth is in keeping with ordinary usage, whereby *ēthos* can cover a wide range of personal traits, including intellectual ones.[11] The fluctuations in Aristotle's own usage depend on the purpose at hand. The *Ethics* is deeply concerned with the nature of "complete" excellence of character, but employs the sharper dichotomy between *ēthos* and *dianoia* for the central task of analyzing its various psychological components (cf. e.g. *NE* 1144a7–9, 20–22), while the broader and more casual sense of *ēthos* is convenient when Aristotle's specialized distinctions are not in play.

With this background in mind, we may turn to the *Poetics*. *Ēthos* is introduced at the beginning of Chapter 2, where Aristotle explains that the different *ēthē* which give rise to action may be distinguished by their *aretē* and *kakia* (excellence and vice) (1448a1–4). The evaluative language here is indeterminate, and could extend to human excellence in the broadest sense (including all excellences of character and intellect).[12] But the association of *ēthos* with excellence and vice recalls the excellence of character of the *Ethics*.[13] The reference is presumably to "complete" excellence, since there is no obvious sign of the narrower dichotomy between *ēthos* and *dianoia*.[14] Note, however, that the wording also allows for degrees of *aretē* and *kakia* which fall short of the fully developed excellences and vices.[15] Aristotle thus leaves space – so necessary in tragedy – for moral imperfection. Indeed perfect virtue is neither necessary nor desirable in tragic characters.[16]

This interpretation accords with Aristotle's detailed recommendations for dramatic *ēthos* (1454a16–36). First he requires *ēthos* to be good of its kind (*chrēstos*). *Chrēstos* is a general word, and does not raise the issue of character as opposed to intellect. But this requirement does implicitly embrace at least one intellectual virtue, namely practical wisdom. For it is the representation of purposeful choice (*prohairesis*) which determines both the presence and the quality of *ēthos* in a drama (1454a17–19; cf. 1450b8–10), and as we have seen, *phronēsis* is indispensable to *prohairesis*. Moreover, when speaking of goodness according to kind, the "kinds" Aristotle mentions are women and slaves, who are good in a different way from men, because of their generic inferiority (1454a19–22). But in both cases this inferiority is one of intellect (*Politics* 1260a2–33). So in this way too, the passage indicates the relevance to dramatic *ēthos* of at least some intellectual qualities. It also confirms that dramatic *ēthos* is not confined to the developed excellences and vices, but includes related or analogous conditions. For intellectual deficiency removes the capacity for full *prohairesis* (cf. *NE* 1111b8–9), making women and slaves incapable of complete excellence of character (*Politics* 1260a2–33; cf. 1277b18–25, *Rhetoric* 1367a16–18).

The second requirement for dramatic *ēthos* is appropriateness to type. A woman, says Aristotle, should not be inappropriately courageous or clever (*deinos*) (1454a23–24). By citing a quality of intellect alongside one of character, he evokes the dichotomy of the *Ethics* (cf. also 1456a21–23).[17] But as we would expect from the broader usage of the *Ethics*, the intellectual attribute in question is one that pertains to action. Cleverness (*deinotēs*) is a close relative of *phronēsis* – it is practical intelligence without virtue to guide its ends (*NE* 1144a23–b1). To exemplify excessive female cleverness, Aristotle adduces the speech of Melanippe in Euripides' *Melanippe the Wise* (1454a31). The fact that this speech includes a disquisition on natural science makes Melanippe's inappropriate cleverness sound more like theoretical than practical wisdom.[18] But her words are aimed at action – she is trying to save her children's life. So it seems that dramatic *ēthos* may embrace not only the practical wisdom needed for "complete" excellence of character, but purely intellectual attributes as well, provided they are deployed in the cause of action. Thus in Euripides' *Bacchae* the wise Teiresias discourses on the nature of Dionysus and Demeter not merely to display his learning, but in an attempt to convince Pentheus of the error of his ways (266–327).

The use of such discourse may also have significant implications for the speaker's practical choices in a more general sense. Dispositions of intellect as well as character help to make a person "of a certain kind in life" (cf. *Rhetoric* 1408a29) – a philosopher or mathematician is dedicated to a way of life founded on certain values.[19] We must therefore distinguish between the transcription of intellectual arguments for their own sake and their use in the representation of persons. As Aristotle says in the *Rhetoric*, mathematical discourses lack *ēthos* because they have no *prohairesis* or goal (*telos*) (1417a18–20; cf. *Poetics* 1450b10–11). But as soon as such arguments are attributed to a speaker, rather than presented in the abstract, they take on implications for character, action and the goals of a human life.[20]

Dramatic *ēthos* thus corresponds roughly to the broadest sense of personal *ēthos* in the *Ethics*, with the addition of theoretical wisdom in so far as it may pertain to choice and action. The sharp dichotomy between *ēthos* and *dianoia*, so prominent in the *Ethics*, is scarcely in evidence. This silence follows naturally from the divergent purposes of the two works. The springs of human action are a central preoccupation of the *Ethics*. (The same concern is betrayed by a parenthesis in the *Poetics* (1450a1–2), thought by most recent editors to have been added as an explanatory gloss composed with an eye to the *Ethics*.) *Ēthos* and *dianoia* as distinct but interrelated aspects of human nature are central to the ethical project of analyzing the nature of human excellence, especially as displayed in purposeful action, and determining the best kind of life.[21] The *Poetics* is also concerned with action, but in a different way. The nature of human excellence, as scrutinized in the *Ethics*, is now presupposed as part of the background for the analysis of drama as an "imitation" of people in action. With the shift of focus from human nature to its representation, the dichotomy between character and intellect within each agent recedes before the distinction between a broader set of human characteristics and the challenge of representing them through language and stage action. It is therefore only to be expected that *ēthos* in the *Poetics* should denote character in the more general sense that lies closer to traditional usage.

This account is confirmed by the one striking counterexample to an inclusive interpretation of *ēthos* in the *Poetics*. In Aristotle's summary derivation of the six "parts" of tragedy, *ēthos* and *dianoia* are introduced in parallel, as the features that enable us to describe a person or action as being "of a certain kind"

(1449b37–38). The language here clearly recalls the paired *ēthos* and *dianoia* of the *Ethics*. But just a few lines later *ēthos* seems to have become inclusive, for now it alone (as a part of the play) makes us call the "people in action" (the *prattontes*) "of a certain kind" (1450a5–6).[22] Dramatic *ēthos* seems to have assumed the task of representing personal *dianoia* as well as *ēthos*, which is just what we would expect from the treatment of *ēthos* elsewhere in the *Poetics*.

This awkward shift, during a single rambling sentence, in the meaning of *ēthos* and its relationship to *dianoia*, is best explained by the change in focus from attributes of (dramatic) persons to attributes of plays (the six "parts" that Aristotle is intent on deriving), that is, from an ethical to a rhetorical perspective.[23] Aristotle begins by thinking of the *prattontes* as persons, and accordingly ascribes to them the parallel *ēthos* and *dianoia* of the *Ethics*, both of which are necessary attributes of persons involved in purposeful action. This perspective also influences the final summary of the six "parts," in which *ēthos* and *dianoia* count as "objects" of imitation (1450a11), and as such must be viewed as distinct aspects of the "people in action."[24] But he is working towards conclusions concerning the attributes (qualitative "parts") of a drama, which is not action but its representation. The focus on dramatic figures as agents, together with the analytic distinction of the *Ethics*, suggests that the drama must have two corresponding parts. But parts of a play are not parts of a person. When the dramatist turns from analyzing the determinants of purposeful choice, to attempting to show an agent making such choices, the dichotomy between *ēthos* and *dianoia* as distinct psychological factors recedes into the background. The perspective is no longer that of the ethical analyst, but that of the artist attempting to produce a convincing representation of a person in action. From this external point of view, personal *ēthos* and *dianoia* are not clearly distinguishable – the bystander observes someone acting, but cannot weigh the internal determinants of either decision or action. The question becomes the more general artistic one of how best to represent the kind of person who would behave in such a way.

Aristotle's argument is also influenced by the fact that *dianoia* is needed for a diferent role. Like *ēthos* it starts out as an aspect of a person, which, in tandem with *ēthos*, is essential to purposeful action. But when this kind of *dianoia* is taken over by dramatic *ēthos*, dramatic *dianoia* can emerge as the "part" of tragedy which uses certain kinds of argumentation (1450a7; cf. 1450b11–12). The shift in the meaning of *dianoia* clearly reveals the dislocation in thought caused by the need to derive aspects of plays from aspects of persons. A person's *dianoia* is what makes him or her intellectually "of a certain kind," but a play's *dianoia* consists of certain types of argument. The derivation of dramatic from personal *dianoia* implies that dramatic *dianoia* will convey the presumed personal *dianoia* of the dramatic figures.[25] But subsuming personal *dianoia* under dramatic *ēthos* allows Aristotle to concentrate on *dianoia* in the broader and less personal sense of rhetorical argumentation (which has obvious bearing on the creation and analysis of Greek tragedy). The emphasis shifts from actions performed by ("real") people, who must have both *ēthos* and *dianoia* but need articulate neither, to the *imitation* of persons in action, who must both appear to have some kind of moral and intellectual character (inclusive personal *ēthos*), and employ various verbal techniques to convey this.[26]

The fluctuating use of both *ēthos* and *dianoia* in this argument thus seems to result from a movement away from the aspects of human nature that necessitate *ēthos* and *dianoia* as two essential "parts" of tragedy and towards those "parts" themselves. This causes considerable confusion, but the inference from persons to plays is not thereby invalidated. It remains true that persons in action must have both *ēthos* and *dianoia*, and that plays (which represent action) must therefore have them too. Personal *dianoia* may become subsumed under *ēthos*, but dramatic *dianoia* is still needed to express it. A similar shift of focus from speaker to speech apears in Aristotle's subsequent definition of *dianoia* as "the ability to say what is available and appropriate, which in speeches is the task of politics and rhetoric" (1450b4–7). *Dianoia* as an *ability* must refer to the personal skill of the orator, dramatist or dramatic character, but the results of this ability are speeches of a certain kind. Such speeches must use the arguments that are "available" – they must employ, in Dale's well-known phrase, "the rhetoric of the situation."[27] But they must also be "appropriate." That this extends to the character of the speaker is suggested by the requirement of "appropriateness" in characterization (1454a22–24; cf. 1454a33–36).[28] The situation to which the speaker's rhetoric must be adapted thus includes not just external circumstances, but the *ēthos* that the dramatist wishes the speaker to project.[29] The *dianoia* of the speech or play both results from and illuminates various aspects of the presumed personal *ēthos* of the speaker, including any pertinent qualities of *dianoia*.

The treatment of *ēthos* and *dianoia* in the *Rhetoric* supports this interpretation of the *Poetics* and suggests further interesting implications for Aristotle's view of dramatic character. In this work, as in the *Poetics*, intellectual qualities are implicit in the strong and repeated association of *ēthos* with purposeful choice (*prohairesis*).[30] The intellectual excellence of *phronēsis* is more explicitly subsumed under *ēthos* in the "ethical proof," or proof "from the *ēthos* of the speaker" (*Rhetoric* 1356a1–13, 1366a8–14, 1377b21–31).[31] To employ this successfully, one must give an impression of *phronēsis* as well as *aretē* and good will (1378a6–20; cf. *Politics* 1309a33–7). *Aretē* here looks like the narrow excellence of character of the *Ethics*, which must be complemented and completed by *phronēsis*.[32] *Phronēsis*, which is defined in the *Rhetoric* very much as in the *Ethics*,[33] is essential to the statesman,[34] and has an obvious relevance to rhetoric. For rhetoric concerns the things we deliberate about; these are not certainties, but things that could be otherwise (1357a1–7) – precisely the field of *phronēsis*.[35] So the orator must not only have but appear to have *phronēsis* as well as *aretē* in the narrow sense, if his advice is to carry conviction (1378a6–19). Both thus form part of his *ēthos*.

Elsewhere in the *Rhetoric*, however, *ēthos* is contrasted with intellect in ways that echo the dichotomy of the *Ethics*. The young, for example, are said to live more by *ēthos* than by calculation (*logismos*),[36] where the former is associated with excellence (*aretē*) and nobility (*to kalon*), and the latter with self-interest (*to sumpheron*) (1389a34–36; cf. 1390a16–18). Here again *aretē* is used in a narrow sense, but this time it is contrasted with intellect rather than complementing it, and linked with *ēthos* to the exclusion of intellect. Later, practical wisdom itself is contrasted with *ēthos*, *aretē* and even *prohairesis*. The orator is enjoined to make the narrative characterful (*ēthikē*) rather than speaking from *dianoia* "as people do now;" the production of *ēthos* involves speaking "as if from *prohairesis*," regardless of self-interest, for the pursuit of self-interest is a sign of a prudent man (*phronimos*),[37] whereas *prohairesis* and self-sacrifice are signs of a good one (*agathos*) (1417a15–26). This passage focuses on the intellectual rather than the moral aspect of *phronēsis*, treating it as a kind of prudence that can be exercised independently of excellence of character, like the "calculation" eschewed by the young, or the amoral faculty of cleverness in the *Ethics*.[38]

But if the good orator must manifest *phronēsis* as well as *aretē*, and *phronēsis* is essential to the good man's *prohairesis*, why are *dianoia* and *phronēsis* here unfavorably contrasted with *ēthos* and *prohairesis*? To resolve this apparent difficulty it is important to observe that Aristotle's warning was not against *dianoia per se*, but against *appearing* to speak from *dianoia* rather than from *prohairesis* (1417a23–24). It is not implied that *prohairesis* is to be conceived of here – in contrast to the *Ethics* – as utterly irrational.[39] But the underlying reasoning or deliberative process should not be displayed, since this might give an impression of calculative self-interest. The need for the orator not only to be but to seem to be a man of practical wisdom must be balanced against his need to appear spontaneously virtuous rather than calculating and clever. For conventional usage sees a conflict between *phronēsis* and *aretē*, between *dianoia* and *ēthos* (1389a34–36, 1417a25–26; cf. *NE* 1145b18–19). In Aristotelian terms there can be no such conflict (cf. *NE* 1144a36–b1), since true self-love coincides with excellence (*NE* 1168a28–69b2; cf. also *Rhetoric* 1390a34–b1). Achilles' decision to avenge Patroclus is paradoxically "selfish," since he is claiming for himself the greater good – the noble (*to kalon*) (*NE* 1169a18–26).[40] But the orator must appeal to an unsophisticated and un-Aristotelian audience,[41] and should therefore avoid unnecessarily displaying the intellectual foundations of his decisions. So in the *Rhetoric* self-love regains its usual pejorative sense, whereby it is aligned with self-interest in opposition to nobility (1389b35–37). The choice of Achilles is no longer "selfish," but a selfless sacrifice of self-interest to nobility (1358b38–59a6). Conventional usage thus constrains the intellectual articulation of the orator's *ēthos*, for the appearance of virtue is more important than precision of argument (1418a37–b1).[42] The good man needs *phronēsis* to complete the "ethical" virtues, but the good orator must understand (whether consciously or as an instinctive result of his internalized craft) when and how far to display each facet of his moral and intellectual character – his *ēthos* in a broad sense – to the audience.

This notion of *display* is fundamental to literary *ēthos*, dramatic as well as rhetorical. Personal *ēthos* is what makes someone "of a certain kind," but a play's *ēthos* is that in virtue of which *we call* the *prattontes* "of a certain kind" (*Poetics* 1450a6).[43] A person may have qualities of *ēthos* without articulating them at any given moment, to others or even to himself (cf. *NE* 1143b11–14), and his motives for action may remain entirely obscure to the outside observer.[44] This opacity does not affect the quality of his character or intellect, nor is he necessarily obliged to explain himself. But the same cannot be said for the orator's persona or the dramatist's characters. The orator's self-representation must not rely on previously known facts about his *ēthos* – he must express that *ēthos* through the speech itself (*Rhetoric* 1356a8–10). The same presumably applies to tragedy, whose principal figures are often broadly delineated by tradition, but are fashioned anew in each poetic treatment.[45] Since the "existence" of dramatic or literary figures (including orators) is confined to and concentrated within the limited span of the work in which they appear, the writer must offer evidence of their characters in the course of that work. Hence the Aristotelian emphasis on *displaying ēthos*: the *ēthos* of the play is "that which *makes clear* what the *prohairesis* is like," when it is not *clear* from the action (*Poetics* 1450b8–10);[46] the play will have *ēthos* if speech or action makes some *prohairesis apparent* (1454a17–19); "those speeches have *ēthos* in which the *prohairesis* is *clear*" (*Rhetoric* 1395b13–14; cf. 1395a26–27, 1417a17, 1367b22); the *gnōmē* or moral maxim – a prime source of rhetorical *ēthos* – is a kind of *declaration* (1394a22; cf. 1395b14–17, *Poetics* 1450a7, 1450b11–12).[47]

So far, we have seen *ēthos* used in the *Rhetoric* both in its narrowest sense, in contrast to *dianoia*, and in the broader sense which corresponds to "complete" excellence of character. But *ēthos* in the *Rhetoric*, as in the *Poetics*, may also indicate a person's total moral and intellectual qualities – not just the excellences of character, and *phronēsis*, but other intellectual attributes as well. In his discussion of types of *ēthos*, Aristotle notes not only that the young are less influenced than the old by calculation, but that they are know-it-alls (1389b5–6), in contrast to the uncertainty of the old (1389b14–19) and the true judgment of the mature man (1390a32–34). Education is likewise treated as an aspect of *ēthos* (1408a31–32; cf. 1395a2–8).[48] Such passages suggest that a broad range of intellectual attributes is relevant to *ēthos*. This is confirmed by the presence of theoretical wisdom (*sophia*) alongside *phronēsis* in Aristotle's list of excellences (1366b1–3), which are included not only for encomiastic purposes, but to enable the orator to characterize the *ēthos* of himself and others (1366a23–28, 1378a16–19). We might expect *sophia* to play a greater role in encomium than in other types of oratory. But though Aristotle does sometimes call theoretical wisdom praiseworthy (*NE* 1103a8–9, *EE* 1220a5–6), virtuous deeds remain the principal material for praise (cf. *Rhetoric* 1367b21–36).[49] The role of *sophia* in rhetorical *ēthos* is therefore perhaps best explained on analogy with the case of Melanippe in the *Poetics*. As in the *Poetics*, however, *sophia* naturally receives less attention than *phronēsis*, since it is less directly relevant to choice and action.

Ēthos in the *Rhetoric* thus has a range of meanings, varying from the narrow technical sense most prominent in the *Ethics* to the inclusive usage of the *Poetics*. Like drama, rhetoric is concerned less with the analysis of action than with its effective representation.[50] Those passages in the *Rhetoric* which adopt the broad usage of the *Poetics* are less preoccupied with the psychological determinants of action than with the persuasive representation of persons with a range of character traits. Even when *prohairesis* is directly involved, the orator will generally be less concerned with analyzing its two complementary aspects than with representing it as being "of a certain kind." From this perspective the more inclusive and traditional sense of *ēthos* is both appropriate and convenient. But when Aristotle does focus on portraying the springs of action, and especially on the relative weight to be assigned to personal *ēthos* and *dianoia* in such representation, he naturally tends to employ the analytical distinction of the *Ethics*. So it is that under the general heading of *ēthos* (in the broad sense) (1388b31–32), he can include an analysis of the relative motivational weight of *ēthos* (in the narrow sense) and calculation (1389a35, 1390a16–17).

These fluctuations in the meaning of *ēthos* in the *Rhetoric* help to clarify Aristotle's usage in the *Poetics*, as distinct from that of the *Ethics*, by showing how he adapts it to the preoccupations of the moment. But there may be a still broader sense of *ēthos* at work in the *Rhetoric*. As we should expect from the *Ethics* and *Poetics*, *ēthos* in the *Rhetoric* is not strictly confined to the settled moral and intellectual dispositions that make up the excellences and vices.[51] But can it also include qualities entirely unrelated to these states? Rhetorical *ēthos* can indeed be indicated not only by the direct representation of *prohairesis*, but by "what follows on each *ēthos*" (1417a21). Cope takes this to mean that "the characteristic peculiarities that accompany each individual character" constitute "another, different, kind of ethical drawing or representation . . . no longer confined to *moral* qualities, but the representation of *character* in general."[52] On this view, *ēthos* in the *Rhetoric* would take a significant step towards those more recent conceptions of literary character which focus not merely upon moral and intellectual qualities, but upon the detailed evocation of individual personalities. Given the close relationship between oratory and drama, this could have important implications not only for the *Poetics*, but for the continuing debate over Greek notions of character and characterization, expecially in tragedy.[53] The evidence therefore deserves careful scrutiny.

To begin with, the "proof" from the *ēthos* of the speaker requires one to convey not only *aretē* and *phronēsis* but also good will (*eunoia*) (1378a6–19). This trait should not be considered a subordinate part of the speaker's *aretē* as such, for Aristotle entertains the possibility that a speaker may display both *aretē* and *phronēsis* but lack *eunoia*, and therefore knowingly fail to advise his audience for the best (1378a12–14). But although *eunoia* is not in itself an excellence, reciprocal good will is the foundation of the excellence of character known as friendship (*philia*) (*NE* 1166a30–67a21; cf. *Magna Moralia* 122a9–12). Similarly in the *Rhetoric*, Aristotle does not discuss the orator's *eunoia per se*, but directs us to his treatment of *philia* (1378a19–20; cf. 1380b34–81b37).[54] The good man will presumably have legitimate reasons for feeling more or less well disposed towards a particular audience, so that *eunoia* in any given case is not a necessary consequence of his *aretē*. But the successful orator must convey the impression that he is well disposed towards whatever audience he happens to be addressing. *Eunoia* must therefore be specified independently of *aretē* as an indispensable ingredient of the orator's *ēthos*.

Aristotle's discussion of various kinds of human *ēthos* introduces further factors which might seem extraneous to the excellences of character and intellect. These *ēthē* are distinguished not only by the emotions,[55] and those settled dispositions which constitute the excellences and vices (cf. *NE* 1105b19–6a13), but by such external determinants as age and fortune (1388b31–34). Similarly style may be made expressive of *ēthos* by following the "signs" not only of the dispositions that make a person "of a certain kind in life," but of such factors as age, sex, and nationality (1408a25–31; cf. Plato *Ion* 540b). These external circumstances are significant, however, not as components of *ēthos*,[56] but as influences upon it.[57] The inexperience of the young, for example, gives rise to optimism (1389a19–26), whereas the old, embittered by experience, are pessimists (1390a4–11). So optimism, but not age, belongs to *ēthos*. This fits in well with the *Ethics*, where appropriate optimism, though clearly distinguished from courage (*NE* 1117a9–15; cf. 1115b3–4), is a feature of the brave man, whereas the coward is a pessimist (1116a2–4). In the *Rhetoric* itself, the optimism of the young contributes to their courage and greatness of soul (1389a26–29, 31–33). And the systematic contrast between the *ēthos* of young and old, as the opposite extremes between which the mature man is the mean (1390a29–b9), shows that Aristotle intended this discussion to be compatible with his ethical theory.

Even the prolix reminiscences of the old (1390a10–11) are germane to the *ēthos* of the *Ethics*. Speech habits fall within the purview of the social excellences and vices (*NE* 1126b11–28b9),[58] and are prominent in the sketch of the great-souled man (1124b28–31, 1125a5–10, 13–14). But linguistic habits and other details of style and behavior are not in themselves aspects of personal *ēthos*. They are "signs" or symptoms of such underlying states of character as flattery (*Rhetoric* 1383b32–35), boastfulness (1384a5–7), rashness and boorishness (1417a22–23, 1408a31–32), all of which number among the vices of the *Ethics* (*NE* 1108a23–26, 1127b33–28b9).[59] Similarly the social excellence of wit (*NE* 1127b33–28b3) is reflected in the *Rhetoric's* contrast between the sour and humorless old (1390a22–23) and the witty and humorous young (1389b10–11). The treatment of the virtues in the *Ethics* itself includes such details of a symptomatic kind, especially in the description of the great-souled man, with his slow gait, deep voice and measured speech (*NE* 1125a12–14). In a collocation likely to strike the modern reader as incongruous, Aristotle says it would be inappropriate for such a man "to flee waving his arms or to act unjustly" (1123b31–32).

This kind of detail (which culminates in Theophrastus' *Characters*) is more prominent in the *Rhetoric* than in the *Ethics*, presumably because of the divergent goals of the two works. The *Ethics* is more concerned with the virtues as such than with their external symptoms, but the *Rhetoric* offers the orator the materials to appeal to a wide variety of audiences, each with its own behavioral and psychological characteristics. The different kinds of *ēthē*, with their identifying features, are therefore catalogued in considerable detail, to help the speaker accommodate his words to them (cf. 1390a25–28). The same features are directly relevant to the representation of *ēthos*. If one uses the appropriate "signs," one's narrative will have *ēthos* (1408a25–27). If one makes someone "say the words belonging to the disposition, one will portray the *ēthos*" (1408a30–31). The "signs" of excellence or vice are sometimes distinguished from their "deeds" (1384a7–8, 1366b27–34), but deeds may themselves serve as "signs" of a disposition (1367b31–33). The same applies to drama: "in the *ēthē* too . . . one should always seek the necessary or probable, so that it is necessary or probable for a person of such a kind to say or do things of such a kind" (*Poetics* 1454a33–35). For representational purposes, then, the saying and the doing are aspects of *ēthos*, but only because such behavioral symptoms are suggestive of the relevant interior states. It does not follow that any feature of rhetorical or dramatic *ēthos* is altogether divorced from the excellences and vices of the *Ethics*.[60]

There remains the question of whether *ēthos* in the *Rhetoric* is confined to character *types*, or allows any room for individuality. The orator could, of course, make cumulative use of the personal traits attributed to the various types – such as walking and talking simultaneously (1417a22–23) – to develop an individual portrait. But Aristotle's treatment of rhetorical *ēthos* shows no concern with personal idiosyncrasy as such. Individual traits do appear, however, in a slightly different context. The narrative should draw on emotion not only by mentioning generic emotional gestures (e.g. "those who are about to weep place their hands on their eyes"), but by introducing details that are peculiarly characteristic of oneself or one's adversary; thus Aeschines describes Cratylus as "violently hissing and shaking his fists" (1417a36–b7). *Ēthos* is not mentioned here, but such displays of emotion are directly relevant to its portrayal (cf. *Politics* 1340a32–35). For the excellences of character consist precisely in the proper feeling and expression of the various emotions (cf. *NE* 1106b16–27, *EE* 1220b7–10, 18–20). The intimate connection between emotion and excellence of character is clear from many passages in the *Rhetoric*, including the extensive treatment of the emotions, which has frequent points of contact with the *Ethics*.[61] We should therefore expect the expression of *ēthos* and emotion to overlap, in both rhetoric and drama, and the emotional gestures adduced by Aristotle to serve double duty as indicators of *ēthos*.

In this same discussion of "accompaniments" of emotion, Aristotle goes on to recommend that the orator introduce himself right from the start as being "of a certain kind," so that the audience "may regard you as being of such a kind, and your opponent too" (1417b7–8). The phrase "of a certain kind" (*poios tis*) has broad reference to anything in the category of quality (*Categories* Ch. 8), but is especially used with reference to *ēthos*.[62] The context here confines the qualities in question to emotional ones,[63] but the reference to the orator's self-representation recalls the "ethical" proof, which requires him to portray himself as being "of a certain kind" (1377b24). This supports the idea that the characteristics mentioned as signs of emotion, whether idiosyncratic or generic, may be symptoms of more permanent qualities of character and thus contribute to the representation of *ēthos*. If we know what provoked Cratylus' behavior, it may shed light on his moral values. It may, for example, characterize him as an irascible man, one of those who "do not hold in their rage but retaliate openly because of their quick temper" (*NE* 1126a16–17) – a type also mentioned in connection with *ēthos* in the *Poetics* (1454b11–13). There is, therefore, room for idiosyncratic detail in the representation of *ēthos*, even though individuality as such is not its province.

Ēthos in the *Rhetoric*, then, though it may include intellectual as well as moral characteristics, does not extend to extraneous generic features or personal idiosyncrasies as such. But such details do enter the discussion, both here and in the *Ethics*, as determinants or symptoms of moral or intellectual character. So in both works certain factors which might superficially seem irrelevant to the Aristotelian excellences of character and intellect turn out to be pertinent to *ēthos* after all. This has interesting implications for *ēthos* in drama. It is often (and rightly) emphasized that Aristotle's conception of dramatic character is a narrow one, compared with many later notions – drama is not an imitation of human beings as such (*Poetics* 1450a16). But this does not mean that his notion of characterization therefore excludes subtle or even personal detail as irrelevant. Halliwell is right to affirm that "*ēthos* . . . is a specific moral factor in relation to action, not a vague or pervasive notion equivalent to modern ideas of personality or individuality – least of all to individuality, since *ēthos* is a matter of generic qualities (virtues and vices) (Halliwell, *Aristotle's Poetics*, 151). But that is not the whole story. Aristotle is not interested in idiosyncrasy as such, but he would admit the importance for dramatic *ēthos* of many details that we would be more likely to ascribe to "personality or individuality." Such details should, however, be viewed as symptoms of moral or intellectual character, rather than as personal traits included for verisimilitude or other artistic purposes.

Greek tragedy is not noted for its subtle delineation of uniquely individualized personalities. But Aristotle's theory can accommodate, for example, such memorable minor characters as the nurse in Aeschylus' *Choephoroi*, with her domestic reminiscences of Orestes' infancy (747–762). These will form part of her Aristotelian *ēthos*, not only because her words give us insight into her moral values, but because the old live on their memories and talk a lot (*Rhetoric* 1390a10–11). The *Rhetoric* suggests that even tragic messengers may have *ēthos*,[64] for Aristotle uses them to exemplify his advice to introduce oneself and one's opponent as being "of a certain kind" (1417b7–10). The introduction of the guard in Sophocles' *Antigone* may be the kind of thing he has in mind (223–236). But even an ordinary messenger may intimate both emotions and moral values in his opening lines (see e.g. Euripides, *Bacchae* 1024–1028). To take a somewhat loftier example, it has often been observed that Creon in *Antigone* is inclined to the use of maxims (*gnōmai*).[65] As we shall shortly see, the content of such maxims makes them an important vehicle of *ēthos*. But according to Aristotle (as well as more recent critics), Creon's *ēthos* is also illuminated by the very fact that he uses them. Since he is portrayed as inexperienced in government (156–157, 175–177), his use of maxims on this subject would appear to characterize him, in Aristotle's pitiless phrase, as "silly and unedu-cated" (*Rhetoric* 1395a2–8).

Creon's maxims return us from *ēthos* to dramatic *dianoia*, of which *gnōmai* form a part. As we saw earlier, *dianoia* in the *Poetics* is primarily used in a rhetorical rather than a personal sense, to refer not to an aspect of the human psyche but to certain kinds of argumentation. This dramatic *dianoia* is defined first as "the ability to say what is available and appropriate" (1450b4–7), then as "all that should be done by means of the *logos*" (i.e. speech as opposed to song), including demonstration and the arousal of emotion (1456a36–b2). Demonstration and emotion are two of the *Rhetoric's* three "proofs through the *logos*" (*Rhetoric* 1356a1–4), and Aristotle directs us to that work for further discussion (*Poetics* 1456a34–36). The connection is confirmed in the *Rhetoric* itself, where the three rhetorical "proofs" (as opposed to style and arrangement) are summarized at the end of Book II as "examples, maxims and enthymemes, and in general the things concerning *dianoia*" (1403a34–b1).

All this suggests that dramatic *dianoia* is coextensive with rhetorical argument in general. But the *Poetics* omits any mention of the third rhetorical "proof," the proof from the *ēthos* of the speaker. Does this mean that dramatic *dianoia* excludes that kind of rhetorical speech which conveys the speaker's *ēthos*?[66] The call for appropriateness in characterization suggests otherwise. Moreover, the summary in the *Rhetoric* also fails to mention the "proof" from *ēthos*, or even the "proof" from emotion. "In general" does provide room for these and other matters treated in the first two books, but the wording suggests that *dianoia* is associated primarily with the third kind of "proof," the proof "in the *logos* itself," whose function is demonstration (1356a3–4; cf. 1356a19–20).[67] This is the aspect of rhetoric that Aristotle considers most important (1354a11–18), and the one to which he devotes the most attention. *Dianoia* is closely associated with such forms of argument in the *Poetics* too, where its functions are specified as demon-stration, maxim and generalization (1450a7, 1450b11–12). The absence of *ēthos* from the fuller list of functions of dramatic *dianoia* (1456a36–b2) presum-ably arises from the presence in this work of *ēthos* as a "part" of tragedy in its own right (a category inapplicable to the *Rhetoric*, where Aristotle does not employ this mode of analysis).[68] But the omission must have been facilitated by the fact that *dianoia*, though embracing all three rhetorical "proofs," is most closely associated with the capacity for argument.[69] The absence of *ēthos* is therefore best regarded as an oversight,[70] and should not be taken to imply that *dianoia* excludes the kind of rhetorical argument which represents the speaker or others as being "of a certain kind." Dramatic *dianoia* is thus broadly the production of rhetorical effects through the techniques discussed in *Rhetoric* I and II, but it focuses more particularly on the kinds of argument summarized at the end of Book II. It is her ability to manipulate such arguments that makes Melanippe, for example, too clever for Aristotle's taste. Too great a share of the *dianoia* of the play can, it seems, be inappropriate to a character's personal *dianoia*, and hence to her *ēthos* in the broadest sense.[71]

Maxim and enthymeme, two of the forms of argument associated with *dianoia* in the *Rhetoric*, provide a clear and significant link between *dianoia* and *ēthos*. Maxims are defined as general statements about "what should be chosen and avoided with regard to action" (1394a21–26). They are an effective vehicle for the expression of *ēthos* (1418a17–18; cf. 1395a18–26), because they declare general preferences about the objects of *prohairesis* (1394a21–26, 1395b13–17). This kind of choice involves personal qualities of *dianoia* as well as *ēthos* (in the narrow sense). But the portrayal of rhetorical *ēthos* evidently does not require one to spell out the intellectual foundations of a choice, or even to declare a specific *prohairesis*. All that is needed is some indication of the general values by which the agent would make such a choice – it is the goal that determines the quality of *prohairesis* (1417a18). (The Socratic dialogues are accordingly granted *ēthos* on the strength of their general subject matter (1417a18–21).) Maxims are thus an effective way of indicating *prohairesis* and *ēthos* with the mimimum of intellectual articulation.

Enthymemes, which make up "the body of the proof" (1354a15), are (typically) incomplete syllogisms concerning probabilities (1356b15–17), which may use maxims for their premises and conclusions (1394a26–31).[72] Aristotle starts his discussion of maxims with an example from Euripides' *Medea*, which serves as the conclusion of an enthymeme and is expanded syllogistically by the addition of a major premise (1394a29–34, 1394b27–31). Major: one should not be lazy or envied (cf. *Medea* 296–297). (Implied minor: education makes one lazy and envied.) Conclusion: one should not educate one's children to be clever (cf. *Medea* 294–295). Such conclusions may help to reveal a speaker's *ēthos* by declaring goals of action.[73] In so far as the enthymeme articulates such goals, this kind of rhetorical *dianoia* will contribute significantly to the expression of personal *ēthos*.[74]

This kind of reasoning bears a close resemblance to the practical syllogism of the *Ethics*, which in turn is intimately connected with *phronēsis*, choice and action. *Phronēsis* guides deliberation so that it results in correct *prohairesis* and hence in right action (*NE* 1140a24–31, 1139a17–35). The practical syllogism represents the underlying structure of such thought processes, and is the form in which practical reasoning may – though it need not – be articulated.[75] Its major premise is a general statement about how one should act (*de Anima* 434a18, *NE* 1140b16–19, 1144a31–33). The minor premise concerns the particular person and situation (*de Anima* 434a18–19). The conclusion is an action (*de Motu* 701a12–23, *NE* 1147a27–28), which may or may not be accompanied by a verbal affirmation of the need to act (cf. *de Motu* 701a19–20, *NE* 1147a31–34). This process can, of course, go wrong in various ways (most of which we would expect to be pertinent to tragedy).[76] The quality of a person's deliberation, when articulated in the practical syllogism with its concluding *prohairesis* and action, reveals that person's moral character in the fullest sense, including not only the ethical excellences, but their essential intellectual accompaniment. The practical syllogism, when explicitly and publicly expressed, thus sheds light on the otherwise opaque interaction between personal *ēthos* and *dianoia*.

The similarities between the enthymeme and the practical syllogism are obvious. Enthymemes concern the things we deliberate about (*Rhetoric* 1357a1–22), and maxims – which may form the premises of enthymemes – are just the kind of general moral statements from which the practical syllogism begins. But there are also significant differences. *Phronēsis* and the practical syllogism must deal with particulars, since this is the sphere of action (*NE* 1141b14–16), and the conclusion of the practical syllogism is itself an action. Rhetoric, by contrast, is a strictly verbal performance, so the rhetorical syllogism may draw its conclusion as a general injunction. Enthymemes may thus have maxims for their conclusions as well as their premises (*Rhetoric* 1394a26–28). Medea's educational enthymeme, for example, ends with a general moral imperative: one should not educate one's children to be clever. The conclusion of the corresponding practical syllogism would be an action – that of refraining from educating one's children. The orator may wish to inspire his audience to act as a result of his syllogizing. He may even spell out a practical syllogism in which he provides the verbal correlate of the conclusion (i.e. expresses a firm intention to act). But he cannot draw a conclusion that *is* an action (though he can describe someone doing so, including himself).

The same restrictions apply to dramatic figures when they are debating or exhorting others to act. As Aristotle's own examples show, it is easy to find such enthymemes in tragedy. But since the playwright portrays people in action, it is also open to him, unlike the orator, to represent both an action and its underlying reasoning in the form of a practical syllogism. In Sophocles' *Ajax*, for example, the hero debates what course of action to pursue (457–480). He begins by posing the fundamental ethical question with which we began, "What should I do?" (457). The major premise, a maxim, is not spelled out until the end of the speech, when Ajax declares, "The well-born man should either live or die nobly" (479–480). (Compare the major premise of the practical syllogism, "a person of such a kind should do a thing of such a kind" (*de Anima* 434a18).) Ajax's intervening ruminations (457–478) spell out what amounts to two minor premises (1) I am not living nobly, and (2) I am well-born. (Compare the minor premise, "this is a thing of such a kind, and I am a person of such a kind" (*de Anima* 434a18–19).) The conclusion (this being a practical syllogism) is not verbally articulated, but is presented some 400 lines later, when the hero falls upon his sword (cf. 854). In reaching this decision, Ajax displays the kind of reasoning from moral premises to purposeful choice and action that qualifies him as the bearer of a well-articulated dramatic *ēthos*. Of course Aristotle would have been unlikely to view Ajax as a model of *phronēsis* (he disapproved of suicide (*NE* 1116a12–15, 1138a4–14), let alone attempted murder). Yet Ajax's speech well exemplifies both personal and dramatic *ēthos* and *dianoia*. For however faulty his premises or conclusion may be in Aristotelian eyes, he "makes clear" to the audience the practical reasoning upon which his decision is based, which in his own terms follows an inexorable syllogistic logic.[77]

Both enthymeme and practical syllogism may thus serve to display the presumed personal *ēthos* and *dianoia* of a dramatic speaker. At the same time, the rhetorical role of the enthymeme forges an inextricable link between *ēthos* and *dianoia* as "parts" of tragedy. Qua form of argument, enthymemes belong to the *dianoia* of the play. But they employ maxims, general statements about what is to be chosen, and are thus indicative of *prohairesis* and hence of personal *ēthos*.[78] By this means they also make the speech itself "characterful." In some cases, simple maxims or other moral statements or symptoms will suffice for characterization.[79] Indeed it is best, other things being equal, to avoid enthymemes when evoking *ēthos*, since demonstration *per se* contains neither *ēthos* nor *prohairesis* (1418a12–17; cf. 1418a37–b1). Enthymemes may also be redeployed as maxims (1418b33–38), thus minimizing the impression that one is speaking "from *dianoia*" (1417a23). But when the *prohairesis* implicit in such simple moral statements is unclear, the underlying reasoning must be spelled out: "One should make the *prohairesis* clear by the language, or if not, append the reason" (1395a26–27).[80] Sophocles "appends the reason" when he makes Antigone explain that she cares more for her brother than for a husband or children because a brother is irreplaceable (1417a27–33). This kind of quasi-syllogistic reasoning belongs to rhetorical *dianoia*, and naturally characterizes the speaker's personal *dianoia*, but it also serves to clarify *prohairesis* and hence to portray personal *ēthos*. The extent to which any given orator or dramatic character is thought to speak "as if from *dianoia*" will be determined by the explicitness and ingenuity of the reasoning.

The relevance of all this to drama is suggested not only by Aristotle's use of tragic exampla,[81] and his explicit association of dramatic *dianoia* with rhetoric, but by the way dramatic *ēthos* and *dianoia* are contrasted in the *Poetics* itself. "*Ēthos* is that [part of the play] which reveals what the *prohairesis* is like . . . whereas *dianoia* is [those parts] in which they demonstrate that something is or is not the case or declare something general" (1450b8–12). This suggests a relationship like that of the *Rhetoric*, whereby *ēthos* in a play consists primarily of declarations of *prohairesis* (by maxims or other means), while *dianoia* provides (among other things) the underlying moral reasoning. The balance between them will determine whether the *ēthos* of the speaker in question is perceived as more "characterful" or "intellectual." Less "intellectual" speakers may eschew dramatic *dianoia* altogether, or confine it to maxims.[82] But the use of more ingenious and explicit argumentation will suggest *phronēsis*, cleverness, theoretical wisdom or other intellectual qualities. When such reasoning is needed to make the *prohairesis* clear (as in the case of Antigone or Medea), then rhetorical *dianoia* becomes a vehicle for the fuller articulation of personal *ēthos* (as well as personal *dianoia*). In such cases, the *ēthos* and *dianoia* of the play will remain logically distinct, but become in practice indistinguishable.[83] It is thus quite natural for Aristotle to speak of "characterful speeches well made in diction and *dianoia*" (*Poetics* 1450a29–30).[84] Even though *ēthos* and *dianoia* are listed as two different "parts" of tragedy, it should not surprise us if they turn out not to be mutually exclusive. The six "parts" are qualitative, not quantitative (1450a8–9), and all of them may overlap. A failure to appreciate this underlies many of the misconceptions surrounding the relationship between these two crucial "parts" of tragedy.[85]

Notes

1. Cf. D. W. Lucas, ed., *Aristotle: Poetics* (Oxford, 1968) ad loc. For a full discussion of *praxis*, see D. Charles, *Aristotle's Philosophy of Action* (London, 1984).
2. On the importance of *praxis* for the logic of Aristotle's argument cf. G. F. Else, *Aristotle's Poetics: The Argument* (Cambridge, MA, 1963), 69–73, 233, 241, 247.
3. The *Ethics, Rhetoric* and *Poetics* intersect at various points, but secure relative dating is impossible (S. Halliwell, *Aristotle's Poetics* (London, 1986), 325–327). Halliwell interprets the *Poetics* in a broad Aristotelian context.
4. Conversely W. W. Fortenbaugh uses *ēthos* and *dianoia* in the *Poetics* and *Rhetoric* to try to elucidate the *Ethics* ("Un modo di affrontare la distinzione fra virtù etica e saggezza in Aristotele," *Museum Patavinum* **5** (1987) 243–258.
5. *NE* 1103a3–10, 1103a14–18, 1138b35–39a3; cf. *EE* 1220a4–6. Health etc. are also excellences (cf. *Rhetoric* 1362b12–18), but human excellence as such is that of the soul, not the body (*NE* 1102a16–17; cf. 1097b33–98a4).
6. Cf. *NE* 1098a4–5, 1102b13–3a10, *EE* 1220a10–11, *EE* 1220b5–7 (with C. Chamberlain, "Why Aristotle called ethics ethics: the definition of *ēthos* in *Eudemian Ethics* 2.2," *Hermes* **112** (1984) 176–183).
7. *NE* 1107a1, 1144b21–24, 1144b30–32, 1178a16–19. On *phronēsis* and its role in deliberation and choice cf. L. H. G. Greenwood, *Aristotle: Nicomachean Ethics Book Six* (Cambridge, 1909), 48–59; R. Sorabji, "Aristotle on the role of intellect in virtue," in Rorty (1980) 205–214; and see further W. F. R. Hardie, *Aristotle's Ethical Theory*, 2nd edn (Oxford, 1980), Ch. 11 and 386–396; N. Sherman, *The Fabric of Character* (Oxford, 1989), Ch. 3; S. Broadie, *Ethics with Aristotle* (Oxford, 1991), Ch. 4.
8. Cf. *NE* 1144a13–20, 1152a15–17, 1163a21–23, *EE* 1228a3–4, 1228a12–21, 1243b9–10, *Topics* 126a35, *Rhetoric* 1367b21–26, 1374b13–14, 1374a9–18, 1368b12–14.
9. 1144b1–17; cf. 1139a17–b5, 1144a6–22, 1144a36–b1, 1144b32–45a6 (for "complete" excellence cf. also 1098a16–18, 1102a5–6). See further Sorabji in Rorty (1980), 201–205. The role of intellect in *prohairesis* is neglected by Fortenbaugh, *Museum Patavinum* 5 (1987). G. F. Held appreciates it ("The meaning of *ēthos* in the

'Poetics'," *Hermes* **113** (1985), 285, 291), but not its implications for *ēthos* in the *Ethics* (cf. E. Schütrumpf, "The meaning of *ēthos* in the *Poetics* – a reply," *Hermes* **115** (1987) 179).

10. See E. Schütrumpf, *Die Bedeutung des Wortes ēthos in der Poetik des Aristoeles* (Munich, 1970), 2–6, 26–28.

11. For the background see O. Thimme, *Phusis Tropos Ethos* (diss. Göttingen, 1935); C. Chamberlain, "From 'haunts' to 'character': the meaning of *ēthos* and its relation to ethics," *Helios* **11** (1984) 97–108; and for intellectual qualities, Held (1985), 290. For the novelty of Aristotle's narrower usage see Schütrumpf (1970), 33–34, 36–38.

12. *Spoudaios* and *phaulos* (1448a2) are common synonyms for *agathos* and *kakos*, and can include intellectual qualities (Held, 1985, 285–287). An ethical interpretation of the value terms in the *Poetics* is now widely accepted. See e.g. C. H. Reeves, "The Aristotelian concept of the tragic hero," *American Journal of Philology* **73** (1952) 172–188; Schütrumpf (1970), 52–63; Halliwell, *Aristotle's Poetics*, 153–154.

13. Cf. also Schütrumpf, *Hermes* **115** (1987) 175–176.

14. Here I agree broadly with Held, pace e.g. A. M. Dale, *Collected Papers* (Cambridge, 1969), 143, and Schütrumpf (1970), 52–63, *Hermes* **115** (1987), who exclude intellectual qualities from dramatic *ēthos* altogether.

15. See Schütrumpf (1970), 51–52.

16. Aristotle does require dramatic characters to be good (1454a16–19; cf. 1448a17–18, 1454b8–9), but they should not be perfect (1453a7–9, 16–17), and may even be bad if strictly necessary (cf. 1454a28–29).

17. Cf. Held (1985), 282–283. Schütrumpf (1970) 126, *Hermes* **115** (1987) 177–179 is unconvincing on this point.

18. On its content, see Lucas, *Aristotle: Poetics*, ad loc.

19. For the various "lives" cf. *EE* 1215a26–b5, *NE* 1095b14–96a10, *Politics* 1324a25–35. Euripides' lost tragedy *Antiope* compared the active and contemplative lives.

20. Cf. the use of mathematical and other abstract arguments in the Socratic dialogues, a genre which does have goals and hence *ēthos* (*Rhetoric* 1417a18–20).

21. An analytical purpose also lies behind most uses of the dichotomy in the *Politics* (cf. 1281b7, 1323b3, 1337a38–39, 1338b4–6).

22. Cf. Held (1985) 283–284 (though contra Held I take *ēthē* in 1450a5 to be parts of plays, not persons; so does Schutrümpf (1970) 90, *Hermes*, **115** (1987) 177).

23. This distinction also helps to explain how there can be "characterless' tragedies (1450a23–27). *Praxis* cannot (logically) take place without some qualities of *ēthos* in the agent. (This is the meaning of 1449b37, not – pace e.g. Lucas, *Aristotle: Poetics*, on 1450a24 – that dramatic figures are inescapably characterized.) But a dramatist may show people in action without clarifying their *prohairesis*. *Ēthos* can thus be both intrinsic to drama yet sometimes missing. Cf. also Else, *Aristotle's Poetics*, 456–457, Halliwell, *Aristotle's Poetics*, 149, 152–153.

24. Cf. Schütrumpf, *Hermes*, **115** (1987) 177. Aristotle is purportedly categorizing the "parts" of tragedy, not of persons, yet such "parts" cannot themselves be the *objects* of imitation. He must therefore mean "parts" derived from/representing personal *ēthos* and *dianoia*.

25. Cf. I. Bywater, *Aristotle on the Art of Poetry* (Oxford, 1909) on 1450a6; contra e.g. Dale, *Collected Papers*, 149, G. F. Else, *Plato and Aristotle on Poetry* (Chapel Hill, NC, 1986), 118–119, 121–122.

26. My argument here implies a substantial overlap between dramatic *ēthos* and *dianoia*. I shall return to this point below.

27. A. M. Dale (ed.) *Euripides: Alcestis* (Oxford, 1954), xxvii. Cf. also *Rhetoric* 1355b10–11, 1396b1–6.

28. For "appropriateness" as a criterion for qualities of *ēthos* in the *Rhetoric*, cf. 1387a27–

32, 1389a29–b2, 1390b6–9, 1394a20–21, 1395a2–8, 1408a26, 1418a39–b1, 1419b6–7. I shall discuss rhetorical *ēthos* further below.

29. Cf. M. W. Blundell, *Helping Friends and Harming Enemies* (Cambridge, 1989), 23–24. Another Aristotelian constraint on the "rhetoric of the situation" is the need to avoid resentment by portraying oneself as virtuous (*Rhetoric* 1418b24–33; contrast Dale, *Euripides: Alcestis*, xxviii).

30. *Rhetoric* 1366a14–17, 1395b13–14, 1417a15–26; cf. also 1367b21–26.

31. The orator makes different use of his own *ēthos* and that of others, but they cover the same range of traits and are portrayed by the same means (cf. 1366a23–28, 1378a16–19, 1417b7–8). There is thus no reason to deny (pace Lucas, *Aristotle: Poetics*, on *Poetics* 1450b9) that here too *ēthos* is connected with *prohairesis*.

32. For this unqualified use of *aretē* cf. e.g. *NE* 1145a4–5, *Politics* 1253a34–35, 1281b4–7, 1323b33, 1339a21–24. Cf. also the use of *ēthos* for the immature character of the young, which still awaits rational development (*NE* 1179b7–10, 29–31; cf. *EE* 1236a40).

33. *Rhetoric* 1366b20–22, *NE* 1140a24–31; cf. also *Rhetoric* 1364b11–19, *NE* 1106b36–7a2.

34. Cf. *NE* 1141b3–42a10, *Politics*, 1289a10–13.

35. *NE* 1141b8–12; cf. 1139a11–14, 1140a24–b4, *Rhetoric* 1366b20–22.

36. For calculation as a function of intellect cf. *NE* 1139a11–15.

37. My uses of the generic "man" and "he" in this paper reflect not only the status of the Greek masculine as the unmarked gender, but Aristotle's own assumption that the male is the complete human being, and the male sex of classical Greek playwrights and orators. Aristotle does use female tragic figures as illustrations in the *Rhetoric, Ethics* and *Poetics*, but to render his masculine forms as "he or she" is to give credit where it is not due.

38. Cf. Held (1985), 292.

39. Even the "unintellectual" *prohairesis* of 1417a24–25 actually contains a germ of moral reasoning ("I wished this; indeed I chose it; even though I did not benefit, it was the better course").

40. Achilles is not named, but there is an unmistakable allusion to his choice between a long and commonplace life and a brief but glorious one.

41. Cf. 1355a24–29, 1357a1–4, 1395b24–96a2, 1404a7–8, 1415b1–8, 1417a35–36.

42. Further constraints are imposed by the rhetorical circumstances – for example whether the speech is deliberative or judicial (cf. 1414a7–17 with E. M. Cope and J. E. Sandys (eds), *The Rhetoric of Aristotle* (Cambridge, 1877) ad loc.).

43. Cf. Else, *Aristotle's Poetics*, 241–242, 244; Schütrumpf (1970), 89–90, *Hermes* **115** (1987) 177; Halliwell, *Aristotle's Poetics*, 151–152.

44. Cf. *NE* 1178a28–34, *EE* 1228a15–18, Sherman (1989), 20 n. 14.

45. Compare e.g. Odysseus in Sophocles' *Ajax* and *Philoctetes*, Creon in *Oedipus the King, Antigone* and *Oedipus at Colonus*, Agamemnon in Aeschylus' *Agamemnon* and Sophocles' *Ajax*. Obviously no personal *ēthos* at all can be presupposed for entirely new characters, or those for whom tradition supplies only a name (cf. *Poetics* 1451b19–21, 1455a34–b13).

46. Some editors exclude 1450b9–10, but see contra Schütrumpf (1970) 92 n. 4; *Hermes* **115** (1987) 177 n. 11; Halliwell, *Aristotle's Poetics*, 152 n. 20.

47. Similarly *dianoia* is *articulated* argument (below, p. 167). On maxims see further below, p. 168.

48. Education is not confined to the intellectual virtues (cf. *NE* 1128a19–27), but certainly includes them (cf. *Politics* 1338b4–6, *NE* 1094b23–28, 1103a14–17).

49. See E. M. Cope, *An Introduction to Aristotle's Rhetoric* (London, 1867), 212–218; Schütrumpf (1970) 76 n. 1; and cf. *MM* 1197a16, 1185b9–12.

50. Rhetoric has a further relationship to action, in that it is normally designed to elicit action from its audience. Drama too may mold character and hence action (cf. Halliwell, *Aristotle's Poetics*, Ch. 6), but less immediately than oratory.

51. Cf. 1386a25, 1388b31–34, 1396b33–34, 1408a25–30.

52. Cope/Sandys, *The Rheotoric of Aristotle*, III. 193 (original emphasis). Cope's commentary makes it clear that he is speaking not of character types but of "the characteristic peculiarities of *individuals*' (original emphasis).

53. For some recent contributions to this vast controversy see C. B. R. Pelling (ed.), *Characterization and Individuality in Greek Literature* (Oxford, 1990).

54. E. Garver, however, argues that the entire treatment of the emotions pertains to *eunoia* ("Aristotle's *Rhetoric* II: deliberative rationality and the emotions," unpublished).

55. The relevance of these to *ēthos* will be discussed further below.

56. Cf. 1386a24–25, where *ēthos* is listed in parallel with such factors.

57. Cf. e.g. 1369a7–30, 1390b14–21, 1390b32–91b7. An exception is the single passage of the *Poetics* where *ēthos* seems to mean *dramatis persona* (1460a9–11). This is best explained as a natural extension of meaning from *ēthos* to its bearers (cf. Bywater, *Aristotle on the Art of Poetry*, on 1454a23).

58. In the *Eudemian Ethics* these lack *prohairesis*, and are therefore not strictly excellences, but they are still related to *ēthos* in the broad sense, for they contribute to the "natural" excellences (*EE* 1234a24–34).

59. Accordingly the orator's delivery will help to convey his *ēthos* (W. W. Fortenbaugh, "Aristotle's Platonic attitude towards delivery," *Philosophy and Rhetoric* **19** (1986) 243–244.

60. Schütrumpf (1970) 30 points out that the piety which is an attribute of *ēthos* in the *Rhetoric* (1391b1–4) has no connection with the *Ethics*. But although this piety is quite different from that of the *Ethics* (cf. *NE* 1179a22–24), it is still a disposition (cf. *Rhetoric* 1391b3), and as such not different in kind from other aspects of *ēthos* in the broadest sense. Moreover conventional religious projects are among the expenditures of the "magnificent" man (*NE* 1122b19–21).

61. *Rhetoric* 2.1–11; cf. also 1386b10–13, 1386b26–34, 1408a16–19.

62. Cf. e.g. *Rhetoric* 1356a10, 1403b11, 18; *Poetics* 1449b37, 1450a1, 5, 19; *EE* 1228a3–4; *Politics* 1340a8. It is also used of the emotional "proof," which renders the hearer "of a certain kind" (*Rhetoric* 1354b20; cf. 1356a3). The present passage, however, concerns the representation of emotion rather than the feelings of the audience (though of course the two are related).

63. The section as a whole concerns signs of emotion, and the second *kai* in 1417b7 ("yourself as well") confirms that this is what Aristotle has in mind (if the text is sound: this *kai* does not appear in all mss.).

64. Pace Lucas, *Aristotle: Poetics*, 107. As Aristotle says, such characterization should be done subtly, so as to "escape the notice" of the hearer (*Rhetoric* 1417b8).

65. See E. Wolf, *Sentenz und Reflexion bei Sophokles* (Leipzig, 1910), 48–53, 126–131.

66. So e.g. Dale, *Collected Papers*, 150.

67. On the meaning of *logos* and demonstration here see W. M. A. Grimaldi, *Aristotle, Rhetoric I: A Commentary* (New York, 1980), ad loc.

68. Cf. Fortenbaugh, *Museum Patavinum* **5** (1987) 246–247.

69. The arousal of emotion is included, since Aristotle does not treat it as a "part" of tragedy (though he might well have done: see *Poetics* xiv). But only here does it join demonstration and maxim as a function of dramatic *dianoia*.

70. Some carelessness here is suggested by the unexpected inclusion of exaggeration and depreciation under *dianoia* (cf. Else, *Aristotle's Poetics*, 564).

71. This is, of course, Aristotle's judgment (as I interpret it), which need not coincide with that of a Greek audience of the fifth or any other century.
72. For the difficulty of defining enthymemes see E. H. Madden, "The enthymeme: crossroads of logic, rhetoric and metaphysics," *Philosophical Review* **61** (1952) 368–376; L. Bitzer, "Aristotle's enthymeme revisited," *Quarterly Journal of Speech* **45** (1959) 399–408; W. M. A. Grimaldi, *Studies in the Philosophy of Aristotle's Rhetoric, Hermes Einzelschriften* **25** (Wiesbaden, 1972), Ch. 3.
73. Not all gnomic enthymemes have such clear implications for action. E.g. major: we are all slaves to money or chance; conclusion: no one is free (1394b4–6).
74. For the ethical implications of the enthymeme cf. 1358a12–17 and see J. H. McBurney, "The place of the enthymeme in rhetorical theory," in K. V. Erickson (ed.) *Aristotle: The Classical Heritage of Rhetoric* (Metuchen, NJ, 1974), 128–130; Grimaldi, *Studies in the Philosophy of Aristotle's Rhetoric*, 136–151; E. Garver, "Making discourse ethical: the lessons of Aristotle's *Rhetoric*," *Proceedings of the Boston Area Colloquium in Ancient Philosophy* **5** (1990) 73–96.
75. See further e.g. D. J. Allan, "The practical syllogism," *Autour d' Aristote* (Louvain, 1955); Hardie, *Aristotle's Ethical Theory*, Ch. 12 and 396–401; and above, n. 7.
76. Cf. *NE* 1142a20–23, 1142b20–33, 1144a31–36, 1146b35–47a10, 1147a25–35.
77. Another good example is Medea's decision to kill her children (*Medea* 1042–1080). In this case wickedness distorts the goal, so that cleverness leads to a corrupt *prohairesis* (pace Lucas, *Aristotle: Poetics*, 107, 108) and villainous action (cf. *NE* 1144a23–b1, *Rhetoric* 1417a18). See further G. Rickert, "Akrasia and Euripides' *Medea*," HSCP **91** (1987) 91–117.
78. Cf. Fortenbaugh, *Museum Patavinum* **5** (1987) 247–248. The claims that maxims in tragedy express *dianoia* "rather than" *ēthos* (S. H. Butcher, *Aristotle's Theory of Poetry and Fine Art*, 4th edn (New York, 1911), 339 n.; cf. Dale, *Collected Papers*, 150), and that maxims expressive of *ēthos* are not part of *dianoia* (T. G. Rosenmeyer, "Aristotelian ethos and character in modern drama," *Proceedings of the IXth Congress of the International Comparative Literature Association* **1** (Innsbruck, 1981, 124 n. 15), seem to be based alike on the arbitrary assumption that *ēthos* and *dianoia* in drama are mutually exclusive.
79. *Prohairesis* and hence *ēthos* may even be expressed through action alone (*Poetics* 1454a17–19; cf. 1454a35–36, *EE* 1228a15–18).
80. Cf. 1357a7–10, 1394b27–29, 1417b16–20.
81. Four of the maxims quoted at *Rhetoric* 1394a26–b6 are from Euripides.
82. Dramatic *dianoia* is by definition verbal (1450a6–7, 1450b4–7, 1456a36–37), but one vexed passage suggests that it may also take the form of action (1456b2–8). Aristotle is probably speaking loosely here, with reference to the so-called "rhetoric of action" (e.g. Bywater, *Aristotle on the Art of Poetry*, on 1456b2) which can produce e.g. emotional effects.
83. Cf. Dale, *Collected Papers*, 153; B. R. Rees, "Plot, character and thought," *Le Monde Grec: Hommages à Claire Préaux*, eds J. Bingen *et al.* (Brussels, 1975), 196; Halliwell, *Aristotle's Poetics*, 155–156; Fortenbaugh, *Museum Patavinum* **5** (1987) 245–246. Most critics, however, assume that Aristotle located the two "parts" in discrete parts of the text.
84. I follow here Vahlen's widely accepted emendation. For a defense of the MS. reading, see Else, *Aristotle's Poetics*, 258 n. 131.
85. I am grateful to Amélie Oksenberg Rorty for urging me to write this paper and guiding its development, and to the following for generously reading and commenting on an earlier draft with little or no advance notice: Eugene Garver, Michael Halleran, Stephen Halliwell, David Keyt and Thomas Rosenmeyer.

Hamartia and Virtue

Nancy Sherman

> Being alive
> Is when each moment's a new start, with past
> And future shuffled between fingers
> For a new game. I'm dealing out
> My hand to them, one more new botched beginning
> There, where we still stand talking in the quad.
> ("One more New Botched Beginning", by Stephen Spender)

Look, a cantaloupe is a hard thing to buy – maybe the hardest thing there is to buy, when you stop to think about it. A cantaloupe isn't an apple, you know, where you can tell from the outside what's going on inside. I'd rather buy a car than a cantaloupe – I'd rather buy a *house* than a cantaloupe. If one time in ten I come away from the store with a decent cantaloupe, I consider myself lucky. I smell it, sniff it, press both ends with my thumb.

I'll tell you about making a mistake with a cantaloupe: *we all do it*. We weren't *made* to buy cantaloupe. Do me a favor, Herm, get off the woman's [back], because it isn't just Lil's weakness buying a cantaloupe: *it's a human weakness*.

> (from *Patrimony: A True Story*, by Philip Roth)

I. Introduction

What nags us in thinking about Aristotle's *Poetics* is that like the tragic protagonist, we too can unwittingly cause our own undoing. Through our own agency, we can bring about our downfall. That we are not in full control of our happiness is a familiar theme in Aristotle's theory of human action. Living well is always subject to contingency and the unexpected. As such, happiness is a matter of both virtuous agency *and* luck. Our capacity for virtuous agency is itself in no small part a matter of luck. But what engages us most as tragic spectators is not simply luck. It is not what befalls the protagonist, either in terms of the hand dealt or the crossroads faced. Rather, it is how the tragic figure contributes to her own misfortune. Even where the action is performed under duress as the

177

result of an external conflict, agency (or causal responsibility) is still implicated.[1] It is agency, or better, failed agency, that draws us in. The point is that individuals make mistakes (*hamartiai*), largely unavoidable, that bring incurable suffering to themselves and those they love. Tragedy works through the agent's own hands. It is a mimetic representation not merely of suffering, but of action.[2] The task of this paper is to explore the nature of tragic mistakes and their relation to the spectators' propensity for pity.

In thinking about *hamartia*, one contrast Aristotle has in mind is reasonably straightforward: the tragic hero is not simply the victim of arbitrary fate or irrational accident.[3] An individual may suffer harm because a tile falls on his head, or even cause harm because his spear hits a spectator who, without warning, runs into its trajectory, or an abnormal gust of wind carries his arrow off course mortally wounding his lover, or the safety catch on the catapult he is using breaks. These are cases of misfortune or bad luck. In some cases they are unlucky coincidences. But they are not the stuff of tragedy. For the *arche* (origin) of the cause of those ill-effects is outside the agent.[4] One is a victim, not an agent. Tragedy, in contrast, is about human action, its circumstances and errors.

It is true, accidents are often like mistaken choices. In both cases one may end up missing the target. Indeed, in Greek, the word *hamartia* is rooted in the notion of missing the mark (*hamartanein*), and covers a broad spectrum that includes accident and mistake,[5] as well as wrongdoing, error, or sin.[6] And Aristotle himself uses the full range. Moreover, certain accidents work through an agent's hands more than others. I pull the drawer out in the usual, unproblematic way and it unexpectedly falls on my leg; I walk over a floorboard and it breaks beneath me; I drop the gun (which I take to be unloaded as it always is) and blow off my daughter's foot; I hurl the spear which wounds my lover. In such cases, I trigger the accident. Unlike walking beneath a falling tile, or being hurled by the wind, I set the chain of events in motion. But still, the overall flavor is happenstance: an agent happens to be doing something at an unpropitious moment.[7]

Tragic *hamartia*, in contrast, focuses on agency. The protagonist is not simply a victim of nature's caprices or faulty mechanics. Rather what matters is that the agent chooses,[8] yet chooses in a way that leads to calamity. The choice goes awry because of ignorance or misjudgment that are *in principle* more within human control than sudden gusts of wind. This need not imply culpability; to be the cause of harm, either through act or omission, may be neither sufficient nor necessary for moral liability.[9] Still it does point to a class of impediments that are internal to the conditions of human agency. On the Aristotelian model, belief and desire together inform choice. More or less innocent defects in either can precipitate disastrous decisions. It is limitations endemic to arriving at a wise choice that yield tragic reversals. So, in self-defense, Oedipus intentionally kills the stranger, and unwittingly becomes a parricide. He mistakes an identity that someone with a more privileged perspective might have gotten right. Phaedra's reluctant choice not to keep silent about her love for her stepson, Hippolytus, is presented as more of a dilemma about what to do, for she is aware in advance of the dangers of baring one's soul to those whose confidence has not been tested. Unlike Oedipus, hers is not a case of mistaken identity (literally, of taking one person for another), but of questionable judgment (of error). Whereas Oedipus makes a mistake, Phaedra errs. But whatever the difference, in each case the agent is causally responsible for the disaster that results. The calamity is made intelligible (rationalized) by some aspect of the agent's own choice. Moreover, the choice has something to do with a condition of character or agency – ignorance, interest, past judgments, passion, and so on. This connection between character, agency, and tragic choice is among the topics I shall be exploring.[10]

In probing the connection between ignorance, choice, and character, I may appear to be reviving the Renaissance and later, Victorian orthodoxy of *hamartia* as "tragic flaw."[11] On this view, the tragic hero comes to ruin through a "great wrongdoing or sin" (*di'hamartian megalen* 1453a16). In short, tragedy comes to embrace the spirit of retribution: having sinned, the protagonist is punished for his errant ways. From the perspective of the spectator, potential feelings of indignation at the sight of wrongdoing and hubris are quieted upon witnessing the punitive effects of self-wrought ruin.

As it happens, I have little interest in restoring this moralistic interpretation. It has little fit with the text of the *Poetics*, and makes fatally wrong turns at crucial moments. As an interpretation of Aristotle's paradigmatic tragedy, *Oedipus Tyrannus*, it fails dismally. It is implausible to claim that Oedipus' illusions about his family identity could have been avoided; that there was information of which he could have availed himself. No one in the play reproaches Oedipus (despite the earnest efforts of critics to find a character flaw in his curiosity, anger, pride, and so on), and in the *Oedipus Colonus*, Oedipus insists he is innocent, that he erred unwillingly.[12]

The alternative notion of *hamartia* as a "mistake of fact" is not a perfect fit either. It may be the right gloss for *Oedipus*, but it works less well for many of the tragedies in the corpus, including those to which Aristotle directly appeals. Brief consideration of the notion of *akrasia* may be instructive here.[13] An explanation of the phenomenon in terms of ignorance of the minor premise (i.e. of the relevant circumstantial facts) is not always apt or adequate. Even where it has a certain plausibility, (as in the case of someone knowing drinking and driving don't mix, but yet failing to see that imbibing this much here and now will adversely affect her driving), we want to know why she failed to apply the principle, what obscured her vision, what beliefs and desires weighed on the other side, how in general, ignorance or misperception relates to aspects of character, such as belief, desire, emotion, and memory. In a comparable way, tragic ignorance does not simply descend upon a character like a sudden blanket of fog. It involves a construal or misconstrual that often has a history in the ends and interests of a character. It is not simply a cognitive matter. Though culpability may be quite different in the cases of tragic *hamartia* and *akrasia*,[14] in both the notion of mistake of fact is at times too sterile, at other times, too restrictive to explain the variety of mistaken choices.

What I shall be suggesting is a range of ways in which tragic characters can err. Like others, I find systematic support in Aristotle's reminder in the *Nicomachean Ethics* that while there is only one way to hit the mark, there are many ways to fall short of it.[15] Still, the point of tragedy is not simply to bear witness to largely innocent but disastrous errors. Its design, Aristotle urges, is for the end of producing tragic pleasure, itself dependent upon the spectator's cathartic experience of pity and fear.[16] For this end, innocent mistakes of fact that bring a character down are not the only means. Pity is directed at undeserved suffering;[17] an agent who is not entirely faultless, but yet who suffers more than her error warrants may appropriately elicit our pity. To concede this does not require a theory of tragic flaw or poetic justice.

This in a rough way sets out the problems. We want to know what the range of tragic mistakes or errors is. And we want to know in what sense pity is an appropriate response to them. But before continuing, I want to comment briefly about the framework in which I place a study of the *Poetics*.[18]

There is no question that Aristotle intended the *Poetics* to form part of an extended inquiry into the nature of human action and happiness. "Tragedy," Aristotle states in the definition of *Poetics* 6, is

> a representation not of human beings but of action and life. Happiness and unhappiness lie in action, and the end [of life] is a sort of action, not a quality; people are of a certain sort according to their characters, but happy or the opposite according to their actions. So [the actors] do not act in order to represent the characters, but they include the characters for the sake of their actions. Consequently the incidents, i.e., the plot, are the end of tragedy, and the end is most important of all (1450a16–23).[19]

There is an obvious analogy with Aristotle's remarks in the *Nicomachean Ethics*. Plot is the most important element of tragedy because it represents the sort of structured action which we know from the *Nicomachean Ethics* constitutes the ultimate end for a human being, namely happiness. While character states make action intelligible, it is not their possession but exercise that is essential for *eudaimonia*. The primacy of excellent activity in the happy life entails that serious and great impediments can frustrate even the virtuous person's realization of happiness. Recovery in a life may be possible, but only after a long and complete period of time in which there have been "many fine successes."[20] Thus, the misfortunes Priam suffers at the end of his life derail his chances for happiness. Granted, truly fine characters may not become morally wretched (*athlios*) as the result of suffering even the most horrible disasters; they bear their misfortune nobly.[21] But still their happiness is vulnerable. In a comparable way, tragedy reveals the dependence of happiness upon successful action. Goodness is not sufficient for happiness.

Thus, I join others in viewing tragic error as an illustration of the fragility of the good life.[22] Aristotle assumes that virtuous individuals have neither divine exemption from contingency nor a stoic attitude toward suffering and disturbance. But as I have been arguing, tragic erors, unlike other impediments that frustrate well-intentioned plans, are impediments of which the agent is the cause. It is in this area of mitigated responsibility that the *Poetics* can contribute to the general discussion of moral luck.[23]

II. *Hamartia* Within the *Poetics*

Despite a long tradition of lively interest within the secondary literature on the notion of *hamartia*, the term itself receives surprisingly little treatment in the *Poetics*. It is introduced rather inconspicuously in Chapter 13 within a discussion of the sort of reversals (*peripeteiai*) that best arouse pity and fear. The question posed is, who is the most appropriate sort of character to suffer the reversals that will excite tragic emotions? Aristotle proceeds eliminatively, as he often does in this treatise. Here is our central text from *Poetics* 13:

> First, it is clear that decent men should not appear undergoing a change from good to bad fortune, for that is not fearful nor pitiable either, but morally repugnant. Nor should wicked men move from bad fortune to good, for this is the most untragic form of all, since it has nothing of what it should, being productive of neither ordinary sympathy, nor of pity nor of fear. Nor again should it show a thoroughly wicked person falling from good fortune to bad. That kind of structure will excite our sense of what is humane [24][*philanthropon*] but neither pity nor fear, for pity is directed toward a person who suffers undeservedly and fear towards someone like ourselves. So that the outcome will be neither pitiable nor terrifying. What is left is the person who falls between these extremes. Such a person is one who neither surpasses [us] in virtue and justice, nor who undergoes a change to misfortune because of evil or wickedness, but who falls because of some error [*hamartian tina*], and who is one of those persons who stand in great repute and prosperity, such as Oedipus and Thyestes, and [other] renowned men from those kinds of families.
>
> Necessarily, then, the finely constructed plot . . . involves a change that moves not from bad fortune to good fortune, but the other way round, from good fortune to bad, not because of evil, but because of a serious error [*di'hamartian megalen*] by a person either like the one mentioned or by someone who is better than worse. (1452b35–53a18)[25]

What is striking is that Aristotle offers no technical definition of the term. In stark contrast to the renderings of reversal and recognition in the chapters before, *hamartia* is slipped in without technical coinage. Still, in light of these chapters, the idea is clear enough that *hamartia* will serve as the causal link that moves the protagonist from ignorance to recognition, and from fortune to ruin. It is the mechanism that initiates the movements of reversal and recognition. "Reversal is a movement or shift [*metabole*] from what is being undertaken to its opposite" (1452a25–27). "Recognition is the movement [*metabole*] from ignorance to knowledge" whereby the protagonist becomes aware of actual or prospective reversals (1452a33). *Hamartia* triggers the reversal which exposes the severity and calamity of the error.[26] An example will illustrate. In the *Trachiniae*, Deianeira's error in mistaking a garment soaked in posion for one soaked in a love charm, is exposed once her unwitting choice (*hamartia*) brings about its disastrous consequences. As her loved one Heracles dons the robe and is consumed by its poison, she brutally recognizes what she has wrought and what she must suffer. The tragic choice precipitates an epistemic change and change of fortune.

The immediate context of *Poetics* 13 is, of course, a broad taxonomy of character types. This has led many down the garden path of associating *hamartia* with a character flaw. But this hardly follows. The point of introducing degrees of virtue and vice in a character is to set constraints on the sort of character who can commit *hamartia* and yet still evoke our pity and fear. Indeed, the whole thrust of the passage is the elicitation of emotions. The claim is that if it were the pre-eminently virtuous who fell, our overwhelming feelings would be of moral disgust and outrage (*miaron*), not pity. We would be offended by the apparent irrationality and senselessness of the downfall. At stake is not some unshakeable belief that the supremely virtuous are exempt from mistake or error – that they are infallible. Rather, it is that within the context of the play, such error is simply not plausible or persuasive. Like caprice or accident, it is unaccountable, unrooted in character and past action. It is still arguable that pity might be the initial response to such a fall and to such an agent. But at some point, pity would appear to yield to moral outrage, the more virtuous the agent and the more undeserving her suffering.[27]

The nugget of the passage, then, is that the ruin of a very good person excites moral outrage; the downfall of someone evil evokes our sense of justice and human satisfaction (*philanthropon*) in witnessing deserved suffering; his rise, again our sense of moral outrage and anger. To feel pity and fear, in contrast, we need to see characters on stage who can err and suffer consequences without our being morally shocked by either the senselessness of the error or the disproportion between it and the calamity. And this requires characters who are more good than bad, but who nonetheless fall short of full perfection. Moreoever, since we tend to perceive ourselves as decent, such characters remind us of ourselves and of our own fallibility. The ability to imagine ourselves in similar straits is requisite for feeling pity: "And in general we feel pity whenever we are in the condition of remembering that similar misfortunes have happened to us or ours, or of expecting them to happen in the future."[28] Still, pity as Aristotle here intends it, is essentially other-regarding – an attending to the suffering of another – in virtue of the capacity to put ourselves in that other's shoes. Fear, in contrast, is self-regarding. We fear for our own lives in virtue of witnessing what others endure.[29]

The literary demand that character be tailored to meet the requirements of pity echoes more general remarks about pity and indignation (*nemesis*) in *Rhetoric* II.8 and 9. The agenda there is naturally different from that of the *Poetics*. There is no mention of the undeserving loss that the pre-eminently virtuous might suffer, or the appropriate response to it. Indignation or *nemesis*, a less virulent emotion than moral outrage, is restricted to the undeserved ascent of the unworthy, and pity, as before, to the undeserved fall of the decent. Still, there is sufficient overlap for the discussion to be instructive about the conditions under which pity is elicited.

We can think of indignation as an emotional protest against prosperity earned through wrongdoing or pretense. In one set of cases, Aristotle suggests, it is a protest against those who have an inflated sense of superiority, brought on by presumptions of new wealth or power, or other sudden changes in status.[30] The protest, registered by those who are deserving or good, is accompanied by a wish to see the undeserving individual defeated and "cut down to size."[31] Moreover, it is a feeling that may be experienced both by one who is directly wounded by another's wrongdoing and gain, as well as by a spectator who from a third person perspective witnesses an offense that yields a morally, illegitimate profit.

Pity, like indignation, according to Aristotle in the *Rhetoric*, is a response toward what is undeserved, specifically, undeserved loss. It "is a feeling of pain at an apparent evil, destructive or painful, which befalls one who does not deserve it, and which we might expect to befall ourselves or some friend of ours, and moreoever to befall us soon" (1385b11–15). Various emotions associated with particular character tendencies and beliefs tend to mitigate against pity.[32] To the *Poetics*' account is thus added the subjective conditions that constrain how an object of the emotions comes to be construed. So, it is argued, pity is unlikely to be felt by those who imagine themselves excessively fortunate, for insolence and security (*hubris*) armor them against the thought of defeat.[33] Similarly, beliefs about one's invincibility and superiority, expressed perhaps by feelings of confidence and militant anger, make it difficult to take seriously the prospect of future misfortune.[34] The thought that "evil cannot strike here" impedes pity, and may encourage further feelings of hostility and denial when it does strike. But equally, excessive fear stifles pity, for it leaves the respondent more self-absorbed in her own circumstances than sympathetic to another's plight.[35] Those who feel pity, Aristotle says, "are between these two extremes." They neither fear in a paralyzing way nor are overly optimistic or dogmatic about what the future may bring. Moderate fear, in contrast, seems to facilitate pity, and is of course fundamental to the cathartic response. Without stifling other-regard, it is an express acknowledgment, close to home, of human vulnerability. Aristotle adds that those who express appropriate pity are not subject to the easy cynicism that "no one is good and that everyone deserves evil fortune" (1386a1). "They must believe that there are some people who are decent" (*ton epieikon*)[36] who may suffer undeservedly. And they must see themselves as among these.

The overall account is a crucial supplement to the enigmatic and brief mention of *hamartia* in the *Poetics*. It confirms the Aristotelian concern for tracking down the conditions conducive to pity, and implies, that the connection between a character's *hamartia* and diminished virtue has more to do with these conditions than with any implicit imputation of culpability in the one who commits *hamartia*.

These remarks also put into perspective Aristotle's response to Plato. In the *Republic*, Plato is concerned with the question of justice, and to a certain extent, poetic justice too. Paideia through the arts requires moralizing: the supremely virtuous must not fall, the vicious must not succeed; in some way or other justice must pay, even if not in Thrasymachean currency. The depiction of divine as well as human action must provide paradigm cases of justice and its rewards. Venerated texts that fail in this regard must be ruthlessly censored. Censorship must be applied too to texts which evoke the more "cowardly" responses of lamentation and grief. These worries are clearly not Aristotle's. He has little interest in moral censorship, and less interest in banning works that provoke affective responses to loss and suffering. Indeed, any hint of moralizing in the *Poetics* is the coincidental effect of an independent concern to design tragedies that arouse precisely the pleasure intrinsic to experiencing pity and fear. In staging optimal conditions for experiencing painful emotions and for enjoying their subsequent relief, Aristotle pays little homage to Plato.

We have discussed at some length the requirement of diminished virtue. Apart from this requirement, however, the nature of the *hamartia* that leads to disaster is left open, and indeed, indefinite. The cause of the fall is *some* error (*hamartian tina* 1453a10) that at very least, is not rooted in malice. But there are foolishnesses that fall short of evil or wrongdoing, self-deceptions that distort, good principles which must, on occasion, yield to others. The sort of errors that can bring an agent down are indefinite and numerous; there are many ways to err, but only way one to get it right.[37] Granted, considerations of pity and fear already restrict *who* can make the error, but not what sort of error they can make. And Oedipus' error, while often relied upon as paradigmatic, is by no means the only kind of *hamartia* Aristotle is willing to entertain. On a more speculative note, there may even be a kind of ignorance in knowingly killing one's own children, as Medea or Agamemnon does. For though each brings about the plan they intend, there are consequences of that plan that are knowable yet are shut out to them by their own myopia, such as, just what values they destroy by the actions they commit. We shall return to the variety of error in tragedy. But before doing so I want to consider the relation of culpability and pardon to *hamartia*.

III. Hamartia in the Ethical Context

According to the familiar, albeit restrictive doctrine of *Nicomachean Ethics* III.1, ignorance (*agnoia*) along with force (*bia*) are the sole excusing conditions from voluntary action.[38] Mixed actions, typically those done under duress, are in some ways involuntary, in other ways not, though on the whole, more voluntary than not, for the cause is in oneself and one acts intentionally, without ignorance.[39] Aristotle goes on to qualify that ignorance which excuses must be ignorance of the particular circumstances of one's actions,[40] not ignorance of what is right and wrong.[41] The errors (*hamartiai*) that arise from the latter sort of ignorance are blameworthy, warranting neither pity nor pardon.[42] Moreoever, for pardon and pity, the agent must be acting not merely *in* ignorance (as when one is drunk or in rage), but *due to* (*dia*) ignorance, where ignorance itself is the cause of the error.[43]

In the early un-Aristotelian *Rhetoric to Alexander*,[44] a plea of ignorance is one of three recommended defense postures in a criminal case. I can deny I committed a certain offense, I can acknowledge it but claim it was lawful, I can acknowledge it but plead mitigating circumstances of error (*hamartema*)[45] or accident (*atuchema*). Aristotle defines the latter distinction as follows: "A harmful act done because of ignorance must be called an error; while the failure to accomplish some good intention, not through one's own fault but owing to someone else or luck, is to be accounted a misfortune" (1427a33–7). Thus, Mereope mistaking his son for the enemy is a *hamartia*. My spear going off course due to a sudden gust of wind is an accident. Aristotle continues:

> The commission of crime [*adikia*] you must declare to be confined to wicked men, while error and misfortune in action are not peculiar to oneself but are common to all men, including those who are sitting in judgment upon you. You must ask for pardon if you are forced to admit that you have committed faults of this kind, pointing out that your hearers are as liable to error and misfortune as you are. (1427a36–b1)

A similar three-way distinction of intentional wrongdoing, error, and accident with equity and pardon applied to the latter two, appears in Aristotle's own *Rhetoric* (I.13, 1374b5–9). The distinction is expanded somewhat in *Nicomachean Ethics* V.8 with intentional wrongdoing now divided into cases due to malice aforethought and those due to passion.[46] At the same time, there is also compression, with both accident and mistake proper (*hamartema*) labeled as kinds of mistakes (*hamartemata*) in that they are both due to ignorance. But on the whole the *Rhetoric* account is preserved. In both, what distinguishes accident from error is whether or not what happens unintentionally is *paralogos* – that is, (in a sense to be clarified), contrary to reasonable expectation:

> There are three kinds of injury in transactions; those done in ignorance are *mistakes* [*hamartemata*] when the person acted on, the act, the instrument, or the end is other than the agent supposed; the agent thought either that he was not hitting any one or that he was not hitting with this missile or not hitting this person or for the sake of this effect, but a result followed other than that which he thought likely (e.g. he threw not with intent to wound but only to prick), or the person hit or the missile was other than he supposed. Now when the injury takes place contrary to reasonable expectation [*paralogos*], it is a *misfortune* [*atuchema*]. When it is not contrary to

reasonable expectation [*me paralogos*], but does not imply vice, it is a *mistake* [*hamartema*] (for a person makes a mistake when the cause originates in him [*he arche en autoi ei tes aitias*],[47] but is the victim of accident when its origin lies outside him). When he acts with knowledge but not after deliberation, it is an *act of injustice* [*adikema*] – e.g., the acts due to anger or to other passions necessary or natural to man; for when men do such harmful and mistaken acts they act unjustly, and the acts are acts of injustice, but this does not imply that the doers are unjust or wicked; for the injury is not due to vice. But when a man acts from deliberate choice, he is an *unjust man* and a vicious man. (1135b10–25)

We can leave to the side the problem of which three kinds of injuries Aristotle means to be marking off among the four that he discusses, as well as the distinction between premeditated and unmeditated wrongdoing. What is crucial for our understanding of *hamartia* in the *Poetics* is the notion that what comes about as the result of accident is contrary to reasonable expectation; what comes about as the result of *hamartia* proper is not. An error can be accounted for; it is not reasonably unexpected. Put differently, in the case of an accident, what as a matter of psychological fact is unexpected, is also normatively so. We don't expect what happens to happen and we are justifed in our surprise. In the case of a mistake, what comes psychologically as a surprise, is, from some more objective perspective, not so surprising. It is not unreasonable that what happened should happen.

The implication drawn by a venerable tradition of commentators and translators is that *hamartia* proper, at least as understood in V.8 and in the parallel *Rhetoric* I. 13, is a kind of culpable negligence. It is a failure to take care, a reproachable ignorance. It corresponds to the Roman standard of liability – *culpa*. Indeed, the claim has been made that the threefold distinction of *adikia*, *hamartema*, *atuchema* is the origin of the three standards of liability much admired in Roman law: *dolus*, evil intent, *culpa*, negligence, and *casus*, accident.[48] The question of provenance cannot be debated here. What is relevant for our purposes, however, is the tendency to detect a standard of *culpa* (negligence) in the *NE* text. *Hamartemata* are taken to constitute a class of negligent injuries.[49] They are less serious in degree of culpability than injuries due to evil intent,[50] though more serious than accidents.

Needless to say, as an interpretation which bears on the *Poetics* there are grave problems. To turn to Oedipus, the claim would be that Oedipus' illusions about his family identity could have been avoided; there was information of which he could have availed himself, possibilities for further application and control which he failed to take. But this is implausible. Similarly, it would be absurd to hold that Thyestes, whose *hamartia* is also cited in *Poetics* 13, was negligent in failing to look for morsels of his children in the plate of meat served up to him.

For these reasons and others, I want to argue against the negligence view, taking the *Poetics* account of *hamartia* as a significant guide post.[51] In so doing

I shift the usual direction of influence in understanding *hamartia*. Before turning to the *Poetics*, however, we need to get a better grasp on the term *paralogos*.

The term is used in a variety of contexts in Aristotle, and can connote what is unexpected, uncertain, strange, paradoxical, or incalculable. In the account of luck in *Physics* II, chance (*tuche*) is described as *paralogos* – unaccountable, "for an account [*logos*] is of things that hold always or for the most part, but luck is of things others than these" (197a17 ff.). In the *Eudemian Ethics* at 1247a33 the same idea recurs, and is followed by Aristotle's helpful definition of luck as "a cause incalculable to human reasoning" (*aitian alogon anthropinoi logismoi* 1247b8). This gives a new dimension to the translation of *paralogos* as contrary to reasonable expectation. The idea is not simply that one is justified in one's surprise, but more fundamentally, that what happens by luck is beyond human reasoning. It is unaccountable, "no human calculation would have hit the mark."[52]

Conversely, what is *not paralogos* is penetrable by human calculation. It is not beyond our reason to account for what happened. Indeed, what happened may be psychologically surprising, even astounding, but at some level it is subject to coherent explanation. But, notice, this makes no commitment to the issue of avoidability, so central to negligence. It says nothing about what care and application could have avoided.[53]

True, to say that some consequence "cannot be reasonably unexpected" pushes one right into the issue of avoidability. It is to suggest that we should have expected what happened, and that had we been adequately enlightened, we could have avoided the disaster. But this is no more than the appeal of the gloss. The alternative connotation does not take us down this path. To be able to see how an agent came to make a mistake, how it followed in a causally coherent way from judgment and character is to show that the mistake is a cause penetrable to human reasoning. Why things turned out unexpectedly can now be explained by what is predictable and repeatable. This, though, does not commit us to saying that the agent ought to have been in a position to see this as he was acting or to have been able to prevent it.[54] Intelligibility and avoidance are separate matters.

It is not difficult to see the impact of the *Poetics* on this interpretation. Tragedy is about action that is causally probable and coherent. The mistake that brings a character to ruin does not emerge like a bolt from the blue but has a causal history in past sequences of actions which follow intelligibly one from the other (*di'allela*) with probability or necessity. What happens is contrary to belief but not contrary to reason (*me doken, me paralogos*). In a good play, the orderliness and flow of the events is inexorably logical. Oedipus sets out uncompromisingly to solve the mystery of Laius' murder. Each clue brings him closer to pinning the murder on himself. And though the discovery turns out to be of the unspeakable, it is not of the rationally impossible. Indeed, it is precisely Oedipus' thirst for truth that forces him to see the unexpected as the logically necessary. Ultimately, humility in recognizing that human reason may reveal but not undo what is done brings him to pity the havoc he has wrought. "There is no tomorrow until one has suffered through the present day."[55]

In *Oedipus*, as in other plays, the tragic mistake bears a universal dimension that appeals to persistent human conditions. We feel pity and fear precisely because as comparable humans we can envision ourselves under a not so dissimilar threat. How avoidable the mistakes may be will vary from case to case. And some mistakes may betray defects of character more than others. But our prevailing response to tragedy is not reproach toward the agent who through error brings herself and loved ones down. It is pity for the failure to see what in principle, in optimal conditions (and sometimes only in hindsight), is accessible to human light. And it is pity for the undue suffering that must be endured.

It is important to say a few words at this point about the relation of pity to regret. "Everything caused by ignorance is non-voluntary" Aristotle says, "but what is involuntary also causes pain and regret [*metameleiai*] . . . hence among those who act because of ignorance, the agent who feels regret seems to be unwilling, and the one who does not feel regret, since he is different, let him be called not willing" (*NE* III.1 1110b18–22). The remark reflects on character and the different attitudes an agent may have to what is done due to ignorance. One agent may feel pleasure or callousness toward an injury she unintentionally causes through accident or error; another pain and regret. The responsibility for the action in each case is no different: mitigating circumstances prevailed. But the person who feels regret displays the more admirable response. Though neither is morally responsible, the agent who feels regret is pained at being causally instrumental, or in the case of accident, the occasion for the injury.[56]

What does this have to do with pity? Regret, as I have conceived it here, is a self-regarding emotion, pity an emotion that may be directed at self, but in tragedy, is directed at others from a third person point of view. Both, however, are pained responses at injury caused by accident or mistake. They are among the emotions unleashed when we witness in the agency of ourselves or others harm brought about through ignorance. But each focuses on a different aspect or moment of the episode. Regret looks back at the crossroads, and is a quiet protest at the moment of choice or accident. What we dwell on is the botched beginning and what we wish to undo is what happened, to replay differently the tragic moment, to clean the slate and start afresh. "If only I'd died then," Oedipus says, ". . . I'd never have come to this" (1485). There is something of disbelief, of the error being too horrible to be allowed entrance.

Pity is a feeling of sadness regarding the consequences of that inauspicious moment. From the point of view of the tragic observer, it is a feeling of pain at what the protagonist suffers, and this requires focusing on the aftermath of the choice rather than on the botched beginning. It is moving beyond the why's and the wherefore's and it is accepting what has happened and the mitigated reasons for the damages now suffered. To feel pity is to dwell on the undeserved suffering. The cathartic advantage depends upon accceptance rather than upon undoing what might, in some possible world, have been avoided.

IV. Varieties of Ignorance

We can conclude from the last section that negligence does not appear to be the standard of liability for *hamartia* in the *Nicomachean Ethics* or the *Poetics*. This is not to deny that the notion of failure to take care (*ameleian*) is appealed to by Aristotle in several places.[57] It is. But in those discussions, it does not represent a separate standard of liability apart from vice or evil. And certainly vice or evil is not implied by *hamartia* in the accounts we have studied. All this is compatible with acknowledging that the tragic protagonist may err out of an ignorance which is not entirely faultless. If only Phaedra were more circumspect in whom she trusted as confidante, Deianeira less jealous of Heracles, Creon not so bound to unflexible political principle. Such are our reactions to these characters. But responses such as these needn't dampen our pity. Rather, they are admissions of the humanity of the protagonists, and the naturalness, though imperfection of certain tendencies and choices. They are not condemnations.

Indeed, in pity, the underlying urge is not to overcome one's own condemnations. One is not condoning, that is, ridding oneself of a judgment that an action is wrong or motivated by malicious intent or carelessness. Condonation, to get clearer, is acceptance of an action or motive as wrong, along with the desire to overcome or "morally compromise" that judgment.[58] But there needn't be any condonation in the leniency of pity. The imperfection that is typically manifest in *hamartia* is not some rottenness that we feel compelled to overlook; rather, it is a defect that even the most decent of persons sometimes falls prey to.

This raises an interesting problem of linkage between the ethical treatises and the *Poetics*. Imperfection of the above sort is a falling short of the mean, a missing of the mark not because of externalities, but because of failure to exercise right reasoning or *orthos logos*. The dimunition of excellence down a notch to mere decency is meant to symbolize that possibility. But this implies that the *phronimos*, the standard of excellence around which the *Nicomachean* and *Eudemian Ethics* rally, is unlikely to be a tragic protagonist. This is not because his life is exempt from external contingency. Rather, it is because error of judgment, misapprehension, mistakes about what is relevant and salient to action, are not easily compatible with what it is to be practically wise. Hitting the mark, getting it right when there are many ways to go wrong, are constitutive of full virtue and wisdom. But even so, this is an idealized conception of virtue that may put ethical standards beyond the reach of humans. Some mistakes, like Oedipus', I would argue, do not reflect badly on character or effort or judgment. Oedipus acts out of an ignorance that is stultifying. There is little he contributed to bring it on, and little he could have done at crucial moments to come to an earlier recognition. His mistake brings him horrible shame, and deadens any hope for his ever knowing joy again. But it does not reflect poorly on character. He acts with dignity and unwavering commitment to discovering the truth. Granted, despite all this, we would be hard pressed to say Oedipus is wise; how can someone who makes a mistake like that be wise? But this tells more against the puzzle he has been given to solve than against his own resolution and conduct in solving it.[59]

The ignorance in the case of other tragic protagonists is different, and may come closer to revealing more obvious blemishes of character. Consider again Deianeira in the *Trachiniae*.[60] She has waited as dutiful wife for the return of Heracles from his labors. The years have been filled with patience, but also fear as he comes and goes "to labor for some master or other." There is steady resentment: "We had children, of course. He sees them the way a farmer sees his back fields: he drops a seed and comes around once in awhile to check the harvest" (38–40).

But Deianeira tries to suppress her anger, even upon learning that Heracles' last labor was a war waged against Eurytos's country solely in order to liberate the ruler's daughter as mistress for himself. Moved both by propriety and the need to take charge, she channels her angry jealousy into a constructive scheme to woo Heracles back. She will send Heracles a robe annointed in the love potion given to her as a dying present by the centaur Nessos, whom Heracles defeated when Nessos showed illicit affection toward Deianeira. Herein lies the tragic error. The potion is not a love charm, but a deathly drug. Heracles is consumed by its poisonous flames when he dons the poison-drenched robe.

Deianeira has been tricked by the centaur who wants nothing more than to revenge his own death on Heracles. But the trick is not entirely lost on Deianeira. It is just that her intense jealousy leads her to minimize the possibility. In this sense, at the very moment of tragic choice, she is less blind than Oedipus; she senses possible trouble ahead yet love rather than caution prevails. To the chorus, she implores:

> [Perhaps] I am being rash . . . Do you think so?
> Say so if you do . . . I'll stop . . . I will.
>
> No, it
>   seems
>   all right
> to do
>   if you think it can
>   work.
>
> I don't know for sure. He said
> it would. I can't tell till I try.
>
> Then you
>   have
>   to
> try. No
>   telling till
>   you try. (580–601)

Deianeira's mistake, more than Oedipus', seems almost avoidable. She took a calculated risk, and lost. And what pity we feel may be calibrated to that. Her ignorance, or more precisely, her willingness to act on her ignorance, is *dia pathos*, rooted in her own passions. Out of jealousy, she moved quickly and less cautiously than she might otherwise have. As such, the ignorance she suffers is simply less systematic and profound than Oedipus'. But still, her mistake has a human proportion that dampens any tendency to reproach her. She acted as a decent and reasonable woman would who wanted to reclaim her husband after all those years of patient waiting. She tried, but then failed in the worst possible way.

Similar thoughts occur in reaction to Euripides' *Hippolytus*.[61] Phaedra, in love with her stepson Hippolytus, keeps her scandalous secret a black mystery to all despite the persistent imploring of the nurse that she empty her soul for thera-peutic counsel. So Phaedra states at (395): "Silence was my first plan. Silence and concealment. For the tongue is not to be trusted: it can criticize another's faults, but on its own possessor it brings a thousand troubles." Yet her resolve breaks as her love festers unbearably inside. She confides in the nurse, with ominous awareness of the risk: "I am afraid of you: I am afraid that you will be too clever for my good. You surely will not tell this to Hippolytus?" The nurse replies, only "Come, let that be."

Thus, there is no naievete here about the dangers of confiding in others, about the risks of bearing one's soul to would-be gossip mongers and those who would gain advantage by betraying others' trust. Yet the pain of living in concealment, in fear of trust yet in need of human support, is equally intolerable. She does what in a sense she must as a fully human being. She unbears herself. And for this *hamartia*, she suffers unduly.[62]

Again, Phaedra's ignorance is not as deeply systematic as that of Oedipus; there is the glimmer that control could have averted disaster. But it would have been control that exceeds reasonable human proportion, that demands us to suspend our trust in others whom we have no real reason to suspect. Averting disasters has its costs too.

To take stock, we have said that some errors of judgment show blemishes of character more than others. Deianeira might have questioned her faith in a love potion given to her by a smitten rival. More than Oedipus, her mistake seems mildly avoidable. Her zeal to regain Heracles' love blinded her from more circumspect judgment. But still she suffers well beyond her desert. Her reversal well exceeds the magnitude of her error. And a similar story can be told for Phaedra. But some tragic acts stretch those limits. Medea's slaying of her own children as revenge against Jason's infidelity seems unpardonable, an act of unnatural and inhuman passion, for which fear and moral outrage rather than pity are aroused.[63] There is nothing great and fine that justifies these base means (*NE* 1110a22), nor any way of construing what she does as forseen but unin-tended. She intends to use her children as means for promoting her own shameful view of honor. Categories of innocence and undeserved suffering don't seem to apply. Still, the story is not quite that simple. The *Medea* seems to force a wedge between pardon and pity. We are reluctant to pardon Medea (for her thirst for revenge is unbridled and deliberate. There is no ignorance of fact or failure to calculate immediate effect). But still we might pity her, pity her for the exercise of a passion we ourselves dread might come unleashed someday,[64] pity her for her a kind of ignorance to see the long-term effects of her action, of what it is to live as a murderer of her own children.[65]

In a related way, Agamemnon, in sacrificing Iphigeneia, acts knowingly, without misapprehension of the immediate circumstances. There is no ignorance of object, instrument, or immediate effect.[66] Yet still, the choice to kill a daughter, though more voluntary than that of Deianeira or Oedipus' killings, involves a kind of ignorance. There is ignorance of how painful the consequences will be, of the magnitude of the disaster, of the wrath of a mother and so on. The conflict itself is no doubt tragic, a dismal hand dealt out that constrains any decent choice. But ignorance too may constrain the choice even more, ignorance of more distant consequences that in some ideal sense, are not foreign to human reason.

This is obviously not the time to embark upon a discussion of tragedies of conflict. But the speculation is that even here, where ignorance is less stark than in the paradigmatic case of Oedipus, a failure to see what is too painful to look squarely in the eye, might be part of the tragedy.

Notes

1. So Aristotle reminds us in *Nicomachean Ethics* (*NE*) III.1, the action is more intentional (*hekon*) than not. Note the term *hekon* is ambiguous between voluntary and intentional.
2. *Poetics* 6, 1449b22–36; 1450a16–23.
3. See T. C. W. Stinton's helpful remarks regarding Aristotle's deemphasis of divine fate (*ate*) in the account of tragic error: "*Hamartia* in Aristotle and Greek Tragedy," *Classical Quarterly* 25 (1975) 221–254; also, L. Golden, "*Hamartia, Ate*, and Oedipus', *Classical World* 72 (1978) 3–12. Contrast J. M. Bremer, *Hamartia: Tragic Error in the Poetics of Aristotle and in Greek Tragedy* (Amsterdam, (1969) and R. D. Dawe, "Some Reflections on Ate and Hamartia," *Harvard Studies in Classical Philology* 72 (1967) 89–123.
4. *NE* V.8 1135b18–19; III.1 1110a17.
5. *NE* V.8 1135b12–20.
6. See Bremer, *Hamartia*, for an impressive lexicological analysis of the word *hamartia* and its cognates, as well as a comprehensive study of the term in the context of the *Poetics*. I believe he overstates his conclusion, however, that Aristotle's usage of *hamartia* in the *Poetics* is that of intellectual error.
7. Consider J. L. Austin's pithy remark: "In an *accident* something befalls: by *mistake* you take the wrong one: in *error* you stray." "A Plea for Excuses" in *Philosophical Papers* (Oxford, 1989), p. 201. See *Physics* II. 4–6 on Aristotle's distinction between chance and spontaneity.
8. The term is *prohairesis*. It is a reasoned choice that reveals character. See Ch. 3 of my *Fabric of Character: Aristotle's Theory of Virtue* (Oxford, 1989).

9. Cf. H. L. A. Hart *Punishment and Responsibility* (Oxford, 1968), esp. 216–218. Also, H. L. A. Hart and T. Honoré, *Causation in the Law* (Oxford, 1985).

10. The above remarks are compatible with holding that when a sudden wind carries my spear off course, it can be said of me that I was *ignorant* of the upcoming gust; had I anticipated it I would have acted differently. But all the same, in hurling the spear, I am not *mistaking* the wind conditions or making a questionable judgment. There is nothing to get right by control. The problem is external.

11. P. Van Braam, "Aristotle's Use of Hamartia," *Classical Quarterly* 6 (1912) 266–272, still remains a useful survey of the debate between *hamartia* as moral flaw or frailty and intellectual error. The translation of *hamartia* as moral "error or frailty" was popularized by S. H. Butcher in his translation of the *Poetics: Aristotle's Theory of Poetry and Fine Art*, 4th edn (London, 1911), 302–333, though in the essays that follow the text Butcher explicitly denies any sharp distinction between moral and purely intellectual error (321). Around the same time, I. Bywater translates *hamartia* as "error of judgment," *Aristotle on the Art of Poetry* (Oxford, 1909). The latter has become the more or less accepted gloss, hence, G. Else *Aristotle's Poetics: The Argument* (Cambridge, MA, 1957), D. W. Lucas, *Aristotle Poetics* (Oxford, 1968), and R. Janko, *Poetics* (Indianapolis, IN, 1987). However, note the Revised Oxford Translation based on Bywater's edition renders *hamartia*: "fault." Butcher's insistence that there cannot be a sharp distinction between the two senses is wisely echoed by T. C. W. Stinton and I. M. Glanville, "Tragic Error," *Classical Quarterly* 43 (1949) 47–56. For further discussion, see S. Halliwell, *Aristotle's Poetics* (Chapel Hill, NC, 1986), esp. Ch. 7.

12. *Oedipus Colonus* 270–274; 437–444; 969–999. See Lucas, *Poetics*, Appendix 4, p. 304 and E. R. Dodds, "On Misunderstanding the *Oedipus Rex*," *Greece and Rome* (1966) 37–49.

13. See *NE* VII 1–3.

14. *NE* VII.1 1145b8–10, 46a3–4; VII.4 1148a2.

15. *NE* I.6 1106b28.

16. *Poetics* 6, 1449b24–28; *Poetics* 14, 1453b10–15.

17. *Rhetoric* II.8, 1385b14, II.9 1386b14.

18. The fundamental rapport between the *Rhetoric* and the *Poetics* has been admirably explored in the recent work of Kathy Eden, *Poetic and Legal Fiction in the Aristotelian Tradition* (Princeton, 1986). One principal claim is that forensic persuasion and tragic *mimesis* share a tradition in legal proof which stresses the depiction of action as causally probable and coherent. In the legal sphere, as in the tragic sphere, rational proof is the more "artful" (*entechnos*) form of persuasion. Thus, she shows that in the *Rhetoric*, preference is give to proofs which rely on the logic of probability (*Rhetoric* I.2 1357a22–31) just as in the *Poetics*, the best technique of recognition "results from the incidents themselves, when our astonishment comes about through probable [incidents]" (*Poetics* 1455a16–22).

19. Unless otherwise noted, I use Janko's translation of the *Poetics* (Indianapolis, IN, 1978), and the Revised Oxford Translation, ed. J. Barnes (Princeton, 1984) of other texts. Note, against Else, I follow Janko in preserving lines a17–18 in the above translation (i.e. the phrase from "happiness" to "quality"). His argument is that with their inclusion, the analogy between action and the representation of action in plot is far more perspicuous.

20. 1101a1–15.

21. 1100b34.

22. Esp. Halliwell and Martha C. Nussbaum, *The Fragility of Goodness* (Cambridge, 1986).

23. Thus, it is misleading to say, as Halliwell does (*Aristotle's Poetics*, p. 207), that tragedy concerns the external conditions of our happiness. For the peculiar task of tragedy is

to show that these external goods are not so external, that they are implicated in our agency.

24. See Richard Janko's helpful notes on this translation of *to philanthropon* in his edition of the *Poetics*, p. 101. Contrast Else, *Aristotle's Poetics*, p. 95. Janko also perceptively notes that *miaron* contrasts both in its literal sense of "filthy" or "disgusting" with *katharsis* as "purification," and in its more figurative sense of "moral outrage" with *to philanthropon*, as "what is humanly satisfying."

25. My own translation, based on Else and Janko.

26. A similar line is adopted by Else, 383–385 and Halliwell, 216.

27. As Stinton has put it: "The point of diminishing virtue is to avoid our sense of outrage which impedes the tragic pleasure" dependent upon feelings of pity and fear: "*Hamartia* in Aristotle and Greek Tragedy," 239. The explanation seems compatible with the general view in the *Rhetoric* that certain feelings can "drive out" other feelings, e.g., intense fear can "drive out" (*ekkroustikon*) the feeling of pity: 1386a23; cf. 1387a1–5.

28. *Rhetoric* II.8, 1386a1–4; a18; a25–28.

29. "Here too we have to remember the general principle that what we fear for ourselves excites our pity when it happens to others" (*Rhetoric* II.8 1386a27).

30. 1387a18–87b6.

31. Relevant here is J. Murphy and J. Hampton's lively discussion of hatred and indignation in *Forgiveness and Mercy* (Cambridge, 1988).

32. *kolutika* at 1387a3; cf. 1387b15–20.

33. 1385b20–21.

34. 1385b30.

35. 1385b32; 1386a23–28.

36. At 1386b4 Aristotle uses the word *spoudaios* to refer to the character of those who elicit our pity. The Revised Oxford translation of the term – "persons of noble character" – seems to obscure the close connection of that phrase with *epieikes*. The terms are often interchangeable in the *NE* and refer to decent and worthy persons, who nonetheless may fall short of absolute perfection; see especially, *NE* IX.12, 1172a10.

37. I rely on Halliwell for this point. See *NE* II.6, 1106b28. Also, note the nontechnical use of *hamartia* a few lines below our cited passage: "Hence those who bring charges against Euripides for doing this in his tragedy are making the same mistake" (1453a25).

38. III.1, 1110a1; Contrast *EE* II.9 where ignorance alone is assumed to be the opposite of voluntary action. Yet overall there is greater leniency in excusing conditions in *EE*; hence action caused by compulsive passion (such as crimes due to irrational love) provide grounds for the involuntary in *EE* II.8 but do not in the *NE*; see 1111a25–1111b3, V.8 1136a5–9.

39. 1110a11–18; 1110b3–5.

40. At *NE* V.8 and *EE* II.9 the same list is repeated: ignorance that marks the involuntary is ignorance of whom, with what means, and for what result.

41. 1110b28–1111a1; cf. 1142a21.

42. 1110b29–30; Cf. 1115b15, 1148a3.

43. 1110b25–27.

44. 1427a24 ff.; see D. Daube for his discussion in *Roman Law: Linguistic, Social and Philosophical Aspects* (Edinburgh, 1969).

45. Note, I am not persuaded by Ostwald's claim of a substantive distinction between *hamartia* (disposition (in ignorance) to make a mistake); and *hamartema* (the mistake). M. Ostwald, "Aristotle on *hamartia* and Sophocles' OT," *Festschrift Kapp* (Hamburg, 1958) 93–108.

46. The latter is nonetheless voluntary, according to *NE* III.1, 1111a25 ff.

47. Note, I do not accept the emendation of *aitias* to *agnoias* found both in J. Urmon's trans. in the Revised Oxford Translation of *The Complete Works of Aristotle* (Princeton, 1985) and H. Jackson, *The Fifth Book of the Nicomachean Ethics* (New York, 1973). Implicit in that rendering is a sense of culpability I reject.

48. I am much indebted to the discussion of these matters in D. Daube's *Roman Law*, esp. "Dolus, Culpa, and Casus," 131–157.

49. This is the view, among others, of Jackson (*The Fifth Book of the Nicomachean Ethics*), Gauthier and Joliff, and most recently, Sorabji: "it is commonly supposed, and correctly I believe, that the second of the four categories is a class of *negligent injuries.*" *Necessity, Cause, and Blame* (Ithaca, 1980), p. 278; see 257–298. R. A. Gauthier and J. Y. Jolif: "Il y a malchance si l'on n'est pas responsable de l'ignorance et erreur si l'on est soi-même cause de l'ignorance." *L'Ethique a Nicomaque* (Louvain, 1970), II.1 *Commentaire* 401.

50. So presumably, that they are without evil (*aneu de kakias* 1135b18), can be more or less acknowledged.

51. I am not alone in my opposition. As I have suggested the classic work is David Daube. I am persuaded by much of his argument, though remain absolutely puzzled by his translation of *paralogos* and *me paralogos* as implying *psychological* reports about what happens contrary and not contrary to expectation. It seems absolutely bizarre to say of Oedipus that things went as intended (read expected) when he slayed the man at the crossroads; see p. 149 as well as M. Schoffield's perceptive study of Daube, "Aristotelian Mistakes," *Cambridge Philological Society Proceedings* **199** (1973) 66–70. Schoffield is also skeptical of the negligence reading of *NE* V.8 though believes it remains a puzzle why Aristotle doesn't discuss the notion more directly in that passage given his remarks elsewhere about failure to take care (*ameleia*). Schoffield, however, does not relate the passage to the concerns of the *Poetics*.

52. Glanville, "Tragic Error," 54. Daube puts it similarly: luck "has nothing to do with my rational self," *Roman Law*, 149.

53. In all this, I do not mean to deny that ignorance may be severely reproachable – on grounds of failure to take care. There is clear evidence to this effect at III.5 and *EE* II.9. Penalties are doubled in the case of drunkenness "for the moving principle is in the individual, since he had the power of not getting drunk and his getting drunk was the cause of his ignorance" (1113b30–34). Again, one is held accountable for ignorance if knowledge is easy to come by or necessary (*EE* 1225b14–17), such as the content of some laws: "We punish those who are ignorant of anything in the laws that they ought to know and that is not difficult, and so too in the case of anything else that they are thought to be ignorant of through carelessness (*ameleian*); we assume it is in their power not to be ignorant, since they have the power of taking care" (*NE* 1113b30–45). From Aristotle's remarks, negligence appears punishable as a kind of vice, and does not represent a lesser degree of liability than vice. My claim is a restricted one, that Aristotle is not concerned systematically to connect negligence with *hamartia*.

54. The pressure to avoid disaster is explicit in the perplexing claim in *Poetics* 14 that the best play is not one in which there is an actual downfall, but rather one in which recognition of the mistake comes just in time to avert calamity. Needless to say, this makes problematic the role of pity and fear at prospective ruin. Still, it may be argued that the *prospect* of ruin, without *actual* ruin (in a play) may be sufficient to elicit in the audience feelings of pity and fear necessary for cathartic relief.

55. So says the nurse in Sophocles' *Trachiniae* (940).

56. See Bernard Williams' notion of agent-regret in "Moral Luck," *Moral Luck* (Cambridge, 1981).

57. See n. 54 above.

58. See Jean Hampton in *Forgiveness and Mercy*, p. 40.

59. While I see the role of divine intervention in the setting of the problem, I do not see it at work as a hostile force that "invades" Oedipus' actual reasoning or conduct. See Leon Golden, "*Hamartia, Ate,* and Oedipus," who argues against Bremer and Dawe.

60. Citations which follows are from the *Women of Trachis*, trans. C. K. Williams and G. W. Dickerson, (Oxford, 1978).

61. *Hippolytus*, trans. D. Greene in *Euripides* I, eds. D. Greene and R. Lattimore (Chicago, 1975). For a discussion of the evidence for ascribing akrasia to Euripides' Phaedra (and Medea), see T. H. Irwin, "Euripides and Socrates," *Classical Philology* (1983) 183–197.

62. There is also the *hamartia* of Theseus, Phaedra's husband, who fatally curses his son Hippolytus on the (false) belief that Hippolytus has seduced Phaedra.

63. Contrast the *NE*'s position that raging anger is not an excusing condition (1136a9 – i.e., passion that is not human or natural) with that of the *EE* in which intense anger or love whose power is "beyond nature" may be thought of as involuntary and as pardonable (II.8, 1225a20 ff.).

64. This is perhaps the sentiment behind the *EE* II.8 pardoning of compulsive emotion.

65. On Medea's monstrous revenge, see B. Knox, "The 'Medea' of Euripides," *Yale Classical Studies* (1977) 193–225. For the claim that Medea acts in full knowledge of the harm she is about to do, see G. A. Rickert, "Akrasia and Euripides' *Medea*," *Harvard Studies in Classical Philology* **91** (1987) 91–117.

66. Cf. *NE* V.8 and *NE* II.9 for this formulation.

Necessity, Chance, and "What Happens for the Most Part" in Aristotle's *Poetics*

Dorothea Frede

I. The Problem

Although they make their entrance at a crucial point in the discussion of the nature of tragedy and remain center stage throughout the *Poetics*, the three concepts that form the title of this essay seem at first sight like actors who have intruded into the wrong play. The reader of Aristotle's other philosophical works is, of course, well familiar with these three actors. They play leading roles in many of his writings, especially in his work on natural science, where they form an indissoluble triad; and they are dealt with extensively in his "tool for science," the *Analytics*. Ideally, the scientist is concerned only with *necessity*, with what cannot be otherwise. Such are the necessary and intrinsic properties of the entities that form the subject matter of his field. But since in most sciences (with the exception of mathematics and astronomy) there are always deviations from the rule, the scientist often has to substitute "what happens for the most part" for what is strictly necessary. Few phenomena in nature are immune to such deviations. These exceptions are dubbed "chance" or "spontaneous" events by Aristotle; they are not the objects of science proper, because they do not allow for scientific explanations. Although accidental events are not tied into the natural scheme of things, as a conscientious scientist Aristotle incorporates even the possibility of exceptions into his scientific apparatus, just as he gives a metaphysical account of them, since "accidental being" constitutes a special sense of "being" (*Metaphysics* E 2–3).

Both the literary critic and the expert in Aristotelian science will wonder about the reason for the transference of such scientific rigor to the *Poetics*. Why does Aristotle insist time and again on the necessary or nearly necessary coherence of the parts of tragedy, to the exclusion of chance, so that they are treated

197

as highly important criteria of judgment?[1] In their proper use, these "modals" would normally demand a homogeneous field, an area where strict generality can at least in principle be expected. Any proper application of Aristotle's "modals" in the *Poetics* would presuppose that the subject matter is a whole *class* or *type* of events or states of affairs, so that it makes sense to look for *uniformity*, while allowing for rare exceptions. No such uniformity would, at least *prima facie*, be looked for in Greek drama, nor in epic, the two forms of poetic art on which Aristotle focuses. Do not both tragedy and epic deal with the exceptional, the singular, rather than the regular? It would seem quite vacuous to demand that the dramatic events that supposedly move us to fear and pity should be of a kind that happen either always, or at least "normally." How could such a theory accommodate *anagnorisis* and *peripeteia*, the unforeseeable recognitions and sudden dramatic reversals of fortune (1450a34 f.), which Aristotle himself praises as essential for a good tragedy? What could, for instance, be the point of asking whether Antigone's decision to bury her brother in defiance of Creon's order – to face disgrace and death rather than the outrage of leaving the corpse of her brother unburied – is a decision of the kind that happens "always" or "for the most part"? Or how could Oedipus' fate, the combination of the highly unusual events that lead to his downfall, be judged by such criteria, especially if the element of chance (*tuchē*) is excluded? Tragedy, it would seem, does not lend itself to such standards of evaluation at all.

There is, of course, the possibility, that the "modalities" are applied in the *Poetics* in a sense which differs in a significant way from the normal conception of the "modalities" in Aristotle. If so, it is strange that he does not give the slightest indication that they carry any unusual meaning. Even if we make allowances for his *insouciance* in stretching the meaning of crucial terms, we would expect at least some explanation of the sense in which he employs the "modals," when he decrees that the proper construction of the backbone of tragedy, the plot, depends on the necessary or natural coherence of beginning, middle, and end: "A beginning is that which is not itself *necessarily* after something else, but after which something else *naturally* is or comes to be; an end, by contrast, is that which is itself naturally after something, either necessarily or *for the most part*, and with nothing else after it; and a middle is that which is after something and also has something else after it. Well constructed plots, therefore, cannot either begin at a *chance* point or end at a *chance* point, but should be constructed in the way just described" (7, 1450b27–34).[2] The very fact that he introduces the concepts of necessity and of "what happens for the most part" together – as an elucidation of what he means by the *natural* sequence in drama, while excluding chance – would suggest that they carry the same meaning as they do elsewhere when used in conjunction.

These cumbersome prescriptions for the unity of tragedy indicate that Aristotle attributes special importance to them. If he omits any specification for the kind of *necessity* or "normality" or "naturalness," which he postulates for the inner coherence of the structure of the plot in tragedy, we have to speculate in what sense the naturalness of this coherence should be interpreted. Our basis must be the explanations Aristotle gives elsewhere for his conception of "what happens either necessarily or for the most part" that excludes chance. For even if he does not presuppose any special meaning for these crucial terms, his customary usage leaves room for quite a wide range of possibilities. Hence an excursion into other Aristotelian writings will be necessary, which will render us at least an overview over the different possibilities, before we can return to the *Poetics* and see to what use he puts them there.

II. Necessity, Normality, and Chance in Aristotle

As he is wont to do with important concepts, Aristotle distinguishes between several senses of "necessary." Although his catalogue of the different senses sometimes varies slightly, he usually speaks of four different types. In his philosophical lexicon in *Metaphysics Δ* 5, he distinguishes between (1) the unqualified necessity of what "cannot be otherwise" (which Aristotle declares to be "in a way" the generic meaning of all that is necessary, 1015a35), (2) the necessity of brute force or compulsion (*bia*), (3) the "apodeictic" necessity of the conclusion of necessary premises, and (4) the hypothetical necessity of the preconditions for some end. Necessary in the primary and privileged sense (*to prōton kai kryiōs anagkaion*). Aristotle adds, is what does not depend on further causes for its necessity. Such are the things which cannot be otherwise at all, things eternal and immobile; they cannot be subject to the necessity of unnatural force either (1015b9–15).[3]

Of these four kinds we can ignore the necessity of force; we can presumably also leave aside without discussion the "apodeictic necessity," since it is highly unlikely that Aristotle assumes either a compulsory or a syllogistically derived necessity for the coherence of drama.[4] Can we also set aside the hypothetical necessity? Under "hypothetical necessity" Aristotle does not understand the "forward looking" kind, which leads from the condition to the consequence, but the "backward looking" one, of what is necessary *if* some purpose or end is *to be* achieved.[5] Although the hypothetical necessity must play some role in drama, since all teleologically determined processes rest on necessary preconditions, it cannot be the necessity Aristotle speaks of in his definition of the necessary unity in *Poetics* 7, quoted above. Not only does he nowhere add any explanation that he is talking of the necessity of the means to a given end, but he actually indicates quite clearly in our passage of the *Poetics* (1450b27 ff.; cf. 1452a18–22) that he has the *forward* looking, unqualified, necessity in mind: the beginning must be such that it leads necessarily or naturally to what follows after it.

Before we engage in any further speculations on the sense of the *forward looking* necessity of "what could not be otherwise" that Aristotle could have envisaged for the development of the tragic plot, we should take note of the second of our "actors," the mitigating "or for the most part." The clause "or what is/happens for the most part" is generally added when Aristotle is concerned with a not quite exceptionless forward-looking necessity. Although the "hōs epi to polu" is therefore defined by the necessity it is attached to, this does not mean that there are not some *shifts* in Aristotle's interpretations of what happens "for the most part." Depending on the context, he emphasizes either its character as an "almost *necessity*" or its character as something that can be otherwise and is therefore *contingent*. So we find what "happens for the most part," or for short, the "usual," either approximated to – or contrasted with – what is necessary.[6] There is no real contradiction here, although the ambiguity in the nature of "what happens for the most part" sometimes causes problems for Aristotle. This emerges especially in contexts where he tries to incorporate the "usual" as a subclass of the contingent in his modal logic, and it has therefore attracted the notice of present-day commentators.[7] But the logical problems of working out a consistent interpretation of necessity and contingency leaves the question we are dealing with unaffected.

We do, however, have to pursue the question what kind of forward looking necessity or at least "usualness" Aristotle can have in mind for the *Poetics*, particularly since we would not, at least *prima facie*, expect any such necessity here. Since the development in tragedy depends on human action, and since Aristotle often contrasts what depends on human decisions with what is necessary, it seems strange that he would postulate a necessity for the development in tragic plots.[8] In what sense could the sequence of events in tragedy be called necessary? We will have to take a closer look at the further determinations Aristotle makes elsewhere for what is unqualifiedly necessary in the sense that it cannot be otherwise (or almost so) in order to see how they could be accommodated to the subject matter of tragedy.

A study of the widespread discussion of what is in principle unqualifiedly necessary (which we have to forego here) would show that Aristotle permits the necessity of this kind in a stricter and in a more relaxed sense, depending on the subject matter he is dealing with. The stricter sense is usually emphasized in the discussion of the first principles of science and in his syllogistics. "Necessary" in the strictest sense is what is part of the essence of whatever entity is in question, i.e. the properties which occur either in the definition or whose definition contains the subject matter (as a definition of "odd" contains a reference to number).[9] But since most entities possess more necessary properties than the ones which are contained in the definition, Aristotle needs further criteria to establish that something is a necessary ingredient.[10] One of the most important tests to determine this kind of necessity is whether the property in question applies to all cases (*kata pantos*) and, moreover, whether this is always (*aei*) so. The temporal condition, that the property should *always* be attributable is given a prominent place by Aristotle. "Always" is at times almost treated as a synonym to "necessary" and contrasted with what happens only "for the most part" and with what happens accidentally or "rarely." This has suggested a statistical interpretation for Aristotle's modal terms.[11] There is indeed a lot of evidence that speaks for such an interpretation, because regularity and continuity must be valuable criteria in natural philosophy, especially when other criteria to determine what "cannot be otherwise" are not available. Whether the relative frequency of the occurrence is more than a heuristic device to determine the modal status of a given state, remains questionable.[12]

But the question of regularity and its exceptions does not seem helpful to the issue in the *Poetics*; what is more pertinent to our question is the confirmation by this resort to "statistics," that Aristotle's conditions for necessity vary in different contexts. While he insists on omnitemporal validity especially in his discussion of the first premises of scientific demonstration in the *Posterior Analytics* and at other places where he discusses the ideal of science (cf. *Metaphysics* E 2),[13] in his dealings with nature and the natural in the sublunary sphere he entertains often a much more relaxed and diversified conception of necessity. First of all, when dealing with natural substances Aristotle does not only acknowledge their essential properties, but also their natural *functions*. So he studies not only what the entities *are*, but also what they *do*.[14] There is no longer any restriction to essential *properties*, but *activities* come in, too. Secondly, since few entities in the sublunary sphere are outside generation and destruction, necessity is not confined to strictly eternal activities, but recurrent events are also regarded as necessary. So the unconditional forward looking necessity becomes a "conditional" one: whenever the circumstances are right, X will happen.[15]

It was clearly the practice of empirical science that drew Aristotle's attention to the need for a more relaxed sense of necessity in nature. He was keenly aware of the fact that there are very few states of affairs or events on earth that do not admit of exceptions. This is, above all, the reason why "what happens for the most part" is not really presented as the opposite of what is necessary in nature, but as a kind of complement. What happens for the most part is, then, not a kind or class of events that differs fundamentally from the events that happen of necessity; it is rather of the same type. For both together are opposed to what happens *by chance*. There are good metaphysical reasons for this approximation: in both cases we are dealing with the realization of a natural potential (*dunamis*), which is actualized necessarily, given the right circumstances. As Aristotle expresses it in *Metaphysics* Θ 5, whenever the corresponding active and passive potentialities are joined together, the one *will* act, the other be acted upon (1048a6). Whether exceptions are excluded or not is, as he explains, a matter of definition; the specification of all the circumstances ("what is possible, and when and how, and under what additional circumstances") will exclude any interruptions. Since such specifications will often be rather cumbersome, Aristotle usually refrains from such precision and concentrates on what "happens by nature," i.e. on the class of events that comprises both the necessary and the "usual." They are the kinds of event that are always realized when nothing interferes with the natural causal development (*Metaphysics* 1048a16; *Physics* 199a11 et pass.).

In nature there is almost everywhere the possibility of an interference with the natural train of events from "outside," so that it does not reach its natural *telos*. Such interferences can be of quite different sorts; they are the causes of *chance events*. Since chance is the *third actor*, or rather the actor who is banished from tragedy, just as it is from the class of "the natural" in his physical writings, we should turn at least briefly to his conception of chance to see what, exactly, is ruled out. Chance events, as he defines them in the second book of his *Physics*, are what happens accidentally within the realm of what normally happens for some *end* (196b21–24; 30). The deviations from the norm do not happen without a cause, however; there is neither any breach of causality nor is there any mystery about where they come from. What happens by accident is rather the result of an unintended overlap of two different causal chains: when someone goes to the marketplace to collect subscriptions for a feast and runs into his debtor, he is said to have retrieved his debt by accident. Because such accidental results were not the intended end, they are not naturally connected with the process in question, and so chance events do not have an account of their own (*Physics* II, 197a18–19). Aristotle calls them "by chance" (*apo tuchēs*) if the interference concerns the *telos* intended in human activities, and "spontaneous" (*apo t'automatou*) if the interference prevents the realization of a natural *telos* (*Physics* II, 6).

That they do not happen for the sake of the naturally intended end, is not a sufficient condition for chance events in nature or human actions, however. Aristotle insists, in addition, that an unintended event is *not* accidental if it is caused by a regular concomitant of the agent's circumstances – it should also not be part of the man's routine activities to go to the marketplace (197a4). What is the point of adding this extra condition? It seems that for Aristotle all the wider normal circumstances of a given causal constellation have to be included in the account to determine whether something is a natural or a chance outcome. Not every factor connected with some action or event is there for the specific purpose; it suffices to make it a necessary or nearly necessary part of it that it should be there usually.[16] This injunction considerably widens the scope of what can be called necessary or natural and limits the scope of *chance* in Aristotle's general ontology. As we will see later, this extra condition plays a significant role in the justification of necessity in tragedy.[17]

Provided that we accept this brief characterization as a sufficient account of the relationship between necessity, chance, and "what happens for the most part," we will still have to return to our initial question, why and in what sense Aristotle can envisage a necessity, or an "almost necessity," for the development in tragedy, and why he excludes chance. So what are our actors doing there, or forbidden to do? To answer this question we will have to see, first of all, how well the qualifications concerning the necessary and the almost necessary can be fitted into the sphere of *human action*, since *praxis* is the main element in Aristotle's discussion of the coherence of tragedy.

The conception of what happens regularly and of what happens by accident is not limited in its application to natural science for Aristotle, as the brief discussion of his conception of chance indicated. Necessity in a more relaxed sense is also attributable to the conditions of human actions. This is due not only to the fact that he regards man as part of nature, and that natural teleology works in human nature as well as in that of animals, plants, and other natural substances. Even the specifically human, the field of morality, has a deterministic character, for Aristotle. Although he does not speak explicitly about necessity in this connection, a necessity of human actions emerges within the causal structure that he assumes for human activities in his ethical writings.[18] Any decision is determined by the agent's inner moral dispositions. Once a person has acquired his/her character, the disposition to choose a certain kind of mean between two extremes will be fixed. The person will find this or that possibility attractive or unattractive, will make the corresponding choices, and will use his/her practical reason to figure out the right means to put them into action, if nothing from outside interferes.[19] To see why Aristotle accepts such a teleologically determined psychological "mechanism," we only have to reflect on the question what the conception of an acquired disposition (*hexis*) for choosing the mean between the extremes of excess and deficiency entails. Every one of us will in every situation of decision envisage this or that end as "the right thing" to aim for, and s/he will employ his or her practical reasoning, *phronesis*, to find the appropriate means to achieve this end. The desire for a certain end and the calculation of the means are necessary functions of the acquired moral disposition ("moral taste") on the one hand, and of practical reason on the other. These are the two factors which will determine how each person will act in any given situation, if no chance event interferes. Hence, given sufficient knowledge, an agent's activities are, at least in principle, as predictable as are the events in nature.

The importance of the psychological determinism at work in Aristotle's ethics has been noticed by various commentators.[20] That Aristotle himself was aware that our inner disposition represents a limitation of the range of human freedom, manifests itself in the fact that he sees the need to justify that we have at least *some* responsibility for our moral or immoral actions. This justification is interesting because Aristotle's "curiously unconfident statement" that we are "co-responsible" emphasizes the limitation of our responsibility for the particular act: we are responsible because we have at least corroborated in the acquisition of our nature or character.[21] The assumption of an inner natural teleological determinism for human actions explains why Aristotle can treat the exceptions from the rule in human action in the same way as he treats accidental events in nature. Both in nature and in human action the accidental is then the only thing that stands in the way of strict regularity, i.e. necessity. It is therefore possible for Aristotle to lump everything that happens "necessarily or for the most part" in human actions together under the title of "the natural," and to oppose it to what happens by chance. This fact explains why he often uses the phrase of "what happens *naturally*" ("*pehpyken*" or some similar construction,[22] as a synonym of "necessarily or for the most part" in connection with human actions, as we find it at the crucial point in the *Poetics* (1450b27–34). The demand for a natural coherence of the parts of tragedy and the exclusion of chance is the demand of a natural coherence within the actions.

As has been emphasized already, Aristotle was aware of the fact that there can always be interferences with human actions, just as impediments are always possible in nonhuman nature, so that a different end than the naturally or humanly intended one can be attained. Since such impediments are incalculable (*aorista, apeira*), exceptions can in fact hardly ever be ruled out ahead of time.[23] Because the accidental is incalculable, it is in the strict sense "unknowable"; there can also be no discipline of what happens outside of the natural (and rational) order of things. The unpredictability of such accidental interferences also explains the tendency in Aristotle's scientific work to prefer the backward looking, hypothetical necessity, to the forward-looking unqualified, necessity. Why he insists on the latter necessity for the coherence in tragedy, a necessity stricter than he demands for most sciences, remains to be seen.

III. The Employment of the "Modals" in the *Poetics*

The fact that there are only three types of states of affairs or events for Aristotle, the necessary, what happens for the most part, and what happens by chance, explains why they play such an, at first sight surprisingly, important role in the *Poetics*, and why Aristotle insists time and again that the development must be necessary and natural. It also explains why he excludes chance: the contingent, in the sense of what happens randomly and for no inherent reason, should not play any prominent role in tragic development, since there is nothing to be known about – or learned from – such occurrences. If tragedy is to teach us anything of universal importance, then the sequence of events must be necessary, or at least nearly so. Since chance is explicitly excluded, this leaves us precisely with the kind of coherence Aristotle prescribes: things must follow "either necessarily or for the most part."[24]

But how well can this classification meet the special conditions presupposed in the *Poetics*, in particular in view of the fact that tragedy does not deal with a whole class or type of events or actions, as was pointed out already at the beginning of this essay? This problem vanishes when we take note of the special kind of universality which Aristotle postulates as essential for tragedy. What he has in mind comes to the fore especially when he turns to the question of the didactic purpose of tragedy: it should represent the universal, even if it lets it appear disguised as the particular. What Antigone does, or what Oedipus undergoes, ought to be presented not as the action peculiar to the individuals they happen to be, but as the action that *a person of such kind* would do or suffer, according to Aristotle.[25] The *personae* in tragedy always represent a *type*, and their actions a type of action. Once this special twist in Aristotle's theory is taken into consideration, it is clear why he must rule out chance events for drama as much as possible and why he decrees that everything that is not strictly motivated is not a natural part but falls "outside of the drama" and should be treated accordingly.[26] Chance solutions, or extraneous interferences like the *dénouement* through a *deus ex machina*, are an embarrassment and result from a weak construction of the plot (1454a36–b2).

But do *all* features of tragedy have to satisfy the condition of being either necessary or "regular?" Since Aristotle once refers to the subject of tragedy as "what might happen" (1451a37), and later mentions the "possible" in a more relaxed sense ("possible because it did happen," 1451b18; cf. 1455a29), there seems room for contingency in a wider sense than the "almost necessary." And at times Aristotle seems, in fact, willing to compromise with respect to certain adornments to the tragic plots; he is ready, for instance, to make some concessions for symbolically significant accidents.[27] But bare possibilities as such cannot be accommodated in purposeful actions; such possibilities would be loose ends and have to count as accidentals. Accidents are not the poet's but rather the historian's concern, as Aristotle decrees, since history is full of unrelated coincidences that have no place in tragedy. In fact, it is the possibility of depicting events undisturbed by accidents that establishes the superiority of tragedy over history and makes it a more philosophical enterprise, because it can depict the universal, i.e. what is not distorted by the incalculable vicissitudes of everyday life.[28] So, given his "ontological scheme" that was lined out earlier, he cannot really relent as far as the structure of the plot itself is concerned. Once chance is excluded, every action must be for an end, and must therefore be well motivated within the context of the play, i.e. presented as necessary. His explanation of the sense of "possible," which he introduces at the beginning of Chapter 9, leaves no room for doubt. The task of tragedy is not to deal with the kinds of things that actually do happen in life, but with "what is possible in accordance with [*kata to*] the likely or necessary" (1451a38).

We may nevertheless wonder whether Aristotle's conformity to his system sets too rigid a framework for tragedy. Does not the strict alternative of "necessity or chance" put too much of a strain on the kind of intuitive coherence we would expect from drama? In short, does not Aristotle's rigor needlessly press the point, so that his "ontological scheme" unduly cuts into poetic freedom of invention and flexibility? And, most importantly, how could there be anything which moves us to fear and pity or touch our human sentiments in any other way, when we witness a development that is necessary and "normal"? It is, of course, quite possible to write didactic tragedies in which all types are flawlessly represented and act exactly in the way a rational spectator with sufficient moral experience and training would expect them to. But though such tragedies might satisfy the conception of theater as a "moral institution" that was entertained by some theorists of the Enlightenment in the eighteenth century, it does not seem to agree with what we see in Greek tragedy. Nor does such rigorous universality even seem to be what Aristotle himself expects, when we take a closer look at his discussion of the elements of tragedy. For he does not, in his detailed recommendations for the construction of complications and solutions in the plot, advocate the obvious and the foreseeable at all.

Before we resign ourselves to the assumption that there is some irreconcilable tension in Aristotle's basic principles for tragedy, a tension that results from his tendency to import the same principles in all disciplines, we should note that these principles in fact allow for quite some flexibility, particularly where human actions are concerned. Not just in practice, but also in Aristotle's ethical theory what is "normal" is not as rigidly regimented as are the principles in other areas. As he asserts himself, the "scientific approach" cannot be applied with the same stringency in all branches of human intellectual activities. Ethics, he likes to repeat, cannot aspire to the same precision as mathematics (cf. *Nicomachean Ethics* (*NE*) I, 3; 7 et pass.).[29] He therefore allows for quite some leeway within the range of human decisions. The choices that a person of a certain type will make can only be roughly of the same kind, and the same imprecision will also apply to the ways and means such a person will choose to bring about the *telos* in question. Ethics, as Aristotle repeatedly asserts, can proceed only in a rough-and-tough way (*pachylōs kai typō*, *NE* 1094b20).

Since drama deals with human action, we can with good reason expect the same kind of flexibility in his *Poetics*, which Aristotle allows in his depiction of human action in his ethics. He, as a matter of fact, gives an unmistakable hint that we have to presuppose a more relaxed sense for the "necessary and the natural" in tragic development than the scientist's strict necessity, which finds its limitations only in rare impediments from outside. We should now take into account a feature in the *Poetics* that has been intentionally passed over so far in this essay. This crucial feature is the fact that Aristotle makes use of the expression "what happens for the most part" only once, namely when he first introduced the "modalities" in Chapter 7 (1450b30). He replaces it in the same chapter by the word "*eikos*," what is *probable* (*plausible* or *likely*), and sticks to that term ever after (1451a12; 51a28; 51b9; 35 et pass.). Since this pairing together of "necessary or likely" is not found elsewhere in Aristotle, the use of "*eikos*" instead of "*hōs epi to polu*" demands some explanation. Before we turn to the question what difference there may be, quite generally, between "what happens for the most part" and the "likely," we should ask ourselves why Aristotle first introduced the "statistical" term in the *Poetics* in the first place, only to drop it immediately afterwards. If it was not a sheer blunder (easily corrected by erasure), we must assume that Aristotle inserts "likely" only afterwards, because he wants to draw our attention to this replacement. It would indicate that by "likely" he means at least in principle the same sorts of events that are usually called "for the most part," but wants to avoid that term in the *Poetics*. So his conspicuously dropping the phrase suggests that the "statistical" connotation of "what happens usually or normally" for some reason brings in a wrong nuance into the discussion of tragedy. Since Aristotle leaves his reasons open for conjecture, we should take a closer look at the normal use of "*eikos*."

As a glance at Bonitz' *Index* (s.v.) shows, *"eikos,"* is not at home in Aristotle's logical writings, nor in his science. As a technical term it is found, besides the *Poetics*, almost exclusively in the *Rhetoric*.[30] The definition that he gives for the meaning of *"likely"* in *Rhetoric* 1357a34–b1, shows that it functions as a replacement of "for the most part" there, too.[31] Fortunately the *Rhetoric* contains some enlightening comments on the difference: "the likely is what happens for the most part, but not unqualifiedly, as it is sometimes defined, but in the sense that it belongs to what can be otherwise." Cryptic as this "explanation" must seem at first sight, it makes sense if we take it as a reference to the ambiguity in the concept of what "happens for the most part," discussed earlier, i.e. that although in principle it belongs to the *contingent*, it is usually approximated to *necessity*. The "almost necessity" of what happens with high frequency, must be what is called the *unqualified* sense of *"hōs epi to polu,"* while "what can be otherwise" must be its *contingent* aspect, i.e. that there is an open possibility of its being otherwise. Why does Aristotle invoke this distinction here? If the "likely" is expressly assigned to "what can be otherwise," then this indicates that it carries a considerably weaker sense than the normal "almost necessity." The "likely" is applied in the *Rhetoric* to cases where the type of event does not *eo ipso* already import an almost necessity, but where, at least in principle, two possibilities are open, one of which is the likely one. Such a more open, or weaker, sense of the "likely" or "probable" fits very well into the context of rhetoric, because necessary premises are hardly available, as Aristotle affirms (*Rhetoric* 1357a22; 26). The rhetorician usually has to deal with a wide open field of possibilities, and can only hope to present the audience with the *subjectively* more likely side of an alternative. In the experience of everyday life cases where everyone will agree on a virtual necessity of what must be assumed, will be much harder to come by, than they are in science. This applies especially to our ordinary assessment of the stringency concerning human actions; the rhetorician has to contend with general views of what is plausible and probable.

But does not this reference to an *open field* of two-sided possibilities contradict the threefold ontological division of the necessary, the nearly necessary, and chance events, which was presupposed for Aristotle in this essay so far? And did we not refer to evidence which expressly included human actions in this division, so that it seemed to be an exhaustive division of all of reality? This apparent contradiction is, fortunately, easily resolved. In the case of human actions *in general* there is indeed a field of wide open possibilities, as long as we are not dealing with a definite kind of agent. There is two-sided possibility while the matter is causally under-determined.[32] Of course, "people" may lie or steal, or refrain from doing so. As soon as we are dealing with a particular *individual*, however, the psychological mechanism is in place, which was discussed above. That is to say, once we are dealing with a specific individual in a particular situation, the two-sided possibilities vanish. The individual will act in accordance with his character necessarily or for the most part, unless some chance event gets in the way.[33]

Because the rhetorician is concerned with the human situation in general, he cannot usually rely on a recognition of "almost necessary" states of affairs by his audience, as the scientist can. So, if he has to try to convince an audience of the likeliness of some accused person's guilt or innocence, he has no such near-necessities at his disposition. He can at best rely on *endoxa* (1402a34), and present his case as the likely one in a situation that might well be otherwise. What is a necessary or highly probable decision for one person to make, may not be so for another, who is not that type of a person. The orator can rely only on a general kind of psychological knowledge, then, and general *statistical* experience will not be sufficient to prove what is the necessary or almost necessary thing that a given individual will do or must have done in a given situation. So the rhetorician's appeals have to be based on the presupposition that for the audience the matter is at the most "plausible" in the sense that it could be otherwise.

The orator and the tragedian have quite a few preconditions of their art in common. Both have to take psychological differentiations into consideration, as well as the fact that in ethics the general rules cannot be as precise as they are in most other sciences. Not only that, the poet, like the orator, also has to count on his audience's psychological knowledge: he has to rely on "the general experience of life," or on what is commonsensically considered as likely. It is this psychological aspect which Aristotle refers to time and again in the *Poetics*, and which makes him agree with certain poets that it is better to depict plausible impossibilities than implausible possibilities (1460a27). For all these reasons the poet's depiction of what is probable and plausible must be very different from the scientist's and resemble much more the rhetorician's, in that both must rely on what is publicly accepted experience.

If the common concerns of the rhetorician and the poet may seem to explain the use of *"eikos"* in both the *Rhetoric* and the *Poetics*, we should not jump too soon to the conclusion that the meaning is the same, however. For we should not forget that there is also a decisive difference between the two cases. The rhetorician is dealing with arguments which must strike a general audience as plausible, even though the audience has no precise knowledge of the facts of the matter. The poet, by contrast, is not concerned with arguments or general plausibilities, but has all the freedom he could wish for, to present his audience with the supposed facts of the matter that explain the decisions and actions of his *personae*. Since it is up to him to create those circumstances, he not only can, he in fact ought to avoid the situation where his hero's actions are causally underdetermined. Though the poet, like the rhetorician, has to rely on psychological knowledge of the human condition, he can use his knowledge to fine-tune all the circumstances, both the inner and outer ones, until the causal constellation looks watertight in a way that must be the orator's dream (cf. *Rhetoric* 1398b21). So the poet can and ought to construct his play in such a way that the hero's actions become a matter of necessity, or nearly so. Aristotle has, therefore, no reason to agree to any weakening of the conditions for the poet.[34]

The fact that he continues to pair off *necessity* and "likeliness" together throughout the *Poetics*, while there is no such combination with necessity in the *Rhetoric*, suggests that the terminological change in the *Poetics* is not one of softening the conditions for similar reasons. So the "plausibility" that the poet is looking for cannot really be the same as the one displayed in a rhetorician's argument, i.e. a probability based on public acceptance.

This argument seems, however, to provide more than we have bargained for. It gives Aristotle good reasons for the imposition of necessity in the *Poetics*, but leaves us without the explanation we are looking for, i.e. the addition of the alternative "*eikos*." It will be of no use to appeal to the insight gleaned from the ethics, that in human affairs there is always only a rough-and-tough likeliness, because this applies only as long as we are concerned with the types of persons in general, while the specifics of the situation of choice are undetermined. As we have seen earlier, Aristotle does believe in a determination of choice for the individual by his character, even if he avoids the use of "necessary" in his ethics. When it comes to the individual's particular decisions in particular, fully specified, circumstances, there is no causal underdetermination. So this general recourse to the basic principles of ethics does not really help us any more to explain the meaning of "*eikos*" in the *Poetics* than the recourse to the *Rhetoric*.

But what different kind of "softening" of the necessity-condition can Aristotle have in mind, especially since interruptions by chance events are ruled out for tragedy? In order to get a better grasp on the tragedian's specific kind of "likeliness" we have to delve more deeply into the peculiarities of the elements of drama to which Aristotle refers, to see what makes "*hos epi to polu*" the wrong term to use in the *Poetics*, but explains the need for some other qualification of strict necessity. What we have said so far shows merely that Aristotle's presuppositions for tragedy are in general agreement with the principles of action in his ethics. He regards it as essential that the tragedian represents the individual as a stand-in for the universal. Furthermore, the hero is not the impersonation of *mankind* in general, but rather of a certain type; the tragedian's aim is to show how a person of a certain kind will act in a particular situation (*tō poiō ta poia* . . . 1451b8; 1454a35). What we have so far ignored is the fact that the poet's striving for universality is of a quite special kind. Firstly, the events and circumstances that form the plot are far from the usual human experience. Secondly, the persons involved, the agents, are not the average types of human beings. It is, rather, the poet's task to present the unusual as necessary or at least as likely. This, to put the cards down finally, must be the peculiarity in tragedy that explains the terminological shift to "*eikos*." A scientific "statistical" conception of what "happens for the most part" would certainly not do to capture the poet's striving for the "unusual likeliness"; nor, of course, could it be replaced by the rhetorician's general probabilities based on *endoxa*. The specific aim of tragedy, to find convincing solutions for unusual problems, explains why Aristotle has to qualify his demand for a *necessary* coherence of the events that form the structure of a plot. Since such events fall outside most of our human experiences, it would often be quite unreasonable to ask for a stronger criterion than the "likely" in our judgment. In extreme cases we may have to stretch all our ethical creative imagination to determine whether a poet has fastened on "the likely" action. To call for necessity may be to ask for the impossible or the meaningless.

The twofold task of combining the unusual and the likely imports certain constraints on the poet, both for the content of the play as well as for its intended effects on the audience.[35] We should look at some of the consequences of this basic conception in Aristotle's further analysis of the requirements for tragedy. It explains to quite some degree the selection of the problems (and the omission of others) in his *Poetics*. If the development must strike the audience as necessary or likely, in spite of its unusualness, both the agents and their situation must remain at least within the range of what is humanly possible, i.e. they cannot fall completely out of the ordinary. So the poet must strike a careful balance to ensure that he remains within the realm of our psychological experience, or at least of our imagination. The development will then have to incorporate what is necessary or likely, in what is in itself an unusual situation, and in agents that are at least somewhat out of the range of the average person: hence Aristotle admits the justification of some poets' claim that the unlikely can be the likely (1456a24–25).

Aristotle's insistence on the compatibility of both these features has the effect that he at times seems to waver when he tries to work out some of the details, as far as the balance between the normal and the abnormal is concerned.[36] The problem of balance becomes apparent, for instance, in the discussion of the magnitude or gravity that Aristotle postulates for tragedy. He indicates that he sees the unusualness of the situation in which the agents find themselves as a necessary condition, and some of the complexities in his prescriptions result from his intention to ensure the "right mean" of unusualness and plausibility. There are, of course, different ways to meet the conditions; as Aristotle indicates, the poet may orientate himself, like a painter, (1) to what *is*, or (2) to what people believe, or to (3) what *ought to be* the case (1460b10 f; 32–b9). While Aristotle's sympathies clearly lie with the last possibility, he acknowledges the poet's need for compromise: the poet must not only aim for the ideal (*kalon*) but respect the particular inner and outer circumstances of his agents (1461a7 f.).

To meet the "unusual-yet-plausible" condition, the protagonists ought not, for instance, to find themselves merely in a situation of enmity or friendship of the ordinary kind. The tragic situation must consist in a more complex constellation that grips the emotions and moral imagination; it demands inescapable enmity arising between natural friends, as between members of the same family, either in ignorance of who they are, or in full knowledge but without obvious solution or escape (1453b15–22). The character of the *personae* must also at least border on the unusual. As Aristotle points out, they must be like us, i.e. recognizable as human beings in the sense that we can identify with them as moral agents, but they must also be raised above the level of the usual to grip our imagination (1452b34; 1453a6–17). In spite of the unusualness of some of the features in drama – the circumstances created by the protagonist's (partial) ignorance and the convoluted family histories – the poet must manage to present the development as natural. To explain the desired combination Aristotle refers to the work of a good painter who remains true to the features of his human models, while idealizing some of their features (1454b9–11). In a similar fashion the tragedian must give his *personae* human features that are compatible with some superhuman qualities.

But it is, of course, not only the unusualness of the person's situation and the (somewhat) larger than life portraits that tragedy demands, which make Aristotle modify his "modals" in such a way that necessity and naturalness take on a slightly different character from the one that they have elsewhere in Aristotle, including the *Rhetoric*. It is the peculiarity of tragic actions that adds to it. When Aristotle demands the coherence or unity of action, then he does not have single actions of a single agent in mind, as he usually does when he analyzes moral actions in his ethical writings. The "action" in drama consists of a sequence of interactions between different agents, in different stages of their comprehension of the situation, since in drama normally no one is in "full control" of the whole development.[37] In tragedy we do not have the moral philosopher's hypothetical sovereign agent whose field of choice is open and transparent. The tragic agents are limited in their knowledge and hampered by the fact that they often act at cross-purposes. Creon and Antigone in Sophocles' play have each their own *telos*, which is incompatible with the other's, and they do not make the decisions they make for the sake of the other. Neither did Creon decree the death-penalty for the burial in order to punish Antigone, nor did Antigone bury her brother in order to be executed.

But does this not make the major reversions accidental or *chance* ones, by Aristotle's own lights? And should not the complexity and opacity of the situation make him lower rather than tighten his demand for necessity and stringency in drama? Why these factors do not introduce an element of chance becomes clear, if we remember Aristotle's explicit condition mentioned earlier, that events are accidental only if they do not result from the agent's own circumstances. Antigone's and Creon's actions do not overlap accidentally; when we ask ourselves whether the outcome of their decisions are "likely" we have to include the conditions ("against whom, when and how . . .") as part of their actions. Furthermore, it is only when we regard their interaction as *the* action around which the drama is centered that we can ask ourselves, in what sense its parts form a necessary or likely progression and whether the action reaches a natural or likely end. The opacity of the situation to the protagonists themselves is no impediment to the demand for stringency either, not because of a relentless rationalism on Aristotle's side, but because of his demand that each agent ought to make the decisions that are the necessary and likely ones for him to make, given his knowledge and character. Such necessity is not at all incompatible with human fragility, vulnerability, or even irrationality. It is the challenge for the artist's ingenuity to forge a necessary and plausible solution to all complications, a solution which makes sense for the interactions of all persons involved. Such wider resolves of complex constellations, the *sustasis* of the play (1453a3), will be regarded as necessary or probable, if the poet has worked out all motives well and provided the appropriate circumstances.

The need to justify the plausibility of the unusual in the actions of the hero seems also to stand behind Aristotle's recommendations concerning the *mistakes*, or even "great mistakes" (*hamartia*), which cause the suffering of great misfortunes (1453a10; 16). This is not the place for a discussion, let alone a decision, of the thorny question of what Aristotle means by "*hamartia*." It is the topic of another essay in this collection. But given the perspective of this essay, we can say without much further debate, that by the "faults" Aristotle attributes to his heroes as a necessary element of tragedy he cannot mean unmotivated slips or mishaps for which they are not responsible. Since *chance events* are banished to the fringes of drama, it must be the protagonist's own actions that lead to his/her downfall, or s/he must at least contribute to it.

To be sure, a "mistake" is defined by Aristotle in *NE* V, 1135b12 as an action committed "with ignorance" (*met' agnoias*).[38] The ignorance involved in a "mistake" is only a *partial* ignorance, however, so that the perpetrator can be excused only as far as the ignorance goes. As Aristotle makes clear in that discussion, he remains culpable to the degree that he is aware or ought to be aware of the circumstances and consequences of his action, because the event is not beyond reasonable expectation. Only if the protagonist does not contribute to the action at all, or the outcome is totally unforeseeable in human terms, is there no responsibility or guilt involved; the result must then be called a "mishap," an *atuchēma*, i.e. an unfortunate chance event (*NE* 1135b17). Such results should, however, clearly be avoided in drama; they fall under the general verdict against "chance" development. If the protagonist is victim to external circumstances only, this would not provoke the appropriate emotional response of the audience, as Aristotle points out. Such a spectacle would at best stir our disgust, but neither pity nor fear (*Poetics* 1452b34–36). Both these emotions presuppose at least some active involvement of the hero, and it is up to the artist's skill to provoke the right mixture of emotional response by meting out the right mixture of the agent's responsibility by letting him commit well-motivated mistakes.

That the perpetrator must be at least partially responsible for his actions in Aristotle's conception explains also why he demands a careful balance for the character of the protagonist: he must be neither a paragon of virtue, nor a consummate villain, but an "inbetween" person – on the whole like ourselves – but preferably better rather than worse than the average person (1453a7). There is the need to find a hero who will commit actions that are of sufficient magnitude, and who will, plausibly or necessarily, end up doing or suffering terrible things (*deina*), that provoke sufficient fear (because he is "like us" and we might suffer the same fate) and pity, because he suffers more than he deserves.[39]

For this reason it also seems wrong to attribute the sudden reversion, the ultimate catastrophe or unexpected salvation, entirely to "external circumstances," as if they did not at least in part follow from the agents', often culpable, misjudgment.[40] Aristotle's choice of terminology, the employment of *eutuchia* and *atuchia* (or *dustuchia*), may suggest that there is an element of *chance* or *luck* involved here. To attribute this to Aristotle would be a clear mistake, however. He has given an unmistakeable indication of why he uses *eutuchia* and *atuchia*: when he first introduces the subject, he explains that it is the agents' *praxeis* (based on character and thought) which makes them succeed (*tugchanousi*) or fail (*apotugchanousi pantes*, 1449b36 ff.). So if it is not inherent evil but error that accounts for the agent's failure, and they get often much more than they deserve, we should not overlook the element of culpable ignorance. It is not only a question of what the protagonist knew and when he knew it, but also of what he *ought* to have known or at least suspected. To avoid harping on Oedipus' failure to find out in time who he really was, we can turn to the Agamemnon in the Aeschylus's play. Of all the persons involved he is the only one without any suspicion or evil forebodings. Yet such obtuseness amounts to moral tone-deafness, when he simply presupposes that all must be quiet on the home front. He steps on the red carpet that leads to his doom without more than general misgivings about a possible inappropriateness of such self-glorification, without asking himself whether *iam tua res agitur*. If the play is about Agamemnon, then it is also about his stubborn ignorance or heedlessness of the consequences of what he has done in the past. So even if a sudden downturn or a sudden recognition is not foreseeable, and rightly deserve our fear and pity, the protagonist can rarely be said to be in entire ignorance of the delicacy of his/her situation. If the development lacks plausibility in all of these respects, it will fail to provoke the right emotional response, which is the proper function (*ergon*) of tragedy (1452a29 ff.).

Aristotle's insistence that the development should be necessary or at least plausible, while the miraculous and surprising should be kept carefully in check, if it is deployed at all,[41] shows that he finds the intelligibility in human terms the most indispensable element of tragedy – and this, rather than his irreligiosity is arguably the main reason why he neglects to discuss the importance of the possibility of divine interference, and the divine element as the background of tragedy in general. If we are to recognize and judge the actions and interactions on the standard of our common human experience, they must fall, at least for the most part, within the terms of what is comprehensible for a morally experienced person. This kind of comprehension of what is necessary or likely cannot include the actions, motives and decisions of the gods, unless they are depicted as rational agents, as we find Apollo, Athena and the Eumenides reason and act in Aeschylus' *Eumenides*. Often the divinities act, and are supposed to act, in ways that are not open for human understanding. It stands to reason that Aristotle in that case would count the divine element as part of the *sustasis*, of the situation of which the human agent must nevertheless make the best sense he can. Orestes in the *Choephori* is brought by divine forces into an inescapable situation, which will provoke our fear and pity; this does not absolve the poet from the task to make his decisions and actions in his assessment of his situation appear as well motivated. It is therefore not only Aristotle's "relentless rationalism" or "secularism" that avoids the question of the divine element almost entirely (cf. 54b5–6), so that he seems deaf to the need for the mysterious in tragedy![42] No matter how strange the circumstances in a drama may be, the progression of the dramatic interaction must remain intelligible, if coherence and motivation are not to fall by the wayside (1455a17).

On the internal coherence rests also the intellectual pleasure that tragedy is supposed to procure in the audience. Aristotle is not very explicit about this point, but the hints that he gives now and then suggest that this is a point of great importance for him. At the beginning of the *Poetics* he once illustrates the pleasure caused by *mimesis* with the example of the pleasure of looking at a painting (1448b14–19).[43] What pleases us is to learn and to "calculate" when we identify the objects ("this one represents that one"). It is not difficult to transfer this very simple model to the experience of watching a drama unfold; we will learn what kinds of persons the agents are from their actions, and we will learn to understand why their actions have the consequences they have. For the critical spectator it is a pleasure to recognize how and why the decisions the agents are making, or the sufferings they have to undergo, are *necessary* or *plausible* ones, so that in the end the tragedy appears as an organic whole (1450b23 ff.; 59a20).[44] This pleasure is enhanced if the situation of the agents, the status of their knowledge or ignorance, as well as their characters, display a certain kind of complexity and unusualness, while the solution turns out to be a necessary and natural one, of an intricacy unforeseen by the spectator. To watch the unfolding of a well-motivated but unusual solution to a difficulty of sufficient magnitude is a pleasure, comparable to the pleasure of listening to a fugue of complex structure.

This *diagnostic* activity is probably not the only reason for the pleasure we derive from mimesis for Aristotle. If he stresses the need to shape tragedy as an organic whole where the beginning is a true beginning, the end a true end, and the middle parts contain the necessary and plausible development that leads from one to the other, he may have more than sheer intellectual artistic pleasure in mind. Tragedy gives the opportunity of studying the kind of complexity and plausibility that *textbook cases* in ethical discussions cannot provide. Since in ethical debates the situations and the persons involved must remain sketchy, such explanations can be no more than rough-and-tough, as Aristotle was well aware. It is then no longer surprising if Aristotle can insist on a necessity for the development in tragedy that he usually avoids in ethics.

If examples in ethics are too general to allow for proofs of necessity, our real-life experiences are usually not general enough. In real life, we have hardly ever the opportunity to experience our or other persons' actions and interactions as meaningful "wholes". Everyday life is a part of *history* with all its little or important accidents and interferences, where agents, their actions and reactions (our own included) are difficult to make sense of, because of all their particular accidental properties that get in the way of a clear development. All these accidental developments and conditions make it difficult to read the "book of life" in a profitable way, or to regard life as bookworthy. We often cannot derive any general insights into ourselves or others from the confused script of the actual occurrences that make up the lives of individuals and the development of history in general. In tragedy all these accidents are stripped away, and so we can learn, and enjoy, to see, what sense we can make of events that are not the products of chance, but are a matter of the individuals' own decisions, not in spite of but *because* they have, as human beings, only limited knowledge and limited power over their own circumstances. This accounts for the nobility and higher philosophical status that Aristotle acknowledges to tragedy over history (1451b5 f.), and it explains why he makes such high demands for the coherence of its parts, so that he can insist on the test that plot and characters be scrutinized *sub specie necessitatis*.

IV. Conclusion

The interpretation of one particular aspect of a work that is as short, complex, and beset by textual difficulties as Aristotle's *Poetics* has certain dangers. It imports the danger of forgetting that this one feature is not the only one, nor perhaps even the most important one for Aristotle himself. It also imports the danger of reading much more into the one feature, than Aristotle himself had intended. Such onesidedness is always difficult to avoid, if the focus is limited. So it is important to remember the need to read this essay in connection with all the other considerations discussed in the other essays. There is no pretense that this particular point of view captures all that is essential about Greek tragedy, or that it even captures all that Aristotle considered as essential.[45] That the discussion has been expository rather than critical of Aristotle's position may well be considered one of its major weaknesses, since it smooths over difficulties that should have rather been worked out. But if the line pursued here may seem overly complimentary to Aristotle, then the intention was to provide a counterbalance to some recent criticism of the justifiability of Aristotle's "cardinal" principles. A counterbalance does not aim at the obliteration of other authors' scruples. If this essay can claim to have thrown a more favorable light on one of the criteria Aristotle considered as important both for the construction and for the critique of tragedies, this should be all it could aim for. I hope indeed to have shown that Aristotle's insistence on necessity or likeliness is not as foreign to the art of tragedy as it may seem at first sight, and that he imposes it on tragedy not only because The Philosopher swoops down with the same scientific spirit on every subject he touches. If we are left with one question to Aristotle, then it will be whether his principle is sound that our actions are a necessary consequent of our character and our assessment of the situation. But this question would force us to review the principles of Aristotlian ethics as a whole, and such a task is clearly a problem that is *allēs pragmateias*.

Notes

1. *Poetics* 1451a12; 27f; 38; b6; 35; 52a20 et pass. In his monograph on the *Poetics* Halliwell calls it the "cardinal principle" or criterion (1986), 161; 220.
2. The text used is the Oxford edition by R. Kassel. All translations are my own. The Greek phrase translated by "for the most part" is "*hōs epi to polu.*" The "*chance beginning*" renders "*hopothen etuchen,*" the "chance end", "*hopou etuchen.*"
3. The lists of the several senses of necessity that we find at other places in Aristotle sometimes contains less than four items; their number depends obviously on the particular point of view under which he approaches the question. Sometimes he contrasts compulsion with all others (cf. *Posterior Analytics* II, 94a36), so we find only two kinds of necessity; sometimes he omits the "apodeictic" necessity because the emphasis lies on the difference between the two natural kinds of necessity, the hypothetical and unconditional one, in contrast to compulsion, so we find three kinds (*Parts of Animals* 639b21; 642a3–7; 32–35).
4. It would be misleading to call it "logical" necessity, because Aristotle has here not the logical form of the argument in mind, but rather the fact that what is concluded is necessary, if it follows from materially necessary premises; so he is more concerned with the *necessitas consequentis*, rather than with the *necessitas consequentiae*. On this topic cf. esp. G. Patzig, 1969, Ch. II. and the notes in J. Barnes, (1975), esp. 127; 222. Since "logical" necessity in general refers to either of these two possibilities in Aristotle, but not to causal necessity, it is advisable to avoid using the term for any of the kinds of non-syllogistic *causal* coherence (cf. Halliwell (1986), 78; 105 (1987), 99 f.; Janko (1987), 88 f.
5. For a comprehensive discussion of hypothetical necessity in Aristotle cf. John Cooper, "Hypothetical Necessity" in ed. A. Gotthelf (1985), 151–167.
6. Cf. *Posterior Analytics* II, 98a8–19. One of Aristotle's favorite examples is the usualness of men growing beards. For an extensive discussion, cf. M. Mignucci, "Ὡς ἐπὶ τὸ πολύ et nécessaire dans la conception Aristotélicienne de la science," ed. E. Berti (Padua, 19810, 172–203.
7. For the literature and a solution of the problem cf. G. Striker, "Notwendigkeit mit Lücken," in (1985), 146–164. Although the "usual" falls under the general definition of the *contingent* as what is neither necessary nor impossible, it does not behave like the contingent in general, because it does not permit negative conversion: if A is *possibly* B, it also holds that A is *possibly not* B; but it is obviously not true to say that if A is *usually* B it also holds that it is *usually not* B (cf. *Prior Analytics* 13, 32a33 ff.).
8. In his ethics as well as in his discussion of rhetoric Aristotle treats what is necessary and what is up to human decision as opposites, cf. *Rhetoric* 1368b33–69a7; *NE* III, 1112b30–34 (cf. *NE* VI, 1140a14; b1 we do not deliberate about what is necessary anyway).
9. Cf. *Posterior Analytics* I 6. For a recent discussion of these issues cf. (ed.) E. Berti, esp. the contributions by R. Sorabji, "Definitions: Why Necessary and in What Way?," 205–244, and J. Ackrill, "Aristotle's Theory of Definition," 359–384.
10. For Aristotle's discussion of essential or *per se* properties in contradistinction to accidental properties cf. *Posterior Analytics* 4, 73a34–24.
11. For the definition of "in all cases" cf. *Posterior Analytics* 4, 73a27–34. The connection

between "necessary" and "always" is further discussed in, *Metaphysics* Δ 5, 1016a14; Θ 8, 105016–24; *Physics* II, 196b12; *De Generatione et Corruptione* 337b35. The "statistical interpretation" owes its prominence most of all to the work of J. Hintikka (1957), 65–90; and (1973), esp. Chs. 2 and 5. Traces of its influence on the interpretation of the *Poetics* can be found in Janko's notes (1987), 89; 218.

12. Uniformity can at best tell us *that* something cannot be otherwise, it is not sufficient to show *why* it should be so, which is the most important condition of knowledge (cf. *Posterior Analytics* 13). Aristotle himself acknowledges at some point that exceptionless occurrence is not a sufficient criterion for necessity (*Posterior Analytics* 75b33).

13. In his "astrophysics" Aristotle even claims that only what is strictly eternal is necessary, cf. *De Gren. et Corr.* II, 11.

14. When conformity to the conditions of the syllogism is at stake, Aristotle focuses on the necessity of *attributes* of substances rather than on the necessity of *events*. But even in the *Posterior Analytics* examples creep in that are not universal *per se* attributes, but events like thunder, greying of hair, the growth of beards, or the twinkling of stars.

15. Aristotle himself mentions the difference between a more stringent and a more relaxed sense of demonstration in *Metaphysics* E 1, 1025b13. At times Aristotle also grants a kind of *de facto* necessity of all that is in actuality when it exists, and calls past events necessary. The necessity of the actual is mentioned in *De Int.* 9, 19a23; 13, 23a21; *Metaphysics* Θ 8, 1050b18. The necessity of the past is mentioned at *NE* 1139b7–9; *Rhetoric* 1418a3–5.

16. Aristotle acknowledges a nonteleological necessity of constant concomitants, cf. my article "Aristotle on the Limits of Determinism," ed. A. Gotthelf (1985), esp. 215–218.

17. This conception of chance is considerably narrower than the notion of "luck" discussed by M. Nussbaum (1986: 3; 318–342; esp. 378–394); because she treats all external interferences not intended by the agent as a matter of luck ("luck is seriously powerful," 384 f.), she can skirt the problem of necessity in her account of Aristotle's *Poetics*. The question of accuracy in terminology does not affect her analysis of the importance of human vulnerability in Aristotle's ethics; it must be pointed out, however, that for Aristotle much less is attributable to *tuchē* in tragedy than she allows for in her "Aristotelian" analysis.

18. Cf. *NE* VI, 2. The necessity of the actualization of the potential, given the right person in the right circumstances, is explicitly extended to human actions in *Metaphysics* Θ 5: everyone will act in accordance with his desires (1048a10–16).

19. This is a rather generous summary of Aristotle's discussion in *NE* II, 1–6 and VI, 1–2; 5. For a more detailed discussion of the interplay between character and action, cf. Ch. 5 in Halliwell's monograph, (1986) and commentary (1987), 93–96.

20. On human self-determination in Aristotle cf. the commentary to the *Nicomachean Ethics* by H. H. Joachim, 108: "We are free, qua self-determined: so far as what we do follows necessarily from our character and from that alone," 108.

21. W. F. R. Hardie (1968), 160. The reference is to *NE* III, 5, 1114a31 ff.: "for we are ourselves also partly responsible (*sunaitioi*) for our states of character, and it is by being persons of a certain kind that we assume the end to be so and so," 1114b22–24.

22. "*Pephyken*," "*physei*" or "*kata physin*"; what "happens naturally" (*Poetics* 1450b28; 29), "by nature" etc. can therefore be treated as a kind of modal operator, a stand-in for "necessarily or for the most part" (cf. *Physics* 200a2). It would in principle be no contradiction to say that something is "up to us" (*eph" hemin*), although the outcome is necessary. In his ethics Aristotle usually avoids speaking about necessity in this sense, since he wants to contrast what is up to choice with the unalterable.

23. Aristotle discusses the reasons for the incalculability of the accidental extensively in *Physics* II, 4–6 (esp. 196b28; 197a8; 17). Cf. also *Metaphysics* E 2; 3.

24. Halliwell seems to underrate the stringency of the general conditions of Aristotlelian ontology, if he regards his insistence as an *overemphasis* of the rational element in tragedy or an overstatement of the required unity of action (1986), 106; 129.

25. *Poetics* 1449a32; b10; 51b5–10. On "universality" in literature, cf. Halliwell (1986), 83; 95; 105; 139 ff.

26. *Poetics* 1453b32. Aristotle mentions such devices as prophecies or messenger's reports to keep what is not well motivated "outside the play," 1454b3; 7; 1455b8.

27. *Poetics* 1452a6–9 he admits wonder-inspiring accidents, *if* they are pedagogically suitable, like the killing of the murderer of Mitys by his statue. But there is at least the *semblance* here that it did not happen by mere chance. He seems also ready to grant some distortion of the plot to good poets, to give an actor the opportunity for a solo aria (1451b33–a1). Such deviations have to be "sweetened over" by other means, however (60b1 f.).

28. On the contrast between history and tragedy, cf. *Poetics* 9, 1451b1–11, where Aristotle stresses the particularity of history, and 23, 1459a21–29, where he focuses on the accidental character of historical events (*"synebē . . . hōs etuche"*). The question raised by Halliwell (1987), 106 why Aristotle does not treat tragedy as feigned history, finds its explanation exactly at this point: history can *by definition* not exclude the accidental or coincidental. This should also settle Nussbaum's query about philosophically minded historians like Thucydides (386): even he could not treat historical coincidences as if they had a *telos* (59b27; 29).

29. Aristotle affirms that we ought not to look for a greater precision than what holds "for the most part" (1094b21–22) and adds that it characterizes a properly educated man not to expect more precision than the subject matter warrants.

30. At the only place where Aristotle uses *"eikos"* as a synonym for *"hōs epi to polu"* in the *Analytics* (*Prior Analytics* II, 27, 70a2 ff.), he is referring to the use of enthymems in *rhetoric*. The few passages in the *Meteorologica* where *"eikos"* is employed, all have a psychological slant; they deal with what it is likely to assume as an explanation (*Mete.* 346a30; 351b19; 352a2).

31. That *eikos* means "for the most part" is confirmed in *Rhetoric* 1402b21: the probable is not what happens always, but what happens for the most part.

32. The two-sided possibility is discussed in *Metaphysics* Θ 2 and 5: for rational agents, in contradistinction to natural potentialities, it is open to act in opposite ways; but Aristotle also makes clear that desire and choice are necessitating principles (1048a10–15).

33. This would include cases of *akrasia*, provided the individual's "reduced state of knowledge" at a given moment has its causes in the particular inner and outer circumstances. It might overtax tragedy's possibilities to show that and why a certain person must act "acratically" in a given situation (especially since tragedy is not a character study, 1450a22), which would explain why Aristotle does not address the question in the *Poetics* (but cf. his demand that inconsistent persons be consistently inconsistent, 1454a26–8).

34. The need for coherence makes the effort of E. Belfiore (1984) futile, to work out a nonmoral sense of *"praxis"* for the *Poetics*. That the bare sequence of events as reported by Aristotle in his summaries of plots (1455b3–23) do not permit any precise moral evaluation, does not mean that the same holds for the development in any particular drama.

35. My claim that the "unusualness" is an important feature of tragedy rests, besides the emphasis on magnitude (*megethos*, 1449a6; b25; 50a25; 51a11 et pass.) and dignity (*semnon*, 1448b25; 49a21), on Aristotle's positive appreciation of the element of the

astonishing or marvelous (*thaumaston*, 1452a1–11; 56a20; 60a11–14, *ekplexis*, 1455a17 coming out of the likely events – *di eikotōn*) and the paradoxical (*para ton logon*, 56b7 55a13; 16; 60a20). That tragedy deals with the unusual, both for the action and the perpetrator, is confirmed in *Rhetoric* 1404b11–14, as a crucial distinction between rhetoric and poetry.

36. The "wavering" does not signify, as Halliwell suggests (1986, 111 f; "delicate issue," 174), that there is a *strain* in Aristotle's theory when confronted with the praxis of tragedy itself. It is not Aristotle's theory that has to balance incompatible demands on account of principles that are difficult to reconcile; Aristotle's theory points up the difficult but challenging demands that a tragedian's high art has to meet.

37. Halliwell rightly reminds us of the fact that *pragmata* are events rather than individual actions (1986, 140 f.), and sometimes refer to the complete dramatic framework and the whole design.

38. Janko (1987, 102 f.) who pleads for the protagonists' ignorance and innocence clearly overlooked the difference between "*di agnoian*" (of *NE* 1110a1; 18 1136a7) and "*met" agnoias*" (1135b12). It would be very strange if Aristotle did not insist on making the *hamartemata* a consequence of the person's character and practical reason (or lack thereof), cf. *Poetics* 1449b37 f.; 50a20 and esp. 1454a33–36; "so that such a one says or does such things either necessarily or plausibly," with *NE* 1104b33; 06b25; 10b29 "*dia toiautēn hamartian adikoi.*"

39. Among such well-motivating character flaws that lead to likely "*hamartiai*" Aristotle mentions irascibility, negligence, and harshness. One can refer to countless examples in Greek tragedy for such faults, for instance Oedipus' irascibility against Teiresias and Creon; or Creon's inflexibility against Antigone. They are indispensable, necessitating factors in these tragedies. It would be interesting to investigate whether any of the extant tragedies that lead to the hero's destruction work without such flaws.

40. Halliwell acknowledges that the pendulum nowadays may have swung too much against attributing responsibility to the faults in the agents (1986, 128), but rules out that there is serious guilt (233 cf. also 1987, 129).

41. The poet should, for instance, never use what is *alogon* if there is no need, 1461b19–20.

42. Cf. esp. the association of the gods with what "people" believe at 1460b35 "what they say about the gods" as the "third best" aim for the tragedian, after "what is or was" and "what ought to be" (60b10/1). It is not clear whether this would include such rational behavior of the gods as the one depicted in Aeschylus" *Eumenides*. On Aristotle's neglect of the special relationship of tragedy to the divine and the specifically mythical, see Halliwell (1987) 12; 111–112. Halliwell is silent about the many divine actions which could well all fit under the "necessary or plausible."

43. As Halliwell works out (1986, 70 ff.), one should not be mislead by the simplicity of Aristotle's analogy to underrate its consequences for his theory.

44. Cf. Aristotle's distinction between different kinds of *orthotēs*; the poet can make certain mistakes that do not reflect on his craft, but not others, *Poetics* 25, 1460b13–32.

45. The question has, for instance, not been raised whether and in what sense Aristotle's discussion of necessity in tragedy stands in relationship to the invincible Necessity of Plato's Myth of Er, the mother of the three fates.

Aristotle's Favorite Tragedies

Stephen A. White

To this day, the winner of the Lyceum Award for the best tragedy remains in doubt. The problem is not, as in Plato's early Academy, that Aristotle was stingy with the laurel, but that he registers a split vote. Twice in the *Poetics* he describes a pattern that the best tragedies follow; but after *Poetics* 13 gives a crown to plays with unhappy endings, *Poetics* 14 gives another crown to plays with happy endings. Or to name the leading contenders, he first favors plays like Sophocles' *Oedipus Tyrannus* (*OT*), and then he favors plays like Euripides' *Iphigenia at Tauris* (*IT*). Scholars have proposed various explanations for this discrepancy, which most consider a flat contradiction: Aristotle may have wavered before what he found an irresoluble tension; or he may have changed his mind without bothering to revise his text; or the two chapters may simply address different questions. But the alleged inconsistency is too plain to miss, and the chapters otherwise cohere very well: Chapter 13 asks what makes for the "finest" tragedies (52b31), and Chapter 14 tries to explain what makes them "fine" (53b26).[1] I am less interested in reconciling the two chapters, however, than in the criteria on which he bases his judgments. More is at stake here than ancient taste or a contest between tragedy and melodrama. Aristotle's preferences are of more than academic interest because they appear as conclusions in a complex argument about the moral dimension of tragedy. My question about his favorite tragedy, in fact, goes to the heart of his ethical theory, and its answer sheds light on a basic moral problem. His ideal Bestsellers, I shall argue, exemplify his views about the relation between luck and morality, and he considers the *OT* and the *IT* best because both highlight what I call "moral fortune," or the way people respond to their luck.

I. Moral Fortune

First, a few words of warning about my use of the term "moral." Some vagueness here is inevitable. But it can also be salutary, for part of the problem here involves the scope of morality in the first place. Roughly, in calling things "moral," I mean to refer quite generally to features of human conduct and character that excite impartial admiration or reproach. I do not mean, for example, to refer only to acts and traits that serve the good (or ill) of others. Though central to my topic, these are only part of what is admirable (or worthy of reproach). In Aristotle's account, moreover, the distance between self and others is not always wide: the virtuous practice altruism with egocentric motives; helping others is often something they want to do. Nor do I mean to limit my subject to obligations and duties, in contrast with what we like or prefer. In Aristotle's account, again, the two tend to converge for the virtuous, and moral conduct includes things people want to do as well as things they or others think they ought to do. One thing I do mean to exclude is didactic moralizing. In saying that Aristotle's criticism of tragedy has a moral basis, I mean only that his analysis makes a moral dimension an essential part of tragedy; he may also think that the theatre can or should be improving or teach us how to behave, but that is not my concern here. In calling things "moral," in fact, I take as my guide the sort of things Aristotle calls *kalon* or "fine." A prime example of what he calls "fine" is virtuous action, and the dominant motive of virtuous people is to do fine things "because they are fine."[2] But the virtuous are not the only ones who do morally admirable things, and as I shall argue, fine action by people of less than perfect virtue plays a major role in Aristotle's favorite tragedies.

The basic principle of Aristotle's ethics, though extremely controversial, is simply stated: happiness, which is much more than an occasional feeling of joy, consists in the exercise of rational virtues in a mature and complete life. He recognizes that we need some of the "external goods" of health, wealth, prestige, and power, but he argues that we can be happy with much less prosperity than traditional and conventional ideals held. Many people saw the virtues as necessary or efficient means to prosperity, but few imagined them sufficient for happiness or thought that the exercise of virtue could guarantee a good life. The principal worry here, dwelt on by poets and philosophers alike, was that external forces seem to have too much influence on our lives, initially in the form of "constitutive luck," and in the form of "incident luck" throughout.[3] First is the luck of the draw: when, where, and to whom we are born can greatly affect our chances of happiness; our physical endowments, our native talents, our upbringing and interests, even our propensities to virtue and vice all owe more to fortune than most of us care to admit. Then, once our character is formed, our lives are continually subject to forces beyond our control or even our ken; good people and others alike, in admirable pursuits and in bad, often succeed or fail with the help and hindrance of lucky events. Even intrepid proponents of theodicy like Hesiod and Solon admit that nothing guarantees that the just will flourish or the wicked receive what they deserve. Zeus, the parable goes, has a great pot of woe beside his pot of weal; he gives freely from the former but is sparing with the latter, so the poets encourage us not to lament our inevitable portion of sorrow, but to be grateful for any good he bestows (*Iliad* XXIV, 527–533; *Republic* II, 379a).

This gap between what we deserve and what we get, between virtue and prosperity, is a recurrent theme in Greek poetry. By itself, however, this unfortunate fact of life has no effect on our moral status, and it is no objection to Aristotle's eudaimonism to complain that virtuous activity cannot guarantee a pleasant and prosperous life. That complaint affects his theory only if a prosperous life is necessary for happiness, which he denies. Nor does he, any more than Plato in his construction of an ideally just society, seek to show that perfected reason and virtue can always, usually, or ever satisfy our every wish and desire; theirs is not the project of Aristotle Onassis. Rather, developing a theme inherited from archaic thought, both he and Plato try to show how the best life humans can live depends on our limiting the range of ends we seek, and how a life dominated by fine and virtuous activities provides the only basis for happiness. The disparity between virtue and fortune threatens eudaimonism only if the effects of luck extend beyond the outcomes of our actions to the very justice and goodness of what we do and how we live. This involves more than the truism that the road to Tartarus is strewn with good intentions; Greek myth and history are full of good men chancing to do bad. Rather, for luck to have a moral effect, it must be able to transform good conduct into bad, and not just by corrupting us, but by determining the "moral success" or failure of our actions. If luck can make our actions right or wrong, we have what is known as "moral luck"; then the moral status of an action can depend on its outcome as well as our intentions, and our conduct will sometimes be admirable and justified only if we actually achieve a just result.

Worries about moral luck derive much of their force from the suspicion that moral assessment sometimes relies too much on intentions, that we are too ready to excuse people for what they only happen to cause. Part of the problem is that we expect people to hold themselves to more exacting standards than they should hold others. Strict liability, though a poor standard for legal disputes, carries more weight in the courts of morality; for given the close link between motives and emotions, we judge people not only by what they do but also by how they feel about what they have done. When people's actions result in serious harm to others, we expect them to feel some regret and to accept some responsibility even if the harm only supervenes on their actions "by accident" – even if the loss is bad luck. Modern roads breed accidental death and injury; but even drivers who are exonerated, though not expected to be contrite, are expected at least to feel regret, and blithe indifference or a denial of any debt for one's part in the causal chain typically indicates a moral lapse or flaw. Yet if it is right not only to be sorry and feel regret but also to attempt some reparation, then it seems right to accept some blame. Unless we are willing to banish these sentiments of regret, it may seem, moral luck has a legitimate place in moral theory.

Worries of this sort seem confirmed by tragedy, where the course of events often upsets the lives of admirable characters. As a result of a highway mis-adventure, for example, Oedipus unwittingly killed his father. But to give Sophocles' familiar tale a novel twist, imagine King Laius of Thebes had fathered an identical twin, Oddipus. As in the play, the twins were spirited away first to Mt. Cithaeron and then to Cornith. But then, when they were taunted by a drunken visitor who denounced them as bastards, only Oedipus left Corinth to seek the truth, and Oddipus remained in what he mistook for his family home, where, after a long and prosperous life as a just and pious ruler, he died on the throne in high honor. But Oedipus, who was warned at Delphi that he would kill his father and marry his mother, who tried to escape his fate by fleeing further from Corinth, who met an imperious stranger he had to slay in self-defense, who delivered Thebes from the Sphinx and restored the royal house of Thebes by siring a family with the widowed Queen, this twin also succeeded as a pious prince and a beneficent ruler. Apart from the single fact, unknown until far too late, that he was himself a child of the Theban Queen, the two lives differ little on purely moral grounds. Or rather, because Oedipus acted to evade his horrible fate, his moral stature may be greater than his brother's. A single unlucky coincidence, however, makes a world of difference for what Oedipus did and who he was: it transforms justified homicide into cursed patricide, loving wedlock into hideous incest, and the joys of virtue and prosperity into abject misery. The tragedy here is not simply that one brother does nothing wrong while the other turns out to have violated the most sacred bonds. Worse, Oedipus himself comes to see his life as morally wanting, entirely by accident and through no fault of his own. He might have avoided his fate at any number of points, as indeed he tried. But his very virtue seems to make him a victim of moral luck: though scarcely culpable, he feels so responsible that he is driven to respond, to make a great gesture at reparation – he blinds himself and accepts the exile which he had himself decreed as punishment for whoever had slain the former King.

Moral luck not only adds to the vulnerability of happiness; it also threatens moral virtue itself. But rather than discuss these two effects, I want to explore a different perspective on tragic misfortune. In particular, I shall argue that Aristotle's analysis of tragedy points to an alternative to moral luck. He agrees that luck can affect both how we feel and what it is that we have done; but that is not enough – at least not always enough – to affect the moral status of action and character. On the contrary, how people react when they find out that their action has led to great harm reveals their moral stature: we retain control over our future actions, and even after chancing to cause great harm, we can still act admirably. Even if we are not responsible for all that we have done, we still have to respond; and depending on how we face imminent or actual disaster, we show ourselves morally better or worse. The strain may be so great, of course, that it undermines our moral convictions. But failing that, fortune does not change the moral status of our character; fortune only provokes us to display it. In that case, the moral significance of fortune stems not from its determining our moral status, but from its revealing our character and concerns. Though related to moral luck, this moral dimension of fortune is quite distinct. Luck affects the outcomes of our actions, and those can affect the moral status of our actions, but the result is "moral fortune" rather than moral luck because our moral stature still depends on how we respond to the effects of luck. My claim, then, is not that moral luck is central to Aristotle's analysis of tragedy, much less that luck makes Oedipus a moral failure who ends up having no way to justify his life and actions. Rather, I shall argue that Aristotle awards the palm to tragedies which portray moral fortune in admirable ways, which show their protagonists overcoming moral luck by responding nobly to bad situations for which they are not strictly responsible. In this respect, Oedipus' moral fortune is no worse than his brother's. Indeed, it may actually be greater, for while Oddipus carries on in ease and comfort, Oedipus shows heroic devotion both to justice when he stands by his decree to exile his father's killer, and to the bonds of love when he still shows great care and tenderness for the family of his incest in the closing scene of Sophocles' play. His fortunes have reached their nadir by the end of the play, but his moral stature remains high, as his tragic fall reveals his noble character and makes him not only more memorable than Oddipus but also more admirable.

II. Admirable Responses

My argument centers on three factors in Aristotle's analysis of tragic *mūthos*, better known as story or plot. One is the difference between the two terms with which he confers the Lyceum awards: Chapter 13 characterizes the "finest" (*kallistai*) tragedies on the basis of our moral admiration for the characters and their actions, but Chapter 14 picks out the "most powerful" (*kratiston*) pattern on a different basis. A second point involves the role of the "tragic emotions" of fear and pity, or anxiety and sympathy; these, he claims, we experience only if we find the protagonists morally admirable. A third factor is the device of "recognition," or the protagonists' discovery during the play of information that decisively affects either what they are on the verge of doing, or what they have already done; the best plays, the *OT* and the *IT* alike, though they place the recognition at different stages in the action, stand apart from all other patterns precisely because they exploit this device. Finally, some support for my argument comes from its consistency, both internal and external: my account avoids any contradiction between *Poetics* 13 and 14, and it also links his analysis of tragedy with his account in the ethical works of the relation between misfortune and virtue.

The last shall be first. Early in the *Nicomachean Ethics*, immediately after equating happiness with the exercise of rational virtue in a complete life, Aristotle tests this thesis against a series of traditional views about happiness.

The topic to which he devotes the greatest attention is the prevailing brief that happiness (*eudaimonia*) depends most on prosperity (*eutuchia*), and the related worry that misfortune (*dustuchia*) makes happiness impossible.[4] First, epic tales about the fate of Priam show that no one is invulnerable to disaster (1.9 1100a5–9); then Solon's dictum, that we should never call people happy before their end, attributes so much power to fortune that the good life would be beyond any mortal's reach (1.10 1100a10–b4); and a fragment of lost tragedy finds human happiness no more constant than a chameleon's colors (b4–7). But echoing Simonides, whose "tetragon" of virtue handles all luck "in the finest way" (b20–22),[5] Aristotle argues first that the virtuous are exceptionally secure against fortune (b7–22), and then, in a passage which illustrates the relevant sense of "fine," that even in great adversity we can act in ways that "shine forth."

> Since many things occur by fortune but vary in importance, it is clear that minor cases of good fortune do not have influence on life, and likewise for minor misfortunes. But when many great things go well, they make life happier, since they enhance life and the exercise of virtue is fine [*kalē*] and noble [*spoudaiā*]; but if many great things go badly, they stifle and damage happiness, since they bring suffering and interfere with many activities. Still, even in these straits the fine [*to kalon*] shines forth when someone bears many great misfortunes with equanimity, not because of an absence of pain, but because of integrity and greatness of soul. So if our activities are sovereign over our lives, as we said they are, none who are happy become miserable, since they will never do anything hateful and bad. For we hold that the truly good and wise bear all fortune gracefully, and they always do the finest [*ta kallista*] out of what is available, just as a good general uses the army at hand in the most effective way, and a cobbler makes the finest [*kalliston*] shoe out of the leather given him. (NE 1.10 1100b22–1101a5)

Aristotle's focus here is on the relation between virtue and happiness and on how the virtuous respond to great adversity, and his primary aim is to defend the thesis that happiness consists in virtuous activity. Without claiming that this guarantees a happy life, he argues that happiness is much more secure than traditional wisdom allows. He readily concedes that luck affects all lives; good luck "enhances" the lives of the virtuous, bad luck "brings them suffering," and serious misfortunes can even put an end to their happiness. But as the craft-analogy is meant to show, the virtuous can still act admirably even when deprived of things they value: like talented artisans, they continue doing fine work even in the face of adversity. The point is not simply that they always do what virtue requires, but that in so doing, they continue to do what they rightly value most. Even if their luck is exceptionally bad and disaster wrecks their happiness, they retain the best part of human life, their virtuous activity.

Aristotle's argument here is elliptical and more would need to be said to defend so close a link between virtue and happiness.[6] But whether or not his conclusions follow, his premises have implications for his analysis of tragedy. He bases the claim that happiness is stable on the claim that virtuous activities are stable. We may doubt that those activities depend on luck as little as he claims, or that they are as satisfying for the virtuous as his argument requires; but the basis for stability here is also the primary object of admiration, and even if the virtuous lose happiness, their action remains admirable. More generally, paragons of virtue are not the only ones who face misfortune nobly, and quite apart from questions about happiness and virtue, anyone who acts as they would act deserves our admiration. This is what transforms moral luck into moral fortune: everyone is exposed to moral luck, as anyone can chance to do something wrong; but how we handle our fortunes determines whether we earn admiration, sympathy, or reproach.[7] We have good moral luck if events never test us and we never chance to do wrong, and bad moral luck if we are tested and fail or if our actions chance to go wrong; but we achieve a good moral fortune if we are tested and shine or if we respond admirably after chancing to do harm. The third possibility is a probability for the virtuous, whose devotion to doing what they should makes them virtually sure to overcome moral luck. But others too can do the same. To develop Aristotle's craft-analogy, Leonidas and his Spartan band showed heroic courage in the desperate straits of Thermopylae, and though few of them exemplified Aristotelian virtue, their valor still "shines forth." Aristotle's view, then, is not that anyone, even the virtuous, can avoid luck entirely or become immune to moral luck; even virtuous actions can have bad consequences. Rather, he holds that a fine response to bad luck neutralizes moral luck, whether the agent is a paragon of virtue or not. Fortune influences our options, the resources we can deploy, and the outcomes of our efforts; but as long as we continue to pursue good ends, we make the best of our luck. Even if our actions happen to result in something "hateful and bad," we can still salvage a good moral fortune. We may regret some results of our actions and wish for better options, but if we continue to choose as we should from the options we have, we can transform even bad moral luck into a good moral fortune.

III. *Poetics* 13

Admirable action is at the center of Aristotle's favorite tragedies. In the first place, the way he draws the boundaries of the genre makes this moral dimension essential. All tragedy, on his account, descends from praise-poetry, and its earliest ancestors were "hymns and encomia" that "represented fine actions and the actions of fine people" (4, 48b24–27). In subject matter, it has the grandeur of epic: the genres differ in form and size, but both portray "noble subjects" (5, 49b9–20; cf. 4, 48b34–49a6 and 25, 61a4–9),[8] and in each, unnecessary badness or vice deserves criticism (15, 54a28–29 and 25, 61b19–21), unless the aim is "parody" (2, 48a11–14). This requirement of admirable subjects also distinguishes tragedy from comedy: despite their common dramatic form, tragedy is closer to epic because it too portrays "noble people" (3, 48a25–28)

who are "better than us" (2, 48a16–18; 15, 54b8–9). The contrast here, while
not exclusively moral (cf. 13, 53a10–12), certainly hinges on virtue and vice (2,
48a1–6; cf. 18, 56a19–23). In his list of four criteria for evaluating "character"
(ēthos) in a tragedy, Aristotle puts this demand for "good" (chrēstoi) protagonists
first, and adds that even less respected characters (he names women and slaves)
should be good "for their kind" (15, 54a16–22). He sets an upper limit on virtue,
as well as a lower one, and the Poetics disapproves of showing what the Ethics
finds best. The "finest" plays are not about paragons of virtue responding nobly
to adversity, because it interferes with the tragic effect if the protagonists are too
bad or too good (13, 52b34–53a7). But if they are less than "outstanding in
justice and virtue" (53a8), they must still be "better than us" (a16; cf. a33). If
the characters are good, however, they act admirably and do fine things, and
that is what good tragedy depicts. It is "fine" when a paragon of virtue handles
misfortune well, but also when people more like us manage to do the same, and
noble actions in adversity are admirable no matter who performs them.

Genre is not the only sign that moral factors are essential. Aristotle's emphasis
on mūthos or "story" has similar implications. First, his interest in admirable
character clearly reflects a deeper demand for admirable forms of action. A
tragedy is above all a representation of action and of life (6, 50a15–20);[9] and its
story, which is simply the pattern of action that it represents, is both its "goal"
(a22) and its principal part – like its "soul," as he adds (a38). Notoriously, this
subordinates character to action (a20–b4), and although Aristotle's precise
point remains obscure, his insistence that "the events and the story are the goal
of tragedy" (a22) implies that the need for admirable characters likewise depends
on the need to portray an admirable action. In particular, the criteria for calling
a tragedy "fine" depend on its story being fine, and the "finest" tragedies portray
especially admirable actions. In the Poetics, in fact, Aristotle uses "fine" almost
exclusively in reference to the story and its parts, hence in reference to the
actions of its protagonists.[10] The one time he calls tragedies "fine" by virtue of
craft or technē, he refers not to diction, for example, but to the kind of plot or story
best suited to incite our fear and pity (13, 53a22–23); and even when he praises
Homer's fine "use" of diction and thought, the point is not that he decked out
his poem with ornamental "finery," but that his imagery and rhetoric serve his
dramatic ends and enhance the effect of his stories (24, 59b11–16). What makes
a tragedy "fine," in short, is not verbal ingenuity or subtle psychological coloring
but the depiction of moral nobility in an intelligible pattern of conduct. Admirable conduct by good people is the essential subject of tragedy, and fine plays
represent fine actions. Tragedians have to master several skills if they are to
represent those actions well, but finding an admirable subject to depict is their
first and most essential task.

This demand for admirable action and character leads to the second of my
topics, the role of the tragic emotions. Tragedy affords a wide range of pleasures,
ranging from musical and visual delights to linguistic and intellectual enjoyment. Its distinctive pleasure, however, which it shares only with epic, turns on

the fear and pity we feel as we follow a play's action.[11] Our text is frustratingly silent about how these painful feelings are connected with our enjoyment of tragedy, but Aristotle clearly has more in mind than the thrill of harmless fright or the comforts of weeping. The "function of tragedy" (13, 52b29), for example, is not only to evoke these painful feelings, but then "through" them to "achieve a *catharsis* of this sort of emotion" (6, 49b27–28). Whatever this phrase means – a question too vexed to address here – it clearly gives fear and pity the decisive role in the distinctively tragic pleasure. Both these emotions, however, presuppose morally respectable characters and action. This is clearest in the case of pity (*eleos*), which Aristotle claims we feel only for those whose suffering we consider undeserved (13, 53a4–6; cf. *Rhetoric* 2.8 1385b13–15). To earn our pity, of course, people do not have to merit forgiveness (*sungnōmē*), much less be wholly innocent. For their suffering to be undeserved, however, they must deserve better, so they must have admirable qualities.[12] A similar point lies behind Aristotle's insistence that tragedies depict people "like us"; just as we feel no pity for protagonists whose suffering seems deserved, so we feel no fear for them if we find them very different and remote (13, 53a4–6). For a story to arouse our fear and pity, then, it must make us morally "involved"; unless we care about what happens to its characters and how they fare, *their* actions and fortunes can hardly affect *our* feelings, or cause *us* to suffer fear or pity *for them*. At the most general level, Aristotle's emphasis on the tragic emotions simply reflects the principle that characters in fiction excite our concern and sympathy only if they earn our respect. In the case of tragedy, however, the need to elicit feelings that are not morally neutral requires that our focus be directed at the suffering of good people acting or intending to act for admirable ends.

It is to find the proper source of fear and pity that Aristotle classifies story-patterns in *Poetics* 13 and 14 (52a28–33), and his aim in the first scheme is to define the pattern that yields "the finest tragedy" (52b31, 53a19, a23; cf. "most tragic" a27–29, "least tragic" 52b37). The basis for his division is twofold: a change in the protagonists' fortunes, and their moral and social status. Initially, these two factors distinguish three patterns: (13a) tales of the just moving from good fortune to bad, (13b) tales of bad people moving from bad fortune to good, and (13c) tales of "very bad" characters moving from good to bad fortune (52b34–53a7). He rejects all three for failing to produce fear and pity. A thorough analysis is beyond the scope of this essay, but three points are important here.[13] First, his claim is not that no tragedies were or could be built on any of these patterns, but only that "the finest tragedies" avoid them. A play built on the rejected patterns may even move an audience to feel the tragic emotions; but if it does, their reaction results not from the moral dimension of the story and action, but from subsidiary devices like graphic diction or lurid staging which cannot produce the distinctive pleasure of tragedy. Second, Aristotle's worry here is not Plato's, that the depiction of unfair suffering in plays fosters injustice in life. Rather, Aristotle's reason for denying that paragons of virtue are fit subjects for tragedy is that their suffering offends our sensibilities too much (13,

52b34–36).[14] Finally, each of these patterns gives only the barest outline of a generic type that can be handled in very different ways, and only further analysis can show how to construct a specimen of the best type. But first, what is the best pattern?

Aristotle concludes that the protagonists in the finest tragedies are of "middle" virtue and status, move from good fortune to bad, and contribute in some way to their fall. Or in his own words, they are "the sort of person who neither excels in virtue and justice, nor moves towards misfortune because of badness or vice, but moves there because of some *hamartia*, and has prestige and prosperity" (53a7–10). The force of the two initial factors of character and fortune is fairly clear: though less than moral saints, the protagonists are better than most of us (a16); and they begin in prosperity but move towards misfortune. But the new element of *hamartia* or error is notoriously elusive. Fortunately, its precise scope does not matter here, provided it introduces a potential for regret. What is crucial is that the protagonists' errors lead them to undertake or accomplish some action, and that their action bring them at least to the brink of misfortune.[15] Whether or not they act intentionally for bad ends that they choose at the start, their action must bring about (or at least threaten to bring about) unwanted results; whether or not their choice is a "moral error," their action has a "moral cost" only if it results in the loss (or imminent loss) of something they rightly value. This may be a cost they are willing to pay, as in Medea's decision to sacrifice her children, or Electra's support for matricide; or it may come as a complete surprise, as when Oedipus discovers his relationship to the man he killed and the family with whom he lives. But unless their error leads them to do something they may regret, unless the protagonists themselves at some point see some undesirable cost in their actions, then their error has no effect on their fortune.

The protagonists in (13a), by contrast, face a loss, but since it does not result from their own choices and actions, they do nothing they regret and have no moral cost to pay. Those in (13b) have nothing to regret at all, as they lose nothing and rise to good fortune. And those in (13c) face a loss that may well result from their own errors, but because they are "very bad," all they regret is their loss and not their choices, so their loss has no moral cost.[16] In Aristotle's preferred pattern, however, a *hamartia* ensures that the protagonists regret their choices as well as the results of their actions. This error, which is lacking in (13a), may or may not exonerate or excuse them; but even if it does, it is a source of regret when they find out what it has led them to do (or almost to do). They may not change their mind or wish they had acted differently, but it at least makes them wish their options had been different. However bad others may think the result (or avoided result), the agents suffer (or come close to suffering) only if they too see it as bad, at least in part. Their error, whether moral or cognitive, makes them regret their actions, and the bad result, whether intended or not, has a "moral cost" which is decisive in the loss they suffer (or narrowly avoid).

Two more points about Aristotle's preferred pattern are important here. After concluding that "the fine story must change from good to bad fortune" (53a12–14), he subdivides this pattern in two ways, according to how a play ends, and how its protagonists stand to one another. The former contrast helps defend Euripides against those who criticized his sad endings (a24–26): far from being a flaw, this makes his plays "most tragic" (a26–30), evidently because they elicit the most intense tragic emotions, the most intense fear and pity. It is worth emphasizing, however, that this is the first mention of endings. In every previous reference to changes in fortune, Aristotle mentions changes both for the better and for the worse; and all four patterns in *Poetics* 13 refer only to moving "into" a good or bad state, not of remaining there and ending in the same state. The "most tragic" plays, then, end unhappily, but they are only a subset of "the finest tragedies."[17] Provided a story involves some serious misfortune, whether actual and ultimate or only prospective, it can end either happily or sadly.

The other division contrasts "simple" stories about the fortunes of a single party like Oedipus or Thyestes, with "double" stories about two opposed sides, either as in the *Odyssey* where the better side meets success in the end by defeating the worse, or as in comic burlesques where even arch enemies end up friends (a30–39). Though others preferred the double type (cf. a13), Aristotle rates it only as "second" (a30). The reason he gives is that its ending yields a pleasure "more at home" (*mällon oikeia*) in comedy than in tragedy (a35–36). But first, double plays can fit his formula for a fine tragedy, as when Odysseus' lapses with the Cyclops lead to a long series of misfortunes before he reaches a good end; and second, they can certainly evoke pity and fear, as his wanderings and trials do (cf. 11, 52a27–29). Moreover, "double" plays are not rejected out of hand: what is "second" can still be quite good,[18] and not only does Aristotle never disparage the *Odyssey* (the closest is 24, 60a35–b2), but he repeatedly treats it as exemplary (as in 4, 48b38–49a2, where he aligns it with tragedy in opposition to comedy). The flaw in tragedies that end as the *Odyssey* does is not the heroes' success but the accompanying ruin of their adversaries, and Aristotle's objection to "double" tales is not to happy endings *per se*, since one party still ends in bad fortune. Rather, he objects to this pattern – in tragedy alone – because of the moral complacency its poetic justice tends to promote. Linking the victory of the heroes with the fall of their adversaries grants an audience's "prayers" (53a34–35), but because it has the flaws of (13c), it diminishes the specifically tragic effect, even if the fall of the wicked is the means to the victory of the just. It is better and "more tragic" to keep the story "simple" and to focus on the fortunes of only one party.

IV. *Poetics* 14

According to the first classification, the "finest" plays portray fine conduct by admirable characters, and what makes them finest involves the potential for regret to which they are exposed. Before introducing the second classification, Aristotle adds two related comments about the proper way to arouse the tragic emotions, both of which highlight the moral dimension of tragedy. First, as if to answer Plato's worry that our interest in tragedy reflects a morbid fascination with the suffering of others, he criticizes poets who rely on visual spectacle to frighten and move us (14, 53b1–14). Merely spectacular plays in the fashion of Hollywood horror-films were no doubt produced; the *Life of Aeschylus* reports that a production of his *Eumenides* made them look so terrifying that women in the audience had miscarriages. But Aristotle denies that theatrics can achieve the distinctively tragic effect. Lurid spectacles thrill many, but unless the structure of action wins our sympathy and respect for the protagonists, the effect is less than tragic. The goal of tragedy is not to shock, but "to provide the pleasure that results from pity and fear by means of representation" (b12). The tragic emotions are only an intermediate goal, the means to a pleasure that results "from" them (b12) and is achieved "through" them (6, 49b27). Unless our reactions grow out of a sense that the characters deserve better than they seem likely to experience, the play fails to provide that pleasure.

The importance of sympathy is underscored by the following observation, that good tragedies depict the interactions of family and friends (*philoi*, 53b14–26). As Aristotle explains, there is nothing to pity if the protagonists are enemies, or neither friend or foe, "except in the suffering itself" (b17–19). The victims, in other words, are the only ones we pity in such a case. By implication, then, we should pity the agents as well. But for them to win our pity, they must not deserve to suffer, so they must be better than their deed alone (or their intended deed) would suggest. A *hamartia* supplies the solution: a son kills a parent, for example, but only by an error (that may range from Oedipus' faultless ignorance to Orestes' mistaking revenge for justice), so even the son wishes he had been able to act differently. The importance of personal ties (*philia*) is that the protagonists harm (or almost harm) people they themselves would much rather not harm. In the better plays, their own horror when they recognize the terrible things they have done, or their joy when they learn in time what they were about to do, dramatizes for us in the audience the moral importance of concerns for *philoi*. For when enemies do (or almost do) terrible things to one another, their actions typically cause them bitter satisfaction, not grief – witness the *Hecuba*. But if the agents fail to recognize the horror of what they do, our sympathy is aroused only by the victims and "the suffering itself." For the proper tragic effect, however, we should be moved by the agents' own anxieties or grief as we understand that they too deserved better than fortune allows (or seems likely to allow).

The second classification of plays grows out of this discussion of the fear and pity aroused by family affairs. In their use of "the traditional stories," Aristotle observes, dramatists are not free to change the basic tales, but it is still up to them to use them "finely" (53b22–26; cf. 9, 51b19–32). Even the best stories can be used badly, and other myths or new stories can be put to fine use. The point of dividing stories anew, then, is to "say more clearly what we mean by finely" (53b26). The basis for his schema is twofold, and unlike the first schema, this one is clearly exhaustive: the protagonists can either do something terrible or only come close to doing it, and they can act either in full knowledge or in ignorance of what is at stake. Four patterns result: (A) the paradigm of Medea, who does exactly what she decides to do; (B) the paradigm of Oedipus, who unwittingly does something terrible and then discovers what he has done; (C) the paradigm of Iphigenia, who stops short of doing something terrible when she discovers what she is about to do; and (D) the paradigm of Haemon, who decides to do something terrible but fails to carry out his decision (53b27–39).[19]

Once the schema is drawn up, Aristotle ranks (D) and (A) as inferior to (B) and (C). First, he calls the Haemon-pattern "worst: it is disgusting, and it isn't tragic since it has no suffering" (53b38–39). Then, without explanation, he ranks the Medea-pattern as "second" (54a2). Most scholars take this to mean "second worst" or "second-rate." But that sense is unparalleled, and as we have seen, when the preceding discussion calls "double stories" like the *Odyssey* "second" (53a30), it ranks them as "second best." Further, some of the examples listed in that chapter show that a play about Medea can use its tale of intentional killing "finely": if tales about Thyestes, Orestes, and Alcmeon exemplify "the finest tragedy" (53a18–22, a point recalled at 54a9–13), then savagery and matricide can surely be used finely.[20] Still, even if Aristotle does consider Euripides' *Medea* "second-rate," his ranking of the other two patterns in the following lines is what generates our crux: first he calls the Oedipus-pattern "better" (*beltion*), then he singles out the Iphigenia-pattern as *kratiston* (54a2–9). If this means that the *IT* is better than the *OT*, or if the *IT* fits the *Odyssey*-pattern, then this ranking contradicts the previous chapter, where plays like the *OT* are "finest" and "most tragic," but plays like the *Odyssey* are only "second." But are these assumptions sound? Obviously, precision is crucial. If, as scholars and translators almost universally agree, *kratiston* means "best," then Aristotle commits one of the great blunders in the annals of literary criticism. But do his terms move on different scales and depend on different criteria?

The first thing to notice is that all of these patterns can be constructed to fit the generic pattern described in *Poetics* 13. Though some fit it more easily, each can be used to show good people moving to misfortune because of some *hamartia*, and each can have the peripety of a complex tragedy.[21] But there are two crucial differences, each of which shows the superiority of (B) and (C) over (A) and (D). First, the kind of error is different. Oedipus and Iphigenia act "unknowingly," so their actions result from factual errors, in each case a mistaken identity. But Medea and Haemon act "knowingly," so their errors are more serious and involve a lapse in moral judgment. Hence, the former pair have better motives. In particular, the *philoi* in (B) and (C) are not just blood-relatives; they also feel *philia* or love for one another. Because any harm the agents cause (or narrowly avoid causing) their loved ones therefore appears more serious to them and hence more undeserved to us, these two patterns evoke greater pity and fear than stories in which the agents knowingly harm (or start to harm) their family. Second, (B) and (C) alone make the full use of the "complex" story which *Poetics* 13 expects of the "finest tragedy" (52b31–32). Both (A) and (D) have a peripety or reversal: Medea's revenge effects a reversal for all, an escape for her but misfortune for everyone else; and Menelaus' decision to postpone any punishment of Helen reverses the fortunes of all the leading women in the *Trojan Women*. But neither pattern has the further complexity provided by a recognition, since *ex hypothesi* the protagonists act knowingly and have nothing to discover. This is crucial because recognition is the major source of regret: a discovery that leads to no reaction is pointless; and if the agent reacts with joy, if Oedipus is delighted to discover what he has done, then our reaction is disgust and the agent's ignorance fails to arouse our tragic emotions. Unless the agents' recognition of their error causes them regret, in short, the error has no tragic effect and does nothing for the story. But when Aristotle defines "recognition," he specifies that it must bear on the agents' fortunes (11, 52a29–32).[22] On two points, then, plays like the *OT* and the *IT*, which show people moving not only from good fortune to bad but from ignorance to knowledge, make a finer use of their story and follow the pattern of "the finest tragedy" more fully.

But what about the verdict of *Poetics* 13 and 14 on the relative merits of (B) and (C)? Does Aristotle prefer the *OT* or the *IT*? One apparent discrepancy is misleading: for the most part, the *Odyssey* depicts agents acting knowingly, so its ending resembles (A) more than (C); but its protagonists are enemies rather than family or friends, so in fact it fits none of the patterns in Chapter 14, and its "second" rank in Chapter 13 is not inconsistent with a preference for the *IT* in Chapter 14. Further, as I argued above, both the *OT* and the *IT* fit the form of the "finest" tragedies in Chapter 13, so even if Chapter 14 favors the *IT*, it is consistent with Chapter 13; (B) and (C) are simply varieties of the best generic pattern. But does Chapter 14 really favor the *IT*? Here we must face the lexical question and settle what Aristotle means by *kratiston* (54a4). If he meant to say what most assume he means, his choice of words is odd: after calling (B) "better" (*beltion*), he could have called (C) "best" (*beltiston*); but instead he risked misunderstanding by varying his terms. Stylistic variation is a possibility; three times in the *Poetics* he uses the comparative *kreittōn*, each arguably synonymous with *beltiōn* (48a6, 62a13, 62b14; but see below). But the intervening lines suggest that his change to *kratiston* reflects different criteria: the reason he finds the *OT* "better" than the *Medea* is that its pattern "has nothing disgusting and its recognition is striking" (54a3–4). The first of these two reasons recalls the argument of Chapter 13 (esp. 52a36), and the second underscores the importance of what (B) and (C) have in common, namely, the most effective way to produce the distinctive tragic emotions. The recognition in the *OT* is "striking," in short, for the same reasons that the recognition in the *IT* is (see 55a16–18): admirable people who have done or are about to do terrible things to those they love earn our pity and fear; and their horror when they discover what they have done, or their relief when they discover what they were about to do, brings our sympathy and admiration for them to a peak. When Aristotle proceeds to call (C) *kratiston*, most scholars assume that he finds it not only better than (B) but also more intense – as if audiences feel more fear and pity for narrow escapes than for disasters or find last-minute recognitions more "striking" than devastating discoveries. But it is doubtful that the proposal is true, or that it is Aristotle's point. Rather, the difference in the two patterns lies in the way the protagonists react to their recognition, with joy or with grief. But if their reactions differ in kind, so do ours: the *IT* answers our wishes while the *OT* does not. Where the two patterns differ decisively, then, is not in the degree or intensity of our emotions; both patterns generate excitement and deliver a "striking" emotional punch. Rather, plays like the *IT* are *kratiston* because they satisfy our normal sensibilities more readily and appease our aspirations for fairness. This is why they are "most powerful."[23]

At the end of the *Poetics*, Aristotle compares tragedy with epic and awards the crown to Dionysus. Others considered epic "better" (*beltiōn*) because it is less "vulgar" and appeals to a "better" audience (26, 61b26–62a4). But Aristotle favors tragedy because it is "clearly more powerful [*kreittōn*] since it achieves its end more [*māllon*]" (62b14–15). His argument is complicated, but at no point does he claim that tragedy is more "striking." What he emphasizes is rather that it is more vivid and more compact (62a17–b11), and in addition to having all that epic has, it provides the added pleasure of music (a14–17). The shared goal which it achieves more effectively, then, is not simply exciting fear and pity, but producing the pleasure which results from those emotions.[24] To call tragedy "more powerful" implies only that it is more satisfying, not that it is more frightening or more pitiful, or even that it is "finer." As Aristotle concedes at the close of *Poetics* 13, the civic audiences of tragedy tend to prefer the happy resolutions that the *Odyssey* and the *IT* share. This, however, is only a result of the audience's "weakness" (13, 53a34), not a sign that the *IT* is superior to the *OT* overall. Indeed, Euripides' unhappy endings, "if constructed correctly, are obviously the most tragic on the stage and in performance" (a27–29). The *IT* may satisfy more of our hopes; but ironically, its avoidance of the actual deed, while exciting a more "powerful" pleasure, deprives it of a scene in which to dramatize the greatest devotion to *philia*. Still, both patterns show admirable responses to misfortune, and both produce a pleasure that stems from our appreciating the protagonists' moral fortune. The verdict of Chapter 14, that (C) is more "powerful" than (B), is thus consistent with the verdict of Chapter 13, that Euripides' unhappy endings are "most tragic." The former answer our prayers, but the latter elicit more pity. Both, however, are species of "the finest tragedy," and what makes them finest is the admirable response to fortune with which they close.

This resolution of our problem can be reinforced by looking again at the topic of recognition. That, not the way a play ends, is what separates the better from the worse patterns in Chapter 14. The decisive feature of both (B) and (C) is that the agents learn in the course of the play something crucial about their own actions. The action in either case hinges on ignorance and a crucial error; whether that issues in disaster or not is less important than how the protagonists respond to their discovery. In his first account of recognition, Aristotle claims that the "finest" form coincides with a reversal, and he names the *OT* as his example (11, 52a32–33). The finest recognition, in short, produces a reversal by itself. For if the protagonists are essentially good people who are *philoi*, as in the *OT*, their discovery reverses their emotions as well as their fortunes. Thus, when he details the different ways to generate a recognition, the kind he finds "best" (*beltistē*) generates a "striking" effect "out of the events themselves"; and this time, both the *IT* and the *OT* are cited as paradigms (16, 55a16–19). In the latter, the hero is struck with regret and remorse when he learns that he has done things that he himself hates having done; and in the former, the heroine greets her discovery with joy because it prevents her from doing something she herself would hate to do. In each case, the recognition forms the climax of the story – the climax but not the end, for in each, the recognition initiates a scene that displays their admirable response to their new situation. Virgil ends the *Aeneid* suddenly with the dying gasp of Turnus and offers no emotional resolution; but by the end of the *Iliad*, the death of Patroclus and Hector has passed, and the survivors have dramatized their love in mourning the lost heroes. Aristotle's favorite tragedies follow Homer here; a recognition ensures that both (B) and (C) end only after celebrating the love which exposes the protagonists to loss, and we leave the theatre admiring them for how they respond to their fortune.

The continuities of *Poetics* 13 and 14 are plain. In each, the moral basis for our emotional reactions is paramount. But in neither does Aristotle single out a pattern as "best." Instead, he first defines the genus he considers "finest," and he then isolates the two species he finds "most tragic" and "most powerful." Neither the *OT* or the *IT* ends up "finest"; both are inherently "better" than other patterns (54a2), but each is used "finely" only if it shows an admirable response to misfortune. What matters most is to construct a story of admirable action. That is the crux, and the same myth can be handled more or less "finely." Alcmaeon, for example, appears in Chapter 13 as a suitable subject for the finest tragedy (53a20), and Astydamas' version is praised in Chapter 14 (53b33). In his analysis of involuntary action, however, Aristotle criticizes Euripides' Alcmaeon for making the "ridiculous" claim that his matricide was a choice of the lesser evil (*NE* 3.1 1110a26–29). The defect in Euripides' version is that it makes an inferior use of pattern (A) and falls short of the *Medea*. Astydamas evidently did better by following pattern (B) and making the matricide depend on ignorance as in the *OT*.[25]

Luck has much to do with the progress and outcome of Aristotle's favorite tragedies, but neither (B) or (C) turns on moral luck. Oedipus is no less admirable for what he has done, and though his life turns out very badly, he is none the worse morally. By the same token, Iphigenia is not morally better or more admirable for what she narrowly avoids doing, though her life is certainly better and more enjoyable. By emphasizing how the protagonists respond to their fortunes, however, Aristotle highlights the power of moral fortune. Oedipus suffers terribly, but his grief is also admirable because it reflects his great concern for the family he turns out to have hurt. Sophocles' final scene, some 200 lines showing a man's deep concern for his family and particularly his daughters, dramatizes not merely the fall of this "child of fortune" (1080), but his rejection of a sort of "moral egotism." Just as egotists value their own desires and interests too much and the interests of others too little, so moral egotists attach too much importance to their own motives and too little to others' needs. But in responding to his luck, Oedipus shows greater concern for the loved ones he has harmed than for defending his motives. Others would be wrong to find him culpable; but if his own first response were to plead innocence on the grounds of ignorance or to argue that the fault lay solely in his stars, he would have revealed himself a paltry soul. Years later he may need to defend his actions to others (see *OC* 265–274, 521–548), but had he denied responsibility initially, he might have earned our pity but not our admiration. By acknowledging his deed with horror, however, he affirms even in his grief the profound love he feels for the progeny of his incest, and his response to misfortune "shines forth."[26]

The nobility of the protagonists' response to misfortune, or to its avoidance, is the focus of the story in all of Aristotle's finest tragedies. Both the *OT* and the *IT* dramatize a movement from *hamartia* to recognition that reveals the depth of the protagonists' concern for the people harmed or threatened by their actions. Aristotle finds the happy endings of (C) more "powerful" because they give us in the audience what we want as well as what we admire. But he finds the unhappy endings of (B) "more tragic" than lucky escapes, not because disaster is more realistic or more moving, but because the affirmation of concern in the midst of disaster is more demanding and typically more admirable than the celebration of a narrow escape. By focusing on moral fortune, both patterns meet the standards of "the finest tragedies": both represent an admirable response to misfortune and both display the human power to overcome fortune morally even when it overcomes our hopes and intentions. The triumph of moral fortune, then, is the hallmark of Aristotle's favorite tragedies. Melodramatic escapes and catastrophic discoveries alike affirm moral concerns in the end, and the pleasure we find in each derives from our admiration for protagonists whose actions are "fine." In the age-old debate over whether enjoyment or edification is the aim of tragedy, Aristotle's answer is a typical "both." Good tragedy is not didactic; it fosters sympathy and admiration rather than rigidity or complacency. But this moral component is also a source of pleasure, for we enjoy seeing moral stamina in others. This is far removed from any morbid fascination with the suffering and misfortune of others. The distinctive pleasure of tragedy results rather from seeing people respond to events admirably, and the importance of fear and pity depends on this goal of eliciting our sympathy and respect for people who uphold their concerns for others no matter what fortune gives them.[27]

Notes

1. In a balanced account, S. Halliwell (*Aristotle's Poetics* (Chapel Hill, NC, 1986), 227–237) emphasizes the many points of agreement in the two chapters. For a lively discussion, see J. Winkler's "An Oscar for Iphigenia" in *The Ephebe's Song* (Princeton, forthcoming); D. W. Lucas (ed.), *Aristotle: Poetics* (Oxford, 1968) outlines the major alternatives on 54a8. For further suggestions, see I. Bywater (ed.), *Aristotle on the Art of Poetry* (Oxford, 1909) on 54a4 (a tension between our emotional response and our moral sensibility); I. M. Glanville, "Tragic Error," *Classical Quarterly* **43** (1949) 47–56 (a new analysis of voluntary action); and J. L. Moles, "Notes on Aristotle, *Poetics* 13 and 14," *Classical Quarterly* N.S. **29** (1979) 77–92 (a jaded palate or seeing a more effective revival).

2. Aristotle's views about "the fine" are central but elusive; see T. H. Irwin, "Aristotle's Conception of Morality," *Proceedings of the Boston Area Colloquium in Ancient Philosophy* **1** (1985) 115–143 (though I think Irwin overstates the importance of acting "for others"), and cf. Lucas, *Aristotle: Poetics*, on 50b37. The following survey of Aristotle's ethics summarizes views defended in T. H. Irwin, "Permanent Happiness: Aristotle and Solon," *Oxford Studies in Ancient Philosophy* **3** (1985) 89–124, and in my *Sovereign Virtue* (Stanford, 1992).

3. See the two papers entitled "Moral Luck" by Thomas Nagel and Bernard Williams: T. Nagel, "Moral Luck," *Proceedings of the Aristotelian Society*, Suppl. 50 (1976) 137–151, reprinted in idem, *Mortal Questions* (Cambridge, 1979), 24–38; B. Williams, "Moral Luck," *Proceedings of the Aristotelian Society*, Suppl. 50 (1976) 115–135, reprinted in idem, *Moral Luck* (Cambridge, 1981), 20–39.

4. On the difference between happiness and prosperity, see n.2 above; Halliwell (*Aristotle's Poetics*, esp. 202–209) rightly underscores the links with Aristotle's ethics here.

5. Solon's maxim appears several times in the remains of tragedy, incl. the closing but probably interpolated lines of the *OT*; see S. D. Olson, "On the Text of Sophocles' *Oedipus Tyrannus* 1524–30," *Phoenix* **43** (1989) 189–195. It has been observed that Aristotle's reference to a chameleon forms an iambic trimeter; and Plato makes Simonides' celebrated ode (fr. 542 Page) the subject of the earliest extant *explication de texte* (*Protagoras* 339–347).

6. Aristotle's reference to "greatness of soul" points to one leg of his defense: those who have this "total virtue" value fine action more than anything else, so they never see any reason to do anything wrong (*NE* 4.3, esp. 1124a1–16); see Irwin, "Permanent Happiness," 120–123, and my *Sovereign Virtue*, Ch. IV.iii.

7. Cf. Aristotle's account of "mixed actions" in *NE* 3.1: circumstances sometimes force us to choose a "lesser evil," and depending on what we choose over what, we may deserve praise (1110a19–21), reproach (a22–23), or forgiveness (a23–26). One way to answer criticism of an action in a play or epic and to show that it is "fine" is to show that its motive is to avoid a greater evil (25, 61a4–9).

8. The moral sense of *spoudaios* is standard; see 2, 48a2 with Lucas' note, *NE* 1100b27 (quoted above), *Categories* 10b5–9. The term also specifies the kind of action required of tragedy in the definition at 6, 49b2, so it contrasts with "laughable." But it means more than "serious": for an action to be serious, it must be important not only to the agent but in fact, so valuable ends must be at stake; but those are precisely what the virtuous seek to preserve and benefit, so an action is *spoudaia* only if the virtuous would do it, hence only if it is admirable in some way.

9. Action is mentioned in 50a15–17, so my point stands even if a17–20 is bracketed; for a defense of these lines, see M. Nussbaum, *The Fragility of Goodness* (Cambridge, 1986), 378–381, and Halliwell, *Aristotle's Poetics*, 203. Many scholars object to the word *kakodaimonia*, which occurs only here in Aristotle's extant works; but it would

be natural for him to use this poetic word instead of his customary but prosaic *athlios* when discussing the subjects and themes of poetry.

10. Of twenty-one instances, three refer to tragedy in connection with its story, six refer directly to the story and its structure, four refer to its "magnitude," three refer simply to actions, one refers to effective diction and thought, and one is an adverb equivalent to "well"; a narrowly "aesthetic" sense appears only in a reference to "pretty" diction (58b21) and in two references outside literature to painting (50b1, 54b11).

11. On the various pleasures of tragedy, see Halliwell, *Aristotle's Poetics*, 62–81. As David Gallop neatly puts it, the distinctive pleasure of tragedy "is distinguishable from the responses of pity or fear felt *while* we are in the theatre . . . since it attends upon our learning or understanding the "universals" about human action and suffering that the work has portrayed" (160–161 in D. Gallop, "Animals in the *Poetics*," *Oxford Studies in Ancient Philosophy* **8** (1990) 145–171).

12. Even if Aristotle recognizes a morally neutral sympathy that we feel for any human suffering, and even if the "humane kindness" associated with *philanthrōpia* is operative at 53a2 and 56a21, the *Poetics* emphasizes pity for undeserved suffering.

13. See Halliwell, *Aristotle's Poetics*, 215–222.

14. Assuming Aristotle expressed himself precisely, (13a) refers to paragons of virtue: the *epieikeis* (52b34) are "fair," which implies they have a species of justice that is "better" than legal justice (see *NE* 5.10 1137b8–25); but then they have "complete virtue" which extends to virtue towards others (5.1 1129b25–34). The point seems confirmed by 53a8.

15. T. C. W. Stinton, "*Hamartia* in Aristotle and Greek Tragedy," *Classical Quarterly* N.S. **25** (1975) 221–254, shows that *hamartia* can refer to a wide range of errors, from blameless ignorance of particulars, through passion and weakness of various sorts, and on to some vice; see esp. 232, and cf. Hallliwell, *Aristotle's Poetics*, 221. I find much of the debate about "moral" *hamartia* misguided: even the most innocent misinformation can lead to results that are not only undesirable but morally horrifying, as in the *OT*.

16. What Aristotle rejects in (13c) is the fall of the "very bad" (53a1); good plays can show the fall of someone with some vices, provided they also display some positive (though not necessarily redeeming) qualities (cf. 15, 54b8–15 and 18, 56a19–23).

17. Imminent loss is already a misfortune: the prospect is painful, whether or not harm finally occurs. Likewise, fear is inherently prospective, and the danger of suffering can evoke pity (note the future tenses in *Rhetoric* 2.8 1386a30–b5). Halliwell (*Aristotle's Poetics*, 204–205 and 218) points out that outside Ch. 13, the *Poetics* always mentions good and bad fortune together.

18. Unless Aristotle uses "second" neutrally to enumerate (e.g. 54b30), it typically has a positive sense, as of the second-best form of recognition (55a20). Thus, the life of moral virtue is the "second" best life (hardly second-rate) to that of intellectual wisdom (*NE* 10.8 1178a9), as Cleobis and Biton are "second" happiest after Tellos (Herodotus 1.31–32), and "being noble" is second best to health in a skolion quoted at *Gorgias* 451e.

19. Pattern (D) is not mentioned initially in any Greek mss. and editors debate whether the clause found in the Arabic tradition at 53b29 is an interpolation. If it is, then the initial omission of (D) supports my claim that Aristotle approves of all three others, though (A) less than (B) or (C); see the next two notes.

20. The text is skeletal: its progression of "worst, second, better, *kratiston*" may mean either "fourth, third, second, first," or "third, second, and two firsts, one *kreittôn* than the other." The former does not imply that "third" is bad rather than good, so it begs the question to assume either interpretation outright. But in favor of the second, it is most unlikely that Aristotle would reject (A) wholesale when he calls it a common

practice of earlier dramatists ("the ancients," 53b27–29), and when he takes his example from Euripides, whose plays he has already defended as "most tragic" (13, 53a24–30). In fact, (A) yields some of "the finest tragedies" in the hands of Euripides: despite some technical flaws (as 53a29 and 56a27 concede; but the flaw noted at 54b1 and 61b20 must be minor as it is shared by the *Iliad*, 54b2), his *mūthoi* arouse pity and fear (53a24–30). Thus, we have pity and fear for Medea as she deliberates how to survive the treachery of Jason, and for Creon's family as they get caught in her web; for a virtually Aristotelian defense of the *Medea*, see A. Burnett, "*Medea* and the Tragedy of Revenge," *Classical Philology* **68** (1973) 1–24.

21. Pattern (D) is hardest to make fit, as Aristotle suggests when he remarks that "no one composes this way, unless occasionally" (54a1). His point, I take it, is that no poet made a habit of using this format, as Euripides made a habit of using (A) and (B); see 53a25. But as Aristotle's mention of Haemon claims, some plays did use (D), as Sophocles presents Neoptolemos in the *Philoctetes* (so Stinton, "Hamartia," 252; cf. the puzzle raised at *NE* 7.2 1146a18–21, and its solution at 7.9 1151b17–22). The problem is that (D) lends itself to bad motives as in (13b), although as the *Philoctetes* shows, they may give way to better motives.

22. Cf. *NE* 3.1 1110b18–24, where Aristotle argues that actions done because of ignorance are involuntary rather than nonvoluntary only if they cause the agent regret.

23. Bywater on 54a4 in *Aristotle on the Art of Poetry* suggests *potissimum* as a gloss. The word means "superior," but it often has the connotations of its etymological cousins, such as "power" (*kratos*), "self-control" or continence (*enkrateia*) and "weakness" or incontinence (*akrasia*). As *Politics* 1.6 shows, "rule by the *kreittones*" is not simply "rule by the better" and the slogan is often rendered as "rule by the stronger"; cf. *Republic* I, 338c–42e.

24. The text does not say explicitly what the end is, but given the similarities of the two genres, "its end" must refer to the pleasure produced by both tragedy and epic (note 62b1 and b13); see Lucas, *Aristotle: Poetics*, on 62b12 and b13.

25. Judicious "use" of inferior materials can produce good results: Homer achieves a "better" use even of the "least artful" form of recognition in the celebrated scene about Odysseus' scar (54b20–30; cf. b1–5).

26. A similar contrast can be illustrated for pattern (A), the other pattern in which a destructive deed is done: Medea earns our respect in part because she agonizes over her deed and views infanticide with horror; but Orestes, who has few scruples either before or after he perpetrates matricide, earns less pity from us in the end because he feels no horror at his deed, and instead, while the Furies demand respect for the bonds of *philia*, he protests his innocence all the way to the Areopagus.

27. Ancestors of this paper were presented in colloquia at the University of California at Berkeley, Carlton College, and the University of Texas at Austin, and I am grateful to those audiences for helpful discussion. I also thank the American Council of Learned Societies and the Institute for Advanced Study for generous support that has allowed me the leisure to revise my argument.

Pleasure, Understanding, and Emotion in Aristotle's *Poetics*

Stephen Halliwell

The purpose of this essay is to argue that the three concepts in my title form an interlocking set of elements in Aristotle's interpretation of the experience of representational (i.e. mimetic) art. The pursuit of this purpose will not, however, involve anything like a comprehensive account of each of these three topics; with many of the *Poetics'* individual remarks about pleasure, for example, I shall not be directly concerned.[1] More strikingly, perhaps, I shall not attempt to explain how the ideas I am addressing, and which I take to be a major part of the foundation of Aristotle's aesthetics, might be related to the perennially contentious issue of *catharsis*. The reason for this silence is my belief that we cannot be confident just what Aristotle meant by *catharsis*; but I am at least prepared to say that, if we had fuller evidence about Aristotle's special use of this term, we would find that it in some way complemented or reinforced the larger view of the experience of art which I ascribe to him.[2]

I start by considering the passage in *Poetics* 4, which has often been wrongly regarded as marginal or digressive, where Aristotle identifies two features of human nature which explain the existence of poetry:

> Poetry in general can be seen to owe its existence to two chief causes that are rooted in nature. First, mimetic activity is instinctive to humans from childhood onwards, and they differ from other creatures by being so mimetic and by taking their first steps in learning through mimesis. [Second],[3] all men take pleasure in mimetic objects. A practical indication of this is that we take pleasure in contemplating the most precise images of things whose sight in itself is painful, such as the forms of the basest animals and corpses. Here too the reason is that learning gives great pleasure not just to philosophers but similarly to all men, though their capacity for it may be limited. Hence people enjoy looking at images, because as they contemplate them they understand and infer each element (e.g. that this is such-and-such a person).

Since, if one lacks familiarity with the subject, the artefact will not give
pleasure *qua* mimetic representation but because of its craftsmanship, color,
or for some other such reason. (1448b4–19)

The pattern of thought here – statement, illustrative attestation, explanation,
further confirmation – is characteristic; one close and particularly germane
parallel is the famous opening of the *Metaphysics* 980a21–27. Also typical of the
philosopher's mentality is his conjunction of poetry with children's imitative
behavior, and his quasi-ethological contrast between man and other animals (a
comparative point, of course, since Aristotle knows of animal mimesis). The first
of these details principally refers not to simple copying (any more than does
artistic mimesis), but to imaginative play-acting, as *Politics* 1336a33–4 helps to
confirm.[4] This gives the context a force which is both anthropological and
psychological. Mimesis, in its artistic but also in some of its nonartistic forms,
involves modelling particular media (in the case of children, their movements
and words) so as to produce an object or a form of behavior which is intentionally significant of a piece of supposed or possible reality. Nothing is said here
which erases the major differences between children's play-acting and, say, a
great painting; yet Aristotle sees a common element between them, which he
identifies as a natural human propensity towards make-believe, and a concomitant pleasure in learning and understanding (for *manthanein* embraces both
these things). The same observation, *à propos* all artistic mimesis, recurs at
Rhetoric 1371a31–b12. But before we can explore the implications of this
important Aristotelian view, some other issues in this section of *Poetics* 4 need
clarification.

If we can take pleasure in even detailed renderings of painful or unattractive
subjects, it would seem that the contemplative attention we give to mimetic
works can in some way convert, override or at least supplement our common
responses to equivalent features of reality. (It does not follow, of course, that we
cannot take pleasure in an art-work because it represents something ordinarily
pleasurable in itself: see p. 245 below; nor that painful emotions altogether lose
this quality when experienced in aesthetic contexts.)[5] Aristotle's point has an
obvious pertinence to tragedy, which affords pleasure through the dramatization
of human failures and sufferings. But we are for the moment concerned, as is
Chapter 4, with the wider aesthetic point. Aristotle clearly supposes that the
pleasure in question depends on the perception of something *known* to be
mimetic and artistic: no-one looking at a painting of a corpse believes himself to
be looking at a real corpse. So we have here a view which has had many
subsequent analogues, perhaps especially in the eighteenth century, when the
problem raised by this passage was a recurrent topic of aesthetic discussion.
Samuel Johnson provides the concisest statement of the tenet: "The delight of
tragedy proceeds from our consciousness of fiction." David Hume, in the short
essay "Of Tragedy" which he wrote in 1757, endorses a similar point from the
French critic Fontenelle, though Hume thinks this only one of a number of

pleasures which convert what would otherwise be painful into pleasurable feelings. Kant, too, cited the capacity of art to produce beautiful descriptions even of the ugly, and his explanation of it seems to have been a variation on the function of fictional representation.[6] Several of these writers made an exception to the principle for disgust and the disgusting. The *Poetics* too contains such an exception in its treatment of tragedy, but that is a matter for a separate enquiry.[7]

The role of artistry in the transformation of painful into pleasurable experience is emphasized by Aristotle's reference to the detail or precision of images at 1448b11.[8] In a related passage, *Parts of Animals* 645a7–15, he talks of the conscious pleasure which we take in the technical skill, "whether pictorial or sculptural,"[9] which produces such images. But it would be wrong to infer that the pleasure envisaged in these passages is pleasure *only* in artistry as such (in, say, the fineness of brush-strokes or of chiselled patterns) – that is actually precluded by the contrast at *Poetics* 1448b17–19: if one is unable to take pleasure in the mimetic significance (see p. 252 below), one may still enjoy certain features of craftsmanship or "finish" (*apergasia*, a term which relates directly to artistic technique),[10] color and texture, or other such features.

To interpret Aristotle's position here, we consequently need to distinguish between two ways in which aesthetic pleasure (pleasure taken in mimetic works) may arise in relation to artistry – the first *mediated* through the artist's skilled accomplishment; the second *restricted* to the material and sensual properties of the artifact. *Poetics* 4 presents this distinction both positively and negatively: positively, by its explanation of the chief pleasure taken in a mimetic work as resting on cognition of the work's significance in relation to the world; negatively, by suggesting, as we have seen, that pleasure in workmanship, color, texture, etc., may be independent of the cognition of what is mimetically represented. In the *Parts of Animals* passage, in fact, we should note the use of the rare compound verb, *suntheōrein* (645a12–13), whose two other occurrences in Aristotle confirm the precise force of the prefix: "contemplate or observe *at the same time.*"[11] What this implies is that when we enjoy a painted or sculpted image, our pleasure *might*, on one level, relate purely to artistry, but on another level, as *Poetics* 4 makes clear but this passage does not, it should supervene upon a sense of how the image relates to the world. The two levels, of course, are able to coalesce in the fullest or richest forms of aesthetic experience. We may well, for example, as Aristotle himself indicates elsewhere, appreciate the use of color in visual art as *integral to*, or partly constitutive of, the mimetic rendering.[12]

Poetics 4 appears to require only this single distinction between two aspects of aesthetic experience and their correlative pleasures. But it has recently been argued by Elizabeth Belfiore that we can take Aristotle actually to be intimating a tripartite scheme of possible stances towards a mimetic work: (1) viewing the object independently of its representational significance; (2) viewing it *qua* (e.g.) animal shape but not *qua* representation of an animal; (3) viewing it *qua* likeness, and grasping the relation between signifier and signified.[13] Of these, (1) and (3) correspond to the two types of response overtly identified in *Poetics* 4, and alluded to, if I am right, at *Parts of Animals* 645a11–13.

It is very difficult to see why we should introduce a third possibility, Belfiore's (2), into this scheme. Belfiore offers two main considerations. The first is that Aristotle's phrase "because of its craftsmanship, color, or for some other such reason" (*Poetics* 1448b18–19) points to "two different ways of viewing an imitation *qua* thing in its own right."[14] But this simply imports a distinction where Aristotle acknowledges none: "or for some other such reason" prompts the inference that various "non-mimetic" pleasures are being bracketed together as a single contrast to the principal pleasure of understanding mimetic significance. Belfiore's second argument depends on a reading of *De memoria* 450b20–31, where Aristotle uses a distinction between an image perceived as a figured or pictured form, *zōon*, and the same image perceived as a "copy," *eikōn* (i.e., here, a portrait of an actual particular), in order to illuminate the difference between a mental image "in itself," and a mental image which is the bearer of a true memory (i.e. which corresponds to particulars in the past). Richard Sorabji, in explaining this distinction, says that "it will be only when we regard a picture as a copy that our attention is directed to the object depicted." Otherwise, "we shall think of the picture simply as a figure."[15] The first part of this comment seems to me perhaps misleading, since we do not, and Aristotle does not argue that we do, any less direct our attention "to the object depicted" (that is, an object in the picture) when we perceive a pictured form. To contemplate a painting as a *zōon* is just to "read" it as a determinate and intelligible form – that of a man, lion, house, or whatever.[16] The difference between the two cases lies not in the form of the depiction as such, but in the referential status of the depiction in relation to reality.

The similarity of this passage to *Poetics* 4 is qualified, then, by the fact that in *De memoria* Aristotle is necessarily interested (for the sake of the analogy with memory images, which can be *only* of particulars) in images that may represent actual instances of things in the world, whereas in *Poetics* 4 his thought *encompasses*, but is not restricted to, the case of portraits. In the latter, in other words, Aristotle needs only to distinguish between apprehending or grasping the representational significance of a mimetic image (whether this significance is or is not related to an actual particular) and viewing the image in some other, nonrepresentational way; while in *De memoria* he is concerned only to separate images related to identifiable particulars from those not so related. There can be no question in *Poetics* 4 of taking Aristotle to be referring solely to portraits. The term *eikōn* is in itself indecisive; it can refer either to portraits ("copies") or to all visual images.[17] Here, however, 1448b11–12 ("images [*eikones*] . . . such as the forms of the basest animals and corpses") shows that it cannot be restricted to the former sense; and although the later example ("this is such-and-such a person") readily suggests the case of a portrait, that sentence as a whole, with the phrase "understand and infer *each element*" (16–17), must have wider applicability. *Eikōn* in this passage, consequently, has to apply to any mimetic image,[18] while in the *De memoria* it specifies only an image of identifiable particulars, e.g. a portrait.

Belfiore's failure to consider the wider and narrower senses of the term *eikōn* causes her to misread the *De memoria* passage as differentiating between seeing a form as (e.g.) an animal but not a representation of an animal, and seeing it as a likeness (i.e. between types (2) and (3) in her tripartition, indicated above). But the term "likeness" cannot be restricted to the narrower use of *eikōn* in the *De memoria*. "Likeness" needs to be correlated with Aristotle's usage of *homoios* and cognates, which can be applied to *any* mimetic work, whether or not it represents independently identifiable particulars. In exegesis of this area of Aristotle's thought, mimesis, representation, and likeness should count as virtually synonymous.[19] Belfiore does indeed equate "likeness" with mimesis when discussing *Poetics* 4, only then to equate "likeness" with *eikōn* in the *De memoria* passage: but this has the unsustainable implication that a painting which is not a portrait (*eikōn* in the narrower sense) is not mimetic either. What this means is that Belfiore's distinction between types (2) and (3) is entirely un-Aristotelian. The notion of "a non-abstract image that does not represent," quite apart from its inherently problematic formulation,[20] has no place in either of the passages in question.

This leaves us, then, with a basic Aristotelian dichotomy between (a) the cognitively[21] grounded pleasure derivable from works of mimetic art; and (b) a range of other pleasures which, though focused on a mimetic work, are independent of its mimetic or representational character. We are now in a position to expand an earlier point. *Poetics* 4 explains that the cognitive pleasure taken in mimesis means that even the representation of painful or ugly objects can be aesthetically satisfying. *Rhetoric* 1371a31–b12 repeats and confirms this: the pleasure in such cases depends on grasping the fact of representation, and is not an unmediated response to *what* is represented. But at *Politics* 1340a23–28 Aristotle states that it is sometimes the case that we take pleasure in the features of the represented reality as such: his example is the beautiful physical form of a person depicted in a painting or statue. The corollary of this, as indicated in this same passage and exemplified extensively by the theory of tragedy in the *Poetics*, is that our response to a representation of the painful should involve emotions of the painful kind we would feel towards equivalent events in life. How, then, are we to combine what look as though they may be two distinct, even potentially incompatible, ideas: first, that our full, cognitive experience of a mimetic work encompasses the fact that it is fictive, not real; second, that in general our responses to mimetic works are closely aligned with those towards equivalent realities in the world?

Far from contradicting the principle of *Poetics* 4 and *Rhetoric* 1.11, this passage from *Politics* 8 actually presupposes that principle. We could not appreciate the form of a beautiful person in a picture *except* by perceiving the mimetic representation or "likeness," i.e. by grasping how the work's form signifies an example or specimen of physical beauty.[22] Between them, accordingly, these passages yield the bipartite view that our response to a mimetic work must always (if it is a response to mimesis as such) rest on the cognitive recognition of representational significance; but that such a response is necessarily a *compound* reaction to the represented reality and to the artistic rendering of it. The compound quality of aesthetic experience, so conceived, has the important implication that it is wrong to regard the two components as properly independent; the separation at *Poetics* 1448b7–19 is presented precisely as a case of defective, incomplete aesthetic experience. When we feel pity and fear at a tragedy, and enjoy the experience because it is focused on an artistic representation, it is not that we *first* feel painful emotions, but then have them tempered by the pleasurable recognition that the events are only mimetic; still less that the latter recognition is followed by the painful emotions. Rather, we only experience the emotions, which may indeed still be in some way painful, because we recognize, in the represented actions and sufferings, human possibilities which call for them. But, equally, grasping the mimetic significance just *is* in part, for Aristotle, apprehending the pitiful and the fearful in the events of the play.[23]

Although, therefore, Aristotle does not spell out the point unequivocally in the *Poetics*, we can, by combining the evidence of the passages so far considered, see that he must take emotion and recognition, and, where appropriate, pleasure and pain, to be somehow *fused* in aesthetic experience. That is entirely consistent with the impression created by his reference to the pleasure we take in contemplating detailed images of unpleasant animals or corpses. More importantly, it fits perfectly with the most specific reference to the appropriate pleasure of tragedy later in the treatise: "the pleasure from pity and fear through mimesis" (1453b12). Aristotle's exploitation of a resource of Greek word-order, enclosing both the qualifying phrases between article and noun (lit.: "the-from-pity-and-fear-through-mimesis-pleasure"), accentuates the unity of the experience described.

We have, then, in passages of the *Poetics*, *Rhetoric* and *Politics*, the highly compressed kernel of a concept of aesthetic pleasure which, in stark contrast to the influential Kantian notion of such pleasure as subjective and noncognitive, can be described as both objectivist and cognitivist, since it seeks to explain aesthetic experience in terms of the features of aesthetic objects (mimetic or representational works) and of the processes of recognition and understanding which such objects require. What we must now address is the attempt to fill out, beyond the spare illustration given in *Poetics* 4, some of the implications of this view. There is no doubt that Aristotle's typical economy of statement carries some responsibility for creating the impression in this passage that he has only an elementary process of cognition in mind. But this does not really excuse those critics who have stressed the simplicity of the illustration and lost sight of the larger purpose – namely, an explanation of the origins and causes (the term *aitiai* embraces both senses) of poetry, and indeed, as the *Rhetoric* passage shows, of mimetic art in general. Thus D. W. Lucas struggles to comprehend what Aristotle might be gesturing towards: "when we have learnt what already familiar thing a picture represents," he writes, "we have not learnt much"; and, after considering further possibilities, he concludes that there is nowhere any hint that Aristotle has a conception of the power of literature to extend our comprehension of life.[24]

But it is interpretatively literal-minded and narrow to restrict Aristotle's point in *Poetics* 4 and *Rhetoric* 1.11 to the mere identification of the subject of a picture, poem, or other mimetic work – as if being able to put some sort of label on the work's content were all that were meant. Martha Nussbaum has rightly observed that *Poetics* 4 can be taken to cover a whole range of possibilities, from simple to much more complex responses to works of art.[25] To try to elucidate the character of these possibilities, I want to use a variety of Aristotelian contexts to create a nexus of thoughts within which to situate the hints we have so far been considering, and to show how some of the major tenets of the *Poetics* can be read afresh in the light of the model of aesthetic experience which emerges.

Mimetic works such as poems and paintings can be said to embody "likenesses": Aristotle is prepared, at *Politics* 1340a23, to use this term generically for the products of artistic mimesis. The cognitive pleasure afforded by the contemplation of mimetic works is accordingly a pleasure in the recognition and understanding of likenesses. But a likeness need not be a copy of an individual or specifiable model. Most mimetic works are not, and are not taken by Aristotle to be, renderings of known particulars; only certain types, especially portraits, fall into this category. Yet all mimetic works are likenesses, and they are so by virtue of having been made to represent imaginable realities in their particular media (colors and shapes, words, rhythms, choreographic patterns, etc.). It is accordingly possible to discern in them features and properties which are possessed by, or can be predicated of, things in the world. When we observe ordinary cases of likeness, we observe common properties or qualities. When we appreciate mimetic works, we recognize and understand the ways in which possible features of reality are intentionally signified in them.[26]

Perceiving and grasping likeness is identified by Aristotle as an important mode of discernment for both philosophers and others. He discusses its relevance to a range of types of philosophical argument (*Topics* 108b7–12), sees it as the essence of producing metaphor (*Topics* 140a8–10, *Rhetoric* 1410b10–19, 1412a9–12, *Poetics* 1459a5–8), and notes its involvement in a variety of other contexts, such as the interpretation of dreams (*De divinatione somniorum* 464b5–12) and the construction of rhetorical analogies (*Rhetoric* 1394a2–9). When Aristotle mentions the observation of likeness in these ways, he clearly does not have in mind a superficial or passive matter of merely registering the existence of similarities: in philosophy, metaphor, the interpretation of dreams, and surely in art too,[27] it is something that not everyone can do, or not equally well. The discernment of likenesses means at its best, then, an active and interpretative process of cognition – a perspicacious discovery of significances in the world, or in representations of the world.[28]

There is perhaps a further and special factor which Aristotle seems to regard metaphors and mimetic works as having in common. A metaphor, as *Rhetoric* 1410b19 puts it, asserts that "this is that." The same phrase is used elsewhere in the *Rhetoric* (1371b9), and a variant of it (lit. "this man is that man") at *Poetics* 4.1448b17,[29] to explain the pleasurable process entailed in the understanding of a mimetic representation. The common point appears to be this: in both cases it is not that a comparison is drawn or a similarity recorded, but rather that something is seen or comprehended *in* something else. In the case of metaphor, Aristotle is analyzing what might be regarded as a dimension of its creativity. At any rate, he expressly denies this capacity to similes at *Rhetoric* 1410b19. If Pericles really said that the death of Athens' young warriors was like the removal of the Spring from the year (which is how Aristotle twice records the saying, though calling it a metaphor in one context),[30] then his audience would be offered a similarity or analogy. But if, speaking of the war dead, he said "the Spring has been taken from one year," then his words might, it seems, have an intensified force: the dead, we could say, become, or are felt as, the disappeared Spring. Aristotle does not, in fact, consistently attach such importance to the difference between metaphor and simile,[31] but this passage may nonetheless give us a hint of something material to the status of mimesis, which does not paradigmatically relate to some independent object or state of affairs, but contains its significance within its own organization.

Whatever we make of these hints regarding metaphor, it is clear that in the case of mimesis we see (or hear, depending on the art) a significance figured in the mimetic object: "this *is* that," "this man *is* that man," etc., is Aristotle's basic way of labeling such cognitive experience, though without thereby implying, as I have insisted, that the experience itself is always rudimentary. As perhaps with metaphor, we do not so much observe or make a connection; we see one thing (the materials of the artistic medium) *as* another (the representational meaning). The important entailment here, if this is right, is that Aristotle's conception of mimesis allows from its very foundations for the necessity and the centrality of the mimetic medium: representational works do not offer us deceptive pseudo-realities, as Plato had sometimes contended, but the fictive signification of possible reality in particular artistic media that can be recognized and judged as such. This dual-aspect view of mimesis seems to me, in fact, to be a premise of the entire argument of the treatise,[32] and it is therefore only to be expected that we should find it presupposed by Chapter 4's reference to the pleasure of mimesis.

Since mimesis need not, and usually will not, represent independently recognizable particulars or individuals, aesthetic understanding cannot be limited to matching a copy with a known original, nor, as I earlier said, can it be reduced to the merely factual and instantaneous registering *that* a certain kind of thing or things has been represented. (To treat a work of art in this way, though common, is to encounter it in only the shallowest of senses.) Aristotle is offering, after all, an account of essential features of the *contemplation*, the complete experience, of mimetic works, and there is a sufficiently marked indication of potential complexity to the process in his phrase, "understand and infer each element" (1448b16–17; cf. *Topics* 140a22). In the case of a tragic drama, the phrase "each thing" will encompass the rich totality of people, actions, emotions, events, arguments, and so forth, with all their various facets and interrelationships; and to "reason," or "infer," will accordingly imply an intricate, unfolding process of attentive comprehension. To understand in this way is to see an accumulating structure of meanings in the work; but while each component may be a "likeness" in the sense of something we require an existing grasp of reality to comprehend, this does not entail that the drama as a whole is straightforwardly similar to anything we have previously experienced.

Moreover, the language of the parallel passages in the *Poetics* and *Rhetoric* gives us two valuable clues to the depth of perspective which lies behind these compressed statements: first, the comparison with philosophy (in the *Poetics* alone); second, the terminology of "reasoning" (*sullogizesthai*),[33] learning and understanding (*manthanein*). At the very least, these two features serve to acknowledge some respectability and seriousness to the phenomenon in question. It is surely no coincidence that a closely similar conjunction of points – a comparison to philosophy, and a use of philosophical terminology for what is involved in mimesis – occurs in a celebrated passage of Chapter 9 of the *Poetics*. We have good warrant, therefore, for using what is said about poetry and quasi-philosophical universals in Chapter 9 to fill out and substantiate the implications of the passage in Chapter 4.

We must start by accepting that, contrary to the common paraphrase, Aristotle does not say unqualifiedly that poetry is a mimesis of universals; he repeatedly says and indicates that it is a mimesis of people and actions (the specific contrast between these two things, at 6.1450a16–17, is a normative principle for tragedy, not a theoretical statement about what mimesis can and cannot show). The characters of poetry are fictive particulars; they have names, perform individual actions,[34] etc.: indeed, one poetic virtue is vividness of the kind which belongs precisely to actualities (17.1455a22–25). Yet the remarks in Chapter 9 suggest that universals are somehow conveyed by poetry, at least more so than in history. This passage has become a *locus classicus* because it looks as though Aristotle is expressing something of supreme interest about poetry; and it seems right to try to do justice to that impression. Equally, however, it would be prudent to take account, as has often not been done, of the comparative and tentative phrasing of the passage.

Three aberrant interpretations can be put rapidly on one side: the universals in question are not quasi-Platonic ideas which transcend the realities of our experienced world; nor are they moralistically formulable truths; nor, finally, are they abstractions.[35] Universals can play a part in human thought in more than one way, or on more than one level. They *can*, in the philosopher's hands, be abstractions, as the subject of definition, for example; and some universals can be arrived at only by fully philosophical procedures: they are remote from sense-perception, as *Metaphysics* 982a24–25 has it. But, equally, other universals are to some degree present, according to *Posterior Analytics* 100a3–b5, even in ordinary sense-perception: they inhere, so to speak, as categories of discrimination and understanding, in perceptual cognition.

The poet does not deal in abstracted universals, as the philosopher does; but nor can the remark in *Poetics* 9 be limited to the minimal sense in which universals are present in sense-perception, since this would give no grounds for the distinction between the material of poetry and the material of history: "poetry speaks more of universals, history of particulars" (1451b6–7). Universals should enter into poetry, therefore, in a way or on a level which is somewhere between abstraction and common sense-experience. Chapter 17 perhaps gives us a clue to what is involved. There Aristotle starts by stressing that the composing poet's search for consistency and vividness will be served by strong imagination (mentally supposing oneself present "at the very events" – a traditional formula). But he then goes on to suggest that one stage in composition – an earlier stage, presumably, than the one which requires such imagination – should involve setting out the skeleton of the plot "in general terms," and only then fleshing it out with episodes. "In general terms," *katholou*, is the same word that Aristotle uses for universals. Some commentators have denied that this connection is pertinent here, but it seems to me that it must be. Confirmation comes from the fact that the passage closely echoes part of Chapter 9 itself: both refer to a process of plot-construction followed by addition of the characters' names (1451b12–14, 1455b12–13); and both relate *katholou* to probability or plausibility (*eikos*), which represents the more-than-particular basis of dramatic conviction.

The universals of Chapters 9 and 17 are built into the plot-structure of a drama – into the causal network of actions and events which it comprises. As such, they also necessarily concern the agents, and Chapter 9 makes this explicit: "the universal means the sorts of things that a certain sort of person says or does according to probability or necessity." So universals are not inherent in the raw stuff of a tragedy or comedy, but become apparent only in and through the shaped mimetic structure of "actions and life" which the poet makes: it is this unified design of the art-work which differentiates poetry, as Aristotle insists, from ordinary events and hence from history. This means that universals are related to causes, reasons, motives, and patterns of intelligibility in the action and characters[36] as a whole. Encouraged by the similar remarks in Chapters 4 and 9, we can infer that whatever Aristotle implies by the pleasure of learning or understanding in the case of mimesis (Chapter 4), it ought, in the case of dramatic poetry, to have something to do with universals.

But it is in any attempt to extrapolate from these spare hints that the dangers of the aberrant interpretations which I mentioned earlier loom up. Above all, perhaps, there is the danger of turning Aristotle's doctrine into some sort of faith in the dramatic type and the typical; this sort of interpretation threatens to take one in the direction of too much *abstraction*, and too little concern with dramatic vividness and conviction. A kindred pitfall is that of supposing the implicit universals of poetry to yield straightforwardly formulable moral truths. Had Aristotle believed this, he would not have failed to say so unequivocally. We can note, moreover, that the example of a plot set out "in general terms" in Chapter 17 gives no support to this hypothesis: there is no trace here of any moralizing thrust to the conception of the plot's sequence of action, only an attention to its coherence. Finally, there is really no ground at all for idealizing Aristotle's universals. Butcher, by doing so with quasi-Hegelian conviction, allows us to see what is so wrong with this: any interpretation which can turn the universal into "nature's ideal intention," "a correction of [nature's] failures," and "the manifestation of a higher truth," seems to have lost sight of the fact that these universals are posited by Aristotle in the substance of *tragedies and comedies*.[37]

It may be useful, as Robert Yanal has suggested, to think of the universals of poetry as "emergent" aesthetic properties – features which are not ready-made, on the surface of the work, but dependent on an active and interpretative apprehension on the part of reader or spectator.[38] Certainly, Yanal's notion that literary texts do not do all the interpretation for us, do not directly tell us their moral, and yet have a rich potential for the learning that Chapter 4 speaks of, seems to accord well with the balance of emphases in the *Poetics*: in particular, 19.1456b2–8 (not cited by Yanal) stresses the way in which dramatic meanings and effects should be inherent *in* the events themselves, and should not require explicit statement, *didaskalia*. (Moral formulae *uttered* by characters or chorus are, of course, a separate matter, and would be covered by Aristotle's notion of "thought," *dianoia*.)

It begins to appear that part of the enterprise of the *Poetics* is the effort to locate a domain for poetry which lies somewhere (though not at some exact midpoint) between other territories whose character, if too closely approximated, would be deleterious to a quality which Aristotle identifies above all with drama. The paradigms of these other territories are philosophy and history, with their associated planes of the pure universal and the contingent particular. Poetry is closer to philosophy than to history, as Chapter 9 asserts, yet at the same time what it offers is the fiction of imagined particulars, and what it must avoid is didactic statement (and, indeed, statement – the authorial voice – *tout court*, which is, for Aristotle, incompatible with mimesis: 24.1460a5–11).

If we now try to combine the readings of Chapters 4 and 9 which I have sketched, it transpires that the two passages can prove mutually illuminating. The cognition of mimetic works entails, in essence, the perception and understanding of their representational content and structure, of the possible or supposed realities they manifest (Chapter 4). But what they represent is not, except in occasional cases, known particulars; and Chapter 9 suggests that, for poetry at least, even the use of such particulars – historical facts – must be transformed by the poet into the material of unified (and, in the process, fictionalized) plot-structures. Hence, to "understand and infer each element" in a mimetic work (4.1448b16–17) cannot be, or cannot be only, a matter of identifying particulars, but must, on Aristotle's account, engage comprehension of how the fictive particulars illustrate, or make sense in terms of, our wider conceptions of reality. And such comprehension cannot take place, as Chapter 9 intimates, without implicit reference to universals, the general categories which structure, and emerge within, our understanding of the world: the process of aesthetic reasoning (*sullogizesthai*) thus bears out the principle that "it is impossible to reason at all without universals" (*Topics* 164a10–11).

I must reiterate my earlier warning that we should not press this participation of universals in the cognition of poetry too hard: we should probably not, for example, assimilate it too closely to the use of likenesses in induction.[39] Perhaps the most prudent conclusion is to see the cognition of poetry as suspended between ordinary processes of intelligent sense-experience and the fully articulated abstractions of philosophy. Poetic fictions offer (or should do: the idea is obviously normative) more than ordinary particulars in the world, since they are constructed in unified patterns of probability or necessity: in this sense, there is more of the universal visible in them, and they are accordingly more intelligible.[40] Appreciative experience of such works will correspondingly draw more on a sense of universals than we always do in much of our common perception of the world. At the same time, poetry falls short of, or cannot – as Aristotle would see it – aspire to, the articulation, system, and surety of good philosophical arguments.

In the case of a complex work such as a tragedy, our sense of universals, or the work's expression of them "through" its fictive particulars, will operate in respect of all three of the "objects" of mimetic significance given in Chapter 6 – actions, character, and "thought" (1450a11). This means that to follow, appreciate and respond to tragedies, we must utilize, and understand how the work itself uses, our wider sense of what it is for people to be agencies in the world, what it is, more especially, for them to be ethically differentiated agencies, and what it is for them to express their thoughts in speech. We require, that is, a fund and a grasp of already existing experience of life which is itself quasi-universal – which has at least the seeds of universals within it.

But does Aristotle imply that poetry can do more than merely confirm or codify such experience? The formulation in Chapter 4 need not preclude the notion that what emerges from our encounters with tragedy is, in part at least, something *new* – something that builds on and enlarges our existing understanding. That is why I have repeatedly translated Aristotle's use of the verb *manthanein* as understanding and/or learning.[41] As with the other elements in this passage, we have to be prepared to do some appropriate extrapolation. The sense of "familiarity with the subject" (lit. "if one has not previously seen [the subject]")[42] is tailored in the immediate context to the rudimentary cases of visual recognition – say, of the figure in a portrait – which Aristotle gives as a token instance of understanding pictorial representation. But if the argument has the strength to explain the roots of poetry and of our responses to it (as it purports to do), the point cannot be restricted to such cases; it needs to be capable of enlargement so as to cover the full scope of the most ambitious types of

mimesis. In the case of tragedy, we need (taking only the most obvious illustrations of the principle) to have sufficient experience of life to understand
various kinds of action, intention and character; to be able to distinguish degrees
of innocence, responsibility and guilt; to know, in an effectively mature way,
what merits pity and fear; to have a grasp of human successes and failures, of
the relationship between status and character, and so forth. All of these things,
and much else besides, would contribute, in other words, to a complex form of
the process which in Chapter 4's general terms is called a matter of understanding and inferring each element in a mimetic work. But tragedy does not just
confirm us in pre-existing comprehension of the world: it provides us with
imaginative opportunities to test, refine, extend and perhaps even question the
ideas and values on which such comprehension rests. Admittedly, Aristotle does
not set himself to pursue all the ways in which tragedy can accomplish this, and
we must accept that he did not attribute to tragic paradox so central a role in the
genre as some modern theories do. But there are nonetheless some clear suggestions in the *Poetics* of an awareness of this dimension of tragic experience.[43]

If we have in *Poetics* 4 and *Rhetoric* 1.11 the kernel of a general conception
of the cognitive pleasure taken in mimetic art-works, we also have in the *Poetics*
as a whole a specific conception of the pleasure arising from the experience of
tragedy, and it should by now be apparent that, on my interpretation, tragic
pleasure – "the pleasure from pity and fear through mimesis" (14.1453b12) –
must instantiate, must be one major species of, the generic pleasure defined in
Chapter 4.[44] And this being so, we can observe how the somewhat schematic
and simplified form of the general statement takes on a richer color and depth
when set in the interpretation of a tradition of mimesis as highly elaborated as
that of tragic poetry. What was stressed in Chapter 4 was the interrelation of
cognition and pleasure; what comes into the foreground in the particular case
of tragedy is the full integration of pleasure, emotion and cognition. The fact that
our passage in Chapter 4 says nothing of emotion in connection with cognition
is due to the concision of Aristotle's argument at that point, though it is possible
to observe how the connection is taken for granted in the ensuing account of
poetic evolution.[45] But the argument anyhow leaves full scope for emotion to be
combined with cognition, and that is precisely what we find provided for in the
details of the theory of tragedy, where Aristotle refers the tragic emotions, in
keeping with his psychological outlook as a whole, to the types of belief which
give them their focus and content (13.1452b34–53a7).

The full experience of a tragedy will necessitate, on the model of Chapter 4,
the understanding of the work's significant structure of "actions and life"
(6.1450a16–17), the ethical characterization of the agents, the content of their
expressed thoughts, and so forth. But this cannot be a drily cerebral process of
understanding; it is the engagement of our imaginations with human actions
and experiences of a deeply serious and, for Aristotle, an intrinsically emotive
kind. It is for this reason that Aristotle speaks interchangeably of the "pitiful"
and "fearful" as features of a tragic plot-structure itself (e.g. 9.1452a2–3) and

of pity and fear as emotions experienced by the spectator (or reader) who attends and submits to what the work offers (e.g. 11.1452a8 f.). These emotional qualities, equally expressible in terms of the work itself or of a fitting response to it, provide the central criteria for the prescriptive treatment of the genre's values and ideals. There is, in this conception of tragic experience, no divorce between thought, or understanding, and feeling, since to feel in the right way towards the right things just *is* one integral dimension of understanding their human sense and meaning.[46] So to suggest, as Jonathan Lear has done, that the cognitive pleasure of tragedy "is a step that occurs en route to the production of the proper pleasure of tragedy," where this pleasure is said to arise "from pity and fear through mimesis,"[47] is to keep apart elements that we should expect to find fused, given his cognitivist view of the emotions, in Aristotle's interpretation.

The tragic experience reflects a duality which we earlier encountered in the *Poetics'* conception of aesthetic experience in general. On the one hand, it matches the principle given in *Politics* 8 that there is a close parallelism between our responses to mimetic likenesses and our responses to events in the world. We can observe this principle precisely in operation, for example, in *Poetics* 13–14, where the ideal aims of tragedy are stated in terms – simultaneously ethical and aesthetic – of the kinds of agents, actions and sufferings which will elicit the requisite emotions. On the other hand, pity and fear are painful emotions, yet the experience of tragic drama is strongly pleasurable: here, then, we have the supreme exemplification of the fact, noted in *Poetics* 4, that the nature of art can transform and integrate painful emotions into aesthetic pleasure. And this transformation, as we earlier saw, is traced back by Aristotle to the root sense of experiencing an artistic representation. So the duality in question both acknowledges the "artificial" status of mimetic fictions, and yet keeps intact their capacity to explore imaginative possibilities of reality.

We are now well placed to see the force of that contention which I indicated at the outset would be central to this paper – that pleasure, understanding and emotion are interdependent concepts in the thought of the *Poetics*. Pleasure in mimesis rests on a cognitive foundation (Chapter 4), and that tenet inevitably points us towards the remarks on poetry and universals in Chapter 9. The "proper pleasure" of tragedy (Chapter 14) aptly conforms to this basic model, for it is a pleasure for which Aristotle specifies the mimetic medium ("*through mimesis . . . ,*" 1453b12). But the pleasure of tragedy also revolves crucially around powerful emotions, and these complete the theoretical circle by drawing us back round to the cognitivist view which Aristotle takes of the emotions. These connections should have emerged clearly enough from the analysis I have offered, but they can be most suitably and conveniently reiterated by way of contrast with an old and still strongly held view about the *Poetics*, namely that it offers a purely hedonistic conception of the experience of tragedy.

The error of the hedonist reading of the *Poetics* can be pinpointed in the treatment of Aristotle's references to the end, *telos*, or the function, *ergon*, of tragedy. Five passages of the *Poetics* belong in the first category (1450a18,

22–23, 1460b24–26, 1462a18–b1, 1462b12–15), and three in the second (1450a31, 1452b29–30, 1462b12–13). Proponents of the hedonist reading typically claim or assume that all these passages corroborate the unequivocal proposition that tragedy's end or function is to give pleasure.[48] But this is misleading. Of course the *telos* and *ergon* of tragedy must incorporate pleasure, but it is as significant as it has often been obscured that Aristotle *nowhere* says without qualification that pleasure is the end or function of tragedy. In fact, he only once says unreservedly what the *telos* is, and that is in Chapter 6: the plot-structure is the end of tragedy (1450a22–23; cf. 1450a18). In two other passages pleasure is mentioned as evidently one dimension of the end and function, but not in such a way as to identify it exclusively with them (1462a18–b1, 1462b12–15). In four other passages there is no explicit mention of pleasure, and every reason to regard Aristotle as thinking of something more than pleasure – either of plot-structure again (1450a31), or specifically of emotive effect (1460b24–26), or of some combination of these and other elements (1452b29–30).

For the point surely is that the end or function of tragedy is not presented as a matter of some single, discrete factor; it involves, rather, the harmonious fulfilment of the "nature" of the genre, and that is something which embraces all the major principles set out in the *Poetics* – principles of form and structure, of action, agency and character. The peculiar pleasure which tragedy affords will thus be of a complex kind ("the pleasure from pity and fear through mimesis"), and one which, as I have argued, exemplifies those general principles of mimetic pleasure which are indicated in *Poetics* 4 and *Rhetoric* 1.11. We should avoid, therefore, ascribing to Aristotle the unqualified view that the aim of tragedy is to give pleasure. It is essential to the whole cast of Aristotelian thought and evaluation that such a proposition *requires* qualification – qualification which situates the idea of tragic pleasure within a fuller conception of the genre: only so will it become clear what differentiates tragic pleasure from other pleasures ("it is not every pleasure, but the appropriate pleasure, that one should seek from tragedy." 1453b10–11).

If we ask, in conclusion, "what, on Aristotle's reckoning, is poetry *for?*," the answer will be (like the ideal tragedy) complex, not simple.[49] We can be confident that Aristotle would wish to stress, with due explanation, that poetry is "for its own sake" in the sense that its aims are not directly instrumental to some externally specifiable goal.[50] Equally, an Aristotelian answer to the question will have to refer centrally to pleasure, since pleasure, as opposed to a biologically necessary or practical purpose, is indispensable to the existence of all mimetic art. This pleasure might be analyzed further into a range of pleasures, many of which I have not been able or concerned to deal with in this essay. But Aristotle speaks firmly of the pleasure peculiar and proper to particular genres, and this is the pleasure which, exemplifying and refining the generic conception sketched in Chapter 4, lies at the heart of his theory of poetry. Such pleasure, I have been contending, is held to arise from the exercise of our capacities for both understanding and feeling in the engagement with the imagined possibilities which art represents. The proper pleasure of an activity, on the mature view of *NE* 10, is the consummation of the nature of the activity: if we wish to grasp a particular pleasure, we must accordingly grasp the activity to which it belongs and which it completes. On the argument of this essay, this means that the best answer we can construct on Aristotle's behalf to the question, "what is poetry for?," must accommodate and integrate all three elements of my title within a composite and subtle notion of aesthetic experience.[51]

Notes

1. See my book, *Aristotle's Poetics* (London and Chapel Hill, NC, 1986), 63–65.
2. J. Lear, "*Katharsis,*" Phronesis **33** *(1988) 297–326, offers a fresh angle on the subject; but cf. n.47 below.*
3. For a defense of this interpretation see my book (n.1) 71 and n.35 there. Note that the phrase "such-and-such" is a place-holder for a particular, not a type.
4. B. Croce, *Aesthetic*, Eng. trans., 2nd edn (London, 1922), 169, accused Aristotle of confusion in linking art with childhood mimesis; but Vico, Croce's hero (ib. 220), makes exactly the same connection: see L. Pompa (ed.) *Vico: Selected Writings* (Cambridge, 1982), 176, §§215–216. The point, to which Plato *Laws* 1.643b–c is germane, remains a serious one: cf. K. Walton, *Mimesis as Make-Believe* (Cambridge, MA, 1990), esp. 21–28, 209–212.
5. That painful emotions remain so even in aesthetic contexts is argued by E. Belfiore, "Pleasure, Tragedy and Aristotelian Psychology," *Classical Quarterly* **35** (1985) 349–361, esp. 349f., 355–358; cf. Lear (n.2) 302. F. Schier, "Tragedy and the Community of Sentiment," in *Philosophy and Fiction*, ed. P. Lamarque (Aberdeen, 1983), 73–92, thinks the experience of tragedy is "not necessarily at all pleasurable" (82, cf. 79–81); but he equivocates on the point, and p. 87 is close to *Poetics* 4. D. Harding, in *Aesthetics in the Modern World*, ed. H. Osborne (London, 1968), 306, challengingly contends that the pleasure of tragedy is a "pseudo-problem."
6. Johnson, *Preface to Shakespeare* (1765), in *Johnson: Prose and Poetry*, ed. M. Wilson (London, 1950), 503; Hume, "Of Tragedy" (1757), in *English Literary Criticism: Restoration and 18th Century*, ed. S. Hynes (New York, 1963), 264–271, esp. 265–266; Kant, *The Critique of Judgement* (1790), §48. On Hume's psychology of weaker reinforcing stronger feelings (anticipated by pseudo-Longinus *De subl.* 15.11) see Shier (n.5) 74–82, 90f. Cf. also the view of Moses Mendelssohn quoted by Lessing in *Laocoon* (1766) §24, and *Thomas Reid's Lectures on the Fine Arts* [1744], ed. P. Kivy (The Hague, 1973), 47. The problem of art's portrayal of the ugly was revived by Nietzsche, e.g. at *Will to Power* §§802, 809, 821.
7. *To miaron, Poetics* Chs. 13, 14, is a notion of moral disgust, comparable to that found in e.g. the passages of Hume (p. 270), Kant and Lessing cited in n.6.
8. Note 1450a36 for the same verb, *akriboun*, applied to literary art; cf. the point at *NE* 1141a9. On art-critical use of this terminology see J. J. Pollitt, *The Ancient View of Greek Art*, Student edn (New Haven and London, 1974), 117ff.; Plato *Critias* 107c–d is also germane.
9. This phrase is one reason why Aristotle cannot be thinking of biological diagrams: an error repeated recently by R. Janko, *Aristotle Poetics* (Indiana, 1987), 74. For contrasting approaches to the *Part. An.* passage see Lear (n.2) 308–309, and G. M. Sifakis, "Learning from Art and Pleasure in Learning: an Interpretation of Aristotle

Poetics 4 1448b8–19," in *Studies in Honour of T. B. L. Webster*, Vol. 1, eds J. H. Betts *et al.* (Bristol, 1986), 211–222, at 214–215.

10. Many Platonic passages illustrate the technical sense of this word-group: e.g. *Republic* 504d7, 548d1, *Laws* 656e, *Sophist* 234b7, 235e2, 236c3, *Protagoras* 312d.

11. The other occurrences are *Prior Analytics* 67a37 and *EE* 1245b4–5; *LSJ* translates correctly. Sifakis (n.9) 215 treats the verb somewhat differently.

12. See *De an.* 440a8–9 (a technique for depiction of water or air); cf. pseudo-Aristotle, *Problemata* 932a30–32. Other, less germane, references to color in painting are *Gen. An.* 725a25–7, *De col.* 792b17, *De mundo* 396b12–15 (a purely sensory quality?).

13. Belfiore (n.5), esp. 351–355.

14. Belfiore (n.5), 351. Belfiore crucially inserts "shape" into her paraphrase of Aristotle, as does Lear (n.2) 309; I too, alas, talked of "form" in this context (n.1) 67, 69: this is misleading, since to perceive the form or shape of a mimetic work is just, for Aristotle, to perceive its representational significance. Cf. the reference to painting at *Poetics* 1450b1–3 (with 1451b23, 26 for the verb *euphrainein*), and n.22 below. Hence Belfiore, 353–354, is also wrong to suppose that *Politics* 1340a23–8 is a case of viewing something "in its own right . . . and not *qua* likeness": Aristotle is there making a point *explicitly* about responses to "likenesses" (*en homoiois*, 23).

15. R. Sorabji, *Aristotle on Memory* (London, 1972), 84.

16. *Zôon*: cf. *Gen. An.* 740a15, *Politics* 1284b9; is *De insomn.* 460b12 pertinent? The term cannot mean an abstract or geometrical configuration: cf. Belfiore (n.5), 352.

17. For *eikôn* as a portrait or copy of a particular see (in addn. to *De mem.* 450b21–51a15) *Rhetoric* 1361a36, 1397b29, *Politics* 1315b19, *Poetics* 1454b9; for the sense "image" *tout court* see *Poetics* 1448b11, ?15, 50b3, 60b9, *Physics* 195b8, *Meteor.* 390a13, *Part. An.* 645a11, *Politics* 1254b36. Ar. fr. 187 Rose[3] (Alex, Aphr. *In Met.* 82.11) shows the term fluctuating between these two senses.

18. Sifakis (n.9) 217–218 produces a quadripartite scheme which contains multiple confusions, including an unwarranted distinction between *mimēma* and *eikōn* in *Poetics* 4. The scheme also depends (cf. 212–213) on rejecting the mss text of *Rhetoric* 1371b6 (for which Kassel's edition is ignored).

19. *Politics* 1340a18 and 33, with 39, shows the synonymity of "likeness" and mimesis. Cf. p. 247 above.

20. Belfiore (n.5) fails to give a clear explanation of this crucial idea. In n.10 she refers to works by E. H. Gombrich and N. Goodman, but the Gombrich essay is concerned with the psychology of *representation* itself (in more than one sense), and therefore does not elucidate the notion of nonrepresentational images; while Goodman's concern is with representations that do not denote. Further obscurity arises in relation to tragedy, where the idea is interpreted as a matter of viewing a play "*qua* people weeping" etc. (354–355): but this seems to imply *belief* (how else could it differ from viewing it as a representation of people weeping?), whereas this was earlier denied on p. 352.

21. Unlike Belfiore (n.5), e.g. 353, I reserve "cognitive" for what Aristotle describes as recognition and learning. A. Nehamas, *Times Literary Supplement* 4371 (9th Jan., 1987) 27, may be right to criticize me for applying too simple a cognitive-sensual dichotomy to *Poetics* 4: I concede that the enjoyment of "workmanship," though necessarily sensual, might also have a cognitive dimension. But Nehamas's claim that the mimetic nature of a work is "very much at issue" in this reference to workmanship, is misleading. It still seems to me legitimate to describe the chief pleasure of mimesis, on Aristotle's account, as strongly cognitivist – i.e. grounded in understanding.

22. The *morphê* in the picture cannot, of course, be an abstract or schematic figure: the noun denotes the form of a certain substance – in this case, the purely sensible form

(cf. *De An.* 424a18) of a person seen as handsome, strong, or beautiful in some other way (note *Rhetoric* 1361b7 ff. for ways in which the perception of human beauty would involve concepts). Cf. n.16 above on *zōon.*

23. Belfiore (n.5) 360 gives the impression of discrete stages in aesthetic experience: "We weep while viewing Oedipus . . . We also view the tragedy *qua* artifact . . . Finally, *because* we shudder and weep . . . we realise that it is an imitation . . ." This seems to me both psychologically and exegetically false, and induced by Belfiore's unnecessarily tripartite reading; her larger argument, that aesthetic pity and fear are still painful emotions, is nonetheless important. I have similar qualms about Lear (n.2) 302: "it is just that *in addition* to the pity and fear . . . one is also capable of experiencing a certain pleasure." (my italics): but "in addition" hardly corresponds to "pleasure *from* pity and fear . . ." at 14.1453b12.

24. D. W. Lucas, *Aristotle Poetics* (Oxford, 1968), 72–73. Likewise Lear (n.2) 308 f.

25. M. C. Nussbaum, *The Fragility of Goodness* (Cambridge, 1986), 388; cf. my book (n.1), 70, E. M. Cope, *The Rhetoric of Aristotle* (Cambridge, 1877), I 218–219, and Sifakis (n.9) 216–217.

26. I elaborate these points in "Aristotelian Mimesis Reevaluated," *Journal of the History of Philosophy* **28** (1990) 487–510.

27. *NE* 1181a19–23 refers to the difference between expert and amateur understanding in fields such as painting and music; the point is in part technical, but it nonetheless suggests the possibility of levels of understanding. On the interpretative *effort* implied by Aristotle's view of mimesis, see H. L. Tracy, "Aristotle on Aesthetic Pleasure," *Classical Philology* **41** (1946) 43–46.

28. Aristotle's comments on mimesis and likeness might be thought to presuppose a strong philosophical realism. I do not share the conviction of J. Derrida, "White Mythology: Metaphor in the Text of Philosophy," Eng. trans., *New Literary History* **6** (1974) 5–74, at 30–46, that such a position is self-deconstructing.

29. There is no reason to follow Gudeman in changing *houtos ekeinos* at *Poetics* 1448b17 to *touto ekeino.* Lear (n.2) 307, and Sifakis 218, mistranslate the former as the latter; *pace* Sifakis, the colloquial idiom *tout' ekeino* is irrelevant.

30. *Rhetoric* 1365a31–33, 1411a1–4; see Cope (n.25) I 145–146 for the historical evidence.

31. *Rhetoric* 1406b20–26, 1407a10–14, assimilate the two figures; cf. M. H. McCall, *Ancient Rhetorical Theories of Simile and Comparison* (Cambridge, MA, 1969), 24–53.

32. See §III of my recent article (n.26). As this article helps to show, my view of Aristotle's mimeticism, as of his entire poetics, involves deep respect and sympathy, along with a commitment to criticism which is itself Aristotelian in spirit: I must therefore rebut the misguidedly strident and inaccurate remarks of R. Janko, *Classical Philology* **84** (1989) 151–159, at 154–155, where I am accused, *inter alia*, of presuming Aristotle guilty of "verbal sleight-of-hand."

33. To find a suggestion of cognitive seriousness and weight in *sullogizesthai*, it is unnecessary (as well as dubious) to take it here in its strictly logical sense, as does, most recently, Sifakis (n.9) 215–220, producing, as he admits (220), a peculiarly jejune form of inference. The medieval Arabic tradition represents the extreme case of the view that Aristotle took poetry to have a quasi-logical status: see e.g. I. M. Dahiyat, *Avicenna's Commentary on the Poetics of Aristotle* (Leiden, 1974), 23. A modern attempt to argue something analogous, though more sensitively, has been made by M. Packer, "The Conditions of Aesthetic Feeling in Aristotle's *Poetics*," *British Journal of Aesthetics* **24** (1984) 138–148, esp. 144. But I prefer a less strict yet richer model of aesthetic understanding: cf. A. Savile, *The Test of Time* (Oxford, 1982), Ch. 5.

34. Actions are particulars: *NE* 1107a31, 1110b6–7.

35. For Renaissance versions of the first two of these distortions see B. Hathaway, *The Age of Criticism* (New York, 1962), Ch. 8. N. Gulley, in *Articles on Aristotle 4: Psychology and Aesthetics*, eds J. Barnes *et al.* (London, 1979), 170, drifts towards abstraction in saying "it is part of [the poet's] job to make generalisations": it would be better to say that certain generalizations *could*, reductively, be used to paraphrase what the poet dramatizes. If it were generalizations as such that were wanted, drama would be redundant.

36. An interesting argument regarding character and universals, though independent of Aristotle, is put by Lamarque (n.5), Ch. IV.

37. S. H. Butcher, *Aristotle's Theory of Poetry and Fine Art*, 4th edn. (London, 1907), 158, 154, 160.

38. R. Yanal, "Aristotle's Definition of Poetry," *Nous* **16** (1982) 499–525. It is instructive that the universal–particular distinction at *De An.* 434a17–19 effectively allows the latter to involve perception of instantiated universals.

39. See e.g. *Rhetoric* 1356b13–14, 1357b28–9, *Topics* 108b7–12.

40. Although one *might* infer from this that good poets need to be people of quasi-philosophical sagacity or insight, Aristotle nowhere indicates that he holds this himself, and I do not know whether he would have agreed with it.

41. *Manthanein* can include the acquisition of new insight: this is certainly so at *Rhetoric* 1410b20–26, where mere confirmation of what one already knows is actually ruled out. Cf. my book (n.1) 73 n.38. For *manthanein* implying the use of existing knowledge, see e.g. *NE* 1143a12–13.

42. A link with the acquisition of universals through experience (e.g. *Posterior Analytics* 100a3–8) may be implicit here, but Aristotle's terseness makes it hard to draw out the point. Cf. Sifakis (n.9) 218–219, with the qualification in n.33 above.

43. Cf. esp. the stress on wonder and surprise, with the high valuation placed on the "complex" plot-structure and its components, reversal and recognition.

44. I take *dia mimēseōs* (1453b12) to overlap in its implications with *hē mimēma* in Ch. 4 (1448b18).

45. The two "causes" of poetry underwrite the account of the course of poetic evolution at 1448b20 ff., where an emotional component is clearly assumed and discernible in the nature of both serious and comic genres.

46. For a modern analogue to this position see Schier (n.5) 89–90 – interestingly, an effectively Aristotelian conclusion to what starts (86), but has difficulty maintaining itself, as a Kantian argument.

47. Lear (n.2) 311; on 310, Lear talks of *catharsis* "*from* pity and fear" (his italics), apparently importing the phrase from 1453b12: the definition, of course, says *through* pity and fear. Although I cannot engage fully with Lear's case on *catharsis*, I note that despite his desire sharply to separate the cognitive pleasure of tragedy from its emotional effect, his ultimate explanation of *catharsis* rests on the "consolation" that tragedy occurs in a world which we perceive, because of the rigorous logic of plot-structure, to be rational not chaotic (325, and cf. 318 on disgust and the irrational). Such perception of a rational world-order would appear to make *catharsis* entail, after all, a significantly cognitive dimension, though Lear had earlier (309–310) described the appreciation of tragic rationality as only a causal antecedent of the proper effect and pleasure of tragedy. Thus a causal antecedent appears to become the central "consolation" of Lear's own solution.

48. A recent instance is M. Heath, *The Poetics of Greek Tragedy* (London, 1987), 9–10; cf. my book (n.1) 81 and n.46 there. Heath, in a forthcoming piece which he has kindly shown me, "Aristotle and the Pleasures of Tragedy," now argues that the peculiar pleasure of tragedy arises from a self-conscious sense of the virtuousness of feeling

pity and fear in appropriate ways. I would consider this factor as, at most, a subordinate dimension, not the essence, of tragic pleasure.

49. When, in a context of political and educational thought, Aristotle poses some such question explicitly for music at *Politics* 1339a11–42b34, his answer encompasses factors of play and relaxation, emotion and ethical character, as well as *diagôgê*, a form of cultivated and pleasurable "leisure" which contributes to happiness: on this, see now Heath's new article (n.48).

50. Cf. Aristotle *Protr.* fr.58 Rose³, = fr.12 Ross, = B44 Düring, where he compares a self-contained justification ("purely for the sake of watching/contemplating") for going to dramatic performances at the Dionysia, with the idea that we need no externally visible reward to justify the study of philosophy.

51. This paper was originally written for a seminar at Brown University, Providence, in April 1989. I am very grateful to all who participated, especially Martha Nussbaum, Alexander Nehamas, and David Konstan.

Tragedy and Self-sufficiency:
Plato and Aristotle on Fear and Pity*

Martha C. Nussbaum

"Honour then the gods, Achilleus, and take pity on me
remembering your father, yet I am still more pitiful;
I have gone through what no other mortal on earth has gone through;
I put my lips to the hands of the man who killed my children."
　So he spoke, and stirred in the other a passion of grieving
for his own father. He took the old man's hand and pushed him
gently away, and the two remembered, as Priam sat huddled
at the feet of Achilleus and wept close for manslaughtering Hektor
and Achilleus wept now for his own father, now again
for Patroklos. The sound of their mourning moved in the house.
Homer, Iliad XXIV 503–512 (trans. Lattimore)

"Give, dear friend. You seem to me, of all the Achaians,
not the worst, but the best. You look like a king. Therefore,
you ought to give me a better present of food than the others
have done, and I will sing your fame all over the endless
earth, for I too once lived in my own house among people,
prospering in wealth, and often I gave to a wanderer
according to what he was and wanted when he came to me;
and I had serving men by thousands, and many another
good thing, by which men live well and are called prosperous . . ."
. . .
Then Antinoos answered him in turn, and said to him:
"What spirit brought this pain upon us, to spoil our feasting?
Stand off, so, in the middle, and keep away from my table . . ."
Homer, Odyssey XVII 415–423, 445–447 (trans. Lattimore)

* This essay will appear in a longer version in *Oxford Studies in Ancient Philosophy*[10] (1992). That version includes more discussion of the ethical-political context of Greek tragic theatre-going, a full analysis of two difficult passages from *Poetics* 13 and *Politics* VIII, a related discussion of Stoic and other views of pity, and fuller discussions of views of other interpreters, including responses to some criticisms of my own earlier work in this area.

I. Reversals

I begin with four tragic situations:

(1) Hecuba and the women of Troy are assigned as slaves to the victorious Greeks. Having already lost her husband and most of her children, she has now endured the loss of her last two possibilities for effective action. For the Greeks have killed her grandson Astyanax, last hope for a rebirth of the Trojan city. And she has failed to secure the just condemnation of Helen. Now, enslaved to the hated Odysseus, unable to act in the spheres in which she had formerly acted well, stripped of the land to which she has given devotion and love, denied even the chance to choose her own death along with that of her burning city, she compares the fortunes of a human life to the reeling gait of a madman, and then walks, empty, to the Greek ships.

(2) King Oedipus has discovered that a life spent trying not to murder his father and marry his mother has been in vain. A tragic ignorance of identities has brought it about that, while (as he saw it) justifiably killing in self-defense, he was actually, in ignorance, committing patricide. And while marrying the queen of the city he has saved, he was in fact also marrying his mother. Stricken with horror at the knowledge of his deed, he puts out his eyes with his wife/mother's brooch-pin, and appears, eye sockets dripping blood, and cries out in pain and horror, invoking darkness.

(3) King Agamemnon has camped with his army on the shore at Aulis. The gods have ordered him to lead a military expedition against the city of Troy. But the winds are still and his ships cannot sail. Already his men are dying of starvation and over-exposure. Now he learns that the gods command a sacrifice: in order for the fleet to sail, he himself must slaughter his young daughter Iphigenia. Do this, and he is a murderer of his own child. Without this, he disobeys the gods' command and all his men die. The king weeps and strikes the ground with his staff, crying out, "Which of these is without evils?"

(4) Hecuba, now a slave, arrives with the Greeks at a deserted shore in Thrace. Her one happy thought is that her youngest child Polydorus remains safe at the home of her close friend Polymestor, very near this place. Soon, however, she learns that this "friend" has murdered the child for his money. Her mind twisted with grief, she vows to dedicate herself to revenge. She murders Polymestor's innocent children and puts out his eyes. As she exults over her crime, it is predicted that she will end her life transformed into a dog with fiery eyes. But, looking at the foul eagerness with which this once noble woman tracks her enemy and delights in his blood, one might well feel that the transformation has already been accomplished.

In each of these terrible examples,[1] we see a good person, a person of good character who has been trying to live well, following his or her commitments as well as possible, given his or her circumstances and information. Yet each of them ends in a condition that is not only miserable, but in some way ethically deficient – either cut off from acting nobly or committing actions regarded as terrible. The cause of their disasters does not seem to lie in bad character, or in character-expressing choices. The Hecuba of the *Trojan Woman* has been a fine queen and a loving mother. The gods and Helen, not she, are to blame for the war that led to her disaster. Oedipus is an upright and courageous man who loves his supposed parents and who has gone to enormous lengths to avoid doing them any harm. He has also been a good ruler and a good husband. He himself insists that his actions were not voluntary,[2] since he was ignorant of the relevant information. Agamemnon is leading his army as well as possible, obeying the command of Zeus. No prior offense of his seems to have caused his dilemma. The Hecuba of Euripides' *Hecuba* has been a loyal mother and a virtuous citizen of her defeated city. She has contrasted good character with the nature of a plant, saying that it is far firmer and will keep its nature no matter what happens. And yet: our first Hecuba ceases to act nobly, because she ceases to act at all. Oedipus kills his father and sleeps with his mother. Agamemnon arranges the slaughter of his daughter. Our second Hecuba kills innocent children in cold blood, and ends the play in a moral condition that resembles that of the vindictive snarling dog she will become. What, then, has happened here?

Human beings have often wished to believe that ethical success, acting and living well, are things that depend only on human effort, things that human beings can always control, no matter what happens in the world around them. Many philosophers and religious thinkers have said as much, and have felt deeply that to insist on this was essential in order to establish that we are dignified beings and not simply the playthings of nature's forces. The idea, most radically explored in Stoic moral thought, originated far earlier in the Graeco-Roman philosophical tradition: if not before, then certainly with Socrates, who is reported in Plato's *Apology* to have said that a good man cannot be harmed, and who urged his audience to rely on this as truth, even though in general he denied that he had moral knowledge.[3]

In saying this, however, Socrates was making a radical departure from prevailing Greek views of these matters, and especially from the thought of Homer and the Greek tragic poets,[4] who were, before Socrates and the moral philosophers who followed him, widely regarded as the central ethical teachers of Greece.[5] The vulnerability of good people to ethically significant reversals is among the central themes of tragedy. It provides the genre not only with much of its *content*, but with its characteristic *form*, shaping its plots and informing the structure of the emotions, pity and fear, through which tragedy characteristic-ally relates to its audience. My purpose in this essay is above all to ask how Aristotle stands on this issue, both in his ethical works and in his account of tragedy in the *Poetics*. What sorts of ethically significant reversals of fortune does he admit, and to what extent are these the same ones that provided tragedy with its plots? How, above all, are his positions on the issue of reversal related to his defense of pity and fear as legitimate and valuable emotions for the spectator? But I shall try to clarify Aristotle's position by looking, as well, at Plato's assault on tragic pity and fear in the *Republic*: for the issues become clearer when we see on what grounds Plato argues that the tragic genre must be eliminated from the good city.

I shall begin by looking at a passage in the *Poetics* where Aristotle makes claims about tragic action that are hard to understand. I shall interpret them by examining the treatment of related issues in the Homeric-tragic tradition and, on the other hand, in the *Republic*. Then, more briefly, I shall examine the arguments on these matters in Aristotle's ethical writings. This will put us in a position to approach the argument of the *Poetics*, and related treatments of fear and pity, asking how, in his explicit treatment of tragedy, Aristotle regards the reversals that are its subject matter, and the emotions that respond to their importance.[6]

II. Tragic Action and *Eudaimonia*

In a controversial passage of the *Poetics*, Aristotle tries to explain why, in thinking about tragedy and its contribution, one should view the plot or action as an element of central importance:

> The most important element is the arrangement of the events. For tragedy is a representation not of human beings but of action and a course of life. And *eudaimonia* and its opposite consist in action, and the end is a certain sort of action, not a character trait. According to their characters people have such and such character traits. But it is according to their actions that they live well or the reverse. (1450a15–20)[7]

Why, it is often asked, does Aristotle assert here that action is "the most important element"? Does he mean to deny the importance of the rich depiction of character?[8]

Clearly he does not. For both in this passage itself and elsewhere in the *Poetics* he insists on the importance of character; and though he allows that there might be a tragedy without characterization (1450a23–5) he clearly believes that this would not be a good sort to aim at (cf. *Poetics* 15, above all). His account of the requirements of pity and fear includes, as we shall see, the stipulation that the hero be a certain sort of character; this indicates that a failure to focus on character would jeopardize the emotional responses that are essential to tragedy. He repeatedly insists, as well, that character and action are very intimately linked: through action the poet "brings in character at the same time" (*ta ēthē sumperilambanousin dia tas praxeis, Poetics* 1450a21–22). Character, furthermore, is what reveals *choice* of what to pursue and avoid (1450b8–10): thus it naturally emerges in action. In the ethical works, similarly, Aristotle understands character to be a "settled state concerned with choice" (*NE* 1106b36); so close is the link between character and action that he doubts whether a person who performs no actions at all could correctly be said to have a certain sort of character (*NE* 1102b5–8). Action is not only *capable* of showing character, it is also the natural expression of character and the best evidence of it (*NE* 1111b4–6, cf. *EE* 1228a3). So by focusing on action here Aristotle does not show a lack of interest in character. Nonetheless, he gives priority to action, claiming that the mere display of character without action would fail to have a relevance to *eudaimonia* that tragic action does have.

We begin to understand the passage better when we ask ourselves what real alternative it rules out. How, that is, might one portray character without action? This question leads us to the character portrait, a literary form made famous by Aristotle's pupil Theophrastus, but attested in some form earlier. It is, in fact, a form of character sketch that Plato's *Republic* endorses as the permissible literature for citizens of the ideal city. Speeches in praise of the goodness of good gods and heroes are allowed, while all tragic action is ruled out. Aristotle, then, is ruling it back in and insisting on its importance with respect to just that goal – illumination about *eudaimonia* – with reference to which Plato thought it pernicious. Tragic plots and tragic action show us something important and true about human life that mere character portraits of good people, by themselves, would not.

To understand this we must, then, turn back to Plato, asking on what grounds tragic action was found ethically objectionable. Plato and Aristotle, as we shall see, agree that tragic action embodies a certain general view about *eudaimonia* and that this view is associated with certain emotions on the part of the spectator. They agree, too, in a general way, about what the view is and what the emotions are. The difference is that Plato believes the view of life to be false and the emotions – based through and through on false belief – to be everywhere inappropriate, whereas Aristotle believes the view to be (with some qualifications) true, and the emotions often appropriate. Let us, then, try to understand this debate – beginning with some observations about the poets themselves.

III. The Reminder of Human Vulnerability

Pity and fear, the emotions at the heart of this dispute, are frequently coupled from a very early date, both in discussions of poetry and in the poets themselves.[9] An implicit general conception of what pity is and requires, and how it is linked to fear, can be found as early as Homer and figures prominently in the tragedians – above all, perhaps, in Sophocles.[10] Pity, as this evidence depicts it, is a painful emotion that takes as its object the suffering of another person. It acknowledges the importance of that suffering and responds to it. (Thus the appeal to pity is often, as in my epigraph from the *Iliad*, a demand for recognition as one whose sufferings matter.) It appears to require (as Aristotle will insist) the belief that the sufferings in question are not merited by the person's own evil deeds. When the sufferings are plainly not the person's fault, as in Priam's case, this need not even be mentioned. Similarly, the horrible suffering of Philoctetes, the result of an accident in which he trespassed unknowingly in a divine precinct, becomes a focus for the characters' pity without further debate, since his innocence has been previously agreed.

Where there is a possible disagreement about culpability, the appeal to pity is often closely linked with the insistence on one's own innocence – as throughout the *Oedipus at Colonus*. At the end of Sophocles' *Trachiniai*, Hyllus insists that the sufferings of Heracles are pitiable where the human actors are concerned, but an occasion of shame for the divine actors (*oiktra . . . aischra*, 1271–1272) – for the human beings were not at fault, while the divine actors showed *agnōmosunē*, culpable lack of concern.[11] Similarly Odysseus, in my second epigraph, follows his appeal by a story showing that his comrades' negligence, not his own wickedness, led to his downfall. When the person's fall does come about in a way for which he or she deserves some blame, the appeal to pity must be accompanied by a claim that the sufferings exceed the amount of due punishment. Thus Cadmus, at the end of Euripides' *Bacchae*, joins to his admission of wrongdoing a claim that the god, by inflicting "unmeasurable sorrow, unbearable to witness" (1244) has exceeded the just penalty (*endikōs men, all' agan*, 1259, and *epexerchēi lian*, 1346). Only this justifies, it seems, his claim to pity from the other characters (1324); and the audience is, in effect, being asked to share that judgment and those feelings. Thus pity may be given either to people whose downfall is altogether blameless or to those who are partly blameworthy. But it always addresses itself to the undeserved nature of the extreme suffering.

It must be emphasized that the appeal to pity, in these and similar cases, requires for its success an acknowledgment, on the hearer's part, of the seriousness of the calamity for the agent's life in general. In making such an appeal, the agent usually insists on the significance of his or her reversal, especially on its connection with the inability to act in admirable or heroic or citizenly ways, or to share in the interactions of *philia*, either familial or friendly. Priam points to the death of his children; Odysseus to hunger and the loss of home and country; Cadmus to the destruction of his house and his own exile. And in granting pity to another, the pitier acknowledges that these sufferings indeed have importance. Hyllus points to the terrible pain and immobility in which his father's heroic career has ended; the *Philoctetes* Chorus speaks of the unlucky man's pain, hunger, friendlessness, and inability to act. The background assumption in all these appeals and acknowledgments is that these things – loss of children, loss of country, immobility, disease, friendlessness – have serious significance, even (perhaps especially?) for a person who is admirable and good.

One further fact about pity that will figure prominently in the debate between Plato and Aristotle is its link with fellow-feeling. Hyllus, asking for pity for his father, asks, as well, for *suggnōmosunē*, "thinking-along-with," or sympathy. And in tragedy generally, pity is the province of humans, rarely of gods. The pitiless countenance of the *Bacchae's* Dionysus, smiling always, reminds both characters and audience that the gods, lacking understanding of suffering as a possibility for themselves, necessarily lack pity also.[12] *Agnōmosunē*, lack of concern, is natural to those who have not shared and can never share the experience of suffering. Thus in pity the human characters draw close to the one who suffers, acknowledging that their own possibilities are similar, and that both together live in a world of terrible reversals, in which the difference between pitier and pitied is a matter far more of luck than of deliberate action.[13] This is where fear fits in: for often the thought of general human vulnerability is accompanied by fear – which, as the expectation of bad things to come, may be directed at the person pitied, if his or her sufferings are thought to be still in the future, but which is often self-regarding as well or instead, as the pitier trembles for his or her own possibilities.

And it is in this that the poets see, I believe, the social benefits of pity. Consider the two Homeric epigraphs of this essay. In the first, a hero who has separated himself in both thought and action from the fate of his fellow human beings is asked to recognize that he too is one to whom terrible life-destroying reversals might come. Priam knows that to appeal for pity he must first move Achilles to fellow feeling: and this he does, reminding him of the sufferings of his father, which might have been far worse than they now are. (As Aristotle emphasizes, concern for a family member often works as a part of self-concern, in giving a basis for pity.) The two men draw close in recognition of the ways in which the afflictions of age and the destructions of war can come to any human, and heroic character proves insufficient to ward them off. Shortly after this, Achilles tells Priam the story of the two urns from which Zeus more or less arbitrarily hands out fortunes to mortals, mixing good and bad – a passage denounced by the Socrates of the *Republic*. Through his pity, Achilles arrives at a new understanding of the shared vulnerabilities of human beings, and becomes able to think of his enemy as a human being like himself.[14] The consequences for social life are enormous: the return of the corpse, the truce, the dignity of the public funeral.

Similar in structure, opposite in outcome, is the case from the *Odyssey*. Here the appeal to pity is, once again, also an appeal to fellow feeling. You are a king, Odysseus says to Antinoos; but so, once, was I. A beggar is not a different species of thing, but a human being subject to fortune as you are yourself. The expected conclusion of the appeal would be compassion and generosity. Antinoos, however, refuses pity, thinking himself above all that and considering a beggar to be a useless "pain," rather than a solemn reminder. The similarity is refused, the beggar dismissed – a grave offense in this society, showing what Aristotle will perceptively call a hubristic disposition (*hubristikē diathesis*, *Rhetoric* 1385b31). Here the failure of pity shows, as its success did in the *Iliad*, the great importance Greek society attaches to pity as a characteristic of the good person and the good citizen. In itself an acknowledgment of true facts about one's own possibilities, it is also a cause of generosity and a cement that binds people to one another.

These patterns remain prominent in tragedy, above all in Sophoclean tragedy. One example must suffice: the *Philoctetes*, where the appeal to pity provides the plot with its entire structure.[15] Philoctetes asks for pity from both the Chorus and Neoptolemus. His sufferings, as I said above, have already been recognized as both innocent and serious. He now asks that the visitors pity him, remembering that everything in human life is risky and one's own fortunes may shift (500–506). Much later, when witnessing an attack of Philoctetes' excruciating pain makes Neoptolemus finally feel the man's suffering, the young hero is moved to pity (965, 1074). He therefore abandons his deceptive plan to steal and keep Philoctetes' bow. The language of the play closely connects the painful experience of pity with a new dimension of ethical responsiveness: for Neoptolemus uses the language of physical suffering to describe his own response (*algō*, 806), and even calls out with the interjection, *papai* (895), that the poor man had used in the throes of his torment – as the pain of pity causes, in turn, the pain of moral distress that leads, eventually, to his generous and noble choice.

IV. Plato on the Self-sufficiency of Goodness

But for Socrates a good person cannot be harmed. And this means, as the *Apology* develops the idea, that many things people usually take to be occasions for fear and pity are not really so: either they are not bad at all, or they are so only trivially, compared to the overwhelming importance of one's own virtue. The downfalls that are worth taking seriously are downfalls in which a person *acts unjustly*. But that, of course, would be occasion not for pity, but for blame and reproach. Undeserved changes of fortune, on the other hand, such as Socrates' imminent death, are not occasions for fear and lamentation because they are not bad at all, or not importantly so.[16]

It is this ethical picture that Plato, like the later Stoics, develops in *Republic* II–III and X to show that the emotion of pity, whenever it occurs, is inappropriate, based on false beliefs, and that tragic poetry is therefore to be utterly rejected.

In *Republic* II–III, Socrates' argument begins from the assumption that the stories we tell the young are very important in shaping their malleable young souls (377BC); he focuses on the danger that the soul will accept false beliefs (*doxai*, 377B, 378D; *pseudos*, 377E). Myths about divine and heroic figures are taken to be influential in behavior through a kind of admiring identification (378B). Therefore it will be forbidden to show the gods causing undeserved suffering either to one another or to humans: if gods are shown causing ill, we must say that what they do is just, and that the mortals are actually being helped by their punishment (379B). Thus one major type of occasion for pity is ruled out from the start: for a class of events that tragedy and Homer characteristically portray as undeserved reversals are now reclassified as both deserved and not really (negative) reversals.

Furthermore, both gods and heroes must be shown as entirely self-sufficient, in need of nothing from the world. The gods are in a condition of such perfection that they do not even have reasons for movement, change, or self-change (380E–81C). As for human heroes, they are not to be shown fearing death or Hades – for the citizens are not to believe that these are terrible impending evils (386B3). Nor will the good man grieve over the deaths of loved ones, lamenting and calling out for pity (387D). This is so because the good man (*epieikēs anēr*, 387D5) does not believe that the death of another good man, his friend, is a terrible thing. Such a person is "most of all himself sufficient to himself with reference to living well, and exceptionally more than others he has least of all need of another . . . Least of all, then, is it a terrible thing to him to be deprived of a son or brother or money or anything of that sort' (387DE). Accordingly, speeches of lamentation and requests for pity – if they are present at all – are to be put in the mouths of women or inferior men, so that the young citizens will "have an aversion to behaving in a similar way" (388A). Numerous Homeric passages are stricken on these grounds. In general, furthermore, literature is required to show that even among non-heroic humans the just live well, the unjust badly (392B).

Book X takes an even stronger stance against tragic poetry, ruling out all *mimēsis*, with the exception of hymns and praises of good men.[17] Once again, the ethical objection against tragedy is that it shows good people (*anēr epieikēs*, 603E, *anēr agathos*, 606B2; and cf. *epieikeis* of the audience at 605C) encountering reversals of fortune and grieving as if these had great significance (603E, 605CD). Again, attention is drawn to the beliefs (*doxas*, 603D) that are associated with this mourning and grieving.[18] Again, the unseemly behavior of the tragic hero is contrasted with the self-sufficient calm demeanor of the truly good man, who recognizes that "nothing among human things is worth much seriousness" (604B12–c1). And here pity explicitly enters the picture. For Socrates points out that tragic poetry leads to fellow feeling (*sumpaschontes*, 605D) and "nourishes the element of pity [*to eleinon*] in us, making it strong" (606B). This has, he alleges, not good but bad consequences: for it makes us less able to achieve a good self-sufficient demeanor in our own sufferings. And this, in turn, impedes rational deliberation (604C, 606D).[19] The right response to such tragedies is not enthusiasm, but disgust (*bdeluttesthai*, 605E6).

In short: tragic action and its scheme of values are both false and pernicious, a source of nothing but lies about *eudaimonia*. The emotions it arouses are based upon lies and subversive of the truly good sort of demeanor, both within oneself and toward others.

Against the disgusting example of tragedy, Socrates in the *Republic* sets the norm of the "wise and serene character, always consistent with itself" (604E); he remarks that it is difficult to represent such a figure in the theatre. Plato's dialogues, however, do represent such a figure, a Socrates who cares little for the prospect of his own death and who pursues his philosophical search regardless of his external circumstances. The *Phaedo* begins from a story that has all the ingredients of tragic action; and its interlocutors remark that, accordingly, they expected to feel pity. But they did not, for Socrates' attitude to his reversal discouraged this response (58E, 59A). Xanthippe is sent away for her tears, Apollodorus sternly admonished for "womanish" behavior (60A, 117D). We might say that we have here the "women or inferior men" of *Republic* 387–388; and the effect of ascribing grieving and lamenting to these inferior figures is indeed, as the *Republic* indicates, to mark these as inferior responses. Socrates the hero, by contrast, confidently continues the search for understanding; and the "drama" in question becomes the drama of argumentation, to be pursued by the intellect alone. This intellect, we are told, reasons best when it manages to avoid the influence of the unhelpful emotions and desires (65E), achieving a state in which, impediments removed, it can see "cleanly" or "clearly" (*katharos*, cf. *Phd.* 65E; and *katharsis, katharmos* at 69C).[20]

V. Aristotle on Fortune and *Eudaimonia*

Aristotle's own views about the possibilities of the good person are distinctly different from Plato's; they admit room for both pity and fear to be legitimate emotions, based on true beliefs. We must begin with the fact that *eudaimonia*, for Aristotle, requires not simply a good character but, in addition, action in accordance with character. This fact, asserted in our *Poetics* passage, is a fundamental starting point in the ethical works (e.g. *NE* 1095a19–20, 1098a16–18, 1098b20–22, *EE* 1219a40–b2). This requirement of activity is used to argue against the view that *being good* is sufficient for *eudaimonia*. Several passages stress that a life with goodness of character might altogether lack conscious awareness (as if someone who was good were to fall into a permanent state of sleep). Such a life, he says, is obviously not *eudaimōn*, and nobody would say that it was "unless he were defending a theoretical position at all costs" (*NE* 1096a1–2, cf. *EE* 1216a3–8; and *NE* 1176a33–35, which insists that *eudaimonia* cannot be a *hexis* since one might have a *hexis* and still live a vegetable's life). Clearly the gap between being good and living well leaves room for luck to enter in: acting from good character has necessary conditions, for example, here, the absence of a disease or accident that would remove consciousness.

Other impediments are explored in other passages. In *NE* VII Aristotle holds that a good person cannot be *eudaimōn* if he is being tortured on the wheel or "has encountered great reversals of fortune": this is so because such circumstances impede activity, and "no activity is complete if it is impeded, but *eudaimonia* is something complete." Aristotle rudely remarks that people who insist that such a person is still *eudaimōn* so long as he is good "are not saying anything – whether that is their intention or not" (1153b16–21).

In *NE* I, Aristotle goes further into the topic of reversal of fortune, choosing as his example the fortunes of Priam. (Thus the discussion has an explicit pertinence to tragedy.) As in *NE* VII, he insists on the importance of external goods such as resources, citizenship, children, and friends, as necessary conditions for virtuous activity (1099a33–b6). (It becomes clear in Books VIII and IX that friends and family members are important in another way as well: as parts of mutual relationships of *philia* that are held to be fine (*kalon*) in their own right, and without which no life would count as *eudaimōn* (1155a29–31, 1155a5, 1169b3 ff., cf. *EE* 1234b32 ff.)). Such resources can fail to be present, through no fault of the person's own, through reversals of fortune. Aristotle's position here, as in *NE* VII, is plainly that such reversals *may* be sufficiently great to prevent a person from being or remaining *eudaimōn*, by impeding his activity (*oudeis eudaimonizei*, 1100a9–10; *lumainetai to makarion . . . kai empodizei pollais energeiais*, 1100b29–30;[21] *ou panu eudaimonikos*, 1099b3; and especially 1101a9 ff., to be discussed shortly). Such reversals can happen, here as in *NE* VII, to any human being, no matter how good – to Priam, who is treated in *NE* VII.1 as an example of outstanding excellence and who is here described as "most especially going well" (1100a6–7), but who is denied *eudaimonia* on account of his misfortune, and is even said to have ended *athliōs*, in a miserable condition (1100a9–10). Such a "shift in the balance of life" (1100b2) will not happen easily. For the good person

> will not be easily dislodged from *eudaimonia*, nor by just any misfortune that happens his way, but only by big and numerous misfortunes; and out of these he will not become *eudaimōn* again in a short time, but, if ever, in a long and complete time, if, in that time, he gets hold of big and fine things. (1101a9–14).

In other words, it takes a great deal of misfortune to step between good character and *eudaimonia*: but sometimes this can happen.

Aristotle makes two further points about a good person in time of misfortune. First, he observes that even when *eudaimonia* is "spoiled" by impeded activity, the person's nobility may still "shine through" in the way in which he bears his misfortunes – not failing to feel their pain (*mē di'analgēsian*), but showing a noble character (1100b30–33). This observation is extremely pertinent to tragedy and the audience's response to it, as we shall see. It is not incompatible with Aristotle's insistence that misfortune can have the power to impede a person from *eudaimonia*: in fact, it is preceded by one statement of that view. But it does show that the catastrophe will not be total: for if character remains, something noble can still be seen, even in the reaction to catastrophe.

A second, closely related, observation is that – given that virtuous activity, and not wealth or status, is the most important thing in life – the good person will be more resistant to catastrophe than a weaker person. For he will always do the best thing possible in the circumstances (1101a3–4). Now this cannot mean that such a person will *always* succeed in being or remaining *eudaimōn*, whatever the circumstances – unless we are to charge Aristotle with an alarming degree of inconsistency; for both before and immediately after this passage, in the same chapter, he insists on the possibility of being dislodged from *eudaimonia*; and his definition of the *eudaimōn* includes a stipulation that the person is "sufficiently equipped with external goods, not for some chance period of time, but for a complete life" (1101a14–15).[22] Furthermore, as we have shown, passages elsewhere provide further solid evidence that being good is not sufficient for *eudaimonia*. Fortunately, however, there is no reason to charge Aristotle with inconsistency: for the passage neither states nor implies that the good person will always retain *eudaimonia*. What it states is simply that the person will always do the best he can. If we combine this with Aristotle's claim that only misfortunes of an especially severe kind will dislodge such a person from *eudaimonia*, we get the conclusion that *often* this doing one's best will in fact be sufficient to guarantee the retention of *eudaimonia*. In the gravest cases, however, it will not be.

Is it possible for good character itself to be undermined by misfortune? In *NE* I, Aristotle answers "no." In the passage quoted above there is one puzzling sentence concerning the length of time it will take to recover when one is dislodged; this sentence may suggest that the damage is imagined to be deeper than the simple absence of external necessary conditions, which could, it would seem, be set right in a moment. But the passage as a whole strongly insists on the firmness of good character. Elsewhere, however, there are some indications that character itself might be affected by reversals. Certainly political surroundings affect character *formation*; and *Politics* II shows how bad governments deprive their citizens of the virtues. The case for adult vulnerability is less obvious. But the books on friendship insist on the importance of friends for the characters of both young and old (esp. 1172a8–14). They insist, too, that one may be deceived by friends, or may lose them to death or old age or absence.[23] Here, then, is an avenue through which it seems possible for damage to good character to occur. The chapters of the *Rhetoric* on old age and the goods of fortune (II.12–14) make it clear that reversals frequently affect character by affecting trust in others and in the future. It is not clear that, or how, the good are exempt from this sort of damage – since these mechanisms of harm are present in good lives as well as bad. In short: Aristotle's position on this question may not be fully consistent across his career. In *NE* I he does indeed (on the whole) seem to reject the possibility of damage to character; elsewhere he suggests that this possibility has not been ruled out.

We may now summarize the debate between Plato and Aristotle, relating it to the disputed passage in the *Poetics*. For Plato there is no use at all for pity, as traditionally conceived: it is built on false beliefs and has bad effects. For good people, people who do not deserve to suffer, do not encounter serious reversals. They do encounter the events of life that most people take to be serious reversals; but to them these things are "not worth much serious concern," and they remain self-sufficient and tearless in the face of loss. When bad events are advancing toward them, they do not fear them; when they happen to a friend, they neither grieve nor pity, since they do not think that anything terrible has happened. If someone *does* react as if something terrible has happened, they feel disgust. Plato does not discuss Aristotle's extreme case of the good person on the wheel: but the Stoics, who do discuss such cases, found in Plato a paradigm for their correct treatment: the case of Socrates in prison, free of fear, repudiating pity.

Aristotle agrees with Plato about some very important things: about the central importance of virtue in the good human life; about the fact that the good person bears disaster better than others, doing the best he can. But because he insists so strongly on the importance of the expression of virtue in action, and because he believes that such action has necessary conditions that may fail to be present through no fault of the person's own, because, in addition, he attaches intrinsic value to types of *philia* that cannot be easily replaced in the event of loss – he does allow that the good person can be dislodged from *eudaimonia*. He opens in this way a space in which both pity and fear are appropriate for and toward good people, and tragic action can show something true about *eudaimonia*. We can see that it is the gap between character and action that is significant here; and thus we can begin to appreciate the importance of our original passage, which insists that tragic action has a relevance to *eudaimonia* that mere character portrayal, all by itself, would not have. Aristotle may or may not agree with every aspect of the Homeric/tragic tradition: we shall pursue that question in Section IX. But he clearly makes room for the reversals characteristic of tragedy to be ethically illuminating, and for pity to be a valuable response.

VI. Aristotle on Fear and Pity

In order to understand Aristotle's brief references to pity and fear in the *Poetics*, we must turn to his extensive discussion in the *Rhetoric*. That discussion shows clearly that these (and other) emotions have, for Aristotle, a cognitive basis: certain beliefs are necessary conditions of the passion in each case.[24] The relevant beliefs, furthermore, are not only a necessary condition, but also a constituent part of each emotion. For emotions are not identified, and distinguished from one another, by some special way they feel – in fact, only two sorts of feeling, pleasure and pain, are recognized in the *Rhetoric* chapters, and are never further subdivided. They are individuated, rather, by the character of the beliefs involved. And the beliefs in question seem to be not just necessary for and constitutive of the complex emotion, but, in most cases, sufficient for the emotion as well. For Aristotle is engaged in telling the young orator how to arouse emotions in his audience; he certainly claims to be giving him a reliable technique. The technique consists in making them believe certain things.

Aristotle's account of the belief-structure of pity and fear lies very close to the Homeric/tragic tradition. Pity is a painful emotion directed at another person's misfortune or suffering (1385b13 ff.). Directly in his initial definition, Aristotle insists that the object of pity must be considered to be *undeserving* (*anaxios*) of the suffering; this judgment he repeats frequently in the discussion that follows. The word *anaxios* is given tremendous emphasis in the passage as a whole; either it or its contrary (negated) occur at 85b14, 85b34–86a1, 86b7, b10, b12, b13. And the judgment is repeated in the *Poetics* (*peri ton anaxion dustuchounta*, 1453a4, and *eleos men peri ton anaxion*, 1453a5). Aristotle's initial definition also insists on the requirement of fellow feeling or identification: pity is felt concerning those misfortunes "which the person himself might expect to suffer, either himself or one of his loved ones" (1385b14–15). He insists, further, that the suffering must be taken to be serious: it must have "size" (1386a6–7).

In the discussion as a whole, Aristotle says more about each of these three requirements. Discussing the requirement of nondesert, he remarks that the pitier must believe to at least some extent in human goodness – he must believe "that there are some *epieikeis* people; otherwise, he will not pity, because he will think that everyone deserves the bad things that happen to them" (85b34–86a1). It is striking that he here uses for the object of pity a word for goodness, *epieikēs*, that Plato had more than once used in the *Republic* in denying that the good person was ever an appropriate object of pity. Aristotle also insists that the goodness of the person (*to spoudaious einai*) is very important in inspiring pity. For it reinforces the belief that the suffering is undeserved (86b6–8). He insists that undeserved sufferings appeal to our sense of *injustice* (86b14–15). Discussing the requirement of fellow feeling, he insists on a certain experience and understanding of suffering (85b24 ff.). He says that it helps if you have parents or children or a wife – presumably because this helps you to sympathize with such losses when they happen to someone else (85b28–29). And he insists that one will not have pity if one thinks that one is above suffering and has everything. Aristotle is not at all friendly to this state of mind: twice he refers to it as *hubris* (85b21–22, b31). Concerning *size*, finally, he enumerates the likely occasions for pity, including most of the serious misfortunes that are the subject matter of tragedy. His list has a close resemblance to the list of potential impediments to good action in *NE* I (1099a33–b6). It includes: death, bodily assault or ill-treatment, old age, illness, lack of food, lack of friends, having few friends, separation from one's friends ugliness (which impedes *philia*), weakness, being crippled, having your good expectations disappointed, having good things come too late, having no good things happen to you, having them happen but being unable to enjoy them (86a6–13).

Fear is closely associated with pity. In the *Rhetoric* he notes that whatever we pity when it happens to another, we fear lest it should happen to ourselves – and conversely (86a22–28, 82b26–27). In fact, his discussions make it clear that this is a slight oversimplification: for many listed occasions for fear are occasions when one is aware that one has done wrong and deserves to be punished. These are not occasions for pity. However, in one direction at least the implication does seem to hold: for all occasions for pity will be occasions for self-directed fear as well.[25] Fear is a painful emotion connected with the expectation of future harm or pain (82a21 ff.). Like pity, it has a requirement of importance (82a28–30); and corresponding, in a sense, to pity's requirement of innocence is a requirement of lack of control or passivity: the person must believe that the bad things cannot be prevented (cf. 82b30–32). Thus people who believe that nothing bad can happen to them will have no fear (82b31–32).

The *Poetics* approaches the topic of fear in a slightly more complex way. For fear, at 1453a5, is still, like pity, directed at the tragic hero, and is presumably a fear of the bad things that are about to happen to the hero.[26] Nonetheless, however, a strong self-referential element remains: for Aristotle says that while pity is directed at the hero as at someone undeserving of suffering, fear takes as its object the hero described as "similar" (*phobos de peri ton homoion*, 1453a5, a6). In fearing the downfall of a person whom we see as similar to ourselves, we are in effect also fearing our own related possibilities.

Aristotle's ethical writings take a very different line from the *Republic* on the topic of both fear and pity. In *NE* I he certainly makes room for the appropriateness of fear, by insisting on the possibility of calamities so great that they can dislodge the person who was "going well" from *eudaimonia* itself. Later, in his account of proper courage, he makes this explicit, insisting that the courageous person will indeed feel fear and pain at the prospect of death. Defining fear in the same way as in the *Rhetoric* (1115a9), he insists that not all fears are appropriate. (For example, one might fear a mouse – 1149a8 – and this is treated as something so absurd as to be pathological.) On the other hand, "there are some things that one must fear, that it is noble to fear, and not to do so is shameful" (1115a12–13). The person who fears, in these cases, is called *epieikēs* (1115a13–14). As objects of proper fear he mentions disgrace, assault on or the killing of one's children or wife, and, above all, one's own death (1115b12–13). In fact, he goes on to assert that the courageous person will be "more pained at the prospect of death the more he has complete virtue and the more *eudaimōn* he is . . . for he will be aware that he is being deprived of the greatest goods, and this is painful" (1117b10–13).

Pity is less frequently discussed, since the *NE* focuses on virtues one should cultivate within oneself more than on responses to the actions and fortunes of others. We can certainly infer from *NE* I, however, that Aristotle does recognize as legitimate a number of occasions for pity; the material we have just discussed implies that the good man who dies will (*pace* Plato) appropriately be pitied by his friends. And in his discussion of voluntary and involuntary action, Aristotle makes two references to pity that have great importance for his understanding of tragedy. In general, he says, we praise and blame voluntary actions; but if they are involuntary we view them with moral indulgence (*suggnōmē*), and in some cases with pity (*eleos*, 1109b30–32). Later in the same discussion, he speaks of actions that count as involuntary because the person acted in nonculpable ignorance, and regretted the act when he knew its true nature. Such ignorance of particulars, he concludes, is deserving of "pity and indulgence" (*eleos kai suggnōmē*). This observation, as we shall see, is central to his understanding of tragedy.

Just as Plato's commitment to the self-sufficiency of the good person led him to reject tragic pity, so Aristotle's commitment to the real importance of *philoi* and other external goods for *eudaimonia* leads him to restore these reactive emotions, and the belief structure that underlies them, to a place of honor. Not all occasions that are ordinarily believed to be occasions for pity and fear will turn out to be so; but the big undeserved disasters on which tragedy focuses are the same ones on which Aristotle also focuses in his account. For tragedies are not written about a mouse running by – and not even, simply, about the loss of money and possessions. They focus on losses of loved ones, country, sphere of action.[27]

VII. The Downfall of the Tragic Hero

The tragic hero, in Aristotle's view, must be an object of both pity and fear. No requirement for tragedy is given such importance and such repeated emphasis in the *Poetics* (1449b27, 52a1–4, 52a38–b1, 52b36, 53a1, a3–7, 53b1, b5, b11–12, b17–18). Tragedy *is* a *mimēsis* of pitiable and fearful things (52a38–b1), and accomplishes its characteristic effect through these emotions (49b27, 53b11–12). The responses of pity and fear are closely connected by Aristotle to the fact that the hero undergoes a change in fortune: a change, he says, is required, either from good to ill fortune or the reverse (51a14–15), and pity and fear are responses to this change. They "come about most especially when things happen contrary to expectation, but on account of one another" (52a2–4). By combining what we know about Aristotle's view of these emotions in general with what he explicitly says in the *Poetics*, we arrive at three requirements for the character of the hero and the nature of his or her change in fortune: (1) the hero must be a generally good person, and undeserving of the suffering he encounters; (2) he must be similar to the members of the audience; and (3) his downfall must be causally intelligible, not simply arbitrary. Let us consider each of these requirements in turn.

First, the hero's goodness. A central requirement for pity, stressed both in the *Poetics* and in the *Rhetoric*, as we have seen, is that the person should be undeserving of the misfortune. The *Rhetoric* stressed, further, that to become an object of pity a person must be thought to be good (*epieikēs, spoudaios*): for if the person is thought to be bad, then it will be assumed that he deserves what he gets. The *Poetics* reinforces this, insisting that the tragic hero should be of good character (*chrēstos*, Chapter 15, where Aristotle makes this the "first" requirement for tragic character, and later calls such characters *epieikeis*, 1454b13). He even says that the hero should be "better than we are" (42b9) and "better than people of today" (48a17–18).[28] (I postpone for a moment the special problems of the opening of *Poetics* 13.) Oedipus is twice mentioned as the sort of hero who would be an object of pity and fear (1452a24 ff., 53b3–7).

It should be stressed that in putting the hero above the audience in character – and even, indeed, in ranking him as *similar* to the best people there – Aristotle is making quite a strong requirement for goodness of character. For unlike the later Stoics, who believed that no fully virtuous person has lived since the deaths of Zeno and Cleanthes, Aristotle does seem to believe that there are good and virtuous people around, and, indeed, that people will become good and virtuous if they have a decent education and no special obstacles. *Eudaimonia* (hence virtue, its necessary condition) is "common to many" (*NE* 1099b18): for it is "open to anyone who is not by nature maimed with respect to virtue, through some sort of effort and care" (18–20).

Second, the hero should be *similar*, or he will not be an object of fear (53a5–6). This theme is further developed in *Poetics* 9, where Aristotle argues that poetry is "more philosophical and more serious" than history (51b5–6), since history shows what has in fact happened, whereas poetry deals in general (*katholou*, 51b8) human possibilities, "things such as might happen" (*hoia an genoito*, 51b5). (Here we see Aristotle agreeing with the Homeric/tragic tradition concerning the generalizing power of pity and fear.) To call poetry philosophical implies that it responds to the desire for understanding that, according to Aristotle, is universal in human beings and that engendered philosophy in the first place (*Metaphysics* I.1). So we may say that the experience of tragic poetry satisfies a desire for understanding of human possibilities. This judgment seems to be developed also in *Poetics* 4, where the pleasure of *mimēsis* is held to be a cognitive pleasure, a pleasure involving recognizing and learning.[29] This cognitive function rests on a bond of similarity between audience and hero that engenders a certain type of identification: we see what happens to the hero as, also, general human possibilities, possibilities for us.[30]

The requirement of similarity is closely linked to the requirement of goodness and nondesert, since Aristotle wants tragedy to have its effect on good citizens as well as less good. Thus we do not feel either pity or fear, he says, at the fortunes of the wicked (53a1, 3–4): for we fail to see them as similar. Even where the person is reasonably good, we need to be convinced that the downfall does not come about through deficiency of character, if we are to have either of the two emotions (53a8–9). Similarity, then, sets a lower limit on goodness that is fairly high up. On the other hand, similarity also suggests an upper limit on the hero's goodness; for the person should not be so far above us as to be no longer a candidate for identification. It is in this way that I would still (as in *Fragility*) understand *Poetics* 13's stipulation that the hero should not be *NE* "surpassing in virtue and justice" (53a8); I would connect this passage with remarks in *NE* VII.1 about a type of excellence" that is "above us" (1145a19). Halliwell takes a similar line.[31] At any rate, the stipulation must be taken in some such way if we are to render that passage consistent with Aristotle's other requirements for the goodness of the hero. (I shall return to the special problems of this section of *Poetics* 13 below.) The idea would then be that the hero is a good case of ordinary available human aspiration – "better than such a one, rather than worse" comments Aristotle just after saying that he is "not surpassing in virtue and justice"; he is also "better than us," but not so far "above us" that we fail to see our own possibilities in his decline.

Third, Aristotle insists that pity and fear will not be felt unless the events of the plot take place according to probability or necessity (51a12). The requirement of causal intelligibility is explicitly connected with the tragic emotions at 52a2–4: they "come about most especially when things happen contrary to expectation, but on account of one another" (52a2–4, cf. above p. 27). The link can best be understood, I think, by referring again to *Poetics* 9. Here Aristotle connects the requirement that plots unfold "according to necessity or probability" with poetry's ability to show general human possibilities. Presumably the connection is as follows. If I witness a person similar to me being struck down in a manner that I find utterly mysterious and arbitrary, I will have no idea whether or not this is the sort of thing that might happen to me; I will simply not understand it, and I will tend to see the events as too weird for identification. If, on the other hand, I see the causal mechanisms at work, and see them as obeying laws of necessity or probability, then the events will strike me as things that could affect my own life.

It is in connection with this requirement of causal intelligibility that a number of interpreters – I believe correctly – have understood Aristotle's insistence that the hero should fall "not through defect and wickedness, but through some error" (*hamartia* 53a8–10). *Hamartia* is contrasted with defeat of character in the immediate context; but it is contrasted as well – implicitly here, explicitly elsewhere, with a causally unintelligible mischance.[32] As Stinton has convincingly shown, *hamartia* is a broad and inclusive notion, including errors both blameworthy and not blameworthy.[33] It is worth remarking that this same inclusiveness is found in traditional ideas of pity – so long as the misfortune exceeds the amount of blame deserved. The unanswered question, however, is why Aristotle insists that the causal mechanism must be an act of the hero's, rather than a (causally intelligible) network of events that bears down on him from outside. Halliwell tends to contrast hero-causality with unintelligibility, as if these were exhaustive options.[34] They are not. There is no mystery about what happens to the Trojan women. War, rape, slavery, murder, are all too easy to understand. But what mistake did *they* make, innocent or otherwise, to bring all this about? To this possible limitation of Aristotle's view I shall return in Section IX.

One passage remains to be discussed. It is one of the most difficult sentences in the *Poetics*, and poses problems for any consistent interpretation of the treatise. In *Poetics* 13, discussing the types of complex plot that will cause pity and fear, Aristotle remarks: "first, it is clear that good men [*epieikeis andras*] should not be shown changing from good to bad fortune – for this is not pitiable or fearful, but disgusting [*miaron*]." I discuss this passage at length in *Fragility*

(p. 502, n. 15),[35] and even more fully in the longer version of this paper. Aristotle's statement is very peculiar indeed to anyone who has closely studied all of his statements about the requirements of pity and fear and about the goodness of the hero. Two possibilities for reconciling it with its context that have frequently been supported are: (1) to say that Aristotle is objecting not to the decline of the good person as such, but only to his *unexplained* decline. This reading, supported by Lear and others, has the merit of connecting the sentence to the chapter's later remarks about *hamartia*, but no reference to causal intelligibility is in the passage itself. (2) One can hold that the passage rules out not ordinary goodness of character, but some sort of extraordinary goodness that would put the hero beyond our moral experience and recognition. This requires giving *epieikēs* a sense it has nowhere else; but it has beeen defended by Lucas, Halliwell, and others as the best hope for saving Aristotle's consistency. As in *Fragility*, I tentatively favor (2), though I see some merit in (1) also, and considerable difficulty in both. The main thing is to realize that watever we say about this sentence, unless we take one of these escape routes or think of a new one, the sentence is inconsistent with a great deal of evidence in the *Poetics* and other works, as the entire argument of this paper has tried to show.

Aristotle shows, then, that the ethically controversial material of pity and fear is not a kernel of content inside the tragic form; it forms the form, and the plots that are its "starting point and soul" (50a38–39). It informs the choice of the hero, the type of story chosen, and the causal structure linking its events. We can add that it also shapes two further features of tragic plot in which Aristotle shows a particular interest: reversal (*peripeteia*) and recognition (*anagnōrisis*). Aristotle connects these features closely to the generation of tragic responses, saying that they are "the greatest things by which tragedy influences the soul" (*psuchagōgei*, 50a33). *Peripeteia* (as contrasted with simple change of fortune) is a reversal of expectations, a change to the opposite of what had been anticipated. We recall that at 52a2–4 a reversal in expectation was taken to be important for pity and fear. This is so, presumably, because in order to pity the hero we have to find him good and undeserving of misfortune; but this response is aided if we are led by the play to expect good things for him, to see him as, like Priam, one who is "especially going well." In reversal it is clearly not always the case that the audience is totally surprised: for the *Oedipus*, Aristotle's central example, shows, instead, abrupt reversal of the *characters'* expectations in a way that the audience would have guessed before them. But even here, in so far as the audience identifies with Oedipus it does not allow itself to know what it knows about the story; and the others characters' good expectations for him, and his for himself, do their work to set him before the audience as a person aiming well, undeserving of catastrophe. Recognition plays a closely related role in showing the hero the true nature of the causal chain that has been unfolding. In all these cases we are dealing with formal literary structures. But they are closely bound up with the tragic emotions and, accordingly, with a controversial ethical content.

In speaking of reversal and recognition, Aristotle does not always prefer an unhappy outcome. In *Poetics* 13 he does, insisting that the direction of change should be "not from bad fortune to good fortune, but, conversely, from good fortune to bad fortune" (53a13–15). He praises Euripides for the unhappy endings of many of his plays, saying that "this is correct," and that "he appears to be the most tragic of the poets" (953a26, 29–30). In Chapter 14, however, he prefers plots like that of the *Iphigenia in Tauris*, where disaster is narrowly averted. It does not seem to me possible to render these two chapters consistent in every respect; but Halliwell is surely right to stress that they are not as much at odds as some have believed. For the second type of plot is, in a sense, a species of the first.[36] Both concern the power of circumstances to bring about the decline of a good person; and it is in this way that both engender pity and fear. It is just that in the latter case the disaster which has all along been the object of pity and fear is averted at the last moment. This, we should insist, does not diminish the sense an audience would have of the vulnerability of the hero's fortunes and, therefore, of their own: for it is very clear that salvation, in such cases, hangs by a thread and is not the hero's to guarantee. Such a double movement of luck would, if anything, heighten the awareness of mutability in the spectator.

The requirements of pity and fear lead Aristotle to downgrade summarily a plot structure favored by Plato in *Republic* II–III, namely one in which the good end happily, the bad unhappily (53a1 ff.). He remarks that this plot does not offer the pleasure proper to tragedy, which he describes as "pleasure from pity and fear through representation" (53b10–12). This is so, presumably, because it lacks the element of the undeserved. Such moralizing dramas, he acknowledges, are popular with audiences, on account of "weakness" (the weakness, presumably, of not facing up to the fact that people do not always get what they deserve). Yet he judges that there is something amiss with them, something alien to the form itself.

So, in his inquiry, Aristotle seeks out the human content of tragic formal structures, seeing the form as governed by its pitiable and fearful content, the content, in turn, as further shaped by the formal structures that seem appropriate to engender these emotions.

VIII. Interpreting *katharsis*

Plato held in the *Republic* that emotions such as pity and fear are powerful impediments to rational deliberation. And in the *Phaedo* he depicted the soul's search for understanding as a process that required *separating* intellect as much as possible from the impeding influence of these and other emotions. He spoke of this process as a "clearing up" or "cleaning up" – using a family of words (*katharōs, katharsis, katharmos*) that were familiar in many different contexts – everyday practical, educational, medical, religious, literary – always, however, with the general sense of "clearing or cleaning up by removal of an obstacle or obstacles."[37] Ancient evidence suggests that Aristotle's idea of poetic *katharsis* is some sort of response to Plato.[38] Therefore, although nothing we have said so far about pity, fear, or even tragic learning and tragic pleasure presupposes any particular interpretation of *katharsis*, and although any interpretation of this difficult material must remain tentative, it seems appropriate to do what we can to make sense of it.

In *Fragility* I studied the *kathairō* word group in some detail, showing its wide range of uses in the sense "cleaning up," "clearing up."[39] There seems to me to be no reason to suppose that the word *katharsis* ever became separated from the rest of the word group and turned into a technical term: it seems to retain both the ordinariness and the range of its cognates. *Katharsis* is just the process that yields a *katharos* result, i.e. one free of dirt or impediment. The word group may of course be used in specialized religious and medical and literary *contexts*. And often in those contexts there will be specialized views about what counts as the achievement of *katharsis*. But there seems to be no reason to think that the word itself has taken on a technical *sense*, no reason not to go on translating it in its ordinary sense of "cleaning" or "clearing up." If there is any group of specialized contexts that seems especially pertinent in understanding Aristotle's use here, it would seem to be the group of rhetorical, philosophical, and literary passages in which the "clearing up" in question is cognitive, a getting clear about obscure matters.[40] But Plato's uses give us an even better reason to investigate a cognitive application of *katharsis* in the *Poetics*, since Plato clearly does envisage the "getting clear" in question as an improvement in understanding by the removal of some obstacles to understanding.

It is also clear that the idea of a *katharsis* produced, as in the *Poetics*, "through pity and fear" (49b27–28) would have been deeply repellent to Plato. Indeed, it would sound to his ears close to an oxymoron (in something like the way in which "military intelligence" is supposed to be an oxymoron). It is, to him, tantamount to saying "cleaning by mud," or "clearing up through disgusting mess." For Aristotle, however, these emotions can be genuine sources of understanding, showing the spectator possibilities that are there for good people. Therefore, what more succinct summary of his difference from Plato could there be, than to speak of a "getting clear through pity and fear"? This interpretation, unlike Leon Golden's variety of the cognitive interpretation,[41] does not require denying that *katharsis* takes place through the emotions themselves. In fact, it insists on this. Once we notice their cognitive dimension, as Golden did not, we can see how they can, in and of themselves, be genuinely illuminating.

As has often been observed, every other element in Aristotle's definition of tragedy picks up some earlier part of his discussion in *Poetics* 1–5. Aristotle emphasizes this fact, saying, "Let us speak of tragedy, taking up from what we have said the definition of its nature that has come into being. Tragedy, then, is . . ." (49b22–24). *Katharsis* is, it seems, the one element in the definition that does not respond to some item in the earlier discussion. In this case, it seems to me that Golden has argued correctly: the *katharsis* reference picks up the discussion of the pleasure of learning in Chapter 4. It is not hard to see how it does so, if we stop hearing _katharsis_ as a weird and mysterious technical term, and start hearing it in its ordinary sense. For "accomplishing through pity and fear a clearing-up concerning experiences of the pitiable and fearful kind"[42] would be easy to connect with Aristotle's general discussion of getting clear and learning in Chapter 4. That was, of course, a general discussion of the pleasure from all _mimēsis_; but its specific tragic variety is later said, precisely, to be "the pleasure from pity and fear through representation" (53b12). I have been arguing that this _is_ a pleasure involving learning, in the way that Chapter 9 suggests.

What does the spectator get clear _about_? Here we face an objection from Jonathan Lear, who rejects the educational interpretation on the grounds, above all, that it does not explain the responses of _good_ people in the audience.[43] But Lear seems to me wrong to assume that for Aristotle a good person never needs to learn anything. Certainly a good adult does not need _paideia_ – but Lear is wrong to think that if we establish that tragic _katharsis_ is not _paideia_ we have ruled out all cognitive and educational functions. _Paideia_, as Halliwell already argued well,[44] is the education of young children; and as Aristophanes' Aeschylus observed (_Frogs_ 1063–1066), tragic poetry is education for grown men, not for children. Good adults in Aristotle do in fact have room to learn something. Experience is cumulative, and there is no reason to think that it ever comes to a stop. Furthermore, Aristotle explicitly imagines good people receiving education and advice from their good friends: "The friendship of the good [_epieikōn_] is good [_epieikēs_], and it increases with their association; and they seem to become better in their activity and their correction of one another" (_NE_ 1172a10–12). So much, I take it, is true of the good members of the tragic audience: however good each person is, there remains room for improvement, advice, further experience.

I imagine this process as functioning in very much the way it functioned in my examples from the poetic tradition. Neoptolemus is good, but capable, as nonomniscient good people are, of making mistakes. Without realizing it, he has diverged from his good character.[45] The sight of Philoctetes' pain removes an impediment (ignorance in this case, rather than forgetfulness or denial), making him clearer about what another's suffering means, about what his good character requires in this situation, about his own possibilities as a human being. The audience, in the midst of wartime, is recalled to awareness of the meaning of bodily pain for another, for themselves. Even good people do need to be reminded – especially in time of war, when military passions run high and awareness of the enemy's similar humanity is easily lost from view in the desire to inflict a punishment. Again, seeing _The Trojan Women_ reminds an audience who had voted for the slaughter of the Mytilenians, the enslavement of women and children – and whose second thoughts were only by sheer luck effective – exactly what it _is_ to lose one's male relatives, to be enslaved and turned out of one's home. Forgetfulness, ignorance, self-preoccupation, military passion – all these things are obstacles (fully compatible with general goodness of charcter) that are "cleared up" by the sharp experience of pity and fear. Is there anyone so good as not to need such reminders, such an emotional house-cleaning? I do not think so, and I do not think that Aristotle thought so.

All of this seems to me to be securely in the argument of the *Poetics*, with or without being attached to the word *katharsis*. I think there are good reasons, however, for connecting it to that word. And this means that it is not such a big surprise that Aristotle does not discuss the *word* again. For on this interpretation he is discussing the *topic* whenever he discusses pity and fear, and what they reveal about human life; whenever he discusses human possibilities; whenever he discusses the pleasure of learning and the philosophical contribution of poetry.[46]

IX. Aristotle's Relation to Tragedy

Let us now return to the paradigms of tragic action set out in the four examples in Section I, asking how they exemplify different ways in which a good person may undeservedly fall from *eudaimonia*. I shall then ask how Aristotle would judge them; and I shall suggest several ways in which his account seems to me to depart from at least some of what ancient tragedy offers.

Our four examples present, it seems, four different structures of tragic action, four different ways in which being good falls short of sufficiency for living well, on account of an undeserved reversal. Although any such classification is bound to run the risk of seeming reductive and overly schematic, we can also say, I think, that they show four major types of tragedy.

(1) The *Trojan Women* is what we might call a *tragedy of impeded action*. We see good people put into a situation of extreme powerlessness, in which, stripped of citizenship, friends, and resources, they can no longer choose the actions that formerly expressed their excellences. We see that they do the best they can, acting well to one another; and yet it seems likely that in losing so much they have lost their *eudaimonia*. This is a common tragic pattern, especially in plays dealing with the end of war.

(2) *Oedipus the King*, by contrast, is what we might call a *tragedy of involuntary action*. Oedipus aims at living well, and chooses as best he can; but ignorance for which he is not to blame brings it about that he commits horrible acts. Oedipus is innocent; and yet his circumstances have prevented him from being *eudaimōn*. Again, this is a central and important tragic pattern.

(3) Agamemnon's case belongs to a different pattern, which we might call the *tragedy of ethical dilemma*. Here chance steps in a different way: not by frustrating action altogether, not by obscuring awareness, but by producing a contingent conflict of two important obligations, in such a way that no innocent course is available. This type arises directly out of ancient Greek polytheism, in which one

must honor all the gods, and yet the gods frequently confront human beings with conflicting requirements. Civil war produces another set of such conflicts.

(4) The *Hecuba* belongs to a small class of plays in which we seem to see *tragedy of eroded character*. Here circumstances do not only impede the heroine's action, they sap the inner structures of trust and motivation that make up her virtue.

Now we must ask which of these types of tragedy Aristotle would admit. The second type is clearly a paradigm case for the *Poetics*. It also accords with the data of the ethical works, as we have seen. One might wonder whether Oedipus is a counterexample to the claim (*NE* 1100b55) that the good person will never do hateful and wicked deeds: but Aristotle, on the whole, individuates actions intensionally, in such a way that Oedipus' killing is not, in the relevant sense, a wicked deed.[47] The third type of tragedy, too, seems compatible with the *Poetics'* analysis of reversal and *hamartia*; and its appearance in the ethical works, though brief, is clear. The class of "mixed actions" in *NE* III.1 includes cases of this sort, in which one may be forced to choose a shameful action because the alternative is ethically worse; Aristotle demands for such cases sympathy, rather than blame.[48]

The first type is central to Aristotle's discussions of reversal in the ethical works, where impeded action is the focus of his remarks about the insufficiency of character for *eudaimonia*. Priam's fate is a major example. (We might, however, take the class of "impeded actions" to include not only cases like Priam's, but also cases like those of Oedipus and Agamemnon, whose actions are certainly impeded by circumstances, though in different ways.) It seems more dubious, however, whether the *Poetics* can include the Priam type, at least as a preferred type. For the reversals that beset the Trojan women, while in no sense mysterious or unexplained, are also in no way caused by their own actions. If we look for a mistake in action that is causally responsible for reversal here, we have to look back to the deeds of Helen – who is not, after all, the heroine. If pressed, we might see *hamartia* in the well-intentioned efforts of Hecuba and Andromache to plan the rebirth of the city through Astyanax, which brings Greek wrath down upon him. But these are "deeds" of speech and imagination only; and one feels, besides, that Astyanax was doomed simply by existing. In short, these heroines are too trapped, too passive, their destinies too independent of their agency, to belong to Aristotle's preferred type. Presumably he would argue that an outcome that is settled from the start will not generate fear and pity as much as a story whose outcome is still in suspense. (Such a passive play may figure in the class of *passive tragedies* recognized in *Poetics* 18.)[49] This is a controversial aesthetic judgment – but it is one we can understand, and one that does not show, on Aristotle's part, any lack of sympathy with the values central to ancient tragedy.

The fourth case is pretty clearly not envisaged in the *Poetics*, which stipulates that the hero must be good and unworthy of misfortune, and that his or her downfall must be an object of pity. Hecuba is indeed good at first, of course, and to an extent, therefore, pitiable – but her change in character generates horror more than pity. In general, the *Poetics* assumes constancy of character, and therefore of audience judgment and emotion. The ethical works insist, on the whole, that this sort of decline does not happen to good people – though, as I have suggested, some material does suggest darker possibilities. We must here admit, then, that Aristotle is usually more optimistic than Euripides – more in tune, I think, with Sophoclean ideas of the hero – in his assessment of what may become of a good person and what may not.[50]

Here another more general question arises. Aristotle insists in the ethical works that, while circumstances may dislodge a good person from *eudaimonia*, they can never push this person into doing base and hateful actions; for this reason, he concludes that this person will never be truly *athlios* (*NE* 1100b34–1101a8, cf. above p. 271). Apparently he means to say that only someone who does wicked deeds has really hit bottom, really become as wretched as one can be. Does tragedy disagree with this estimate? The word *athlios* all by itself gives us no solid information: for a little earlier in that same passage of the *NE*, Aristotle actually uses that every word to describe the end of Priam's life after he is topped from *eudaimonia* by misfortune (1100a10). Presumably in the first (Priam) case, he means "miserable, pitiable" and, in the second, something like "at the bottom of the scale, basely wretched." *Athlios* has both senses. So the question cannot be the simple question whether tragic poets use the *word athlios* of their pitiable good heroes – for they do, of course, much as Aristotle does of Priam – but it must rather be what they *mean* by this. Do they depict their heroes as pitiable and miserable, not *eudaimones*, but still showing nobility by their good efforts and firm character? Or do they show them as lowest of the low, on account of their circumstantial reversal alone? If the former, they agree with Aristotle. If the latter, they are more pessimistic about human possibilities, or less inclined to judge that virtue makes a crucial difference when so much else has been lost.

Any general answer to this question will be bound to seem too simple; and yet I think we can say something useful here. It seems to me that Aristotle's characterization of the good person in adversity fits very well with Sophoclean tragedy – in which the hero's nobility does "shine through" in calamity, and in which his or her unshaken disposition to do the best is a source of honor, even if he is not, finally, *eudaimōn*. While Oedipus is clearly *athlios* (*OT* 1204) in the sense in which Aristotle calls Priam *athlios*, he also has the nobility and firmness of which Aristotle speaks. On the whole Sophoclean tragedy is dedicated to the assertion of unbending virtue in the fact of a hostile and uncomprehending world, and dedicated, too, to manifesting that human virtue has not in fact been altogether extinguished by the obstacles that menace it. Thus the ending of the *Trachiniai*, with its strong distinction between the situation of the human characters, which deserves pity, and that of the gods, which deserves shame. Euripidean tragedy, on the other hand, seems in some instances more open to the darker possibilities of decline that are ignored or ruled out in Aristotle's universe; and even where virtue is retained it does not seem to count for as much, in a world where its expression is drastically curtailed.

In another way as well, Aristotle seems closer to Sophocles than to Euripides. In Sophoclean tragedy, where there is divine causation it follows causal laws that are usually intelligible in human terms, and does not seem to threaten Aristotle's demand that the causal structure of the plot should be fully comprehensible. And in so far as gods are shown to be different from humans, they are not different in a way that calls into question human norms of virtue. In fact, the perception of the human characters that they live in a world in which the gods may act in cruel and pitiless ways only reinforces their commitment to the human virtues of friendship and fellow-feeling, the human emotion of pity. Thus it seems to me that Aristotle's failure to say very much about the divine is not a grave deficiency in his account, if we are thinking of Sophocles; for the presence of divine agency in the plot will not alter the demands the *Poetics* makes for certain types of character, emotion, and causal structure.

In the case of some dramas of Euripides – I think above all of the *Bacchae*[51] – the situation is different. For the presence of the divine in the human world does radically alter expectations of what a human being should be – not just in the obvious sense that all humans should honor the gods – this is equally true in Sophocles – but in the sense that honoring this strange new god requires departures from reasoned norms of good character into conduct that is volatile and mysterious, inconstant and sometimes deadly. Even the notion of character itself is threatened, as the god demands, and exemplifies, a fluidity of identity that links the human with the bestial on the one hand, the divine on the other. To refuse these influences is to become, like Pentheus, both impious and bestial; to accept them is to accept a loss of control over oneself, and the risk of doing terrible things. This strange and transfigured world does not seem easy to reconcile with Aristotle's categories of analysis – either with his demand for causal intelligibility or with his assumption of firm character. Thus I would agree with Halliwell, up to a point, that Aristotle secularizes tragedy. I do not think his mode of analysis impoverishes our understanding of many major dramas, including most of those of Sophocles; but it is not complete, and it does not fare well with Dionysus.

The world of Sophoclean tragedy is a world in which nobility (like Philoctetes' island)[52] is surrounded by dangers, both natural and divine. The gods lack compassion for human suffering and can cause terrible misfortunes (often through chains of human agency) that dislodge good people from *eudaimonia*. In disaster, these good people retain heroic dignity and stature. Both the presence of pity in the play and the arousal of pity in the spectators assert the undeserved nature of the hero's fall, the worth of his or her efforts. Hero and friends, sharing in lamentation, insist on the importance to human life of the things misfortune has spoiled, and on the fact that human beings do not fully control them. Spectators, sharing in the hero's suffering, become aware of the importance of these elements in their own lives, and of their vulnerability. According to the tradition, this should have a tendency to increase generosity and concern for the sufferings of others. The world of Plato's ideal city, by contrast, is a world in which such lamentation will be greeted with disgust, as a sign of ethical deficiency. Spectators will either not see such things at all (X), or will learn not to identify with characters who behave this way (II–III). No human things are worthy of such great concern. Aristotle, I claim, though not agreeing with all tragedies in all respects, accepts the general elements of the Sophoclean picture and makes them the basis of his account of tragedy. Tragic action gives rise to pity and fear. Through their pity and fear, indeed *in* those responses, spectators attain a deeper understanding of the world in which they must live, the obstacles their goodness faces, the needs each has for the help of others.[53]

Notes

1. These cases are, of course, respectively: Euripides' *Trojan Women*, Sophocles' *Oedipus the King*, Aeschylus' *Agamemnon*, and Euripides' *Hecuba*. I discuss the last two in Martha Nussbaum, *The Fragility of Goodness*, Chs. 2 and 13, the second in Nussbaum, "The *Oedipus Rex* and the Ancient Unconscious," forthcoming in *Freud and Forbidden Knowledge*, eds. P. Rudnytsky and E. Spitz (New York, 1993).
2. This description is given in the *Oedipus at Colonus*: see 270–274, 521–549, 960–987, and cf. 1565; for pity in connection with this, see 536–537. There is no reason to suppose the *Oedipus the King* to be in these respects different: see Nussbaum, (n.1).
3. *Apol.* 41D, and cf. 30CD. For one interpretation of the denials (and assertions) of knowledge, see G. Vlastos, "Socrates" Disavowal of Knowledge." *Philosophical Quarterly* **35** (1985) 1–31.
4. Plato treats Homeric together with tragic examples, and even calls Homer the leader of the tragic poets: see *Republic* 598D, 605C, 607A, and II–III *passim*.
5. For a representative example, see Aristophanes' *Frogs*, where the decision to resurrect an outstanding ethical teacher is without further discussion understood to require bringing back one of the great tragic poets. See esp. Aeschylus' claim at 1063–1066: "Little boys have a teacher who tells them what to do; grown men have the poets." Plato's examination of the poets presupposes their great influence as teachers, and in fact begins by granting that some form of *mousikē* is best for the education of the soul (376E). See further Nussbaum, *The Fragility of Goodness*, Interlude 1.
6. For related discussions, see Nussbaum, *The Fragility of Goodness*, esp. Chs. 11–12 and Interlude 2; also Ch. 13, pp. 418–419 on Aristotle's relation to Euripides, Ch. 5 on Platonic self-sufficiency, Interlude 1 on the antitragic structure of the Platonic dialogue. For discussion of some criticisms of my arguments, see Nussbaum, " 'Reply' to Papers on *Fragility*," *Soundings* **72** (1990) 725–781, and the longer version of this paper. On Stoic attitudes to these questions, see Nussbaum, "Poetry and the Passions: Two Stoic Views," in *Passions & Perceptions*, eds., Brunschwig and M. Nussbaum (Cambridge, 1992).

   On all these issues, see the illuminating discussion in S. Halliwell, "Plato and Aristotle on the Denial of Tragedy," *Proceedings of the Cambridge Philological Society* **30** (1984) 49–71; *Aristotle's Poetics* (London and Chapel Hill, NC, 1986); *The Poetics of Aristotle*, trans. and comm. (London and Chapel Hill, NC, 1981); and *Plato: Republic X*, trans. and comm. (Warminster, 1989). See also the perceptive discussions and criticisms of my arguments in Halliwell, "Review of M. Nussbaum, *The Fragility of*

Goodness," *Ancient Philosophy* **8** (1988) 313–319; and "Settling a Quarrel: Philosophy and Literature," *Philosophical Investigations* (forthcoming).

7. For the Greek text of the passage and a comprehensive discussion of philological issues, see Nussbaum, *The Fragility of Goodness,* pp. 500–501, n.2, with refs.

8. See D. W. Lucas, *Aristotle's Poetics* and J. Jones, *On Aristotle and Greek Tragedy* (London, 1962), discussed in Nussbaum, *The Fragility of Goodness,* p. 379.

9. See refs in Halliwell, *Aristotle's Poetics,* p. 170, n.3, with further bibliography.

10. See the acute discussion in R. P. Winnington-Ingram, *Sophocles: An Interpretation* (Cambridge, 1980), esp. pp. 321, 328.

11. On this passage, see Nussbaum, "Transcending Humanity," in *Love's Knowledge: Essays on Philosophy and Literature* (New York, 1990) and Nussbaum "Introduction" to Euripides' *Bacchae,* trans. C. K. Williams (New York, 1990); on the absence of pity in the Sophoclean gods, Winnington-Ingram, *Sophocles,* Ch. 13.

12. On the *Bacchae,* see Nussbaum, *Bacchae,* with other references.

13. I am assuming here that both pitier and pitied are good, and more or less equally good.

14. There are many good treatments of this passage: e.g. J. Griffin, *Homer on Life and Death* (Oxford, 1980); J. Redfield, *Nature and Culture in the Iliad* (Chicago, 1975); J. B. White, *When Words Lose Their Meaning* (Chicago, 1984).

15. On the play in general, see Nussbaum, "Consequences and Character in Sophocles' *Philoctetes,"* *Philosophy and Literature* **1** (1976–77) 25–53. Pity words occur 16 times in the play, more often than in any other play of Sophocles. For other examples of appeals to pity that allude to the general possibility of a shift in fortune, see esp. *Ajax* 121–126, where Odysseus grants pity "thinking no more of his situation than of my own," and *Trachiniai* 296–301, where Deianeira's pity is accompanied by self-regarding fear.

16. See *Apol.* 35E ff. on the fear of death, 28A ff. on the overwhelming importance of virtue, 34C on the refusal to plead for pity by bringing his family into court.

17. It is clear that these hymns and praises are taken to be mimetic; on this, and in general on differences between II–III and X, see Halliwell, *Plato: Republic V;* see also Halliwell, "Plato and Aristotle on the Denial of Tragedy."

18. There may, however, be serious differences about the psychology of the emotions between II–III (with IV) and X. X recognizes only two parts of the soul, and seems to treat grief like a bodily appetite that demands gratification, rather like hunger (cf. esp. 606A, *pepeinēkos tou dakrusai . . . kai apoplēsthēnai*); IV insists on the particular responsiveness of emotions to belief, a fact that figures importantly in the discussion of poetry in II–III.

19. Cf. also *pimplamenon kai chairon,* 606A, *trephei ardousa,* 606D.

20. For fuller discussion of this material, see Nussbaum, *The Fragility of Goodness,* Interlude 1 and Ch. 5. On the Stoic use of Socrates as exemplum, see Nussbaum, in *Passions & Perceptions.*

21. In Nussbaum, *The Fragility of Goodness,* Ch. 11 I argue at length that *eudaimon* and *makarion* are interchangeable in these and other contexts. This lets in much more evidence about the vulnerability of the good person, which I discuss, as well, in that chapter.

22. Cf. 1100b19–22, where he says of the good person, "He will always or more than anything (anyone?) else do and consider the things according to excellence" – qualifying his remark so as to show that in doing the best one can one might not always succeed in fully doing the things according to excellence.

23. For the evidence, see Nussbaum, *The Fragility of Goodness,* Ch. 12.

24. I have argued this in Nussbaum, *The Fragility of Goodness,* Interlude 2, in Nussbaum, "The Stoics on the Extirpation of the Passions," *Apeiron* **20** (1987) 129–177, and in

greater detail in Ch. 3 of *The Therapy of Desire: Theory and Practice in Hellenistic Ethics*, the Martin Classical Lectures 1986 and forthcoming. See also Leighton, "Aristotle and the Emotions," *Phronesis* **71** (1982) 139–158. On the connection between *Poetics* and *Rhetoric*, see also Halliwell, *Aristotle's Poetics*, Ch. 6, and Lear, "Katharsis," *Phronesis* **33** (1988) 297–326.

25. There is also, clearly a temporal asymmetry: one fears only so long as the bad thing is approaching; and Aristotle even insists that one must have hope of salvation.

26. Here I am in agreement with Halliwell, *Aristotle's Poetics*, p. 176, and believe that in *The Fragility of Goodness* I did not express myself precisely enough on this issue.

27. On Stoic continuations of this debate, see Nussbaum, "The Stoics on the Extirpation of the Passions" and "Serpents in the Soul: A Reading of Seneca's *Medea*," in *Pursuits of Reason: Essays in Honor of Stanley Cavell*, eds. T. Cohen, P. Guyer, and H. Putnam (Lubbock, 1992).

28. Halliwell, *The Poetics of Aristotle*, pp. 75–76 tentatively suggests that these references from Chs. 2 and 15 refer to traditional heroic qualities, rather than to ethical qualities that Aristotle himself would recognize; he does, however, hold that *beltion* in Ch. 13 refers to ethical qualities. In *Aristotle's Poetics*, pp. 152–153, 160, 166–167, however, he does take Ch. 2's categories to be ethical. I see no reason to charge Aristotle with inconsistency of usage here – or, indeed, to take him to say "better" when what he means is "not really better, but what some have believed to be better." In Ch. 15 the focus is on ethical qualities, and before this passage Aristotle has already said that the first requirement of tragic characterization is that it shows ethical goodness – *chrēstos*, a word one would not link with mere wealth or status; the ethical word *epieikēs* is also used. When Aristotle wants to talk of wealth and status, he does so plainly: e.g. 53a10–12: "those who are in great repute and good fortune . . . and well-known men from those families."

29. On the links between Chs. 4 and 9, see Halliwell's essay in this volume.

30. Aristotle's negative example in *Poetics* 9 is "what Alcibiades did or suffered" – presumably because he believes Alcibiades' character and career are so *sui generis* that one would not be likely to see his fortunes as possibilities for oneself.

31. Halliwell, *Aristotle's Poetics*, Chs. 5 and 6.

32. For the contrast with *atuchēma* see *EN* 1135b16–22, where *hamartēma* is also contrasted with *adikēma*, or unjust action, in a way that is pertinent to *Poetics* 13. For a detailed discussion of these passages, see Nussbaum, "Aristotle," in *Ancient Writers*, ed. T. J. Luce (New York, 1982), Vol. I, pp. 377–416.

33. T. C. W. Stinton, "*Hamartia* in Aristotle and Greek Tragedy," *Classical Quarterly* N.S. **24** (1975) 221–254; a similar line is taken by Halliwell, *Aristotle's Poetics*, Ch. 7.

34. Halliwell, *Aristotle's Poetics*, Ch. 7, esp. p. 229, where he holds that an ethically infallible person could fall only by "some accidental or quite external cause." I would insist that the accidental or arbitrary and the external are crucially distinct: the latter includes the former, but also includes many sorts of causally comprehensible sequences.

35. This discussion is neglected by both Lear, "Katharsis" and T. H. Irwin, "Review of M. Nussbaum, *The Fragility of Goodness*," *Journal of Philosophy* **85** (1988) 376–383; the latter asserts that I do not discuss the passage. For an excellent summary of the issues, see Lucas, *Aristotle's Poetics*; also Halliwell, *Aristotle's Poetics*.

36. Halliwell, *Aristotle's Poetics*, Ch. 7, p. 222 ff. He insists, however, that averted catastrophies will not bring about the same full expression of pity and fear: pity is a response to undeserved misfortune, not to the prospect of such misfortune.

37. See the fuller investigation of this, with examples, in Nussbaum, *The Fragility of Goodness*, Interlude 2.

38. For the evidence, see Halliwell, *Aristotle's Poetics*, p. 2, n.2.

39. See also the parallel development of the English word "defecation," discussed in *The Fragility of Goodness*, pp. 502–503, n.17.

40. See the examples assembled in *The Fragility of Goodness*, pp. 389–390. Typical is Epicurus, who refers to his letter to Pythocles as a *katharsis phusikōn problēmatōn*, a "clearing up of the difficulties of natural philosophy," especially by the removal of obscuring false beliefs.

41. L. Golden, "Catharsis," *Transactions of the American Philological Association* **93** (1962) 51–60; "Mimesis and Catharsis," *Classical Philology* **64** (1969) 43–53.

42. Here, without much conviction, I continue to translate *pathēmatōn* as "experiences" ("experiences of the pitiable and fearful sort") rather than as "emotions" – in which case *toiouton* would indicate that other related emotions, too, are at work. Both *pathos* and *pathēma* can mean either "experience" or "emotion," and nothing in my interpretation hangs on the choice. The only puzzle in the latter case would be why no other emotions were mentioned elsewhere; and indeed, apart from grief, it is difficult to know which ones Aristotle might have intended.

43. Lear, "Katharsis".

44. Halliwell, *Aristotle's Poetics*.

45. See my analysis of the role of character in the play in Nussbaum, "Consequences and Character in Sophocles' *Philoctetes*"; also M. W. Blundell, "The *phusis* of Neoptolemus," *Greece and Rome*.

46. For a full discussion of the problems of *Politics* VIII.7, see the longer version of this essay.

47. On this issue, see J. L. Ackrill, "Aristotle on Action," *Mind* **87** (1978) 595–601 (repr. in *Essays on Aristotle's Ethics*, ed. A. O. Rorty, Berkeley, 1980); and Nussbaum, *The Fragility of Goodness*, Ch. 9 and Ch. 11, pp. 334–335.

48. See Nussbaum, *The Fragility of Goodness*, p. 335, with Ch. 2; also M. Stocker, *Plural and Conflicting Values* (Oxford, 1990).

49. I owe this point to Halliwell, in conversation.

50. See Nussbaum, *The Fragility of Goodness*, pp. 418–419.

51. See Nussbaum, *Bacchae*.

52. See Nussbaum, *The Fragility of Goodness*, Interlude 2, and Nussbaum, "Consequences and Character in Sophocles' *Philoctetes*."

53. I am extremely grateful to Stephen Halliwell for discussions that helped me a great deal in writing this essay. I also wish to thank Julia Annas, David Konstan, Amélie Oksenberg Rorty, Christopher Rowe, and Gregory Vlastos for their helpful comments.

Pity and Fear in the *Rhetoric* and the *Poetics*[1]

Alexander Nehamas

I

Even when he feels his case has been very strong, Aristotle is unlikely to resist introducing an additional argument into a philosophical discussion if one is available to him. Perhaps the best example of this consists of Chapters 2–3 of *Physics* I: having claimed that, as a natural philosopher, he need not argue against Melissus and Parmenides (since their monism and their denial of motion put them outside the domain of natural philosophy strictly speaking), Aristotle proceeds to argue against them anyway – *echei gar philosophian hē skepsis* (185a20). But his criticisms of the theory of Forms in *Metaphysics* A 9 and M 4–5, as well as his dispute with Plato over the Form of the Good in *Nicomachean Ethics* I.4, are also good cases in point. It is therefore relatively surprising that in cases which involve not simply disagreement about particular views on a specific topic, but the more general issue whether a whole field of inquiry is or is not legitimate, he often seems to be avoiding a direct confrontation with his opponent.

This is true both in the *Rhetoric* and in the *Poetics*, works which articulate in detail the structure of fields and practices against whose very existence Plato had argued vigorously. The *Gorgias* and the *Phaedrus* denied that rhetoric as traditionally conceived could be an art, though the latter allowed for the possibility of a rhetoric which turns out to be straightforwardly a part of philosophy (259e–271c). The *Ion* and the *Republic* produced a list of accusations against poetry in general, and tragedy and epic in particular. Yet the exact nature of Aristotle's answer to Plato's charges against the poets can still, as I hope to show, provoke dispute: Does Aristotle argue that poetry benefits the emotions or that it is cognitively important (or both)?[2] And what are the considerations that entitle him to begin the *Poetics* on the assumption that poetry (along with poetics itself, which is its study, 1447a12) is an art in the first place?

The *Rhetoric* raises similar questions. Where, exactly, does Aristotle argue that rhetoric is a real *technē*? Does he believe, and on what explicit grounds, that the ability to persuade other people of one's views, independently of those views' content, is ethically acceptable? In his argument with Gorgias, Socrates had claimed that rhetoric could not be an art unless it addressed a specific subject-matter of its own. When Gorgias finally stated that rhetoricians teach justice and injustice to their students, Socrates countered that if that were the case then, contrary to Gorgias' own earlier insistence, rhetoric could never be used for unjust purposes (449a–461b). Both the question of its subject-matter and the nature of its ethical status were therefore left unresolved. In the *Phaedrus*, Socrates argued that rhetoricians, if they are to have an art and to produce true beliefs in an audience about matters of right and wrong, must meet two con-ditions: they must themselves possess strict knowledge of those matters (259e–260a) and they must be experts on the nature of the human soul; otherwise they will not know how best to address the particular sort of people they are confronted with on each particular occasion (270e–271c).

Yet Aristotle's *Rhetoric* begins with the bald statement that rhetoric is parallel to dialectic because, "in a way" (*tropon tina*), both concern all topics – thus completely sidestepping Socrates' original argument in the *Gorgias* to the effect that each art must have its own particular subject matter – and goes on immediately to characterize it as a methodical practice (*hodos*). Aristotle returns to this point and insists on it at 1355b25–34. He does, in fact, a little later concede to Plato that the subject of rhetoric can be more narrowly construed as similar to that of *hē peri ta ēthē pragmateia* (1356a26); he agrees with Gorgias, in other words, that rhetoric is concerned with justice and injustice broadly conceived (cf. 1359b10–11). But he denies that the rhetorician needs to have knowledge of ethical matters in anything like the strict sense which Plato had considered necessary. He also leaves the question of the rhetorician's own ethical character unanswered.[3]

Both the *Rhetoric*, then, and the *Poetics* begin by presupposing that their subjects – oratory and fiction, respectively – are *technai* which can be studied systematically, though in neither case does Aristotle promise the precision Plato had demanded. Both works give the strong impression that the practices with which they are concerned are of significant benefit both to individuals and to society, though in neither case does Aristotle make his reasons for thinking so uncontroversially clear. In what follows I propose to ask, in an oblique manner, whether Aristotle did in fact face the challenges Plato had issued against both fields, how he proceeded to meet them and how successful he was in his endeavor.

I will approach the set of questions regarding the technical status of oratory by means of an examination of Aristotle's treatment of the emotions (*pathē*) in *Rhetoric* II. Aristotle, I believe, is prompted to discuss this issue in detail by the requirement expressed in the *Phaedrus* that orators know enough about the soul in order to be able to tailor their presentations to the emotional needs of the different kinds of audience which they find themselves addressing on different occasions. His detailed examination of the emotions is intended to show that orators possess appropriate knowledge about the emotions even though they are not, and need not be, philosophers. They need not, that is, have the synoptic and systematic understanding of the soul, of its place in nature, and of its various kinds that Plato had required of them (*Phdr.* 270d ff.).

Rhetoric II, then, is an indirect attempt on Aristotle's part to disarm one of Plato's main criticisms of the claims of oratory to be a *technē*. To the extent that Aristotle answers Plato, he does not do so by means of an explicit argument but rather by the texture of his demonstration of the sort of knowledge about emotion that orators need and in fact have. Before I turn to this text, however, let me anticipate one of the implications of my reading. After looking at emotions generally, I shall focus on pity (*eleos*) and fear (*phobos*) in particular. We shall then see that the structure of Aristotle's discussion does not fit at all well with our most usual ways of understanding the *Poetics*. For we shall find first that, in general, Aristotle envisages that the emotions can be refined and improved by considerations and processes that are essentially rational. No such factors appear to be involved in the famous last clause of his definition of tragedy in the *Poetics* (1449b24–29), which is most often read as concerning either the elimination or, more plausibly, the purification of pity and fear. Second, we shall also discover that the structure Aristotle attributes to the emotions generally and to pity and fear in particular – that is, both the objects toward which they are directed and the reactions they produce in those who experience them – makes it impossible to maintain that the *catharsis* to which that definition refers is a process which involves the emotions in any way.

But if this is so, then it is unlikely that the definition of tragedy contains a reply to Plato's charge in the *Republic* that poetry "feeds and inflames" the passions (606d3–6). And this in turn suggests that Aristotle may be avoiding a direct confrontation with Plato not only on the status of poetry as a *technē* but also on the question of the benefits and harms it is capable of conferring upon us. At the very least, it suggests that even if Aristotle is confronting Plato on this latter problem, he is not doing so through his very definition of tragedy itself. We shall then have to raise two questions, neither one of which can be easily answered: Where does Aristotle address Plato's ethical challenge? And is this a challenge which has, or can be, successfully met?

In short, both on the technical and on the ethical level, neither the *Rhetoric* nor the *Poetics* seem to me to offer the direct opposition to Plato's views which in so many other cases characterizes Aristotle's response to his teacher in particular and to his opponents in general. Why Aristotle's approach is more indirect in these cases is a question as important as it is difficult to answer: it is, in fact, at least as difficult to answer as the general theoretical question, still in my opinion unanswered, whether the confrontation of Plato and Aristotle on these topics has ever been resolved.

At the beginning of the *Rhetoric* Aristotle distinguishes three "technical" (*entekhna*) modes of persuasion (*eidē pisteōs*) orators can use: speaking itself, which proves or appears to prove the conclusions we wish to reach; the presentation of our character in a way that will advance our credibility and our cause; and the creation in the audience of the proper frame of mind, disposing them toward judging in our favor (I.2, 1356b35 ff.).

It may seem that the Aristotle introduces both the second and the third of these kinds of persuasion as a response to the *Phaedrus*, since both involve the proper treatment of the audience. Still, it is clear that only the third provides an answer to Socrates, who was concerned not with the speaker's character but with the fact that the true orator should know what kinds of soul, what kinds of people, would be affected by what kinds of speech and, accordingly, produce the appropriate oration in each instance (271b1–5). Characteristically, and consistently with his general views on the status of rhetoric, Aristotle does not think that it is necessary for the orator to possess anything that even approaches the rigorous exactness (*pasē akribeia*) of the scientific knowledge of the soul and its affections (*pathēmata*) which Socrates had demanded. But equally characteristically, instead of making the general programmatic remarks Plato had considered sufficient regarding that knowledge, Aristotle devotes a long stretch of his work (II.2–17) to a detailed examination of the emotions and character types to be found in various audiences. In this way he supplies the orator with highly specific advice on how to address each audience effectively.

The connection between the *Rhetoric* and the *Phaedrus* is therefore complex. Though Aristotle refuses to require the exact knowledge Plato demanded of the orator, he takes the necessity of being acquainted with the affective side of one's audience extremely seriously and discusses it in exhaustive detail: in rather vague terms, Plato calls for detailed knowledge; in very detailed terms, Aristotle articulates a rough and ready familiarity.[4] In so doing he also provides us with extremely valuable information about the emotions of pity and fear, whose importance to the theory of tragedy in the *Poetics* is matched only by the allusiveness with which they are treated in that work.

It is also important to note that the *Rhetoric* gives special emphasis to the requirement that both the speaker's character and the audience's emotions be manifested and affected, respectively, by elements of the *oration itself* (*dia tou logou*, 1356a9; *hupo tou logou*, 1356a14). This shows two things. First, that Aristotle is consistent when he attacks his predecessors in the opening pages of the treatise for concerning themselves with topics which are really not part of the subject-matter of rhetoric (*exō tou pragmatos*, 1354a15–16, 1355a19): unlike them, he does not recommend the *independent* manipulation of the audience, but he does know that speaking can in fact affect its hearers, and considers it a part of *rhetoric itself* to know how to deliver speeches which will themselves have the appropriate effects.[5] Second, Aristotle's insistence that the audience be influenced emotionally through the speech itself shows something very significant about his theory of the emotions generally. Human beings are, in various degrees, rational. On a particular occasion, an appeal to our reason can move our emotions in a particular direction. Habitual manifestation of an emotion in a particular direction affects its scope and intensity. In other words, emotions can in the long run be shaped, directed and redirected, by essentially *rational* considerations. I now want to amplify this view and to defend it against a recent criticism.

II

Aristotle introduces his discussion of the emotions at the end of the first chapter of Book II of the *Rhetoric* (1378a19 ff.). An emotion is, he writes, whatever so changes us as to affect our judgment and is also attended by pain and pleasure (*esti de ta pathē di' hosa metaballontes diapherousi pros tas kriseis hois hepetai lupē kai hēdonē*), "for example, anger, pity, fear, and whatever is like them and all that is opposite to those" (this is a list to which we shall return).[6] It is true that this definition, like every definition of the particular emotions in the following chapters, refers only to what we might call the psychological aspects of our emotional life. It thus corresponds to what in the *De Anima* is described merely as "a dialectician's" account being contrasted with a fuller definition that would also make reference to the bodily states which are part of what each emotion is (I.1, 403a3–b19). We should not think, however, that this is a straightforward rejection of the account given in the *Rhetoric*: the *De Anima*, rather, offers a supplementation necessary for the sake of the full, physical investigation of the emotions which forms part of its own subject-matter. For the rhetorician's purposes, the account of anger, for example, as "a painful desire for revenge," etc. (II.2, 1378a30–32), which appears in the *De Anima* as "a desire for returning pain or something like that" (*orexis antilupēseōs ē ti toiouton*, 403b30–31), can be perfectly adequate. The bodily component of the emotions is not relevant to the questions of character and responsibility with which rhetoric is concerned.

This is not to say, however, that in serving the rhetorician's purposes Aristotle is simply presenting commonplace views of the emotions which do not correspond in any way to his own considered judgment concerning them. The claim has often been made. But I believe that, in the absence of evidence to the contrary, the discussion of emotion in the *Rhetoric*, even if not definitive, should still be taken seriously as a source of information about Aristotle's considered views.[7] Even if Aristotle is presenting and exploiting commonplace attitudes toward the emotions, there is no reason to believe that he considers such attitudes to be fundamentally misguided.

Now, in a serious sense of the term, *ta pathē* are, according to Aristotle, nonrational. We do not choose them: *orgizometha men kai phoboumetha aproairetōs* (*NE* II.5, 1106a2–3). More importantly, they are coordinate with the two kinds of nonrational desires, appetitive and "spirited" (*epithumiai kai thumos*), in respect of which the virtues are exercised. For the virtues are defined as states (*hexeis*). A state, in turn, is said to be "that according to which we are well or badly disposed in relation to the emotions" (*NE* II.5, 1105b25–26). The connection between emotions and nonrational desires is established as follows. Human ethical virtue belongs to the soul's nonrational part (*NE* I.13, 1102b11 ff.; cf. *EE* II.1, 1220a10). Aristotle introduces this nonrational element into his picture of the human soul in the first place by means of distinguishing its desires from those of reason (*NE* I.13). These nonrational desires, therefore, which are what reason controls in the case of the self-controlled and of the temperate agent, are connected closely, though in a way not made clear by Aristotle, with the emotions. For it is the proper occurrence of the emotions that the virtues aim to regulate, and the *Eudemian Ethics* had already connected the two to each other in its claim that reason rules not reason but "desire and emotion" (*orexin kai pathēmata*, II.1, 1219b40–1220a1).

Despite the fact that the emotions are nonrational, however, they are, in a sense which we will have to explain, subject to reason. This emerges both as a general principle in Aristotle's writings and as a direct implication of his treatment in the *Rhetoric*. For our purposes it does not matter whether Aristotle divides the nonrational, nonnutritive part of the soul itself into two further parts (*orgē* or *thumos* on the one hand and *epithumia* on the other, *Rhetoric* I.10, 1369a4), or considers it as unitary (*to epithumētikon*, *NE* I.13). The important point is that this nonrational part is said, on a number of occasions and in a number of ways, to be amenable to reason: it partakes in (*metekhei*), obeys (*peitharkhei*), agrees with (*homophōnei*), listens to (*katēkoon*), and is persuaded by (*peithetai*) rational considerations.[7]

Apart from this general theory, however, and as one of its consequences, the treatment of the emotions in the *Rhetoric* yields the same result. In connection with each emotion, Aristotle distinguishes three aspects: how people are disposed who (are likely to) feel that emotion (*pōs diakeintai*, 1378a23; *pōs ekhousin*, 1379a10); who are those toward whom they feel it (*tisin*, 1378a23); and on what grounds the emotion is felt (*epi poiois*, 1378a25). And what is perfectly clear in connection with each of these three factors, in turn, is that their description and analysis bristles with what we would without hesitation call "cognitive" factors.

Fear, for example, is defined as "a pain or disturbance due to imagining (*phantasia*) some destructive or painful evil in the future. For there are some evils, e.g. wickedness or stupidity, the prospect of which does not frighten us: only such as amount to great pains or losses do. And even these only if they appear not remote but so near as to be imminent" (II.5, 1382a21–23). Similarly, those of whom we tend to be afraid are described in particularly detailed terms, easily giving rise to the inference that fear involves complex considerations regarding the situation in which one finds oneself. Not only, for instance, are we likely to be afraid of those who are both unjust and powerful (1383a35): we also, as a result of a syllogistic process, are to be afraid of those of whom people stronger than we are, are themselves afraid, since (*gar*) they will be able to do to us even greater harm than they can do to those more powerful (1382b14–16). Finally, "fear is felt by those who believe something to be likely to happen to them, at the hands of particular persons, in a particular form, and at a particular time" (1382b32–34) – felt, that is, by people as a result of a set of complex and detailed discriminations.

Furthermore, throughout his discussion of fear (and of pity as well in II.8) Aristotle consistently describes the object of the emotion as something which appears (*phantasia, phainomenon*) evil: its value is therefore part of the grounds for having the emotion in question. Aristotle's whole approach to these two emotions (and, in fact, to all the others he discusses here) is guided by the idea that a value judgment is inherently involved in every emotional reaction.

In seeing that the emotions essentially involve cognitive and evaluative, that is, rational elements, Aristotle presents a picture of our mental life which is in fact continuous with Plato's.[9] For Plato, too, refused to separate the emotions very radically from the other aspects of the psyche: even the "civic" courage of the Guardians, which is discussed at *Republic* 429a–430c, is brought about by education (though, it must be admitted, education in *mousikē kai gumnastikē*) and results in their coming to be persuaded (*peisthentes*) to accept the laws and to develop correct and proper views about what is and is not to be feared (*doxan orthēn te kai nomimon deinōn te peri kai mē*, 430b3).

It is important in this context to realize that the cognitive and the evaluative are only part of the rational. For Plato and Aristotle, to have propositional content and to contain an evaluation of the object which provokes them are not features which are by themselves sufficient to turn the emotions into *rational* states of mind. Aristotle's whole discussion of the nonrational parts of the soul and of the desires and feelings associated with them presupposes, and expresses, the view that they all involve both content and evaluation but are still to be distinguished from reason.

But if the emotions have both complex propositional content and contain evaluations of their objects, what is it that prevents them from being fully rational? What distinguishes *boulēsis* on the one hand from *thumos* and *epithumia* on the other? The answer, I believe, is that rational desires are essentially based on considerations concerning the correctness, the *truth*, of our evaluation of a situation as good or bad (*NE* VI.2, 1139b12). In other words, what makes a desire or emotion rational is not its content, which can have a complex propositional and evaluative structure, but the *grounds* on which that structure depends. Our states are rational if what causes us to be in them includes reasons for considering them appropriate.[10]

It is important to repeat, once more, that all desire, rational and nonrational, involves both thought and evaluation.[11] The reason this, in turn, is important is that it allows us to understand the sense in which Aristotle believes that emotions and nonrational desires in general are ultimately subject to reason. Reason, as we have seen, can "persuade" the nonrational desires. The nonrational desires are somehow "convinced" to abandon their own, more or less immediate, evaluations of the goods and evils in every situation and to accept instead the evaluations of reason, which take into account the long-term welfare of the agent as a whole. In particular, virtue consists in the cultivated ability consistently to give priority to these evaluations and, accordingly, in having the *appropriate* emotions and desires in each particular case.

It is important to emphasize that, as this formulation implies, Aristotle envisages that the emotions will form an integral part of the virtuous life.[12] Emotions persist in the soul in which reason rules and their motivating force (*hormē*) is preserved. This force, however, consistently conforms to one's *boulēsis*; it therefore regulates the intensity of the felt emotion and guides the behavior of the agent in the direction established by the agent's considered judgment.

When reason, then, "persuades" the emotions, it does not eliminate them; it simply aligns them with its own judgment concerning each situation. Now the combination of these factors may appear to create a serious problem for Aristotle's view. For if the "educated" emotions which cooperate with reason continue to supply each agent with their own independent motives for action, then each of these emotions may appear to involve not only cognitive and evaluative aspects, but also a strong decision-making element. If the emotions are to maintain their independent motivating force and not to be absorbed into reason, as the Stoics later were to urge, then, it might be claimed, they must possess

> something perilously akin to decision. In experiencing full-fledged anger . . . a person *assents* to the idea that some act of retribution is to be done, and it is only in consequence of that that she is actually moved to do it. Can one give an acceptable account of what this assent is, without being forced to admit that *it*, at least, comes from the very rational power that Aristotle wanted to set clearly apart from the non-rational desires as a separate, competing source of impulses to action?[13]

The charge, made by Cooper, is serious. But I believe that the *Rhetoric's* discussion of the emotions may provide us with the beginnings of an answer to it, and that its ability to do so, incidentally, is another indication that we should pay close attention to the views Aristotle expresses in that work.

Partly on the basis of Aristotle's view that the function (*ergon*) of both practical and theoretical reason is "the truth" (*NE* VI.2, 1139b12). Cooper defines nonrational desires as those whose causal history nowhere involves an investigation "into the truth of what is good for onself," that is, into whether or not something really is or is not good, whatever appearance it may present to an agent. Once we note this, however, we cannot avoid noting that all the definitions of the emotions in the *Rhetoric* essentially involve a reference to an *apparent* good and evil: we have already seen that fear involves a *phantasia kakou* and that pity is caused by a *phainomenon kakon*. But we should also give appropriate emphasis to the fact that a reference to appearance is made in each and every definition of emotion in Book II of the *Rhetoric*. Aristotle's consistency in this respect is remarkable.[14]

Accordingly, I would like to suggest that the distinction between rational and nonrational desires or emotions is to be made on the grounds that the former involve in their causal history an investigation of whether something really is or is not good for the agent while the latter exert their motivating power and produce the feelings associated with them on the basis of what appears good or bad to the agent as a function not of deliberation concerning the good but as a result simply of natural inclination, acculturation, socialization or habituation. The real problem for Aristotle, in my opinion, is that unless he shows how exactly one becomes habituated into virtue without relying on a literal model of reason persuading the emotions to agree with its choices, their nonrational status will remain in question; the precise mechanism by which emotion is trained into virtue needs to be made explicit. If the emotions can be straightforwardly convinced by reason, then there is no reason to think that they are not rational to begin with. If, on the other hand, persuasion plays no role in their habituation, we must provide an account which distinguishes their treatment from coercion.[15]

But even though the mechanism through which the emotions are "persuaded" by reason remains obscure, we can at least say what the process produces once completed. Training for virtue ensures that what appears as good and evil to the emotions will one day come to coincide with what is in fact good and evil – not, again, as the result of their own investigation into the truth concerning these matters but simply because, having followed reason and *boulēsis* sufficiently in the past, what becomes apparent to them is what the former have determined is in fact the case. The apparent good and evil and the real good and evil coincide, though the manner in which each is determined is not the same: the emotions are still directed toward appearance, that is, their object is still determined by them in whatever the way was in which it was always determined in the past; no part of their "deliberation" is an effort to establish what is good for the agent. It is just that the emotions have listened to *logos* (the *logos* of one's own, or of one's family, or of one's fellow-citizens, including, in all likelihood, the orators among them), as one listens to one's father or friends (cf. *NE* I.13, 1102b32–1103a3). They thus have become habituated to being provoked by those objects and on those grounds which reason, independently, has determined to be in reality the right objects and grounds of provocation. This, I think, preserves the distinction between the rational and the nonrational and allows the emotions to exist, to be felt and to have motivating force even in the virtuous person. The difference is that the considered judgment of the virtuous is never altered on account of their emotions: emotional response follows the course set by reason. Even if the emotions are in themselves nonrational, they are felt rationally by the virtuous person.

Significantly, the *Rhetoric* gives advice on how to influence the emotions of one's audience but does not limit itself (as it should not, in view of the sort of manual that it is) to showing how to alter the emotions and their apparent objects in the right direction only: its instruction is, we might say, ethically neutral (cf. I.1, 1377b31–1378a5). Even though, however, the result of the *Rhetoric's* instruction concerning the emotions is ethically neutral, its method of instruction is in a serious if broad sense rational. For, apart from the minor concession Aristotle makes in connection with pity (which we have already noted) his advice concerns how to affect the emotions of one's audience *dia tou logou*. His text provides detailed analyses of the emotions precisely because orators are to provide reasonable grounds on which their audience is to become emotionally disposed in the manner that is advantageous to their own cause. These analyses characterize the state of people who experience or are likely to experience a particular emotion, the people toward whom they are likely to feel it, and the grounds on which the emotion is felt. They aim to supply the orator with knowledge of the appropriate information that an audience needs in order to be put into a particular mood. And this information is relevant and efficacious because the nonrational elements in the soul possess, as we have seen, complex propositional structure. Accordingly, we can accept the view that the *pathē* represent nonrational elements in the soul. And though they are subject to reason, they are not ultimately to be absorbed by it.[16]

III

I now want to apply the conclusions we have reached about emotions in general to Aristotle's discussion of fear and pity in the second Book of the *Rhetoric* (Chapters 5 and 8). If we can assume, as I have suggested above, that the views Aristotle discusses here are relevant to his own attitudes toward the emotions, then we can appeal to these texts in order to understand, as much as this is possible, the function of pity and fear in the *Poetics*.[17]

Both in the *Poetics* and in the *Rhetoric*, pity and fear are closely associated with one another. Though in the former work this is mostly accomplished by their constant conjunction,[18] the *Rhetoric* demonstrates their connection both through its definitions and through its subsequent elaboration.

Fear is defined as "a pain or disturbance due to imagining some destructive or painful evil in the future. For there are some evils, e.g. wickedness or stupidity, the prospect of which does not frighten us: only such as amount to great pains or losses do. And even these only if they appear not remote but so near as to be imminent" (II.5, 1382a21–25). Pity, in turn, is defined as "a feeling of pain at an apparent evil, destructive or painful, which befalls one who does not deserve it, and which we might expect to befall ourselves or some friend of ours, and moreover to befall us soon" (II.8, 1385b12–16).

In both cases, the objects are serious harms. In the case of fear, they are harms to ourselves, prospective and near. In the case of pity, they are harms that threaten others, who do not deserve them; but they are the sorts of harm that we might expect to threaten us or our own as well, especially if they seem imminent. By referring these harms to ourselves, the second clause in the definition of pity connects the emotion with fear, and Aristotle makes this connection explicit in two parallel passages, one in each chapter. "Speaking generally," he writes in his discussion of fear (1382b24–26), "anything causes us to feel fear that when it happens to, or threatens, others causes us to feel pity." In the case of pity, "we have to remember the general principle that what we fear for ourselves excites our pity when it happens to others" (1386a24–26). The relation is symmetrical: We fear for ourselves what we tend to pity others for, and we pity others for what we would fear for ourselves.

It is important to note that Aristotle believes firmly that we can feel pity not only on account of something which has happened or is happening to someone else, but also on account of the threat of its occurrence: pity, like fear, can be prospective; we can pity those who are in situations in which something terrible is likely to happen to them even if in the end it doesn't. We can feel pity on account of what might happen. And since fear is by definition wholly prospective (cf. 1382b29),[19] it is clear that Aristotle builds into his very conception of these emotions the possibility that the evils they involve may not in fact occur. The reason this is important is that it coheres perfectly with his view in *Poetics* 14 that plays like *Iphigenia in Tauris*, *Cresphontēs* and *Hellē* exhibit the best kind of plot even though they are all plays of averted catastrophe: all end with a happy resolution (1453a4–8).[20] The tragic emotions are prompted by tragic prospects: not only by tragic endings.

But though the prospective nature of the tragic emotions fits well with some of the views expressed in the *Poetics*, the coordinate nature of pity and fear creates a serious problem for the relevance of the *Rhetoric's* account of these emotions to their function in the theory of the *Poetics*. We have seen that the *Rhetoric* argues that both pity and fear are caused by the prospect of one's own suffering (or, also, of the suffering of one's own). Yet the fear involved in tragedy does not seem to be self-regarding in this manner. In the theater, at least part of our fear is directed at the sufferings of the characters: we fear *for* them and not, at least not primarily, for ourselves. The *Rhetoric's* account of fear and pity is essentially self-regarding. Can such an account shed any light on their significance to fiction, where sympathetic feeling for the suffering of others seems to be primary?[21]

We might try to answer this question affirmatively by insisting that, strictly speaking, the *Rhetoric's* definition of fear does not say explicitly that the emotion is concerned with oneself.[22] But the trouble is that, though this is not stated in so many words, it is directly implied by Aristotle's statement that "there are some evils, e.g. wickedness of stupidity, the prospect of which does not frighten us: only such as amount to great pains or losses do" (*ou gar panta ta kaka phobountai, hoion ei estai adikos ē bradus, all' hosa lupas megalas ē phthoras dunatai,* 1382a22–24). This statement makes an unmistakable reference to evils one expects for oneself. And since Aristotle offers it as a direct explication of the definition of fear, it seems that though it does not logically rule out the possibility that the objects of fear can sometimes be the sufferings of others, Aristotle considers that possibility very remote indeed.[23]

To preserve the connection between the *Rhetoric* and the *Poetics* we might also try to appeal to *Rhet* 2.5.15, 1383a8–12. Aristotle here advises orators, "if it is advisable that the audience should be frightened," to make them feel that they themselves are in danger by reminding them that the relevant harms have occurred to others, both stronger than and similar to them. This does indeed involve a reference to the misfortunes of others, but it seems clear to me that Aristotle does not advise orators to inspire fear *on behalf of* those others in their audience. Rather, this idea is simply that they should instill in their audience the belief that such things can happen or have happened to others: this, he believes, will make the audience afraid that similar misfortunes are likely to happen *to themselves* as well, and to fear that possibility. And though friends and relatives, who are in a sense an extension of oneself (*Rhet* 2.8.1–2, 1385b14–18; 2.8.13, 1385b27–29), do constitute a class on behalf of which one can indeed be afraid, this is not relevant to the question at issue: the characters of tragedy are not the friends or relatives of the audience.

Nevertheless, and despite these difficulties, the fact that fear is essentially self-regarding does not prevent us from appealing to the *Rhetoric* for an elucidation of the *Poetics*. We have seen that Aristotle writes that what we fear (for ourselves) is what, when it happens to others, causes us to pity them. Now it is quite possible that what occurs in tragedy is that we have brought before us sufferings of characters like us (*homoioi*), who do not deserve them (*anaxioi*, *Poetics*, 13, 1453a3–6).[24] We feel pity for these characters because they are suffering evils they do not deserve and which, as the *Rhetoric* says, we might ourselves be subject to. In addition, the fact that the (proper) tragic characters are similar to us reminds us (just as the orator was advised to remind the audience, 1383a8–12) that the prospect of being faced with such misfortunes is quite likely; and the likelihood of those misfortunes makes us afraid – for ourselves.

Does this mean that we can no longer attribute to Aristotle a view to the effect that the theatrical audience imaginatively or sympathetically feels fear on behalf of the characters of tragedy? Is there no sense in which I can fear for Oedipus as I see him rushing headlong, though totally unaware, into destruction? There is indeed a sense in which I can. I can imagine what *I* would feel like if I were in Oedipus' place, *with the knowledge I now possess*: knowing what I know and also seeing myself doomed to perform the actions he is destined for, I will indeed be very much afraid. This is really an imaginative fear for myself. But it is a fear for myself which is based on seeing myself as someone relatively similar to Oedipus or, rather, as someone of whom the character of Oedipus is a part. For, as I have argued elsewhere, Oedipus is not a person who *has* a character but *is himself* a character, a type, which we may recognize as a type to which we ourselves belong.[25] It is precisely in order to account for this phenomenon that Aristotle insists on the philosophical nature of poetry and on the universal status of the situations it depicts despite its giving particular names to the characters it represents (1451a36–b15). In recognizing Oedipus or Medea in ourselves we recognize that what can happen to that sort of person can happen to us as well, since we have just come to recognize that we ourselves are that sort of person, that we are, to that extent, Oedipus or Medea ourselves.

This in fact is a serious aspect of the fear of fictions. It is not precluded by my interpretation of Aristotle's view of fear as essentially self-regarding. My interpretation, therefore, does not deny the occurrence of strong fear in the tragic audience, nor does it assert that all fear has a direct and explicit reference to the self – my fear "for" Oedipus is in fact fear for me, though in a highly indirect and mediated manner. And if this is so, it is not obvious that considering fear as always self-regarding prevents us from attributing to Aristotle a view to the effect that the tragic audience does experience *some* "imaginative" or "sympathetic" fear after all.[26] The *Rhetoric* explains how speeches can affect and channel the emotions of their audience precisely by showing how orators can manipulate them directly. To that extent, then, there may be a series asymmetry between the way in which speeches affect and channel the directly-felt emotions of their listeners and the way in which fictions reform, if at all, the emotions they generate in their audience.

IV

I would now, in the little space that remains to me, like to turn to a brief examination of a frighteningly complex problem, knowing well that my attempt is bound to be an instance of boldness and not of courage, of *thrasos* and not of *tharsos*. I believe that though the *Rhetoric* generates a clearer picture of the nature of pity and fear as Aristotle understands them, the picture it produces, perhaps paradoxically, actually obscures our already minimal understanding of the *catharsis*-clause in the definition of tragedy in the *Poetics* (6, 1449b27–28) even further. The reasons for this are complex: I mentioned one at the very end of the previous section, and I will detail some others shortly. The subject is altogether overwhelmingly difficult. I will therefore have to be both short and dogmatic, hoping to begin a discussion worth continuing in a longer study.

To start with, I depart from the current consensus that *catharsis* in the *Poetics* is to be understood, in light of *Politics* VIII, primarily as "purgation" in a medical sense, as the discharge of unwanted and unneeded substances from the body or the soul.[27] In addition, I have a number of reservations regarding the view, recently supported in different versions by Halliwell and Nussbaum, that *catharsis* refers primarily to a homeopathic "purification" or "clarification" of the emotions of pity and fear by means of their expression in the theater.[28] Though I consider this view vastly superior to its predecessor, I am unable to accept it. My reasons are the following.

First, the discussion of the *Rhetoric* shows that pity and fear are emotions which are exhibited in a vast variety of situations. All of these, of course, involve the expectation of serious harms, but the specific nature of the harms in question varies tremendously. We are afraid of the anger and enmity of powerful and unjust people, of outraged virtue, of anyone who knows that we have done something wrong, of those we have wronged, of those who have done something wrong themselves, of our rivals in general, and of much more besides (1382a33–b26). The grounds of pity are similarly diverse. Aristotle lists, among other candidates, death in its various forms, bodily injuries and afflictions, old age, diseases, lack of food, friendlessness, deformity, and so on (1386a4–16).[29]

And yet when Aristotle comes to discuss the pleasure proper (*oikeia*) to tragedy in *Poetics* 14, and having said that this pleasure derives from pity and fear, he seems to think that the situations which are likely to produce those emotions are limited to horrible deeds within particular families: "What must be sought are cases where suffering befalls bonded relations – when brother kills brother (or is about to, or to do something similar), son kills father, mother kills son, or son kills mother" (1453b19–22).[30] Now it could perhaps be argued that these are cases where the extreme of pity is called for: since they are in this sense paradigmatic, our reaction to them shows us how to respond properly to other pitiful situations in life. We must still remember, however, that the pity felt in the tragic situation is felt sympathetically, and it is not obvious how this latter experience can be transferred to life: the point is not that it cannot, but that neither we nor Aristotle can assume that the phenomenon needs no further elucidation.

Yet even if we assume that the experience of pity can be transferred from fiction to life, it is not at all clear that the situation is similar in regard to fear. In the case of fear, a "purification" or "clarification" of the emotion would have to be an improvement in our ability to discriminate between what is and what is not fearful. It would bring about a set of more refined, more perceptive and more apt reactions, and the effect of such improved reactions would in turn be to make us more courageous than before. Yet Aristotle insists explicitly that courage is best exhibited in displaying the appropriate feelings and engaging in the appropriate behavior *when in danger of dying at war* – a situation which, as he knows well, is not germane to most tragedies.[31] If, therefore, pity and fear have a nature as variegated as the discussion of the *Rhetoric* indicates, it becomes very difficult to see how it could be one of the most crucial functions of tragedy, which prompts these emotions only in relation to very special – and not always paradigmatically central – situations, to refine their experience and expression in relation to everyday life.

A second reason for feeling uneasy with this approach to the role played by pity and fear in tragedy is that, as we have seen both in connection with the *Nicomachean Ethics* and with the *Rhetoric*, the emotions are generally refined and habituated to react correctly to the appropriate situations by means of their coming to be "persuaded" by reason. This may in fact be a problem, as we have seen, for Aristotle's moral psychology: but that it is his view is undeniable. By contrast, the *catharsis*-clause in the *Poetics*, read in the manner we are presently discussing, seems to envisage a directly homeopathic process which can be found nowhere else in Aristotle's writings. Reason is not involved in any serious manner in the "education" of any emotions to which the clause may be referring. If Aristotle is concerned with the *catharsis* of emotions here, then he seems to be thinking that simply being in a particular emotional state in perhaps appropriate circumstances in itself leads to more refined experiences of the same kind. Perhaps this is possible, and perhaps Aristotle believes that it is. But we have little or not evidence to that effect, and we cannot just assume that this is his considered judgment.[32]

I believe that some kind of homeopathic interpretation of *catharsis* will continue to appear as the most satisfactory approach to this question if we begin with the assumption, which is nearly universal,[33] that the final clause of Aristotle's definition of tragedy constitutes his answer to Plato's charge against the poets. This assumption, made explicitly by Halliwell, who in so many other ways revises traditional approaches to the *Poetics*, is that "[w]e can set out with moderate assurance . . . from the premise that Aristotelian *catharsis* is intended in some way to produce an answer to Plato's objections to the psychological effects of tragic poetry" (pp. 184–185).[34]

This is precisely the assumption I want to call in question. I have just given two reasons for thinking that Aristotle's analysis of the education of the emotions in the *Nicomachean Ethics* as well as of the nature of the emotions in general and of pity and fear in particular in the *Rhetoric* makes it difficult to see how he could think that tragedy refines the latter. But there are other reasons as well.

One is that it is an undisputed fact that the association of pity, fear and poetry is not original with Aristotle; we can easily trace it back to Homer, Sophocles, Gorgias and, of course, to Plato.[35] To that extent, then, Aristotle's introduction of pity and fear in his definition of tragedy is part of a long tradition. But need it, just for that reason, also be a response to the Platonic component of that tradition? Aristotle has long been supposed to provide an answer to the famous charge against poetry at *Republic* 606a–d.[36] Now *Republic* 606a2–b8 does accuse tragedy of making its audience enjoy inappropriate manifestations of pitiful behavior in the theater and so of predisposing them to similar behavior in real life. But it is important to note, first, that fear is not mentioned in this passage and, second and much more important, that the case of pity (along with ridicule in the case of comedy, 606c2–9), is *only a special case of all the emotions and passions*:

> So too with sex, anger, and all the desires, pleasures, and pains which we say follow us in every activity. Poetic imitation fosters these in us. It nurtures and waters them when they ought to wither; it places them in command of our soul when they ought to obey in order that we might become better and happier instead of worse and more miserable.[37]

But this is a very *general* challenge. It is not answered in the *catharsis*-clause, which, much more specifically, is only concerned with pity and fear. Unless, against good grammar, we are prepared to believe that by the words *toiauta pathēmata* Aristotle intends to refer to all the emotions and passions with which Plato was preoccupied, his answer to Plato will be, at best, partial and lame: to Plato's claim that poetry perverts *all* the passions, Aristotle would in this case be replying that, by a mechanism he cannot explain, tragedy improves two.

And even if we did take Aristotle to be thinking of all the passions in his definition of tragedy, the answer we would then attribute to him would still be psychologically shallow and unsatisfactory. For it is not at all clear how a refinement of our reactions to pity and fear specifically can be generalized to the refinement of all these other emotions as well. Perhaps the exercise of pity in proper circumstances in the theater may allow us to know better when to indulge in it in real life. But the idea that exposure to fiction and to the sexuality it contains and represents is bound to improve our actual inclinations toward *ta aphrodisia* (*Rep.* 606d11) is a view extraordinarily difficult to accept, especially in the absence of an explicit and detailed account of the mechanism through which such a result can be produced.

Furthermore, there is good reason not to read *toiauta pathēmata* as referring to all the passions Plato, and the tradition, had in mind. This is because Aristotle himself gives no indication at all that pity and fear, or fearful and pitiful events (*ta phobera kai eleeina*), are representative of emotions in general: in none of his ten references to these two pairs in connection with the dramatic plot and with tragic pleasure is there any suggestion that they head an open-ended list, that they stand for anything other than themselves. By contrast, when in Chapter 19 he comes to discuss "thought" (*dianoia*), which he connects with rhetoric, he claims that one of its functions is the arousal of emotion (in the play's characters) and refers to emotion by one of his usual lists, headed by pity and fear, and going on to anger "and all such things" (1456a38–b1). When Aristotle is using a particular emotion as an example of emotion in general he is perfectly capable of showing that that is just what he is doing. That he does so in none of the cases that are of interest to us now is very strong evidence that he is not thinking of fear and pity as representative of the emotions in general and that therefore he is not appealing to them in order to show, against Plato, that poetry can be of broad emotional benefit.

In view of all these considerations, then, we may at least question whether the *catharsis*-clause is meant as a direct answer to Plato in the first place. That it is not is suggested by the specific considerations I have discussed so far as well as by the general strategy of not engaging directly with Plato which I have attributed to Aristotle both in the *Poetics* and in the *Rhetoric*. And if the *catharsis*-claim is not interpreted in this way, then new ways of approaching it become possible.

In particular, it now becomes easier (though by no means easy) to construe *pathēmata* no longer as emotions but, rather, as the incidents of the drama itself.

This is exactly the sense of the word at *Republic* 393b4–5, where it refers to the incidents in the *Odyssey*. In the *Poetics* itself, the term is used at 1459b11 as one of the three components of the tragic plot along with *peripeteia* and *anagnōrisis*. At 1452b11–12 it is defined, in the form *pathos* (its identity with *pathēma* at 1459b11 is assured by its being said to be part of the plot and, again, coordinate with *peripeleia* and *anagnōrisis*) as a *praxis phthartikē ē odunēra* – precisely the sort of action that is connected, as we saw in our discussion of the *Rhetoric*, with the definition of both pity and fear.[38] On the other hand, the connection between *pathos* and pity and fear is not exclusive: it is also the case that the right "combination of recognition and reversal will produce pity or fear (and it is events of this kind that tragedy, on our definition, is a mimesis of)" (*Poetics* 11, 1452a37–b1).[39]

This last phrase is particularly important: *hē gar toiantē anagnōrisis kai peripeteia ē eleon hexei ē phobon* (*hoiōn praxeōn hē tragōidia mimēsis hupokeitai*). This must refer in the first instance back to 1452a1–3, where tragedy is said to be not only an imitation of a complete action but also of pitiful and fearful events. But where, in turn, is the justification for this claim? The only plausible candidate (as Halliwell's translation, quoted above, concedes) is the very definition of tragedy in Chapter 6. But the definition is such a plausible candidate only if *pathēmata* are construed as incidents and not as emotions. If *pathēmata* are emotions, then the definition of tragedy gives us no information about the plot beyond the fact that it concerns an action "which is serious, complete and of a certain magnitude."

My claim, therefore, is that *pathēma* in the definition of tragedy is coordinate with *praxis* and that it bears the generic sense of "incident" rather than the specific sense given it at 1452b11–13. Accordingly, I propose to construe *toianta* as referring to *praxis spoudaia kai teleia megethos ekhousa*. Aristotle is saying that the *catharsis* of the sort of action of which the tragic plot consists is reached only through a series of incidents that are themselves pitiful and fearful – characteristics which it is quite reasonable to attribute to the events that constitute the tragic plot.

All this, however, still leaves the issue of the sense of *catharsis* unresolved.[40] My own inclination is to accept Nussbaum's approach to the term, to take its primary sense as that of "clarification" and to accentuate the sense of "resolution" or "explanation" which can be found in Epicurus' phrase *kata tēn tōn allōn phusikōn problēmatōn catharsin* in the *Letter to Pythocles* (D.L. x. 86), in several uses of the adverb *catharōs* in Aristotle himself, and in a number of other contexts and authors.[41] However, instead of claiming that the clarification involved in Aristotle's definition of tragedy primarily concerns the emotions of pity and fear themselves, I want to suggest that it is a clarification of the pitiful and fearful incidents of the drama itself. That is, I propose that we consider *catharsis* as the "resolution," "dénouement," or "solution" of the tragic plot,[42] the *lusis* to which Aristotle refers at 1454a37, 1455b24 ff. and 1456a9 ff.[43] And keeping in mind that "clarification" never leaves the sense of "purification" far behind, we should also recall that the resolutions of tragedy are not, for Aristotle, ethically neutral: plays end as they should. Whether a tragedy does or does not result in affliction (*eis dustukhian*, 1453a25), the evils it does or was about to involve are not undeserved. Their occurrence or imminence teaches its audience something important about life and fate, even if, as I believe, it is not clear whether we can say in general terms what this lesson is or, indeed, whether there is a single lesson that tragedy teaches beyond expanding our sense of the factors which can affect the shape of our life.[44]

Tragedy, then, is an imitation of an action which is serious, complete, and of a certain magnitude, using language embellished in various ways in its different parts, through action and not through narration, and carrying such incidents to their appropriate resolution through a course of events that provoke pity and fear. The emotions are provoked by the action of the drama. But though pity and fear are also products of drama, they are primarily part of its content and their inclusion in the definition of the genre does not function to provide an answer to Plato's objection at *Republic* 606d – which, in view of its generality, they could not have accomplished in any case. Nothing in Aristotle's account prevents him from having a theory about the importance of tragedy for the cultivation or refinement of the emotions. But I believe that, whether he does or not, he does not include a reference to that theory in his definition of the genre. Aristotle may well agree with Plato that the ethical significance of drama is relevant to its overall evaluation, and may believe, contrary to Plato, that drama can be at least on occasion ethically beneficial. But that is not how he chooses to answer Plato on this issue, on this occasion.

V

How then does Aristotle respond to Plato's attack on poetry? Does he face it at all? I would like to make two comments concerning this issue. The first is that not all of Plato's objections against poetry concern the arousal of emotion. Though he pays great attention to emotion at *Republic* 605c–607a[45] and some at *Laws* 658d–660a, he often attacks poetry on cognitive grounds alone. This is so, for example, in the *Ion* as well as in the *Apology* (22a–c); and the *Phaedrus*, which gives pride of place to emotion, still assigns the mimetic poet's life a very low status (248e1–2). And there is evidence in the *Poetics* that Aristotle is concerned to offer an account of poetry which allows it to yield knowledge despite Plato's denials (1448b5–17, 1451b5–19).[46] What needs to be investigated further is the nature of the knowledge in question. If this knowledge has a practical dimension, then Aristotle's response may in the end include a rebuttal of Plato's claim that poetry can only feed and not shape the passions. But there is no reason to assume that his rebuttal must be made explicitly in the very definition of tragedy.

My second comment will allow me finally to bring this essay to a close by returning to a point I made at the beginning. Plato accuses both rhetoric and poetry of not being *tekhnai*. He accuses them both of having profoundly harmful effects on their audience. Each one of these is a serious charge and each depends at least partly on the fact that the activities in question do not have a specific subject-matter and are addressed primarily to the emotions and not to reason. It is fascinating that Aristotle begins both the *Rhetoric* and the *Poetics* with the assumption that oratory and its study (*hodos*, 1354a8; *tekhnē*, a11) on the one hand and poetry and its study (*tekhnai*, 1447a21; *methodos*, a12) on the other are all arts, without an explicit argument against Plato's objection. In fact, he opens the *Rhetoric* with the admission that at least in a manner of speaking rhetoric has no particular subject-matter at all (1354a1–6; cf. 1355b25–27) and qualifies the claim only later (1356a25–27, 1359b9–11). Similarly, his first reference to the subject-matter of poetry as human action in general (*mimountai hoi mimoumenoi prattontas*, 1448a1) construes it broadly enough to appear to concede Plato's point: *prattontas ti?* is Plato's obvious retort. It is only subsequently that he spells out in more detail the specific subject-matter of tragedy, though still not in a way that would have been certain to leave Plato satisfied.[47] It is equally fascinating that though Aristotle clearly believes that both fiction and rhetoric have immense importance in our lives and actually allow us to live better than we could without them, he simply does not articulate in detail his reasons for holding this view in the manner that so often characterizes his procedure.

I would like to end by suggesting that both the *Poetics* and the *Rhetoric* defend the view that their subjects and their study are in fact *tekhnai* not so much by explicit argument but by their own very practice. Aristotle is not in total disagreement with Plato about their lack of a specific subject-matter in a strict sense of the term. But his argument against the view that this prevents them from being *tekhnai* consists in his actual and detailed elaboration of the ways in which both poetry and oratory can be followed more or less systematically, can be practiced more or less well, and can result in products which can be evaluated more or less rationally. This is a very powerful argument. But it is not clear that it does not beg Plato's question, which depends on certain explicit criteria for what constitutes a *technē*, and which Aristotle does not meet directly. Similarly, Aristotle obviously believes in the value of both rhetoric and fiction. But it is not clear what the reasons are that enable him to feel confident that his positive evaluation is correct.

The problem, then, whether or not Aristotle has met Plato's criticisms successfully has not yet, to my knowledge, received a satisfactory answer. The issue of the nature, the status and the ethical character of rhetoric and fiction remains disturbingly unresolved. Plato's questions, like most of the other questions he asked, are still our own.

Notes

1. This essay was originally prepared for the *XIIth Symposium Aristotelicum*, which was held in Princeton in August of 1989. I am particularly grateful for the response, on that occasion, of Martha Nussbaum, who was my commentator, as well as for the comments of Stephen Halliwell and Gisela Striker. Amélie Oksenberg Rorty read an earlier draft of the essay and gave me detailed and valuable suggestions. Sarah Broadie's criticisms of two earlier versions led to a number of serious alterations and additions. I am particularly grateful to her.

2. The former alternative is very firmly entrenched. But a recent account, offered by S. Halliwell in *Aristotle's Poetics* (London, 1986), is now under attack by Nikolas Pappas, who, in 'The *Poetics*' Argument Against Plato' (unpubl. ms.), argues in favor of the second.

3. 1355a14–18, 1359b12–16. The former passage sounds very much like Socrates's argument to the effect in order to know what the truth is like, and therefore be plausible to an audience, the rhetorician must first know what the truth itself is. But Aristotle's point goes exactly in the opposite direction: Because the truth and what has verisimilitude are similar, he argues, the latter is all the rhetorician needs to know. Cf. John Cooper, "Ethical-Political Theory in Aristotle's *Rhetoric*," forthcoming in *Proceedings of the XIIth Symposium Aristotelicum*. For Aristotle's text, here and elsewhere in this essay, I rely on Rudolf Kassel, *Aristotelis Ars Rhetorica* (Berlin, 1976).

4. Sarah Broadie has pointed out to me the relevance to this issue of *Nicomachean Ethics* 1.4, 1094b26–27. In his discussion here of the various appropriate standards of exactness in the various disciplines, Aristotle explicitly says how wrong it would be to ask the theorists of rhetoric to supply demonstrative proofs for their views.

5. This was already noticed by W. D. Ross, *Aristotle* (London, 1964), p. 270: Aristotle himself recognizes the part played by the appeal to emotion, but insists that the emotion must be produced by the speech itself and not by adventitious devices common to the Greek law-courts. J. Cooper presents detailed arguments in favor of the view in "Ethical-Political Theory in Aristotle's *Rhetoric*," pp. 3–8. Yet we should also admit that Aristotle's advice (1386a32–b4) on how best to produce pity in an audience includes, for example, bringing "the clothes of those who have suffered" to the podium: and it is not clear that *this* procedure does not fall outside the business of rhetoric itself.

6. The translation, here and elsewhere in this essay, is from Jonathan Barnes (ed.), *The Complete Works of Aristotle: The Revised Oxford Translation* (Princeton, 1984).

7. William Fortenbaugh, "Aristotle's *Rhetoric* on Emotions," in *Articles on Aristotle: Psychology and Aesthetics*, eds. J. Barnes, M. Schofield and R. Sorabji (London, 1979), pp. 133–153. Fortenbaugh reviews the relevant literature on pp. 134–141, and should be consulted for the various approaches that have been taken toward the subject. Leighton also identifies *pathē* with emotions, but bases his view on different, even incompatible, and quite sophisticated considerations; see Stephen R. Leighton, "Aristotle and the Emotions," *Phronesis* 27 (1982) 144–174.

8. *NE* I.13, 1102b25–33; cf. VII.7, 1149a26 ff., where the point is made in connection with *thumos*, to which *epithumia* is now contrasted as totally beyond reason.

9. For an emphasis on the cognitive aspects in Aristotle's conception of the emotions, see Halliwell, *Aristotle's Poetics*, p. 173. Halliwell, however, tends to find a much sharper contrast on this issue between Aristotle and Plato than I believe justified.

10. Cf. John M. Cooper, "Some Remarks on Aristotle's Moral Psychology," *Southern Journal of Philosophy*, **17** (Suppl.) (1989) 31: "Non-rational desires will be desires no part of the causal history of which is ever any process (self-conscious or not) of

investigation into the truth about what is good for oneself: whatever the cause of the value judgment such a desire may nonetheless contain may be, the cause is never any reason the agent might think there is for *making* this judgment. Non-rational desires have other causes than reason, and these are the origin of whatever value-thoughts the desires may contain."

11. Cf. Cooper, "Some Remarks on Aristotle's Moral Psychology": "The difference . . . consists solely in whether or not the source of these thoughts lies in *reasons* one thinks there are for having them" (p. 33).

12. This is also apparent from the definition of virtue at *NE* II.5, 1105b25–26. On the issue in general, see L. A. Kosman, "Being Properly Affected: Virtues and Feelings in Aristotle's Ethics," in *Essays on Aristotle's Ethics*, ed. A.O. Rorty (Berkeley, 1980), pp. 103–116. Cf. Martha Craven Nussbaum, *The Fragility of Goodness* (Cambridge, 1986), pp. 308–309.

13. Cooper, "Some Remarks on Aristotle's Moral Psychology," p. 39.

14. Anger (*phainesthai*, 1378a31), calm (implicitly, through its definition as the opposite of anger, 1380a9), friendship (*oiesthai*, 1380b37), enmity and hatred (*hupolambanein*, 1382a4), confidence (*phantasia*, 1383a17), shame and shamelessness (*phainesthai*, 1383b13), indignation (*phainesthai*, 1387a8), envy (*phainesthai*, 1387b23), "emula-tion" (*phainesthai*, 1388a32).

15. I believe this is also a problem for Plato's division of the soul in the *Republic*. It is, in addition, a problem for his account of how cooperation between the different classes of citizens in his ideal state is accomplished. That this is indeed a problem is suggested by his having to rely on characterizing the relationship between the Guardians and the producers by means of any oxymoron: the latter are both friends (*philoi*) and slaves (*douloi*) of the former (*Republic* 589cd).

16. My sense is that if there is indeed a problem about the ultimate rationality of the *pathē* for Aristotle, it springs not so much from the fact that he considers them to be directly motivating factors, *hormai*, which involve the agent's assent (this is Cooper's central contention), but because of their susceptibility to reason (which Cooper also mentions, but not as prominently). This is true especially because of Aristotle's use of *peithein* and associated verbs in connection with the emotions' education (he uses such vocabulary not only on the occasions we have noted, but also in connection with his discussion of desires and pleasure in *Rhetoric* I.11, 1370a18–27).

17. Halliwell, *Aristotle's Poetics*, Ch. 6, provides the best defense of this procedure. See pp. 172–173, 175–176, for Halliwell's justification.

18. Cf. 1449b27, 1452a2, b32, 1452b1, 1453a1, a4, a5 (where a distinction between them is also drawn), a6, 1453b1, b12.

19. The present-tense *gignomena* at 1382b25 does not refute this point, for the fearful is here being addressed from the point of view not of the sufferer but of the person who is to feel pity on the sufferer's account.

20. For this reason, I cannot fully agree with Halliwell that it is a "paradoxical result" of Aristotle's moral psychology "that it focusses tragic pity and fear on a movement towards misfortune, but does not require that movement, the *metabasis* of the plot, to be irreversible; pity and fear, so the theory posits, can be successfully aroused by a clear glimpse of 'incurable' suffering" (p. 182). It is not paradoxical that we fear what is still in the future or that we take pity on someone who has not yet suffered evil because we recognize that we would be terribly afraid of the threat of the evil in question to ourselves.

21. Cf. Halliwell, *Aristotle's Poetics*: "It has appeared to some this fact invalidates any attempt to use the *Rhetoric* to elucidate the tragic emotions of the *Poetics*" (p. 176). Rejecting that appearance, Halliwell claims that though "tragic fear differs from ordinary fear by virtue of being focussed on the experience of others . . . this does not

take it outside the conception of the emotion expounded in the *Rhetoric*" (p. 176). I agree with Halliwell's conclusion, though my reasons, as I explain in the text, are different.

22. Cf. Halliwell, *Aristotle's Poetics*, p. 176, where the concession that "this is for the most part assumed" is also made.

23. Accordingly, I find it hard to accept Halliwell's view that the account of fear in the *Rhetoric* clearly allows for this possibility (*Aristotle's Poetics*, p. 176). Cf. also *EE* III.1, 1228a10 ff., which suggests that what is fearful to someone is never the object of fear for the brave and, by implication, for any other agent.

24. For the text of the *Poetics* I rely on R. Kassel, *Aristotelis de Arte Poetica Liber* (Oxford, 1965).

25. Cf. "Mythology: The Theory of Plot," in *Essays on Aesthetics: Perspectives on the Work of Monroe C. Beardsley*, ed. J. Fisher (Philadelphia, 1983), pp. 180–197.

26. Some of the complexities of having specific feelings toward fictional characters, though only obliquely related to this issue in the *Poetics*, are discussed in Kendall Walton, *Mimesis as Make-Believe* (Cambridge, MA, 1990), pp. 185–204, 241–249.

27. The view, originally introduced by J. Bernays, *Zwei Abhandlungen über die aristotelische Theorie des Drama* (Berlin, 1880), partly translated in Barnes, Schofield, and Sorabji (eds.), *Articles on Aristotle*, pp. 154–165, is well discussed by Halliwell, *Aristotle's Poetics*, pp. 191–197. Both Halliwell and Nussbaum have distanced themselves from this consensus as well. Halliwell does not state that the passage in the *Politics* (1341b32–1342a19) is totally irrelevant to the *Poetics*, but issues enough qualifications to block any easy transference of the view of the former to the text of the latter. His main point is well stated in his *The Poetics of Aristotle: Translation and Commentary* (Chapel Hill, NC, 1987), p. 90, n.2: In "*Politics* 8.7 . . . *katharsis* involves a highly excited emotional experience followed by relief. But Aristotle is there discussing abnormal emotions, and the implications of the passage therefore need to be adjusted to take account of the very different nature of pity and fear." Halliwell wants to keep the sense of "purgation" in the background, but gives the sense of "purification" significantly greater emphasis. Nussbaum, in *The Fragility of Goodness* (pp. 389–390), interprets *catharsis* as "clarification," but claims that both "purgation" and "purification" are elements in this manner of understanding the term. A recent allopathic version of the purgation-view, to the effect that the experience of pity and fear in tragedy allows us to discharge harmlessly feeling contrary to them, is offered by Elizabeth Belfiore in a paper presented at Princeton University in 1989, "An Allopathic View of Tragic Katharsis." Belfiore also presents an excellent overview of alternative views on the subject. The main objection to Belfiore's interpretation, apart from the general considerations militating against the purgation-view, is that it forces us to construe *toiouton* at 1449b27 not as *touton* ("these," which is itself implausible, and provokes a central objection to homeopathic versions of the purgation-interpretation) but as equivalent to *tōn enantiōn* ("contrary"), which seems quite impossible.

28. Though neither Halliwell nor Nussbaum wants to exclude the sense of "purgation" completely from *catharsis*, they both prefer to understand *catharsis* to refer primarily to a homeopathic refinement of the emotions of pity and fear. Thus Halliwell concludes his discussion by writing that "tragic *katharsis* in some way conduces to an ethical alignment between the emotions and the reason: because tragedy arouses pity and fear by appropriate means, it does not, as Plato alleged, "water" or feed the emotions, but tends to harmonise them with our perceptions and judgments of the world" (*Aristotle's Poetics*, p. 201). Similarly, Nussbaum argues that "tragedy contributes to human self-understanding precisely through its exploration of the pitiable and the fearful. The way it carries out this exploratory task is by moving us to respond

with these very emotions . . . [T]he function of tragedy is to accomplish, through pity and fear, a clarification (or illumination) concerning experiences of the pitiable and fearful kind" (*The Fragility of Goodness*, pp. 390–391). But though I consider both views significantly more attractive than any version, homeopathic or allopathic, of the purgation-interpretation, I am still uneasy with them. My reasons are detailed in the text.

29. Nussbaum, in *The Fragility of Goodness*, pp. 383–384, links all the cases Aristotle refers to as falling "under the inclusive notion of injuries caused by luck." I am not sure this can easily apply to death or bodily injury, which may well be the result of choice. A general discussion of the "inclusive notion" in question, though valuable and important, is far beyond the scope of this essay.

30. The translation is from Halliwell, *The Poetics of Aristotle*.

31. *NE* III.7, 1115a24–b6; cf. *EE* III.1, 1229b2–13 on the issue of death in general.

32. Nussbaum correctly stresses the interrelation of feelings and beliefs in emotion, p. 383. If a belief on which a feeling is based proves false, the feeling does not persist. But this process seems to me more complicated that the simple phrase *di' eleou kai phobou* suggests: reason is involved. In construing *catharsis* as "clarification," Nussbaum writes that "clarification, for [Aristotle], certainly takes place *through* emotional responses" (italics in the original). But this is supported merely by the claim that this is what "the definition [of tragedy] states" (p. 390). An investigation into whether the emotions can clarify themselves, and of the exact manner in which this is accomplished in Aristotle, would be, I believe, an important undertaking.

33. But see the essay by Pappas mentioned in n.1 above.

34. As Halliwell points out (p. 185, n.19) the assumption goes all the way back to Proclus, *in Platonis rempublicam*, I.42.

35. See Halliwell, *Aristotle's Poetics*, p. 170 and n.3. In view of the argument I am about to make concerning Plato, it is relevant to note that Gorgias also does not mention only pity and fear in this connection (*Helen*, 8–9). The audience of poetry, he writes, experiences horrible terror (*phrikē periphobos*), tearful pity (*eleos poludakrus*), but also mournful longing (*pothos philopenthēs*) and whatever other emotion is involved in the fate of poetry's subjects.

36. Halliwell, *Aristotle's Poetics*, p. 185, n.19.

37. *Republic* 606d1–5, trans. G. M. A. Grube (Indianapolis, 1974).

38. This, of course, is also the view of Gerald F. Else, *Aristotle's Poetics: The Argument* (Cambridge, MA, 1967), pp. 227–232. However, I am in disagreement with much of the rest of Else's construal of the *catharsis*-clause. I should also point out that the passage quoted above, which defines *pathos* as a kind of *praxis* shows that Aristotle does not always have to construct *pathos* or *pathēma* on the one hand with *praxis* on the other. This indicates that he can well refer to the "action" of which tragedy is an imitation as also "something which is undergone," which is what my reading of the definition of tragedy implies.

39. The complicated nature of the relationship between the terms *pathos*, *pathēma* and emotions or incidents, especially, of course, painful ones and the connections between *pathos* and "passion", both suffering and event suffered, are well discussed in Thomas Gould's recent book, *The Ancient Quarrel Between Poetry and Philosophy* (Princeton, 1991). See particularly chapters 7–10. Gould's discussion shows that the words themselves seldom settle the issue as to what – an event or an experience – is being referred to in a text, and that understanding each of their occurrences in context is crucial for understanding their sense.

40. Else takes *catharsis* as purification of a *miasma*, connects it with his view of hamartia, writes that "I can pity [a murderer or would-be murderer] if I judge that he did not intend the parricide, matricide, or whatever, as such," and concludes that "[t]he

spectator . . . is the judge in whose sight the tragic act must be "purified," so that he may pity instead of execrating the doer" *Aristotle's Poetics*, p. 437). The problem with this view, however, is obvious: it makes the generation of pity the very end and goal of tragedy and thus goes against the wording of the definition and it makes fear (which is not itself part of that goal) inessential to the drama.

41. See Nussbaum, *The Fragility of Goodness*, pp. 388–389 and n.17 and *LSJ* s.v. III.2. See also Bonitz, s.v. *katharos*, refs to *Rhetoric* I.2, 1356a26, *Rhet. ad Alex.* 31, 1438a7, *Apr.* I.44, 50a40.

42. The terms are respectively used by D. W. Lucas, *Aristotle: Poetics* (Oxford, 1968), p. 182, Halliwell, *The Poetics of Aristotle*, pp. 113–114, 149, and Richard Janko, *Aristotle: Poetics* (Indianapolis, 1987), p. 119.

43. As all three authors point out, the *lusis* does not signify simply the very close of the drama as "dénouement" as "resolution" in particular imply, but a much broader range of events, perhaps even, in the case of a "simple" tragedy, the whole development of the drama; cf. Halliwell, *The Poetics of Aristotle*, pp. 113–114.

44. I believe that Else noted something like this in his discussion of *catharsis*, but pushed the point much too far in arguing that all tragic heroes are in the end purified in that they are shown not to have deserved the evils that befall them and thus become the objects of pity on the part of the spectators (see *Aristotle's Poetics*, pp. 422–439).

45. The earlier arguments in Books II and III, though they also address emotion and character, are exclusively concerned with the education of the young and involve fundamentally different considerations. Cf. my "Plato on Imitation and Poetry in *Republic* 10," in *Plato on Beauty, Wisdom, and the Arts*, eds. J. M. E. Moravcsik and Philip Temko (Totowa, NJ, 1982), pp. 47–78.

46. This is the claim of Pappas, "The *Poetics'* Argument Against Plato."

47. The reason is that Plato's view that poets merely imitate the practitioners of crafts of which they themselves are ignorant is not explicitly denied or neutralized in the *Poetics*.

Katharsis

Jonathan Lear

I

(1) Tragedy, says Aristotle, is a mimesis of a serious and complete action, having magnitude, which through pity and fear brings about a katharsis of such emotions.[1] But what Aristotle meant by what he said, in particular, what he meant in claiming that tragedy produces a katharsis, is a question which has dominated Western philosophy and literary criticism since the Renaissance.[2] In the last hundred years it has been widely accepted that by katharsis Aristotle meant a purgation of the emotions.[3] Now there is a sense in which the interpretation of katharsis as purgation is unexceptionable: having aroused the emotions of pity and fear, tragedy does leave us with a feeling of relief; and it is natural for humans to conceive of this emotional process in corporeal terms: as having gotten rid of or expelled the emotions.[4] But at this level of generality, the interpretation is an unhelpful as it is unexceptionable. For what we wish to know is how Aristotle conceived of the process of katharsis as it occurs in the performance of a tragedy. Even if we accept that Aristotle drew on the metaphor of purgation in naming this emotional process "katharsis," what we want to know is: did he really think that this process was an emotional purgation or did he merely use the metaphor to name a process that he understood in some different way? At the level of mere metaphor there seems little reason to choose between the medical metaphor of purgation and its traditional religious competitor, purification, not to mention more general meanings of "cleansing," "separation," etc.[5] In fact, the preponderant use which Aristotle makes of the word "katharsis" is as a term for menstrual discharge.[6] As far as I know, no one in the extended debate about tragic katharsis has suggested the model of menstruation. But why not? Is it not more compelling to think of a natural process of discharge of the emotions than of their purging?

It is only when we shift from the question of what metaphors Aristotle might have been drawing on to the question of what he took the process of katharsis in tragedy to be that there is any point in choosing among the various models.

315

Of course, the task of figuring out what Aristotle meant by katharsis is made all the more alluring, as well as frustrating, by a passing remark which Aristotle makes in the *Politics* while discussing the katharsis that music produces: "the word 'katharsis' we use at present without explanation, but when later we speak of poetry we will treat the subject with more precision."[7] We seem to be missing the section of the *Poetics* in which Aristotle explicitly set out what he meant.[8]

In this essay I will first isolate a series of constraints which any adequate interpretation of katharsis must satisfy. These constraints will be derived from a consideration of Aristotle's extended discussion of the emotions, of the effect of tragedy, and of how tragedy produces this effect. The constraints may not be tight enough to delimit a single acceptable interpretation, but I shall argue that they are strong enough to eliminate all the traditional interpretations. Second, I will offer an interpretation of tragic katharsis which satisfies all the constraints.

(2) Let us begin with the suggestion that a katharsis is a purgation of the emotions. To take this suggestion seriously one must think that, for Aristotle, katharsis is a cure for an emotionally pathological condition: tragedy helps one to expel or get rid of unhealthily pent-up emotions or noxious emotional elements.[9] The only significant evidence for this interpretation comes from Aristotle's discussion of the katharsis which music produces in the *Politics*:[10]

> We accept the division of melodies proposed by certain philosophers into ethical melodies, melodies of action, and passionate or inspiring melodies, each having, as they say, a mode corresponding to it. But we maintain further that music should be studied, not for the sake of one, but of many benefits, that is to say, with a view to education, to katharsis (the word katharsis we use at present without explanation, but when hereafter we speak of poetry we will treat the subject with more precision) – music may also serve for intellectual enjoyment, for relaxation and for recreation after exertion. It is clear, therefore, that all the modes must be employed by us, but not all of them in the same manner. In education the most ethical modes are to be preferred, but in listening to the performances of others we may admit the modes of action and passion also. For emotions such as pity and fear, or again enthusiasm, exist very strongly in some souls, and have more or less influence over all. Some persons fall into a religious frenzy, whom we see as a result of the sacred melodies – when they have used the melodies that excite the soul to mystic frenzy – restored as though they had found healing and katharsis. Those who are influenced by pity or fear, and every emotional nature, must have a like experience, and others in so far as each is suscept- ible to such emotions, and all receive a sort of katharsis and are relieved with pleasure. The kathartic melodies likewise give an innocent pleasure to men. Such are the modes and melodies in which those who perform music at the theatre should be invited to compete.[11]

It does seem that Aristotle distinguishes kathartic melodies from those "ethical melodies" which help to train and reinforce character – and thus that the point of katharsis cannot in any straightforward way be ethical education.[12] But the only reason for thinking that katharsis is a cure for a pathological condition is that Aristotle's primary example of katharsis is as a cure for religious ecstacy.[13] However, even if we accept that religious ecstacy is a pathological condition, the idea that katharsis is meant to apply to a pathological condition can only be sustained by ignoring an important claim which Aristotle makes in the quoted text. Having begun his discussion of katharsis with the example of those who are particularly susceptible to religious frenzy, Aristotle goes on to say that the same thing holds for anyone who is influenced by pity and fear and, more generally, anyone who is emotionally influenced by events.[14] In case there should be any doubt that Aristotle means to include us all under that category he continues: "and a certain katharsis and lightening with pleasure occurs *for everyone*."[15] But everyone includes virtuous people and it is absurd to suppose that, for Aristotle, virtuous people were in any kind of pathological condition.

Nor does the idea of a purgation seem like a plausible analogue for tragic katharsis. In a medical purge, as the Aristotelian author of the *Problems* says, "drugs are not concocted – they make their way out carrying with them anything which gets in their way: this is called purging."[16] The idea of a purgation seems to be that of the introduction of a foreign substance, a drug, which later gets expelled from the body untransformed along with the noxious substances. But the idea of a purgation as it is suggested by the commentators is of a homeopathic cure: we introduce pity and fear in order to purge the soul of these emotions.[17] The problem is that though the idea of a homeopathic cure was available in Aristotle's time, there is no evidence that he was aware of it and lots of evidence that he thought that medical cure was effected by introducing contraries.[18] But once we abandon the idea that for Aristotle a medical purgation was a homeopathic cure, there seems to be little to recommend the medical analogy. What foreign substance is introduced to expel what contrary noxious substance in the soul? Why should one think that the virtuous man has any noxious elements in his soul which need purging?

Indeed, if we look to Aristotle's account of the emotions, they do not seem to be the sort of things which are readily conceived as purgeable. Fear, for example, is defined as a pain or disturbance due to imagining some destructive or painful evil in the future.[19] That is, the emotion of fear is not exhausted by the feeling one has when one feels fear. In addition to the feeling, the emotion of fear also requires the belief that one is in danger and a state of mind which treats the danger as worthy of fear. All three conditions are required to constitute the emotion of fear.[20] If, for example, one believes one is in danger but one's state of mind is confidence in being able to overcome it, one will not feel fear.[21] An emotion, then, is not merely a feeling, it is an orientation to the world. But if an emotion requires not merely a feeling, but also a belief about the world one is in and an attitude toward it, then it is hard to know what could be meant by purging an emotion. An emotion is too complex and world-directed an item for the purgation model to be of significant value.

(3) I do not wish to spend time on the idea that tragic katharsis effects a

purification of the emotions, for though this view has had proponents since the Renaissance, it is not seriously held today.[22] The major problems with the idea of purification are, first, that virtuous people will experience a certain katharsis in the theater, but their emotional responses are in no sense impure; second, it is not clear what is meant by purifying the emotions. One possibility was suggested by Eduard Muller: "Who can any longer doubt that the purification of pity, fear and other passions consists in, or at least is very closely connected with the *transformation* of the pain that engendered them into pleasure?"[23] The fact that we do derive a certain pleasure from the pitiable and fearful events that are portrayed in tragedy is, I think, of the greatest importance in coming to understand tragic katharsis. However, it is a mistake to think that, in tragedy, pain is *transformed* into pleasure. Pity and fear are not abolished by the tragedy; it is just that in addition to the pity and fear one feels in response to the tragic events, one is also capable of experiencing a certain pleasure. Moreover, even if there were a transformation, to conceive of it as a purification is to assume that the original emotional response of pity and fear is somehow polluted or unclean. But this isn't so. Aristotle makes it abundantly clear that pity and fear are the appropriate responses to a good tragic plot.[24] The pain of pity and fear is not an impurity which needs to be removed, it is the emotional response which a virtuous man will and ought to feel.

(4) Perhaps the most sophisticated view of katharsis, which has been powerfully argued for in recent years, is the idea that katharsis provides an education of the emotions.[25] The central task of an ethical education is to train youths to take pleasure and pain at the right sort of objects: to feel pleasure in acting nobly and pain at the prospect of acting ignobly.[26] This is accomplished by a process of habituation: by repeatedly encouraging youths to perform noble acts they come to take pleasure in so acting. Virtue, for Aristotle, partially consists in having the right emotional response to any given set of circumstances: feeling pain at painful circumstances, pleasure at pleasurable ones, and not feeling too much or too little pain or pleasure, but the right amount.[27]

Tragedy, it is argued, provides us with the appropriate objects towards which to feel pity and fear. Tragedy, one might say, trains us or habituates us in feeling pity and fear in response to events that are worthy of those emotions. Since our emotions are being evoked in the proper circumstances, they are also being educated, refined, or clarified. By being given repeated opportunities to feel pity and fear in the right sort of circumstances, we are less likely to experience such emotions inappropriately: namely, in response to circumstances which do not merit pity and fear. Since virtue partially consists in having the appropriate emotional responses to circumstances, tragedy can be considered part of an ethical education.

There are two overwhelming advantages to this interpretation which, I think, any adequate account of katharsis ought to preserve. First, this interpretation relies on a sophisticated, and genuinely Aristotelian, conception of the emotions.

Tragedy provides (a mimesis of) certain objects toward which it is appropriate to form certain beliefs and evaluative attitudes as well as feel certain pains. Second, this interpretation offers an account of the peculiar pleasure we derive from a performance of tragedy.[28] Aristotle, as is well known, believes in an innate desire to understand, and a special pleasure attends the satisfaction of that desire.[29] If tragedy helps to provide an ethical education, then in experiencing it we come better to understand the world, as fit object of our emotional responses, and better to understand ourselves, in particular, the emotional responses of which we are capable and which the events portrayed require. It is because we gain a deeper insight into the human condition that we derive a special cognitive pleasure from tragedy.

This interpretation does have a genuinely Aristotelian ring to it: it is a position that is consonant with much that Aristotle believed and it is a position he might have adopted. But I don't think he did. First, as we have seen, a virtuous person will experience a certain katharsis when he sees or hears a tragedy performed, but he is in no need of education.[30] Second, the *Politics'* discussion of music clearly distinguishes music which is educative of the emotions and should be employed in ethical training from music which produces katharsis.[31] The best attempt I have seen to meet this problem is by arguing that the type of katharsis which Aristotle is contrasting with ethical education is only an extreme form derived from orgiastic music:

> Once attention is shifted to types of katharsis connected with more common emotions and with those who do not experience them to a morbidly abnormal degree (and both these conditions are true of the tragic variety), it is possible to discern that katharsis may after all be in some cases compatible with the process which Aristotle characterizes in *Politics* 8 as a matter of habituation in feeling the emotions in the right way and towards the right objects (1340a16–18) . . . Simply to identify tragic katharsis with a process of ethical exercise and habituation for the emotions through art would be speculative and more than the evidence justifies. But to suggest that these two things ought to stand in an intelligible relation to one another (as the phrase "for education and katharsis" at *Pol.* 1341b38 encourages to see them), is only to argue that tragic katharsis should be capable of integration into Aristotle's general philosophy of the emotions, and of their cognitive and moral importance, as well as into the framework of his theory of tragedy as a whole.[32]

Of course, tragic katharsis and ethical education might stand in an "intelligible" relation to each other even if they served completely different purposes, but when one sees the phrase "for education and katharsis" quoted out of context, it is tempting to suppose that education and katharsis are part of a single project. Unfortunately, the text will not support this supposition. Aristotle explicitly says that although one should use all the different types of melodies, one should not use them for the same function.[33] And when he says that music may be used "for the sake of education and of katharsis,"[34] he is unambiguously listing different benefits that may be derived from music.[35] Nor is it true that, in this passage,

Aristotle is only contrasting education with an extreme orgiastic form of kathar-sis. For although, as we have seen, he begins by talking about the katharsis of religious frenzy, he very quickly goes on to mention a certain katharsis had by everyone, and the fact that two lines before he explicitly mentions those who are susceptible to pity and fear suggests that he had tragic katharsis in mind.[36] Thus the contrast which Aristotle draws between ethical education and katharsis cannot easily be brushed aside.

Moreover, Aristotle continues by saying that vulgar audiences will have vulgar tastes and that professional musicians ought to cater to those tastes, since even vulgar people need relaxation.[37] But if even some melodies are ethically educative, why doesn't Aristotle insist that the vulgar be confined to such uplifting tunes? The answer, I think, is that it's too late. Aristotle contrasts two types of audience: the vulgar crowd composed of artisans and laborers on the one hand, and those who are free and *have already been educated* on the other.[38] In each case the characters of the audience have been formed and ethical education would be either futile or superfluous.

Aristotle clearly thinks that tragedy is among the highest of art forms. Aside from the fact that tragedy is the culmination of a teleological development of art forms which began with dithyrambs and phallic songs,[39] and aside from the fact that Aristotle explicitly holds it in higher regard than epic, notwithstanding his enormous respect for Homer, Aristotle critizes certain forms of inferior plots as due to the demands of a vulgar audience. For example, Aristotle crticizes those allegedly tragic plots which end with the good being rewarded and the bad being punished: "It is ranked first only through the weakness of the audiences; the poets merely follow their public, writing as its wishes dictate. But the pleasure here is not that of tragedy . . ."[40] This would suggest that a proper tragic plot would be appreciated and enjoyed above all by a cultivated person. It is hard to escape the conclusion that, for Aristotle, education is for youths, tragic katharsis is for educated, cultivated adults.

The third reason why the education-interpretation of katharsis ought to be rejected is that there is a fundamental sense in which tragedy is not evoking the proper responses to events portrayed. Should we be spectators to tragic events which occur not in the theater but in real life to those who are close to us, or to those who are like us, the proper emotional response would be (the right amount of) pity and fear. To take any kind of pleasure from these events would be a thoroughly inappropriate response. Thus there is a sense in which tragedy provides a poor training for the emotional responses of real life: first, we should not be trained to seek out tragedy in real life, as we do seek it in the theater; second, we should not be trained to find any pleasure in real life tragic events, as we do find pleasure in the tragic portrayals of the poets. Although a mimesis of pitiable and fearful events must to a certain extent be like the real life events which they represent, the mimesis must, for Aristotle, also be in an important respect *unlike* those same events. For it is precisely because the mimesis is a mimesis that a certain type of pleasure is an appropriate response to it. Were it not for the fact that Aristotle recognized a salient difference between mimesis and the real life events it portrays, Aristotle would have had to agree with Plato that poetry should be banned from the ideal state. Aristotle disagrees with Plato not over whether tragedy can be used as part of an ethical education in the appropriate emotional responses, but over whether a mimesis is easily confused with the real thing. Aristotle's point is that although the proper emotional response to a mimesis would be inappropriate to the real event, a mimesis is sufficiently unlike the real event that there is no danger of it having an improper educational effect on the audience. From the point of view of ethical education alone, poetry is allowed into the republic not because it has any positive educational value, but because it can be shown to lack any detrimental effects. If poetry has positive value, it must lie outside the realm of ethical education.

"There is not the same kind of correctness in poetry," Aristotle says, "as in politics, or indeed any other art."[41] The constraints on the poet differ considerably from the constraints on the politician. The politician is constrained to legislate an education in which youths will be trained to react appropriately to real life events; in particular, to feel the right amount of pity and fear in response to genuinely pitiable and fearful events. The tragedian is constrained to evoke pity and fear through a mimesis of such events, but he is also constrained to provide a katharsis of those very emotions. It is in the katharsis of those emotions that the emotional response appropriate to poetry goes beyond that which is appropriate to the corresponding real life events. Thus in coming to understand what katharsis is, we will be approaching an understanding of the special contribution poetry makes to life.

The final reason why the education interpretation of katharsis ought to be rejected is that in the end it does not explain the peculiar pleasure of tragedy.[42] Of course, a proper appreciation of tragedy does require a finely tuned cognitive appreciation of the structure of the plot and there is no doubt that the exercise of one's cognitive faculties in the appreciation of tragedy does afford a certain pleasure. But the pleasure we derive from tragedy is not primarily that which comes from satisfying the desire to understand.

In fact, there is little textual support in the *Poetics* for the hypothesis that the peculiar pleasure of tragedy is a cognitive pleasure. The main support comes from *Poetics* 4, where Aristotle explains the origins of poetry:

> It is clear that the general origin of poetry was due to two causes, each of them part of human nature. Imitation [*mimesis*] is natural to man from childhood, one of his advantages over the lower animals being this, that he is the most imitative creature in the world, and *learns at first by imitation. And it is also natural for all to delight in works of imitation.* The truth of this second point is shown by experience; though the objects themselves may be painful to see, we *delight* to view the most realistic representations of them in art, the forms for example of the lowest animals and of dead bodies. The explanation is to be found in a further fact: *to be learning something is the greatest of pleasures not only to the philosopher, but also to the rest of mankind, however small their capacity for it; the reason of the delight in seeing the picture is that one*

is at the same time learning and reasoning [sullogidzesthai] what each thing is,
e.g. *that this is that;* for if one has not seen the thing before, one's pleasure
will not be in the picture as an imitation of it, but will be due to the execution
or coloring or some similar cause.[43]

It is important to note that Aristotle is here concerned with the *origins* of a
process which culminates in the development of tragedy. Children begin
learning by their early imitations of the adults around them, and in learning they
derive a rudimentary form of cognitive pleasure: but this is only an explanation
of how elementary forms of imitation naturally arise among humans. It is not
an explanation of the peculiar pleasure of tragedy.

One must also be cautious in interpreting Aristotle's claim about the pleasure
in learning. Aristotle is trying to explain why we take pleasure in viewing
imitations of objects that are themselves painful to look at. Now it is tempting
to assimilate this passage with Aristotle's admonition in the *Parts of Animals* that
one should not shy away "with childish aversion" from studying blood and guts
and even the humblest of animals: for the study of even the lowest of animals
yields a pleasure which derives from discovering the intelligible causes of its
functioning and the absence of chance.[44] For Aristotle there contrasts the
cognitive pleasure derived from coming to understand causes from the pleasure
derived from an imitation:

> For even if some [animals] are not pleasing to the sense of sight, nevertheless,
> creating nature provides extraordinary pleasures for those who are capable
> of understanding causes and who are by nature philosophical. Indeed, it
> would be unreasonable and strange if mimetic representations of them were
> attractive, because they disclose the mimetic skill of the painter or sculptor,
> and the original realities themselves were not more interesting, to all at any
> rate who have eyes to discern the reasons that determined their formation.[45]

Aristotle is saying that there are two distinct pleasures to be derived from
animals that are in themselves unpleasant to look at: a cognitive pleasure in
understanding their causes, and a "mimetic pleasure" in appreciating an artist's
skill in accurately portraying these ugly creatures. It is this distinctively
"mimetic pleasure" that Aristotle is concentrating on in *Poetics* 4. The reason
why he focuses on the artistic representation of an ugly animal is that he wants
to be sure he is isolating the pleasure derived *from the mimesis,* rather than the
pleasure one might derive from the beauty of the animal itself. In explaining this
"mimetic pleasure," Aristotle does allude to the pleasure derived from learning.
But that Aristotle has only the most rudimentary form of "learning" in mind is
made clear by his claim that this pleasure in learning is available not only to the
philosophically minded, but to all of mankind *however small their capacity for it.*
What one is "learning" is that *this is that*: i.e. that *this* (picture of a dead mouse)
is (an accurate representation of) *that* ([a] dead mouse). The "reasoning" one is
doing is confined to realizing that one thing (an artistic representation) is an
instance of another. The pleasure, Aristotle says, is precisely that which would

be unavailable to someone incapable of formulating this elementary realization: that is, to someone who had never seen a mouse.[46] Such a person would not be able to recognize representation *as a representation*, and thus his pleasure would be confined to appreciating the colors and shapes in the painting. Thus it is a mistake to interpret this passage as suggesting that the reasoning is in any sense a reasoning about causes. *Poetics* 4, then, is about the most elementary pleasures which can be derived from the most elementary of *mimeseis*. Although this is a first step towards an understanding of tragic pleasure, it does not lend support to the thesis that tragic pleasure is a species of cognitive pleasure.

Now Aristotle does repeatedly insist that a good tragedy must have an intelligible plot structure. There must be a reason why the tragedy occurs: thus Aristotle says that the events must occur plausibly or necessarily,[47] that the events must occur on account of one another rather than in mere temporal succession,[48] and that the protagonist must make a certain mistake or error (*hamartia*) which is responsible for and explains his downfall[49] And I think there is no doubt that the proper effect of tragedy on an audience is brought about via the audience's cognitive appreciation of the intelligible plot structure. The question, then, is not whether an audience must exercise its cognitive faculties, nor whether it may find pleasure in so doing; the question is whether this cognitive exercise and its attendant pleasure is the proper effect of tragedy. Is this cognitive pleasure the pleasure appropriate and peculiar to tragedy? To see that the answer is "no," consider one of Aristotle's classic statements of the demand for intelligibility: "Tragedy is a *mimesis* not only of a complete action, but also of fearful and pitiable events. But such events occur in the strongest form when they occur unexpectedly but in consequence of one another. For the events are more marvellous [*thaumaston*] when they occur thus than if they occur by chance . . ."[50] Aristotle's point is that a plot structure in which the events do not merely succeed each other in time, but stand in the relation of intelligible cause to intelligible effect, albeit a relation in which the intelligibility only comes to light with a reversal and recognition, is the best plot structure for protraying truly pitiable and fearful events. What it is to be a pitiable and fearful event is to be an event capable of inducing pity and fear in the audience. But pity and fear is clearly not the proper effect of tragedy: it is merely a necessary step along the route towards the proper effect. For Aristotle says that it is *from* pity and fear that tragedy produces a katharsis of these emotions.[51] Therefore, the audience's cognitive appreciation of the plot's intelligible structure and attendant pleasure are important, but they are *causal antecedents* of the proper effect and proper pleasure of tragedy.

Aristotle does say that events are more marvelous (*thaumaston*) when they occur unexpectedly but in an intelligible relation to each other. And this fact is invoked by those who wish to argue that tragic pleasure is a cognitive pleasure. For in the *Metaphysics* and *Rhetoric*, Aristotle links the wondrous or marvelous with our desire to understand.[52] It is owing to wonder, Aristotle says, than man first began to philosophize: the rising and setting of the sun, for example, provokes man's wonder and this wonder sets him on a journey to explain why this phenomenon occurs.[53] Thus it is suggested that the wonder that is produced in a tragedy provokes the audience to try to understand the events portrayed and the pleasure that attends coming to understand is tragic pleasure.[54]

If there were already a strong case for thinking that tragic pleasure was cognitive pleasure, then the link between the marvelous and tragedy, on the one hand, and with the desire to understand, on the other, would be suggestive. However, in the absence of a strong case, there are three reasons why Aristotle's remarks on the marvelous cannot be used to lend any significant support to the idea that tragic pleasure is cognitive. First, in the *Poetics* passage just quoted Aristotle seems to be suggesting that the relation between wonder and understanding is precisely the opposite of that suggested by the *Metaphysics*: it is by cognitively grasping that the events, though unexpected, are intelligibly linked to one another that wonder is produced in us. So while in the *Metaphysics* wonder provokes us to understand, in the *Poetics* understanding provokes us to experience wonder. Second, although in the quoted passage Aristotle associates intelligibility with wonder, towards the end of the *Poetics* Aristotle also associates wonder with irrationality.[55] One advantage of epic over tragedy, he says there, is that it is better suited to portraying irrational events (*to alogon*). For since the audience of an epic narrative does not actually have to see the irrationality acted out on stage, it is less likely to notice it as irrational. However, Aristotle says, it is the irrational which chiefly produces wonder (*to thaumaston*). And he says that *the experience of wonder itself is pleasant*.[56] So in this case it cannot be that wonder provokes understanding which is pleasant – for irrationality ultimately resists understanding. And at the end of the *Poetics*, Aristotle suggests that the pleasure proper to epic and the pleasure proper to tragedy are of the same type,[57] even though tragedy is a higher form of the art. Yet if the pleasure proper to epic can be derived from a plot containing irrationalities, it hardly seems that this pleasure can be cognitive. Finally, even if one grants a link between wonder and cognitive pleasure, this in itself does nothing to support the thesis that tragic pleasure is cognitive. For an anticognitivist like myself does not believe that there is no role for cognition and its attendant pleasure in the appreciation of a tragedy; he only denies that cognitive pleasure is to be identified with tragic pleasure. For the anticognitivist, cognitive pleasure is a step that occurs en route to the production of the proper pleasure of tragedy.

The final text which is cited in support of the cognitivist thesis is Aristotle's claim that poetry is "more philosophical" than history:

> Poetry is more philosophical and more serious than history: for poetry speaks more about universals, while history speaks of particulars. By universal is meant what *sort* of thing *such a sort* of person would plausibly or necessarily say or do – which is the aim of poetry though it affixes proper names to characters; by a particular, what Alcibiades did or had done to him.[58]

Of course, philosophy is an exercise of man's cognitive faculties and, as is well

known, Aristotle repeatedly insists that it is universals which man understands.[59] However, even if we interpret this passage just as cognitivists would
like us to – as suggesting an intimate link between the appreciation of tragedy
and the exercise of our cognitive abilities – nothing in this passage would help
us decide between the cognitivist and the anticognitivist theses. For, as we have
seen, the anticognitivist does not deny that a cognitive understanding of the plot
is essential to the proper appreciation of a tragedy, he only denies that tragic
pleasure can be *identified* with the pleasure that attends understanding.

But, more importantly, I don't think we should interpret this passage as the
cognitivists would like us to. There is a certain plasticity in the idea of a universal
which facilitates the transition from poetry to cognition. The true objects of
knowledge, for Aristotle, are essences and these essences are "universal" in the
sense that two healthy human beings will instantiate the same essence: human
soul. But the reason that essences are linked with knowledge is that in coming
to understand a thing's essence we come to understand what that thing is *really*
like. In coming to understand human essence, we come to understand *what it
is to be* a human being. Now when Aristotle says that poetry is "more philosophical" than history because it deals with universals, it is tempting to read him as
saying that poetry provides us with deeper insights into the human condition.
This is a temptation which ought to be resisted.[60] If we look to what Aristotle
means by "universal" in the passage under discussion, it is clear that he does not
mean "universal which expresses the essence of the human condition," but
something much less grandiose: that poetry should refrain from describing the
particular events of particular people and instead portray the *sorts* of things a
given *type* of person might say or do. Aristotle gives an example of what he
means by the universal element in poetry later on:

> The following will show how the universal element in *Iphigenia*, for instance,
> may be viewed: a certain maiden having been offered in sacrifice, and spirited
> away from her sacrificers into another land, where the custom was to
> sacrifice all strangers to the Goddess, she was made there the priestess of his
> rite. Long after that the brother of the priestess happened to come; the fact,
> however, of the oracle having bidden him go there, and his object in going,
> are outside the plot of the play. On his coming he was arrested, and about
> to be sacrificed, when he revealed who he was – either as Euripides puts it
> or (as suggested by Polyidus) by the not improbable exclamation, "So I too
> am doomed to be sacrificed as my sister was"; and the disclosure led to his
> salvation. This done, the next thing, *after the proper names have been fixed* as
> a basis for the story, is to turn to the episodes.[61]

Aristotle's point is simply that poetry deals with types of actions and type of
persons, even though the poet, after having constructed the "universal" plot
later assigns names to the characters.[62] Aristotle does say that such a universal
plot is "more philosophical" than history, but by this he did not mean that poetry
gives us ultimate understanding of humanity. Rather, he meant that it has
emerged from the mire of particularity in which history is trapped and thus has

taken a step along the way towards philosophy. Whether fairly or unfairly, Aristotle had a very low opinion of history (he seemed to hold history in the same regard as we hold newspapers) and thus something doesn't have to be very philosophical to be more philosophical than history.[63]

What then is the point of Aristotle's requirement that poetry deal with universals if it is not to insist upon poetry's ultimate cognitive value? If we read *Poetics* 9 through to the end it becomes clear that Aristotle's overall concern is with the formation of a plot that effectively produces pity and fear in the audience.[64] But in order for an audience to feel pity and fear they must believe that there is a certain similarity between themselves and the character in the tragedy: and the reason they must believe in this similarity is that they must believe that the events portrayed in the tragedy might happen to them. For a person to feel pity and fear he must believe that he himself is vulnerable to the events he is witnessing. That is why Aristotle says that the poet's function is not to portray events that *have* happened, but events that *might* happen – and that these possible occurrences seem plausible or even necessary.[65] The point of portraying plausible events that might happen is that the audience will naturally come to believe that these events might happen *to them*. And this is a crucial step in the production of pity and fear in their souls. Poetry uses universals for the same purpose. Because poetry is not mired in particularity, but concerns itself with types of events which occur to certain sorts of people, it is possible for the audience to appreciate that they are the sort of people to whom this sort of event could, just possibly, occur. The universality Aristotle has in mind when he talks about the universality of poetry is not as such aiming at the depth of the human condition, it is aiming at the universality of the human condition.[66]

Enough has been said, I think, to make it clear that the education-interpretation, however attractive it is, must be rejected as an account of what Aristotle meant by tragic katharsis. But having already rejected the purgation- and purification-interpretations, we have abandoned all the important traditional accounts. What, then, did Aristotle mean by tragic katharsis? It is to this question that I now turn.

II

(5) Although the work so far has been largely critical, I think something of positive value has emerged. For in seeing how previous interpretations fall short, we have isolated a series of constraints which any acceptable interpretation of katharsis must satisfy. These constraints may not be so constraining as to isolate a single, definitive interpretation, but they at least set out a field in which the truth must lie. In this section I would like to state the constraints on any acceptable interpretation of katharsis and I would like to offer an interpretation which fits those constraints.

One of the major constraints on any interpretation is:

(1) There is reason for a virtuous man to experience the performance of a tragedy: he too will experience a katharsis of pity and fear.[67]

Precisely because of (1), it follows that

(2) Tragic katharsis cannot be a process that is essentially and crucially corrective: that is, it cannot be a purgation, in so far as purgation is of something pathological or noxious; it cannot be a purification of some pollution; it cannot be an education of the emotions.

This is not to deny that a kathartic experience may be corrective. Aristotle, as we have already seen, thought that kathartic melodies can help to restore those who are particularly susceptible to religious frenzy; and one might similarly suppose that a tragic katharsis could restore those who are particularly suscpetible to the tragic emotions of pity and fear. Nor do I mean to deny that a virtuous person may experience relief in a kathartic experience – a relief that it is natural to conceive of in terms of the release of pent-up emotions. However, the virtuous man is not in a pathological condition, nor is he polluted with some impure element which needs to be removed. Nor is he in need of any further training of the emotions: indeed, it is because he is already disposed to respond appropriately to the situations of life, both in judgment, action and emotion, that he is virtuous. The idea that provides an education of the emotions suffers further from the fact:

(3) What one feels at the performance of a tragedy is not what one *would* or *should* feel in the real life counterpart.

For although tragedy provokes pity and fear in the audience, it also elicits an appropriate pleasure: this pleasure would be thoroughly inappropriate to real life tragic situations. But the fact that a good person (at least) feels pleasure in the performance of a tragedy, but would not do so in real life, suggests

(4) A proper audience does not lose sight of the fact that it is enjoying the performance of a tragedy.

Although the audience may identify emotionally with the characters in the tragedy, this identification must remain partial. Throughout its emotional involvement, the audience keeps track of the fact that it is an audience. For in a real life tragedy a person would feel fear and, if he stood in the right relation to the tragic event, pity, but he would derive no pleasure from the tragic event. This implies:

(5) The mere expression or release of emotions is not in itself pleasurable.

For Aristotle, pity and fear are unadulterated pains.[68] The mere opportunity to feel these painful emotions does not in itself provide relief: everything depends on the conditions in which these painful emotions are to be felt. Those who have assumed that a katharsis, for Aristotle, was a release or discharge of pent-up or unexpressed emotions have assumed that the mere experience of emotions, even painful ones, has a pleasurable aspect to it. There is pleasure to be had in a good cry. Such an idea may have a certain plausibility to it, but it is foreign to Aristotle. For him, it depends on what one is crying about. If one is crying in the theater, a certain pleasure may ensue, but there is, for Aristotle, no pleasure to be had in crying over real life tragic events. This is the problem with taking katharsis to be the mere release of emotion. For Aristotle there is nothing pleasurable about experiencing pity and fear *per se*.

These conditions under which we can derive pleasure from pity and fear and the conditions under which a katharsis of pity and fear occurs are intimately linked, for

(6) Katharsis provides a relief: it is either itself pleasurable or it helps to explain the proper pleasure that is derived from tragedy.[69]

Constraints (3)–(6) together suggest that if we are to understand tragic katharsis, we should look to the special ways in which tragedy produces its emotional effects.

Aristotle, as we have seen, defines tragedy in part by the effect it has on its audience: it is a mimesis of an action which by arousing pity and fear produces a katharsis of those emotions.[70] It might seem odd to a modern reader to see Aristotle *define* tragedy in terms of its effect, for in a modern climate we tend to think that a work of art should be definable in its own terms, independently of whatever effect it might have on its audience. But it would be anachronistic to insist that Aristotle could not have been defining tragedy in terms of its effect on the audience. Poetry (*poiesis*), for Aristotle, is a type of making (*poiesis*), and the activity of any making occurs *in* the person or thing towards which the making is directed.[71] For example, the activity of the teacher teaching is occurring, not in the teacher, but in the students who are learning; the activity of the builder building is occurring, not in the builder, but in the house being built. It stands to reason that, for Aristotle, the activity of the poet creating his tragedy occurs ultimately in an audience actively appreciating a performance of the play.[72]

Not only does Aristotle define tragedy in terms of its effect, he thinks that various tragic plots can be evaluated in terms of their effects on an audience.

> We assume that, for the finest form of tragedy, the plot must be not simple but complex; and further, that it must imitate actions arousing fear and pity, since that is the distinctive function of this kind of imitation. It follows, therefore, that there are three forms of plot to be avoided. A good man must not be seen passing from good fortune to bad, or a bad man from bad fortune to good. The first situation is not fear-inspiring or piteous, but simply

disgusting. The second is the most untragic that can be; it has no one of the
requisites of tragedy; it does not appeal either to the human feeling in us, or
to our pity, or to our fears. Nor, on the other hand, should an extremely bad
man be seen falling from good fortune into bad. Such a story may arouse the
human feeling in us, but it will not move us to either pity or fear; pity is
occasioned by undeserved misfortune, and fear by that of one like ourselves;
so that there will be nothing either piteous or fear-inspiring in the
situation.[73]

The important point to note about this passage is that Aristotle is evaluating
plots not on the basis of *feelings*, but on the basis of the *emotions*. The reason we
do not feel pity and fear in witnessing the fall of a bad man from good to bad
fortune, is because pity requires the *belief* that the misfortune is undeserved, fear
requires the *belief* that the man who has suffered the misfortune is like ourselves.[74] (Presumably Aristotle assumed that the proper audience of tragedy
would not believe themselves to be sufficiently like a bad person to believe that
the things that befall him (most likely as a consequence of his badness) might
befall them.)

Similarly with the disgust we feel when watching a good man fall from good
to bad fortune: such disgust isn't a pure feeling which can be identified on the
basis of its phenomenological properties alone. Disgust requires the belief that
there is no reason *at all* for this good man's fall. It is sometimes thought that
Aristotle contradicts himself for he elsewhere seems to suggest that tragedy is
paradigmatically about admirable men falling to bad fortune.[75] But if we take the
rest of Chapter 13 as explicating what Aristotle means when he denies that the
fall of a good man can be the basis of a properly tragic plot, I think we can see
a consistent point emerging. In tragedy, Aristotle insists, the central character
must make some mistake or error (*hamartia*) which leads to his fall.[76] The
hamartia is a mistake that rationalizes the fall. So what Aristotle is excluding
when he prohibits the fall of a good man is a totally irrational fall: one that
occurs through no fault of the good man at all. Aristotle certainly does allow the
fall of a good man to be the subject matter of tragedy: but not of a man who is
so good that he has made no mistakes which would rationalize his fall. This
distinction illuminates what is meant by disgust: disgust is an emotion that is
partially constituted by the belief that there is no reason at all for the misfortune.
Disgust is something we feel in response to what we take to be a total absence
of rationality.

Aristotle thinks that the mere fact that tragedy must arouse pity and fear in
the audience justifies him in severely restricting the range of tragic plots.

It is not necessary to search for every pleasure from tragedy, but only the
appropriate pleasure. But since it is necessary for the poet to produce the
pleasure from pity and fear through a mimesis, it is evident that he must do
this in the events in the plot. We should investigate, then, what sorts of
events appear to be horrible or pitiable. In respect to such actions, it is
necessary that the people involved be either friends with each other or
enemies or neither of these. But if enemy acts on enemy, there is nothing

pitiable about this – neither in the doing of the deed, nor in intending to do it – except in relation to the terrible event itself [*kat' auto to pathos*]. The same is true when the people stand in neither relation. But whenever the terrible events occur among loved ones [friends, kin], for example if a brother should kill or intend to kill or do some other such thing to a brother, or a son to a father, or a mother to a son, or a son to a mother: we should search for these things.[77]

Aristotle is clear that the peculiar pleasure of tragedy is produced by evoking pity and fear in the audience and that this is accomplished by constructing a mimesis of a special type of terrible event (*pathos*). Aristotle uses the same word, "*pathos*," both to signify a terrible event, catastrophe or serious misfortune and to signify emotion. When, for example, Aristotle cites *pathos* as one of the three ingredients needed in a plot, along with reversal and recognition, in order to produce pity and fear, he is not requiring a certain motion to be portrayed on stage, he is requiring that there be a destructive act.[78] So one might say that, for Aristotle, there is an objective *pathos* and a subjective *pathos*: and the two are related. For what Aristotle is trying to do in this passage is delimit the precise type of objective *pathos* which is adequate to bring about a particular type of subjective *pathos* – pity and fear – in response.[79]

The objective *pathos* required to produce the tragic emotions is a terrible deed done between kin or loved ones. That is why the great tragedians have correctly focused in on just a few families that have been ripped apart by terrible deeds.[80] But what is it about the portrayal of a terrible deed done *among kin* that makes it particularly well suited to evoking pity and fear?

Perhaps a start may be made in answering this question by recognizing that at least a necessary condition for the audience feeling pity and fear in response to such terrible deeds is that they believe that such events could happen to them. For fear this is obvious. Aristotle, as we have seen, defines fear as a pain due to imagining some painful or destructive event befalling one. And he further requires that the fearful event be both imminent and capable of causing great pain.[81] For we do not fear distant pains, for example death, nor do we fear imminent but minor pains: "From the definition it will follow that fear is caused by whatever we feel has great power of destroying us, or of harming us in ways that tend to cause us great pain."[82] Aristotle is explicit that we feel fear only when we believe that we are ourselves vulnerable to an imminent and grave danger: "we shall not fear things that we believe cannot happen to us."[83] A further condition on fear is that we must believe that there is at least a faint possibility of escape from the danger.[84]

At first sight, it appears that pity is the paradigm of an other-regarding emotion. We feel pity for others when they suffer what we believe to be undeserved pain.[85] However, Aristotle makes it clear that in order to feel pity for others we must also believe that the terrible event which has befallen them might befall us or our loved ones and, moreover, might befall us soon. Thus in order for us to feel pity for others, we must believe that the others' situation is significantly similar to our own. One might at first think that pity can be felt for those who are in some relevant respect like us – either in social standing, character, or age – even though we do not believe we could end up in their situation, but Aristotle denies this. We do feel pity for those who are like us, but the reason we do, Aristotle thinks, is because in such cases we think it more likely that the misfortune that has befallen them can befall us.[86] This explains Aristotle's otherwise puzzling remark in the *Poetics* that we fear for someone who is similar to us.[87] Why, one might ask, should one fear for someone else – even if he is like us? The appropriate emotion to direct towards another, especially toward another who is similar to us, should (we might think) be pity. Aristotle's point is that fear is an appropriate emotion to feel in response to a similar person's misfortune: for through his similarity we recognize that we stand in the same danger he did.

Likewise with pity. Aristotle's only caveat is that the perceived danger cannot be too immediate: for in that case fear (for oneself) will drive out pity (for others).[88] Pity will also be driven out of the souls of those who, already ruined, believe that no bad can further harm them, and of those who believe themselves omnipotent and impervious to harm.[89]

> Those who think they *may* suffer are those who have already suffered and have safely escaped from it: *elderly men, owing to their good sense and their experience*; weak men, especially men inclined to cowardice; and *also educated people, for they are able to reason well.*[90]

Aristotle clearly recognizes pity as a reasonable emotion for an educated and thoughtful person: and since good tragedy is ideally for an educated audience, it follows that, for Aristotle, the pity which good tragedy evokes is a reasonable emotional response to the events portrayed.

(6) It follows that a normal, educated audience, going to a performance of a good tragedy, believes that the terrible events portrayed – infanticide, parricide, matricide, the tearing apart of the most primordial bonds of family and society – could happen to them. Had they lacked that belief they would, in Aristotle's eyes, be incapable of experiencing the tragic emotions. This allows us to impose a further constraint, at least upon the emotions from which a tragic katharsis is produced:

(7) The events which in a tragedy properly provoke the pity and fear from which a tragic katharsis occurs must be such that the audience believes that such events could happen to them.

Before proceeding, I would like to dispose of two objections which might be raised against this conclusion. The most serious objection is that the audience need not believe that the terrible events could happen to them: they are able to experience the tragic emotions because they are able to identify imaginatively with the central character and thus empathically feel what we feels. Within Aristotle's world, it is clear that the objection has the situation the wrong way around: for Aristotle, it is only because we think ourselves to be sufficiently like another that we can identify with him.[91] For Aristotle, we cannot identify with the very bad or with the gods: it is precisely because we are so distant from such beings that our emotions must retain a similar distance from theirs. That is why, for Aristotle, there is no important distinction to be made between our feeling our fear and our feeling Oedipus's fear. The very possibility of our imaginatively feeling Oedipus's fear is grounded in the recognition that we are like him: that is, it is grounded in the possibility of our fearing for ourselves.[92] Moreover, this objection does not take seriously the emotion of pity. We cannot feel pity in imaginatively identifying with Oedipus: part of what makes Oedipus such a remarkable and admirable figure is his lack of self-pity, his willingness to accept responsibility for his acts. But if our pity isn't an imaginative re-enactment of Oedipus's self-pity, then it must, as we have seen, be grounded in the belief that his fate could be ours.[93]

The less serious objection is that the audience doesn't come to the performance believing that the terrible events portrayed in the tragedy could happen to them: they are persuaded that this is so by the performance itself. The shortest answer to this objection is also the best: tragedy is not rhetoric, it is poetry. Because fear sets us thinking about how to escape from the perceived danger, an orator may wish to persuade his audience that they are in danger,[94] but a tragedy doesn't try to persuade its audience of anything. The only effect on the audience that a tragedy aims to produce is a certain emotional response (the content of which we are trying to uncover). Of course, if tragedy is to succeed in this, it must portray events which are convincing, plausible, events which plausibly could occur.[95] But Aristotle's point in insisting that the poet construct plausible, convincing plots is not so that he may persuade the audience of anything but so that he may portray an event which the audience can recognize as one that could, just possibly, happen to them.

Now if a normal, educated audience, going to the performance of a good tragedy, believes that the terrible events to be portrayed could, just possibly, happen to them, there *seems to be* a striking fact which is true of them both before they enter and after they leave the theater: they are missing the feelings which together with their beliefs would constitute the emotions of pity and fear. One might like to say that they are cut off from their emotions, but that can't be quite right. Since, for Aristotle, emotions are partially constituted by beliefs, it is more accurate to say that the distinct elements that conjointly constitute an emotion – belief and feeling – seem split off from one another. Another way of putting it is to say that normal educated people in normal circumstances and outside of the theater seem to have certain beliefs that they do not feel.[96]

A misleading way of putting an important truth is this: that when a normal, educated person experiences a performance of a good tragedy, he is able to unify certain beliefs he has with feelings that are appropriate to those beliefs. He came to the theater believing that he could commit or suffer terrible deeds. In the theater he is able to feel those beliefs. but before we jump to the conclusion that katharsis is a unification of belief and feeling, a unification of the tragic emotions, let us stop to consider why this mode of expression is misleading. It is misleading because it suggests that what we feel in the theater is what we ought to feel in real life: that in real life the appropriate feelings are somehow kept at bay from the beliefs which would rationalize them.

But this cannot be right. For constraint (1) requires that the virtuous person experience a katharsis in the performance of a tragedy, but his emotional reactions are already appropriate to the real life situations in which he lives; and constraint (3) requires that our emotional response to tragedy is not what we would or should feel in response to real life counterparts. Tragic pleasure depends crucially on the belief that one is emotionally responding to a *mimesis* of tragic events.[97] Without this belief, tragic pleasure is impossible. Therefore, constraint (7) – that the audience believe that tragic events could happen to them – must be interpreted in a way which does not suggest that the virtuous person, in not feeling pity and fear in ordinary life, is somehow cut off from a proper emotional response to his situation. It is completely un-Aristotelian to suppose that what we feel in the theater is what we ought to feel in real life, but for some reason do not. In real life the virtuous man feels just what he ought to feel. But, then, how could he believe that terrible, tragic deeds could, just possibly, befall him and not feel fear and dread?

Everything depends on the strength of the modal operator. The virtuous man believes that terrible, tragic events could happen to him, true, but the possibility of those things happening is, in his opinion, too remote for the actual feeling of fear to be warranted.[98] Although a tragic breakdown of the primordial ties of human life is possible, the virtuous man also recognizes that this is less likely to happen to him than almost anything else. That is why it is misleading to say that tragedy restores the appropriate feelings to our already existing beliefs. Our belief that tragic events could, just possibly, befall us already has the appropriate feeling attached to it outside the theater. No unification is needed for, at least in the case of the virtuous person, there is no split that needs to be overcome.

And yet the belief that tragic events could, *just possibly*, happen to us does exert some pressure on our souls – even on the souls of us virtuous people. This is precisely the pressure which takes us to the theater. For in the theater we can imaginatively bring what we take to be a remote possibility closer to home. As Aristotle himself said: ". . . those who heighten the effect of their words with suitable gestures, tones, appearance, and dramatic action generally, are especially successful in exciting pity: they thus put the disasters before our eyes, and make them seem close to us, just coming or just past."[99]

The tragic poet, for Aristotle, plays a role in the world of emotions somewhat similar to the role of the skeptic within the world of beliefs. The skeptic awakens us to the fact that we ourselves believe in certain epistemic possibilities which in ordinary life we ignore: for example, that we could be asleep, dreaming, or perhaps deceived by an evil demon. On the one hand, these possibilities are extremely remote, so we are justified in ignoring them in ordinary life; on the other hand, they lend content to the idea that in ordinary life we are living "inside the plain": and they fuel our desire to get outside the plain of everyday life and see how things really are, absolutely.[100]

The tragic poet awakens us to the fact that there are certain emotional possibilities which we ignore in ordinary life. On the one hand, these possibilities are remote, so it is not completely unreasonable to ignore them in ordinary life; on the other hand, they lend content to the idea that in ordinary life we are living "inside the plain": and they fuel our desire imaginatively to experience life outside the plain. Even if tragedy does not befall us, it goes to the root of the human condition that it is a possibility we must live with. And, even if remote, the possibility of tragedy is not only much more imminent than the skeptical possibilities, it is much more threatening. For while skeptical possibilities are so designed that they make no difference to the experience of our lives, in tragedy our lives are ripped asunder.

But there is a genuine problem about how to experience tragic possibility. On the one hand, the possibility of tragedy in ordinary life is too remote to justify real fear, on the other hand, it is too important and too close to ignore. Tragic poetry provides an arena in which one can imaginatively experience the tragic emotions: the performance of a play "captures our souls."[101] However, it is crucial to the pleasure we derive from tragedy, that we never lose sight of the fact that we are an audience, enjoying a work of art. Otherwise the pleasurable katharsis of pity and fear would collapse into the merely painful experience of those emotions.[102] Aristotle is keenly aware of the important difference between a mimesis of a serious action and the serious action of which it is a mimesis. The emotional response which is appropriate to a mimesis – tragic pleasure and katharsis – would be thoroughly inappropriate to the real event.

It is this experience of the tragic emotions in an appropriately inappropriate environment which, I think, helps to explain our experience of relief in the theater. We imaginatively live life to the full, but we risk nothing. The relief is thus not that of "releasing pent-up emotions" *per se*, it is the relief of "releasing" these emotions in a safe environment. But to say that it is this experience of relief to which Aristotle gave the name "katharsis" is not to characterize it fully: one needs also to know the content of our relief, what our relief is about.

Here I will only mention briefly certain consolations which are integral to Aristotle's conception of tragedy. The world of tragic events must, Aristotle repeatedly insists, be rational. The subject of tragedy may be a good man, but he must make a mistake which rationalizes his fall.[103] The mere fall of a good man from good fortune to bad fortune for no reason at all, isn't tragic, it's disgusting.[104] The events in a tragedy must be necessary or plausible, and they must occur on account of one another.[105] In so far as we do fear that tragic events could occur in our lives, what we fear is chaos: the breakdown of the primordial bonds which links person to person. For Aristotle, a good tragedy offers us this consolation: that even when the breakdown of the primordial bonds occurs, it does not occur in a world which is in itself ultimately chaotic and meaningless.

It is significant that, for Aristotle, *Oedipus Rex* is the paradigm tragedy rather than, say, *Antigone*.[106] For the point of tragedy, in Aristotle's eyes, is not to portray a world in which a person through no fault of his own may be subject to fundamentally irreconcilable and destructive demands. In Aristotle's conception of tragedy, the individual actor takes on the burden of badness, the world as a whole is absolved.[107] And there is further consolation is recognizing that even when they are responsible for their misfortunes, humans remain capable of conducting themselves with dignity and nobility.[108] Even in his humiliation and shame, Oedipus inspires our awe and admiration.

In the *Rhetoric* Aristotle says that those who have already experienced great disasters no longer feel fear, for they feel they have already experienced every kind of horror.[109] In tragedy, we are able to put ourselves imaginatively in a position in which there is nothing further to fear. There is consolation in realizing that one has experienced the worst, there is nothing further to fear, and yet the world remains a rational, meaningful place in which a person can conduct himself with dignity. Even in tragedy, perhaps especially in tragedy, the fundamental goodness of man and world are reaffirmed.[110]

Notes

1. See *Poetics* 6, 1449b22–28.
2. See Baxter Hathaway, *The Age of Criticism: The Late Renaissance in Italy* (Ithaca, NY, 1962), pp. 205–300.
3. This is largely due to Jacob Bernays' influential *Zwei Abhandlungen über die aristotelische Theorie des Drama* (Berlin, 1880, first published Breslau, 1857). A chapter of this book has been translated as "Aristotle on the Effect of Tragedy" by Jonathan and Jennifer Barnes in *Articles on Aristotle*, Vol. 4, (J. Barnes, M. Schofield and R. Sorabji eds. London, 1979). Bernays' interpretation had a wider influence than on Aristotelian scholarship alone; for Bernays was Freud's wife's uncle and it seems that Freud and Breuer were aware of the interpretation and relied on it when formulating his conception of catharsis in the early stages of the formation of psychoanalytic theory. (See Bennett Simon, *Mind and Madness in Ancient Greece* (Ithaca, NY, 1978, pp. 140–143).) The katharsis-as-purge metaphor is used by Plato in the *Sophist* (230C–231E) where the Socratic *elenchus* is represented as purging one of false beliefs.
4. See e.g. Sigmund Freud, *The Standard Edition of the Complete Psychological Works of Sigmund Freud* (London, 1981), X: 233–234, XII: 218–226; XIII: 78–90; XIV: 73–102; XIX: 235–239; Wilfrid Bion, *Learning From Experience* (London, 1984) and *Second Thoughts* (London, 1984); Melanie Klein, *Narrative of a Child Analysis* (London, 1961) pp. 31 ff., *Contributions to Psycho-Analysis* (London, 1948), pp. 140–151, 303, *Developments in Psycho-Analysis* (London, 1952); W. R. D. Fairburn, "Schizoid Factors in the Personality," in *Psychoanalytic Studies of the Personality* (London, 1984); Richard Wollheim, "The Mind and the Mind's Image of Itself," in

On Art and the Mind (Cambridge, MA, 1974), "Wish-Fulfilment," in *Rational Action*, ed. Ross Harrison, (Cambridge, 1979), *The Thread of Life* (Cambridge, 1984).

5. The idea that purgation and purification need not be treated as contraries is argued by Humphrey House, *Aristotle's Poetics* (London, 1956), pp. 104–111, and by Stephen Halliwell, *Aristotle's Poetics* (Chapel Hill, NC, 1986), pp. 184–201.

6. See e.g. *Generation of Animals* I.20, 728b3, 14; IV.5, 773b1; Iv.6, 775b5; *History of Animals* VI.18, 573a2, a7; VI.28, 578b18; VII.2, 582b7, 30; VII.4, 584a8; VIII.11, 587b2, b30–33, 588a1. For the use of "katharsis" to describe seminal discharge, *Generation of Animals* II.7, 747a19; for the discharge of urine: *History of Animals* VI.18, 573a23; for birth discharge: *History of Animals* VI.20, 574b4.

7. *Politics* VIII.7, 1341b37–39.

8. Aristotle uses the word "katharsis" only twice in *Poetics*: once, as we have seen, in the definition of tragedy and once to refer to the ritual of purification at which Orestes is recognized by his sister, Iphigenia, *Poetics* 17, 1455b15).

9. Bernays is explicit that katharsis is a cure for a pathological condition.

10. See *Politics* VIII.5–7. Bernays argues persuasively that to understand the concept of tragic katharsis, we must look to Aristotle's discussion in the *Politics* of the katharsis which music produces; though, as we shall see, he is less persuasive in his interpretation of that discussion. G. R. Else and, following him, Leon Golden have argued that one should not look outside the *Poetics* for the meaning of tragic katharsis. (G. F. Else, *Aristotle's Poetics: The Argument* (Cambridge, MA, 1957), pp. 439 ff.; Leon Golden, "Catharsis," *Transactions and Proceedings of the American Philological Association* **93** (1962) 51–60; and "Mimesis and Catharsis," *Classical Philology* **64** (1969) 145–153.) This, I believe, is a misapplication of a principle from new criticism. The *Poetics* was not meant to be a self-contained universe; it was an integral part of Aristotle's philosophy. If, for example, we were trying to determine what Aristotle meant by art (*techne*) or poetry (*poiesis*) in the *Poetics*, there would be no plausibility to claiming that we should completely restrict ourselves to the *Poetics'* discussion. Of course, Aristotle does use '*poiesis*' in a special way in the *Poetics*: it is to be translated as "poetry" rather than as a "making" which is the appropriate translation in the *Metaphysics*. However, if we ignore all other Aristotelian works we remain blind to the philosophically important fact that, for Aristotle, poetry is a special type of making. There is no doubt that we must approach other texts with care, for, to return to our current concern, Aristotle's use of "katharsis" when discussing medical purging may be different in significant respects from his use of the term when discussing tragedy. But such interpretive difficulties are not sufficient grounds for ignoring other texts altogether. (Indeed, Else's and Golden's stricture led them to formulate a highly implausible account of katharsis, in which katharsis is not an effect on the audience of tragedy, but a resolution of the events in the play. This implausible interpretation depends upon an even more implausible translation of Aristotle's definition of tragedy. For an excellent criticism of this interpretation, see Stephen Halliwell, *Aristotle's Poetics* Appendix 5, esp. pp. 354–356.)

11. *Politics* VIII.7, 1341b32–42a18. Here I have made a few changes in the revised Oxford translation: I use "ethical melodies" rather than "melodies of character" for "*ta ethika*"; I use a transliteration of "*katharsis*" rather than translate it as "purgation"; I translate "*pathos*" as "emotion" rather than as "feeling"; and I translate "*kouphidzesthai meth' hedones*" as "relieved with pleasure" rather than as "lightened and delighted."

12. Bernays makes this point. Halliwell interprets this passage so as to diminish Aristotle's apparent contrast between education and katharsis. For a criticism of this interpretation, see Section 4, below.

13. See esp. *Politics* VIII.7, 1342a4–11. Bernays takes religious ecstasy to be a pathological condition.

14. 1342a11–13: *tauto de touto anagkaion paschein kai tous eleemonas kai tous phobetikous kai tous olos pathetikous.*

15. "*Kai pasi gignesthai tina katharsin kai kouphidzesthai meth' hedones*" 1342a14–15; my translation and emphasis. (By the way, this statement seems to me to provide absolutely conclusive evidence against Humphrey House's claim that, for Aristotle, a phronimos at the theatre would experience no katharsis. See his *Aristotle's Poetics*, Ch. VIII.)

16. *Problems* 42, 864a34.

17. See e.g. Franz Susemihl and R. D. Hicks, *The Politics of Aristotle* (London, 1894), p. 651, n.1), who along with Humphrey House *Aristotle's Poetics*, p. 110) quote Milton's preface to Samson Agonistes. Cp. Halliwell, *Aristotle's Poetics*, pp. 192–194.

18. Halliwell is aware of this: *Aristotle's Poetics*, p. 193, n.37. See *Nicomachean Ethics* 1104b17 f., *Eudemian Ethics* 1220a36.

19. *Rhetoric* II.5, 1382a21 ff.

20. See *Rhetoric* II.1 and II.5. In addition, Aristotle believes there are certain physiological changes which accompany an emotion. *On the Soul*, 403a16–19.

21. *Rhetoric* II.5, 1382b30 ff.

22. See Hathaway, *The Age of Criticism*.

23. Eduard Muller (*Theorie der Kunst bei den Alten*, Vol. 2, pp. 62, 377–388) quoted by Bernays, *Zwei Abhandlung*, p. 156.

24. See e.g. *Poetics*, 13–14 where plots are evaluated on the basis of the type of emotional response they tend to evoke in an audience. Those that do not produce pity and fear, but, for example, disgust are rejected as inadequate for tragedy.

25. See Humphrey House, *Aristotle's Poetics*, Stephen Halliwell, *Aristotle's Poetics*, Leon Golden, "Catharsis" and Martha Nussbaum, *The Fragility of Goodness*. Golden and Nussbaum speak of a "clarification" of the emotions.

26. *NE* II.

27. *NE* II.6, 1106b6–28. This is Aristotle's famous doctrine of the mean.

28. Aristotle is clear that one need not actually see a performance on stage in order to experience the effect of tragedy; simply hearing it read out loud is sufficient. See *Poetics* 14, 1453b4–7; 6, 1450b18–19; 26, 1462a11–12. For Aristotle's mention of the peculiar and appropriate pleasure of tragedy, see *Poetics* 14, 1453b10–14; 23, 1459a17–24; 26, 14652b12–14, cf. 1462a15–17.

29. *Metaphysics* I.1.

30. Nor, contra Golden and Nussbaum, do his emotions need to be clarified.

31. *Politics* VIII.7, 1341b32–1342a18 (quoted above).

32. Halliwell, *Aristotle's Poetics*, pp. 195–196.

33. 1342a1–2.

34. My translation of 1341b38.

35. This is made clear by 1341b36–38: . . . *ou mias heneken opheleias tei mousikei dein alla kai pleionon charin (kai gar paideias heneken kai katharseos* . . .). But in case there is any doubt, it is settled by "*triton*" at 1341b40: clearly, education, katharsis, and intellectual enjoyment are being listed as three distinct benefits obtainable from music.

36. 1342b11–15.

37. 1342b18–29. This passage is also cited by Bernays as part of his argument that katharsis is not meant by Aristotle to be morally educative.

38. *Ho men eleutheros kai pepaideumenos* (1342b19). Cp. also *Poetics* 26 (esp. 1461b27–28) which suggests that tragedy will be appreciated by a better sort of audience.

39. *Poetics* 4, 1449a10–15.

40. *Poetics* 13, 1453a33–36.

41. *Poetics* 25, 1460b13–15.

42. Here I am particularly indebted to Giovanni Ferrari.

43. *Poetics* 4, 1448b4–19, my emphasis. I have altered the revised Oxford translation of 1448b14–15: *sullogidzesthai ti hekaston, hoion hoti houtos ekeinos* which is rendered there as "gathering the meaning of things, e.g. that the man there is so-and-so." My translation is more literal which I think is important to the interpretation of this passage.

44. *Parts of Animals* I.5, 645a4–37.

45. *Parts of Animals* I.5, 645a8–15.

46. *Poetics* 4, 1448b17–19. Such a person, presumably, would not have heard a sufficient description to recognize a mouse: the person Aristotle has in mind, I think, is someone who has *no idea* of a mouse: so he is in no position to recognize of any painting that it is a painting of a mouse.

47. See e.g. *Poetics* 9, 1451a37–38; 10, 1452a17–21; 15, 1454a33–36; 16, 1455a16–19; 25, 1461b11–12.

48. E.g. *Poetics* 9, 1452a3–4; 10, 1452a20–21.

49. *Poetics* 13, 1453a8–30. Nussbaum argues that the point of a hamartia is to render the protagonist sufficiently like us that we can identify with him to the extent required to experience the tragic emotions of pity and fear (*The Fragility of Goodness*, pp. 382 ff.). Her reasoning is based on her more general interpretator that, for Aristotle, the point of tragedy is to explore the gap which inevitably exists between being good and living well. I do not think that the general interpretation can be correct. Although Aristotle does accept that being virtuous is not sufficient for happiness and that external misfortune can ruin a thoroughly good man (*NE* I.10), it is quite clear that Aristotle does not think that such an event could be the basis for a tragedy. Consider the example *Poetics* 13, 1452b30–36, where Aristotle says that tragedy cannot portray the fall of a good man from good to bad fortune, for such an event does not arouse the tragic emotions of pity and fear but a thoroughly nontragic emotion of disgust. Aristotle does reluctantly admit that a virtuous man can be destroyed *for no reason at all*, that is, through misfortune, but he denies that this is the stuff of tragedy. Tragic events always occur for a reason.

50. *Poetics* 9, 1452a1–6 (my trans. except for two phrases from Oxford).

51. *Poetics* 6, 1449b27–28. Literally, Aristotle says a "katharsis of *such* emotions" (*ton toiouton pathematon*), but Bernays has argued convincingly that "such" should be understood demonstratively, as referring exclusively to pity and fear.

52. *Metaphysics* 982b12 ff., 983a12 ff.; *Rhetoric* 1371a31 ff.

53. *Metaphysics* 982b12 ff. I discuss this at some length in *Aristotle: The Desire to Understand* (Cambridge, 1988).

54. See e.g. Halliwell, *Aristotle's Poetics*, pp. 70–74.

55. *Poetics* 24, 1460a11–17.

56. *Poetics* 24, 1460a17.

57. *Poetics* 26, 1462b13–14. See the note on the passage in D. W. Lucas, *Aristotle's Poetics* (Oxford, 1968), p. 257.

58. *Poetics* 9, 1451b5–11.

59. At *Metaphysics* XIII.10, 1087a10–25, Aristotle does qualify his claim that episteme is of universals. See my "Active Episteme" (in *Mathematics and Metaphysics in Aristotle: Proceedings of the Xth Symposium Aristotelicum*, ed. A. Graeser (Ber, 1986)) for an analysis of this passage.

60. Although I am certainly willing to accept that Aristotle thought that tragedy provides deeper insight into the human condition than history does, I don't think that is the immediate point he is making in the passage under discussion.

61. *Poetics* 17, 1455b2–13 (Oxford trans.). See also Aristotle's description of the plot of the *Odyssey* at 1455b16–23.
62. *Poetics* 17, 1455b, 12–13; cf. 9, 1451b8–16.
63. Aristotle does not seem to have been familiar with Thucydides. One cannot but wonder how Aristotle would have changed his mind about history if he had carefully read the History of the Peloponnesian War.
64. As we have seen, that is why Aristotle says at the end of Chapter 9 that the events in a tragedy should occur unexpectedly but on account of one another.
65. *Poetics* 9, 1451a36–38, repeated again at 1451b4–5, just before Aristotle claims that poetry is more philosophical than history because it deals with universals (1451b5–7).
66. Among humans, that is.
67. See *Politics* VIII.7, 1342b14; and the numerous references in the *Poetics* in which the plot of a good tragedy is distinguished from that which will appeal to a vulgar audience: e.g. *Poetics* 13, 1453a30–36 (cp. 9, 1451b33–1452a1 and 6, 1450b16–19) and *Poetics* 26, in which Aristotle seems to accept the principle that tragedy is a higher art form than epic precisely because it appeals to a better audience.
68. See *Rhetoric* II.5, 8; cp. the account of anger as a composite of pain and pleasure: *Rhetoric* II.2.
69. Aristotle, as we have seen, says that everyone undergoes a "certain katharsis and lightening with pleasure": *Politics* VIII.7, 1342b14–15.
70. *Poetics* 6, 1449b24–28; see p. 297 above.
71. *Physics* III.3.
72. I say "ultimately" because there is a two step process involved: (1) the poet's creating the *muthos* and writing the play, (2) the performance of the play before an audience. I am using the word "performance" widely to cover both the enactment of the play on stage by actors and the simple reading or recital of the play out loud. Aristotle is explicit that a tragedy can have its proper effect even when it is not acted out on stage: a person who merely hears the tragedy read out loud will experience pity and fear. See *Poetics* 14, 1453b3–7; 6, 1450b18–19; 26, 62a11–12, a17–18.
73. *Poetics* 13, 1452b30–1453a8 (Oxford trans. except that I use "disgusting" for "*miaron*" rather than Oxford's "odious").
74. *Poetics* 13, 1453a4–6.
75. See e.g. *Poetics* 15, 1454b8–13.
76. *Poetics* 13, 1453a8–17.
77. *Poetics* 14, 1453b10–22 (my trans.).
78. *Poetics* 11, 1452b10–11. For other objective uses of "*pathos*" in the *Poetics*, see e.g. 13, 1453b18, b19–20, b39, 54a13. See also *Rhetoric* II.5, 1382b30; *Metaphysics* V.21, 1022b20–21; *NE* I.11, 1101a31.
79. It is tempting to speculate that, for Aristotle, there is also an objective as well as a subjective katharsis. For the katharsis referred to in the definition of tragedy is clearly subjective – i.e. something that goes on within the souls of the members of the audience; while the katharsis at which Orestes is saved (17, 1455b14–15) is clearly objective: viz. a ritual sacrifice. It goes beyond the evidence of the texts to construct a theory of the relation of objective to subjective katharsis. But it is worth noting in passing that if Aristotle believed that a subjective katharsis occurs in response to an objective katharsis, then the entire debate over where the katharsis is occurring, within the play itself or in the audience, would be idle. It would be occurring in both places (albeit in different forms).
80. *Poetics* 13, esp. 1453a17–22; 14, 1454a9–13.
81. *Rhetoric* II.5, 1382a22–30.
82. *Rhetoric* II.5, 1382a28–30.

83. *Rhetoric* II.5, 1382b31–31; cp. b28–1383a12.
84. *Rhetoric* II.5, 1383a5–8. Those who have lost all hope of escape grow resigned and callous.
85. *Poetics* 13, 1453a5; *Rhetoric* II.8, 1385b14 ff.
86. *Rhetoric* II.8, 1386a24–27.
87. *Poetics* 13, 1453a5–6.
88. *Rhetoric* II.8, 1386a24–25.
89. *Rhetoric* II.8, 1385b19 ff.
90. *Rhetoric* II.8, 1385b23–27. Cp. *Politics* VIII.7, 1342b19, where an educated audience (*hoi pepaideumenoi*) is contrasted with a vulgar one.
91. Since it is an incredibly complicated subject, I would like to reserve for another occasion a discussion of the general conditions required for emotional identification.
92. *Poetics* 13, 1453a5–6; *Rhetoric* II.5, 1383a10–13.
93. One might lamely try to keep the objection alive by saying that when we feel pity we are identifying with the chorus. But then the question arises: why should we identify with the chorus? The only plausible answer is that the chorus is in some way expressing our views. And if that is so, we are again led back to the conclusion that we believe that what happened to Oedipus could happen to us.
94. *Rhetoric* II.5, 1383a7–12.
95. E.g. *Poetics* 9, 1452a36–38, b5–7, b15–19.
96. I use "outside the theater" in the widest possible way: even the oral recitation of a tragedy counts for the purposes of this essay as going on "inside the theater."
97. See constraints (3)–(6).
98. If I may for a moment indulge my desire to be droll, let me put this in the language of modal semantics: In the virtuous man's opinion (and thus: in truth) the worlds in which he kills his mother, is killed by his mother, etc. are possible worlds and thus stand in an accessibility relation to the real world. All tragic worlds are possible worlds. However, all such tragic worlds are sufficiently removed from the actual work of a virtuous person (in ordinary circumstances) that they do not fall within the set of legitimately feared worlds.
99. *Rhetoric* II.8, 1386a32–35. Of course, Aristotle is here talking within the context of rhetorical persuasion, but his point obviously carries over to the theatre.
100. See Thompson Clarke, "The Legacy of Skepticism." *Journal of Philosopy* **69** (1972) 754–769.
101. *Psuchagogei*: cf. *Poetics* 6, 1450a33–36.
102. See constraints (4)–(6) above.
103. *Poetics* 13, 1453a7–17; 15, 1454b8–13.
104. *Poetics* 13, 1452b30–36.
105. *Poetics* 9, 1452a3–4; 10, 1452a20–21; 15, 1454a33–36; 16, 1455a17; 9, 1451a36–38.
106. Which was, of course, Hegel's choice.
107. See W. R. D. Fairbairn's account of "the moral defense" in "The Repression and the Return of Bad Objects," *Psychoanalytic Studies of the Personality* (London, 1984).
108. Aristotle makes a related (though different) point at *NE* I.10: he reluctantly admits that even a virtuous person can suffer great misfortune however he offers the consolation that the virtuous person will at least bear his misfortunes nobly and with greatness of soul.
109. *Rhetoric* II.5, 1383a3–5.
110. For another treatment of skepticism and its relationship to tragedy see, of course, Stanley Cavell, *The Claim of Reason* (Oxford, 1979). I would like to thank Giovanni Ferrari both for the many lovely evenings in which we translated and discussed the *Poetics* together and for his criticisms of an earlier draft.

From Catharsis to
the Aristotelian Mean*

Richard Janko

In this essay, I shall argue that Aristotle believed that catharsis can lead to virtue: our responses to the representation (*mimēsis*) of human action can habituate us to approximate more closely to the mean in our ordinary emotional reactions. Literature, and especially drama, can contribute to the formation and continuing education of mature citizens. Aristotle's views are central to continuing debates about public control over artistic representation and the mass media, and the role of art and the artist in education and society.

My argument builds on recent revisions of the influential view of catharsis as the purgation of undesirable emotions set out by J. Bernays.[1] An analysis of Aristotle's general theory of the emotions shows that there is a close connection between Aristotle's views on representation and catharsis. New textual evidence[2] clarifies how watching representations of actions can enable us to approach the virtuous mean.

I

The notion of catharsis was of fundamental importance to Aristotle's theory of literature. Although he ends his definition of tragedy with the statement that

* This essay was written in Fall 1990 while I held a Fellowship provided by the Andrew W. Mellon Foundation at the National Humanities Center. I wish to thank both these institutions for their support. I am also grateful to the staff at the Center and to audiences at the Center, at the University of North Carolina, Chapel Hill, and at Wellesley College, to whom I presented versions of this paper. I also benefitted from the advice of Marco Fantuzzi, Michele Hannoosh, Amélie Oksenberg Rorty, Ian Rutherford and Paul Vander Waerdt. All translations are my own (see my *Aristotle: Poetics*, Indianapolis, 1987).

tragedy "accomplishes by means of pity and fear the catharsis of such emotions" (1449b27), he gives us no full analysis of the concept. In the absence of such an analysis, scholars have relied primarily on *Politics* VIII and the extant *Poetics* to reconstruct Aristotle's views, supplementing these with his discussions of the emotions in the *Rhetoric* and *Nicomachean Ethics*.[3]

Because the definition of tragedy makes the catharsis of pity and fear essential to the genre, the plots of tragedies are best structured in such a way as to represent the kinds of actions that are best suited to arouse those emotions (1452b32). A good tragedy should not depict the fall of decent men from good fortune into misfortune, since this does not excite pity or fear, but is *miaron*, "disgusting" (1453b36), literally "dirty" or "polluted," provoking feelings of shock or revulsion. This evidently constitutes the opposite of catharsis, whether we take that term to mean "cleansing," "purification," "purgation" or "clarification" (see below, Section IV).

The *Poetics* also specifically connects catharsis with *mimēsis*: the pleasure proper to tragedy is "the pleasure that comes from pity and fear by means of representation" (*tēn apo eleou kai phobou dia mimēseōs hēdonēn*, 1453b12). Aristotle distinguishes between feeling pity and fear because of real events (which is not pleasant), and feeling these emotions because of a representation (which *is* pleasant). This distinction is confirmed by 1448b10–12: we derive pleasure from looking at representations even of things that are in actuality painful to contemplate, like the most despised animals and corpses; these objects are "impure" – once again evoking the idea of catharsis.[4]

II

Aristotle's response to Plato's attack on poetry is also a response to Plato's view of the emotions.[5] Indeed, when Socrates challenges those defenders of poetry "who are not poets but love poetry" to prove in prose that poetry is beneficial to society (*Republic* X 607d), Plato may already have had Aristotle in mind.[6] One of Plato's main objections to mimetic poetry is that it can nourish emotions – such as pity, lust and indignation – which would be better suppressed or restrained by the reasoning part of the soul (*Republic* X 605d–606d). Mimetic and dramatic poetry is dangerous because the arousal of such emotions may make it difficult to restrain them in one's everyday circumstances, putting the appetitive part of the soul in charge (606a–c). Even the temporary experience of being under the control of such emotions can permanently affect the soul of the spectator, since nurturing feelings of pity for others' sufferings on the stage makes it difficult to restrain such a reaction toward one's own misfortunes in life (606b).

If Aristotle's theory of catharsis is to hold, he needs to refute Plato on this point. Aristotle explains tragic catharsis by comparing it with the healing of people suffering from ecstatic outbreaks of emotion (*enthousiasmos*); these people are cured by "cathartic songs," which excite their souls and thereby relieve their excessive emotions (*Politics* VIII 1342a2–16). Bernays argued that the catharsis which we obtain from watching a tragedy operates similarly, arousing and releasing undesirable feelings of pity and fear.[7] The weakness of his approach is his assumption that Aristotle held the same wholly negative opinion of the emotions that Bernays attributes to Plato, and would therefore regard them as needing to be cleaned out periodically. Aristotle recognized that well-balanced emotional reactions are a crucial factor in making correct choices and thus in forming and maintaining a settled good character.[8] Sometimes one *should* feel such emotions as pity, anger or fear, if they are felt towards the right object, to the proper degree, in the correct way and at the right time. Proper compassion, justified anger and the right degree of courage can and should affect moral choice (see e.g. *NE* III 1115b11–20). We must feel the emotions rightly for the circumstances: if we have too much fear, we are cowardly; if too little, we are foolhardy. Only if we feel the correct amount of fear relative to the situation do we attain courage. Virtue lies in our having such appropriate reactions, reaching the mean between the extremes relative to ourselves.

A disposition to feel emotion correctly in this way is essential to the development of good character.[9] If we force ourselves to act justly, but in fact long to act otherwise, we are self-controlled (*enkrateis*) but not fully virtuous, since our desires are not in tune with our actions.[10] Just as we become good by habitually doing good, until good action becomes a "second nature" to us, so too by feeling emotion appropriately we become habituated to having the correct emotional responses. Because the emotions also have a cognitive component, such reactions help us to take the correct decisions, so that we approach nearer to the virtuous mean.

III

Aristotle's analysis of the educational role of *mousikē* in *Politics* VIII clarifies how poetry can contribute to virtue,[11] since by "*mousikē*" he means not only music, but also the poetry which was usually performed along with it, including drama (1340a14 ff.).[12] *Mousikē* has three functions – education, amusement and educative entertainment (*diagōgē*), which contributes to intelligence.[13] He goes on to ask whether *mousikē*

> . . . contributes to the character and the soul. This would be clear, if we become of a certain sort in character by means of it. Actually, the fact that we do become of a certain sort [sc. because of it] is obvious for many reasons, especially the songs of Olympus. For it is agreed that these arouse the soul to ecstasy (*enthousiasmos*), and ecstasy is an emotion of the character connected with the soul. Again, when listening to representations (*mimēseis*) everyone comes to share in the emotion, even apart from rhythms and songs themselves. (1340a5–13)

Aristotle compares songs which arouse ecstasy in some people to "representations" which arouse a wider range of emotions in everybody; this comparison recurs in the later passage on catharsis. Among "representations" he includes unaccompanied mimetic poetry and even prose (e.g. mime), since *mimēseis* need not have "rhythms and songs" to accompany them (*Poetics* 1447a28–b23). He then introduces both the habituation of our emotions and the concept of *mimēsis* so central to the *Poetics*:

> Since music happens to belong among pleasant things, and virtue is concerned with feeling delight correctly and loving and hating [sc. correctly], clearly one should learn, and become habituated to, nothing so much as judging correctly, i.e. feeling delight in decent characters and fine actions. Rhythms and songs contain especially close likenesses [*homoiōmata*] of the true natures of anger and mildness, bravery, temperance and all their opposites, and of the other character-traits: this is clear from the facts – we are moved in our soul when we listen to such things. Habituation to feeling pain and delight in things that are like [sc. the truth] is close to being in the same state regarding the truth. (1340a14–24)

If listening to music can habituate us to feel the proper emotional reactions in real life, because it contains "likenesses" of emotions like anger or indeed pity, then dramatic poetry, which arouses emotion, must have the same effect. That Aristotle believed this is clear from the only place in the *Politics* where he refers explicitly to catharsis, VIII 1341b34 ff.:

> We accept the division of songs proposed by some people engaged in philosophy into songs relating to (a) character, (b) action and (c) ecstasy . . . We can therefore state that the art of music should be used not for a single beneficial purpose but for several. In fact it should be used (a) for education and (b) for catharsis (as for what we mean by "catharsis," we shall speak without qualification now, but more clearly in the *Poetics*), and thirdly (c) for educative entertainment [*diagōgē*], for both rest and relaxation from tension. (1341b32–41)

By "songs relating to character," Aristotle apparently means non-narrative didactic poems like the moral maxims of Theognis; by "songs relating to action" he certainly means those which represent action, as do tragedy, comedy, and epic. He next matches up the three different types of songs with the purposes to which they may be put:

> It is therefore obvious that one must use all the [sc. kinds of] melodies, but not use them all in the same way. (a) Those most related to character must be used for education, but (b) those related to action and to ecstasy must be used for listening to while others play them. (1342a1–4)

"Education" (*paideia*) here means the education only of boys (*paides*); Aristotle has been discussing which instruments boys should learn to play during their schooling. But *everyone* may benefit from the other two kinds of song, *both* of which arouse emotion (the "songs relating to catharsis" arouse ecstasy, while those "relating to action" arouse a wider range of feelings, as he stated above):

> For the emotion that arises violently in some souls exists in all, but differs in its degree, e.g. pity and fear as well as ecstasy. Some people tend to be taken over by this agitation [sc. ecstasy], but we can see that, as a result of the holy songs which they use to rouse the soul to a frenzy, they settle down as if they had attained healing, i.e. catharsis. It follows that this very same thing happens to people who are prone to pity, fear and emotion in general, and to the rest [sc. of us] to the degree that each participates in such [sc. emotions], and a sort of catharsis and relief, accompanied by pleasure, comes about for everyone. Likewise cathartic songs too afford people harmless delight. For this reason, those performers who are concerned with music for the theatre must be allowed to use such melodies and songs. (1342a5–18)

The repeated mention of "pity and fear" shows that Aristotle has tragedy specifically in mind. His argument runs as follows. We are all subject to the emotions to some degree, pity and fear (A) as well as ecstasy (B). Wild "cathartic" songs arouse ecstasy and bring about catharsis in the extreme case of people prone to this emotion (B′). "Songs relating to action" (specifically tragedy) have just such an effect on people who tend to feel pity and fear, to which we all are prone to some extent (A′). Just as this effect of tragedy is accompanied by pleasure (A″), so the "cathartic" songs too provide a "harmless delight" (B″).[14] The legislator must allow both kinds of *mousikē* to be performed in the theater. Thus tragic catharsis has a part to play in the functioning of the state.

Aristotle clearly regards *both* types of song as appropriate for both catharsis and educative entertainment (*diagōgē*), which contributes to intelligence; *diagōgē* is for adults what play or amusement (*paidia*) is for children (*paides*) (1339a30).[15] He asked whether we should participate in music for (a) amusement and relaxation, or (b) to habituate our characters to feel delight correctly and become virtuous, or for (c) "*diagōgē* and practical wisdom" (*phronēsis*) (1339a15–24). Since he now omits to specify which songs (those relating to action or those relating to ecstasy) provide *diagōge*, he probably took it for granted that both kinds of song do so. He has to argue for the more debatable proposition that songs relating to action can produce a "kind of" catharsis no less than do the "cathartic" songs in the extreme case of people prone to *enthousiasmos*.

The relation between catharsis and *diagōgē* may be closer than first appears. This passage suggests that they combine to perform for adults the function which *paideia* performs for children, i.e. the training of both the emotions and the intelligence, with the theater regarded almost as a form of adult education.[16] The emotions and the intelligence are interdependent: the emotions can play an important part in cognition, and *vice versa*. Thus catharsis and *diagōgē* seem to be negative and positive aspects of one and the same process: via *catharsis*, we moderate our tendency to feel inappropriate emotional reactions, and via *diagōgē* we make intellectual progress towards intelligence. Both aspects of this process are needed if we are to achieve virtue.

IV

There is now general agreement that catharsis affects the spectators' emotions rather than the actions represented in the play.[17] Only by denying the relevance of the *Politics*, with its reference to the *Poetics* (VIII 1341b30), is it possible to regard catharsis as a "clarification" of the plot, i.e. the causal structure of the action.[18] A modified version of this theory applies catharsis to the emotions of both the characters and the spectators.[19] The *dramatis personae* of a tragedy may well come to recognize the cause of their misfortunes, and to feel regret when the nature of the *hamartia* which brought about disaster is made plain; and the depiction of their enlightenment on the stage will certainly contribute to the enlightenment of the spectators. But Aristotle lays little emphasis on this. For him, the final cause of the tragic action is its effect on the audience (cf. *Poetics* 1453b3–5), not on the *dramatis personae*, although the latter must certainly face a misfortune for the spectators to be moved.

The followers of Bernays[20] hold that catharsis consists in removing the spectators' excessive emotions, which are inherently undesirable. The best audience for a tragedy will then be composed of people pathologically disposed to feel excessive emotions, i.e., for those interpreters who relate catharsis to the theory of humors, with an excess of black bile. But Aristotle was strongly opposed to such physiological reductionism.[21] More importantly, Bernays' interpretation seems to imply a consequence that Aristotle would certainly reject: that the wise and virtuous do not benefit from the process.

Bernays' view that catharsis is a homoeopathic process has also been criticized. E. Belfiore[22] has argued that the pity and fear aroused by a representation differ from those aroused by real events; the process of catharsis must therefore by allopathic, whereby different emotions drive out the normal ones, rather than homoeopathic, whereby pity and fear drive out pity and fear. But the medical analogies in *Politics* VIII are nothing more than analogies.[23] Moreover, Aristotle regarded the emotions evoked by representations as "likenesses" of the real emotions (1340a18 ff.). Like the translation of the term *catharsis*, the question of allopathy versus homoeopathy is not a central issue: only when we can form a clear picture of Aristotle's theory on other grounds can we establish which of the many connotations of "catharsis" were more important to him, since in his time it could connote medical purgation, religious purification and intellectual clarification.

Catharsis is, as we saw, related to the concept of *mimēsis* itself. Golden[24] has argued that the representation of universal patterns of human action by means of fiction permits us to see those patterns more clearly, leading to a "clarification" (*catharsis*) that operates on a purely intellectual level. He equates the pleasure we gain from tragedy with our cognitive pleasure when we recognize a representation of something as representing that thing (1448b9). But Golden goes too far in denying the importance of the emotions for catharsis. On the other hand, the many scholars who hold that catharsis is a purification or clarification of the emotions, by means of the *mimēsis*,[25] do not go far enough, since they neglect the way that practical wisdom involves feeling appropriate emotions in an appropriate way.[26] Like Plato, Aristotle thought that witnessing representations and having emotional responses to them can have habit-forming effects (*Republic* X 606a–c; *Politics* VIII 1340a14–24). The average Athenian citizen had the opportunity to see at least nine tragedies yearly at the City Dionysia. Because Aristotle puts such a heavy emphasis on our ability to learn from *mimeseis* (including visual images and sketches, 1448b10 ff.), particularly when they arouse strong emotions, there is good reason to suppose that he thought that the experience of tragic catharsis could affect our emotional habits. Hence the end-result of catharsis is to dispose us to feel emotion in the right way, at the right time, towards the right object, with the correct motive, to the proper degree, etc.[27] H. House extended this view to its logical conclusion: he argued that catharsis "brings our emotions nearer to those of a good and wise man," i.e. nearer to virtue, which is the mean between the extremes relative to us.[28]

This approach resolves many difficulties. First, we need not ascribe to Aristotle a Platonizing view of the emotions which he did not hold. Nor should we attribute to him the kind of incoherence within his highly systematizing philosophy which is implied by a failure fully to exploit the *Politics* and *Ethics* in interpreting the *Poetics*. Instead, we obtain a deep and rich account of human psychology,[29] which answers the main criticisms leveled by Plato against literary representation, and draws on many interdependent strands of Aristotle's ethics, psychology, politics and aesthetics.

V

Other ancient sources for Aristotle's doctrine confirm our view of the educative function of catharsis.[30] In his *Commentary on Plato's "Republic"* I (p. 49 Kroll), Proclus states that Aristotle's *On Poets* rebutted Plato's proposal to expel the dramatic and mimetic poets from his ideal state:

> It has been objected that tragedy and comedy are expelled illogically, since by means of these it is possible to satisfy the emotions in due measure [*emmetrōs*] and, by satisfying them, to keep them tractable for education [*paideia*], by treating the discomfort in them. Anyway it was this that gave Aristotle, and the defenders of these genres in his dialogue against Plato [*en tois pros Platōna logois*], most of the grounds for their accusation [sc. against him].

An echo of this same doctrine appears in Iamblichus, *On the Mysteries* I 11:[31]

> The potentialities of the human emotions that are in us become more violent

if they are hemmed in on every side. But if they are briefly put into activity, and brought to the point of due proportion [to symmetron], they give delight in moderation (metriōs), are satisfied and, purified (apokathairomenai) by this means, are stopped by persuasion and not by force. For this reason, by observing others' sufferings (pathē) in both comedy and tragedy, we can check our own emotions (pathē), make them more moderate (metriōtera) and purify them (apokathairomen). So too in holy rites, when we watch and hear shameful things, we are freed from the harm that derives from them in actuality.

Iamblichus does not name Aristotle as his source, but was familiar with some of his other lost dialogues. Both Neoplatonist testimonies confirm several important points about catharsis, for which Iamblichus (but not Proclus) uses the related terminology:

(1) The emotions are not in themselves educated, but are to be kept "tractable for education," i.e. emotional excesses will no longer stand in the way of correct ethical choice.
(2) The emotions are to be led to the point of due proportion, i.e. they will better correspond to the Aristotelian mean between the extremes.
(3) The process involves mimēsis: by watching a representation of others' sufferings/reactions/emotions (pathē can mean all three things), we can attain the catharsis of our own.
(4) Catharsis applies to both tragedy and comedy.
(5) Catharsis is compared to the effect of certain sacred rituals which involved obscenity. Aristotle speaks of such rites in the same context as comedy (Politics 1336b13 ff.); it seems reasonable to suppose he also made this connection in the On Poets.

A third Neoplatonist, Olympiodorus,[32] preserves in his peculiar testimony the Platonic view of the emotions as inherently evil, but gives the same account of the aim of catharsis: "Aristotelian catharsis cures evil with evil, and, by the conflict of opposites, leads to due proportion [symmetria]." (Commentary on Plato's First Alcibiades, p. 54).

Finally, the Tractatus Coislinianus (TC), which I have argued to be a summary of Aristotle's lost Poetics II,[33] concurs:

Tragedy reduces the soul's emotions of ⟨pity and⟩ fear by means of compassion and dread. It wishes to have a due proportion [symmetria] of fear . . . There wishes to be a due proportion [symmetria] of fear in tragedies, and of the laughable in comedies. (TC III, IX)

Although these passages speak of symmetria, the Tractatus uses the term "catharsis" in its definition of comedy (IV).

Previous scholars' uncertainty about the Aristotelianism of these texts, their lack of detail and their tendency to speak of symmetria rather than catharsis explains why they have been neglected. But a new text from Herculaneum reinforces the connection between catharsis and virtue. Herculaneum papyrus 1581 derives from the *On Poems* V of Philodemus, but the opinions expressed in it are clearly not those of the Epicurean philosopher. Although their author's name is not preserved, the language and content point to Aristotle or someone very close to him; their source is probably the *On Poets*.[34]

The opening fragments let us glimpse an argument that a poet represents a complete action, and that in a complete drama there arises, from the representation of fearful and pitiable events happening to others (*allotria*), a "tragic catharsis of pity, i.e. cathartic of pitiable things" (fr. 3). Someone (the poet?) "reveals in the story (*logos*) the catharsis of *hamartiai*" (fr. 4); and mention is made of "spiritedness" (*thymos*) and "correcting an error with a small correction" (fr. 5). We finally reach two fully readable scraps, separated by a sizable lacuna:

> . . . Folly is present in the wisest of souls, and intemperance in the most temperate. Likewise there are fears in brave souls and jealousies in magnanimous ones. One can observe, regarding the [pleasures(?)] of life, that, during sleep [and when one is] in drinking-bouts [and] fevers and [in] emotional states [even the wise can fall into error(??) . . .][35] (fr. 6)

> . . . [We have concluded from] what we have agreed [that] a poet represents a complete action. It must be understood that poetry is useful with regard to virtue, purifying, as we said, the part [*to morion*, i.e. *the related part of the soul?*]. It must be added that every art can become [the origin] of what is best among the things that are in them [i.e. *the arts*] by nature . . . [*two lines lost*] . . . and produces catharsis . . . (fr. 7)

Here we have many elements of our interpretation of catharsis. The representation of universalized patterns of action apparently brings about a "clarification [*catharsis*] of *hamartiai*." The cathartic process can benefit everyone, even the wisest and most temperate of souls; we are all imperfect. Catharsis "purifies" part of the soul, probably its "spirited" part (cf. the reference to *thymos*);[36] hence poetry contributes to virtue. The last fragment presumably went on to say that the purpose of mimetic poetry is to produce catharsis, as one expects from the inclusion of catharsis in the *Poetics*' definition of tragedy. The fragments do not mention "habituation," "education" or *diagōgē*. However, the presence of folly (*aphrosynē*), the opposite of *phronēsis*, in the list of weaknesses common to everybody confirms that catharsis is related to *phronēsis*.

VI

If we are to see how completely Aristotle aimed to rebut Plato's attack on poetry, two further questions must be addressed. These are (1) the range of emotions subject to tragic catharsis, and (2) the functioning of comic catharsis.

Plato criticized mimetic poetry for arousing a whole gamut of emotions, including pity, laughter, lust and indignation (*Republic* X 605d–606d). Although

Aristotle regards pity and fear as the emotions most essential to tragedy, there is evidence that he too thought tragedy (and indeed epic) arouses a wider range of feelings, which can all be the object of catharsis:

(a) Aristotle says tragedy accomplishes "by means of pity and fear the catharsis of such emotions" (1449b27). "Such" (*toioutos*) is in this context as ambiguous in Greek as in English: it may mean "the aforementioned emotions," but can equally well mean "the aforementioned emotions and others like them."

(b) He says that "all [sc. the effects] that have to be produced by speech fall under reasoning [*dianoia*]; these are . . . the production of emotions, e.g. pity, fear, anger etc." If the characters' rhetoric can arouse diverse emotions, so can their actions (1456b1).

(c) He lists pity and fear as emotions aroused by tragedy and epic, specifically by Odysseus' tales in *Odyssey* IX–XII (*Rhetoric* III 1417a12).[37] Now a scholiast on *Iliad* I 1, discussing why Homer begins his epic with the word "wrath," explains that he does this "in order that, as a result of this emotion, the relevant part of the soul may be purified[38] and he may make the hearers more attentive to the bulk [sc. of the poem] and accustom us to endure our *pathē* nobly." The expression "the part," *to morion*, recalls the Herculaneum papyrus (fr. 7). If this opinion goes back to Aristotle's *Homeric Questions*, we can add anger as an emotion subject to catharsis in epic poetry.

(d) Finally, "pity, fear and emotion in general" are the feelings which are aroused in everyone, and given a catharsis, by watching performances in the theater (*Politics* VIII 1342a10 ff.).

Now pity, fear and anger are all emotions accompanied by pain (*lypē*, cf. *Ethics* II 1105b21, *Rhetoric* II 1382a21, 1385b13); the kind of suffering (*pathos* in its other sense) which arouses these emotions is painful. Thus, in Aristotle's view, tragedy and epic arouse, and lead to a catharsis of, painful feelings in general.

VII

With this in mind, let us turn to the emotions associated with comedy, notably laughter. Plato had specified laughter and jokes as the undesirable pleasure in which we indulge when we watch comedies (*Republic* X 606c); he also lists laughter among a whole range of emotions, including anger and fear, at *Philebus* 50a–b. Aristotle thought the emotion aroused by comedy is laughter,[39] because he relates comedy to the nature of the laughable, just as he later relates tragedy to actions which arouse pity and fear (1449a33 ff.):

> Comedy is, as we said, a representation of people who are rather inferior –
> not, however, with respect to every [sc. kind of] vice, but the laughable [*to
> geloion*] is [sc. only] a part of what is ugly. For the laughable is a sort of error

[*hamartēma*] and ugliness that is not painful and destructive, just as, evidently, a laughable mask is something ugly and distorted without pain.

Proclus and Iamblichus indicate that comedy, like tragedy, produces a catharsis (see above, Section VI). But the main evidence is the *Tractatus Coislinianus*, which defines comedy as "accomplishing by means of pleasure and laughter the catharsis of such emotions," as well as saying that comedy aims at "a due proportion of the laughable" (*TC* IV, IX). I have argued[40] that "pleasure" denotes the pleasurable emotions in general, including laughter, just as if Aristotle had said that tragedy achieves a catharsis of "pain and fear," i.e. the painful emotions including fear. In the *Nicomachean Ethics* he lists the emotions as "anger, fear . . . and pity, and generally whatever is accompanied by pleasure or pain," but continues by restating these emotions as "being angry or being *pained* or feeling pity" (my emphasis) (II 1105b21 ff.). We have no right to emend the *Ethics* to remove his shorthand expression for "feel painful emotions."[41] My interpretation entails the unobjectionable proposition that tragedy depends for its effect on painful emotions, comedy on pleasant ones.[42]

The *Nicomachean Ethics* helps to clarify the "catharsis of pleasure and laughter" (IV 1127b34–1128b9) . Aristotle discusses how we may best attain the mean relating to "intellectual entertainment together with play" (*diagōgē meta paidias*, 1127b5). This involves achieving the mean, wit, which is the middle way between the extremes of boorishness and buffoonery (*bōmolochia*):

> Those who go to excess in the laughable are thought to be buffoons and vulgar persons, striving after the laughable by any means and aiming more to arouse laughter than to speak decorously and avoid paining the butt of their jokes. (IV 1128a4–7)

Aristotle concludes his discussion by resuming the three ways of attaining virtue in social behavior. One should aim at the mean (1) between obsequiousness and surliness, (2) between boastfulness (*alazoneia*) and understatement ("irony," *eirōneia*) regarding one's own merits, and (3) between buffoonery and boorishness (1128b5–9):

> The ways which we have mentioned of attaining the mean are three. They all concern social intercourse in words or actions of some kind, but differ in that one of them [sc. boastfulness] relates to truth, the others relate to what is pleasant [*to hēdu*]. Of those relating to pleasure [*hēdonē*], one [sc. buffoonery] is displayed in our amusements [*paidiai*], the other [sc. obsequiousness] in our social contacts in the rest of life.

Here, then, is the explanation of the *Tractatus'* comic catharsis of "pleasure and laughter" – we can attain the mean concerning *to hēdu* or *hēdonē*, by purifying our tendency to excess or deficiency in laughter and amusement. This is confirmed by *TC* XIV, where the characters of comedy are given as "the buffoonish, the ironical and the boasters," traits discussed here in the *Ethics*. Both irony and buffoonery appeared in the "lost" continuation of the *Poetics*.[43]

VIII

These arguments suggest the following conclusions. Tragedy depicts people who are *spoudaioi*, meaning both "good" and "serious." Comedy represents the opposite kind of "inferior" people, *phauloi*, but within them only a subcategory, those who are laughable (*geloioi*); some "inferior" types are so evil that they are not funny. A good tragic plot hinges on a great *hamartia* committed by a *spoudaios*, which leads to a painful or destructive event. Comedy too depends on a *hamartēma* (the word means the same as *hamartia*), but one without painful or destructive results (1449a35). The *mimēsis* of the *hamartia* arouses the appropriate emotion to the proper degree; its catharsis enables us to moderate our own tendency to err in life in respect of that emotion.[44]

Since, in watching tragic dramas, we are watching the sufferings of characters who are only represented, we derive no harm from this experience, as we might from "real" events. Instead, we benefit, because our propensities to diverge from the mean in feeling the emotions are reduced. Moreover, dramatic mimesis leads us to the correct emotional response to the characters' plight via our moral and cognitive judgments about them, since their personalities and actions are vividly represented as universal patterns of action. Our enhanced perceptions can improve our capacity for moral judgment, practical wisdom and virtue. The drama we watch is no evanescent experience. On the contrary, feeling such appropriate emotional reactions can habituate us to achieve and maintain the proper standard in our moral choices, leading toward the mean in emotional terms and hence to practical wisdom and virtue.

The catharsis of the pleasant emotions in comedy offers similar benefits: we learn to laugh at the right objects and to the proper degree. Moreover Aristotle would add, with his usual optimism, that we learn not to laugh at actions which cause excessive pain to others, whereas the buffoon does not mind whether his jokes injure their object.[45] For the mature citizen, both tragedy and comedy are a civilizing force. The pity and fear aroused by watching *Oedipus the King* might lead a timorous man to realize that his own fears are exaggerated, and that his own misfortunes are not so terrible; yet the same play might arouse in a powerful and confident person, prone to feel and behave arrogantly toward others, the thought that even the mightiest ruler may one day need the sympathy and help of those weaker than himself. Similarly, laughing at a comedy might make a real-life buffoon realize how foolish he seems at the dinner-table, but might make a prude relax from his prissiness. All these reactions conduce to the mean.

This theory of catharsis provides a subtle and effective response to Plato. The essential difference between the two lies in Plato's pessimism about the way ordinary people are liable to confuse imitation and reality, mistaking the extreme situations portrayed on the stage for everyday social norms, to be followed in life. Aristotle is more sanguine, believing that people can distinguish representation from reality. He denies that they will naively carry their emotional reactions to representations over into their lives. Far from becoming habituated, as Plato fears (*Republic* X 606a–c), to the emotional weaknesses which drama depicts and evokes, Aristotle's spectators will, through the process of catharsis, come to acquire appropriate emotional reactions.

These contrasting attitudes have very different implications for the relationship between society and the arts. The Platonic legislator would maintain strict control over the content of literature, and would ban Homer, tragedy and comedy from the ideal state; these forms of popular entertainment are too corrupting, not only for the emotionally immature but even for the Guardians.[46] Although the Aristotelian legislator will not control the content of these arts, he must protect the young from their effects (*Politics* VIII 1336b1 ff.). Since he proposes to ban indecent talk which minors might hear, he thinks that the legislator must also forbid them

> to observe either pictures or speeches [*logoi*] that are indecent. Let the authorities take care that no sculpture or painting is a representation of such [sc. indecent] actions, unless in the temples of those gods before whom custom allows even scurrility . . . But as for younger people, they must not be allowed to be spectators of either lampoons or comedy until they attain the age at which they may already share in reclining at supper and getting drunk, and education has made them all immune to the harm arising from such things. (*Politics* VIII 1336b13–24)

Aristotle regards minors as Plato regards the whole populace – immature and impressionable. He might even have endorsed Plato's critique of drama, if it had concerned only the young. But, since he has more faith in education than does Plato, he not only rejects controls over the literary forms available to adults, but also values the emotional and intellectual enlightenment which they can bring; he trusts in the mature and educated judgment of the better class of spectators to discriminate good from bad art, and to award the prizes accordingly. Portrayal of extremes of action is necessary for the adult audience to experience the appropriate emotional reactions to the full; but it may mislead minors who lack enough experience of life to distinguish *mimēsis* from reality.

This passage implies that Aristotle expected comedy to include obscenity and invective. By his own poetic criteria, "the contents of comedy must deviate from the ethical norms of polite social intercourse," since, "if one is to represent morally inferior people, one must (logically) represent them doing and saying morally inferior things."[47] It is striking – and perhaps telling – that Aristotle delayed his account of catharsis to the second book of the *Poetics*, which analyzed the rumbustious comedy of Aristophanes.[48]

Notes

1. *Grundzüge der verlorenen Abhandlung des Aristoteles über Wirkung der Tragödie* (Breslau, 1857), reprinted in *Zwei Abhandlungen über die aristotelische Theorie des Drama* (Berlin, 1880), and trans. in *Articles on Aristotle: 4. Psychology and Aesthetics*, eds. J. Barnes, M. Schofield and R. Sorabji (London, 1979), pp. 154–65.

2. See esp. M. L. Nardelli, "La catarsi poetica nel *P. Herc.* 1581," *Cronache Ercolanesi* **8** (1978) 96–103.

3. A cross-reference in the *Politics* (1341b40) suggests that Aristotle's main discussion of catharsis was in *Poetics* Book II; there was another account in the dialogue *On Poets*, a work more widely read than were the lecture-notes which comprise the *Poetics*. Cf. G. F. Else, *Aristotle's Poetics: the Argument* (Cambridge, MA, 1957), p. 337n. For annotated translations of the fragments see R. Janko, *Aristotle: Poetics* (Indianapolis, 1987), pp. 56–65, 175–195; R. Laurenti, *Aristotele: I Frammenti dei Dialoghi* (Naples, 1987), pp. 211–300.

4. So J. M. Redfield, *Nature and Culture in the* Iliad (Chicago, 1975), p. 68.

5. For defenses of Plato's position see Alister Cameron, *Plato's Affair with Tragedy* (Cincinnati, 1978); J. A. Elias, *Plato's Defense of Poetry* (Albany, 1984); A. Nehamas, "Plato and the mass media," *The Monist* **71** (1988) 214–234. See further J. Moravcsik and P. Temko (eds), *Plato on Beauty, Wisdom and the Arts* (Totowa, 1982); G. F. Else, *Plato and Aristotle on Poetry* (Chapel Hill, 1986), pp. 3–64. Aristotle makes no direct criticism of Plato in the *Poetics*, since all his students would recognize the *Tendenz* of his lectures, but named him explicitly in *On Poets* fr. 72–73 Rose (cf. M. W. Haslam, "Plato, Sophron and the dramatic dialogue," *Bulletin of the Institute of Classical Studies* **19** (1972) 17–38).

6. So G. F. Else, *The Structure and Date of Book 10 of Plato's* Republic, *Abhandlungen der Heidelberger Akademie der Wissenschaften* (Phil.-Hist. Klasse 1972), Abh. 3, pp. 53 f.; idem, *Plato and Aristotle on Poetry*, pp. 69 f.

7. Bernays (see n.1).

8. See W. W. Fortenbaugh, *Aristotle on Emotion* (London, 1975); L. A. Kosman, "Being Properly Affected: Virtues and Feelings in Aristotle's Ethics," in *Essays on Aristotle's Ethics*, ed. A. O. Rorty (Berkeley and Los Angeles, 1980), pp. 103–116.

9. See M. F. Burnyeat, "Aristotle on Learning to be Good," in Rorty (ed.), *Essays on Aristotle's Ethics*, pp. 69–92; cf. R. Sorabji, "Aristotle on the Role of Intellect in Virtue," in Rorty (ed.), *Essays on Aristotle's Ethics*, pp. 201–219, esp. 214 ff.; N. Sherman, *Aristotle's Theory of Moral Education* (Diss. Harvard, 1982), esp. pp. 102–151.

10. See A. O. Rorty, "Akrasia and Pleasure," in Rorty (ed.), *Essays on Aristotle's Ethics*, pp. 267–284.

11. The relevance to catharsis of this neglected passage was shown by C. Lord, *Education and Culture in the Political Thought of Aristotle* (Ithaca, 1982), pp. 82–89, and Sherman, *Aristotle's Theory of Moral Education*, pp. 162 f.; cf. A. Rostagni, "Aristotele e Aristotelismo nell'estetica antica," *Studi Italiani di Filologia Classica* II (1922) 1–147, esp. 43–53 (reprinted in his *Scritti Minori* I: *Aesthetica* (Turin, 1955), pp. 76–237); Janko, *Aristotle's Poetics*, pp. 58, 181 f.

12. Lord, *Education and Culture*, pp. 85–89.

13. On *diagōgē* see A. E. J. Schendler, *An Aristotelian Theory of Comedy* (Diss. Michigan, 1954), pp. 84–97; Lord, *Education and Culture*, pp. 75–85; C. Wagner, '"Katharsis" in der aristotelischen Tragödiendefinition," *Grazer Beiträge* **11** (1984) 67–87, esp. 79–81; and S. G. Salkever, "Tragedy and the Education of the *Dēmos*: Aristotle's response to Plato," in *Greek Tragedy and Political Theory*, ed. J. P. Euben (Berkeley and Los Angeles, 1986), pp. 274–303, esp. p. 286.

14. Since scholars have not understood that the first half of this sentence deals with the "songs relating to action," many have accepted Sauppe's emendation of *kathartika* to *praktika* at 1342a15, which forces into the text the reference of these songs which is rightly felt to be needed. Lord lists the scholars who have adopted or rejected this emendation (*Education and Culture*, p. 132, n.49), rightly dismissing it himself, as did Rostagni (*Scritti Minori* I: *Aesthetica*, p. 54).

15. Cf. above, n.13.
16. Cf. Lord, *Education and Culture*, pp. 102–104, and Salkever, in Euben (ed.), *Greek Tragedy and Political Theory*. Schendler, *An Aristotelian Theory of Comedy*, pp. 97–118, implausibly argues that catharsis is the aim of tragedy, *diagōgē* that of comedy.
17. For surveys of older work on catharsis see the references in Else, *Aristotle's Poetics*, p. 225, n.14; for more recent work see P. Somville, *Essai sur la Poétique d'Aristote* (Paris, 1975), pp. 78–95; L. Golden, "The Clarification Theory of Catharsis," *Hermes* **104** (1976) 437–452; D. Keesey, "On some recent interpretations of Catharsis," *Classical World* **72** (1979) 193–205; D. E. White, *A Source Book on the Catharsis Controversy* (Diss. Florida State University, Tallahassee, 1984); S. Halliwell, *Aristotle's Poetics* (London, 1986), pp. 350–356.
18. So Else, *Aristotle's Poetics*, pp. 224–232, 423–447; H. D. F. Kitto, "Catharsis," in *The Classical Tradition: Literary and Historical Studies in Honor of Harry Caplan*, ed. L. Wallach (Ithaca, 1966), pp. 133–147. Cf. too H. D. Goldstein, "Mimesis and Catharsis Reëxamined," *Journal of Aesthetics and Art Criticism* **25** (1966) 567–577.
19. So D. Keesey, *Classical World* **72** (1979) 193–205; J. P. Anton, "Mythos, Katharsis and the Paradox of Tragedy," *Proceedings of the Boston Area Colloquium in Ancient Philosophy* **1** (1985) 299–326; and eventually Else himself, in *Plato and Aristotle on Poetry*, pp. 158–162, esp. 161 f.
20. Bernays' view (above, n.1) was anticipated by H. Weil, "Ueber die Wirkung der Tragödie nach Aristoteles," *Verhandlungen der 10. Versammlung deutscher Philologen und Schulmänner in Basel 1847* (Basel, 1848), pp. 131–140. He is followed by, e.g., D. W. Lucas, *Aristotle: Poetics* (Oxford, 1968), pp. 273–290; C. Gallavotti, *Aristotele, Dell'arte poetica* (Verona, 1974), pp. 230 ff.; E. Flores, "La catarsi aristotelica dalla *Politica* alla *Poetica*," in *Poetica e Politica fra Platone e Aristotele, Annali dell'Istituto Universitario Orientale di Napoli*, Sezione Filologica-Letteraria **6** (1984), pp. 37–49.
21. Cf. M. Nussbaum, *The Fragility of Goodness* (Cambridge, 1986), pp. 264–289, 502 n.17.
22. E. Belfiore, "Pleasure, Tragedy and Aristotelian Psychology," *Classical Quarterly* **35** (1985) 349–361; "Wine and *catharsis* of the emotions in Plato's *Laws*," *Classical Quarterly* **36** (1986) 421–437, esp. 432 ff. For another attack on the idea of homoeopathy, see J. Lear, "Katharsis," *Phronesis* **33** (1988) 297–326, esp. 301.
23. Cf. M. Nussbaum, "Therapeutic arguments: Epicurus and Aristotle," in *The Norms of Nature: Studies in Hellenistic Ethics*, eds. M. Schofield and G. Striker (Cambridge and Paris, 1986), pp. 31–74, esp. pp. 53 ff.
24. L. Golden, "Catharsis," *Transactions and Proceedings of the American Philological Association* **93** (1962) 51–60; (with O. B. Hardison), *Aristotle's Poetics* (Englewood Cliffs, 1968), pp. 114–120; "Mimesis and katharsis," *Classical Philology* **64** (1969) 145–153; "Katharsis as Clarification: An Objection Answered," *Classical Quarterly* **23** (1973) 45 f.; "The Purgation Theory of Catharsis," *Journal of Aesthetics and Art Criticism* **31** (1973) 473–479; "The Clarification Theory of Catharsis," *Hermes* **104** (1976) 437–452; "Aristotle on Comedy," *Journal of Aesthetics and Art Criticism* **42** (1984) 286–298. S. G. Salkever in Euben (ed.), *Greek Tragedy and Political Theory*, simply equates the effect of tragedy with the sort of *catharsis* of false opinions provided by dialectic in Plato's *Sophist* 230b–d. On the *Sophist* see also Wagner, *Grazer Beiträge* **11** (1984) 75.
25. Cf. P. Somville, *Essai sur la Poétique d'Aristote*, pp. 92 ff.; idem, "Katharsis et ésthétique chez Aristote," *L'Antiquité classique* **40** (1971) 607–622; Redfield, *Nature and Culture in the* Iliad, pp. 52–68; R. Dupont-Roc and J. Lallot, *Aristote: La Poétique* (Paris, 1980), pp. 188–193; Belfiore, *Classical Quarterly* **35** (1985) 349–361 and **36**, 421–437; Lear, *Phronesis* **33** (1988) 297–326.
26. The view that poetry conduces to virtue was widespread in antiquity. The brilliant

reconstruction by D. Delattre of Philodemus, *On Music* IV (*Cronache Ercolanesi* **19** (1989) 49–143) shows that the Stoic Diogenes of Babylon adapted to his own purposes Aristotle's whole theory of catharsis as reconstructed here; see further R. Janko, "A first join between *P. Herc.* 411 and 1583 (Philodemus, *On Music* IV)," forthcoming in *Cronache Ercolanesi* **2** (1992).

27. Cf. (in order of date) Rostagni, *Scritti Minori* pp. 123 ff.; H. House, *Aristotle's Poetics: A Course of Eight Lectures* (London, 1956), pp. 105–112; Lord, *Aristotle's Theory of Moral Education*; Sherman, *Education and Culture*; I. Smithson, "The Moral View of Aristotle's *Poetics*," *Journal of the History of Ideas* **44** (1983) 3–17; A. Paskow, "What is Aesthetic Catharsis?," *Journal of Aesthetics and Art Criticism* **42** (1983) 59–68, substantially repeated in "A Meditation on Aristotle's Concept of *Catharsis*," in *Philosophy and Culture: Proceedings of the XVIIIth World Congress of Philosophy* (Montreal, 1988), III, pp. 709–714; R. Janko, *Aristotle on Comedy* (London and Berkeley, 1984), pp. 139–151; idem, *Aristotle: Poetics*, pp. xvi–xx, 181–190; Wagner, "Katharsis"; Nussbaum, *The Fragility of Goodness*, pp. 378–391; Halliwell, *Aristotle's Poetics*, pp. 184–200, 350–356; P. Simpson, "Aristotle on Poetry and Imitation," *Hermes* **116** (1988) 279–281; D. J. Depew, "Politics, Music and Contemplation in Aristotle's Ideal State," in *Aristotle's Politics: A Cultural Reader*, eds. F. D. Miller and D. Keyt (Oxford, 1991). For pre-Bernaysian holders of this view see Halliwell, *Aristotle's Poetics*, pp. 352 f.; for a recent critique of it see Lear, *Phronesis* **33** (1988) 297–326.

28. House, *Aristotle's Poetics*, pp. 112 f.; cf. Smithson, *Journal of the History of Ideas* **44** (1983) 17; Janko, *Aristotle's Poetics*, pp. xviii–xx; Laurenti, *Aristotele: I frammenti dei Dialoghi*, pp. 266–268. The connection is understood by Halliwell, *Aristotle's Poetics*, pp. 352 f., but is not made explicit in his main account of catharsis.

29. The striking parallels with modern cognitive psychology merit deeper investigation. For starting points see Belfiore, *Classical Quarterly* **35** (1985) 358, n.26.

30. For more extensive commentary on the relevant passages see Janko, *Aristotle: Poetics*, pp. 186–90; Laurenti, *Aristotele: I frammenti dei Dialoghi*, pp. 264–268.

31. Both passages are wrongly included among the fragments of the *Poetics* by R. Kassel, *Aristotelis De Arte Poetica* (Oxford, 1965), p. 52 (he omits Iamblichus' last sentence). They are both dismissed by Lord, *Education and Culture*, pp. 176 f., apparently because they agree with the *Tractatus Coislinianus*! Lord assigns this theory to the Neoplatonists, but it is already parodied by Lucian, *Vera Historia* I 1 (cf. Janko, *Aristotle on Comedy*, 148).

32. Cf. A. Ničev, *L'Enigme de la catharsis tragique dans Aristote* (Sofia, 1970); "Olympiodore et la catharsis tragique d'Aristote," in *Studi in Onore di A. Ardizzoni* (Rome, 1978), pp. 641–659; *La Catharsis tragique d'Aristote* (Sofia, 1982). See also Lord, *Education and Culture*, pp. 164 f., and Janko, *Aristotle on Comedy*, p. 147. Ničev's own interpretation of catharsis is an unacceptable variant of the theory that it means intellectual clarification (cf. the critique by Halliwell, *Aristotle's Poetics*, p. 355).

33. *Aristotle on Comedy*, with the comments of J. Barnes, *Phronesis* **20** (1985) 103–106. Not the least of the ironies surrounding my book on the *Tractatus* was the simultaneous publication of an article by V. Janković, "Tractatus Coislinianus," *Živa Antika* **34** (1984) 87–94, arguing (in Serbian) that the question ought to be reopened. Nonetheless, the importance of the *Tractatus* is often disparaged. M. Heath, while "willing to believe that the *Tractatus* descends from an epitome of *Poetics* II", dismisses it as "an obscure and contentious little document" ("Aristotelian Comedy," *Classical Quarterly* **39** (1989) 344–354, esp. 344). The sheer difficulty of this epitome is no reason to neglect it.

34. Nardelli, *Cronache Ercolanesi* **8** (1978) 96, n.4, shows that the doctrines are those of Aristotle, not Theophrastus, but does not suggest from which work they derive. She

assigns the text to *On poems* Book IV (p. 99), but see R. Janko, "Philodemus' *On Poems and Aristotle's *On Poets*,*" Section VI, forthcoming in *Cronache Ercolanesi* **21** (1991). For the numeration and sequence of the fragments see Janko, *Aristotle: Poetics*, p. 187. The moral elements in the theory led D. F. Sutton to assign it not to Aristotle, but to a successor who turned Aristotle's (Bernaysian) tragic catharsis into "a moralizing defence of poetry" ("*P. Herc.* 1581: the Argument," *Philosophia: Epetēris tou Kentrou Ereunēs tēs Philosophias Athēnōn* **12** (1982) 270–276).

35. For this last point cf. *NE* I 1102b4, VII 1151a1 ff. and further parallels in Nardelli, *Cronache Ercolanesi* **8** (1978) 102.

36. Cf. Lord, *Education and Culture*, pp. 160–164, who argues that the emotions affected by tragic catharsis are those associated with the spirited part of the soul. P. A. Vander Waerdt develops this point, showing that the harnessing of citizens' *thymos* (which results in a desire to rule) is a major question in Aristotle's *Politics*, and that intelligent and thymoeidetic citizens may find the locus of their happiness in the leisured enjoyment of music, poetry and the arts ("Kingship and Philosophy in Aristotle's Best Regime," *Phronesis* **30** (1985) 249–273, esp. 258–260).

37. The terms used are *oiktos* and *deinōsis*, but these are synonymous with *eleos* and *phobos* (Janko, *Aristotle on Comedy*, pp. 136 f.).

38. *Hin' ek tou pathous apokathareusēi to toiouto morion tēs psuchēs* (schol. ADT). H. Erbse reads *apokatarreusēi* with schol. AT, but the verb is paralleled (*Scholia Graeca in Homeri Iliadem* I (Berlin, 1969), p. 3). The bT scholia ascribe part of the same opinion to Zenodotus (ibid., p. 4).

39. *Contra*: Halliwell, *Aristotle's Poetics*, p. 275, n.1, and in G. A. Kennedy (ed.), *The Cambridge History of Literary Criticism*. I: *Classical Criticism* (Cambridge, 1989), pp. 182 f. But at 1453b5 Aristotle speaks of tragedy as arousing "shivering and pity," referring to a *physical* symptom of fear. On the cathartic function of comic laughter see Lane Cooper, *An Aristotelian Theory of Comedy* (New York, 1922), pp. 60–76; Schendler, *An Aristotelian Theory of Comedy*, pp. 97–118; D. F. Sutton, *Self and Society in Aristophanes* (Washington DC, 1980), pp. 69–79.

40. *Aristotle on Comedy*, pp. 156–160. *Contra*: D. Lanza, "La Simmetria impossibile," in *Filologia e Forme Letterarie: Studi offerti a Francesco della Corte* V (Urbino, 1987), pp. 65–80, esp. pp. 67 f.; L. Golden, "Aristotle on the Pleasure of Comedy," (this volume).

41. Among others T. H. Irwin, *Aristotle: Nicomachean Ethics* (Indianapolis, 1985), p. xxiii, reads *phobēthēnai* for the manuscripts' *lupēthēnai*, the *lectio difficilior*, which is printed by I. Bywater in his Oxford Classical Text (Oxford, 1894).

42. Cf. Janko, *Aristotle on Comedy*, pp. 150, 160 f., on *TC* III–IV. Plato, perhaps already responding to Aristotle, seeks to complicate this by seeing a mixture of pleasure and pain in comedy, in that we are pleased at others' pains (*Philebus* 50b–c); on this see M. Mader, *Das Problem des Lachens und der Komödie bei Platon* (Stuttgart, 1977), and C. Hampton, *Pleasure, Knowledge and Being* (Albany, 1990), pp. 64–67. Some who dispute the value of the *Tractatus* suggest that Aristotle held this Platonic theory (e.g. Halliwell, in *Classical Criticism*, p. 182 f.). Aristotle might well have approved of it as an explanation of why we enjoy invective, but could not have applied it to comedy as he defines that genre at *Poetics* 1449a33 ff. Golden, "Aristotle on the Pleasure of Comedy" (this volume), identifies righteous indignation as the emotion aroused by comedy, but, since this is a painful emotion (*Rhetoric* II 1386b9–11), it is incompatible with the requirement that the laughable in comedy exclude pain and destruction (*Poetics* 1449a32–7).

43. See *Rhetoric* III 1419b2 ff. with Janko, *Aristotle on Comedy* pp. 216 f.

44. Lucas, *Aristotle: Poetics* pp. 288 f., proposed that comic catharsis, especially in the Old Comedy of Aristophanes, worked by means of "the imaginary suspension of many among those restraints and restriction which make civilized life possible," comparing

the testimony of Iamblichus. But he rejected this because the emotions purified by comedy are common to everyone, whereas only a few benefit from enthusiastic music; and because, on this theory, the emotions aroused by the representation are undesirable ones in the case of pity and fear. Lucas' ascription to Aristotle of a Platonic view of the emotions prevented him from developing his insight.

45. This was Plato's complaint against comedy at *Philebus* 48a–50e.

46. Nehamas, *The Monist* **71** (1988) 214–234, suggests that, in Athenian society, poetry held the same place as does television in ours; Plato's views are closely comparable to those of modern critics of the mass media. He indicates that the proper response to the critics of television is to follow Aristotle: to classify and explain the different genres of programs.

47. M. Heath, *Classical Quarterly* **39** (1989) 344–354, esp. 345. In *Aristotle on Comedy*, pp. 204–206, I represented Aristotle as concerned to ban indecent speech generally, overlooking the importance of the exemption which he grants to comedy and iambus. My error was to assimilate his thought too closely to Plato's.

48. As Heath remarks (*Classical Quarterly* **39** (1989) 353f), his argument discredits the frequent claim that Aristotle could not have approved of Aristophanic comedy, despite *Poetics* 1448a25–28, where he names Sophocles, Homer and Aristophanes as if they were the best exponents of the three major genres he intends to discuss (cf. Janko, *Aristotle on Comedy*, p. 249, versus Halliwell, *Aristotle's Poetics*, p. 273 and n.30). The *Tractatus*, of course, uses Aristophanes as the basis of its analysis of comedy.

Aristotle and Iphigenia

Elizabeth Belfiore

In Chapter 14 of the *Poetics*, Aristotle writes that the best kind of tragedy is exemplified by Euripides' *Iphigenia in Tauris* (*IT*): "the best is the last; I mean for example in the *Kresphontes* Merope is about to kill her son, but she recognizes him and does not kill him, and in the *Iphigenia* sister [is about to kill] brother . . ." (1454a4–7).[1] Few modern readers have agreed with Aristotle about the superiority of this tragedy. In the view of most scholars, the *IT* is either an inferior tragedy, or it is not really a tragedy at all. H. D. F. Kitto calls the *IT* a "romantic melodrama," a kind of drama in which the emotions are "lightly engaged," and in which there is no "tragic theme" or "intellectual profundity."[2] M. Platnaur, ignoring Aristotle, remarks that the *Iphigenia* "has never been ranked as among its author's greatest plays," and that it "is not a tragedy at all."[3] Bernard Knox sees the *IT* plot type as the ancestor of Western melodrama, in which we have "not tragic catastrophe but hairsbreadth escape from it."[4] T. B. L. Webster says that this play is "light-hearted,"[5] and according to Anne Burnett[6] and Dana Sutton, it closely resembles the comic satire play.

Why are modern evaluations of Euripides' play so radically different from that of Aristotle? The question is an important one, especially since we cannot dismiss Aristotle's admiration for the *IT* as mere individual eccentricity. Because Aristotle's preference for the dramatic type modern readers tend to scorn as "melodrama" appears to have been shared by Greek playwrights and audiences,[7] a study of Aristotle's reasons for preferring the *IT* can tell us much about Greek tragedy as a whole, as well as about the philosopher's own views. In attempting to see Euripides' *IT* through Aristotle's eyes, this essay begins by examining some modern assumptions about tragedy that can lead us to focus on very different aspects of the *IT* from those that were of central importance for Aristotle. These differences in perspective mean, in effect, that our *IT* is not the same play as Aristotle's. After a brief discussion of Aristotle's theory of the tragic plot in general, and his comments in the *Poetics* that are directly applicable to the *IT* plot in particular, I conclude with an analysis of Euripides' play according to Aristotelian criteria. On an Aristotelian reading, I argue, the *IT* is a better-constructed, more serious, and more "tragic" play than modern scholars often believe.

Some of the differences between our *IT* and Aristotle's are strikingly apparent in modern studies comparing Euripides' *IT* with his *Helen*. It is a commonplace in modern criticism that the structures of these two plays are nearly identical. Henri Grégoire, for example, calls them "twins," and remarks that "one can make a résumé of one of these tragedies that is perfectly suited to the other."[8] In both plays, according to Grégoire:

> A Greek princess, belonging to the illustrious house of the Artrides, is kept against her will, far from the Hellenic land, by a barbarian king who slaughters all the strangers who reach his domain. The sorrow of the unfortunate woman is at its peak when she acquires the certainty that the man she loves most has perished. Suddenly this man is before her . . . After a touching recognition, both people examine their chances for escaping together. The woman, who shows herself to be the more ingenious, devises a ruse that succeeds beautifully: the Barbarian, tricked by the Greek woman, consents and agrees willingly to the execution of this plan. Pretending that she has the greatest zeal for the interests of the monarch, and alleging as a pretext certain rites that can only be celebrated in the sea, the princess goes away with her accomplice and an escort furnished by the king himself. The two Greeks are aided by some compatriots, who were waiting for them, hidden in an irregularity of the coastline. The king's people at last discover the betrayal; one of them runs to alert his master, who orders all-out pursuit of the fugitives. But a divinity appears, who orders the king to submit, and to respect the power of destiny and the will of the gods.[9]

Aristotle would certainly not have agreed that this résumé is "perfectly suited" to the *IT*, for his own plot outline of this play is very different. In *Poetics* 17, Aristotle summarizes the "universal" (1455b2–3) of "the Iphigenia," that is, the plot common to Euripides' and Polyidos' versions of the story:

> A certain girl after being sacrificed and disappearing from the view of those sacrificing her was settled in another land where the custom was to sacrifice strangers to the goddess, and she came to hold that priesthood. A while later, it happened that the brother of the priestess arrived. The fact that the oracle commanded him to go there, for some reason that is outside the universal, and his purpose [in going], are outside the plot.[10] He arrived, was seized, and when about to be sacrificed, he made himself known, either as Euripides or as Polyidos wrote it, saying, as was plausible, that not only his sister but himself also had to be sacrificed. Thence is salvation. (1455b3–12)

It is obvious from these two plot outlines that Grégoire's *IT* is not at all the same as Aristotle's. In fact, if we did not know that both are based on the same play, we would not be likely to guess that this is so. Among the many differences, a few are especially significant. Aristotle notes the relationship between

Iphigenia and Orestes, and he writes that recognition prevents brother from being sacrificed by sister. He explicitly excludes divine intervention (the oracle) from the plot, and he omits entirely the "intrigue," the means by which brother and sister escape, concluding, in three words: "thence is salvation." This "intrigue" is not part of the plot, but only an episode, for, immediately after the plot outline just quoted, Aristotle goes on to write: "After this, having set down the names [the poet should] 'episodize.' The episodes should be appropriate, as is, for example, in the case of Orestes, the madness by means of which he was captured, and the salvation by means of the purification" (1455b12–15). Grégoire, on the other hand, does not mention any relationship between "the princess" and "the man she loves most." Nor does he note that in the *IT*, but not in the *Helen*, relative is about to kill relative. Most of Grégoire's outline concerns the "intrigue" omitted by Aristotle, and he pays particular attention to the final *deux ex machina*, which is also not part of Aristotle's outline.

Grégoire is typical of modern scholars in emphasizing "intrigue" and neglecting aspects of the *IT* plot that most concern Aristotle. Other scholars who compare the *IT* with the *Helen* also fail to note that the threat of kin murder in the *IT* distinguishes this plot from that of the *Helen*, or they mention this difference between the two plays only in passing.[11] Seen from their point of view, the *IT* plot does not, indeed, differ essentially from that of the *Helen*: both are "intrigue plays."[12] Aristotle, on the other hand, focuses on kin murder and recognition, while ignoring "intrigue." Seen from his point of view, the threat of kin murder in the *IT* sharply distinguishes this play from the *Helen*, in which there is no such threat. According to Aristotle, the *IT* is one of the best tragedies because in it, sister is about to kill brother, recognizes him and does not do so (*Poetics* 14.1454a4–7, quoted at the beginning of this essay). Because there is no danger of kin harming kin in the *Helen*, this play would be, by Aristotelian standards, a very poor tragedy.[13]

These different points of view, ancient and modern, are bound up with very different concepts of tragedy. While Aristotle believes plot to be of central importance in tragedy, modern concerns instead center on characterization and psychology.

Aristotle admires plays like the *IT* because they have excellent plots. He defines tragedy as "imitation of action" (*Poetics* 6.1449b24), and states that the plot (*muthos*) is the imitation of action (1450a3–4). A plot is a formal structure, a "composition of events" (1450a4–5), having a beginning, middle, and end (*Poetics* 7.1450b21–31), and proceeding, according to probability or necessity, from good to bad, or from bad to good fortune (7.1451a13–15). A good Aristotelian tragedy also has "character" (*ēthos*), a part of tragedy something like our "characterization." Character is what gives people in the play certain ethical qualities (6.1450a19), and "shows what kind of choice someone makes" (6.1450b8–9; cf. 15.1454a17–19). In Aristotle's view, however, character is strictly secondary to plot, which alone is essential to tragedy: "Without action there could be no tragedy; without character there could be" (6.1450a23–25).

The plot is "the first principle and as it were the soul of tragedy; character is second" (6.1450a38–39). This concern with plot leads Aristotle, in giving his outline of the Iphigenia plot, to concentrate on the major events that forward the movement of the action from bad to good fortune: the arrival and capture of Orestes, the threat of kin murder, recognition, and salvation.

Grégoire's résumé, on the other hand, shows that his main concern, like that of moderns generally, is with psychology and character. He mentions the princess' "sorrow" and "the man she loves most"; he states that she is "ingenious," and "devises a ruse" that tricks her enemy, "pretending" to have his interests at heart. For Grégoire, the character of Iphigenia, and in particular, her cleverness and ability to trick and deceive, is of most interest in this play. This one reason why he concentrates on the "intrigue," in which her clever character is most clearly revealed.[14]

Another example can help us see more clearly the difference between Aristotle's plot-centered view of tragedy and modern psychologically oriented expectations. In *Poetics* 17, just after the plot summary quoted above, Aristotle gives a similar outline of the story (*logos*) of the *Odyssey*, that is, its plot:

> The story of the *Odyssey* is not long. A certain man is away from home for many years, carefully watched by Poseidon and alone. Moreover, things at home are in such a state that his possessions are wasted by the suitors and his son is plotted against. He himself arrives, storm-tossed, and making himself recognized by some, attacks and is himself saved while he destroys his enemies. This is what is proper [to the story]; the rest is episode. (1455b16–23)

This outline carefully excludes all the psychological aspects of Homer's poem that modern readers often find most interesting: "the man of many ways" who encounters the cities and minds of many people, and who suffers many pains as he strives to reach home (*Odyssey* I.1–5). Instead, Aristotle focuses only on the main events that forward the progress of the action from bad to good fortune: Odysseus' return home, the recognitions, his punishment of the suitors.

Before we laugh at Aristotle's simple-minded account of the story of the man of many ways, however, we would do well to reexamine our own prejudices. John Stuart Mill wrote that "story-telling" is most honored by societies "in a rude state," and by "rude minds."[15] The same bias, somewhat less crudely expressed, is found in Otto Brendel, who notes, without further discussion: "Implicit in the modern reaction [to the *IT*] is the axiom that a good drama should do more than tell a story, however exciting."[16] This modern prejudice against plot goes along with the assumption that tragedy is centrally concerned with character: with the individual as a psychological entity that wills and desires, strives and fails. For example, D. D. Raphael writes that tragedy represents "a conflict between inevitable power, which we may call necessity, and the reaction to necessity of self-conscious effort."[17] According to William Chase Greene, "The greatest Greek drama . . . rests on the interplay between fate and character, between what man cannot change and what remains within his power."[18] And, in Martha Nussbaum's view: "The great tragic plots explore the gap between our goodness and our good living, between what we are (our character, intentions, aspirations, values) and how humanly well we manage to live."[19]

This character-centered view has important consequences for studies of Greek tragedy, and for interpretations of the *Poetics*. For one thing, it often leads scholars to attempt to find a psychological realism in Greek tragedy that the dramatic conventions of this genre did not allow and that the extant plays do not display. The inappropriateness of the view that characters in Greek drama are psychological entities much like their real-life counterparts is now widely recognized, as scholars from Tycho von Wilamowitz to Thomas Rosenmeyer have argued against the idea of "a constant dramatic personality existing independently of the sequence of scenes in which the playwright develops the action."[20]

Another consequence of the modern character-centered view of tragedy, however, is less well understood. This is the tendency of many modern scholars to incorporate character into plot. R. S. Crane explicitly argues for the integration of plot and character when he states that we should see plot as a "particular temporal synthesis . . . of the elements of action, character, and thought."[21] This view of plot and character may well be appropriate to a study of the modern novel, Crane's primary concern. It is, however, a serious mistake to attribute this view to Aristotle, as do many scholars. This is what John Jones, for example, appears to do when he writes that in the *Poetics* Aristotle has a concept of "characterful action," in which "the human self is present in its acts."[22] Stephen Halliwell also appears to confuse the Aristotelian distinction between character and plot when he writes that the *Poetics* has an "agent-centred perspective."[23] Halliwell's statement that "we must be able to identify it [sc. Aristotelian character] as a specific dimension of the action" is quoted with approval by Simon Goldhill.[24] This "agent-centred perspective," however, is modern rather than Aristotelian.[25]

To a great extent, it is this modern bias in favor of character and against plot that is responsible for negative evaluations of Euripides' *IT*. There is no significant conflict between characters,[26] or within a single character,[27] or between the characters and fate: indeed, the play ends happily. Iphigenia and Orestes are not torn and twisted; they make no agonizing decisions; they engage in little questioning of the human and divine order; they are not long deluded. Because Euripides' play frustrates modern expectations about what tragedy should be, scholars tend to view it as something other than a tragedy. To understand Aristotle's admiration for the *IT*, then, we must make a conscious effort to see it from his plot-centered point of view.

A brief study of Aristotle's theory of the tragic plot in general is an essential preliminary to an analysis of his views on the *IT* plot in particular.[28] As we have seen, plot, imitation of action, is, according to Aristotle, "the first principle and as it were the soul of tragedy" (6.1450a38–39). To create a good tragedy, then, one that arouses pity and fear (6.1449b27), the poet must create a good plot. Such a plot need not be "tragic" in the modern sense, for a good tragedy may end in either bad or good fortune (7.1451a13–14). What is essential, in Aristotle's view, is that the plot have certain formal properties, and that it deal with certain important subjects.

The most important rule for plot construction, according to Aristotle, is that events should proceed "according to probability or necessity" (*kata to eikos ē to anagkaion*).[29] Poetry is "more philosophical and more serious than history" because it states "the universal," that is, "what kinds of things a certain kind of person says or does according to probability or necessity" (9.1451b5–9). This principle of probability or necessity governs the plot as a whole. A good tragic plot represents a change from good to bad fortune, or from bad to good fortune, in which events succeed one another according to probability or necessity (7.1451a12–14). Such a plot proceeds from beginning, to middle, to end according to this principle:

> The beginning is that which is not itself after something else by necessity, but after it something else is or comes to be by nature. The end, on the contrary, is that which is itself after something else by nature, either by necessity or for the most part, but after this there is nothing else. The middle is that which is itself after something else, and after it there is something else [by necessity, or for the most part]. (*Poetics* 7.1450b27–31).[30]

The principle of probability or necessity also governs the individual parts of the plot. The most important of the events that make up the tragic plot, or "composition of the events," are the three "parts of the plot": *pathos*, recognition, and reversal (11.1452b9–13). These three parts of the plot contribute to its function by arousing pity and fear (see, e.g., 11.1452a38–b1, 14.1453b14–22). Every tragedy, simple and complex, has a *pathos*, defined as "a destructive or painful action" (11.1452b11–12). In addition to a *pathos*, the best plots, the complex, also have recognition, reversal, or both (*Poetics* 10, with 13.1452b30–32). Aristotle defines "reversal" (*peripeteia*) as "the change to the opposite of the things done" (11.1452a22–23).[31] That is, reversal occurs when the action changes direction, and goes towards good fortune when it had been heading towards bad, or towards bad fortune when it had been going towards good fortune. Aristotle defines "recognition" in Chapter 11: "Recognition, just as the word also indicates, is a change from ignorance to knowledge, either to *philia* [kinship] or to enmity, of those defined with respect to good or bad fortune" (1452a29–32). Aristotelian recognition is not simply a mental state in which one comes to acquire knowledge. Because it is a part of the plot, it is an actual event affecting the movement of the action between good and bad fortune. Recognition, like reversal, results in good or bad fortune, and arouses pity and fear for this reason (1452a38–b3). Aristotle explicitly states that recognition and reversal should occur according to the principle of probability or necessity at

10.1452a18–21, and at 11.1452a23–24. While the *pathos* is not explicitly said to follow this principle, it must clearly do so, since it is one of the three parts of a plot (11.1452b10) that is itself constructed according to this principle.

When recognition and reversal occur together, as they do in the best plots, this point in the play is its structural and emotional focal point, marking the beginning of the change from good to bad (or from bad to good) fortune. Aristotle calls attention to this focal point in Chapter 18, where he says that every tragedy has two sections, a complication and a solution: "By 'complication' I mean the [tragedy] from the beginning until the last part from which it changes to good or bad fortune. By 'solution' I mean the [tragedy] from the beginning of the change until the end" (1455b26–29). The complication often includes some of the action represented on stage (1455b25). In the Iphigenia story, for example, Orestes' arrival, capture, and his being about to be sacrificed are part of the complication. The complication also includes the "things done before" (*ta prope-pragmena*: b30), and thus "outside" (b25) the stage action, that are nevertheless essential to the plot.[32] These events outside the stage action are a part of the beginning, because other events follow them according to probability or necessity. For example, in the Iphigenia plot, the sacrifice at Aulis, and Iphigenia's settlement in the Taurian land, form part of the complication and the beginning, and are therefore mentioned in Aristotle's plot outline in Chapter 17, even though they are not represented on stage. These events make necessary or probable the action of the Iphigenia plot, but do not themselves follow other events by necessity or probability, in this plot. The solution begins, in the Iphigenia story, at that point in the plot at which reversal and recognition coincide. Here, the action changes direction and heads towards good fortune, for recognition is itself good fortune, and it also makes salvation probable or necessary.

In contrast to the plot itself, the episodes of a good tragedy are not probable or necessary, but only plausible (*eikos*, in this sense).[33] Aristotle's distinction between plot ("the universal": 1455b1) and episode is clearest from the examples he gives in Chapter 17, two of which are from Euripides' *IT*: Orestes' madness "by means of which he was captured," and the "salvation by means of the purification" of Orestes. These are "episodes" that are "appropriate" to the story (1455b13–15). Orestes' capture and the salvation are included in the plot outline as events of the plot itself: they follow by probability or necessity from the previous events in this plot. There are, however, a number of different plausible ways, besides madness and purification, in which the capture and salvation might be brought about by the poet. Orestes might be captured as he attempts to break into the temple, and Iphigenia might give a drug to the Taurians to effect the escape. A play in which capture and rescue are brought about in these ways would have the same probable or necessary events, and therefore the same plot, but it would have plausible episodes different from those of the *IT*. Aristotle's outline of the Iphigenia plot gives us examples of two different plausible episodes that bring about the probable or necessary recognition. Orestes is recognized,

Aristotle states, "either as Euripides or as Polyidos wrote it, saying, according to what is plausible [eikos] . . . ." Here, eikos occurs without its usual companion "the necessary." Orestes' speech, in Polyidos' version of the Iphigenia story, is again called "plausible" (eikos, without "necessary") at 16.1455a7. This speech is plausible, and not probable or necessary, for Euripides' way of bringing about the recognition, by means of the letters Iphigenia wishes to send, is equally "plausible" (eikos, again without "necessary"), as Aristotle makes clear in 16.1455a18–19.

If the episodes in a good tragedy are plausible and appropriate to the story, though not a part of the plot, other elements are even more extraneous, as Aristotle's outline of the Iphigenia plot makes clear. These are events "outside the universal," that is, "outside the plot," such as the oracle, and Orestes' reasons for going to the Taurian land (16.1455b7–8). Orestes' arrival is an essential part of the plot, for the other events follow from it by probability or necessity. However, if this arrival itself followed anything else, such as a divine command, by probability or necessity, it would not be part of the beginning of the Iphigenia story, but part of the middle of another story.

According to Aristotle, a good plot not only follows the principle of probability or necessity, it also deals with certain significant human actions. This point emerges from his statements about the parts of the plot. The three parts of a good tragedy arouse pity and fear not only because they follow one another according to probability or necessity, but also because they are concerned with philia (kinship) relationships.[34] The importance of philia in the tragic plot is clearest in Aristotle's statements about the pathos. Not just any destructive or painful event, for example, one in which enemies or neutrals kill one another, arouses pity and fear in the best way (14.1453b17–19). A pathos is truly pitiable and fearful only if it is one between philoi (relatives): "When the pathē take place within philia relationships, for example, when brother kills or is about to kill brother, or son father, or mother son, or son mother, or does something else of this sort, this is to be sought [by the poet]" (1453b19–22). Such an event need not actually take place in order to arouse pity and fear in the best way: it need only be "about to occur" (mellon), like the sacrifice in the Iphigenia story.

Philia is also of central importance in the two other parts of the plot. While reversal, a change to good or bad fortune, is not explicitly said to be concerned with philia, Aristotle believed that philia is essential to good fortune, and that loss of philoi is the most terrible bad fortune (Eudemian Ethics (EE) 1234b32–33, Nicomachean Ethics (NE) 1155a4–6). Moreover, in the best tragedy, reversal occurs together with recognition (Poetics 11.1452a32–34), and a good recognition, like a good pathos, concerns philoi. The best recognition, Aristotle writes, is recognition of persons (1452a29–38), and, as Aristotle's definition indicates, is a change "to philia or enmity" (1452a31). That recognition is concerned with philia is also clear from Aristotle's remark in Chapter 14 that in one kind of plot people "recognize philia" after doing a terrible deed (1453b30–31).

In Aristotle's view, then, the tragic plot is a formal structure governed by the principle of probability or necessity, and dealing with the most important human actions. Its function is the arousal of pity and fear. The three parts of the plot – *pathos*, recognition, and reversal – are the most important elements in the formal structure, the universal. This plot structure is a composition of events, proceeding according to probability or necessity from beginning, to middle, to end. Character and the merely plausible episodes are not part of this plot structure. In the best tragedies, the *pathos* is a destructive or painful event in which *philos* kills or is about to kill *philos*. The best tragedies also have recognition (a change to *philia* or enmity), and reversal. Their focal point, their emotional and dramatic climax, is the beginning of the solution, when reversal and recognition occur together, and a change begins from good to bad, or from bad to good fortune. Thus, the best tragic plot, in Aristotle's view, is not just an exciting story. It is instead a story, with the compelling force of probability or necessity, that concerns *philia* relationships.

In focusing on *philia*, Aristotle's theory reflects the actual practice of the tragedians, for *philia* is a central theme in the plots of nearly all of the extant tragedies.[35] The view that tragedy concerns *philia* is also deeply rooted in Aristotle's views on the importance of *philia* in human society. According to his *Politics*, "the human being is by nature a political animal," that is, one whose nature it is to live in communities consisting of kin and other *philoi*.[36] This concept of human nature is the basis for Aristotle's belief that "lack of *philoi* and isolation [is] most terrible" (*EE* 1234b32–33). In his view, Oedipus is pitiable not so much because he suffers blindness, pain, and the loss of wealth and power, as because he is irrevocably cut off from the *philia* relationships that make him part of the human community.[37] Because it deals centrally with *philia* relationships, Greek tragedy, in Aristotle's view, is concerned with the basis for society and civilization, for our very humanity, our nature as political animals. Seen from Aristotle's point of view, then, a tragedy in which plot is of central importance certainly need not show "a lack of depth in the dramatic handling."[38] On the contrary, a drama that is concerned with terrible events that threaten our very humanity is essentially serious, important, "tragic."

Within this context of Aristotle's views on tragedy as a whole, his preference for Euripides' *IT* is readily understandable. Aristotle admires this play because it is a story about *philia* relationships, with the formal plot structure best suited to arouse pity and fear. His explicit statements about this play, and other statements in the *Poetics* that are directly applicable to it, help us to see that this is so.

Aristotle explicitly mentions Euripides' *IT*, or a play about Iphigenia among the Taurians, in six passages in the *Poetics*.[39]

(1) In *Poetics* 11.1452b3–8, after stating that the best kind of recognition is that of persons, Aristotle cites the recognitions in the *IT* as examples of this best kind: "Since recognition is recognition of persons, some of them are [recognitions] only of one person by the other, when it is clear who the

other is. At other times, it is necessary for both people to recognize [each other], for example, Iphigenia was recognized by Orestes as a result of the sending of the letter, but it needed another recognition for him to be recognized by Iphigenia."

(2) In Chapter 14, Aristotle ranks plot types in order from worst to best (1453b37–1454a9). The worst plot is that in which someone is about to act (that is, as Aristotle's examples show, to kill a *philos*), knowing of the relationship, but does not act (1453b37–38). Next to the worst is a plot in which someone is about to act, knowing of the relationship, and does act (1454a2). Still better is a plot like that of Sophocles' *Oedipus the King*, in which someone acts in ignorance, and then recognition of *philia* occurs (1454a2–3, with 1453b29–31). The best plot, writes Aristotle, is one like that of "the Iphigenia," in which someone is about to kill a *philos*, but does not do so because recognition occurs (1454a4–7, quoted at the beginning of this article).

(3) In *Poetics* 16.1454b30–36, in a ranking of kinds of recognitions, Aristotle classifies the recognition of Orestes by Iphigenia as next to the worst: "Second [from the worst] are those [recognitions] made up by the poet, because they are lacking in art. For example Orestes in the *Iphigenia* is recognized as Orestes. She [is recognized] by means of the letter, but he himself says what the poet and not the plot requires. So that this is much like the error previously mentioned [sc. recognition by signs], for it would also have been possible to bring in some [signs]."

(4) In 16.1455a6–8, in giving examples of the fourth kind of recognition, that "from reasoning" (1455a4), Aristotle writes of "the [sc. recognition?] of Polyidos the sophist concerning the *Iphigenia*. For he said that it was plausible [*eikos*] for Orestes to reason that his sister was sacrificed, and that it happened to himself also to be sacrificed." While this statement most probably refers to an *Iphigenia* written by Polyidos (cf. 17.1455b10–11: "as Polyidos wrote it"), it might also be a suggestion made by Polyidos the sophist about how Euripides' play could have been better written.[40] In any case, this statement does not characterize a recognition that actually occurs in Euripides' play.

(5) At 16.1455a16–19, Aristotle gives the recognition of Iphigenia by Orestes in the *IT* as an example of the best kind of recognition: "The best recognition of all is that which results from the events themselves, when emotion comes by means of plausible things [*eikotōn*], for example, in the *Oedipus* of Sophocles and in the *Iphigenia*. For it was plausible [*eikos*] for her to want to send letters."

(6) In Chapter 17.1455b3–15 (quoted above), Aristotle gives an outline summary of "the universal" of the Iphigenia plot, and states that the episodes should be "appropriate," as are Orestes' madness and purification in the *IT*.

Aristotle also makes a number of statements that do not explicitly concern the *IT*, but that are nevertheless relevant to an understanding of his views on the plot of this play.

(7) In Chapter 11.1452a32–33, Aristotle writes that "the best recognition occurs together with reversal." While Aristotle's example is *Oedipus the King*, he could also have cited the *IT*, in which recognition marks the beginning of the change from bad fortune to good fortune. This change is the beginning of the solution, the point "from which it changes to good fortune" (18.1455b27). Aristotle's words in the plot outline in Chapter 17 indicate the coincidence of recognition with reversal and with the beginning of the solution in the Iphigenia plot: "thence [sc. from the recognition] is salvation" (1455b12).

(8) In Chapter 13, Aristotle praises Euripides for his unhappy endings: "Most of his [tragedies] end in bad fortune. This, as has been said, is the correct way" (1453a25–26). While the *IT* is not mentioned, it clearly does *not* end in bad fortune.

(9) In Chapter 14, as noted above, Aristotle writes that the best *pathos* is one in which *philos* harms or is about to harm *philos* (1453b15–22). That the *IT* contains such a *pathos* is clear from passages 2 and 6.

(10) In Chapter 15, Aristotle writes that the *deus ex machina* should not be used to solve difficulties in the plot, as it is in the *Medea* (1454a37–1454b2). Instead, writes Aristotle, "the *mēchanē* should be used for things outside the drama, either for things that came before it that it is not possible for a human being to know, or for things that come afterwards that require prophecy or a messenger report. For we attribute to the gods the power of seeing everything" (1454b2–6). This best way of using the *mēchanē* is clearly the one employed by the *IT*: Athena appears to explain events that will occur after the play itself.

Most of these statements in the *Poetics* reflect favorably on the *IT*. In the first place, its plot as a whole is well constructed. Because the Iphigenia plot is given as a paradigm of "the universal" in Chapter 17 (passage 6), it is reasonable to suppose that this plot is a good example of a sequence of events proceeding from beginning, to middle, to end, according to probability or necessity. Each of the individual parts of the *IT* plot – *pathos*, recognition and reversal – is also best of its kind. Both the Chapter 17 outline (passage 6), and passage 2 show that the *IT* contains the best kind of *pathos*, that in which *philos*, rather than enemy or neutral, kills or is about to kill *philos*, and that it is a plot of the superior, complex kind, since it contains recognitions. The outline of the Iphigenia plot in Chapter 17 also shows, as we have seen, that this play contains reversal together with recognition. The *IT* contains two recognitions, both of which are of the best kind in that they are recognitions of persons (passage 1). Of these, the recognition of Orestes by Iphigenia is of an inferior subcategory, one "made up by the poet" (passage 3), while the recognition of Iphigenia by Orestes is praised in passage 5 as the best kind, that arising "from the events themselves." The *IT* is also a good tragedy because the episodes are "appropriate" to the story (passage 6). Moreover, this play makes good use of the *mēchanē* (passage 10).

A notorious problem, however, arises in connection with Aristotle's statement in Chapter 14 (passage 2) that the *IT* is an example of the best plot, one in which recognition prevents kin murder. While this plot necessarily ends happily, Aristotle states, in Chapter 13, that the best tragedy ends unhappily (passage 8).[41] While it may not be possible to reconcile these apparently inconsistent passages completely, it is important to realize that they do not simply contradict one another. While Aristotle praises the unhappy ending in Chapter 13, in Chapter 14 he makes no mention of a happy ending. Instead, he praises the *IT* for its good use of *pathos* and recognition. In this play, pity and fear are aroused by a *pathos* that is about to take place between *philoi*: sister is about to kill brother. Emotion is also aroused by the recognition of the relationship (see 1453b31: "to recognize *philia*"), which, by probability or necessity, prevents the terrible event from occurring. Thus, recognition in the *IT* coincides with a reversal and with the beginning of the solution, the point in the play at which the change to good fortune begins. It is, then, Euripides' creation of this dramatic and emotional focal point that Aristotle praises, and not the happy ending as such.

In summary, then, Aristotle's statements in the *Poetics* tell us that the *IT* is a good play because it has the excellent formal structure that allows it to deal in an emotionally powerful way with events that are of primary importance for our nature as human beings: those that concern *philia* relationships. The threat of kin murder (a *pathos* about to take place) arouses pity and fear that reach an emotional climax in the powerful dramatic moment in which recognition of *philia* prevents murder and brings about salvation. These events, this plot, make the *IT* a good tragedy, while "intrigue," characterization, psychological conflict, and religious questions, as well as meter and diction, are of purely secondary importance and interest.

Not only do Aristotle's plot-centered views on tragedy in general, and on the *IT* in particular, make good sense in theoretical terms, his statements also provide an excellent commentary on Euripides' text. In this case, at least, Aristotle's theory reflects and explains the facts to perfection, showing that he knew Euripides' play, and especially the recognition scene, thoroughly and in detail, and that he read it intelligently and sensitively.[42] I conclude this essay by analyzing Euripides' play, from beginning, to middle, to end, according to the Aristotelian criteria just discussed.

I. The Beginning

In Aristotle's view, the beginning of a tragic plot comprises (a) the *propeprag-*

mena, "the things done before" the events represented on the stage, and (b) some of the events represented on stage (18.1455b24–30). The "things done before" in the Iphigenia story are set forth as follows in Aristotle's plot outline:

> A certain girl after being sacrificed and disappearing from the view of those sacrificing her was settled in another land where the custom was to sacrifice strangers to the goddess, and she came to hold that priesthood. (17.1455b3–6)

This information, essential to the plot, includes the fact that a girl was supposedly sacrificed, but actually came to the Taurian land, the fact that it is the law to sacrifice strangers to a goddess in this country, and that the girl holds this priesthood. This background information constitutes part of the beginning of the plot because, while it is not made probable or necessary by anything else, it makes other events in the plot probable or necessary. Because the girl was supposedly sacrificed, but actually rescued, she is alive but her brother does not know this. And because the girl must sacrifice strangers, her being about to sacrifice her brother is probable or necessary.

In Euripides' play, this essential background information is given in Iphigenia's speech in the prologue (1–41), where she tells us who she is, what happened at Aulis, and what her duties are in the Taurian country. The importance for the plot of this background information is shown by Iphigenia's repetition of much of it in the recognition scene. Here, she states more clearly that those in Argos believe her dead (771), and that Artemis saved her and settled her in the Taurian land (784–786). In the prologue, we also learn that Iphigenia has had a dream, which she interprets as an indication of her brother's death (42–64). This dream, however, is not mentioned by Aristotle, even as a plausible episode.

The arrival of Orestes is the only part of the Aristotelian beginning of the plot to be represented on stage, in Euripides' play. This arrival, together with the "things done before," makes the events of the middle of the plot probable or necessary. Aristotle mentions the arrival as follows:

> A while later, it happened that the brother of the priestless arrived. The fact that the oracle commanded him to go there, for some reason that is outside the universal, and his purpose [in going], are outside the plot. He arrived . . . . (1455b6–8)

Orestes' past history, unlike Iphigenia's, is not an essential part of this plot, in Aristotle's view. All we need to know is that he is the priestess' brother, and that he arrives.

In Euripides' play, Orestes' arrival takes place in the second half of the prologue (67–122). Here, we also learn that Orestes is going to attempt to steal the statue of Artemis, as commanded by the oracle (77–103). In addition, we meet Pylades, and learn that Orestes is still pursued by Furies (79–84). None of this, except the arrival itself, figures in Aristotle's plot outline, which in fact explicitly excludes the oracle and Orestes' purpose in going to the land of the Taurians.

II. The Middle

The middle of the Iphigenia story, in Aristotle's outline, comprises the brother's capture, his being about to be sacrificed by his sister (the *pathos*), and the recognitions:

> [He] was captured, and when about to be sacrificed, he made himself known, either as Euripides or as Polyidos wrote it, saying, as was plausible, that not only his sister but himself also had to be sacrificed. (1455b9–11)

In Euripides' play, Orestes' capture is recounted in the Herdsman's speech (238–339). He is "about to be sacrificed" by Iphigenia as a probable or necessary result of this capture and of the circumstances and events that constitute the beginning. That the sacrifice is imminent is also clear from the preparations made by Iphigenia at 467–471 and 725–726. Orestes remarks, if we accept A. Seidler's emendation, that Iphigenia is "about to kill" (*mellōn ktanein*) him at 484.[43] These are, interestingly, the very words Aristotle uses in *Poetics* 14 to characterize a plot in which kin kills or is about to kill kin: *apokteinē ē mellē*: 1453b21.

While Aristotle does not give an account of Euripides' recognitions in the Chapter 17 outline, he does so in other passages, as we have seen. At 16.1455a16–19, (passage 5 in the list above), he praises the recognition of Iphigenia by Orestes, stating that "emotion [*ekplēxis*] comes by means of plausible things." In Euripides' text, this recognition occurs at 769 ff., when Iphigenia says, "Tell Orestes . . . ." In this passage, Orestes experiences the same strong emotion (*ekpeplēgmenos*: 795; cf. 773: *ekplēsse*) that Aristotle mentions in his account of Orestes' recognition. This recognition scene also has a quality Aristotle calls "the marvellous" (*to thaumaston*), for events occur "contrary to expectation [*para tēn doxan*] because of one another" (9.1452a4–5). Although Aristotle does not mention the *IT* in this connection, he uses the same words Orestes does in Euripides' play. Orestes says that Iphigenia's revelations are "marvellous" (*thaumast*: 797, cf. 839), and that she now has the brother whom she never expected (*ou dokous'*) to have (802). The other, inferior, recognition mentioned by Aristotle (passage 3) takes place, in Euripides' play, immediately after the first recognition, when Orestes first states, and then proves, his identity to his sister (795–826). When Iphigenia asks Orestes for a proof or token (*tekmērion*: 808; cf. 822) of his identity, we remember Aristotle's statement that this, inferior, recognition "made up by the poet" is much like recognition by signs (1454b35–36). Recognition in the *IT* is coincident with reversal and with the beginning of the solution, the point "from which it changes to good fortune" (*ex hou metabainei eis eutuchian* 1455b27–28). Aristotle's words are very similar to those of Pylades in Euripides' play, who remarks, just before the recognition: "It is possible, it is, for great bad fortune/to have great changes" (*all' estin, estin hē lian duspraxia/lian didousa metabolas* 721–722). In Euripides' play, the reversal clearly occurs at the same time as the recognition. The reunion of brother and sister is in itself good fortune, as both Iphigenia and Orestes remark (*eutuchousa*: 837; *eutuchoimen*: 841), and, immediately following the recognitions, at 874, Iphigenia and Orestes begin to plan their escape.

On the other hand, Aristotle's plot outline excludes much in the central section of Euripides' play that is of great interest to modern readers. The means by which Orestes' capture takes place (his madness) is a plausible episode rather than part of the plot (*Poetics* 17.1455b13–14), and the means by which the recognition occurs (Iphigenia's desire to send the letter: 16.1455a18–19) is also an episode. Because these episodes are appropriate to the story, they enhance the emotional effect of the events they bring about in the plot, but they are not themselves part of the plot. Other passages in the *IT* are not even Aristotelian episodes: all of the choral odes; Iphigenia's speech at 342–390, in which she theologizes and expresses her emotions; the dialogue between brother and sister at 472–642, in which Iphigenia's growing sympathy with Orestes is apparent; the dialogue between Orestes and Pylades in which each offers to die in the other's place (674–722). Many of these passages are important for characterization (*ēthos*), but they are inessential to "the soul of tragedy."

III. The End

The end of the Iphigenia story, in Aristotle's outline, is summarized in three words: "thence is salvation" (*Poetics* 1455b12). While Aristotle goes on to praise the episode by means of which salvation occurs ("the salvation by means of purification": 1455b14–15), he is careful to distinguish this episode from "the universal," the essential plot. According to Aristotle, then, most of the entire last section of Euripides' play (873 to the end) is episode rather than part of the plot: the "intrigue" in which Thoas is deceived, the Messenger's speech about the wave that pushes the ship back to shore, and the appearance of Athena *ex machina*. Here, of course, is where Aristotle's analysis of the play differs most profoundly from that of mdoern scholars, for whom the "intrigue," and other aspects of the last part of the play are of supreme importance. According to Aristotelian criteria, these scholars err in focusing on episode and on even more extraneous material, while ignoring plot.

According to Aristotle, then, the essential elements in Euripides' play are: (1) the circumstances (the events at Aulis, Iphigenia's priesthood, the relationship between Iphigenia and Orestes) that make the events of the plot probable or necessary; (2) Orestes' arrival, capture and his being about to be sacrificed by his sister; this in turn makes (3) recognition and reversal probable or necessary, and these events make (4) salvation and good fortune probable or necessary. The play is about these events, and it derives its most powerful emotional effects from them. Other material in the play is also important and interesting, but its function within the play as a whole is to enhance the emotional effects of the essential plot, or to provide "color" (*Poetics* 6.1450a39–b3) and "sweetening" (6.1449b28–29).

This plot-centered reading of Euripides' *IT* has several advantages. First, it illuminates the underlying structure of this play, focusing as it does on a few important events, and considering the rest as material of secondary interest. The plot of the *IT* is, according to Aristotle's analysis, a tightly-knit unity of events that follow one another according to probability or necessity, rather than a loose combination of two or more distinct sections, such as, for example, the recognition and "intrigue" of many modern scholars.[44] Second, Aristotle's reading locates the climax of the plot, in which recognition and reversal occur, and fortune begins to change from bad to good, in the recognition scene, the emotional impact of which is obvious to any reader. Finally, if the *IT* is not an intrigue play, or a psychological drama, or a thriller, or a melodrama, but a play about *philia*, and therefore about our essential nature as political animals, it has a serious, important, "tragic" theme.

There are some indications in Euripides' play that he, like Aristotle, thought of the *IT* as a play about *philia*, and about relationships that are political in a broader sense. According to Aristotle, human beings are political animals because it is their nature to live in communities of *philoi*, and the person who is by nature not political is "a lover of war" (*Politics* 1.1253a3–7). Similarly, in Euripides' play, harm to *philoi* is closely connected with war, for it was the sacrifice of daughter by father at Aulis that marked the beginning of the Trojan War. On the other hand, avoidance of kin murder in the *IT* leads to a peaceful solution of difficulties between Greeks and barbarians: Thoas is persuaded to cease attacking the Greeks, and they in turn leave without shedding blood. Avoidance of human sacrifice also has wider religious and political implications, in Euripides' play. In Artemis' new rite to be established in Attica, a priest will not kill but merely draw blood from a man's neck. Athena ordains this rite when she tells Orestes:

> Establish there this custom: at the festival,
> to atone for your uncompleted sacrifice,
> let a sword be held to a man's throat, and blood be drawn,
> for religion's sake, so that the goddess may have her rights. (1458–1461)[45]

The new, Greek Artemis is to be a more peaceful goddess, who no longer demands human sacrifice. Athena's words suggest, however, that Artemis will remain peaceful only so long as she is compensated and honored in a rite that commemorates human sacrifice by actually drawing blood. While her statement, of course, provides an *aition*, an explanation of the causes, for the rites of Artemis Tauropolos,[46] the idea that lies behind it is also applicable to the *IT* itself.

As a play that arouses fear and pity at the threat of sacrifice of brother by sister, the *IT* is itself a ritual in which human sacrifice and kin murder are commemorated and averted. This tragedy can be seen, then, as a kind of symbolic sacrifice that helps to avert real murder. By providing an emotionally powerful reminder of the dangers of kin murder, the *IT* teaches the audience to fear and avoid the terrible deeds against *philoi* that lead not only to personal disaster but also to war. When this play was produced, at the bitter end of the Peloponnesian War of Greeks against Greeks, this lesson would have been an especially powerful one.[47]

Whether we believe with Aristotle that the *IT* is an emotionally powerful and formally well-constructed tragedy, or see it instead as a light-hearted tragi-comedy or melodrama depends ultimately on our subjective reactions as we read or see the play. If we realize, however, that these reactions are conditioned in large part by our expectations about what tragedy is and should be, we will not reject an Aristotelian reading simply because it focuses on plot rather than on psychology and character. The plot of the *Iphigenia in Tauris* surely is, in its Aristotelian essentials, universally tragic and significant. What matters most profoundly and fundamentally for our existence as human beings is whether we, like Iphigenia, will recognize our brothers in time to avoid killing them. The rest, as Aristotle puts it, is episode.[48]

Notes

1. Unless otherwise noted, for the *Iphigenia in Tauris* I follow the text of J. Diggle (Oxford, 1981; rpt. with corrections, 1986), and for the *Poetics* that of R. Kassel (Oxford, 1965; rpt., with corrections, 1966). All translations are my own unless otherwise noted. Hereafter, these and the following works will be cited by author's last name, or last name and date only: O. J. Brendel, "*Iphigenie auf Tauris*," in *Goethe Bicentennial Studies*, ed. H. J. Messen (Bloomington, IN, 1950), 1–47; G. F. Else, *Aristotle's Poetics: The Argument* (Cambridge, MA, 1967); S. Goldhill, *Reading Greek Tragedy* (Cambridge, 1986); H. Grégoire (ed.), *Iphigénie en Tauride*, in *Euripide*, Vol. 4 (Paris, 1968); G. M. A. Grube, *The Drama of Euripides* (London, 1941); B. Knox, "Euripidean Comedy," in *The Rarer Action: Essays in Honor of Francis Fergusson*, eds. A. Cheuse and R. Koffler (New Brunswick, NJ, 1970), rpt. in *Word and Action: Essays on the Ancient Theater* (Baltimore, 1979), 250–274 (refs are to the rpt. edition); R. Lattimore (trans. and ed.), *Euripides: Iphigenia in Tauris* (Oxford, 1973); C. B. R. Pelling (ed.), *Characterization and Individuality in Greek Literature* (Oxford, 1990); G. Perrotta, "L' 'Elena' e l' 'Ifigenia Taurica' di Euripide," *Studi italiani di filologia classica* N.S. **6** (1928) 5–53; M. Platnauer (ed.), *Euripides: Iphigenia in Tauris* (Oxford, 1938); M. Pohlenz, *Die griechische Tragödie*, 2d edn. (Göttingen, 1954); F. Solmsen, "Zur Gestaltung des Intriguenmotivs in den Tragödien des Sophokles und Euripides," *Philologus* **87** (1932) 1–17, and "Euripides Ion im Vergleich mit anderen Tragödien," *Hermes* **69** (1934) 390–419; D. F. Sutton, "Satyric Qualities in Euripides' *Iphigeneia at* [sic] *Tauris and Helen*," *Rivista di studi classici* **3** (1972) 321–330; A. W. Verrall, *Essays on Four Plays of Euripides* (Cambridge, 1905).
2. H. D. F. Kitto, *Greek Tragedy* (London, 1939), 311, 315, 316.
3. Platnauer, "Introduction," v.

4. Knox, 256.

5. T. B. L. Webster, *The Tragedies of Euripides* (London, 1967), 187.

6. A. P. Burnett, *Catastrophe Survived* (Oxford, 1971), 71–72.

7. This was argued by J. J. Winkler in "An Oscar for Iphigeneia," Martin Classical Lecture 4, Stanford, 1988 (forthcoming in *Rehearsals of Manhood*, Princeton).

8. Grégoire, 85. Among others who see a close similarity between the two plots are Lattimore, 3–4; K. Matthiessen, *Elektra, Taurische Iphigenie und Helena, Hypomnemata* 4 (Göttingen, 1964); Perrotta; Pohlenz; Sutton; Verrall, 51–52. An exception is H. Strohm, *Euripides: Interpretationen zur dramatischen Form* (Munich, 1957), 77–78.

9. Grégoire, 85; ellipsis in original.

10. I adapt R. Janko's translation of 1455b7–8 (*Aristotle: Poetics I*: [Indianapolis, 1987]), which makes excellent sense of the text, without need for bracketing *dia . . . katholou*, with Kassel.

11. Most of the scholars who stress the similarities between the two plots (see n.8, above), play down this crucial difference. It is not mentioned at all by Lattimore, Perrotta, Sutton, or Verrall.

12. On the *IT* as "intrigue play" see esp. Solmsen's articles.

13. See *Poetics* 14.1453b14–22, discussed further below.

14. Cf. Solmsen's description of "intrigue plays" in terms of characterization: 1932, 3–4.

15. J. S. Mill, "Thoughts on Poetry and Its Varieties" (1833), in *Collected Works of John Stuart Mill*, eds. J. M. Robson and J. Stillinger (Toronto, 1981), 1: 345.

16. Brendel, 3. Cf. Grube, 329.

17. D. D. Raphael, *The Paradox of Tragedy* (Bloomington, IN, 1960), 25.

18. W. C. Greene, *Moira* (Cambridge, MA, 1944), 92.

19. M. C. Nussbaum, *The Fragility of Goodness* (Cambridge, 1986), 382. Cf. N. Frye, *Anatomy of Criticism* (Princeton, 1957), 214–215; and Knox, 250.

20. T. G. Rosenmeyer, *The Art of Aeschylus* (Berkeley and Los Angeles, 1982), 211, summarizing the view of T. von Wilamowitz-Moellendorff expressed in *Die dramatische Technik des Sophokles* (*Philolg. Untersuchungen* **22**, Berlin, 1917). Good accounts of the modern controversy about "character" in Greek drama are given by P. E. Easterling, "Presentation of Character in Aeschylus," *Greece and Rome* **20** (1973) 3–19, and "Constructing Character in Greek Tragedy," in Pelling, 83–99, and by Goldhill, 168–172.

21. R. S. Crane, "The Concept of Plot and the Plot of *Tom Jones*," in *Critics and Criticism*, ed. R. S. Crane (Chicago, 1952), 620; cf. 618. See also P. Brooks, *Reading for the Plot: Design and Intention in Narrative* (Oxford, 1984), 12. I am indebted to Thomas Clayton for calling my attention to these works.

22. J. Jones, *On Aristotle and Greek Tragedy* (London, 1962), 33.

23. S. Halliwell, *Aristotle's Poetics* (London, 1986), 146.

24. Halliwell, 152, quoted by S. Goldhill, "Character and Action," in Pelling, 119.

25. I argue for a strict interpretation of Aristotle's plot–character distinction, and against the tendency of many modern scholars to blur this distinction in Ch. 3 of *Tragic Pleasures: Aristotle on Plot and Emotion* (Princeton, 1992).

26. This point is made by Brendel, 2.

27. See Grube, 329–330.

28. I discuss Aristotle's theory of the tragic plot in greater detail in *Tragic Pleasures* (n.25, above).

29. This phrase, or a close variant, is used in connection with the events of the plot at 7.1451a12–13; 8.1451a27–28; 9.1451a38, 1451b9, 1451b35; 10.1452a20; 11.1452a24; 14.1454a34, 1454a35–36.

30. It is clear from 1450b29–30 that "by nature" means "either by necessity or for the most part." Throughout this passage, Aristotle uses the equivalent expression "for

the most part" in place of "the probable" [*eikos*]. On the equivalence of *eikos* and "for the most part" in Aristotle's thought, see the passages cited by R. Sorabji, *Necessity Cause, and Blame* (Ithaca, 1980), 55, n.36: *Prior Analytics* 70a5; *Rhetoric* 1357a34, 1402b16, 1403a1. Also see, on this equivalence, R. Dupont-Roc and J. Lallot, *Aristote, La Poétique* (Paris, 1980), 211–212.

31. On *peripeteia* see Belfiore, "*Peripeteia* as Discontinuous Action: Aristotle *Poetics* 11.1452a22–29," *Classical Philology* **83** (1988) 183–194.

32. In other passages (e.g. 15.1454b3, 17.1455b7) "outside" refers to events that are outside the plot.

33. Good accounts of the meaning of "episode" in the *Poetics* are those of K. Nickau, "Epeisodion und Episode," *Museum Helveticum* 23 (1966) 155–171, and M. Heath, *Unity in Greek Poetics* (Oxford, 1989), 49–55. I disagree with them in some important respects, however.

34. Else argues against translating *philia* as "love," or "friendship" in the *Poetics* and shows that *philoi* are relatives rather than merely friends: 349–350, 391–398, 414–415. In Aristotle's other works, of course, friends, are often included among *philoi*.

35. The importance of the theme of *philia* relationships within the actual tragedies is widely recognized. See Else, 391–398; A. Gudeman, *Aristoteles: Peri Poiētikēs* (Berlin and Leipzig, 1934), 257–258; B. Vickers, *Towards Greek Tragedy* (London, 1973), 230–243; Goldhill, 79–106; M. W. Blundell, *Helping Friends and Harming Enemies* (Cambridge, 1989).

36. *Politics* 1.1253a2–3; cf. *EE* 1242a22–28.

37. On Oedipus and Aristotle's *Politics* see J.-P. Vernant, "Ambiguity and Reversal," in J.-P. Vernant and P. Vidal-Nquet, *Tragedy and Myth in Ancient Greece*, trans. J. Lloyd (Sussex and New Jersey, 1981), 107.

38. Grube, 329.

39. Aristotle names Euripides in the last of these passages. His mention of the letter-sending episode allows us to infer that passages 1, 3 and 5 also concern Euripides' particular version of the Iphigenia plot. Passage 2 concerns other versions of this plot as well as Euripides'. On passage 4 see below.

40. The text and sense of 1455a6–7 are uncertain. On the problem of Polyidos' identity see Else, 509–510, who suggests that Polyidos wrote a criticism of Euripides' play.

41. A good survey of the controversy surrounding the problem of consistency of Chapters 13 and 14 is given by J. Moles, "Notes on Aristotle, *Poetics* 13 and 14," *Classical Quarterly* 29 (1979) 82–92.

42. Further proof of this is Aristotle's citation of *IT* 727 in *Rhetoric* 3.1407b34–35, which establishes the reading *poluthuroi*.

43. J. Dingle defends this reading in *Studies on the Text of Euripides* (Oxford, 1981), 82–83.

44. Among those who hold this view of the play are Solmsen, 1932, 2; 1934, 400; Pohlenz, 399; and G. Zuntz, 'Die Taurische Iphigenie des Euripides," *Die Antike* **9** (1933), 245–254, 248–249.

45. Lattimore's translation.

46. On this rite see Grégoire, 88–97; Platnaur, vii–xi; E. Simon, *Festivals of Attica* (Madison, WI, 1983), 83–88.

47. While the precise date of the *IT* is much disputed most scholars agree in placing it within a year or two of 414, around the time of the Sicilian Expedition.

48. I am indebted to Thomas Clayton for helpful comments on an earlier draft of this essay.

Aristotle on the Pleasure of Comedy

Leon Golden

In the *Poetics*, Aristotle designates the kind of action that is represented in comedy as the "ridiculous" (*to geloion*). There is no reference in the *Poetics*, however, to the appropriate emotion that is associated with the representation of such action.[1] The *Tractatus Coislinianus*, which has been defended as an authentic witness to Aristotelian doctrine on comedy, offers the phrase "through pleasure and laughter" as the appropriate emotional responses to the action of comedy.[2] The question then arises as to whether "through pleasure and laughter" accurately describes Aristotle's view of the emotions which we feel in response to the ridiculous action which Aristotle defines as the basis of comedy. Janko argues that this is the case (158–160) but I believe that he is in error on this important point.

What we will be searching for and how we will proceed are strongly influenced by the following passage (1453b10–14) which is only partially quoted by Janko in his argument in favor of the validity of the "through pleasure and laughter" clause in the *Tractatus Coislinianus*:[3] "For it is not necessary to seek every pleasure from tragedy but only the one which is appropriate to it. Since it is necessary for the poet to provide pleasure *through mimesis* [italics mine], it is apparent that this most be introduced into the action." Now Aristotle also tells us (1448b15–17) that we take pleasure in viewing all mimetic representations because it turns out that we learn and make inferences from them. It is important to note here that Aristotle's unambiguous identification of mimetic pleasure with learning and inference challenges traditional views of the key concept of *katharsis* as either "purgation" or "purification." As I have argued elsewhere, only an interpretation of *katharsis* as "intellectual clarification" can establish a harmony between this term and the *telos* of *mimēsis* which Aristotle explicitly defines for us in this passage.[4] Since *mimēsis* qua *mimēsis* generates intellectual pleasure, we know that comic *mimēsis* must necessarily also provide this kind of

pleasure. Comic intellectual pleasure will not, of course, arise from the representation of pity and fear, the incidents and emotions associated with tragedy,
but rather from the kind of incident represented in comedy (1449a34). Tragic
and comic *mimēsis* must be essentially similar in regard to the intellectual
pleasure which they offer as forms of *mimēsis* but must differ from each other in
content and emotional response because one is concerned with pity and fear and
the other with the ridiculous. Pity and fear, as we have noted, refer to both the
incidents represented in tragedy and to the emotions evoked by those incidents.
The comic parallel to incidents involving pity and fear is "the ridiculous" and we
are in the process of identifying Aristotle's view of the appropriate emotional
response to such action.

In the first clause of the definition of tragedy, Aristotle recognizes that this
genre is a *mimēsis* of a *praxeos spoudaias*, a phrase which should be translated
"noble action" and not "serious action."[5] This phrase stands in direct contrast
with Aristotle's explicit identification of comedy as a *mimēsis phauloteron*, a
representation of baser types of human beings. We see that it is Aristotle's
purpose in the first clause of the definition of tragedy to identify the type of
character that is represented in that genre and that he has explicitly supplied us
with the information we need for establishing the parallel definition of comedy
which must accomplish the same purpose.

The phrase *praxeos spoudaias* does not, as we have just shown, speak to the
issue of the type of *character* represented in comedy, but it does have a different,
and quite important, role to play in a genuine Aristotelian definition of comedy.
We have seen that Aristotle identifies "the ridiculous" as the kind of *incident*
which is represented in comedy. This makes "the ridiculous" a precise analog of
pity and fear in the catharsis clause of the definition of tragedy. Thus "the
ridiculous" belongs in the catharsis clause of the definition of comedy (if that
definition is to parallel Aristotle's definition of tragedy) in partial substitution for
the phrase "through pleasure and laughter" which does not describe the kind
of incidents represented in comedy.

The intellectual pleasure that arises from *mimēsis* qua *mimēsis* is, of course, as
important a component of comic pleasure as it is of tragic pleasure. What we
must now establish is the way in which this intellectual pleasure is conditioned
by the kind of incident that is characteristic of comedy, "the ridiculous," in the
same way as the pleasure of tragedy is conditioned by the pitiable and fearful
incidents of tragedy. If we are successful in this final phase of our inquiry we will
provide a theoretical basis in Aristotelian theory for the emotion evoked by
comedy that is parallel to the emotions of pity and fear in tragedy. Thus our task
will be to construct the comic parallel to Aristotle's explicit description of the
pleasure of tragedy at *Poetics* 1453b10–13. Earlier I argued that "pity and fear"
in the definition of tragedy had to refer to both the incidents depicted in tragedy
and to the emotions evoked by those incidents. I pointed out that Aristotle had
clearly identified the kind of action or incident that is depicted in comedy as being
"the ridiculous" but that he had not, anywhere in the *Poetics*, described the

emotions that are evoked by this type of incident. The *Tractatus Coislinianus* fills this lacuna with "through pleasure and laughter" but, as we have noted, the claim of this phrase to stand as the authentic comic parallel to tragic pity and fear in Aristotelian literary theory been the subject of considerable scholarly dispute.[6] There are a number of places in Aristophanes where indignation, but not laughter, is appropriate. We have such a scene in the *Clouds* (1476–1477) when Strepsiades comes to the realization that he made a profound mistake in renouncing the gods and entrusting himself to Socrates and goes on to atone for his error by burning down the Phrontisterion. We find a similar experience in the *Lysistrata* (588–592) where the play's heroine responds to the commissioner's arrogant dismissal of women's claim to a share in the burdens of war with the sharp reminder of the heavy price women pay for the war effort: their dead sons and husbands. Thus it appears that indignation with or without laughter is intimately involved in our apprehension of "the ridiculous."

My hypothesis is that Aristotelian comic theory requires the representation of action that is "ridiculous" and that such action evokes, as the appropriate comic emotion, a form of "indignation" whether or not that indignation is accompanied by laughter. It is now my task to show that Aristotle could have reasonable intended this view of the incidents and emotions that are characteristic of comedy.

Thanks to explicit discussions in the *Poetics* and the *Rhetoric* we know quite precisely what "pity and fear" are and how they function in tragedy. We also know that at *Rhetoric* 1386b9 Aristotle explicitly designates *nemesan* as the emotion directly opposed to pity. Since tragedy and comedy are placed by Aristotle in polar opposition concerning the kind of action and character they represent, the identification of *nemesan* as the antonym of pity provides a suggestive clue for uncovering an important aspect of the Aristotelian theory of comedy. I propose to develop an argument here that illuminates the role of *nemesan* as the essential comic parallel to pity.

At *Poetics* 1453a2–7 Aristotle identifies pity and fear as the emotions we feel toward anyone who is like ourselves and undeservedly falls into misfortune. In this passage, pity has a primary reference to the undeserved nature of the misfortune and fear to the recognition of our own vulnerability to such misfortune. This bare reference to the central emotions of tragedy, pity and fear, is developed more fully in the *Rhetoric*. At 1385b13–16 Aristotle defines pity as a painful experience caused by a destructive evil that occurs to someone who does not deserve it. Moreover, at 1386a26–28 he tells us that whatever we fear in regard to ourselves, we pity when it occurs to others. A similar point is made in the discussion of fear at 1382b26–27, where we are told that those things are fearful which are designated as pitiable when they occur to others than ourselves.

Aristotle's doctrine of tragic emotion contains the following essential elements:

(1) pity and fear are painful emotions;

(2) pity and fear are evoked by destructive evil such as death or injury;

(3) pity and fear occur under circumstances of undeserved misfortune affecting people like ourselves;

(4) pity and fear are the obverse and reverse of the same emotional experience; pity designating the pained recognition of undeserved misfortune occurring to others than ourselves, and fear designating a recognition of such misfortune occurring, or threatening to occur, to ourselves.

Aristotle tells us (*Rhetoric* 1386b9) that directly opposed to pity is *nemesan*[7] and he defines this term as the painful feeling that arises because of the occurrence of undeserved good fortune. This point is confirmed at 1387a8–11. Aristotle goes on to specify the categories of undeserved good fortune that elicit *nemesan*. After noting that the just, brave, and virtuous man would not be subject to *nemesan*, he identifies wealth and power as the proper subject matter for *nemesan*. At 1387a18–32 he calls attention to the fact that *nemesan* arises only when such characteristics as wealth and power are found in circumstances that violate the laws of proportion and appropriateness (*analogia kai to harmotton*). He strongly emphasizes this point when he states that *nemesan* has the same reverse side as pity, i.e. fear (1387a31–32). He notes that both envy and *nemesan* become fear when something harmful threatens oneself from the good fortune of another. He emphasizes that *nemesan* arises in the face of the undeserved good fortune of someone other than ourselves.

Aristotle's doctrine of *nemesan* has the following essential elements:

(1) *nemesan* is the emotion that is directly opposed to pity;

(2) the reverse side of *nemesan* is the same as the reverse side of pity, i.e. fear;

(3) *nemesan* is a painful feeling that arises because of the undeserved good fortune of someone else;

(4) *nemesan* is directed not at all kinds of undeserved good fortune but at certain specific types such as wealth and power;

(5) *nemesan* occurs in circumstances that violate the laws of proportion and appropriateness.

Pity and fear are dependent for their expression on the kind of character that Aristotle designates as essential for tragedy. Aristotle explicitly defines (*Poetics* 1453a4–17) the requirements for the evocation of pity and fear. He states here that the only kind of hero who can properly evoke these emotions is the individual who is not exceptional in virtue and justice, nor one who suffers from vice or depravity, but rather someone who is in between these opposite poles or who is better rather than worse than such a person (1453a16–17). Elsewhere in the *Poetics* Aristotle refers to this appropriate hero of tragedy as *spoudaios* ("noble") while the hero of comedy is the human being who is *phaulos* ("ignoble") [*Poetics* 1449a32–33]. We see that *spoudaios* and *phaulos* are precise antonyms. I stress their antonymic relationship in this context because of the explicit emphasis placed by Aristotle on their role in differentiating tragedy from comedy. This significant opposition between the essential character required for tragedy and the essential character required for comedy leads to the following hypothesis that I wish to propose concerning the Aristotelian theory of comic action and comic emotion:

(1) We know that pity and fear are painful experiences that are evoked by the representation of the *undeserved misfortune* (italics mine) of a *spoudaios* hero (pity arising when such misfortune affects others than ourselves and fear when we contemplate our own vulnerability to them).

(2) We know that *spoudaios* and *phaulos* are antonyms and that Aristotle explicitly associates the *spoudaios* hero with tragedy and the *phaulos* hero with comedy.

(3) We know that Aristotle explicitly recognizes *nemesan* as a painful feeling that is evoked by *undeserved good fortune* (italics mine) that occurs to another person and that he understands that this *nemesan* turns into fear when the undeserved good fortune of another person is seen as a direct threat to oneself (*Rhetoric* 1386b22–25).

(4) Our hypothesis is, then, that just as the emotions of pity and fear are appropriate responses to the *spoudaios* hero of tragedy, so *nemesan* is an appropriate response to the *phaulos* hero of comedy.

We propose to test this hypothesis, derived from the argument that has been cited in the *Rhetoric*, by comparing it to the brief but quite explicit discussion of comedy in the *Poetics* 1449a32–37. In this passage Aristotle makes the following points concerning the essential nature of comedy:

(1) Comedy involves the representation of the more ignoble (*phauloteroi*) type of human being.

(2) These are represented not in accordance with every kind of vice but in accordance with the "ridiculous" (*to geloion*), which is a subdivision of "the ugly" (*aischos*).

(3) *To geloion* is further defined as an "error" (*hamartema*) or "ugliness" (*aischos*) that is without pain and not destructive.

We argue that the passages from the *Rhetoric* and the *Poetics* are both relevant to, and consistent with, each other and, when taken together, provide a persuasive basis for an Aristotelian theory of comedy. The explicit antonymic opposition, "noble/ignoble" (*spoudaios/phaulos*), which has never been called into question and which essentially differentiates tragedy and comedy, is linked by us in the present argument to the explicit antonymic opposition, "pity/indignation" (*eleos/nemesan*), which has, up to now not played any major role in the scholarly attempt to understand Aristotle's theory of comedy. Moreover, we call attention to the fact that the explicitly recognized opposition, *undeserved misfortune/*

undeserved good fortune, determines for Aristotle whether pity or *nemesan* is to be experienced. Finally, we must address the question of whether Aristotle's explicit recognition of *to geloion* as the object of comic *mimesis* has a parallel in the passages of the *Rhetoric* that deal with *nemesan*.

After reviewing the ancient evidence for *nemesis* Cope writes: "According to Aristotle's definition of *nemesis*," a feeling of pain at undeserved good fortune," it represents the "righteous indignation" arising from a sense of the claims of justice and desert, which is aroused in us by the contemplation of success without merit, and a consequent pleasure in the punishment of one who is thus undeservedly prosperous."[8]

We must now ask how "indignation" (*nemesan*) and the concept of (*nemesis*) can be related to the concept of "the ridiculous" (*to geloion*) which Aristotle explicitly identified as the object of comic representation in the *Poetics*. We recall that *to geloion* refers to an error or ugliness committed by or found in an ignoble (*phaulos*) character. In such a play as the *Clouds* and in much other comic literature, we see that such error and moral ugliness lead to the kind of prosperity which Strepsiades and Socrates enjoy temporarily until righteous indignation takes effect to rectify the moral order of the play. Aristotle has also told us that such error and ugliness in comedy is painless and not destructive. Now the righteous indignation which is involved in *nemesan* as that term is defined by Aristotle in various works is a painful emotion just as "error and ugliness" would be in ordinary life. If, then, we find that "error and ugliness" are presented *without pain* when they are the objects of comic *mimēsis*, are we also justified in transferring this important qualification to our intellectual and emotional response to their comic representation, i.e. to "indignation" (*nemesan*)? If we can, then we have located in *nemesan*, in "righteous indignation" that is *without pain and not destructive*, the precise emotion that is generated by "the ridiculous" (*to geloion*) which Aristotle identifies as the essential object of comic *mimēsis*. We have argued that Aristophanes intended us to respond with *nemesan*, devoid of pain to the major incidents of the *Clouds* and especially to the temporary and very unjustified good fortune of Socrates, the charlatan intellectual, and Strepsiades, the eager swindler of his creditors until his conversion at the end of the play. We should note that in the case of some dark comedies and tragicomedies some pain may actually be evoked by the incidents of the play and in our resultant emotional response to those incidents but that such painful experiences in comedy are regularly limited and counteracted by the immediate intervention of farcical events.

We must, however, understand that there is no fully adequate translation of *nemesan* into English. The translation "indignation" will be misleading if we fail to remember that this emotion, like all emotions, admits of degree and nuance. If we focus on Aristotle's precise association of the term *nemesan* with the recognition of (1) *unjustified good fortune and* (2) *whatever violates the laws of proportion and appropriateness*, we will understand what the word means and how it applies to comedy. *Nemesan* is that emotion which we feel whenever we recognize *inappropriateness* in human behavior as Aristotle indicates at *Rhetoric* 13872a31–32 where he says that "if someone, although he is a good human being, does not meet with what is fitting, we must feel indignation."

The ridiculous, *to geloion*, which for Aristotle is the essential object of comic *mimēsis*, should be understood as an important special case of "the inappropriate" since the "error" or "ugliness" it represents must, by definition, fall below expected norms. The "ridiculous" must generate the same emotion we experience toward any other dimension of "the inappropriate" and this, then, would be that form of *nemesan* which, like the constitutive elements of *to geloion*, "error" and "ugliness," is "painless and not destructive." In that part of the spectrum of comedy that we know as "Old Comedy," the *nemesan* that arises is almost always precisely described by the English term "indignation." This feeling of "indignation" is also present in the spiritual descendants of Old Comedy, the tragicomedies and dark comedies which allow some degree of pain but immediately limit or arrest that emotion. In other parts of the spectrum, such as in ancient and modern examples of "New Comedy," we find different kinds and degrees of the inappropriateness that is inherent in *to geloion* and these evoke related but quite varied and subtly nuanced responses to representations of the ridiculous in plot, character, and thought.

Notes

1. By a happy terminological accident Aristotle's widely known description of tragic emotion, "through pity and fear," can refer to both incidents and emotions. *To geloion* cannot serve this double purpose for comedy and so we will have to reconstruct Aristotle's theory of comic emotion from indications he gives in the *Poetics*, the *Rhetoric*, and from the actual practice of comedy.
2. See R. Janko, *Aristotle on Comedy: Towards a Reconstruction of Poetics II* (Berkeley and Los Angeles, 1984), 156–160.
3. The fully quoted passage supports the view of Tierney cited and rejected by Janko (*Aristotle on Comedy*, 157) that pleasure (*hedone*) is the end and not the means of both tragedy and comedy.
4. For a statement of the argument concerning the pleasure of *mimesis*, in general, and of my views of *katharsis* as "intellectual clarification," see my article "The Clarification Theory of *Katharsis*," *Hermes* **104** (1976) 443–446.
5. For arguments in favor of interpreting *praxeos spoudaias* as "noble action" in opposition to "serious action," see my article, "Is Tragedy the Imitation of a *Serious Action?*" *Greek, Roman and Byzantine Studies* **VI** (1965) 283–289.
6. Aristotle recognized at *Rhetoric* 1372b33–35 that we respond with laughter to manifestations of "the ridiculous." W. W. Fortenbaugh, *Aristotle: On Emotion* (New York, 1975), p. 21 specifies the nature of that laughter as follows: "He [Aristotle] came to see that the emotional response appropriate to comedy is neither the laughter of an envious man nor the laughter which follows upon personal abuse. Rather it is the laughter that follows upon perceiving mistakes and deformities which do not cause pain or destruction and only those plays which present such mistakes and deformities are satisfactory comedies capable of evoking the comic emotion of finding something funny." I would add that finding something funny often means taking it very seriously indeed as in the case of the themes treated by Aristophanes. Janko,

Aristotle on Comedy, recognizes this point when he quotes K. Mcleish's view (159) that because comedy (unlike farce) "springs from character rather than action, its effect is seldom hilarious, but more often a kind of serious pleasure, an inward smile at the frailties and foibles of humanity . . . Whereas farce eschews serious themes, comedy very often embraces them."

7. Aristotle's precise words are "especially opposed to pity is what people term 'indignation'" and he goes on to say that the act of feeling pain at undeserved good fortune is opposed "in some way" (*tropon tina*) to the act of feeling pain at undeserved bad fortune. The phrases "especially" (*malista men*) and "in some way" (*tropon tina*) suggest important, but not unambiguous, nuances in this passage. In interpreting these phrases I follow E. M. Cope, *The Rhetoric of Aristotle* II, rev. and ed. by J. M. Sandys (Cambridge, 1877) *ad loc.* who indicates that the sense of the passage "is this: – Pity is *most* opposite to righteous indignation, though envy *seems* to be as much so, but *is* not."

8. E. M. Cope, *The Rhetoric of Aristotle* II, pp. 107–109. He thinks that the best Aristotelian definition of *nemesan* is to be found in *Eudemian Ethics* III 7. 2: ". . . and what the ancients called *nemesis* is the feeling of pain at undeserved bad and good fortune and feeling pleasure in deserved bad and good fortune."

The *Poetics* for a Practical Critic

Wayne Booth

I see something strange and wonderful in the fact that the single most important influence on literary criticism has been a puzzling fragment written almost two and a half millennia ago, a work over which Greek scholars quarrel endlessly. Although the *Poetics* comes to me, as it does to most practising critics, through multiple translations that carry meanings Aristotle would no doubt repudiate, I have found – and continue to find – that it "proves" itself in its use.[1] I want to show how – despite changes in critical and literary fashions – the *Poetics* enables us to understand the complexities of complex and difficult works, and thus helps us answer a range of critical questions in a profoundly illuminating way.

My way of using Aristotle can make no scholarly claims for itself: this is "my" *Poetics*, reconstructed as if Aristotle were our contemporary, addressing us moderns as "you," and referring to himself in the first person. Though he thinks of us as somehow alien, my Aristotle is brought up to date. He knows all the genres and species within genres and particular works that we know. His project requires him to repeat what some readers will think banal, but he knows from twenty-four centuries of experience that many other readers need to hear his main points repeated again and again. Indeed much of what he says is intended to convince some "Aristoteleians" that they have been corrupted by modern influences. Needless to say, my "Aristotle" does not dwell on the likelihood of *my* having gone astray.

Artistic Quality as a Subject for Study

The point of our turning to *poetics* now, and thus away from politics and ethics and rhetoric and metaphysics and biology and physics and logic and dialectic and all the other sciences we have pursued, is to explore the twin arts of making and of judging the quality of makings: How can we talk *usefully* about both the art of *making well* and the art of *judging well?* How can we come to an understanding of what we make that will unite makers and judges in a perception of excellence that will prove useful to future makers and judges?

It should surprise no one that we insist here on being useful, as we insist in our *Ethics* on learning to act well rather than simply learning the truth about what constitutes right action. The end of poetics for the poet is to improve in making well; the end of poetics for the critic is to improve in judging makings – and perhaps to assist the poet to create better makings.[2] You English-speaking readers might better call the first of these "poeming," since your English doesn't have a word for it. If you call the second "criticizing," you must remember to limit the term to its root sense of judging quality, leaving to one side – though not necessarily condemning – much of what you in your time *call* criticism.

Distinction Between the Primary World and Imitations

Our experience shows[3] that the human makings we prize and appraise are of two kinds: those that are made and experienced as a direct contribution to what might be called "life itself" or "the primary world" of utility (*our* plows and chairs and soup bowls, *your* bicycles and toothbrushes and army tanks); and those that are "imitations" of whatever actions go on in that primary world. In the primary world, people plow, sail the oceans, kill one another, using objects other people have made. Artists *qua* artist do not sow or reap, make love or beget children, murder or punish; instead they create a "second" nature of representations – an "alternative world" or "secondary reality" – of imagined experience. Artists paint, dance, sing, compose poems, imitating actions people have performed or might have performed in the primary world. Poetics is concerned only with makings of this second kind, makings that reflect, represent, re-make, re-shape materials provided by "life itself": both the kinds our two cultures share (statues, paintings, tragedies, comedies, lyric and satiric poems, philosophical dialogues) and the kinds history has added (novels, movies, TV serials and commercials, comic strips, symphonic music, jazz . . .)[4]

This distinction does not mean that imitations have no practical effect on "life"; indeed some of them, like your TV commercials and magazine ads, are designed specifically to have immediate practical effects (see the "Fourth Distinction" below). Nor does it mean that makings in the primary world will never borrow from the domains of imitation: you have telephones shaped like animals and Woolworth flower pots shaped like some of our most prized nude statues. Please always remember that all of my borderlines are likely to present fuzzy cases; indeed, it is out of the fuzzy cases that many of the most interesting inventions of new genres and species of makings will spring, through the millenia leading to your species-crowded time. Indeed, the interpretations we most like of our work are those that see the distinctions that follow as heuristic, not fixed divisions among essences; but of course we are aware that most interpreters have seen us as among the worst of the essentializers.

First Distinction among Imitations: Means (Medium)

Our experience shows that there are many kinds of re-makings, re-tellings of the usually bungled stories that the primary world creates in its daily round, and that it is not the critic's job to set limits on kinds of making. We live among imitations in language, in music, in dance, in the graphic arts; the possibilities within each of these media are unlimited, and we are happy to see that by now you have invented media and mixtures of media that we could never have dreamed of (though we must confess that some of your inventions, such as rock video and violent TV cop shows stretch our tolerance beyond the breaking point.)[5]

For *useful* criticism – only one of the tasks that "criticism" in your sense will want to perform – we must choose which medium, or mixture of media, we want to dwell on. Principles of making or judgment that apply to painting often do not apply to verbal or musical works, and even when they do it is usually in the most general way: discussions of Phidias or Rembrandt, or comparisons of them with Sophocles or Shakespeare, can never tell us much about whether or why a particular tragedy or dithyramb or comic novel or lyric poem is well composed. Constructional questions of the kind specific to appraising *makings* can be asked usefully only about works that belong to a specific medium, or specified mixture of media. Here we attend to works made primarily in words, with the words occasionally assisted by music, dancing and acting.

In making such relatively sharp distinctions of media, however, we do not mean to deny the usefulness of collapsing those distinctions, when critics wish to pursue questions not directly related to compositional excellence.

Second Distinction: A Further Consideration of End (Function, Purpose, "Final Cause")

Our experience shows that the *verbal* arts can remake the primary world in many different ways, with many different effects, emotional and intellectual. We should thus distinguish diverse *functions* of imitations, just as we have already distinguished imitations from objects in the primary world. It is only in relation to their functions, or ends, that we can ever hope to distinguish good from poor makings. We must, then, search for just the right degree of particularity of ends according to which our judgments are to be made.

It would be folly, for example – one would say "obvious folly" had not so many critics fallen into this foolishness – to judge a tragedy as if it were designed to do precisely what a Platonic dialogue is designed to do. Consequently we must first distinguish those verbal re-makings constructed to be useful or persuasive as truth (stories included in political speeches, say; TV commercials; gospels; hagiographies; philosophical dialogues) from those that exhibit the mysterious, hard to define, somehow "higher purpose-without-purpose" that we discover in works made for the sake of our simply having, or living with, the thing made: disinterested *supplements* to the primary world.[6] Such makings do of course produce practical effects, quite possibly the most powerful effects of any verbal works: the mysterious catharsis, for example, that we experience in attending our tragedies, or the gloriously transformative bliss you and we have experienced when attending to the best of Shakespeare's comedies. That experience can, as every spectator knows, make a great difference in how one copes with life the morning after the play, at the office, or on the farm. But the main "practical" effect pertinent to a properly *poetic* study of imitations-for-imitation's-sake is the quality of the experience itself: the life lived with the work, not the life lived after that living. Those who want to pursue the ethical and political consequences of living with imitations will have to turn to the sorts of study we hint at in our *Politics* and *Ethics.*[7]

Of course it will always be true that politicians and pedagogues will find reason to use poetic imitations as rhetoric to produce practical changes in the primary world. But in turning to poetics proper we want to know, following our invariable practice of pursuing first the distinctive function of each art and science rather than its resemblances to the others, just what is *added to* "primary life" when we re-make it and then enjoy together the act of re-making, of imitating. We'll want to think about just what would be missing if we had only the primary world. That question will prove interesting both when we ask it about the practical uses of imitation, as when the orator turns to *narratio* or the maker of telephones chooses animal shapes, and when we ask it about works that ostensibly claim no immediate usefulness but that were considered by our teacher and friend Plato as spiritually dangerous.

We are aware that our interpreters have disagreed about just how far to push the distinction between practical (or "didactic") imitations and those that are "pure", "aesthetic," "disinterested." Some, like Sheldon Sacks, have claimed vast differences between two kinds of narrative. The first, works like your *Pilgrim's Progress*, or *Gulliver's Travels*, and *1984*, or most of our comedies, imitate an "idea" or structure of ideas; details are selected or rejected as they strengthen or weaken the idea. The second, works like our *Oedipus Rex* or your *King Lear*, imitate an "action"; details are selected or rejected as they strengthen or weaken the experience of characters acting and suffering the consequences of action.[8] For them, the effects produced by the two kinds can overlap, the first (if they're any good) being pleasurable as well as educational, the second (whether they're any good or not) producing educational results, intended and unintended.

Others have gone beyond admitting to the overlap and have simply rejected the distinction, emphasizing rather the shared principles of organization that are found in all highly-articulated narratives. For them the didactic/mimetic distinction is troublesome at best.[9] Others still have claimed that no such distinctions of function can be found *in the works themselves:* they are all the product of varying interests of diverse readers.[10]

Whatever the outcome of any such disputes, we must insist that all appraisals of any composed form must be referrable to the distinctive end that dictated, however mysteriously, its making. Particular tragedies and comedies and satires and spiritual journeys will be mutilated if they are appraised according to inappropriate ends. In short: the *end* of the experience of making and re-making will for us be everywhere dominant.

Third Distinction: the Object Imitated

Our experience shows that such differences of functional organization are closely tied to differences we observe in the diverse *objects* whose *shapes,* or *forms,* are imitated. The form of an *idea* or assemblage of ideas will largely determine how Dante, Swift, Johnson, and Orwell organize their imitations; the form of an *action,* or sequence of deeds-with-consequences, choices made by characters of relatively determinate moral quality – choices leading from here to there (from beginning to ending) – will deterine how Sophocles or Shakespeare or Dickens make *their* choices. Similarly, the ethical quality of the character experiencing a given plot-trajectory will relate reciprocally to whether the end of the work is to be tragic or comic or farcical or lyrical – or whatever.[11]

Fourth Distinction: Manner and its Resources

Your experience has shown that the "above-average" qualities we find in the heroes of our Greek tragedies by no means exhaust the poets' possibilities in producing serious actions with tragic potential. In principle a character can be made, through transformations of *manner,* to appear better than the norm on any dimension of human value. Many of your modern novelists have mastered the art of revealing, in characters whose every external sign would place them, if portrayed on our stage, as far "worse than ourselves," signs of a superior internal sensitivity or charitable spirit completely hidden to other characters within the story.

Experience thus shows that when poets choose what to show as open action or speech, what to tell about what someone said or did, and *whether to show or just tell about or not even to mention the internal condition of thought and feeling* that accompanies overt action and speech, they can turn "the imitation of a serious action with a proper magnitude" into a farce, or "the imitation of a seemingly comic or farcical or loathsome action" into pathos or even something very close to tragedy. In writing the *Poetics* we were seriously handicapped by not having at hand the immensely diverse instances of manipulations of *manner* of the kind that your history offers you. Had we known, say, about the many rich possibilities of stream-of-consciousness, our paragraph at the beginning of Chapter III and our scattered notes later on about the superiority of *showing* over *telling* would have been greatly elaborated. Indeed, we can see now that in our energetic pursuit of how to discern (or create) excellence in tragic drama, we seriously overlooked many revealing subtleties of *manner* even in our own epics.[12] What is a worse oversight, as we view it now, is that we allowed our emphasis on the action imitated, conceived of as something determinate and objective, to lead us to underplay the whole role of the chorus and the power they exercised in our tragedies – as a special form of "shown-telling" – in determining the audience's view of the object.

How to Discern a Species

We have now reached the point, somewhat laboriously, where we can gather together – not the four marks of tragedy, as we originally did at the beginning of Chapter 6, but the four marks of *any* defined species, always remembering that though "end" comes last in the listing, it is ultimately and always formally determinative of the others. Any species will be defined (1) as a given kind of imitated "object" (pattern of life, whether an action in our sense or other quite different patterns, with or without casual connections among the events; in principle our methods can apply to the most paratactically "emplotted" works as well as to those that have a temporal plot of the kinds developed in our tragedies; the only works that can ever escape us would be certain of your modern stochastic, aleatoric non-*works* which in fact have no order to be experienced or analyzed); (2) represented (imitated) in a definably specific manner (telling, showing, *style indirect libre*, stream of consciousness, mixed-or-consistent, etc.); (3) embodied in a specifiable means (language that is metaphor-laden or spare, sentence structure plain or ornate; diction high or low, music-laden, as in Joyce, or prosaic; verbal language or dance or film – any distinctions among media will apply here if they are likely to *affect the effect*); (4) all three of these both determining – in the reader's or spectator's experience – the *effect*, as *end*, or *purpose*, and yet, for the creator, determined in every detail by an intuition of the whole: the end, function "purpose" or "final cause." From the receiver's perspective, the "end" is the total experience of a pattern of hopes, fears, expectations, inferences, thoughts, desires, surprises and fulfilments, a pattern sharing general features with other members of the species, even though each instance of the species is in another sense unique. From the author's perspective, the end is the realization of an "imitated object" that is unified, whole, coherent in its power to fulfil in every detail the potential of the species. For both creator and re-creator, the power of the integrated whole, the "end," will appear to have dictated every choice of detail, regardless of the actual historical path followed by the author in the total act of creation.

If what we have said so far makes sense, it follows that almost nothing we have to say after we have explained why plot is the soul of tragedy (1450b) can be applied directly to any but a very few of the species your criticism addresses. Even when you discuss works that seem to belong to the species of tragedy, you will find, as we do at 1455b, that few of them fall even loosely within the same species as our admired *Oedipus Rex*. You will make hash of your *Othello* or *The Mayor of Casterbridge* or *Death of a Salesman* if you apply, unmodified, our criteria for the best tragedy.

It should now be obvious that a poetic species is, in our view, entirely different from the large loose lumpings that your critics usually try to deal with – what might better be called *genres* or families: "the novel," "the lyric," "poetry," or even "pure poetry." What's more, a species – a poetic kind that can be defined as we define tragedy – is entirely different from the amorphous lump of disparate species ordinarily covered in your time with the word "tragedy." It is neither as general as most of your generic terms nor as particular as the unique work of art: it is what we find when we have *specified* the means (medium), the object (the stuff imitated), and the manner, all three with sufficient precision to further the effect, or "end," or total distinctive power of any particular poem. The re-made piece of life belongs to a *species* of re-making that is *experienceable in some relatively determinate way*. A defined species will thus obviously in principle accommodate more than one member, though usually when artists attempt new instantiations they in fact produce quite different species – a point that could well justify a full treatise in itself.

Especially in times like yours, when novelty seems for many a supreme good,[13] it is probable that poets will invent not just new members of a pre-existing species but works that are *sui generis*, unique instances at their birth of utterly unprecedented species: for example, your James Joyce created, in a fusion of Swift and Sterne and Burton and untold others, a new species of fiction in *Ulysses*. Inevitably, such a fabulous novelty stimulated "imitators" – in a different sense of that much abused word: what we might call piecemeal imitations of object, or of manner, or of means. Thousands of your novelists worldwide have copied devices from *Ulysses*, but even works like Pynchon's *V* or *Gravity's Rainbow*, or William Gaddis's *The Recognitions*, so *Ulysses*-like in some respects, can hardly be said to be of precisely the same species. Yet other species invented in modern times – for example the detective story in which crimes are solved by an eccentric but brilliant central character – have yielded many thousands of exemplars.

Not Form *vs.* Content or Style *vs.* Meaning but Formed Matter as Unified Experience

Working as we are doing here, we treat a poem neither as an abstract form nor as a statement of ideas or themes or meanings – not as form on the one hand

and content on the other, but rather as *a composition to be experienced (or recomposed)*: a created object, a piece of *enformed matter.* The matter is the human stuff; the form is not something separable from the matter but is the matter's own shape.[14]

Seeing poems in this light enables us to escape, if we are careful, the two kinds of criticism that have so badly deflected many moderns from a full appreciation of the marvel that is poetic creation. On the one hand, your critics have dwelt on abstract forms – linguistic patterns, "plots" as mere intrigue, manipulations of point of view. On the other, they have been ideologues, treating the ideas found in poems as themes that might as well have been expressed discursively. Indeed, a great deal of your criticism has consisted simply of prose restatements of what the critics think poems mean. Most of your recent deconstructors of meanings do not escape this reduction: to find meanings evaporating or proving to be inconsistent is still to abstract the ideas of the poem from the human stuff it is made of, and from the reader's or spectator's *experience* of that stuff as *formed in this way.* Nevertheless, it has been encouraging to us to note certain new efforts to develop a more sophisticated ideological critique, one that attends fully to the ideology of the form and not just to extracted doctrines.[15]

The Question of Quality Once Again

Once we have clarified the species of a given poetic form, we can ask with some precision, "Was the making of this form a special achievement, an outstanding instance of the human capacity to make forms – an especially valuable moment in the history of human making?" More precisely, we can ask, "*How* does the invention and ordering of parts here contribute to its success in fulfilling its end – and hence to our deciding whether the making is indeed successful in realizing this specific end?" In short, we can now ask not only "Was this reforming of the universe of forms worth the former's effort – and ours?" but also, "How does the way it is done lead to our experiencing it as we do?"

What this means in practice is that we pick out made forms in the world that, *in our direct experience,* have proved pre-eminently admirable.[16] Everyone who has come to prize some art works over others knows that we value those forms that do something for us or to us that we know, intuitively, to be good. We may go wrong in our loves and hates – that should go without saying. But we come to care about any form that seems to work upon us in ways that feel important, or healing, or purging, or enlightening or just plain pleasant or entertaining – and so on. In the light of such workings, we can – if we wish – explore the parts or elements that are doing the work – just as we would study the detailed features of admired creatures in the primary world, asking what makes them tick when they tick well. We thus find ways of performing a "part/whole analysis" that can at least partially explain how, in this species of poem, the choice and ordination of parts contributes to what is finally admirable – or, in our Greek experience of tragedy, prizeworthy.

When this seemingly subjective criterion – do I admire this form, does it do something to me that I'm glad to have done, does it seem *to me* to succeed? – is treated to such a part/whole analysis, it calls into play criteria that are not merely subjective, because they can now be tested in open discussion. When the lover of tragedy says, or implies, that this or that tragic form is prizeworthy because it does an especially good job of rousing pity and fear and then purging those emotions, it is not easy, and it may be impossible, to convince doubters that this experience is in itself valuable: unless they have had something like the same experience, the lover will find no beginning point for discussion. But when any two people have shared an experience of any form, whenever their sense of its general value in any way overlaps, they can then begin to talk quite rigorously, rationally, objectively, about how the parts work or fail to work toward that experience. And they can then compare *this* specific work that seems to belong in this species with *that* work of the same species, real or merely imagined, for the sake of comparison, and thus compare their relative success within the possibilities of the species.

In short, they can begin to discuss the quite precise question: In this form – this comedy, this tragedy, this meditative sonnet, this tragic opera . . . – do the *parts* do their job fittingly, have they been *made* to fit, to fit better than the parts fit in that other comedy or tragedy or meditative sonnet or tragic opera?

One more point about vocabulary before moving on to our criteria of excellence: When we say, in Chapter 6, that every tragedy necessarily has "six constituent *parts*," your English word, like our Greek *meros*, is full of ambiguities. Writing now in English, we would use the word "elements" or perhaps even the word "materials," for the six general requirements for the very existence of a tragedy of our kind; plot, character, thought, diction, spectacle and melody. Remove any one of these (with the possible exception of spectacle and melody) and you don't simply make a worse tragedy: you eliminate the tragedy entirely, perhaps turning it into some other species of art or praxis. Nobody ever says "This work fails because it has no diction." Rather we point to flaws *in* the diction. If we say "the play has no plot," we really mean that it has a poor plot. In other words, we find in every presented tragedy that all of these elements are by definition present at every moment. The "parts" that we appraise in criticism are those infinitely various moves that poets can make in fulfilling the essential job of the six "elements." Obviously, none of this means that other species exhibit the same six elements, or order their elements in the same way.

The Search for Specific Criteria

What we've said so far suggests that bad criticism is usually bad because it is too general. It is just too easy for the critic to say, this poem is wonderful because it is packed with lovely alliteration and rhymes, or because it has sympathetic characters, or because it expresses this or that deep truth, or because the plot is true to life, forgetting that there are lots of bad poems that are packed with alliteration and rhyme, or sympathetic characters, or deep truths, or realistic details. Indeed, most general criteria for parts/wholes just don't work when we want to appraise particular poems: clarity, beauty, simplicity, complexity, depth, accessibility, originality, universality, coherence, capacity to shock or comfort – each of these can be an artistic virtue, but only when realized in a specific work of a kind that profits from "parts" that help realize the experience of the special virtue.

In contrast to these, what criteria can be useful when we move beyond our first intuitive experience and ask whether an analysis of how parts fit confirms or qualifies our first intuitive responses?

We find only three. (1) Is the given part in any way needed or useful – that is, can it be scrapped without reducing the effectiveness of the whole implicitly aspired to by the other parts, or do we need some others that are not here (the engineer built a marvelous sportscar except for one thing: he forgot to include power brakes)? (2) Are the parts here in the best possible order, or could the working of the whole be more powerful with a different ordering (would this marvelous family camper be improved by putting the refrigerator where the toilet is, and *vice versa*)? (3) Are the parts the right size (does this particular dune buggy need a lower chassis, to lower the center of gravity)?

These three criteria, addition/deletion, transposition, and expansion/contraction, will always – yes, always – give us something worthwhile to say about any form we meet, especially whenever we are challenged to make explicit our intuitive likes and dislikes. [In our talking, in the *Poetics*, about expungability and transposability (end of Chapter 8) and about magnitude (Chapter 7) we surely should have given a fuller account (1451a).]

Addition/Deletion

The first criterion is what we had in mind when we gave the essential "quite short" story of the *Odyssey* and then said, "the rest is episodes": much as we may come to love one or another of all those little side trips on the ten-year journey home, each of them is fungible (that is, substitutable) because the essential experience of the epic would not be destroyed if another episode *of the same general kind* were substituted. (If our original passage is not fresh in your memory, have a look at our shameless commission of the heresy of paraphrase at 1455b; XVII. 6.) We are aware that what we have just said will seem like sacrilege to any New or Newer critic who interprets the work as an embodiment of meanings, or as an inevitably incoherent "text," rather than as a proffered experience; Odysseus's visit to Hades, for example, can be replaced with some other wild descent into some other kind of profundity, without destroying the "epic story," (or plot in our sense). But if the critic has decided that the work is essentially an exploration of the meaning of life, to eliminate Hades would maim it intoleraby. Indeed the real point in our brief argument for the superiority of tragedy over epic just following 1462 (XXVI to the end) is that too much of the *Odyssey* could be expunged or altered without destroying the whole. On the other hand it is clear that the *Odyssey* requires a great number of such episodes if it is to work as it does, and it is superior to other epics just because its episodes are comparatively integrated into the "story" as viewed in "general outline." Though any one of them could be dropped, as a group they are inexpungable.[17]

Suppose we explore what happens when we think along these lines about one of your enduring tragedies, *Othello*. The first step, not an easy one, is to arrive at the same level of confidence about the essential "little story" of *Othello* as we expressed about the *Odyssey*. In doing so we are in effect performing an abstraction from the *soul* of the work – the object imitated and the end aimed for – postponing questions about manner and means.

> A great and generous-spirited general who lacks political and social experience woos and wins a lovely, innocent woman who belongs to a family and culture that feels contempt for *his* culture and deplores the secret marriage [to substitute "race" for "culture" is not essential to this tragic plot, but Shakespeare's choice of race is a brilliant one because it heightens the promise of tragedy]. His wicked lieutenant, who hates him, convinces him that his new wife is betraying him with another officer, using as evidence the claim that no innocent woman would marry a member of his repugnant culture. Maddened with jealousy, the general then kills her, immediately discovers her innocence, and in his anguish kills himself.

Note that we have employed moral epithets here – great, generous, innocent, wicked – of the kind we did not feel the need to apply explicitly to Odysseus when we summarized his story; from your point of view that was an unfortunate oversight in the *Poetics*, since to talk of "a man" does not adequately specify, as all true accounts of species require, the human qualities of the "object imitated." But of course every Greek reader of our text would have imported, silently, the understanding that Odysseus is a significant, "serious," essentially sympathetic character. Obviously the story we outline for the "man" would, according to our own principles, be an entirely different story if our summary could have read, "A wicked, contemptible man is for many years away from home . . ." and so on.

Our "little story" about Othello obviously in one sense mutilates the real *Othello* even more than we mutilated the *Odyssey* by paraphrase. But it does have implicit in it – and that is all we require – the tragic quality that must be heightened by whatever choices the playwright makes if the play is to realize that quality. With this summary and our experience of tragedy in hand, we can ask precise questions about the quality of each artistic choice: the contribution of each part to the whole. A way of putting such questions is this: could we improve the play by adding to or subtracting from the parts Shakespeare pulled out of his almost unbelievably capacious parts-bag?

We must first complicate our earlier distinction (toward the end of 1455b) between the essential story, constructed of essential incidents – for example, there *must* be an encounter between "the man," Odysseus, and the threat to his hearth, the suitors – and what are "episodes." In appraising episodic materials (the word "episodic" has for you moderns taken on a somewhat more pejorative meaning than we intend here), we can distinguish four levels of resistance to cutting: those incidents that are *essential* if the experience is to be what it is; those that are perhaps replaceable but at least useful – something *like* them is required; those that while not especially useful are at least *appropriate;* and those that, because they are neither essential nor useful nor appropriate, not only can be dropped without a trace, but *should* be, because they are in fact harmful to the whole.[18]

Experience teaches about *Othello* (most evidently in contrasting productions) that a good many of its parts can be cut, or replaced with similar parts, without the changes being noticed by anyone but scholars. For example, a very large proportion of the individual lines could be written somewhat differently, and many have been now and again simply dropped, without noticeable harm. Even those quotable quotes that fill the books of famous quotations cannot be said to be absolutely essential: "Virtue? A fig! 'tis in ourselves that we are thus or thus. Our bodies are our gardens, to the which our wills are gardeners." Having come to know such wonderful lines we don't want to lose them, but how could we argue that they are irreplaceable? They are instead what I have called fungible: replaceable with others like them.

What our little summary teaches us, by contrast, is that some parts are absolutely essential – and thus the soul of the work – and that Shakespeare has proceeded brilliantly, whether consciously or unconsciously, in his provision of the essentials and in heightening their power. To have a tragedy formed from this basic story of disastrous jealousy as borrowed and transformed from the novella by Cinthio, at least four characters are essential: you just can't have *this* tragedy without two lovers and a third person as the object of jealousy, and though you could have a play about jealousy with only three characters, you couldn't have a powerful or plausible one without an extraordinarily rich character like Iago to play upon the triangle and make jealousy do its work.

Turning from the essential to the useful, we find a host of minor characters who are brilliantly chosen to heighten the power of the "soul": an attractive, sensitive and somewhat obtuse Casio to help arouse the jealousy; an Emilia and a Roderigo to be manipulated by the villain, so that he can continue to gull the chief victims without their knowing it and without our thinking Othello's gullibility implausible; a Brabantio to get things started with his angry demonstration of Othello's cultural status, thus effectively threatening the doom to come; a duke – on down the line of disposability – to order Othello to Cyprus, where he is in a sense unprotected from his own disastrous will; a couple of noble Venetians to come into the chaos of Cyprus and restore order.

None of these is in any way essential; in fact all but Emilia were wiped out by

Verdi, as you know, when he did his opera *Otello*. Indeed, he found the whole first act unnecessary, since he had available the musical rhetoric needed to get our feelings roused. We do not mean to imply, however, by this introduction of a second version of the play, that the two works are finally of the same species; they are not, not only because of the difference in medium but because the "object imitated" is changed by Verdi away from the plot of a "great good man brought down (in part) by his own weakness" toward the somewhat more romantic plot of "true lovers innocently destroyed." Our essential "little story" for Verdi's work would read quite differently, if we took time to do it right.

The significant point, as we turn to the third level in our pursuit of this play's true quality, is that we find almost nothing that is *merely* "appropriate" or "ornamental." We find only one character whose loss we would not lament: the clown. A picker of nits might add the sailors, or Bianca, another woman Verdi found no use for. Notice again how the standard of what is essential depends on our notion of the species, the special experience of this specific form. If we conducted the same search for what is essential, useful, or appropriate, in discussing a novel by Jane Austen, Dickens, George Eliot, Tolstoy, or Dostoevsky, we would find our standard of necessity established not by the desire for a taut, concentrated tragic effect produced in two or three hours, but rather by the quite different effects of a prolonged and profound entry into larger, more leisurely and more diverse worlds.[19] Far more parts, in such works, seem merely useful or appropriate, far fewer absolutely essential; this is one reason your Henry James concluded, rightly or wrongly, that too many of them were inferior works of art: "great fluid puddings," not possessing the tightly-knit form we are finding in *Othello* and that James created in his best fictions.

Even the parts of *Othello* that we might say are fungible, because at best only appropriate, are so *wonderfully* appropriate, so pat to the point of our experience, that we could not even think of saying, "Your friend Ben is right: You should have blotted that one, old man." Though we would never miss them if they had never been invented, we could not bear to lose them now.

Consider Iago's prolongation of "put money in thy purse." Tight economy, as an abstract criterion, would dictate getting on with the intrigue against Othello. Iago says that he spends time with Roderigo just for his own sport and profit – then he does get on with what is essential explanation: a further promise of his intended villainy. Clearly if we had never experienced the elaborate talk about money and purses we would never miss it. Yet it is entirely appropriate, as ornament to Iago's character, and it adds to our fun and terror as we observe the mounting signs of his rhetorical skill and consequent threat to our hero.

When we descend finally to the fourth level, seeking parts that are not just expungable but harmful, we find nothing whatever. In contrast, when we attend your modern plays, we encounter in many of them entire second acts that seem to weaken effects sought by the first and third. In *Othello* (though not in all of Shakespeare's plays) we find hardly a line that does not seem either necessary, useful, or appropriate. He just is too good to give any opening to our cutting scissors, which in our terms means he is near perfection in making every detail *function* toward heightening the shattering tragedy of Othello's destruction. In this play it's as if he had written to stand up under *our* closest scrutiny.

We should stress again both that our method has led to demonstrable assertions of quality, and that those assertions are demonstrable only in reference to a clearly specified tragic form. If we tried, for example, to appraise the play as a dramatized theodicy, or as a treatise on feminism, most of which we now consider essential or useful could simply be scrapped in production and ignored or deplored in criticism. This is in fact what much of your criticism does to parts of Shakespeare's plays plucked for the purpose clean out of the functioning wholes.[20]

Size of Parts

Turning to the criterion of amplification, let us shift to *Oedipus Rex*. *Oedipus* has been famous since my time for its ability to stand up under the first criterion: every step, every character, every moment seems essential, as it is obviously organized to build and build and build to the greatest realization not just of Oedipus's disaster, but to the tragedy of his family and of the whole city. This tautness is obviously what led Coleridge to call it one of the greatest plots of all time – one that can stand up under questions about expungability with greater pride even than *Othello* can.

But how does it look when we ask whether the right elements have been amplified to just the right degree, with just the right heightening of diction, thought, or character, to make the plot work at the highest possible level.[21] If we placed *Oedipus* in the wrong species, we would be led to questions that would almost certainly mutilate the play. For example, if Greek tragedy were treated as only an interesting but heavy-handed early beginning toward the full glories of the sub-species of tragedy realized by Shakespeare, you would surely want to reduce the role of the chorus by about two-thirds. Some of our own more secular contemporaries have indeed complained, after our annual festival, that they have been bored by the constant interruptions of "the plot" with prolonged speculative comments. Only when we sense the full *religious* tragedy of a city, even of a culture, and sense how in that culture that kind of tragedy entails grappling with the gods and what they mean in the life of the city, do we see just how, for that effect, a large dose of choral speculation and lament and generalization is not just useful but required. Here we must admit that our *Poetics* appears, in retrospect, shockingly silent on the special religious qualities of this species. If we had known *Othello*, its individualized difference would have led us to say more about the centrality of explicit and prolonged religious and philosophical commentary in the *Oedipus* kind of tragedy.

Transposability

The third criterion, placement, or sequencing or "ordination," deserves more space than we can give it here, since it is the source of so many wonderful effects created by the artists of your time: Proust, James, Faulkner, and their followers. Too much of your criticism could be applied unchanged if the works discussed had been composed backwards, or scrambled: so little account do the critics take of excellence in ordered sequence.

Of course this criterion, like the others, becomes applicable in radically different forms in different genres: in plays and novels, it appears in choices of what should be shown dramatically, as scene, and what should merely be narrated. In poems it appears both in the sequencing of stanzas and lines within stanza and in the sequence and tempo of what is revealed. In short, all works that succeed have some kind of "suspension," but the kind varies with the needs of the work. In *Othello* Shakespeare could have kept us guessing about Iago's wickedness until Act V; instead he gives us an early scene that removes all of *that* kind of suspense once and for all. In *Oedipus* there is even less mystery, since "we" all know the facts before the play begins: the entire emphasis of the ordering is on dramatic irony.[22]

Note that transposing parts seldom if ever changes the nature of the object imitated; it changes mainly the audience's apprehension of that object. The chronological events of *Othello* remain the same whether Iago's character is revealed to us early or late, but our experience can be transformed by the slightest transformation. In this respect our *Poetics* can be seen as frequently rhetorical: asking not just "how are beautiful verbal objects organized?" but "how are they made to move audiences in specific ways?"

If the editor had granted us twice as much space, we should have been delighted to take this rare chance to consider one by one the main objections that critics over the millenia have raised about the *Poetics*. Instead we can mention only a few of them and hint at how we might reply:[23]

CRITIC: *You lead to pigeonholing*, shoe-horning the living work into pre-ordained slots.

ARISTOTLE: Not at all: that's only what some of our misguided readers have done, eager to find a crutch to lean on. For us it is the poet who invents the species, requiring the critic to be endlessly alert in the effort to allow *experience*, not schemata, to guide the inquiry. You have missed the point of our insistence on working *a posteriori*.

CRITIC: You belabor the obvious. Most careful critics achieve, intuitively and without all this apparatus, a precision of family-placement sufficient for all practical purposes.

ARISTOTLE: Well, yes, we do believe that careful readers often arrive intuitively at what we here spell out laboriously. A sensitive critic without any such scheme as we have recommended will commit fewer ravages on individual works than some "Aristotelian" who carefully traces the object, manner, means, and end of a work without every having experienced its workings. But even "sensitive readers" tend to be sensitive only in certain dimensions, and they fall into habits of placement that do great injustice to new works belonging to hitherto unknown species. The degree of system that we hope for – seeking always only that degree of precision that is appropriate to the subject matter[24] – can be a fine protection against one's over-confident intuitions.

CRITIC: You treat works as if each of them aspired to only one "end," but we moderns have learned that the works we care for do not have some single "soul" that controls everything the poet has done and everything the careful reader discovers. Surely it takes no passionate commitment to the deconstructionist enterprise to recognize that every work we care about bursts the seams of any formulation of the central intention that we might attempt, whether of the species or of the particular work.

ARISTOTLE: Granted: dogmatic soul-labeling in poetics, like soul-labeling in life, can freeze the enterprise. But the fact remains (see n. 10) that any one reader or viewer *experiences* only one work at a given time (even if that work is experienced as ambiguous). If the objection is simply that different readers and viewers respond in different ways, who has ever denied it? If it is that there is in fact nothing in common among the diverse responses of different readers, then the objector should engage in more careful observing. If we are ever given a chance for fuller debate with modernist celebrations of difference, we shall be able to show, quite easily, that there is more common ground among *experienced* readers than is generally acknowledged. Critics dispute only what they dispute about, and their disputes are mutually intelligible only to the degree that they share some sense of the disputed objects. Reading even the wildest deconstructionist on *Oedipus* (with the title and author's name expunged), one would never suspect that the work being discussed might actually be *Aucassin et Nicolette* or *Beowulf*.[25]

If on the other hand the objection is that our method abstracts from the full vitality of the actual literary works, then of course we can only concur. All critical methods are inherently reductive, when their results are compared with what happens when any great art work is engaged with fully.

CRITIC: You neglect the most important questions, the questions that really interest readers and spectators: about the meaning of life, about ethical and political and cultural and historical issues.

ARISTOTLE: Read our other works. Then, when you come back to read the *Poetics* more carefully, you'll be surprised at how many of those "more interesting" questions are implicitly addressed, once you face constructional questions with a determination to attend to the ethical qualities that are inescapably present in any effective plot. Appraisals of the relative ethical value of different works and different species are implicit, for example, in what we say about the superiority of certain characters and plot forms over others.

CRITIC: You hardly mention the grand differences in quality and effect to be found among large-scale diverse *genres* of imitation: the novel, for example, as opposed to drama or lyric poetry.[26] Your scrappy talk in the *Poetics* about the differences between tragedy and epic does not even mention possible differences of *ethical* effect. Yet surely there are qualitative differences in the effect of the private reading of novels and epics (say) and the public attendance at plays or the family viewing of TV.

ARISTOTLE: True enough, but such questions are even more difficult to grapple with than the ethical differences among species and among individual works within a species. We always hope to formulate our sciences in such a way as to produce the possibility of shared intellectual or practical progress. Should we not be allowed to do one thing at a time?

CRITIC: You just assume, without hard proof, that differences of quality are real. You ignore our modern discovery that all judgments of quality are contingent upon the culture and psychology of the judge.

ARISTOTLE: We not only ignore it, we reject it, and we refuse to repeat here our many reasons for rejecting it.[27]

CRITIC: Your bias for construction of "imitations" that are unified as *actions* leads you to ignore or underplay a multitude of other kinds of structure or anti-structure that in fact have merit. Your rather spurious effort to bring your work up-to-date still fails to face up to the challenge presented by the many anti-genres and mixed genres of modern times?

ARISTOTLE: Yes of course: we have always had to concentrate on the most impressive art works that we have experienced. For example, had we known even a fraction of your fictional works we would have insisted that the soul of many of them is not a plot or action at all, in our sense of the words, but an *action of telling,* a kind of intricate dance-of-manner performed through a special relation between an ironic, playful, elusive implied author and the attentive reader. The various species of this kind of *imitation of the act of imitation* pursue the end (final cause) not of catharisis of tragic emotions but of various kinds of wonder, amusement, or despair appropriate to different kinds of authorial struggle, success, or failure, and different views of the world in which the telling occurs. The various kinds of intricacy and skill in the dance of telling become the *dynamis* of each of the various species in this "reflexive" genre. To admit as much is not, however, a violation of our inductive method: it is just an invitation to construct other *poetics* based on what experience of these other species reveals. (Perhaps we should underline a point implicit here throughout: you have not written a "poetics" of any species until you can be sure that someone reading your account could go away and compose another recognizable instance of the kind, simply on the basis of your account.)

We might also have gone on to speculate about such exploitations of manner-as-central, asking about what is gained, and lost, when actions in my sense are cast aside and the dance of manner becomes central. The temptation to tell a story that imitates the action of telling a story has been prominent for at least two millenia,[28] though it has been succumbed to so frequently in the late twentieth century as to threaten, at least from our perspective, total burnout.

We would also note again that many of your modern works that appear to be actions in our sense are really not imitations of an action but imitations of an idea as represented in a pseudo-action.[29] Your poets have become increasingly skillful, over the centuries, in disguising works that are actually apologies, organized as patterns of ideas, making them appear to be actions depending on probable and necessary linear connections among characters' choices. And others depend on new forms of satire – deliberate assaults on reader's beliefs – as the "soul" of the work, even though the "surface" looks totally non-didactic. Still others have introduced deconstructions of concepts like "character" and "sympathy" that would require analytical efforts radically different from most of what we have said here. In this respect one might well want to consider . . .

Obviously once my Aristotle gets wound up, he will never stop, so I must cut him off arbitrarily. But where am I, Wayne Booth, in all this? Obviously I cannot expect that many readers will turn from fashionable current interests to explore with me, once again, just what can be learned from the "constructional" mode recommended here. I do not myself intend to occupy a major part of my critical time writing as I have done here about *Othello* and *Oedipus;* though I happen at the moment to be doing a constructional analysis of James's *The Wings of the Dove,* I shall move next to "ideological" subjects like a theoretical defense against political torture, a probing of the literature of fundamentalism, and a comparative study of how people talk about conversion experiences.

But the truth is that something like the thinking reported on here, at the risk of obviousness and tedium, will precede and perhaps underlie everything I shall want to say about specific literary works in those ideological enterprises. Any criticism of any artistic work's ideology that is not preceded by the care with form that "Aristotle" has tried to illustrate here can teach us little about the work, however much it may tell us about the critic.

An uncomfortable personal way of putting my continuing debt would be to assert that I could never have written *The Rhetoric of Fiction,* or any of the evaluative portions of subsequent works, without pursuing a version of the method I extract from the *Poetics,* especially the first six chapters. In the mid-1950s I looked up, as it were, from a decade of trying to understand both the *Poetics* and the fiction I loved, and I discovered that just about everybody was lumping together huge heaps of works – the novel, "fiction," the true novel, the-novel-as-poetry – and then lashing away at individual works because they violated rules about point-of-view that were really applicable, at best, only to some items in the heap. Working with only one or at best two of the "causes" Aristotle dwells on, ignoring too often the differences among the "objects imitated" and the question of divergent poetic ends, they had discovered single tests for all comers.[30]

Now – more than three decades later – as I look at other inquirers into ideological significance I see too many of them as lacking a clue about what is entailed before one pronounces on the ideology of a work – before one can claim to have reconstructed what current fashion calls its "values." A primary motive in attempting to reinstate the study of compositional excellence is the hope of enabling ideological critics to address one another more productively: we can't manage genuine debate about our judgement of a work unless we find ways to talk together in *some* sense about *the same work.*

Notes

Those notes that are in italics are by "Aristotle"; all others are by WCB.

1. I was introduced to the *Poetics* four decades ago by the "Chicago neo-Aristotelians." The works that have been most important to me are *Critics and Criticism: Ancient and Modern,* ed. Ronald S. Crane (Chicago, 1952), Crane's *The Languages of Criticism and the Structure of Poetry* (Toronto, 1953), and Richard McKeon's "Rhetoric and Poetic in the Philosophy of Aristotle," in Bibliography below.

2. I remember Ronald Crane saying, in about 1955: "What pleases me most about the work of the Chicago school on the *Poetics* is the number of responses I get from novelists and playwrights thanking us for our help." Not long ago I met a producer of TV dramas who said: "The most important single influence on my success here has been Sheldon Sacks' teaching of the *Poetics.*" This is not the place to give a full account of the so-called Chicago School, not just the first generation but the many who, under their influence, have made the *Poetics* central to their criticism. In "Between Two Generations: The Heritage of the Chicago School" (*Profession 82,* Modern Language Association of America, 1982, pp. 19–26), I once gave a brief – and by now sadly outdated – account of some of those who openly confess some affiliation with or indebtedness to the "School": Walter Davis, Robert Denham, Homer Goldberg, Arthur Heiserman, Elizabeth Langland, Richard Levin, Richard McKeon, Norman Maclean, James Malek, Robert Marsh, Elder Olson, Peter Rabinowitz, Ralph Rader, Mary Doyle Springer and Austin M. Wright. You can look them up. It is often said, by people who are bored with careful inquiry into forms, that the Chicago School had little influence: their closest rivals, the New Critics, won the day. But I would claim – naturally enough – that my Aristotle would take far more pleasure and pride in reading the works of these men and women than in reading the vastly larger pile of explications and thematic readings springing from the New Critics – and I haven't even listed those who owe more to the "School's" pluralistic philosophy and emphasis on a special kind of literary and intellectual history.

3. I am always surpised at how little is made, by most commentators and borrowers, of Aristotle's habitual testing of his claims against "what our experience shows." Even when his argumentative steps look like logical deductions one can often see that the logic is an empirical consultation of what the experience of tragedy necessarily

entails: "Since the representation is performed by living persons, *it follows* at once that one essential part of tragedy is the spectacular effect . . ." (6.5. Loeb ed.).

4. *Of course on another occasion we might get around to writing a "poetics" of industrial design. I am told that you have developed schools of design that claim to do for coffee pots what we claim to do for poems. See, for example, Richard Buchanan, "Wicked Problems in Design,"* Thinking Design Issues VIII *(Spring 1992) No. 2.*

5. I (WCB) must confess that Aristotle seems to me somewhat too sure of his opinions here. What kind of objective inquirer would lash about him like this?

6. *Our great-great-great-great grandson, I. Kant, will have a lot to say about this.*

7. *See the gratifying use that my pupil, W. Booth, makes of my work on friendship (Books VIII and IX of my Ethics), as applied to the time lived in the company of re-makings of this "impractical" kind:* The Company We Keep: An Ethics of Fiction *(Berkeley, 1988), Chs 6–7. See also Martha C. Nussbaum's* Love's Knowledge: Essays on Philosophy and Literature *(New York, 1990).*

8. Sheldon Sacks, along with some other "Chicago Critics," in fact expanded this twofold division to three, dividing didactic works into satires and apologues. What organizes the parts of satires, he claims, is the satiric purpose – a pattern of ideas, in one sense, but with that pattern determined by an aim at an "external" target. What organizes the parts of apologues, he says, is of course the "apology": the truth to be taught. His favorite example was always Johnson's *Rasselas*, which, though it clearly in one sense imitates an action in which some events lead, consequentially, to other events, is overtly and clearly organized overall according to a limited number of possible roads to happiness. Each possible path is knocked down in turn by events obviously invented for the sake of illustrating a final truth about life, not for the sake of completing an intelligible action. See Sheldon Sacks, *Fiction and the Shape of Belief: A Study of Henry Fielding, with Glances at Swift, Johnson, and Richardson* (Berkeley, CA, 1964).

9. See Zahava Dorinson McKeon, *Novels and Arguments: Inventing Rhetorical Criticism* (Chicago, 1982).

10. *Your contemporary love affair with indeterminacy depends for its appeal on noting just how many meanings a given reading-culture, or even a given reader, can find in any great work. But when one thinks of EXPERIENCE rather than MEANING, one finds that a given reader can have only one experience of a work at a time, an experience that is always to some degree "determinate": it is just this experience (however manifold) and no other. The experience will immediately grow and change as the reader re-reads and talks with other readers, as W. Booth has insisted with his concept of "coduction"* (The Company We Keep, *pp. 70–75). But still, AT ANY ONE MOMENT, it can be only what it is and not what some other reader's happens to be. Any reader's appraisals will carry weight, in discussion, only to the degree that others are persuaded to agree to something like his or her view of its "end."*

11. *We are not concerned about whether the artist's choices are made consciously or unconsciously. You will have noticed that our* Poetics *has nothing whatever to say about the differences between conscious intentions and unconscious or Muse-directed choices. It is the "intention" of the emerging art work, as invented by the perhaps totally muse-dominated poet's intuition of its emerging possibilities, that determines the choices; in this highly specialized kind of* qualitative *inquiry it is only in rare circumstances that we can hope to find much use for research into a poet's stated "intentions" – quite a different sense of the word.*

12. These are what I thought I was elaborating when I began writing *The Rhetoric of Fiction* (Chicago, 1962; rev. ed., 1983). It actually grew into a work that in a sense "rhetoricized" not just what the *Poetics* says about "manner" but all of the "causes" and "parts" that Aristotle covers.

13. I like the saying that the Chinese have recently developed in criticizing young

novelists too eager to pursue "Western" novelties: "They are so hotly pursued by the mad dogs of innovation that they cannot find time to go to the side of the road to piss" (private report of visitor to China, 1991).

14. *We hoped to have established this truth from the beginning. But everybody chose, soon after our demise, to revert to making the rhetorical form/content distinction basic, leaving us to twist and turn in our grave. Indeed, we feel that Booth often commits the same heresy.*

15. For examples of how this can be done, see Barbara Foley, "Race and Class in Radical African – American Fiction of the Depression" *Nature, Society and Thought* III (1990) 305–324 and James Phelan, *Reading People, Reading Plots; Character, Progression, and Interpretation of Narrative* (Chicago: 1989).

16. *Some interpreters – we note especially Booth – have tended to use the word "love" in this context: we find that we love a creation and then we try to explain it. But to me to use such language would be to sell out to the sentimental views of my mentor, Plato.*

17. Of all the claims made in the *Poetics*, the evaluations of epics versus plays seems to me, WCB, one of the shakiest. There is surely something wrong with Aristotle's application of the criterion of "unified action" to works like the *Odyssey*, leading to "his" claim here that the Hades scene is fungible!

18. *Many of the disharmonies uncovered by your deconstructionists are indeed disharmonies. But often enough they are not caused by* écriture *or culture or whatever but simply by the inattention or lack of genius in their authors. Would that all the second-and third-generation deconstructionists were as given to close reading as their masters, who can be more penetrating about forms than many a critic who claims to rely on my work! And would that all of them would look for harmonies of experience rather than harmonies of meaning; since every great work is necessarily packed with clashes of meanings, their search for incoherencies can never fail!*

19. It is this difference, elaborated, that leads Martha Nussbaum to the claim that long fictions are the most powerful of all literary works in their ethical effects. See esp. *Love's Knowledge*, pp. 236–237.

20. See the work of another prize pupil of mine, Richard Levin, for example *New Readings of Old Plays: Recent Trends in the Reinterpretation of English Renaissance Drama* (Chicago, 1979).

21. *We should not need to underline the point that our first four elements are in a hierarchical order of form and matter: plot enforms the matter of character; character enforms the matter of thought; thought enforms the matter of diction. The pattern breaks down, of course, as we come to spectacle and melody, both of which, like the others, are found at every point in the play but are enformed by all the other four, not just by diction. You see, we do work both with system and with attention to WHAT EXPERIENCE SHOWS.*

22. *Needless to say, had we been able to know the work of critics like Gérard Genette, and the novels they discuss with great rigor, our own hints about transposability would have been expanded. See* Narrative Discourse: An Essay in Method, *Trans. Jane. E. Lewin (Ithaca, 1980). Original, 1972.*

23. *The most telling objections have been aimed, we want to emphasize, at misreadings and misguided "Aristotelian" practices that we in fact never advanced and strongly repudiate.*

24. *Ethics* I. 3.

25. For a careful argument about the sharings on which our differences are built, see Ralph Rader, "Fact, Theory, and Literary Explanation," *Critical Inquiry* I (Dec. 1974) 245–272.

26. See Bakhtin's elaborate encomium to "the novel," a "genre" not defined by any list of actual novels, though represented by the greatest novelist, Dostoevsky. Michael M. Bakhtin, *The Dialogic Imagination: Four Essays*, ed. Michael Holquist, trans. Caryl Emerson and Michael Holquist, (Austin, TX, 1981).

27. *We cannot resist, however, citing once again Booth's valiant demonstration, in Chapters 3 and 4 of* The Company We Keep, *of the absurdity of attributing all judgments of value to the judges only, leaving no powers whatever to the poems judged.*

28. *We must say that we are much impressed by Booth's early dissertation, which no one but ourselves seems to have read, in which he struggles to identify the species of the earliest great success of this kind:* "Tristram Shandy *and Its Precursors: The Self — Conscious Narrator"- (Diss. Univ. of Chicago, 1950); "Did Sterne Complete* Tristram Shandy?" *Modern Philology 48 (1951), 172–183; "The Self-Conscious Narrator in Comic Fiction before* Tristram Shandy," *Proceedings of the Modern Language Association, 67 (1952) 163–. 185. But it is surely significant that Booth himself claims to have worked, dealing with that "formless" novel, strictly according to principles learned from our* Poetics.

29. See David Richter, *Fable's End: Completeness and Closure in Rhetorical Fiction* (Chicago, 1974).

30. A dramatic instance of this can be found in Caroline Gordon's letters of advice to Flannery O'Connor, telling her just what rules of point of view must be obeyed if one is to write good fiction.

Epilogue:
The *Poetics* and its Interpreters

Stephen Halliwell

Aristotle's *Poetics* . . . is at once the first work entirely devoted to "literary theory" . . . and one of the most important in the canon. The simultaneous presence of these two features is not without paradox: it is as if a man with an already greying moustache were to emerge from his mother's womb . . .

(T. Todorov)

Historical culture is indeed a kind of inborn grey-hairedness . . .

(Nietzsche)[1]

The recurrently, indeed tenaciously, significant status of the *Poetics* within the long vista of literary criticism, is a remarkable phenomenon whose ramifications, both positive and negative, can be evaluated from numerous standpoints. If we are today relatively well placed to understand some of the complexities of the work's role in this unfinished story, it remains doubtful whether this gives us anything like a supreme vantage point from which to review our own relationship to the contents of Aristotle's small yet tersely challenging treatise. We have reached a point at which our technical equipment, in terms of linguistic, historical and philosophical scholarship, allows us to achieve a consistent and defensible view of many of the *Poetics'* major ideas and emphases, as well as to identify the shape of the ground on which disagreements over some of its still controversial implications must be pursued. But there seem to be at least two striking respects in which we fall short of being able to settle our relations to the *Poetics*. In the first place, the work continues to confront us with what might be described as a difficult mixture of the explicit and the implicit, a combination of crisply stated arguments with elusively exploratory hints and suggestions, thus generating a peculiarly intriguing stimulus to interpretative interest. In addition, there is perhaps now less intellectual consensus than ever before about the uses we might aim or desire to make of the writings of the past, especially where those writings bring with them so large an inheritance of cultural attention, and so many accretions of contentious exegesis, as does the *Poetics*.

409

If this last point alerts us to a sharp tension between attitudes of detachment and assimilation (even "appropriation") towards the texts of classical antiquity, it might be argued – and this is a theme which will reappear – that this is not an entirely new predicament, but only an exacerbated version of a dilemma at least as old as the Renaissance. Whatever verdict might eventually be reached on that larger question, it seems at any rate plausible to suppose that the enterprise of coming to terms with as familiar yet distant an object as the *Poetics* can only benefit from a heightened and strongly comparative awareness of how, on a cultural rather than purely material level, we have come to possess this work at all: an awareness, that is to say, of the fluctuating ways in which earlier periods have addressed themselves, and adjusted their own critical concerns, to the arguments of the *Poetics*. It is something more than an automatically defensive gesture to observe that an awareness of this kind needs to be fostered by detailed and thorough work on a large number of topics; it cannot be achieved to any very extensive degree, only perhaps encouraged, by the summary and limited considerations which I shall sketch in this closing chapter.[2] Such a caveat is of course a necessary acknowledgment of the size and multiplicity of the questions which loom up once we try to hold in a steady frame of reference the interpretation and reception of the *Poetics* over half a millennium. But it is also an admission that what strikes us as significant about that long and intricate history will depend on the points of view implicit in the assumptions and concerns which we call our own. It is certainly easy enough to find fault with many features, in particular, of neoclassical Aristotelianism; I have done so myself elsewhere. In this essay, however, I want to try and draw out some strands of positive import concerning the motivation of those involved in the different phases of the work's fortunes. The *Poetics* has been, and continues to be, approached from a considerable variety of angles, each of which brings its own priorities and pressures of understanding with it. It may make a real difference not just to our reading of the work itself, but also to our assessments of earlier readings, how we estimate the comparative importance of such aims as situating the *Poetics* within Aristotle's larger system of thought; judging its success as an account of certain genres and works of Greek literature; treating it as the basis of a full-blown theory of poetry or literature; considering its (potential) relevance to types of writing practised in our own culture; or extracting from it germinal ideas which are capable of further development and elaboration in the terms of more recent styles of criticism.

One temptation to be avoided is the assumption that the treatment of the *Poetics* by successive commentators, translators and critics can be definitively judged by the standards or methods, whether philological or critical, of our own day. That there has been substantial and coherent, though scarcely unilinear, progress in the technical exegesis of the treatise, between the time, say, of Averroes' twelfth century "middle commentary" (which, in its Latin translation,[3] exercised strong influence on many Renaissance readers, until displaced by the major sixteenth century works of Robortello, Castelvetro and others) and the scholarship of the past century or so, is impossible to deny. One of the results of this progress is a basis of common comprehension and evidence with which it would be absurd to dispense. But it would be exceedingly partial and unilluminating to view five hundred years of *Poetics'* interpretations purely in this fashion; such an angle of vision would fail to notice many ideas and preoccupations which have persistently motivated significant and interesting attitudes towards the work. Equally, however, it will hardly do to regard this same vista as no more than a demonstration of the irredeemably relativist character of all interpretation, or to believe that we have no secure historical basis on which to order and estimate the disparate claims that have been made about the treatise. It is possible for us to draw some essential discriminations between the arguments of the *Poetics* and the concerns of its interpreters, and to discriminate too between the diverse implications of the demands which these interpreters, ourselves included, make of the treatise. In short, we can hope to blend historical judgment with a considerate sensitivity to the shifting critical and ideological currents in which the interpretation of the *Poetics* has often become caught up. And the purpose of doing so will be to achieve, at the same time, an improved grasp of what the *Poetics* may have to offer its readers, and a sharper alertness to some of the factors which are capable of affecting our own stance towards it.

The *Poetics* seems, on the face of it, an unlikely work to have achieved so seminal a status. Incomplete; substantially afflicted by textual corruptions; somewhat disproportionate in its treatment both of types and of aspects of Greek poetry; rarely as full as we might like it to be in elucidation of its leading ideas, and sometimes brief and inchoate to the point of deep obscurity – all these features make the small treatise a work which is frequently elusive and tantalising. Yet it requires little reflection to see that the spareness of the *Poetics'* fabric of argument is, in fact, also a key part of the explanation for two of the salient characteristics of its cultural afterlife, at least since the Renaissance: first, for the fascination which it has repeatedly exercised over readers and critics; second, for the degree to which the work has been found valuable in the creation of literary creeds, and in the prosecution of aesthetic controversy. The condition of the treatise is such that its structure of ideas consists of a peculiarly thought-provoking combination of prominent emphases (on mimesis, on genre, on poetic form and unity, on the central tragic emotions), intriguingly terse and inconclusive formulations of certain cardinal points *(katharsis, hamartia)*, and an admixture of suggestive *aperçus* (e.g. on the relation between character and action, the difference between poetry, history and philosophy, or the range of "objects" of mimesis available to the poet).

One result of this configuration of elements has been the capacity of the work to make itself available to a large diversity of literary interests, from the sometimes academic classicism of the sixteenth or seventeenth centuries to the post-Freudian psychology or the structuralist poetics of recent times. Another, kindred result has been the discrepant and, at times, keenly contested nature of the verdicts that have been passed on the *Poetics*. Aristotle's approach to poetry has been equally often judged to be modestly empirical or theoretically comprehensive and systematic (at least in its ambitions). His aesthetic stance has been found by some to be essentially moralistic, by others a model of pure formalism or aestheticism. His pronouncements have been praised and followed as instructively authoritative (or condemned as narrowly authoritarian), but also admired for what as shrewd a reader as Goethe called their "Liberalität"[4] and what many have seen as their notably tolerant and patient response to the absolutism of Plato. In each of these respects there is something of interest to be said on either side, though it would be facile to infer that the striking of a balance would necessarily get us closest to the truth in every case. What can fairly safely be said is that the assortment of views historically held about the character of the work reflects a subtle interplay between its own attributes and the needs brought to their reading of it by critics of many different schools.

These considerations can be given further substance by observing that the centuries of repeated translation, interpretation and appraisal of the *Poetics* since the Renaissance have been marked by a complex, overlapping pattern of both continuity and change. Let us start from the sketchy but convenient simplification that reduces this pattern to a succession of three main periods; first, the establishment, in sixteenth century Italy and subsequently in other parts of Europe, of a body of putatively Aristotelian principles and standards within the movement of literary neoclassicism; secondly, in the eighteenth and early nineteenth centuries, a growing disparagement and neglect of a work now heavily tarnished by its association with institutionalized and academic constraints; finally, the modern recovery of interest in the treatise, albeit interest of a now more temperate, modified and eclectic variety. As we follow the elaboration of this historical development in greater if severely selective detail, a number of necessary qualifications will emerge, and the most important of them will serve to show that the simple contrasts of this skeletal scheme disguise the many instabilities of use and evaluation in which the *Poetics* has repeatedly become caught.

In the first place, I wish to stress that the understanding of the *Poetics* in the era of neoclassicism was not a static phenomenon; it evolved with the changing phases, and was affected by the conflicting strains, through which the movement as a whole passed. The book assumed a central yet disputed significance for this movement principally as a result of the extraordinarily intense half-century of Italian literary argument and practice between approximately 1530 and 1580. It was at this time that its contents were widely disseminated in educated circles, in both Latin (especially Pazzi's, 1536) and Italian (especially Segni's, 1549) translations; that a series of large and elaborate commentaries were devoted to it (including those of Robortello (1548), Vettori (1560) and Castelvetro (1570)); and, no less importantly, that reference to the *Poetics* became a salient feature of the controversies pursued in the literary treatises, as well as the prefaces to individual works, which were produced in such profusion in this period. But these dry data inadequately communicate the strikingly serious nature of the struggles for artistic values which were conducted within this whole phenomenon of revived Aristotelianism. In the literary ferment and the critical debates of sixteenth century Italy, historical interpretation of the *Poetics* as a set of arguments tied to their own, highly particular cultural milieu, was not completely unknown to the most careful of the commentators; but it was overwhelmingly subordinated, in the period as a whole, to an engagement with the *Poetics* as a document thought to contain concepts and values of great relevance to the culture of the present. The *Poetics* mattered so much to writers and critics, in an age of evolving classicism, above all because it was read and interpreted in relation to the literature, and the possibilities of literary production, in the contemporary world.

But it would be highly misleading to claim that this cultural state of affairs turned the *Poetics* easily or automatically into an unquestioned source of doctrinal orthodoxy. Three points can be highlighted here to counteract any such oversimplification: first, the *Poetics* was not usually a self-sufficient or exclusive basis for classical principles, but contributed to a compound and varying body of doctrine which derived its components from a broader range of ancient texts; second, its weight and authority were far from uniformly accepted, but were subject to constant reassessment; third, its standing was always open to special contention in relation to the debates which surrounded the production of new literature and the fostering of genres not discussed by Aristotle (lyric, pastoral, romance, tragicomedy). The *Poetics* was rarely an isolated object of attention or source of critical tenets. Not only was it regularly interpreted alongside, and in the light of, Horace's *Ars Poetica,* in such a way as to dilute many of its own distinctive ideas into a kind of homogenized rhetorical classicism; but there was constant, if unsystematic, reference and comparison to other ancient sources (Plato, Cicero, Quintilian, as well as classical poets, Latin much more often than Greek) whose interests and aims were not always consistent with Aristotle's. Particularly widespread was the application to the *Poetics* of two fundamental ideas from Horace: decorum or propriety as the indispensable requirement of all literary practice; and a mixture of moral purpose with pleasure, "utile dulci," as the essential aim of literature. But there were more specific conflations of disparate views. As regards tragedy, to give a token instance, the surviving formulae of Latin grammarians (Diomedes, Donatus, Evanthius), as well as the practice of Senaca, were influential in spreading a conception of the genre which focused on both the necessarily high social status of tragic figures and the externally appalling nature of their sufferings,[5] in contrast to the *Poetics'* stricter emphases on tragic agency, ethical character and the progressive logic of an integrated plot-structure. The simplified definition of tragedy, heavily promoted by Scaliger and others, was, at best, a pale reflection of Aristotle's account of tragedy; yet it was very rarely challenged by supposedly Aristotelian critics before the eighteenth century (the *Discours* of Corneille being one of the few exceptions).

Furthermore, it is a common misapprehension to suppose that Aristotelian authority was ever really straightforward or undeviating in the neoclassicism of the sixteenth to eighteenth centuries. Excessively familiar appeals to the slogans of the Unities and "les règles" represent only those points at which the conflicts and arguments aroused by literary classicism hardened into academic shibboleths of orthodoxy; they are a far from sufficient or reliable guide to the whole range of interpretative positions and commitments taken up by critics, writers and readers in this period. Similarly, assertions of Aristotle's infallibility as a regulator of literary standards tend to acquire a somewhat fideistic character, and they certainly illustrate only one extreme of the actual deployment of the *Poetics* in the manifold artistic disputes of the time. The underlying and urgent impetus behind the tradition of neoclassical reference to the treatise derives from the pressures that had built up within the larger cultural matrix created by Renaissance humanism, especially at the advanced stage of antiquarian self-consciousness that had been reached by the sixteenth century. These pressures were engendered above all by the dynamics of a search for cultural identity and esteem; and Aristotle's involvement in this process was just one element in an often contentious and delicately balanced re-engagement with the art and ideas of antiquity.[6]

From the beginnings of the renewed attention to the *Poetics* in later sixteenth century Italy, there has, in fact, never been a time when the work has received a largely unanimous reverence, though there have sometimes been rigid individuals or small, purist circles for whom this was so. Extreme statements of Aristotelian authority were often either polemically motivated moves in tense struggles for artistic success and critical standing, or avowals of faith rather than of thorough conviction. One striking example of this is the fact that Scaliger's description of Aristotle as "dictator perpetuus" in all artistic matters – a description which later generated the inaccurate idea of Scaliger as the chief propagator of the *Poetics'* doctrines – is the pronouncement of a theorist whose actual Aristotelianism is often no more than slight and superficial. Scaliger's views diverge from or supplement those of the *Poetics* itself in numerous ways: in their strong Latinate coloring; their heavy concern with style and diction; their overtly moralistic assumptions; their rejection of mimesis as fundamental to poetry; their restriction of the chorus to an act-dividing role; and much besides. Even critics with more extensive or detailed interest in Aristotle's ideas rarely took these over in anything like a pure or unqualified form. Trissino, in his expanded *Poetica* of 1563, as well as in his influential neoclassical tragedy, *Sophonisba* (1514–15), adopts a literary stance which is actually more hybrid and mixed in its sources than the explicit allegiance to Aristotelian ideals would suggest. Another important poet-critic, Giraldi (Cinthio), in the middle of the same century, demonstrates that strong respect for the *Poetics* was entirely compatible with something more than unquestioning adherence to orthodoxy. Giraldi is an Aristotelian and a classicizer in many of his basic literary standards, yet he is prepared to make and defend choices among the various classical models available to him: this leads him not only to diverge from certain points in Aristotle's conception of tragedy (e.g. on the exclusion of the divine from the dénouement of a tragic plot), but also to insist, in his discourse on the romance (1554), that a postclassical genre could not be expected to conform to classical principles which had not been made for it. This last point, which was not peculiar to Giraldi, contains the seed of what would eventually become the kernel of eighteenth and nineteenth century opposition to the complete enterprise of critical Aristotelianism.

The *Poetics'* involvement in controversy – about its own contents, about its relation to competing conceptions of poetry (not least, those of a Platonizing tendency), and about its direct bearing on urgent issues within the interpreting culture (new genres, uses of the vernacular, choices of literary models) – can be seen as early as the contrast between the attitudes of two such significant commentators as Robortello and Castelvetro. Although these figures share certain humanistic concerns and broadly philological methods, there is a sharp and telling discrepancy between the essentially positive attitude of Robortello, focused on the elucidation of Aristotle in such a way as to work his ideas into an already existing fabric of rhetorical and moralizing criticism, and the much more iconoclastic approach of Castelvetro, whose manner towards the contents of the *Poetics* is more independent, free-moving and captious. Castelvetro's best known doctrine, the first full and explicit formulation of the three Unities, is a good illustration of this. Not only is it un-Aristotelian in its inclusion of place and its emphasis on time; it also brusquely inverts Aristotle's own priorities by making unity of action secondary to, and only derivative from, the others, and it rests its whole case on an insistence, quite contrary to the *Poetics,* on the unavoidably theatrical conditions of drama, as well as on a cynical view (perhaps showing Platonic influence) of the deficiencies of popular audiences.[7]

Although Castelvetro's naturally polemical temperament and cast of intellect were factors in his attitudes to the *Poetics,* his divergences from Aristotelian ground are a further index of the constant impingement of contemporary issues and needs upon the reading of the treatise. Castelvetro was extensively and strongly interested in vernacular literature, as well as in the status of poetry, not least drama, in his own society; his views were ultimately driven and shaped by a determination to bring his understanding of Aristotle to bear upon these matters. In more diffuse ways, as I have already emphasized, this was a persistent trend in the entire neoclassical context of sixteenth century Italy, where debates over modern and ancient genres, over choices of literary models, and over the relationship between the vernacular and the classical languages, were already underway when interest in the *Poetics* revived. Indeed, it was clearly the existence of a climate in which the formation of modern literature was intimately involved with the reinterpretation of the classical past that prompted and sustained criticism's recourse to the *Poetics,* and which largely predetermined the needs which writers and theorists brought with them to their inspections of the work.

The involvement of the *Poetics* in contemporary debates continued to be a defining feature of neoclassicism in its succeeding phases elsewhere in Europe, especially in France and England. Most notably, the struggles over literary practice, linguistic purity and critical authority that centred on the newly permanent Parisian theatres from the 1630s to the 1670s, in many ways re-enacted the pattern of artistic ferment, and the quest for stable cultural standards, that had taken place a century earlier in Italy. So too, though much less tidily and with less institutional drawing of battle-lines, did the tension between classical and native norms in seventeenth and eighteenth century English criticism, which came increasingly to focus itself on the character of Shakespearian drama (the same subject as would eventually form the crux of German Romanticism's challenge to Aristotelianism). But the role of the *Poetics* in this expansion of neoclassicism gradually came to lose something of the variousness of its deployment by *Cinquecento* critics; French theorists moved somewhat away from the broader poetic and rhetorical concerns of their Italian predecessors, and concentrated more intensively on drama. Yet there is, in the seventeenth century, an increasing sense of second-hand Aristotelianism in the realm of literary polemics. Many French and English critics were most directly influenced not by the *Poetics* itself, but by existing Italian discussions of it, as well as by the important successor to those discussions in Heinsius's edition of 1610 (reprinted in 1611 with a treatise on tragedy). Classicism by now almost inevitably involved a relationship to antiquity that was routed via Italy, and this was true even for those who could and did read ancient texts: when Milton explains his models of tragedy, in the preface to *Samson Agonistes* (1671), it is the precedent equally of "the ancients and Italians" that he cites. Indicative of the seventeenth century's often less direct approach to the *Poetics* is the scarcity of vernacular translations or new editions of the work in France and England: the first influential French translation (after Norville's little-used version of 1671) was André Dacier's, of 1692; and the first at all in English, published anonymously in 1705, was significantly rendered not from the Greek but from Dacier.

French classicism's re-enactment of some of the critical disputes of the Italian culture to which it turned for guidance and sanction may in time have produced a hardened and somewhat stereotyped Aristotelianism, and one which was obsessed by polemics over the Unities to a degree that had never been true of the Italians. But this is not to say that we should accept the easy judgment (easy for post-Romantics) that the continuing mediation of literary controversies through categories and principles drawn from the *Poetics* was a complete misdirection of critical energies. Such a judgment overlooks the essential ways in which reference to classical models and arguments suited, and became embedded in, the artistic processes of the time, and was capable of supplying a set of terms in which fundamental debates over poetic aims and values could be advanced. Issues such as verisimilitude, decorum, the unities and poetic morality, were no mere academic distractions; they were points of precise relevance to the design and influence of contemporary poetry, and they represented one particular way of approaching matters which can be seen to have had a recurrent importance in the history of criticism. If this had not been so, it would be impossible, above all, to account for the extent to which playwrights of the stature of Corneille and Racine could have formulated, explained and defended their individual understandings of dramatic classicism within terms that were heavily indebted to the preceding century's discussions of the *Poetics*. It was principally by choice and inclination, not through compulsion from an oppressive climate of opinion, that both writers supplemented their theatrical practice by engaging in active and independent reflections on the Aristotelian terms of contemporary dramatic criticism: Corneille in, above all, the three *Discours* written for the 1660 edition of his works, and Racine in his personal notes on the *Poetics*, as well as in his prefaces to *Iphigénie* and *Phèdre*.[8]

Corneille and Racine, in their somewhat different ways and styles, attest to the possibility of discovering simultaneously creative and classical commitments within the framework of literary Aristotelianism. But the broader current of arguments that attended the development of seventeenth century French theater, especially tragedy, perhaps inevitably produced some highly polarized responses to the key question of how a document such as the *Poetics* could contribute to the creation of a modern literature in a very different social and artistic environment. Symptomatic of such polarization is the gulf between the views promulgated in the same decade, the 1670s, by Rapin and Saint-Évremond. Rapin, in his *Réflexions sur la Poétique d'Aristote* (1674), offers a kind of summation of the tenets of the most doctrinally stringent wing of literary classicism. He finds a perfect consistency between Aristotle's treatise and the values of "nature," "reason" and "good sense." The rules of literary practice which are stated by Aristotle, or can be extracted from his book, are thus treated as a kind of codification of universal, indispensable and permanent standards of art (though not so permanent that Rapin cannot contradict Aristotle on as large a question as the respective merits of tragedy and epic). And these standards are in turn reducible to a single overriding canon, that of propriety or "la bienséance" – a criterion which, in fact, appears only occasionally in the *Poetics*, but lies at the heart both of Horace's *Ars Poetica* and of the tradition of classical rhetoric. Opposed to such edicts of a final orthodoxy was the dissenting view of Saint-Évremond, who, without deriding the merits of the *Poetics* in its own terms, contends that the poetry of one age should never be regulated by the poetics of another, and that many crucial changes in religion, in ethics and in social practices, make it wrong to base modern works on ancient models.[9] Here, in the cast of Saint-Évremond's arguments, which are partly reflective of a trend of thought soon to find polemical expression in the *Querelle des anciens et des modernes*, but are nevertheless unusually radical for their time, we already have much of what was to become, a century later, the platform for a rejection of Aristotelian classicism.

If we glance back over the whole movement of literary neoclassicism, there were, as I have emphasized, only a minority of critics who were content to regard the jurisdiction of the *Poetics* as intrinsically definitive. It is an old travesty, and a regrettably lingering one, to suppose that this was the spirit which predominated among classicizing theorists. Much commoner was the attempt to produce a stable harmonization of contemporary aesthetic concerns with a view of what the *Poetics* seemed, or could be taken, to stand for. Of course, many writers used Aristotle to legitimize some particular principle or commitment, and in doing so they can often be seen now to have interpreted his book in drastically tendentious ways: the prevailing habit of understanding *katharsis* as a mechanism of moral didacticism is as good an instance of this as any. But the process was nonetheless, for the most part, something much more than an empty invocation of authority: it was a constantly reargued attempt, which motivated important creative artists as well as critics and scholars, to work out a *rapprochement* between cultural forces from the past and artistic challenges in the present.

The reductive view which, by contrast, sees the whole of this movement as a tradition of unthinking subservience to pseudo-Aristotelian dogmas, was strongly promoted during the Romantic and subsequent reaction against neoclassicism. Yet the treatment of the *Poetics* in this later period is itself a much more complex matter than this stance of opposition, or the simplified historical scheme which I earlier mentioned, would lead us to believe. It is undoubtedly true that the period from around 1750 onwards did, as a whole, see a relative decline in interest in Aristotle's treatise, as well as the growth of a marked skepticism about ideas of classical authority in general. But there was also a sufficient realization that Aristotle could not simply be identified with the adaptations of his ideas by sixteenth and seventeenth century interpreters. This realization was gradually to become a common one; in England, we find it, for instance, in the attitudes of Coleridge, whose lectures on Shakespeare dismiss French pieties about Aristotle the "infallible censor," but whose *Biographia Literaria* claims to find in the *Poetics* – neither for the first nor the last time in post-Renaissance interpretations of the work – a congenial view of poetry as "essentially ideal."[10] But the separation of Aristotle from his recent spokesmen is best exemplified in Germany, where neoclassicism had established itself latest and where the recoil from it was correspondingly sharpest, and by a trio of major figures – Lessing, Herder, and August von Schlegel – who all vehemently repudiated French classicism of the seventeenth century, but who nonetheless differed considerably in what they perceived as the consequences of this repudiation for their appraisal of the *Poetics*.

Of the three, Lessing occupies the most ambiguous position in this respect, and perhaps more generally in his relation to the conflict between classical and proto-Romantic values. In his *Hamburgische Dramaturgie* (1767–68), Lessing seems simultaneously to wish to escape from the rigidities of French Aristotelianism, and yet to retain for Aristotle's critical standing the kind of prestige with which neoclassicism had endowed it. It is significant that he does this by concentrating attention upon psychological rather than formal or moral questions. He offers, in particular, a lengthy reappraisal of the nature of tragic pity and fear, and the connected concept of *katharsis,* and in doing so he combines insights, not always acknowledged, drawn from previous writers on the treatise (above all, perhaps, Heinsius's recognition of the Aristotelian relation between emotion and virtue), with a fresh and incisive line of argument of his own devising. This leaves Lessing, in many of his conclusions, delicately suspended between old and new; his reading of *katharsis*, for example, breaks away from the simpler moralism of many earlier critics, while still insisting on the ethical implications of the doctrine in terms of Aristotle's psychology of the mean. A generation later, and with the force of Romanticism now expanding rapidly, Lessing's continuing reverence towards Aristotle already looked somewhat dated. August von Schlegel, a figure of central significance in the diffusion of Romantic ideas, was able, in his influential Vienna lectures on drama (1808), to dismiss Lessing's view of *katharsis* not simply as a poor interpretation but as an outmoded appeal to a work of whose value for the understanding of poetic imagination and feeling – cardinal concepts for the new aesthetic – Schlegel formed a generally low estimate.[11]

But between the widely divergent positions of Lessing and Schlegel, a third and more promising way was discerned by Herder, whose passionate essay on *Shakespeare* (1773) opens up the possibility of a radically new framework for modern dealings with the *Poetics*. Herder writes under the influence of a powerful sense of cultural relativism – a sense both of the deep differences between cultures, and of the organic unity of individual cultures. He therefore regards any attempt to fashion the art of the present in the likeness of that of the past as doomed to sterility, and he is in no doubt that the "rules" of French classicism, whether in criticism or in dramatic practice, represent a disastrous dead-end. But Herder fully exculpates Aristotle himself for what he regards as the perversion of his real views; he is confident that if Aristotle were alive today, he would produce a very different work of poetics to accommodate the distinctive nature of "northern," i.e. Shakespearian, drama. Given his philosophical model of human culture, Herder is able to avoid the pressure to set the art or the criticism of past and present in competition with one another. He regards Sophocles and Shakespeare as both having achieved dramatic greatness, but in necessarily very different forms. And, from the same basic premises, he is similarly able to adumbrate a new view of the *Poetics* as a document which, while it cannot furnish the grounds for a contemporary aesthetic, has a real value for the understanding of its own culture.[12]

The cases of Lessing, Herder and Schlegel, even in this abbreviated presentation, all serve to demonstrate how the rejection of the "old order" of classical tenets, in the later eighteenth century and especially under Romanticism, constituted a crucially transitional phase in the fortunes of the *Poetics*. Aristotle's book had perhaps lent itself to the kinds of controversy which, in the cultural climate created by the Renaissance, had characterized attempts to shape and define modern literary ideals by constant adjustment to the approved models of antiquity. But as the momentum of a traditional and increasingly conservative classicism faded, it began to become both feasible and reasonable to approach the *Poetics* with greater interpretative flexibility. When Goethe and Schiller corresponded about the *Poetics* in April and May 1797, they were certainly both free of strong neoclassical prejudices, though the thoughts of both men were subtly poised between ancient and modern ideals; and they were consequently able to reappraise some of Aristotle's arguments at a distance from earlier orthodoxies.[13] Now that, at Goethe's prompting, he had read the work for himself, Schiller found that it had been "monstrously misunderstood," and suggested that it was "fear" of Aristotle which had had such a bad effect on the French. Both he and Goethe reached conclusions that mixed admiration with reservations. Goethe praised Aristotle's rationality (perhaps a trace, here, of older neoclassical values), but also his closeness to experience, and his "liberalism" in the defense of poets against carping critics; what he principally missed was an adequate account of epic, and Schiller agreed with this. Schiller found the work satisfying *despite* Aristotle's clear-headed character, and among a variety of other observations he shrewdly judged that the *Poetics* was on the side neither of those who value merely "external" form in poetry, nor of those who ignore form altogether. One further remark of Schiller's, that Shakespeare, despite some particular discrepancies, has more in common with the spirit of the *Poetics* than does French classical tragedy, matches the arguments of Lessing much more closely than those of Herder, and shows that if Aristotle's reputation as a literary theorist was waiting, we might say, to be *reclaimed* from neoclassicism, it might even be used to add weight to very different casts of aesthetic principles.

Such reclamation was hardly, as it turned out, to be a major preoccupation of Romantic and nineteenth century critics, but it was a nonetheless continual process by which attitudes towards the work were both reorientated and opened up in ways that are still with us. Perhaps the most paradoxical part of this process was the attempt to discover aspects of one kind of literary Romanticism within Aristotle himself. This could only be done either by ignoring salient emphases and large tracts of the work, or at least by heavily selective elaboration of a small number of its ideas. In fact, though, this was not an entirely new type of reading, since it had been anticipated by an occasional tendency in *cinquecento* Italy to offer platonized (or neoplatonic) accounts of mimesis and "universals" in the *Poetics;* such views were echoed in England, for example, by Sir Philip Sidney, and we have already noticed their later recurrence in Coleridge. It is even possible to find traces of this attitude in Herder, who, notwithstanding his radical separation of northern from Greek culture and drama, nevertheless cites the *Poetics* itself for the concept of organic unity which he invokes in his account of Shakespeare's genius.[14]

The most sustained and influential attempt of this kind in the nineteenth century has proved to be that of a scholar, not a critic. It is S. H. Butcher's widely used edition with interpretative essays, *Aristotle's Theory of Poetry and Fine Art* (1895), which has done most to make and keep available a reading of the *Poetics* as a work which, first, rests on a sense of art as spiritually creative and idealistic, and, second, offers a concept of aesthetic pleasure untainted by moral considerations of the kind over which neoclassicists had expended so much anxiety. These are not views which will now recommend themselves equally to all readers of the treatise, though Butcher shows some finesse in coaxing his interpretations from Aristotle's laconic phrases. Like earlier idealist interpreters, Butcher makes much of the inclusion, in a sentence in *Poetics* 25 (1460b8–11), of "things as they should be" among the possible objects of poetic, and indeed all artistic, representation. His platonizing extrapolation from this to things "which never can be," or "the true idea," may be scarcely defensible as an elucidation of Aristotle's critical position, but it illustrates two factors of broader significance: first, that the *Poetics* contains many statements of a pregnancy that lends itself to speculative elaboration (a point to which Castelvetro long ago drew attention); second, that Butcher was perpetuating an old tradition, and one which crosses the dividing line between neoclassical and Romantic, of interpreting the *Poetics* in the hope of locating in it attitudes at harmony with current conceptions of poetry.

If we combine these two factors with the unprecedented pluralism of movements of literary theory and criticism in the present century, we have an essential part of the explanation for the fact that the status of the *Poetics* in recent times has proved to be one of openness to a wider diversity of uses and revaluations than ever before. This is not to ignore the diffusion of a reasonable scepticism – as we have seen, something practically as old as the post-Renaissance "rediscovery" of the work – about the relevance of the *Poetics* to the reading and understanding of modern genres and contemporary works of literature: "in the face of modern literature we simply cannot go back to Aristotle, however refurbished and updated."[15] Such scepticism has not, however, done much to dampen recurrent, if often markedly eclectic, appeals to the work by modern critics, and for a disparate range of purposes: the early Eliot's anti-Romantic doctrine of poetic "impersonality," for instance; the genre- and form-centered systems of the Chicago school and Northrop Frye; or the interest of some Structuralists in typologies of literary modes and conventions.[16] All such appeals represent, in one way or another, continuing attempts to align Aristotelian ideas with the critical preoccupations of the present; the three I have cited, whatever their substantial differences (in relation, say, to the mimeticist view of art), all affirm a commitment to some conception of the autonomous poetic artifact. But alongside these enterprises persists the very different conviction, inherited from thinkers such as Herder but intensified by the larger forces of cultural relativism in modern times, that to seek such alignment is to transgress the radical distinctions which exist between cultures, and schemes of thought, greatly separated in space and time.

Yet it is an inescapable paradox for this form of cultural relativism that it can only establish its cogency by engaging in historical enquiry and argument; without that, it can scarcely claim to know that there are such things as distinct cultures, still less to be sure that their artistic practices and values are inevitably incommensurable. But once the need for historical perspective is accepted, not only does this in itself imply a basis of understanding, a pragmatic realism, which runs beneath cultural differences; it also opens up the many problems pertaining to the (self-)definition of an intellectual and aesthetic culture, including the complex relationship between culture and tradition. Herder believed that "northern" and Greek culture had utterly incompatible standards; but he seems to have experienced no difficulty in holding a series of beliefs for which the grounds could not but be historical: first, that he and Shakespeare, despite differences of time, place and language, really did belong to the same culture; second, that there had been such a thing as a common Greek culture which embraced both Sophocles and Aristotle; third, that this Greek culture, though remote, could still be comprehended and appreciated by an eighteenth century German. It is as though Herder tacitly accepts that there are, in practice, many forms, strands and degrees of tradition which preserve contact, and at least some measure of intelligibility, between the present and those stages of the past that are embodied in literature. But it is in his insistence on cultural difference, and the denial of the kind of universalism presupposed by much neoclassicism, that Herder seems a thinker for his own times. So, however, does his contemporary, Winckelmann, who believed that cultural health depended on a recovery of Greek values and vitality, and whose ideas were spurned by Herder.

We are the heirs, among much else, both of Herder's relativism and of Winckelmann's Romantic Hellenism. This means that our relationship to ancient Greek culture (or cultures) remains a matter for constant and always provisional reassessment. But it also means that such reassessment is under-pinned by a deep sense, however cautiously it now needs to be formulated, of the importance and usefulness of the past to the present. Where the *Poetics* is concerned, no-one is any longer likely to dispute the need for an awareness of certain kinds of historical distance between ourselves and the mental world of this document, nor for a corresponding respect towards the integrity of the work's original context in its place, time and intellectual setting: we need, that is, the history both of Greek literary culture, and of Greek philosophy, if we are to give ourselves the best chance of keeping both a reliable and a vivid grasp of Aristotle's meanings. But because the *Poetics* has become important and conten-tiously formative within the development of literary criticism since the Renais-sance, our understanding of it, on the broadest level, needs also to engage with many of the implications and ramifications of that development. So we need too, for the fullest perspective on the work's significance, the history of criticism, a history which is evidently not something that simply waits to be told, but one whose patterns and dynamics need an actively interpretative definition. Criti-cism, in this connection, needs to be taken in the widest of applications, for part of the protean character of Aristotle's concepts and arguments has proved to be the attention they have received over a much broader field than that of literary criticism in the narrower sense. Since the mid-eighteenth century, the *Poetics* has been often cited, as well as challenged, both for particular doctrines (mimesis, *katharsis*, unity) and as a paradigmatic structure of principles, by theorists concerned with aesthetic issues in the arts in general. The resulting transmission of the work's ideas through a multiplicity of discourses inevitably influences part of the framework within which we continue to read and evaluate it. That amounts to saying that comprehension of the *Poetics*, and comprehension of the tradition of its interpretation, are no longer entirely separable. To approach the work, we are obliged, whether or not we are always consciously aware of it, to discover new paths through that tradition – to participate in the tradition, but also to extend and change it. And that is a relationship to the past, combining both indebtedness and independence, which the suitably reflective interpreter is likely to conclude is only as it should be.

Notes

1. F. Nietzsche, *Untimely Meditations*, trans. R. J. Hollingdale (Cambridge, 1983), 101, alluding to the image at Hesiod, *Works and Days* 180–181. T. Todorov, *Introduction to Poetics*, Eng. trans. (Brighton, 1981), xxiii.
2. I have attempted a fuller analysis of the *Poetics'* afterlife in Ch. 10 of my book, *Aristotle's Poetics* (London and Chapel Hill, NC, 1986), and supplemented this in the introduction to my translation, *The Poetics of Aristotle* (London and Chapel Hill, NC, 1987), 17–28. In the present essay I have deliberately abstained from repeating references to secondary literature and specialist works given in the notes to those two books: I do not intend this to conceal my grateful indebtedness to many of the authors cited on those previous occasions.
3. A useful translation of Hermann's version of Averroes is now available in A. J. Minnis and A. B. Scott (eds.) *Medieval Literary Criticism c.1100–c.1375* (Oxford, 1988).
4. On Goethe see p.418 and n.13 below.
5. The tradition represented by these definitions is discussed at length by A. P. McMahon, 'Seven Questions on Aristotelian Definitions of Tragedy and Comedy,' *Harvard Studies in Classical Philology* 40 (1929) 97–198, though I do not fully accept his attempt to link them to Aristotle's own views.
6. An exaggerated account of the rigidity of Aristotelianism is given by e.g. J. E. Spingarn, *A History of Literary Criticism in the Renaissance*, 2nd edn. (New York, 1908), esp. 136–148. For a more sympathetic approach, see T. B. Jones and B. de Bear Nicol, *Neo-Classical Dramatic Criticism 1560–1770* (Cambridge, 1976).
7. L. Castelvetro, *Poetica d'Aristotele vulgarizzata et sposta*, 2nd edn. (Basle, 1576), 57, 107–109, 179, 297, 534–535, 687.
8. On Corneille and Racine see P. Somville, *Essai sur la Poétique d'Aristote* (Paris, 1975) 146–159, and my 1986 book (n. 2 above) 305–308; what I say here modifies the emphasis of those earlier comments on Corneille.
9. See especially *De la tragédie ancienne et moderne* (1672).
10. *Biographia Literaria* Ch. 17; cf. Ch. 22, where we can recognize the Coleridgean origin of the earlier misstatement of Wordsworth's in the 1800 Preface to *Lyrical Ballads*: "Aristotle, I have been told, has said that poetry is the most philosophic of all writing . . ."
11. A. W. von Schlegel, *Vorlesungen über dramatische Kunst und Literatur*, ed. E. Lohner (Stuttgart, 1966–67), I 63 (Lessing and *katharsis*), II 9–29 (Schlegel's main discussion of Aristotle), II 273 (criticism of Lessing's 'faith' in Aristotle).
12. Herder's essay is conveniently translated by J. P. Crick in H. B. Nisbet (ed.) *German Aesthetic and Literary Criticism: Winckelmann etc.* (Cambridge, 1985), 161–176.
13. See Goethe's letters of 28th April, 3rd and 6th May, with Schiller's of 5th May, 1797; further references to the *Poetics* in Schiller's letters of 24th November and 8th

S. Halliwell

December, 1797, 24th August 1798, 18th June 1799, 6th July 1802. Goethe of course returned to the *Poetics* in his *Nachlese zu Aristoteles' Poetik* (1827).

14. E. Shaper, *Prelude to Aesthetics* (London, 1968), 122–134, offers some reflections on Romantic organicism in relation to the ideas of both Plato and Aristotle.

15. R. Wellek, *The Attack on Literature* (Chapel Hill, NC and Brighton, 1982), 108.

16. On Eliot see my translation (1987), 25–26: Eliot was 'flattered' when Leonard Woolf reviewed *The Sacred Wood* under the heading, 'Back to Aristotle': V. Eliot (ed.), *The Letters of T. S. Eliot*, Vol. I 1898–1922 (London, 1988) 427. For Structuralist interest in Aristotle, see e.g. the references to him in G. Genette, *Figures of Literary Discourse*, Eng. trans. (Oxford, 1982).

Selected Bibliography

This selective listing has been compiled from the bibliographies provided by contributors to this volume, and from comprehensive bibliographies in Elizabeth Belfiore's *Tragic Pleasures: Aristotle on Plot and Emotion* (Princeton, 1992); Stephen Halliwell's *Aristotle's Poetics* (Chapel Hill, NC, 1986), pp. 357–364; and *Articles on Aristotle*, Vol. IV, edited by Jonathan Barnes, Malcolm Schofield and Richard Sorabji (New York, 1979), pp. 187–190. For further references, consult the notes for each essay and the bibliographies in Belfiore's and Halliwell's books.

Editions and Translations

Barnes, J. (ed.), *The Complete Works of Aristotle. The Revised Oxford Translation* (Princeton, 1984).

Butcher, S. H., *Aristotle's Theory of Poetry and Fine Art*, 4th edn (New York, 1911; rpt. New York, 1951).

Bywater, I., *Aristotelis Ethica Nicomachea* (Oxford, 1894).

——, *Aristotle on the Art of Poetry* (Oxford, 1909).

Christ, W. von, *Aristotelis De Arte Poetica* (Leipzig, 1913).

Cope, E. M., *The Rhetoric of Aristotle*, 3 vols, rev. J. E. Sandys (Cambridge, 1877).

Dupont-Roc, R. and Lallot, J., *Aristote, La Poétique* (Paris, 1980).

Else, G. F., *Aristotle: Poetics. Translated with an Introduction* (Ann Arbor, MI, 1970).

Epps, Preston (trans.), *Poetics* (Aristotle) (Chapel Hill, NC, 1967).

Fuhrmann, M., *Aristoteles: Poetik*, 2nd edn (Stuttgart, 1982).

Golden, L. and Hardison, O. B., *Aristotle's Poetics* (Englewood Cliffs, 1968).

Gudeman, A., *Aristoteles. Peri Poiētikēs* (Berlin and Leipzig, 1934).

Halliwell, S., *The Poetics of Aristotle* (Chapel Hill, NC, 1987).

Hardy, J. (ed. and trans.), *Aristote: Poétique* (Paris, 1952; 4th edn Paris, 1980).

Hicks, R. D., *Aristotle, De Anima* (London, 1907).

Hubbard, M. E. trans. of *Poetics* in D. A. Russell and M. Winterbottom (eds), *Ancient Literary Criticism* (Oxford, 1972).

Hutton, J. (trans., intro.), *Aristotle's* Poetics (New York, 1982).

Irwin, T. (trans.), *Aristotle. Nicomachean Ethics* (Indianapolis, 1985).

Janko, R. *Aristotle: Poetics* (Indianapolis, 1987).

Jowett, B. and Twining, T. (trans.), *Aristotle's* Politics *and* Poetics, intro. Lincoln Diamant (New York, 1957).

Kassel, R., *Aristotelis De Arte Poetica* (Oxford, 1965; rpt. with corrections, 1966).

Lucas, D. W., *Aristotle: Poetics* (Oxford, 1968; rpt. with corrections, 1972).

Newman, W. L., *The Politics of Aristotle*, 4 vols (Oxford, 1887–1902).

Potts, L. J., *Aristotle on the Art of Fiction*, 2nd edn (Cambridge, 1959).

Ross, W. D., *Aristotle's Metaphysics*, 2 vols. (Oxford, 1953).
—— (ed.), *Poetica (Aristotle)* (Oxford, 1957).
Rostagni, A., *Aristotele. Poetica*, 2nd edn (Turin, 1945).
Sinclair, T. A. (trans.), *The Politics*, rev. T. J. Saunders (Harmondsworth, 1981).
Susemihl, F. and Hicks, R., *The Politics of Aristotle: Books 1–5* (London, 1894).
Telford, K. A. (trans. and comm.), *Poetics (Aristotle)*, (Chicago, 1961).
Vahlen, J. (ed.), *Aristotelis de arte poetica liber*, 3rd edn (Leipzig, 1885).
Woods, M. (trans. and comm.), *Aristotle's Eudemian Ethics, Books I, II, and VIII* (Oxford, 1982).

Commentaries

Bonitz, H., *Index Aristotelicus*, 2nd edn (Berlin, 1870).
Butterworth, C. E. (ed., trans.), *Averroës' Three Short Commentaries on Aristotle's Topics, Rhetoric and Poetics* (Albany, 1977).
——, *Averroës' Middle Commentary on Aristotle's Poetics* (Princeton, 1986).
Dahiyat, I. M., *Avicenna's Commentary on the* Poetics *of Aristotle* (Leiden, 1974).
Grimaldi, W. M. A., *Aristotle, Rhetoric I. A Commentary* (New York, 1980); and *Rhetoric II* (1988).
Joachim, H. H., *Aristotle, The Nicomachean Ethics; A Commentary*, ed. D. A. Rees (Oxford, 1951).
Wartelle, A., *Lexique de la Poétique d'Aristote* (Paris, 1985).

Bibliographies

Cooper, L. and Gudeman, A., *A Bibliography of the Poetics of Aristotle* (New Haven, 1928).
Else, G. F., "Survey of Work on Aristotle's Poetics, 1940–1954," *Classical Weekly* **48** (1954) 73–82.
Herrick, M. T., "Supplement to Cooper and Gudeman (1928)," *American Journal of Philology* **52** (1931) 168–174.
White, D. R., "A Sourcebook on the Catharsis Controversy," Diss., The Florida State University (1984).

Books and Articles

Ackrill, J., "Aristotle on Action," *Mind* **87** (1978) 595–601. Repr. in *Essays on Aristotle's Ethics*, ed. A. O. Rorty (Berkeley, 1980).
——, "Aristotle's Theory of Definition," in *Aristotle on Science: The Posterior Analytics*, Proceedings of the 8th Symposium Aristotelicum, ed. E. Berti (Padua, 1981), 359–384.
Adkins, A. W. H., *Merit and Responsibility* (Oxford, 1960).
——, N.S. 'Friendship' and 'Self-Sufficiency' in Homer and Aristotle," *Classical Quarterly* N.S. **13** (1963) 30–45.
——, "Basic Greek Values and the Interpretation of Greek Literature," *Proceedings of the Classical Association* **62** (1965) 29–31.
——, "Aristotle and the Best Kind of Tragedy," *Classical Quarterly* N.S. **16** (1966) 78–102.
Allan, D. J., "Some Passages in Aristotle's *Poetics*," *Classical Quarterly* N.S. **21** (1971) 81–92.
——, "*Eidê Tragôdias* in Aristotle's *Poetics*," *Classical Quarterly* N.S. **22** (1972) 81–88.

——, "Two Aristotelian Notes," *Mnemosyne* **27** (1974) 113–122.

——, "Peripeteia quid sit, Caesar occisus ostendit," *Mnemosyne* **29** (1976) 337–350.

Anderson, W. D., *Ēthos and Education in Greek Music* (Cambridge, MA, 1966).

Anton, J. P., "*Mythos, Katharsis* and the Paradox of Tragedy," in *Proceedings of the Boston Area Colloquium on Ancient Philosophy* **1** (1985) 299–326.

Armstrong, D. and Peterson, C., "Rhetorical Balance in Aristotle's Definition of the Tragic Agent: *Poetics* 13," *Classical Quarterly* N.S. **30** (1980) 62–71.

Atkins, J. W. H., *Literary Criticism in Antiquity*, 2nd edn (London, 1952).

Baldry, H. C., "The Interpretation of *Poetics* 9," *Phronesis* **2** (1957) 41–45.

Bambrough, R., "Aristotle and Agamemnon," *Philosophy and Literature* (Suppl. to *Philosophy* 1983), *Royal Institute of Philosophy Lecture Series* (Cambridge, 1984).

Barnes, J., *Aristotle's Posterior Analytics*, trans. with notes (Oxford, 1975).

——, Schofield, M. and Sorabji, R. (eds), *Articles on Aristotle*, Vol. 2 (New York, 1977): Vol. 4 (New York, 1979).

Battin, M. P., "Aristotle's Definition of Tragedy in the *Poetics*, Part I," *Journal of Aesthetics and Arts Criticism* **33** (1975) 155–170.

Belfiore, E., "Aristotle's Concept of *Praxis* in the *Poetics*," *Classical Journal* **79** (1983/4) 110–124.

——, "Plato's Greatest Accusation Against Poetry," *Canadian Journal of Philosophy* (Suppl.) **9** (1983) 39–62.

——, "Pleasure, Tragedy and Aristotelian Psychology," *Classical Quarterly* N.S. **35** (1985) 349–361.

——, "Wine and *Catharsis* of the Emotions in Plato's *Laws*," *Classical Quarterly* N.S. **36** (1986) 421–437.

——, "*Peripeteia* as Discontinuous Action: Aristotle, *Poetics* 11. 1452a22–29," *Classical Philology* **83** (1988) 183–194.

——, *Tragic Pleasures: Aristotle on Plot and Emotion* (Princeton, 1992).

Bernays, J., *Grundzüge der verlorenen Abhandlung des Aristoteles über Wirkung der Tragödie* (Breslau, 1857).

——, "Aristotle on the Effect of Tragedy," trans. J. and J. Barnes from *Zwei Abhandlungen über die aristotelische Theorie des Drama* (Berlin, 1880, first published Breslau, 1857) in Barnes *et al.* (1979) *Articles*, Vol. 4, 154–165.

Berti, E. (ed.), *Symposium Aristotelicum* (Padua, 1981).

Blundell, M. W., *Helping Friends and Harming Enemies* (Cambridge, 1989).

Booth, W., *The Company We Keep: An Ethics of Fiction* (Berkeley and Los Angeles, 1988).

Bremer, J. M., *Hamartia: Tragic Error in the Poetics of Aristotle and in Greek Tragedy* (Amsterdam, 1969).

——, *Miscellanea Tragica in honorem J. C. Kamerbeek*, eds S. L. Radt and C. J. Ruijgh (Amsterdam, 1976).

Broadie, S., *Ethics with Aristotle* (Oxford, 1991).

Brower, R., "The Heresy of Plot," in *Aristotle's Poetics and English Literature* (Chicago and London, 1965).

Burke, K., "Rhetoric and Poetics," in *Language as Symbolic Action* (Berkeley, 1966), 295–307.

Burnett, A. P., *Catastrophe Survived. Euripides' Plays of Mixed Reversal* (Oxford, 1971).

Burnyeat, M. F., "Aristotle on Learning to be Good," in *Essays on Aristotle's Ethics* ed. A. O. Rorty (Berkeley, Los Angeles and London, 1980), 69–92.

Cameron, A., *Plato's Affair with Tragedy* (Cincinnati, 1978).

Cave, T., *Recognitions* (Oxford, 1988).

Chamberlain, C. T., *The Meaning of the Word* Ethos *in Aristotle's* Poetics *and Its Interpretations in Three Renaissance Commentaries on the* Poetics, Diss., University of California at Berkeley (1979).

Charles, D., *Aristotle's Philosophy of Action* (London, 1984).

Charlesworth, M. J., "Aristotle on Beauty and *Katharsis*," *Philosophic Studies* 7 (1957) 56–82.

Cooper, J. M.,*Reason and Human Good in Aristotle* (Cambridge, MA, 1975).

——, "Aristotle on the Forms of Friendship," *Review of Metaphysics* 30 (1977) 619–648.

——, "Friendship and the Good in Aristotle," *Philosophical Review* 86 (1977) 290–315.

——, "Aristotle on the Goods of Fortune," *Philosophical Review* 94 (1985) 173–196.

——, "Hypothetical Necessity," in *Philosophical Issues in Aristotle's Biology*, eds A. Gotthelf and J. G. Lennox (Cambridge, 1987), 243–274.

——, Review of Martha Nussbaum's *The Fragility of Goodness*, in *Philosophical Review* 97 (1988) 543–564.

Cooper, L., *An Aristotelian Theory of Comedy* (New York, 1922, rpt. 1969).

—— (ed.), *Aristotle on the Art of Poetry* (Ithaca, 1947, rev. edn 1962).

——, *The Poetics of Aristotle, Its Meaning and Influence*, (New York, 1927, rpt. Westport, 1977).

Cope, E. M. and Sandys, J. E. (eds), *The Rhetoric of Aristotle* (Cambridge, 1877).

Crane, R. S. (ed.), *Critics and Criticism: Ancient and Modern* (Chicago, 1952).

Dacier, A., *Preface to Aristotle's Art of Poetry* (Los Angeles, 1959).

Dawe, R. D., "Some Reflections on *Atē* and *Hamartia*," *Harvard Studies in Classical Philology* 72 (1967) 84–123.

Depew, D. J., "Politics, Music and Contemplation in Aristotle's Ideal State," in *A Companion to Aristotle's Politics*, eds D. Keyt and F. Miller (Oxford, 1991), 346–380.

Dētienne, M., *Mythe et Langage. Les Maîtres de la Verité dans la Grèce archaïque* (Paris, 1967).

Devereux, G., "The Structure of Tragedy and the Structure of the *Psychē* in Aristotle's *Poetics*," in *Psychoanalysis and Philosophy: Essays in Memory of Ernest Jones*, eds C. Hanly and M. Lazerowitz (New York, 1970), 46–75.

Dirlmeier, F., "*Katharsis pathēmatōn*," *Hermes* 75 (1940) 81–92.

Dodds, E. R., "On Misunderstanding the *Oedipus Rex*," *Greece and Rome* 13 (1966) 37–49; rpt. in *Twentieth Century Interpretations of Oedipus Rex*, ed. M. J. O'Brien (Englewood Cliffs, 1968), 17–29. References are to the rpt. edn.

Dover, K. J., *Greek Popular Morality in the Time of Plato and Aristotle* (Oxford, 1974).

Downing, E., "*Hoion Psychē*: An Essay on Aristotle's *Muthos*," *Classical Antiquity* 3 (1984) 164–178.

Düring, I., *Aristoteles. Darstellung und Interpretation seines Denkens* (Heidelberg, 1966).

Dyer, R. R., "*Hamartia* in the *Poetics* and Aristotle's Model of Failure," *Arion* 4 (1965) 658–664.

Eden, K., "Poetry and Equity: Aristotle's Defense of Fiction," *Traditio* 38 (1982) 17–43.

——, *Poetic and Legal Fiction in the Aristotelian Tradition* (Princeton, 1986).

Else, G. F., "Aristotle on the Beauty of Tragedy," *Harvard Studies in Classical Philology* 49 (1938) 179–204.

——, "'Imitation' in the Fifth Century," *Classical Philology* 53 (1958) 73–90 and addendum: 245.

——, *The Origins and Early Form of Greek Tragedy* (Cambridge, 1965).

——, "Imitation," in *Encyclopedia of Poetry and Poetics*, ed. A. Preminger (Princeton, 1965).

——, *Aristotle's Poetics: The Argument* (Cambridge, MA, 1957).

——, "Persuasion and the Work of Tragedy," in *Tragique et Tragédie dans la Tradition Occidentale*, eds P. Gravel and T. J. Reiss (Montreal, 1983), 63–68.

——, *Plato and Aristotle on Poetry*, ed. P. Burian (Chapel Hill and London, 1986).

Euben, J. P. (ed.), *Greek Tragedy and Political Theory* (Berkeley and Los Angeles, 1986).

——, *Tragedy and Political Theory* (Princeton, 1990).

Falus, R., "Some Remarks on Aristotle's Theory of Catharsis," *Homonoia* **2** (1980) 57–88.

Foley, H. P., *Ritual Irony, Poetry and Sacrifice in Euripides* (Ithaca, 1985).

Forte, D. F., "Injustice and Tragedy in Aristotle," in *Georgetown Symposium on Ethics* (Lanham, 1984), 175–184.

Fortenbaugh, W. W., "Aristotle and the Questionable Mean-Dispositions," *Transactions of the American Philological Association* **99** (1968) 203–231.

——, *Aristotle on Emotion* (London, 1975).

——, "Aristotle's *Rhetoric* on Emotions," in Barnes *et al.* (1979) *Articles*, Vol. 4, 133–153.

Frede, D., "Aristotle on the Limits of Determinism," in Gotthelf (1985).

Freeland, C., "Aristotelian Actions," *Nous* (1985) 397–414.

——, "Revealing Gendered Texts," *Philosophy and Literature* **15** (1991) 40–58.

——, "Accidental Causes and Real Explanations," in *Essays on Aristotle's Physics*, ed. L. Judson (Oxford, 1991) (forthcoming).

——, "Nourishing Speculation: A Feminist Reading of Aristotelian Science," in *Critical Feminist Essays on the History of Western Philosophy*, ed. Bat-Ami Bar On (Albany, 1992) (forthcoming).

Gagarin, M., *Aeschylean Drama* (Berkeley, 1976).

Gallop, D., "Animals in the *Poetics*," *Oxford Studies in Ancient Philosophy* **8** ed. J. Annas (1990) 145–171.

Gellrich, M., *Tragedy and Theory* (Princeton, 1988).

Gill, C., "The *Ēthos/Pathos* Distinction in Rhetorical and Literary Criticism," *Classical Quarterly* N.S. **34** (1984) 149–166.

Glanville, I., "Note on *Peripeteia*," *Classical Quarterly* **41** (1947) 73–78.

——, "Tragic Error," *Classical Quarterly* **43** (1949) 47–56.

Golden, L., "Is Tragedy the 'Imitation of a Serious Action'?" *Greek, Roman and Byzantine Studies* **6** (1965) 283–289.

——, "The Purgation Theory of Catharsis," *Journal of Aesthetics and Art Criticism* **31** (1973) 473–479.

——, "Aristotle and the Audience for Tragedy," *Mnemosyne* **29** (1976) 351–359.

——, "The Clarification Theory of *Katharsis*," *Hermes* **104** (1976) 437–452.

——, "Epic, Tragedy and Catharsis," *Classical Philology* **71** (1976) 77–85.

——, "Towards a Definition of Tragedy," *Classical Journal* **72** (1976) 21–33.

——, "*Hamartia, Atē* and Oedipus," *Classical World* **72** (1978) 3–12.

Goldhill, S., "The Great Dionysia and Civic Ideology," *Journal of Hellenic Studies* **107** (1987) 58–76, rpt. in *Nothing to Do with Dionysos?*, J. Winkler and F. Zeitlin, eds (Princeton, 1990), 97–129.

——, *Reading Greek Tragedy* (Cambridge, 1986).

Goldschmidt, V., *Temps Physique et Temps Tragique chez Aristote* (Paris, 1982).

Goldstein, H. D., "*Mimēsis* and Catharsis Reexamined," *Journal of Aesthetics and Art Criticism* **25** (1966) 567–577.

Gomme, A. W., *The Greek Attitude to Poetry and History* (Berkeley, 1954).

Gomperz, T., "Zu Aristoteles' Poetik; ein Beitrag zur Kritik und Erklärung der Capitel 1–6," *Sitzungsberichte der philosophisch-historischen Klasse der kaiserlichen Akademie der Wissenschaften zu Wien* **116** (1888) 543–582.

——, "Die Kunstlehre des Aristoteles," in *Griechische Denker* (Leipzig, 1909), Vol. 3, 316–329.

Goodman, N., *Languages of Art. An Approach to a Theory of Symbols*, 2nd edn (Indianapolis, 1976).

Gotthelf, A. (ed.), *Aristotle on Nature and Living Things* (presented to David Balme on his seventieth birthday) (Pittsburgh, PA, and Bristol, 1985).

—— and Lennox, J. G., *Philosophical Issues in Aristotle's Biology* (Cambridge, 1987).

Gould, T., "The Innocence of Oedipus. The Philosophers on Oedipus the King," *Arion* **4** (1965) 363–386; 582–611.

Grenot, L., *Recherches sur le Développement de la Pensée Juridique et Morale en Grèce* (Paris, 1917).

Grube, G. M. A., "A Note on Aristotle's Definition of Tragedy," *Phoenix* **12** (1958) 26–30.

Gulley, N., "Aristotle on the Purposes of Literature," in Barnes *et al.* (1979) *Articles*, Vol. 4.

——, "The Concept of *Historia* in Aristotle's *Poetics*," *Trivium* **15** (1980) 1–9.

Halliwell, S., "Plato and Aristotle on the Denial of Tragedy," *Proceedings of the Cambridge Philological Society* **30** (1984) 49–71.

——, *Aristotle's Poetics* (Chapel Hill, NC, 1986).

——, *Plato: Republic X*, trans. and comm. (Warminster, 1988).

——, "Aristotelian *Mimēsis* Reevaluated," *Journal of the History of Philosophy* **28** (1990) 487–510.

——, "Philosophy and Literature: Settling a Quarrel?" in *Philosophical Investigations* (forthcoming).

Hardie, R. P., "The Poetics of Aristotle," *Mind* **4** (1895) 350–364.

Hardie, W. F. R., *Aristotle's Ethical Theory*, 2nd edn (Oxford, 1980).

Hardison, O. B., "The Place of Averroes' Commentary on the Poetics in the History of Medieval Criticism," in *Medieval and Renaissance Studies*, ed. J. L. Lievsay, Vol. 4 (Durham, NC, 1970), 57–82.

Hathaway, B., *The Age of Criticism* (Ithaca, 1962).

Heath, M., *The Poetics of Greek Tragedy* (Stanford, 1987).

——, *Unity in Greek Poetics* (Oxford, 1989).

——, "Aristotelian Comedy," *Classical Quarterly* N.S. **39** (1989) 344–354.

——, "Aristotle and the Pleasures of Tragedy" (forthcoming).

Held, G. F., *Aristotle's Teleological Theory of Tragedy*, Diss., University of California at Berkeley (1981).

——, "*Spoudaios* and Teleology in the *Poetics*," *Transactions of the American Philological Association* **114** (1984) 159–176.

——, "The Meaning of *Ēthos* in the '*Poetics*'," *Hermes* **113** (1985) 280–293.

Herington, C. J., *Poetry into Drama* (Berkeley, 1985).

Herrick, M. T., *The Poetics of Aristotle in England* (New Haven, 1930).

Hintikka, J., "Necessity, Universality and Time in Aristotle," *Ajatus* **20** (1957) 65–90.

——, *Time and Necessity, Studies in Aristotle's Theory of Modality* (Oxford, 1973).

Horn, H.-J., "Zur Begründung des Vorrangs der '*praxis*' vor dem '*ēthos*' in der aristotelischen Tragödientheorie," *Hermes* **103** (1975) 292–299.

House, H., *Aristotle's Poetics: A Course of Eight Lectures*, rev. C. Hardie (London, 1956 and 1961).

Hume, D., "Of Tragedy," 1757, in *English Literary Criticism: Restoration and 18th Century*, ed. S. Hynes (New York, 1963), 264–271.

Irwin, T., "The Metaphysical and Psychological Foundations of Aristotle's *Ethics*," in *Essays on Aristotle's Ethics*, ed. A. O. Rorty (Berkeley, 1980).

——, "Permanent Happiness: Aristotle and Solon," *Oxford Studies in Ancient Philosophy* **3** (1985) 89–124.

——, *Aristotle's First Principles* (Oxford, 1988).

Janko, R., *Aristotle on Comedy. Towards a Reconstruction of Poetics II* (Berkeley and Los Angeles, 1984).

——, "Philodemus' *On Poems* and Aristotle's *On Poets*," *Cronache Ercolanesi* **21** (1991), 1–60.

Janković, V., "Tractatus Coislinianus," *Ziva Antika* **34** (1984) 87–94.

Joachim, H. H., *Aristotle, The Nicomachean Ethics; A Commentary*, ed. D. A. Rees (Oxford, 1951).

Jones, J., *On Aristotle and Greek Tragedy* (Stanford, 1962).

Keesey, D., "On Some Recent Interpretations of Catharsis," *Classical World* **72** (1979) 193–205.

Kennedy, G. A. (ed.), *The Cambridge History of Literary Criticism. I: Classical Criticism* (Cambridge, 1989).

Kitto, H. D. F., "Catharsis," in *The Classical Tradition: Literary and Historical Studies in Honor of Harry Caplan*, ed. L. Wallach (Ithaca, 1966), 133–147.

——, "Aristotle and Fourth Century Tragedy," in *For Service to Classical Studies. Essays in honor of Francis Letters*, ed. M. Kelly (Melbourne, 1966), 113–129.

Knox, B. M. W., *Oedipus at Thebes* (New York, 1957).

Kokolakis, M., "Greek Drama: The Stirring of Pity," in *Studies in Honour of T. B. L. Webster*, eds J. H. Betts, J. T. Hooker and J. R. Green (Bristol, 1986), 170–178.

Kommerell, M., *Lessing und Aristoteles* (Frankfurt, 1940).

Kosman, L. A., "Being Properly Affected: Virtues and Feelings in Aristotle's Ethics," *Essays on Aristotle's Ethics*, ed. A. O. Rorty (Berkeley, Los Angeles and London, 1980), 103–116.

Kraut, R., *Aristotle on the Human Good* (Princeton, 1989).

Lamberton, R. D., "*Philanthropia* and the Evolution of Dramatic Taste," *Phoenix* **37** (1983) 95–103.

Lane, R. E., "The Catharsis of Pity and Fear," *Classical Journal* **50** (1955) 309–310.

Leighton, S. R., "Aristotle and the Emotions," *Phronesis* **27** (1982) 144–174.

Lesky, A., *Greek Tragic Poetry*, trans. M. Dillon (Yale, 1983).

Levin, S. R., "Aristotle's Theory of Metaphor," *Philosophy and Rhetoric* **15** (1982) 24–46.

Lloyd, G. E. R., *Aristotle: The Growth and Structure of his Thought* (Cambridge, 1968).

——, *Science, Folklore and Ideology* (Cambridge, 1983).

Lock, W., "The Use of *Peripeteia* in Aristotle's *Poetics*," *Classical Review* **9** (1895) 251–53.

Loraux, N., *Tragic Ways of Killing a Woman*, trans. A. Foster (Cambridge, MA, 1987).

Lord, Carnes, *Poetry and the City: An Interpretation of Aristotle's Poetics* (Ithaca, NY, 1972).

——, "Aristotle's History of Poetry," *Transactions of the American Philological Association* **104** (1974) 195–229.

——, *Education and Culture in the Political Thought of Aristotle* (Ithaca and London, 1982).

Lord, Catherine, "Tragedy Without Character: Poetics VI. 1450a24," *Journal of Aesthetics and Art Criticism* **28** (1969–70) 55–62.

Lucas, D. W., "Pity, Terror, and *Peripeteia*," *Classical Quarterly* N.S. **12** (1962) 52–60.

Lucas, F. L., "The Reverse of Aristotle," *Classical Review* **37** (1923) 98–104.

——, *Tragedy, Serious Drama in Relation to Aristotle's Poetics* (Totowa, 1981).

McKeon, R., "Literary Criticism and the Concept of Imitation in Antiquity," in *Critics and Criticism: Ancient and Modern*, ed. R. S. Crane (Chicago, 1952), 147–175.

——, "Rhetoric and Poetic in the Philosophy of Aristotle," in *Aristotle's Poetics and English Literature*, ed. E. Olson (Chicago and London 1965), 201–236.

McMahon, A. P., "Seven Questions on Aristotelian Definitions of Tragedy and Comedy," *Harvard Studies in Classical Philology* **40** (1929) 97–198.

Mignucci, M., "*Hōs epi to polu* et necéssaire dans la conception aristotélicienne de la science," in Berti (1981), 173–203.

Modrak, D. K. W., *Aristotle. The Power of Perception* (Chicago and London, 1987).

Moles, J., "Notes on Aristotle, *Poetics* 13 and 14," *Classical Quarterly* N.S. **29** (1979) 77–94.

——, "*Philanthropia* in the *Poetics*," *Phoenix* **38** (1984) 325–335.

——, "Aristotle and Dido's *Hamartia*," *Greece and Rome* **31** (1984) 48–54.

Moravcsik, J., "On Correcting the Poets," *Oxford Studies in Ancient Philosophy* **4** (1986) 35–47.

—— and Temko, P. (eds), *Plato on Beauty, Wisdom and the Arts* (Totowa, 1982).

Moulinier, L., *Le Pur et l'Impur dans la Pensée des Grecs* (Paris, 1952).

Nagy, G., *The Best of the Achaeans* (Baltimore and London, 1979).

Nardelli, M. L., "La Catarsi Poetica nel *P. Herc. 1581*," *Cronache Ercolanesi* **8** (1978) 96–103.

Nehamas, A., "Plato on Imitation and Poetry in *Republic* 10," in *Plato on Beauty, Wisdom and the Arts*, eds J. Moravcsik and P. Temko (Totowa, 1982), 47–78.

——, "Mythology: The Theory of Plot," in *Essays in Aesthetics: Perspectives on the Work of Monroe C. Beardsley*, ed. J. Fisher (Philadelphia, 1983), 180–197.

——, "Dangerous Pleasures," review of Halliwell, *Aristotle's Poetics* 1986, *Times Literary Supplement* 4371 (9th January, 1987) 27–28.

Ničev, A., "Aristot. *Poet*. 25, 1460b16," *Helikon* **3** (1963) 490.

——, "*L'Énigme de la Catharsis Tragique dans Aristote* (Sofia, 1970).

——, "Aristotle's *para ten doxan* and the Modern Detective Story," in *Studi Classici in Onore di Quintino Cataudella* (Catania, 1972), 2: 265–278.

——, *La Catharsis Tragique d'Aristote. Nouvelles Contributions* (Sofia, 1982).

Nietzsche, F., *The Birth of Tragedy* (1st edn 1872), trans. W. Kaufmann, *Basic Writings of Nietzsche* (New York, 1968).

North, H., *Sophrosynē* (Ithaca, 1966).

Nussbaum, M., "Aristotle," in *Ancient Writers*, ed. T. J. Luce (New York, 1982), I, 377–416.

——, *The Fragility of Goodness. Luck and Ethics in Greek Tragedy and Philosophy* (Cambridge, 1986).

——, "Therapeutic Arguments: Epicurus and Aristotle," in *The Norms of Nature: Studies in Hellenistic Ethics*, eds M. Schofield and G. Striker (Cambridge and Paris, 1986), 31–74.

——, "Nature, Function, and Capability: Aristotle on Political Distribution," *Oxford Studies in Ancient Philosophy* (1988) Suppl. Vol. 145–184.

——, *Love's Knowledge: Essays on Philosophy and Literature* (New York, 1990).

Olson, E. (ed, intro.), *Aristotle's Poetics and English Literature. A Collection of Critical Essays* (Chicago, 1965).

——, *The Theory of Comedy* (Bloomington, 1968).

——, "The Poetic Method of Aristotle: Its Powers and Limitations," *On Value Judgments in the Arts* (Chicago, 1976).

Østerud, S., "*Hamartia* in Aristotle and Greek Tragedy," *Symbolae Osloenses* **51** (1976) 65–80.

Ostwald, M., "Aristotle on *Hamartia* and Sophocles' *OT*," in *Festschrift Kapp* (Hamburg, 1958), 93–108.

Pappas, N., "The *Poetics*' Argument Against Plato," unpubl. ms.

Parker, R., *Miasma: Pollution and Purification in Early Greek Religion* (Oxford, 1983).

Paskow, A., "What is Aesthetic Catharsis?" *Journal of Aesthetics and Art Criticism* **42** (1983) 59–68.

——, "A Meditation on Aristotle's Concept of *Catharsis*," in *Philosophy and Culture: Proceedings of the XVIIth World Congress of Philosophy* (Montreal, 1988), III, 709–714.

Patzig, G., *Aristotle's Theory of the Syllogism* (Dordrecht, 1969).

Pearson, L., "Characterization in Drama and Oratory – *Poetics* 1450a20," *Classical Quarterly* N.S. **18** (1968), 76–83.

Pelling, C. B. R., *Characterization and Individuality in Greek Literature* (Oxford, 1990).

Perrin, B., "Recognition Scenes in Greek Literature," *American Journal of Philology* **30** (1909) 371–404.

Pfeiffer, R., *History of Classical Scholarship: from the Beginnings to the End of the Hellenistic Age* (Oxford, 1968).

Philippart, H., "La Théorie Aristotélicienne de l'Anagnorisis," *Revue des études greques* **38** (1925) 171–204.

Pickard-Cambridge, A. W., *Dithyramb, Tragedy and Comedy* (Oxford, 1927).

——, *The Theatre of Dionysus in Athens* (Oxford, 1946).

——, *The Dramatic Festivals of Athens*, 2nd edn, rev. J. Gould and D. M. Lewis, with suppl. and corrections (Oxford, 1988).

Redfield, J. M., *Nature and Culture in the* Iliad: *The Tragedy of Hector* (Chicago, 1975).

Rees, B. R., "*Pathos* in the *Poetics* of Aristotle," *Greece and Rome* **19** (1972) 1–11.

——, "Aristotle's Theory and Milton's Practice: *Samson Agonistes*," Inaugural Lecture, Birmingham (1972).

——, "Plot, Character and Thought," in *Le Monde Grec. Pensée, Littérature, Histoire, Documents. Hommages à Claire Préaux*, eds J. Bingen, G. Cambier and G. Nachtergael (Brussels, 1975), 188–196.

——, "Aristotle's Approach to Poetry," *Greece and Rome* **28** (1981) 23–39.

Roberts, J., "Political Animals in the *Nicomachean Ethics*," *Phronesis* **34** (1989) 185–204.

Rorty, A. O. (ed.), *Essays on Aristotle's Ethics* (Berkeley, Los Angeles and London, 1980).

——, "Akrasia and Pleasure," in *Essays on Aristotle's Ethics*, ed. A. O. Rorty (Berkeley, Los Angeles and London, 1980), 103–116.

——, "The Place of Psychology in Aristotle's *Rhetoric*," in *Proceedings of the Boston Area Colloquium in Ancient Philosophy*, 1991–92, ed. J. Cleary (New York, 1992).

Rosenmeyer, T. G., "Design and Execution in Aristotle *Poetics* Ch. 25," *California Studies in Classical Antiquity* **6** (1974) 231–252.

——, "Aristotelian *Ēthos* and Character in Modern Drama," *Proceedings of the IXth Congress of the International Comparative Literature Association* (Innsbruck, 1981).

——, "History or Poetry? The Example of Herodotus," *Clio* **11** (1982) 239–259.

Rosenstein, L., "On Aristotle and Thought in the Drama," *Critical Inquiry* **3** (1976–1977) 543–565.

Ross, W. D., "Rhetoric and Poetics," in *Aristotle* (London, 1923; 1956), 276–290.

Russell, D. A., *Criticism in Antiquity* (London, 1981).

Saïd, S., *La Faute Tragique* (Paris, 1978).

Salkever, S. G., "Tragedy and the Education of the *Dēmos*: Aristotle's Response to Plato," in *Greek Tragedy and Political Theory*, ed. J. P. Euben (Berkeley and Los Angeles, 1986), 274–303.

——, *Finding the Mean* (Princeton, 1990).

Sambursky, S., "On the Possible and the Probable in Ancient Greece," *Osiris* **12** (1956) 35–48.

Schaper, E., "Aristotle's Catharsis and Aesthetic Pleasure," *Philosophical Quarterly* **18** (1968) 131–143.

Schendler, A. E. J., *An Aristotelian Theory of Comedy*, Diss., University of Michigan (1954).

Schofield, M., "Aristotelian Mistakes," *Proceedings of the Cambridge Philological Society* **199** (1973) 66–70.

——, "Aristotle on the Imagination," in *Aristotle on Mind and the Senses*, eds G. E. R. Lloyd and G. E. L. Owen (Cambridge, 1978) 99–129; rpt. in Barnes *et al.* (1979) *Articles*, Vol. 4, 103–132.

Schrier, O. J., "A Simple View of *Peripeteia*," *Mnemosyne* **33** (1980) 96–118.

Schütrumpf, E., *Die Bedeutung des Wortes "ēthos" in der Poetik des Aristoteles*, Zetemata 49 (Munich, 1970).

——, "Traditional Elements in the Concept of *Hamartia* in Aristotle's *Poetics*," *Harvard Studies in Classical Philology* **92** (1989) 137–156.

Segal, E. (ed.), *Greek Tragedy* (New York, 1983).

Sherman, N., *Aristotle's Theory of Moral Education*, Diss., Harvard University (1982).
——, *The Fabric of Character* (Oxford, 1989).
Sifakis, G. M., "Learning from Art and Pleasure in Learning: an Interpretation of Aristotle, *Poetics* 4.1448b8–19," in *Studies in Honour of T. B. L. Webster*, eds J. H. Betts, J. T. Hooker, and J. R. Green, Vol. 1 (Bristol, 1986), 211–222.
Simon, B., *Mind and Madness in Ancient Greece: The Classical Roots of Modern Psychiatry* (Ithaca, 1978).
Simpson, P., "Aristotle on Poetry and Imitation," *Hermes* **116** (1988) 279–291.
Smithson, I., "The Moral View of Aristotle's *Poetics*," *Journal of the History of Ideas* **44** (1983) 3–17.
Solmsen, F., "The Origins and Methods of Aristotle's *Poetics*," *Classical Quarterly* **29** (1935) 192–201.
Somville, P., *Essai sur la Poétique d'Aristote* (Paris, 1975).
Sorabji, R., "Aristotle on the Role of Intellect in Virtue," *Proceedings of the Aristotelian Society*, N.S. **74** (1973–1974) 107–129; rpt. in *Essays on Aristotle's Ethics*, ed. A. O. Rorty (Berkeley, Los Angeles and London, 1980), 201–219; references are to the latter.
——, *Necessity, Cause, and Blame* (Ithaca, 1980).
——, "Definitions: Why Necessary and in What Way," in Berti (1981), 205–244.
Sörbom, G., *Mimēsis and Art* (Stockholm, 1966).
Sparshott, F., "The Riddle of *Katharsis*," in *Center and Labyrinth. Essays in Honor of Northrop Frye*, ed. E. Cook (Toronto, 1983).
Spiegel, N., "The Aesthetic, Intellectual and Moral Effects of Tragedy According to Aristotle," *Rivista di Filologia e di Istruzione Classica* **94** (1966) 415–423.
Stanford, W. B., *Greek Tragedy and the Emotions* (London and Boston, 1983).
Stevens, E. B., "Some Attic Commonplaces of Pity," *American Journal of Philology* **65** (1944) 1–25.
——, "Envy and Pity in Greek Philosophy," *American Journal of Philology* **69** (1948) 171–189.
Stinton, T. C. W., "*Hamartia* in Aristotle and Greek Tragedy," *Classical Quarterly* N.S. **25** (1975) 221–254.
Striker, G., "Notwendigkeit mit Lücken," *Kontingenz, Neue Hefte für Philosophie* 24/5 (Göttingen, 1985).
Süss, W., *Ēthos: Studien zur älteren griechischen Rhetorik* (Leipzig, 1910).
Taplin, O., *Greek Tragedy in Action* (Berkeley and Los Angeles, 1978).
Tracy, H. L., "Aristotle on Aesthetic Pleasure," *Classical Philology* **41** (1946) 43–46.
Tracy, T., *Physiological Theory and the Doctrine of the Mean in Plato and Aristotle* (The Hague and Paris, 1969).
Twining, T., *Aristotle's Treatise on Poetry* (London, 1789, rpr. Farnborough, 1972).
Vahlen, J., *Beiträge zu Aristoteles' Poetik* (Berlin and Leipzig, 1914).
Van Braam, P., "Aristotle's Use of *Hamartia*," *Classical Quarterly* **6** (1912) 266–272.
Verdenius, W. J., "The Meaning of *Ēthos* and *Ēthikos* in Aristotle's *Poetics*," *Mnemosyne* **12** (1945) 241–257.
——, *Mimesis: Plato's Doctrine of Artistic Imitation and its Meaning to Us* (Leiden, 1949; rpt. 1972).
——, "Katharsis tōn Pathematon," in *Autour d'Aristote. Recueil d'études de philosophie ancienne et médiévale offert à A. Mansion* (Louvain, 1955), 367–373.
——, "Arist. *Poet*. 1452a25," *Mnemosynē* **18** (1965) 281.
——, "The Principles of Greek Literary Criticism," *Mnemosynē* **36** (1983) 14–59.
Vernant, J.-P. and Vidal-Naquet, P., *Myth and Tragedy in Ancient Greece*, Engl. trans. (New York, 1981).
Vickers, B., *Towards Greek Tragedy* (London, 1973).

Von Fritz, K., "Tragische Schuld und poetische Gerechtigkeit in der griechischen Tragödie," *Studium Generale* **8** (1955) 194–237.

——, "Entstehung und Inhalt des neunten Kapitels von Aristoteles' Poetik", in *Antike und Moderne Tragödie. Neun Abhandlungen* (Berlin, 1962).

Walton, K., *Mimesis as Make-Believe* (Cambridge, MA, 1990).

Webster, T. B. L., "Fourth Century Tragedy and the *Poetics*," *Hermes* **82** (1954) 294–308.

Weil, R., *Aristote et l'histoire: Essai sur la "Politique"* (Paris, 1960).

Weinberg, B., *A History of Literary Criticism in the Italian Renaissance*, 2 Vols (Chicago, 1961).

Whalley, G., "On Translating Aristotle's *Poetics*," *University of Toronto Quarterly* **39** n.2 (1970) 77–106.

White, S. A., "Is Aristotelian Happiness a Good Life or the Best Life?," *Oxford Studies in Philosophy*, 1990.

——, *Sovereign Virtue* (Stanford, 1992).

Will, F., "Aristotle and the Source of the Art-Work," *Phronesis* **5** (1960) 152–168.

——, "Aristotle and the Question of Character in Literature," *Review of Metaphysics* **14** (1960–61) 353–359.

Wilson, J. C., "Difficulties in the Text of Aristotle," *Journal of Philology* **32** (1913) 138–147; 164.

Wimsatt, W. K., "Aristotle and Oedipus or Else," in *Hateful Contraries* (Lexington, KY, 1965).

Winkler, J., "An Oscar for Iphigenia," in *The Ephebe's Song: Athenian Drama and the Poetics of Manhood* (Princeton, 1992) (forthcoming).

Winnington-Ingram, R. P., "Tragedy and Greek Archaic Thought," in *Classical Drama and Its Influence* (London, 1965), 31–50.

——, *Sophocles: An Interpretation* (Cambridge, 1980).

Yanal, R., "Aristotle's Definition of Poetry," *Nous* **16** (1982) 499–525.

Young, C., "Aristotle on Temperance," *The Philosophical Review* **97** (1988) 521–542.